Philosophic Inquiry in SPORT

Philosophic Inquiry in SPORT

William J. Morgan, PhD
University of Tennessee

Klaus V. Meier, PhD
University of Western Ontario

Editors

Human Kinetics Publishers, Inc.
Champaign, Illinois

Library of Congress Cataloging-in-Publication Data

Philosophic inquiry in sport.
   Includes bibliographies.
   1. Sports--Philosophy. I. Morgan, William John,
1948-   .   II. Meier, Klaus V., 1945-   .
GV706.P478 1988   796'.01   87-2767
ISBN 0-87322-119-2

Developmental Editor: Jan Progen, EdD
Production Director: Ernie Noa
Assistant Production Director: Lezli Harris
Assistant Editor: Julie Anderson
Proofreader: Linda Purcell
Typesetter: Sonnie Bowman
Text Layout: Floyd Brewer
Cover Design: Jack Davis
Printed By: R.R. Donnelly and Sons

ISBN: 0-87322-119-2

Printed in the United States of America

10 9 8 7 6 5 4 3 2 1

Human Kinetics Publishers, Inc.
Box 5076, Champaign, IL 61820
1-800-DIAL-HKP
1-800-334-3665 (in Illinois)

Contents

Preface

The field of sport philosophy is still a very young one. Although the sixties marked the first flurry of genuine academic interest in this subject, it was not until 1972 that a scholarly society devoted to this area of inquiry (the Philosophic Society for the Study of Sport) was formally ratified in conjunction with the annual meetings of the Eastern Division of the American Philosophic Association. Further, it was not until 1974 that a scholarly vehicle exclusively devoted to sport philosophy (namely, the *Journal of the Philosophy of Sport*) commenced publication.

Be that as it may, in this relatively short period of time, particularly the last decade, a significant and increasingly sophisticated corpus of literature on the philosophy of sport has emerged. The publication of anthologies that attempt to organize and capture the best of this literature, however, has not kept pace with either the quantity or the quality of this scholarly production. In fact, of the three major anthologies that focus on sport philosophy, one is out of print (Gerber and Morgan's *Sport and the Body*, 1979) and the other two are significantly dated (Osterhoudt's *Philosophy of Sport*, 1973; and Allen and Fahey's *Being Human in Sport*, 1977). Although Vanderwerken and Wertz's recent anthology (*Sport Inside Out*, 1985) is a welcome addition to the field, its contributions are split between literature and philosophy. Consequently, there is not a single, current anthology available that has the philosophy of sport as its exclusive theme.

It is in response to this serious gap in the literature, a gap that impedes both the teaching and the advance of sport philosophy as an academic subject, that we present the following collection of articles. Our aim in this regard has been an ad-mittedly ambitious one. Although we are well aware of the difficulties entailed in serving diverse clientele, we have attempted to select essays that are appropriate for undergraduate and graduate students in particular, and for scholars interested in sport in general. Our guide in this process has been the level of sophistication of the material, and our perceptions of the philosophic background of the prospective readers. We have also tried to present a balance of analytical, existential and phenomenological, and critical research essays, which reflect the breadth of contemporary Anglo-American and Continental philosophy. Finally, we have attempted to offer a blend of classical essays, works of long-revered standing by major philosophers, and new essays that reflect the rigor and acumen of the current essay literature.

The terse introductions to each section are intended simply to introduce the essays to the readers, to suggest points of agreement and dispute between and among the essays, and to suggest possible avenues of resolution and philosophical advancement. The bibliographies at the end of each section offer further readings that readers might profitably pursue in preparing for class discussions and writing papers.

The division of sections reflect the major branches of philosophic inquiry itself, running the gamut from metaphysics (theory of reality) to aesthetics (theory of value). Two exceptions, one notable and one more minor, should be mentioned here. First, there is no section dealing with epistemological (theory of knowledge) issues in sport. This is most assuredly not because epistemology is an unimportant branch of philosophy, but because the literature on sport is not especially strong in this area. We mean *strong* here principally in a quantitative and not a qualitative sense. That is, although some fine pieces have been written concerning the epistemic status of sport, a sufficient number have not been published to warrant a separate section. Second, for similar reasons, treatments of sport from the perspective of Eastern philosophy (for example, zen and sport) are also excluded. No doubt, these deficiencies will be rectified in the near future as the body of philosophic writings on sport continues to expand.

There will be those, of course, who will object to some of our selections, or who will be troubled by some of our omissions. As always, such disputes reflect the philosophic inclinations, classroom experiences, and overt prejudices of all those concerned. As editors, we can only hope that we have sufficiently tempered our own tastes and biases, and have produced a volume of wide appeal. That, at any rate, was our foremost intention.

William J. Morgan
Klaus V. Meier

Part
I

The Nature of Sport, Play, and Game

The various claims made about the social, moral, and aesthetic significance of sport presuppose an understanding of its basic nature. Indeed, the only way to sort out such claims is to be clear about the subject (sport) that bears them. This is the job of conceptual analysis. Accordingly, the aim of the present section is to examine the essential characteristics of sport. What are its necessary and sufficient conditions? How is it to be likened to or distinguished from other kindred phenomena such as play and game? These, and other related questions, make up the central theme of the present section.

Huizinga's classical account of play argues that it is a rather special human undertaking whose spirit infects most of the cultural forms of human life. In particular, play has, he argues, its own sense of seriousness and meaning, and stands outside the confines of immediate, everyday life. It is, therefore, not dominated by either a mercenary or practical disposition. Caillois' essay attempts to classify the various types of games. He divides games into four categories: games of competition (*agon*), games of chance (*alea*), games of simulation (*mimicry*), and games of vertigo (*ilinx*). Games can be further categorized, argues Caillois, along a continuum between two opposites: On the one end we have carefree exuberance and improvisation (*paidia*), and on the other, binding constraints and conventions (*ludus*).

Suits offers a more restrictive account of play, which argues against the common tendency to characterize play as merely autotelic activity. He regards autotelicity to be a necessary but not a sufficient condition of play. Hence, Suits defines play additionally as the temporary reallocation to autotelic activities of resources primarily committed to instrumental activities. He also disputes the notion that play and game-playing are logically linked in some fashion. Suits concludes that although game-playing is often playing, it need not be. In contrast, Schmitz, although suggesting no strict logical entailment between play and sport, argues nonetheless that an important ontological connection exists between them. That is, he argues that if sport is to be all that it is capable of being, it must be conducted in a play-like manner. The suspension of the ordinary world accomplished by play is therefore, in Schmitz's argument, crucial to the preservation of sport as a legitimate human enterprise. Severing this connection between play and sport, he claims, can only occur at the expense of sport itself, of its central, most endearing values.

In his essay on sport, Suits advances the thesis that the elements of sport are essentially, but not totally, the same as the elements of game. He defines game as the attempt to achieve a specific state of affairs,

1

using means permitted by the rules, where the rules prohibit use of more efficient in favor of less efficient means, and where the rules are accepted just because they make the playing of the game possible. Suits defines sport more particularly as a game that is based on skill, where the skill involved is of a physical sort, and where a certain level of institutional stability and following is apparent.

Although McBride regards Suits' account of game to cover a goodly share of the game-playing universe, he does not regard it, as Suits does, as a definition that captures all of the necessary and sufficient conditions of game-playing. Such an ambitious claim, McBride charges, opens Suits' definition to refutation by a single counterexample. McBride suggests one such counterexample in the form of a game played by no less than Wittgenstein, Norman Malcolm, and his wife—a game called *Sun, Earth, and Moon* (SEM). McBride argues that SEM is a game despite its being deficient in all of the elements Suits cites as indispensable elements of game-playing. McBride further suggests that Suits' definition of game is, in addition to being too narrow, too broad. For in suggesting that sports like footracing are games, Suits goes against the grain of ordinary language usage, which seldom, if ever, refers to footracing in such terms.

Suits' response to McBride seeks to disarm McBride's charge of both broadness and narrowness. With respect to the former, Suits argues that the charge misses the mark because his definition was not intended to account for all *uses* of the word game, but rather for what games *are*. The latter requires that an activity that meets all the criteria of game-playing, say footracing, be acknowledged as a game, regardless of whether or not it is commonly called one. With respect to McBride's charge of narrowness, Suits shows that under certain conditions SEM is indeed a game precisely because it does satisfy all of the conditions he cited as crucial to game-playing. Hence, he concludes that McBride's counterexample fails.

In the final essay of this section, D'Agostino argues against formalist accounts of game and sport of the sort authored by Suits. Formalist accounts of games, he claims, view games solely in terms of the formal rules that govern them. But D'Agostino considers such a rider to be suspect because it fails to see that games have an ethos as well as a set of rules. He defines the ethos of game as those conventions that determine how the codified rules of that game are applied in concrete circumstances. Only by considering the formal rules of games and their social contexts, D'Agostino concludes, can we adequately explain, for instance, the prevalence of physical contact in a supposedly noncontact sport such as basketball.

Further reading in this area is still rather sparse. Tangen (1985) offers a pragmatic–contextual definition of sport. Reddiford (1985) re-examines the distinction between constitutive and regulative rules as it bears on the nature of sport question. Hyland's (1984) monograph on play seeks a more fundamental grounding of play that goes beyond the limitations of sociological, psychological, and historical approaches. Similarly, Meier (1981) brings to light the deficiencies of sociological definitions of sport. Champlin (1977) discusses the need for developing a critical definition of sport and sets out the notion of *universe of discourse* as a tool for constructing such a definition. Thomas (1976) examines concepts closely tied to the conceptual ken of sport (game, rules, competition, and the like). Paddick (1975) provides an insightful analysis of physical activity, arguing that what makes an activity a physical activity is not its lack of mental involvement, nor its simple dependence on gross movement, but rather its express valuation of certain bodily movements. There is also an extensive, but somewhat tangential, body of literature on game theory that contains useful analyses of various characteristics of game theory.

The Nature of Play

JOHAN HUIZINGA

First and foremost . . . all play is a voluntary activity. Play to order is no longer play: it could at best be but a forcible imitation of it. By this quality of freedom alone, play marks itself off from the course of the natural process. It is something added thereto and spread out over it like a flowering, an ornament, a garment. Obviously, freedom must be understood here in the wider sense that leaves untouched the philosophical problem of determinism. It may be objected that this freedom does not exist for the animal and the child; they *must* play because their instinct drives them to it and because it serves to develop their bodily faculties and their powers of selection. The term "instinct", however, introduces an unknown quantity, and to presuppose the utility of play from the start is to be guilty of a *petitio principii*. Child and animal play because they enjoy playing, and therein precisely lies their freedom.

Be that as it may, for the adult and responsible human being play is a function which he could equally well leave alone. Play is superfluous. The need for it is only urgent to the extent that the enjoyment of it makes it a need. Play can be deferred or suspended at any time. It is never imposed by physical necessity or moral duty. It is never a task. It is done at leisure, during "free time". Only when play is a recognized cultural function—a rite, a ceremony—is it bound up with notions of obligation and duty.

Reprinted from *Homo Ludens* (pp. 18–21) by Johan Huizinga, 1950, London: Routledge & Kegan Paul. Copyright 1950 by Routledge & Kegan Paul Publishers. Reprinted by permission.

Here, then, we have the first main characteristic of play: that it is free, is in fact freedom. A second characteristic is closely connected with this, namely, that play is not "ordinary" or "real" life. It is rather a stepping out of "real" life into a temporary sphere of activity with a disposition all of its own. Every child knows perfectly well that he is "only pretending", or that it was "only for fun". How deep-seated this awareness is in the child's soul is strikingly illustrated by the following story, told to me by the father of the boy in question. He found his four-year-old son sitting at the front of a row of chairs, playing "trains". As he hugged him the boy said: "Don't kiss the engine, Daddy, or the carriages won't think it's real". This "only pretending" quality of play betrays a consciousness of the inferiority of play compared with "seriousness", a feeling that seems to be something as primary as play itself. Nevertheless, as we have already pointed out, the consciousness of play being "only a pretend" does not by any means prevent it from proceeding with the utmost seriousness, with an absorption, a devotion that passes into rapture and, temporarily at least, completely abolishes that troublesome "only" feeling. Any game can at any time wholly run away with the players. The contrast between play and seriousness is always fluid. The inferiority of play is continually being offset by the corresponding superiority of its seriousness. Play turns to seriousness and seriousness to play. Play may rise to heights of beauty and sublimity that leave seriousness far beneath. Tricky questions such as these will come up for discussion

3

when we start examining the relationship between play and ritual.

As regards its formal characteristics, all students lay stress on the *disinterestedness* of play. Not being "ordinary" life it stands outside the immediate satisfaction of wants and appetites, indeed it interrupts the appetitive process. It interpolates itself as a temporary activity satisfying in itself and ending there. Such at least is the way in which play presents itself to us in the first instance: as an intermezzo, an *interlude* in our daily lives. As a regularly recurring relaxation, however, it becomes the accompaniment, the complement, in fact an integral part of life in general. It adorns life, amplifies it and is to that extent a necessity both for the individual—as a life function—and for society by reason of the meaning it contains, its significance, its expressive value, its spiritual and social associations, in short, as a culture function. The expression of it satisfies all kinds of communal ideals. It thus has its place in a sphere superior to the strictly biological processes of nutrition, reproduction and self-preservation. This assertion is apparently contradicted by the fact that play, or rather sexual display, is predominant in animal life precisely at the mating-season. But would it be too absurd to assign a place *outside* the purely physiological, to the singing, cooing and strutting of birds just as we do to human play? In all its higher forms the latter at any rate always belongs to the sphere of festival and ritual—the sacred sphere.

Now, does the fact that play is a necessity, that it subserves culture, or indeed that it actually becomes culture, detract from its disinterested character? No, for the purposes it serves are external to immediate material interests or the individual satisfaction of biological needs. As a sacred activity play naturally contributes to the well-being of the group, but in quite another way and by other means than the acquisition of the necessities of life.

Play is distinct from "ordinary" life both as to locality and duration. This is the third main characteristic of play: its secludedness, its limitedness. It is "played out" within certain limits of time and place. It contains its own course and meaning.

Play begins, and then at a certain moment it is "over". It plays itself to an end. While it is in progress all is movement, change, alternation, succession, association, separation. But immediately connected with its limitation as to time there is a further curious feature of play: it at once assumes fixed form as a cultural phenomenon. Once played, it endures as a new-found creation of the mind, a treasure to be retained by the memory. It is transmitted, it becomes tradition. It can be repeated at any time, whether it be "child's play" or a game of chess, or at fixed intervals like a mystery. In this faculty of repetition lies one of the most essential qualities of play. It holds good not only of play as a whole but also of its inner structure. In nearly all the higher forms of play the elements of repetition and alternation (as in the *refrain*), are like the warp and woof of a fabric.

More striking even than the limitation as to time is the limitation as to space. All play moves and has its being within a play-ground marked off beforehand either materially or ideally, deliberately or as a matter of course. Just as there is no formal difference between play and ritual, so the "consecrated spot" cannot be formally distinguished from the play-ground. The arena, the card-table, the magic circle, the temple, the stage, the screen, the tennis court, the court of justice, etc., are all in form and function play-grounds, i.e. forbidden spots, isolated, hedged round, hallowed, within which special rules obtain. All are temporary worlds within the ordinary world, dedicated to the performance of an act apart.

Inside the play-ground an absolute and peculiar order reigns. Here we come across another, very positive feature of play: it creates order, *is* order. Into an imperfect world and into the confusion of life it brings a temporary, a limited perfection. Play demands order absolute and supreme. The least deviation from it "spoils the game", robs it of its character and makes it worthless. The profound affinity between play and order is perhaps the reason why play, as we noted in passing, seems to lie to such a large extent in the field of aesthetics. Play has a tendency to be beautiful. It may be that this aesthetic factor is identical with the impulse to create orderly form, which animates play in all its aspects. The words we use to denote the elements of play belong for the most part to aesthetics, terms with which we try to describe the effects of beauty: tension, poise, balance, contrast, variation, solution, resolution, etc. Play casts a spell over us; it is "enchanting", "captivating". It is invested with the noblest qualities we are capable of perceiving in things: rhythm and harmony.

The element of tension in play to which we have just referred plays a particularly important part. Tension means uncertainty, chanciness; a striving to decide the issue and so end it. The player wants something to "go", to "come off"; he wants to "succeed" by his own exertions. Baby reaching for a toy, pussy patting a bobbin, a little girl playing ball—all want to achieve something difficult, to succeed, to end a tension. Play is "tense", as we say. It is this element of tension and solution that governs all solitary games of skill and application such as puzzles, jig-saws, mosaic-making, patience, target-shooting, and the more play bears the character of competition the more fervent it will be. In gambling and athletics it is at its height. Though play as such is outside the range of good and bad, the element of tension imparts to it a certain ethical value in so far as it means a testing of the player's prowess: his courage, tenacity, resources and, last but not least, his spiritual powers—his "fairness"; because, despite his ardent desire to win, he must still stick to the rules of the game.

These rules in their turn are a very important factor in the play-concept. All play has its rules. They determine what "holds" in the temporary world circumscribed by play. The rules of a game are absolutely binding and allow no doubt. Paul Valéry once in passing gave expression to a very cogent thought when he said: "No scepticism is possible where the rules of a game are concerned, for the principle underlying them is an unshakable truth. . . ." Indeed, as soon as the rules are transgressed the whole play-world collapses. The game

is over. The umpire's whistle breaks the spell and sets "real" life going again.

The player who trespasses against the rules or ignores them is a "spoil-sport". The spoil-sport is not the same as the false player, the cheat; for the latter pretends to be playing the game and, on the face of it, still acknowledges the magic circle. It is curious to note how much more lenient society is to the cheat than to the spoil-sport. This is because the spoil-sport shatters the play-world itself. By withdrawing from the game he reveals the relativity and fragility of the play-world in which he had temporarily shut himself with others. He robs play of its *illusion*—a pregnant word which means literally "in-play" (from *inlusio, illudere* or *inludere*). Therefore he must be cast out, for he threatens the existence of the play-community. The figure of the spoil-sport is most apparent in boys' games. The little community does not enquire whether the spoil-sport is guilty of defection because he dares not enter into the game or because he is not allowed to. Rather, it does not recognize "not being allowed" and calls it "not daring". For it, the problem of obedience and conscience is no more than fear of punishment. The spoil-sport breaks the magic world, therefore he is a coward and must be ejected. In the world of high seriousness, too, the cheat and the hypocrite have always had an easier time of it than the spoil-sports, here called apostates, heretics, innovators, prophets, conscientious objectors, etc. It sometimes happens, however, that the spoil-sports in their turn make a new community with rules of its own. The outlaw, the revolutionary, the cabbalist or member of a secret society, indeed heretics of all kinds are of a highly associative if not sociable disposition, and a certain element of play is prominent in all their doings.

A play-community generally tends to become permanent even after the game is over. Of course, not every game of marbles or every bridge-party leads to the founding of a club. But the feeling of being "apart together" in an exceptional situation, of sharing something important, of mutually withdrawing from the rest of the world and rejecting the usual norms, retains its magic beyond the duration of the individual game. The club pertains to play as the hat to the head. It would be rash to explain all the associations which the anthropologist calls "phratria"—e.g. clans, brotherhoods, etc.—simply as play-communities; nevertheless it has been shown again and again how difficult it is to draw the line between, on the one hand, permanent social groupings—particularly in archaic cultures with their extremely important, solemn, indeed sacred customs—and the sphere of play on the other.

The exceptional and special position of play is most tellingly illustrated by the fact that it loves to surround itself with an air of secrecy. Even in early childhood the charm of play is enhanced by making a "secret" out of it. This is for *us,* not for the "others". What the "others" do "outside" is no concern of ours at the moment. Inside the circle of the game the laws and customs of ordinary life no longer count. We are different and do things differently. This temporary abolition of the ordinary world is fully acknowledged in child-life, but it is no less evident in the great ceremonial games of savage societies. During the great feast of initiation when the youths are accepted into the male community, it is not the neophytes only that are exempt from the ordinary laws and regulations: there is a truce to all feuds in the tribe. All retaliatory acts and vendettas are suspended. This temporary suspension of normal social life on account of the sacred play-season has numerous traces in the more advanced civilizations as well.

Everything that pertains to saturnalia and carnival customs belongs to it. Even with us a bygone age of robuster private habits than ours, more marked class-privileges and a more complaisant police recognized the orgies of young men of rank under the name of a "rag". The saturnalian licence of young men still survives, in fact, in the ragging at English universities, which the *Oxford English Dictionary* defines as "an extensive display of noisy and disorderly conduct carried out in defiance of authority and discipline".

The "differentness" and secrecy of play are most vividly expressed in "dressing up". Here the "extra-ordinary" nature of play reaches perfection. The disguised or masked individual "plays" another part, another being. He *is* another being. The terrors of childhood, openhearted gaiety, mystic fantasy and sacred awe are all inextricably entangled in this strange business of masks and disguises.

Summing up the formal characteristics of play we might call it a free activity standing quite consciously outside "ordinary" life as being "not serious", but at the same time absorbing the player intensely and utterly. It is an activity connected with no material interest, and no profit can be gained by it. It proceeds within its own proper boundaries of time and space according to fixed rules and in an orderly manner. It promotes the formation of social groupings which tend to surround themselves with secrecy and to stress their difference from the common world by disguise or other means.

The Structure and Classification of Games

ROGER CAILLOIS

In 1933, the rector of the University of Leyden, J. Huizinga, chose as the theme of his solemn speech, "the boundaries of play and of work in culture." He was to take this subject up again and to develop it in a powerful and original work published in 1938, *Homo Ludens*. Most of the statements in this book are debatable. Nonetheless, it opens the way to extremely fertile research and reflection. It is to Huizinga's lasting credit that he masterfully analyzed the fundamental characteristics of play and that he demonstrated the importance of its role in the development of civilization. He wanted on the one hand to find an exact definition of the essential nature of play; on the other hand, he attempted to shed some light on that part of play that haunts or enlivens the principal manifestations of all culture, the arts as well as philosophy, poetry as well as juridical institutions, and even certain aspects of war.

Huizinga achieved brilliantly what he set out to do. However, if he discovered play, whose presence and influence had until then been overlooked, he deliberately neglected to describe and classify the games themselves, as if all play represented an answer to the same need and explained the same psychological attitude. Thus a study of his first formulae helps us to understand the strange lacunae in his inquiry. We recall that he defined play in the following manner:

Summing up the formal characteristics of play we might call it a free activity standing quite consciously outside "ordinary" life as being "not serious," but at the same time absorbing the player intensely and utterly. It is an activity connected with no material interest, and no profit can be gained by it. It proceeds within its own proper boundaries of time and space according to fixed rules and in an orderly manner. It promotes the formation of social groupings which tend to surround themselves with secrecy and to stress their difference from the common world by disguise or other means.[1]

Such a definition, though all the words have value and meaning, is both too broad and too narrow. It is meritorious and fruitful to have grasped the affinity between play and secrecy or mystery, but this relationship should not enter into a definition of play, which is almost always ostentatious. Undoubtedly secrecy, mystery, and disguise lend themselves to an activity of play, but it should be immediately added that this activity necessarily takes place at the expense of secrecy and mystery. It exposes, publicizes and in a way expends secrecy, tending, in a word, to deprive it of its very nature.

Then again, that part of Huizinga's definition which alludes to play as an action devoid of any material interest entirely excludes betting and games of chance—that is, gambling houses, casinos, horse races, lotteries which, for good or

Reprinted from *Diogenes*, 12, (Winter, 1955), pp. 62–75. Copyright 1955 by *Diogenes*. Reprinted by permission.

evil, occupy an important place in the economy and in the daily life of different peoples, under an infinite variety of forms which makes the constancy of the relations between risk and profit all the more impressive. Games of chance, which are also money games, figure almost not at all in Huizinga's work. This deliberate exclusion is not without consequence.

Under these circumstances, it would be better to address ourselves to another formula of Huizinga's, less fruitful than the preceding one, but which, in my opinion at least, does not give rise to any major difficulty:

> Play is a voluntary action or occupation executed within certain fixed limits of time and place, according to rules freely accepted but absolutely binding, having its aim in itself and accompanied by a feeling of tension, joy and the consciousness that it is "different" from "ordinary" life.[2]

Although this second definition does not deliberately ignore games of chance, neither does it attribute a sufficient place to them. Moreover, the last part of it not only advantageously replaces the too explicit mention of secret and of mystery, but also gives one to understand that play could consist in the representation of something. Here, it is no longer the world of betting that is taken into consideration, but that of spectacle and interpretation, of dramatic play.

These observations, which extend very markedly the domain explored by Huizinga, still overlook such things as kites, crossword puzzles, and rocking horses, and to some extent dolls, games of patience, Chinese puzzles, hoops, most toys, and several of the more widespread diversions.

What do we get from these summary observations? First, that play is certainly an activity that is

1. Free: the player cannot be forced to participate without the game immediately changing its very nature.

2. Separate: circumscribed within boundaries of time and space that are precise and fixed in advance.[3]
3. Regulated: subject to conventions which suspend ordinary rules and temporarily establish a new law which alone counts.

However, these three attributes—whose prime importance I in no way challenge—imply, perhaps because of the fact that they do not affect the structure of the data they define, that such data should in turn be made the object of a distribution which attempts, this time, to take into account, not the characteristics which oppose them as a whole to the rest of reality, but those which confer upon them, among other things, their decidedly irreducible originality. In other words, once the *genus proximum* has been determined, it becomes urgent to state precisely the *differentia specifica* of each subsidiary category.

To this end, I suggest a division under three principal headings in accordance with whether, in the different games, the role of competition, luck, or disguise predominates. For all practical purposes only one of these, the first, attracted Huizinga's attention. I shall call them, *agôn, alea* and *mimicry,* respectively. All three definitely belong to the realm of play. One *plays* football or billiards or chess (*agôn*); roulette or the lottery (*alea*); pirates or Nero or Hamlet (*mimicry*). However, these terms do not cover the world of play in its entirety. Perhaps one should also single out the existence of a common principle of diversion, of turbulence, of free improvisation and of insouciant self-expression whereby a certain uncontrolled fantasy, which we shall call *paidia,* manifests itself. It likewise seems necessary to define a complementary tendency that is the inverse of this instinct in certain respects but not in all: the penchant for adapting play to arbitrary, imperative, and deliberately hindering conventions in order to obtain a perfectly useless although strictly determinate result. I shall call this last component *ludus.*

It is not my intention, in employing this foreign nomenclature to establish some sort of pedantic mythology, totally devoid of meaning. But, because I had to assemble disparate manifestations under a single rubric, it seemed to me that the most economical way of so doing was to borrow from this or that language both the most significant and the most comprehensive term possible in order to keep each ensemble studied from being uniformly marked by the particular characteristic of one of the elements that compose it; this could not fail to happen if the name of one element was used to designate the entire group. Besides, as I proceed with my attempt to establish the classification which I have fixed upon, everyone will have the opportunity to appreciate for himself the necessity of utilizing a nomenclature that does not refer too directly to concrete experience, which it is partly designed to break down according to a hitherto unstated principle.

Agôn

A whole group of games appears in the form of competition, as a struggle in which equality of chance is artificially created in order to make sure that the antagonists confront each other under ideal circumstances. This will give a precise and incontestable worth to the victor's triumph. Each time, therefore, the contest hinges on a single quality—speed, endurance, vigor, memory, deftness, ingenuity, etc.—operating within defined limits and without any external help. The winner will therefore appear to be the best in a precise category of feats. Such is the rule for athletic contests and the *raison d'être* of their multiple subdivisions, whether two individuals or two teams are competing (polo, tennis, football, boxing, fencing, etc.), or whether an indeterminate number of competitors are participating (races of all kinds, riflery, golf, athletics, etc.). Games in which each contestant begins with the same number of identical elements also belong to this category.

Draughts and chess are perfect examples. The quest for equality of chance from the start is so obviously the essential principle of the contest that it is reestablished by assigning a handicap to players of superior ability. In other words, within the equality of chance established from the start, a second inequality, proportional to the supposed relative strength of the participants, is created. It is significant that such a system exists for the muscular type of *agôn* (sports matches) as well as for the most cerebral type of *agôn* (chess, for example, in which the weaker player is given an extra pawn, knight or rook).

For each contestant the mainspring of the game is his desire to excel and win recognition for his ability in a given domain. Furthermore, the practice of *agôn* presupposes concentration, appropriate training, assiduous effort, and the will to win. It implies discipline and perseverance. It makes the champion rely solely on his own resources, encourages him to make the best possible use of them and forces him to utilize them fairly and within fixed limits which, being the same for everyone, result in rendering the superiority of the winner indisputable. The *agôn* appears as the pure form of personal merit and serves to demonstrate it.

Outside often on the periphery of play, one observes the notion of *agôn* in other cultural phenomena that conform to the same code: the duel, the tournament, certain constant and remarkable aspects of what we call polite warfare.

Alea

In Latin this is the word for the game of dice. I use it here to designate all games—in contrast to *agôn*—that are based upon an inequality external to the player, over which he has not the slightest control. Consequently, it is far less a question of triumphing over an adversary than over destiny. To put it more plainly, fate is the sole agent of victory, and where rivalry exists, victory means only that the winner was luckier than the loser. Dice, roulette, heads or tails, baccarat, lotteries, etc. provide unmistakable examples of this category of games. In this case not only is no attempt made to eliminate the injustice of chance, but it is the pure arbitrariness of luck that constitutes the sole mainspring of the game.

Alea signalizes and reveals the boons of fate. The player's role is an entirely passive one. He does not display his abilities or his propensities, the resources of his skill, of his muscles, or of his intelligence. All he does is to wait for the decision of fate. He gambles a stake. Justice forever sought after, but this time differently, and, here again, prone to operate under ideal circumstances —rigorously accurate, the proportionate reward for his gamble. All the efforts referred to above to equalize the contestants' chances are employed in this case to scrupulously balance *alea* and profit.

In contrast to *agôn, alea* negates work, patience, skill, qualifications. It eliminates professional endowments, order, and training. In one instant it abolishes accumulated results. It is either total failure or absolute favor. It bestows upon the lucky player infinitely more than a lifetime of work, discipline, and hardship could procure for him. It seems like an insolent and supreme mockery of merit.

Agôn is a vindication of personal responsibility, *alea* a resignation of the will, a surrender to destiny. Certain games like dominoes, and most card games combine *agôn* and *alea*: chance governs the way the "hands" of each player are composed and they then do their best, according to their lights, to exploit the lot that a blind fate has assigned to them. In a game like bridge, science and reason constitute the only means a player has to defend himself, and it is these that permit him to make the very most of the cards dealt to him; in a game like poker the attributes of psychological insight and human understanding are more likely to count.

Generally speaking, the role of money is all the more important, as chance plays a greater part and consequently the player's opportunities to defend himself are less good. The reason for this is very clear: *alea's* function is not to make the most intelligent person win the money, but, on the contrary, to abolish the natural or acquired superiority of individuals in order to place everyone on an absolute and equal footing in the face of luck's blind verdict.

As the result of *agôn* is necessarily uncertain and must, paradoxically, relate to the effect of pure chance, given the fact that the contestants' chances are, in principle, as even as possible, it then follows that any encounter that possesses the characteristics of an ideally regulated competition can be the object of betting, in other words of *aleas*: to wit, horse races, or greyhound races, football or Basque pelota matches, cock-fights. It even happens that the stakes vary constantly during the game, according to the ups and downs of *agôn*.[4]

Agôn and *alea* represent contrasting attitudes, and in some way, symmetrical ones, but they both conform to the same law: the artificial establishment of conditions of absolute equality among the players, which reality denies mankind. For nothing in life is clear unless it is precisely that everything in it, luck as well as merit, is always disorder in the beginning. Play, *agôn* or *alea,* is therefore an attempt to substitute perfect situations for the normal confusion of everyday life. These perfect situations are such that the role of merit or of luck appears clear and unequivocal. They also imply that everyone must enjoy exactly the same possibilities to prove his worth, or, on the other scale, the exact same chance to win. In one way or another one escapes from the world by making *it* other. One can also escape from it by making *one-self* other. This is what we call mimicry.

Mimicry

Every game presupposes the temporary acceptance, if not of an illusion (although this last word means nothing more than entry into play, *inlusio*), at least of a closed, conventional, and, in certain respects, fictitious universe. The play can consist not in the unfolding of an activity or in experiencing one's fate in an imaginary setting, but in becoming an illusory person oneself and in behaving accordingly. One then finds oneself confronted by a diversified series of manifestations whose common characteristic is that they rest on the fact that the subject plays at believing, at pretending to himself, or at making others believe that he is someone other than he is; he temporarily forgets, disguises, strips his own personality in order to be another. I choose to designate these manifestations by the term *mimicry* (which, in English, is the word for the mimetism of insects), in order to emphasize the primitive, elementary and quasi-instinctive nature of the impulse which produces them. They include, first of all, the behavior of a child who pretends he is an airplane (and acts like one by stretching out his arms and imitating the roar of a motor), who plays soldier, pretends he is a musketeer or a gangster, etc. They also embrace any diversion that requires a mask or a costume and consists in the very fact that the player is disguised and in the consequence of this. Finally, it is clear that theatrical representations and dramatic interpretations rightfully belong to this group.

The pleasure resides in being someone else or in making others think you are someone else. But as this is play we are discussing, it does not essentially involve fooling the spectator. A child who pretends to be a train will readily refuse his father's kiss, saying that one shouldn't kiss a locomotive. He does not attempt to make his father believe that he is a real locomotive. At a carnival, a masked person does not try to convince others that he is a real marquis, or a real toreador, or a real Indian, any more than an actor tries to make people believe that he "really" is Lear or Charles V.

The spy or the fugitive, however, disguises himself to really fool people because he is not playing a game.

Activity, imagination, interpretation, *mimicry* can scarcely have a relation to *alea,* which imposes upon the player the immobility and the chill of mute expectancy. *Agôn,* however, is not necessarily excluded. At the very moment when an actor plays a part, he tries, more indistinctly but also more profoundly, to be a better actor than the others, or to interpret a role that was created before him better than the others have done. He knows that he is subject to the public's judgment and to criticism. He plays, in the sense that he represents such or such a hero, but he also plays because he expects a prize in a prolix but unceasing competition with living or dead rivals.

Mimicry contains most of the characteristics of play: freedom convention, suspension of the real, circumscribed time and space. But continuous submission to precise and imperious regulations is less obvious here than elsewhere. I know of course that on the stage the actor must adhere to his lines, but one can hardly compare this servitude to the observance of fixed regulations which define the structure of a game. In the latter, it is a matter of a *framework* always necessarily identical with itself; and in the former, a matter of a *content* which may vary in each case, which is not a limitation but rather the substance, the very being of the character to be invoked. The frame work is, in truth, nothing more than the text.

Rules are inseparable from play as soon as it acquires what I shall call an institutional existence. From that moment on, they become a part of its nature, transforming play into a fertile and decisive instrument of culture. But it remains true that a primary freedom, which is the need for relaxation and the whole field of diversion and fantasy, resides at the source of play. This freedom is the indispensable prime mover of play, and remains at the origin of its most complex and rigidly organized forms. Such primary power of improvisation and gaiety, which I call *paidia,* is fused with the taste for gratuitous difficulty, which I propose to call *ludus,* in order to bring about the different games to which, without exaggeration, a civilizing property can be attributed. They illustrate, in fact, the moral and intellectual values of a culture. Moreover, they help to fix and define them.

I chose the term *paidia* because its roots signify the word "child" and because I do not wish to disconcert the reader needlessly by using a term borrowed from an antipodal language. But the Sanskrit word *krēdati* and the Chinese word *wan,* as far as I can judge by the indications that Huizinga provided and reproduced, seem to me both richer and clearer. *Krēdati* denotes the play of adults, of children, and of animals. It applies more specifically to gambols, that is to say, to sudden and capricious movements which a super-abundance of gaiety or vitality engenders. It is also used to signify erotic, illicit relations, the ebb and flow of waves, and all things that undulate to the caprice of the wind. The word *wan* is even more explicit, as much in regard to what it defines as to what it does not: it means essentially childish play, but also all the varieties of carefree and frivolous diversion which, for example, the verbs to frolic, to frisk, to jest,[5] to trifle, etc., evoke. Besides, and this is more revealing, it also means to examine, to manipulate, to fashion into trinkets, which connects it with the modern category of *hobbies,* in other words, the collector's mania. It evokes, as well, the peaceful and soothing soft-ness of moonlight.[6] Finally, *it is not used* to denote either competition, games of skill, dice games, or dramatic interpretation; in other words, it excludes equally all three categories of institutional games: *agôn, alea,* and *mimicry.*

In the light of these relationships and of these semantic exclusions, what can be the scope and the significance of the term *paidia?* I, for one, would define it as the word that encompasses the spontaneous manifestations of the instinct of play: the cat entangled in a ball of yarn, the dog licking himself, the infant laughing at his rattle—all these represent the first identifiable examples of this kind of activity. It occurs in all joyous exuberance, the kind that is expressed by an immediate and dis-ordered agitation, by an impulsive, relaxing, and deliberately immoderate pastime, whose im-promptu and unruly character remains its essential, if not its sole *raison d'être.* We do not lack per-fectly clear illustrations of this kind of sudden movement, of color, or of noise, from pencil marks to daubing with paint, from squabbling to uproar.

Such manifestations generally have no label and cannot have one, precisely because they remain within the bounds of stability of every distinctive

sign, of every clearly differentiated existence which would enable our vocabulary to sanction its autonomy by a specific appellation. Besides, soon the conventions, the techniques, the tools appear, and with them the first games: leap-frog, hide and seek, the hoop, blind man's bluff, dolls. Here the contradictory paths of *agôn, alea,* and *mimicry* branch off. The pleasure one feels in resolving a difficulty occurs here too; we are speaking of the complication that is deliberately created, arbitrar-ily defined, so that the fact that one has finally seen it through brings no advantage other than the inner satisfaction of having solved it. This mainspring which is clearly *ludus* also can be observed in the different categories of games, with the exception of those that depend entirely upon a decision of fate. It appears as both complement of an instruc-tion for *paidia,* which it disciplines and enriches. It provides the opportunity for training and nor-mally results in the conquest of a determined skill in the acquisition of a particular mastery, in the management of such or such an apparatus, or in the capacity to find a satisfactory answer to prob-lems of a strictly conventional order. It differs from *agôn* in that the player's tension and his talent function without any sense of competition or rival-ry: he struggles against the obstacle and not against one or several contestants. Games like *bilboquet* (cup and ball), *diabolo* and yo-yo can be classi-fied as manual skills. These simple instruments readily make use of natural, elementary laws; for example, in regard to the yo-yo, weight and rota-tion are involved and the skill consists in convert-ing alternate, rectilinear movements into a continuous circular one. Inversely, the hoop rests on the exploitation of a concrete atmospheric con-dition. One can easily see that the possibilities of play are almost infinite. Games like solitaire or *baguenaude* (ring puzzle) belong to another category of games: they make a constant appeal to the turn for computation and combination. Fi-nally, crossword puzzles, mathematical pastimers, anagrams, logographic verse of all sorts, the kind of active detective-story reading that is an attempt to discover the guilty party, chess or bridge problems—all these, devoid of instruments, constitute so many variations of the most widespread and the purest form of *ludus*.

One also observes a situation that in the beginning has a tendency to repeat itself infinitely, but on the basis of which new combinations can develop. They inspire the player to compete with himself and enable him to observe the stages of his progress on which he prides himself vis-à-vis those who share his taste. The relationship of *ludus* with *agôn* is evidenced in this way. Moreover, it is possible that, in the case of chess or bridge problems, the same game may appear sometimes as *agôn* and sometimes as *ludus*.

The combination of *ludus* and *alea* occurs just as frequently; it is particularly evident in games which one plays alone and where the ingenuity of the maneuvers influence the result to some extent, and in which the player can, to a slight degree, calculate how much impetus to give to the ball that marks the points and attempt to direct it. Nonetheless, in both these examples, it is mainly luck that determines the outcome. However, the fact that the player is not entirely helpless and that he knows he must rely on his skill or talent, even though this counts for very little, is enough to combine the character of *ludus* with that of *alea*.

Here, too, the player is competing with himself in a way, because he expects the next effort to succeed where the last failed, or he hopes to accumulate a higher number of points than his last score yielded. It is in this way that the influence of *agôn* is manifest, coloring, in fact, the general atmosphere of *ludus*. And even though both these games are played alone and, in principle, do not call for competition, it is quite simple to start a match at any time, with or without a prize, the kind, for example, that newspapers occasionally organize. Nor is it pure accident that slot machines are to be found in cafés—places where it is the custom for people to gather in groups, thus forming the embryo of a public.

There is one characteristic of *ludus* which, in my opinion, can be explained by the presence of *agôn,* and which is a constant burden: the fact that it depends largely upon fads of the moment. The yo-yo, the *bilboquet,* the *diabolo,* the *baguenaude,*

came into being and then disappeared as if by magic. They took advantage of a certain passing fad that was to disappear without a trace and that was quickly replaced by another. Although somewhat more stable, the fad for intellectual pastimes is nonetheless a transitory one: riddles, anagrams, acrostics, charades—all these have had their hour. It is quite probable that crossword puzzles and mystery stories will suffer the same fate. Such a phenomenon would be enigmatic if *ludus* represented as individualistic a pastime as it appears to; in reality, it is steeped in an atmosphere of competition. It can subsist only to the extent that it enjoys public favor, which transforms it into a virtual *agôn.* Lacking this, it is powerless to survive. In truth, it is not sufficiently supported by an organized spirit of competition, which is not essential to its practice, and neither does it provide material for any kind of spectacle capable of attracting the attention of a crowd. It remains uncertain and diffuse. It provides *paidia* with perpetually renewed forms. It invents a thousand opportunities and a thousand structures in which are to be found man's desire to relax and mainly his need, of which he apparently cannot be quit, to utilize the science and concentration, the skill and intelligence he possesses in the cause of pure uselessness.

In this sense, it represents that element in play whose cultural importance and fertility seem to be the most striking. It does not express as decided a psychological attitude as *agôn, alea,* or *mimicry,* but in disciplining *paidia,* it works behind the scenes to give to the three fundamental categories their purity and their excellence.

There remains a last species of games which does not seem to belong to those already mentioned and which can be considered the only truly modern innovation in this domain; games which are based upon the pursuit of *vertigo.*

Without question, people have for a long time deliberately sought out the confusion that a slight giddiness provokes, for example, the activities of the whirling dervishes and the Mexican voladores (flying fish). Nor must we overlook, in the realm of the most anodymic play, the merry-go-round and the ancient swing. Every child knows well, how, in turning rapidly around and around, he is able to attain a centrifugal state of flight, and wild prankishness in which his body has difficulty regaining its place and perception its clarity. Unquestionably he does it for fun and delights in it.

I suggest the term *ilinx* to include these different manifestations. It is Greek for whirlpool, from which is derived, precisely, and in the same language, the word *vertigo* (lingos). This designation also includes the *vertigo* to be found in certain animals, particularly in sheep, many of the effects of intoxication, some dances like the waltz, and finally, the giddiness induced by high speed, the kind one experiences on skis, in a motorcycle, or in an open car. Powerful machines are necessary to give these sensations the kind of intensity and brutality that can cause giddiness in adults. It is therefore not astonishing that we had to await the industrial age to see *vertigo* really become a category of play. Actually, it is dispensed to an avid multitude by a thousand implacable machines set up in the market places and in the amusement parks. Here, small wagons run on rails whose outline forms an almost perfect semi-circle, so that the vehicle, before it uprights itself, seems about to fall into space and the passengers, tied to their seats, feel as if they are falling with it. Elsewhere, other enthusiasts are locked in a series of cage-like seats which balance them and keep them upside down at a certain height above the crowd. In a third kind of machine, the sudden release of a giant spring catapults a car, which slowly returns to take up its position in front of the mechanism that will catapult it once again. Everything is calculated to incite visceral sensations of terror and of psychological panic: speed, fall, shocks, accelerated gyration combined with alternating climbs and descents. A final invention makes use of centrifugal force. This force is applied to the wall of a gigantic cylinder of unsupported bodies, immobilized in all kinds of postures, paralyzed, while the floor slips away and descends a few inches. The bodies remain ''stuck together like flies,'' as the establishment's publicity reads.

These machines would obviously have exceeded their purpose if it were merely a question of ex-

acerbating the organs of the middle ear upon which one's sense of balance rests. But the entire body is subjected to the kind of treatment that anyone would fear if he didn't see others falling all over each other in similar fashion. Indeed, it is worth our while to observe people as they leave these machines. They are pale, they stagger, they are on the verge of nausea. They have been shrieking with fear, they have been breathless, and they have had the terrible sensation that all their insides, their very vitals, were afraid, were curling up in an attempt to escape from some horrible attack. Yet, even before they have calmed down, most of them rush off to another ticket-window to purchase the right to suffer once again the same torture from which they expect enjoyment.

I say enjoyment because I hesitate to call such rapture inversion; it is far more akin to a spasm than to a pastime. Thus pleasure and the quest for vertigo exist when the latter is the object of *play,* when, in other words, it occurs under precise and fixed circumstances, isolated from the rest of reality, and when one is free either to accept or refuse it.

It seems legitimate, therefore, to inscribe the term *ilinx* next to *agôn, alea,* and *mimicry,* in order to complete the picture of the motives of play. The penchant for vertigo must be added to those that are expressed, first, by an ambition to succeed solely through the meritorious agency of fair competition; second, by a resignation of the will in exchange for an anxious and passive awaiting of the decree of fate; and third, by the illusion of being cloaked in another's personality. In *agôn,* the player relies only on himself and he bends all his efforts to do his best; in *alea,* he relies on everything except himself and he surrenders to forces that elude him; in *mimicry* he imagines that he is other than he really is and invents a fictitious universe; *ilinx,* the fourth fundamental tendency, is an answer to one's need to feel the body's stability and equilibrium momentarily destroyed, to escape the tyranny of perception, and to overcome awareness.

The variety and fertility of the games that tend to satisfy these cardinal temptations attest to their

Table 1

	AGÔN (COMPETITION)		ALEA (CHANCE)	MIMICRY (PRETENSE)	ILINX (VERTIGO)

PAIDIA
 	
noise
agitation
laughter
dance
hoop
solitaire
games of
  patience
crossword
  puzzles
 	
LUDUS
	races
	combats
	etc.
	athletics
		not regulated	*comptines*
			heads or tails
				childish imi-
				tation
				masks
				costumes
					children's
					swings
					merry-go-round
					teeter-totter
					waltz

	boxing
	fencing
	football
	checkers
	chess
			betting
			roulette
			
			lotteries
			  compounded
			  or parlayed
				theatre	outdoor sports
					skiing
					mountain-
					  climbing

Note: In each vertical column, the games are classified very approximately in such order that the *paidia* element constantly decreases, while the *ludus* element constantly increases.

importance and to their permanence. It is certainly not rash to suggest that psychology, along with sociology, will derive useful additions and instructive lessons from a study of games.

Notes

1. *Homo Ludens,* London: Routledge & Kegan Paul, 1949, p. 13.
2. *Ibid.,* p. 28.
3. As for space: the hopscotch diagram, the checker-board, the chess board, the stadium, the playing field, the track, the ring, the dueling ground, the stage, the arena, etc. . . . As for time: the beginning and the end of a game, the complications of a pos-

sible prolongation, the kind of disgrace entailed by a default, which the fact of calling "I give up," represents or by any withdrawal during the course of a game or of a match, unless it is caused by a physical accident.
4. For example, in the Balearic Islands at a game of pelota, or in Colombia and the Antilles, at cock-fights.
5. It goes without saying that this last need is to be understood in its actual sense, because the baguenaude is really an assemblage of things, the manipulation of which is complicated and demands the player's extreme concentration and which, therefore, belongs to the category of *ludus.*
6. Information which Duyvendak communicated to Huizinga, of *Homo Ludens,* p. 32.

Words on Play

BERNARD SUITS

I propose to advance and defend a tentative definition of play. This may not strike all of you as a
terribly exciting prospect. For I am well aware that
there are topics the very contemplation of which
induces in some people definite—and sometimes
violent—rejective reactions. There are those, for
example, who display acute anxiety whenever they
are obliged to understand something in abstract
symbols. Others are overcome by a kind of profound melancholy when invited to consider a new
proof for the existence of God. But some of the
most extreme reactions come from those who are
incurably opposed to the construction of
definitions—persons I think of as terminal Wittgensteinians. For when a terminal Wittgensteinian
realizes that you are seriously trying to define
something, he exhibits anxiety *and* melancholy,
and then he calls you bad names.

Why do I want to define play? Because it's there?
Partly, no doubt. But chiefly because a definition
is a kind of restriction or limitation, and I believe
that, ever since Huizinga began to find play under
nearly every rock in the social landscape, quite
a bit too much has been made of the notion. I suspect, indeed, that there is somewhat less to the entire subject than meets the eye—or at least than
has met the eye of many a practicing *paidia*trician.
For there is little now that someone or other has
not called play, from a cat chasing its tail to
Aristotle contemplating the Unmoved Mover.

Now, at least to the uninitiated, the word "play"
seems too small and fragile a vessel to contain such
a volume of meaning without spilling over or
bursting apart. What does a cat chasing its tail have
in common with Aristotle contemplating God?
Well, more than one might think, it turns out. Both
the cat and Aristotle are engaged in autotelic
activities—that is, activities which are ends in
themselves. For Aristotle attending to his God and
the cat attending to his tail would give the same
answer to the following question:

"What is chasing your tail good for?"

"It isn't good for anything," the cat would reply. "It's good in itself."

"What is contemplating God good for?"

"It isn't good for anything," Aristotle would
reply (and in fact did reply). "It's good in itself."

And so if one defines play as any autotelic activity whatever, the cat chasing his tail and Aristotle contemplating God are both playing.

But I am far from convinced that play *is* the
same as *any* autotelic activity whatever. For notice
that two steps are required in order to arrive at
that conclusion. The first step is to acknowledge
that Aristotle contemplating God and a cat chasing his tail are both engaged in autotelic activities. I accept that as a perfectly legitimate step.
But the second is not. For the second step consists
in assigning the word "play" to both of these activities. What is the justification for that assignment? Let us pause for a moment and ask how the
word "play" got into the discussion in the first
place. Is it not because a cat chasing his tail is already called "play"?

"Is the cat playing?" we inquire.

Reprinted from *Journal of the Philosophy of Sport,* IV, (1977),
pp. 117–131. Copyright 1977 by the Philosophic Society for
the Study of Sport. Reprinted by permission.

"No," is the reply. "He's ripping out the postman's throat."

"Oh," we say, and then presently:

"Is the cat playing *now?*"

"Yes," is the reply. "He's chasing his tail."

"Ah," we say.

But now notice that a human contemplating God also is already called something. It is called a religious experience. We can, then, with precisely the same justification we had for calling Aristotle's contemplation of God "play," now call the cat's chasing his tail a religious experience. Please don't respond that for all we know a cat's chasing his tail *is* a religious experience—for a cat. I'm entirely willing to grant that it may be. You never really know with cats. But even if a cat's chasing his tail *is* a religious experience, surely we cannot establish that fact by the method that is proposed for establishing the fact that the contemplation of God is play. For all we agree that Aristotle and the cat have in common is that they are performing autotelic activities. We have certainly not agreed that all autotelic activities are religious experiences. And in precisely the same way, we should not agree that both Aristotle and the cat are *playing* unless we can first establish the fact that all autotelic activity is play.

Or are we really concerned with facts here? Perhaps we are not. Perhaps it's just a case of *calling* all autotelic activities play, as when a writer on the subject explains himself in the following way: "By the word 'play' I shall mean to signify any autotelic activity whatever, even though that activity is not normally called 'play'." In other words, perhaps what is wanted is the Humpty-Dumpty approach to the problem. You remember the exchange between Humpty and Alice in *Through the Looking Glass:* Humpty-Dumpty has just concluded his argument that in a year's time one can receive 364 *un*birthday presents to only one birthday present and, commenting on this remarkable conclusion he exclaims: "There's glory for you!"

"I don't know what you mean by 'glory,' " said Alice.

"Of course you don't," said Humpty, "till I tell you. I meant 'there's a nice knockdown argument for you.' "

"But," Alice objected, " 'glory' doesn't mean 'a nice knockdown argument.' "

"When *I* use a word," Humpty-Dumpty said in rather a scornful tone, "it means just what I choose it to mean neither more nor less."

"The question *is*," said Alice, "whether you can *make* words means so many different things."

"The question *is*," said Humpty-Dumpty, "which is to be master—that's all.".

Rational discourse can tolerate a certain amount of Humpty-Dumptyism. It is, for example, intellectually permissible to stipulate a usage for the sake of expository simplicity. Humpty-Dumptyism becomes intolerable only when it is forgotten that a stipulation one has made is not a statement of fact. But because the memories of stipulators are no better (and often worse) than the memories of other people, such forgetfulness sometimes happens, and sometimes very quickly indeed, as in the following fabled exchange between Abraham Lincoln and a heckler.

Lincoln. Tell me sir, how many legs does a horse have?

Heckler. Four.

Lincoln. Right. But suppose we call a horse's tail a leg. Now how many legs does a horse have.

Heckler. Five.

Lincoln. Wrong. Calling a tail a leg does not make it one.

Furthermore, while stipulating that something is so seems to be a much more cautious move than does boldly asserting that something *is* so, that is not always the case. If I were to inform the Dean of my Faculty, for example, that I was willing to stipulate, but not to assert, that he was of sound mind, this would be an act not of caution but of foolhardiness. And so to stipulate that play is the same as any autotelic activity whatever could be incautious in two different ways. If that identification is factually *incorrect,* we have constantly to be on guard against the bad memory of the stipulator. And if the identification is factually *correct,* then it is misleading to call it a stipulation. Part of my purpose today is to try to provide enough words on play to persuade you that the identification of play with autotelic activity is at best a stipulation. That is, I shall deny the claim that if any x is an autotelic activity, then that x is *ipso facto* play.

However, I also want to affirm—at least for the sake of argument—that the converse of that proposition *is* true. That is, I shall assume that *all* instances of play *are* instances of autotelic activity. In other words, I regard autotelicity as necessary but not sufficient for an adequate definition of play. What we have at the outset of our quest, therefore, is a genus in search of a difference. That difference, I shall presently argue, has to do with *seriousness.* And the kind of seriousness at issue, I shall further argue, is best illuminated by the much quoted and much neglected observation of Schopenhauer that the play of animals consists in the discharge of superfluous energy.

But first, as a way of getting into the subject, let me say something about games—for the following three reasons: (1) I know more about games than I do about play. Or at least I believe that I do. (2) It has seemed intuitively obvious to many writers on the subject that games are a subspecies of play, and it will be instructive to see why that intuition is false. (3) We can begin to see what play is like, I believe, precisely by seeing how it is *un*like games.

Let me begin, then, with the apparently outrageous assertion that there is no logical relation whatever between playing and playing games. Why does this appear outrageous? Well, look at the words I myself have just used: *playing* and *playing* a game. Surely this indicates that playing a game is a *kind* of playing. But of course it indicates nothing of the kind. The word "play" is highly ambiguous. Still, without undertaking a long and tedious philological inquiry, I think we can non-contentiously separate out and eliminate from consideration several uses of the word "play" which would otherwise pointlessly com-plicate our search. I suggest that we ought not concern ourselves with the word "play" when it is used as equivalent in meaning to such words as "perform," "operate," or "participate in." Thus, we can play the violin, but this means simply to perform upon the violin. We can play a pinball machine, but this means simply to operate it. And, finally, we can play a game, but this means simply to participate in it. These uses, I suggest, are not uses which affect the present discussion, since it is clear that in each of these uses another expression can be substituted for the expression "play" without any loss of meaning. It may very well be that these uses of the word "play" are—or originally were—metaphorical, and there will be occasion a bit later on to say something about play and metaphor. But for now it is clear, I think, that the existence of the expression "playing a game" is not by itself a compelling reason for insisting that there is a logical relation between playing and playing games.

In contending that playing and playing games are logically independent, I mean that, even though game-playing very often *is* playing, one cannot conclude that *because* x is an instance of playing that x is therefore an instance of game playing, and also that one cannot conclude that *because* y is an instance of game playing that it is therefore an instance of playing. Such absence of logical entailment between play and games seems to receive at least *prima facie* support from the following examples taken from everyday life. "Johnny," says Johnny's mother, "stop playing with your mashed potatoes." It surely would be straining usage to conclude that Johnny is engaged in playing a *game* with his mashed potatoes. And Thomas Aquinas gives as an example of play a man idly stroking his beard. Again, this fact evidently does not permit us to infer that the man is playing a *game* with his beard. If Johnny and the beard stroker *were* playing games (and not simply playing), then presumably the following questions would be answerable: What are the goals of these games? What are the rules? What counts as winning? What counts as cheating?

That one has to be playing in order to be playing a game seems equally implausible. When professional athletes are performing in assigned games for wages, although they are certainly playing games, we are not at all inclined to conclude from that fact that they are without qualification playing. For we think of professional athletes as working when they play their games and as playing when they go home from work to romp with their children.

Some very common usage, then, seems to treat play and games as independently identifiable kinds of behaviour. What follows are my reasons for concluding that this usage is entirely correct. I suggest that when the word "play" is used to designate the kind of thing Johnny does with his mashed potatoes when he is not getting down to the serious business of eating them, what is being designated is the kind of thing that is inherently relative to something else, but that "game," when it is used to refer to such things as chess and baseball, is not. In this respect, the word "play" is like the word "light" when it is used to refer to the shade of a colour, and "game" is like the word "blue," the name of a colour. There is the same kind of logical independence, I suggest, between "play" and "game" that there is between "light" and "blue." Thus, although it is the case that some blues are light and also (therefore) that some light coloured things are blue, it clearly does not follow that the lightness of a colour can be inferred from its blueness, nor its blue-ness from its lightness. And just as lightness inherently has an opposite, darkness, so play has an inherent opposite—seriousness, or perhaps a certain kind of seriousness. But neither *blue* nor *game* is the kind of thing that has an opposite. What is the opposite of blue? Green? Red? What is the opposite of chess? Handball? Poker?

Thus, in saying that Johnny is playing *with* his supper, and that the beard stroker is playing *with* his beard, we are implying that these objects normally have, or are involved in, purposes that are foreign to, and perhaps on occasion inconsistent with, the purposes to which Johnny and the beard stroker are putting them. When we use the word "light" of a colour there is a tacit "instead of dark" in our meaning, and, similarly, in the expression "playing *with*" there is a tacit "instead of treating it seriously" in our meaning. So I feel justified in entertaining the following hypothesis about play: playing always means playing *with* some x or other, although this prepositional addition is not always, and perhaps not even usually, expressed. We thus say simply that Johnny is playing. But if, I suggest, we want to *test* an assertion that Johnny is playing, then we must be able to come up with some x that Johnny is playing *with:* beards, mashed potatoes, whatever.

I think that this is an illuminating hypothesis. It also appears to be a false hypothesis. It is not false, as a matter of fact, but it does appear to be. For, returning to Johnny, we see that he has, at long last, ingested the last of his mashed potatoes and has gone outside to play. Well, now, what do we mean when we say that he has gone outside to play? We certainly do not appear to mean that he is playing *with* anything in particular, nor even that he is *doing* anything in particular. We mean, very likely, that he is doing one or another of a number of certain things, but that he is not doing one or another of a number of other things. He is playing ball, or rolling in the grass, or pulling the wings off flies, or just hollering out of sheer exuberance. But he is *not* doing his homework or weeding the garden or writing a letter to the *Times*. Johnny does not appear to be playing *with* anything at all—well, maybe the fly, but for the most part he is simply playing.

Perhaps it is this kind of consideration that has made plausible the view that play is the same as any autotelic activity whatever. For it seems that the *only* feature common to all of the things Johnny may be doing when he is at play is that they are all things he does because he wants to do them in themselves rather than because he must do them for some further purpose. From this point of view listening to a Beethoven quartet is as much play as is playing baseball or hollering in an exuberance of spirits, or stroking your beard. In fact, the efforts of Kant, Schiller, and Santayana, for example, are directed to showing that aesthetic enjoyment is not only play, but the highest and best kind of play.

Still, I am disturbed by the fact that it is almost exclusively *philosophers* who want to call listening to Beethoven play, and also by the fact that these philosophers are really much more interested in aesthetics than they are in play. And so I still suspect that there *is* something common to Johnny's prandial and post-prandial playing, in addition to the fact that both kinds of play are autotelic activities, and that this additional element is a reference to something that is being played *with*. Schopenhauer can help us try to discover what this played-*with* thing is, I believe, if we take a close look at his observation that the play of animals consists in the discharge of superfluous energy.

This observation has usually been treated by others interested in play as a mere physiological comment. But even if that was all Schopenhauer intended by the remark, its implications go far beyond physiology. They point, I think, to the basic logic of the idea of play. We shall see that the word "superfluous" does not tell the whole story, but it does imply precisely what is at issue if *play* is the kind of relative term that I have suggested is the case. For the superfluous, or the more-than-enough, necessarily refers to the *enough*; its meaning is inherently related to another term. Now, what did Schopenhauer mean by superfluous energy? Superfluous for what? Presumably for surviving, or perhaps for surviving at an acceptable level of safety and comfort. Broadly speaking, then, play here appears to be contrasted with work, or, in general, with the performance of primarily instrumental activities. Play, accordingly, must be the expenditure of energy in actions which are not instrumental, for if some supposed surplus energy were used for the performance of instrumental activities it would not really be surplus. There is, however, a difficulty. When Schopenhauer and others talk about animals in this way they attribute to them an instinctive rationality, in very much the way that theoretical economists postulate economically rational decision makers in the operation of markets. Thus, it is *not* supposed that animals continue to pursue food, shelter, and safe-

ty beyond the point at which such pursuit continues to provide a pay-off. And animals are in this respect sometimes compared favourably with humans, who are often thought of as not knowing when to stop in their pursuit of instrumental goods, most notably, money and power. In the kind of philosophical zoology practiced by thinkers like Rousseau, for example, it is civilized men but not animals or noble savages who become hoarders, gluttons, and cowards.

Why do I raise this point? Because it suggests that although animals are instinctively capable of distinguishing the enough from the more-than-enough, human beings often are not. But if that is so, then the proposal that play involves the expenditure of surplus energy, while it may tell us something about the play of animals, can tell us nothing —or at least nothing very reliable—about the play of humans. For suppose we know that Smith is secure enough financially to take a much needed vacation from his thriving business. Smith, however, erroneously believes himself *not* to be sufficiently secure, and so continues working. He is now in fact expending surplus energy, and so if Schopenhauer's view is correct, he must be playing. But he isn't playing; he's working harder than ever.

But let us not dismiss Schopenhauer's thesis on that account. Let us just add the proviso that for human beings the energy at issue must not only *be* superfluous, but that it must also be *believed* to be superfluous. Still, if this addition takes care of one difficulty, it appears to raise another. For it simply is not the case that humans play *only* when they have, or believe that they have, energy left over from their instrumental pursuits. To the contrary, unlike the highly rational animals that inhabit the forests of philosophers, humans are well known for letting play *interfere* with their productive enterprises. But in such cases play is not the discharge of surplus energy; it is the usurpation of scarce energy. It is just this kind of practice that killed the legendary grasshopper.

Is Schopenhauer's observation, then, completely irrelevant to human play? Not at all. He was perfectly correct as far as he went; it is just that he did not go far enough, and he did not generalize sufficiently from his original insight. He did not go far enough because he thought that play had to do only with superfluity. In fact, it is concerned just as much with scarcity. For we now see that the energy expended in play must be either over and above the store needed for instrumental pursuits (Schopenhauer's view), *or else* that it must steal from that store. And this confirms, if it is true, the hypothesis that play must be understood by reference to something else—on the Schopenhauerean view, to a store or quantity of energy whose initial commitment is to activities which are not play.

With one further modification of Schopenhauer's principle we shall have laid the ground for a definition of play. The word "energy" in Schopenhauer's formulation is, I suggest, unduly narrow. I think it is both necessary and permissible to substitute for that word the word "resource." If we are concerned only with animals, then "energy" will do, more or less, since that is the only resource—or at least the most obvious resource—that animals have. But, if we are seeking a definition that will include human as well as animal play, we will want to include resources additional to human energy—mashed potatoes, for example, and beards.

What emerges from our expansion of Schopenhauer's observation about play is that play is concerned with a use of resources for which those resources were not initially intended, where the original allocation was for instrumental activities and the new allocation is for autotelic activities. This may all be summed up in the following statement, which I now offer as a definition of play:

x is playing if and only if x has made a temporary reallocation to autotelic activities of resources primarily committed to instrumental purposes.

Food, for example, is a resource which is primarily committed to the purpose of bodily nourishment; that is its first priority. But food can also be used as a resource for a quite different kind of purpose, as when one makes hills, valleys, and rivers out of mashed potatoes and gravy. And when, as in this case, the activity to which an instrumental resource is diverted is regarded as an end in itself, we say that it is play. Primarily instrumental resources can, of course, also be rechanneled into other instrumental, rather than into autotelic, activities. Thus, mashed potatoes, in an emergency, can be used to stop up a crack in the wall against the winter winds, but this is not a case of playing with food because the diversion is from one instrumental use to another instrumental use. However, it should be noted that sometimes such diversion (instrumental to instrumental) *is* referred to as "playing." Smith, for example, observes that Jones is lying to Robinson, and Smith takes Jones to task with the following comment: "Jones, what are you playing at?" This, it seems clear, is a figurative use of the word "playing," and its force is that it captures *one* aspect of play, namely, that there has been a diversion of an instrumental resource to some other purpose. But the use is figurative rather than literal just because it does not capture all aspects of play; in this instance, it does not capture the fact that the diversion must be into an autotelic activity. For when Jones lies to Robinson he is diverting the resource of verbal utterance from one instrumental use—communication—to another instrumental use—deception. Such metaphorical use of "play" and "game" is, of course, very common, and it very often can be a serious impediment to analysis, as in Eric Berne's systematically misleading use of the word "game" in his book *Games People Play*. On the other hand *awareness* that such uses are figurative can be of great help in analysis, since an explanation of *how* they are figurative requires a sorting out of the respects in which the thing at issue is, and the respects in which it is not, play or a game.

But this is something of a digression from our main concern, and it is time to return to a question we earlier left unanswered. Granted that Johnny's trifling with his mashed potatoes can be called play because it involves that reallocation of resources which the definition requires, what about the case where Johnny is simply outside playing, but where he is not, at least obviously, playing with any object at all. (And here I must interrupt myself to insert a parenthetical caution. If Johnny is, for example, playing baseball, we must not say that he is *playing* just by virtue of the fact that he is playing *with* his baseball. That *with* is a different kind of *with* than the *with* that is required by the definition. For playing the game of baseball *with* a baseball is not a diversion or reallocation of the ball to a secondary use: playing baseball with the ball is the ball's primary use. In order to illustrate the kind of thing I mean by playing *with,* Johnny would have to be using the ball for some purpose other than baseball, and this other purpose would have to consist in some activity that Johnny would find intrinsically worthwhile, like seeing how much of the ball he could shove up his nose.) End of parenthetical caution and back to Johnny after supper, outside, playing, but where he is not toying with mashed potatoes, or fondling bears, or putting baseballs to unorthodox uses. He is, as a matter of fact, gamboling about on the greensward. And so our question remains. If Johnny is indeed playing, what on earth is he playing *with*?

The answer, you will no doubt be relieved to hear, is not very hard to find. Beards, mashed potatoes, and baseballs are not the only kinds of things that can be played with. *Any* resource, remember, which has or can be given a primarily instrumental allocation will meet our requirement. Well, there is one resource that is always required for every pursuit. This universal resource is time. *Whatever* it is we wish to do, we are always in need of enough time in which to do it. And in the non-Utopian condition of man that has always existed—and thus in the social context that has produced all of our linguistic usages—the first priority in the allocation of time has been to instrumental activities, basically to the maintenance and betterment of the conditions of existence. But when there has been more than enough time for those pursuits, time has been temporarily allocated

to intrinsically valued pursuits, such as gamboling on the greensward. Johnny, therefore, is seen to be playing both during and after supper in the same sense of playing. For in both cases he has allocated instrumental resources to intrinsically valued activities. It is just that the allocation of one resource—the mashed potatoes—is prohibited (or at least frowned upon), because of a scarcity, while the other resource—the time after supper—is permitted because of a surplus. It is perhaps unnecessary to point out that it is not always things like mashed potatoes which are in short supply and time which is abundant. Johnny may, on another occasion, point out to his mother that there is a good deal of mashed potatoes left over at the conclusion of supper, and she may permit him to play with this surplus. On the other hand, time better spent in study is sometimes frittered away in idle pastimes: "Get down to work, young man. Playtime comes *after* school."

There are, therefore, conditions under which it is proper to call various kinds of aesthetic enjoyment play; not, however, merely because they are intrinsically valued pursuits, but because of the conditions under which such intrinsically valued activities are pursued. The conditions must be such that the time used for such pursuits is viewed in contrast to a situation in which that time *ought* to be used for an activity which has a higher claim upon it.

Consider Nero's alleged fiddling while Rome burned. We know, of course, that we should not say that Nero was playing on the ground simply that he was playing the fiddle, because that means merely that he was performing upon the fiddle. But we certainly may say that he was playing by fiddling *around* while Rome burned, for we mean that he was trifling with his time instead of allocating it to the implementation of important executive actions which the situation clearly required. And so we non-metaphorically say that Nero played while Rome burned, and we say it disapprovingly, for we regard this as a misallocation of time. But now consider Nero under more normal conditions. Having put in a full and productive day administering the laws and policies of the empire, he withdraws to the music room to play upon the lyre. We may in this case, too, say that he is playing, because we are viewing his aesthetic enjoyment in contrast to the claims which more important activities make upon his time. But on this occasion there is no disapproving tone when we utter the word "playing," because Nero has met the more important claims upon his time and thus has a surplus which he may legitimately use for his own amusement. Still, we call this use of his time play *only* because we view it in contrast to a more important use of time which tacitly or in principle—continues to assert its claim. Thus, if a new crisis arose—say an unexpected fall in the number of available Christians for the coliseum—the prior claims against his time would be reasserted, and would be transformed from claims in principle to claims in fact.

I thus suggest that those philosophers who have claimed that things like aesthetic and religious experiences are instances of play are partly right and partly wrong. Such things are play not just because they are intrinsically valued activities (and in this respect they are wrong), but from the perspective of scarce time they *are* play, for to reallocate time from an instrumental to an intrinsic use is to play with time. But from the perspective of unlimited time—as in Utopia—listening to Beethoven and contemplating God are not play, for from this perspective there is no reallocation of time from an instrumental to an intrinsic use, since in Utopia time *has* no instrumental use. And so those philosophers who have supposed that Utopia, or the ideal of existence, must necessarily consist in play are quite wrong. Autotelic activities, yes; play, no. Whatever it is that a Utopian is doing, playing cannot be one of those things, for play must have an opposite, and in Utopia that opposite is eliminated by definition.

It follows from these considerations that one and the same activity—e.g., listening to Beethoven, contemplating God—can correctly be designated "play" by designator x at the same time that it is correctly designated "not play" by designator

y. How can this be? Well, it is of the nature of relative terms to behave in this fashion. Is this shade of blue correctly designated "light"? Yes, because it is surrounded by much darker blues. Is this same shade of blue now correctly designated "dark"? Yes, because now it is surrounded by much lighter blues. Very well, what are the relevant surroundings which must be present before we can correctly designate something as "play"? The answer lies in that part of our definition which refers to "resources primarily committed to instrumental purposes."

For whether any given resource is primarily committed to instrumental purposes or to other purposes is a matter not of necessity or obdurate fact, but of choice. Primitive man evidently chose to give first priority among his resources to pursuits which were instrumental for survival.

But, primitive man did not *have* to do that. He could have made a first priority commitment of his resources to autotelic activities. He could have allocated virtually all of his energy and time not to securing food, shelter, and safety, but to art and creative social relations, say cave painting and kinky sex. Admittedly, if primitive man had chosen that priority he would not have been around very long, and we would not be around at all.

However, the point I wish to make is not about our survival, but about our language. And in aid of making that point let me put to you the following question. If primitive man *had* devoted himself exclusively to the pursuit of autotelic activities —wantonly burning his candle at both ends and, like the fabled grasshopper, perishing in a single season—would he have been at all likely to call such activity "play"? And I submit that the answer to that question ought clearly to be in the negative. He would have had no more reason to call such activity play than we would have to call a robin's egg light blue if robin's eggs were the only blue objects in the universe.

This aspect of play, and indeed the whole burden of my argument, can be summed up and illustrated by a curious development in an even more curious tennis match that you may not have heard about. It was a mixed doubles event, and Team A was made up of Tommy More, a visitor to our world from Utopia, and Prudence Paidia, a highly gifted amateur. Tommy, we might note in passing, was neither a professional nor an amateur, since in Utopia the distinction between the two has no application. Team B consisted of Chrissie Rich, top women's professional, and the Grasshopper of ancient fable. All were playing for the fun of it except Chrissie, who would receive a prize of one hundred thousand dollars if her team won. (It's not that Chrissie is greedy, that's not the point. It's that she is a professional, and if my story is to make its point she must be made to behave like one.) All four were superb players—so superb, in fact, that the match never got beyond the first game. They arrived at deuce and stuck there. For a solid month. Then the officials called a time out, and asked the players whether they would like to stop playing and declare the match a stalemate. (Curiously, it did not occur to anyone to invent and introduce a game tie-breaker—but then these were tennis players, not organizational geniuses.) The suggestion that the match be terminated was put to each of the players in turn, and these were their responses:

Chrissie Rich: Let's continue, by all means. This is no temporary re-allocation of my time, but precisely the activity to which my time has a first priority commitment.

Tommy More: No, there's no reason for me to quit. Although I could, of course, be doing other things—playing bridge, listening to Beethoven, contemplating God—I enjoy playing tennis every bit as much as I enjoy doing those things—*more* than contemplating God, to be honest about it. So this is not a temporary reallocation of my time. It is just the kind of thing I do with all of my time.

The Grasshopper: I admit that if I were *not* the Grasshopper I would want to quit, since no ordinary person of limited financial resources can afford to remain unemployed as long as this match promises to last. But, just because I am the Grasshopper, my devil-may-care attitude about my future welfare makes irrelevant to me the concerns of ordinarily prudent people. All of my time is taken up with non-productive activities, even though the heavens fall, so this is no temporary reallocation of my time. In this respect, I am just like Tommy More, the Utopian, except that for him the heavens *won't* fall.

Prudence: I alone, then, my friends, will have to quit. I understand why each of you is willing to continue, but none of your reasons applies to me. I'm an assistant professor of physical education supporting a husband in graduate school and the term begins tomorrow. If I don't show up for work I'll be fired. This month has been a temporary reallocation of my time, and I must now return that resource to its primary allocation. Unlike the rest of you, I've been at play.

"How dreadful for you," said Tommy. "You ought to move to Utopia."

"I hope," replied Prudence, "that we are all moving in that direction, however slowly."

"Come, come, Prudence," put in the Grasshopper, "why not play on anyway. What do you care if you get fired?"

"I care," replied Prudence.

"Well," exclaimed Chrissie impatiently, "at least let's try to get a substitute. Isn't there anyone in the audience with a lot of time on his hands?"

"*I* have," came a voice from the grandstand in a somewhat smug tone.

"Who are you?" Chrissie demanded.

"A full professor of philosophy," was the no less smug response.

The substitution was quickly made. Two serves later Chrissie and the Grasshopper had won the first game.

Although I have used a game to illustrate what I conceive to be the basically contextual nature of play, it is clear, I hope, that precisely the same characteristic responses of our representative foursome would be evoked by a number of other activities as well—certain aesthetic and religious pursuits, for example. The only requirement is that the activity at issue be capable of being pursued as an end in itself. If, for example, the members of the foursome were required to decide whether to discontinue listening to Beethoven or contemplating God, they would make the same decisions they made about the tennis match, and for the same reasons. And thus, while I would not want to maintain that pushpin is, without qualification, as good as poetry, I do want to submit that poetry is as good a candidate to be play as pushpin, and that religious contemplation is as good a candidate as poetry.

Still, a nagging doubt remains. Perhaps, even though we may be willing to grant—or at least seriously to entertain—the possibility that a number of things are, and ought to be, called play by virtue of conforming to the definition that I have advanced, we may be quite unwilling to give the same assent to a number of other things which also conform to the definition. And I suspect that aesthetic appreciation and religious experience may rank very high in such a list of doubtful contenders. So let me try to remove such doubt or, failing that, at least to blunt its edge.

It should be remembered that I wish to maintain that aesthetic and religious experiences are suitable candidates for the denomination "play" only when they are, in fact, cases of autotelic behaviour. Thus, if a given instance of aesthetic appreciation or religious devotion is *really* (although perhaps scarcely consciously) valued because of its usefulness for some further purpose, then it is not *really* autotelic behaviour, and so it does not *really* qualify even as a candidate for the name "play." Now, I suggest that activities that are very highly valued—which aesthetic and religious pursuits are, by those who value them at all—are very nearly always valued at least in part because they are thought to be, in one way or another, good *for* us, and not solely because they are thought to be good in themselves. At the very least, aesthetic and religious activities are thought to *improve* us. Dedication to aesthetic pursuits can, for example, improve our social standing with the ladies and gentlemen of the Opera Society; and dedication to religious pursuits can improve our standing with God, or at least with our religious neighbors. Such mildly contemptible advantages as these, of

course, are not the only advantages thought to attach to these activities. Often such activities are valued just because they are thought of as making us better—by making us more complete—human beings. But whatever the improvement thought to result from these pursuits, it is still *improvement* that is at issue, and so the pursuit is still valued because of its instrumental, not its autotelic, character.

Now, I think it is very hard for us to think of such things as aesthetic appreciation and religious devotion as *purely* autotelic, for it is very hard for us to remove from our conception of these pursuits all trace and tinge of instrumentality, of some respect in which we hope that they will make us better, or at least better off; whereas, it is very easy to remove such undertones of betterment when we think of things like pushpin—or it would be if anyone knew what pushpin was. Still, I believe it *is* possible to think away the usefulness of aestheic and religious pursuits if we really put our minds to it. And, I suggest, that if we are successful in that attempt, we will be much less inclined—and perhaps not inclined at all—to deny that such pursuits ought *ever* to be called play.

I have constructed the following short classical drama as an aid to successful completion of that intellectual exercise. The place is Rome—that's what makes it a classical drama—and as the curtain rises we find that the Hun is at the gate and that the Roman legions are making a last ditch defense of civilization against the invading hordes. The stage setting focuses on a small part of this activity. Close inside the city wall, Sergeant Salvatorius is loudly exhorting his troops to make a firm stand, and all are heeding his shouted orders to man the battlements, to shore up the gates, to tip baskets of paving blocks on to the barbarians below, and so on. But now we see that not quite all are engaged in these pursuits. One very fat soldier is sitting upon a small stool a short distance from the center of activity. His eyes are unfocused and he seems quite oblivious of the frenzied goings on nearby. He is, as a matter of fact, contemplating God, which is what he customarily does with all of the time he can spare or steal from his military duties. Perhaps because of this propensity to spend so much of his time in a sitting position, he is known to his comrades as Gluteus Maximus. Sergeant Salvatorius, freed for a moment from the requirements of command, approaches Gluteus.

"Private Maximus," he says politely, for this is the *new* Roman army, "are you contemplating God again?"

Gluteus's eyes come back into focus and he looks up at his superior.

"Yes, Sergeant, I was."

"Well, Private, don't you think, things being the way they are, that putting out those fires over there or helping out with the boiling oil is more important just now than contemplating God?"

"Well, Sergeant," Gluteus responds, minimally shifting from his right maxima to his left, "it seems to me that contemplating God is pretty important."

"Suppose we test that assertion, Gluteus," says the sergeant, who studies philosophy at night school.

"How?" Gluteus asks.

"I think a few simple questions will do the job. First, what do you hope to accomplish by sitting there contemplating God?"

"Nothing whatever," replies Gluteus. "Contemplating God is not good for anything. It is good in itself."

"You're quite sure that you expect to accomplish nothing by your contemplating?"

"Quite sure, Sergeant."

"You aren't, for example, seeking God's assistance in saving civilization from the invaders?"

"Certainly not, Sergeant Salvatorius. The question is laughable." Gluteus's body begins to quiver unpleasantly here and there in silent mirth. "The God that I spend all of my time contemplating," he continues, "is not *that* kind of God. He does not bustle about in the world trying to fix up this and fix up that, as though He were some kind of overworked service man. He, like me, spends all of his time contemplating the only really perfect thing in the universe—Himself."

S. So your contemplating God will not help save Rome. But will it help save you? Are you trying to get into heaven, perhaps?

G. Certainly not. Even if there is a heaven, God has no interest in seeing me there. He is not interested in me at all. It is I who am interested in Him.

S. And your contemplating God is not for the purpose of earning his good opinion of you?

G. Obviously not.

S. Then perhaps you are spending your time in religious contemplation in order to secure the good opinion of your neighbors.

G. Hardly, my dear fellow. If I wanted that I'd go to the temples and make expensive sacrifices. Most of Rome regards me as more or less a hopeless imbecile.

S. Yes, well, I can see you're no slave to public opinion. But come now, Gluteus, are you not contemplating God so that you will become a better human being?

G. Certainly not. If I wanted to become a better human being I'd take up jogging.

S. Very well, then here is the last question. Think carefully before you answer it, for with your answer the test will be completed. There is one last thing which you may, without realizing it, hope to accomplish by contemplating God, even though you believe that there is no advantage in your contemplating beyond the contemplating itself.

G. That certainly is my belief. But if you think it is a mistaken belief, by all means ask your question.

S. Here it is. Even though you hope for no additional advantage, either on earth or in heaven, from your contemplation of God, don't you expect to become a better God-contemplator the more you contemplate? If that is so, then your contemplation would not be a purely autotelic activity, but would have an instrumental aspect as well.

G. I can put your mind at rest, Salvatorius. I believe with an unshakeable conviction that I am as good at contemplating God as I shall ever become.

S. In that case, Private, please, please get your gluteus up to the battlements with maximum speed and lend us a hand. Playtime comes *after* we save civilization.

Sport and Play:
Suspension of the Ordinary

KENNETH L. SCHMITZ

Sport and play are familiar, but their meaning is not obvious. Play is perhaps as old as man himself, and some will say older. Sport has undergone a remarkable development in some civilizations. It is pursued today by millions in the highly technological societies. Sport is sometimes firmly distinguished from play, and it certainly contains other factors. Nevertheless, the following reflection will suggest that sport is primarily an extension of play, and that it rests upon and derives its central values from play. On this basis it will be maintained that a generous acceptance of the play element in sport is essential for the full realization of this latter form of human behaviour.

The variety of play poses a grave difficulty in understanding it. Its very unity is problematic. Is there a single phenomenon of play which has sufficient unity to be called a special form of human behaviour? The present reflection moves within the context of certain uses not exclusive to English in which the word "play" occurs. Children play in the yard, waves play on the beach, lovers engage in erotic play, an actor plays a part, a musician plays an instrument, a footballer plays a game, a bettor plays the horses, and the gods play with men. The meanings are various; some are peripheral, extended or metaphorical uses. I think,

however, that a central core of meaning remains which points towards an indeterminate yet coherent form of human behaviour. This complex structure I call the phenomenon of play.

Wittgenstein poses the difficulty when he lists a wide range of uses of the word "game." He thinks that the variety shows that there is no essence common to all games but only a family resemblance which permits a chain of different uses. I sympathize with much of what Wittgenstein says about the search for a common essence at all costs. Nevertheless, I think that he assumes too strong a doctrine of essence and too exacting a conception of language before he goes on to his refutation. He seems to tie the doctrine of essence to the doctrine of substance. Now this is an understandable conjunction in the light of much of traditional philosophy, but I do not think it is a necessary or a wise one. It might be said that I set out here to clarify the "essence" of play, but I certainly do not think that I will have established a "substance" of play. I have mentioned a "central core" and a "structure," but it may be more helpful to bear in mind more fluid and dynamic metaphors than the traditional figure of a static structure, idea or form. Gabriel Marcel often speaks of a phenomenon as present in varying degrees along a continuum. Or we might even picture an element as more or less present and more or less pure in a series of chemical solutions.[1] But these are only metaphors.

Nor should we be surprised if the same word is extended to activities which do not share an im-

Reprinted from *Sport and the Body: A Philosophical Symposium* (pp. 22–29) edited by Ellen W. Gerber and William J. Morgan, 1979, Philadelphia: Lea & Febiger. Copyright 1979 by William J. Morgan. Reprinted by permission.

portant central meaning. Ordinary usage is the usage of ordinary men, and not that of scientists or philosophers. Family resemblances suffice. It is enough in ordinary speech that one important similarity hold between a clear instance of play, such as children's frolic, and an extended usage, such as piano playing. Thus we speak of ball-players and easily transfer the vocabulary of play and sport to events such as war-games where the factor of contest so heavily weighs. Although the usage is clear enough, further thought may uncover reasons for the frequent association of contest with play but not its necessity for all forms of play. Then, too, the contest in war-games may prove alien in meaning and psychological tone to the contest which occurs in sporting games.

When reflective analysis seeks to isolate the phenomenon of play it must recognize still other hazards. The difficulty of bringing play to reflective clarity is a difficulty which all immediate and obvious phenomena share. Just as in emotion, for example, so too in play, we live under the spell of peculiar immediacy. We throw ourselves into the spirit of the frolic or game, and when reflection itself becomes an ingredient in playfulness it takes on the character of immediacy, serving the values and objectives of the game. Moreover, play compounds the difficulty by revealing itself in a way that is secretive and shy. It can dodge the determined attentions of reflection by encouraging an amused contempt for it, or by permitting itself to be banished to the years of growing-up. An adult and work-oriented thought finds it easy to neglect or to misrepresent it, as though it were not worthy of "serious" attention. It resists analysis and preserves its essential meaning by turning our accounts of it away from itself to some alien value. Of course, we must recognize the biological and psychological value of play, in relaxation and escape, in rest and exercise, in education and character-formation. But unless play is nothing but these functions, we cannot understand them fully without understanding *it*. The present intent, then, is to clarify the spirit of play, to determine its appropriate forms, and to characterize the element of play in sport.

There is a thicket of other difficulties, too. Play hides obscurely within a host of very complex phenomena and behaviours and is subtle enough to be easily confused with other forms. For a full analysis, it would be necessary to say what play is not. It seems easiest to see that play is not work, and yet it may call sometimes for very great effort. War may highlight the difference, for like work, war is serious, but like play it is non-productive. The words "conquest" and "victory" belong to the vocabulary of war. The first is said easily enough of work, and the second of play. Some forms of play also resemble war in having the element of contest in them; but the essence of war is deadly contest, it is heavy with death. The grave risk of life is not excluded from play, but if life is risked for some alien value, no matter how high, or if death is certain, the spirit of play is extinguished. There is a certain lightness about play which it shares with other forms of leisure. To be sure, play is not the same as good humour, for although it may be fun, it is not necessarily funny. G. K. Chesterton caught the mood when he remarked that certain affairs were too important to be taken seriously. Play consists in what we may call "non-serious" importance. Still, it cannot be equated simply with pleasure or amusement. Indeed, a full analysis of play would have to make room within it for ingredients of pain and discomfort. It would have to be asked, too, whether a high degree of cruelty, as in the ancient bear-baiting or the gladiatorial games, crushes, perverts or merely tempers the spirit of play.

Such an extended analysis of play is not appropriate here, and I turn instead to sketch out, briefly and tentatively, the positive character of this elusive blithe spirit.

The Varieties of Play

Play can be considered under four general varieties: frolic, make-believe, sporting skills and games. The least formal play is simple spontaneous frolic, and this is associated especially with the very young. It is that aspect of play which is found also in young animals, and its occasional appearance in adult humans seems to manifest the feature of neoteny so pronounced in man. Such play among kittens and puppies, or something very like play, may well be a kind of training along with a desire to satisfy curiosity and to express plain high spirits. It is usually intense and brief and tends to dissipate itself with the outburst of energy that makes it possible. It is an immediate and unreflecting expression of a kind of animal joy, a kicking off of the normal patterns of behaviour, purposeless and without constraint. "Horsing around" illustrates the manner in which the play-world can erupt for a brief moment. A practical joke can trigger a spontaneous display. Someone from the group splashes cold water upon the others lying at leisure in sun and sand, and an impromptu "battle" begins, with little or no declared object and with fluid changing of sides. It is a quicksilver form of play, dashing off now in one direction, now in another, fragmenting and rejoining forces in new combinations for new momentary objectives.

A second more or less informal variety of play is that of make-believe or "just pretending." This, too, is commonest with children but not exclusive to them. There is, of course, daydreaming, a sort of playing with images, roles and situations, though this tends to diminish with adult life or is translated into artistic creativity. Among adults the carnival such as the Mardi Gras, the parade such as the Santa or homecoming parade, and costume parties are examples of this variety of play, intermixed with elements of frolic. It is interesting that some form of the mask or costume is used as a means by which the adult can enter the play-world. In its secular shape as in its religious origin, the mask is a device for suspending the everyday world. The child, on the other hand, needs no such device and with nothing at all can create for himself the world which his playful imagination gives to him. There are usually no well-defined and explicit rules for pretending games, though the roles assumed determine a rough and approximate fittingness. One child is quick to tell another that

she is out of character, and the adult who goes to a ball dressed as Bugs Bunny will find his part already somewhat defined for him. Such playfulness, however, is quite different from a theatrical role in which the part is already drawn *a priori* and the actor is expected to interpret and manifest it by using the words and situations provided beforehand by the playwright. What is uppermost in the play of the theatre is representation, whereas in play itself a rough approximation serves merely to suggest and maintain the illusion proper to it. On stage the play is for the sake of presentation, whereas in make-believe the representation is for the sake of play. More generally, it may be said that art and aesthetic experience centre upon the embodiment and expression of meaning, whereas play is for the sake of a certain form of action. In the ballet, for example, action is subordinated to gesture, but in genuine play, mimicry and expression are either incidental or for the sake of the action.

The more formal varieties of play take two styles: skills and games. The first style includes surfboarding, sailing, horse-riding, mountain-climbing, hiking and similar play activities. It calls for knowledge, skill and a certain endurance; so, at least in an elementary way, does the bouncing of a ball, jumping with a pogo stick, yawing a Yo-Yo and skipping rope. The final style of play is completely formal, such as the games of baseball, card-playing and the like. Both styles of play are contests. The former require the mastery of a skill in conformance with natural forces, such as the behaviour of wind and water or the motion of ball and rope. They may even have rudimentary rules. In the truly formal games, however, rules predominate, and although they are determined by agreement, they are held as absolutely binding. Even in solitaire one cannot actually *win* the game if he cheats. Cheating in play is the counterpart of sin in the moral order. It seeks the good of victory without conforming to the spirit of the game and the rules under which alone it is possible to possess it. In the flowery language of a bygone era: the crown of victory sits hollow upon the head of a cheat, who has excluded himself from the values of the game-world and can only enjoy the incidental fruits that sometimes attend a victory. This is quite apart from any moral do's or don'ts, and is written into the very texture of the game-world. In any case, the rules of play differ from those of morality. We can take up the game or leave it, but the rules of morality oblige without any conditionality. Moral rules apply within a context of human action and values that is not that of play and that may touch directly upon the issues of life and death.

In each of these four varieties of play different features predominate: in the frolic the aspect of spontaneous celebration, in imaginative pretense the aspect of creativity, in skill and game the aspect of contest. These aspects are met with in non-play situations too: celebration in worship, creativity in art and contest in work and war. It remains, therefore, to mark out their peculiar quality in the play-world and to indicate its ontological character.

Play as Suspension of the Ordinary World[2]

The spirit of play may be carried over into many activities and even subordinated to other purposes, but it is manifested and realized most perfectly in the four varieties distinguished above. The essence of play comes into existence through the decision to play. Such a constitutive decision cannot be compelled and is essentially free. Through it arises the suspension of the ordinary concerns of the everyday world. Such a decision does not simply initiate the playing but rather constitutes it. That is, it does not stand before the playing as winding a mechanical toy stands before its unwinding performance, but rather it underlies and grounds the entire duration of play. This duration may be interrupted or ended at any time, and in this sense the play-world is fragile, ceasing to be either because of the intrusion of the natural world of ordinary concerns, the loss of interest on the part

of the players, or the completion of the play-objective. Devices are sometimes used for entrance into and maintenance of the play-spirit, but they are subordinate to the essential demands of play. In a prevalent adult form of contemporary play, nightclubbing, which intends to resemble the frolic, alcohol is almost methodically used to make the transition from the ordinary world somewhat easier. The constant threat of the price tag at the end of the evening naturally makes the suspension of ordinary concerns rather more difficult. It goes without saying that too much alcohol brings about the demise of play, as do drugs, for play seems to demand a deliberate maintenance of itself in keeping with the voluntary character of its founding decision. Play may be a kind of madness, but it is self-engendered and self-maintained.

Inasmuch as the play-decision suspends ordinary concerns, it breaks open a new totality. The world of play with its own non-natural objectives and formalities may be said to transcend the natural world and the world of everyday concern. Of course, it must reckon with natural laws and cannot suspend their real effective impact. Players tire and drop out of the game or are injured; or there just isn't time for a last set of tennis or bridge; or the little girls playing house are called in for supper. Moreover, some forms of play, such as surfboarding or mountain-climbing, deliberately set for their objectives the conquest of natural forces. What is common to these and all forms of play is that natural processes do not determine the significance of the play. The player does not follow natural forces as such. Whereas the worker often follows them in order to redirect them as in cultivation, the player may resist them, ignore them as far as possible or create a new order of significance whose elements are non-natural, as in word-games. The surfer follows them in order to wrest from them a carefree moment of exhilarating joy; the archer takes them into account in order to hit a target of his own proposing; and the chess-player moves within a set of spatial possibilities that are ideal in themselves and only indicated by the board and chessmen.

Religion, art and play are rightly spoken of as ways of transcending the strictly natural world. Religion, however, does not suspend the world of nature. Quite the contrary, in its historical forms, it turns back from a sacred and alien distance towards nature in order to reawaken and restore it to its original freshness and creativity. Art and aesthetic experience transcend the natural world in the embodiment and expression of concrete, symbolic meaning. Art suspends the natural and puts it out of play when it gives ultimate value to transnatural objectives. Kant, of course, speaks of a certain detachment or disinterestedness. The sign of the transcendence of play over the natural world is manifest by a certain excess which characterizes its spirit. There is in it an uncalled-for exhilaration, a hilarity in the contest and in the mood of celebration. Like art and religion, play is not far from the feast, for art celebrates beauty and religion celebrates glory, but play celebrates the emergence of a finite world that lies outside and beyond the world of nature while at the same time resting upon it.

The Play-World as a Distinctive Order

The space and time of play are not contiguous with natural space and time. The little child creates an area in the room in which battles are fought, seas sailed, continents discovered, in which animals roam and crops grow. Adults create the playing field which is a space directed according to the objectives and rules of the game. A ball driven to the right of a line is "foul," another landing beyond a certain point is "out of play." In chess the knight alone can jump and the bishop can only move diagonally. Play-space is not at all relative in most games and to the extent to which arbitrary rules are invented to that extent the space becomes more determinate and more absolute. Players hold willingly to the rules or those who do not have officials to encourage them in the most formal

sports. This maintenance of the absolutely binding force of the rules is a free acceptance flowing out of and essentially one with the play-decision, and with the suspension of the natural ordinary world and the substitution of a new order. The laws of natural forces are put to use in an extraordinary way within an extraordinary world inspired by a motive that has suspended the ordinary interests of everyday life.

The structured order of play-space is especially evident in those games in which a single or double point in the play-space is the key to the contest, the privileged space of the goals, target or finishing-line. So, too, play-time is not contiguous with ordinary time, though it must frequently bow to it. In ice hockey sixty minutes of play-time are not sixty minutes of clock-time, and in baseball play-time is simply nine innings or more. Of course, natural space and time are the alien boundaries that ring about and mark the finitude of human play, but the play has its own internal boundaries set by the objectives and rules of the game. When a ball is out of bounds in many games the game-time stops also. Men set the objectives and rules of play and yet there is a certain sense in which the play-objective, freely chosen, sets its own basic rules. Play seems to begin by abandoning forms of everyday behaviour, but it maintains that abandonment in a positive and determinate way by creating a new space and time with new forms and rules of behaviour that are not determined by or functional within the everyday world but which nevertheless have a positive meaning of their own. Within its boundaries and objectives the play-world exhibits a totality of meaning and value that is strikingly complete and perfect. Play reveals itself as transnatural, fragile, limited perfection.

The suspension of the natural world and its subordination to the game or its sublimation into the play context can be described as the suppression of the real, where "reality" is restricted to the natural and ordinary world. Play then builds an illusion. Huizinga notes that the Latin word for play (*ludus*) is closely related to the word for illusion (*inlusio*).³ The "inactuality" of play is most evident in the imaginative play of make-believe. This suspension of the "real" world by means of a play-decision releases a world of "unreality" which needs no justification from outside itself. It is a self-sealed world, delivering its own values in and for itself, the freedom and joy of play. As a piece of fine art needs no other defence than itself, and as the feast need exist for no other reason than its own values, so too play, though its claims must be balanced within the whole man against those of "reality," receives justification only through and in itself. As colour cannot validate its existence and meaning except to one who sees, so play cannot vindicate itself except to one who plays. To anyone else it appears superfluous. The stern Calvin Coolidge, it is said, once snorted that going fishing was childish, which only proved to fishermen that he was absurd. Play has its own built-in finality. It is in this sense objectless; it has no other object than itself.

Nevertheless, an adequate philosophy can free the mind from an exclusive preoccupation with the natural world and open it out onto all the modes of being. Each is seen to have its value. Like religion and art, play embodies a significance that is not fully grasped in clear concepts. As an analysis does not replace a poem or a painting, so a description of its rules is no substitute for play. But an analysis may open the mind to the genuine reality of play. The proper vehicle of meaning in play is action and in this it is much closer to ritual and myth than to scientific concepts. Play is meaning embodied in action; it is "significant form"⁴ precisely as human behaviour. The world which opens out through the play-decision is a world of possibilities closed off from the natural and ordinary world. Measured against the ordinary world the world of possibility opened up by play seems inactual and illusory; but measured in terms of being itself, it is a radical way of being human, a distinctive mode of being. It is a way of taking up the world of being, a manner of being present in the world in the mode of creative possibility whose existential presence is a careless joyful freedom.

I suggest, then, that there is a phenomenon of play which is an indeterminate yet coherent mode of human behaviour. It comes to be through a decision which does not simply initiate or occasion play, but which founds and underlies it. It is a decision which is freely taken and maintained, either spontaneously or deliberately. It is a decision which seeks to secure certain values for human consciousness and human existence, a certain meaning and a certain freedom. It may be called an activity of maintaining an illusion, if we speak in terms which still give primacy to the natural world. But it may also be called an activity of suspension, whereby the natural forces while not abrogated are dethroned from their primacy. More positively, it may be called an activity of constitution, which breaks open distinctive possibilities of meaning, freedom and value. It has no other essential objective than those implicit in the founding decision. It has its own time and space, boundaries and objectives, rewards and penalties. It is a distinctive way, voluntary and finite, of man's being-in-the-world. Playing in the world, man recovers himself as a free and transcendent being.

The Play-Element in Sport

Two factors are especially prominent in sport: the first is the emphasis on good performance, and the second is the element of contest. If sport consisted simply of performance and contest, however, scholarship examinations would be reported in the sporting pages. Examinations are liable to be deadly serious and to be related directly to educational objectives which are part of the natural and social world.

Sport may be carried on at various levels of competence and preparedness, from the unplanned street game to the carefully planned amateur or professional sporting event. In the former, natural ability and past experience determine the proficiency of the maneuvers. Planned events are usually preceded by exercises for general conditioning and precise training. These preparations are directed towards the performance of activities within a non-natural space and time and in accord with more or less formally specified rules. The excellence of the performance is judged within a matrix of values that flow from the decision to play this or that kind of game.

The performance, moreover, is for the sake of the contest, either against natural forces, such as in the high jump, or against other players, as in track meets. In some sports, there is only one contestant, as in hunting; but in most, as in team games, a contestant pits himself also against other players. The performance is tested by the contest of player against player, and the verdict is sealed by the victory.

It may seem that the play element is not essential to sport. Thus, for example, the sport of hunting lies very close to the natural needs of man. Moreover, it has little of formal rules. The various game laws are not to be confused with sporting rules, for they are meant to conserve the natural supply of game as a condition for further hunting. They are laws, not rules. Of course, if two huntsmen vie with each other for the largest or the quickest bag, we say that they have made a game out of it. Here again, they have imposed upon the natural value, namely, the food procured, a game-value, the prize of victory. Such a contest, however, is to be distinguished from the contest of bucks seeking a mate or tycoons seeking a fortune. It is imaginable that the latter might be taken up in a *spirit* of play, but it is not properly playful in its *form*. We see here a distinction between the forms of play and the spirit which inhabits them. This spirit can sometimes animate certain other forms of behaviour. Thus a man may bet in order to win and pay off the mortgage, or he may bet in order to risk something valuable to him. Only the latter is animated by a spirit of play. Even it is no longer play if it is compulsive, for it may then be the sublimation of the wish to totter between life and death.

In addition to good performance and contest, then, spontaneous creative freedom is inherent in play. This suggests that sport can be carried out without the spirit of play. Nevertheless, in the life of individuals and in the history of the race, sport emerges from play as from an original and founding existential posture. Sport is free, self-conscious, tested play which moves in a transnatural dimension of human life, built upon a certain basis of leisure. Sport is in its origin and intention a movement into transcendence which carries over from the founding decision to play and which builds upon that decision an intensified thrust towards the values of self-consciousness tested through performance, competition and victory. There is certainly a return to seriousness in the discipline of formal sport. There is training, performance and competition. But the objectives of sport and its founding decision lie within play and cause sport to share in certain of its features— the sense of immediacy, exhilaration, rule-directed behaviour, and the indeterminacy of a specified outcome.

Sport can be demanding, but its essence is as delicate as any perfume and can be as readily dissipated. There are three abuses which can kill the spirit of play within sport and reduce sport to something less than its fullest human possibilities.

The first abuse is the exaggeration of the importance of victory. I do not refer to the will to win, which must be strong in any highly competitive sport. Still, such a will must be situated within a more generous context—the desire to perform as well as it is humanly possible. Many factors not under the control of players or judges may determine the ultimate victor. Such an awareness does not tarnish the prize, but situates it properly within a limited and qualified texture. Victory in sports is not absolute, and it should not be allowed to behave like the absolute. The policy of winning at all costs is the surest way of snuffing out the spirit of play in sport. The fallout of such a policy is the dreary succession of firings in college and professional sport. Such an emphasis on victory detaches the last moment from the whole game and fixes the outcome apart from its proper context. It reduces the appreciation of the performance, threatens the proper disposition towards the rules and turns the contest into a naked power struggle. The upshot is a brutalization of the sport.

And so, the sport which issued from the play-decision, promising freedom and exhilaration, ends dismally in lessening the humanity of players and spectators.

The second abuse stems from the rationalization of techniques within a sport when the rationalization is promoted by an exaggerated sense of the value of efficiency. Good performance is important and the best performance is a desirable ideal. A coach has always to deal with a definite group of individual players. He must assess their potential for the game, combining firmness with good judgment and enthusiasm with restraint. Hard coaching is to be expected, but under pressure of competition it is tempting to let moderation give way to an uninterrupted drive for limitless proficiency. An abstract tyranny of the possible may drive players beyond what they should be asked to give, compelling them to spend what they neither have nor can afford. Driven beyond their natural capacities, they lose the spirit of play, and the values which are supposed to be the initial and perhaps even the paramount reason for taking up the sport. There is a subtle and difficult difference between such tyrannic proficiency and the will to excel which every competitor must have and which leads him to pit his body and personality with and against others. There is a difference between a tyrant and a coach who rightly demands the best his players can put forth. There is a difference, too, between a rationalization which sacrifices everything to technical competence and a reasonable improvement of techniques of training and performance which lift a sport to new accomplishments. Such a merely technical drive is more than likely in our age which tends to over-rationalize all life in the name of technical perfection. The deepest problems in our technological society centre about salvaging, promoting and developing truly human possibilities. Sport stands in a very sensitive position. It can be part of the drive to dehumanization, or in a very direct and privileged way, to the recapture of human values and human dignity. An ultimate and limitless demand for proficiency forced upon players and sport at the cost of all other values including those of play will diminish all who participate—players, staff and spectators.

The first and second abuses are internal threats which arise from detaching victory or performance from the context of play. The third abuse arrives from outside what is essential to sport. It arises with the presence of spectators and threatens to alienate the sport from its play-objectives and values. Such an alienation becomes even more likely when the commercial possibilities of a sport are exploited. The genuine essence of play cannot be present when it is play only for the spectators, as in the gladiatorial contests of the Roman circus in which contestants were often compelled against their wishes to face wild beasts or even one another. One of the requirements is that the participants also take up the activity in a spirit of play. In commercial sport, the spectators usually attend the game in a spirit of play, though some attend simply with friends or to be seen. The players, on the other hand, are under contract, though it is under contract precisely "to play." It seems an oversimplification, however, to discount professional sport as play merely because the players are paid. We do not call a work of fine art non-art simply because it is commissioned. Moreover, the distinction between amateur and professional is a social one, distinguishing those who pursue a vocation from those who pursue an avocation. Olympic sport claims to reflect the time when some games were part of the culture of a "gentleman." Amateurs today are of three kinds: the occasional players who are not very serious in their pursuit of the sport; those who, like many bowlers or curlers, are serious devotees of the sport but not under contract to play it; and those would-be pros who are not yet skilled enough to play the sport under contract. On the side of the professional player what threatens the purity of the spirit of play is the compulsion implied in the contractual obligation to render services at given times, to practise in order to maintain and improve skills, and to participate in games as required. But these demands are intrinsic to many games. The threat lies even more in the nature of the binding force. In professional sport it does not lie in interest in the game itself but rather is reinforced and ultimately enforced by values not intrinsic to the game. Perhaps the clearest distinction is between the wage the pro earns and the win or loss of the game. Win or lose, for a time at least he is paid a wage for services delivered; but he gets the victory only when "the gods of the game" smile upon him. Play ceases when the primary reasons for undertaking it are alien to the values of the play-world itself. Values intrinsic to the play-world include not letting down one's own teammates in team games, not begging off the contest because of personal discomfort, taking pleasure in performing activities within the rules of the game, prizing the victory and its symbols. Values that lie outside the play-world include agreement to deliver services for wages earned, abiding by a contract because of fear of being sued, playing out games in order not to be barred from further league participation, finishing out a sports career in order to achieve social and economic standing upon ceasing to play. These motives are not unworthy; they are simply not motives of play. A player may respect the values of play without directly experiencing them, as when he finishes out his sports' career as ably as possible in order to fulfill the possibilities of the game and thereby allow other participants and spectators to share in the values of the game. Heroism in sport often arises through the determination of a player to maintain the importance of the play-world even in the face of disturbances from the "real" world, such as painful injuries, private worries, physical exhaustion, or even fading interest, although the fan tends to look upon the latter as a betrayal. On the side of the spectator in professional and even in other organized sport, what threatens the purity of the spirit of play is the reduction of the players to hirelings, and the game to something which is expected to deliver to the spectator a period of pleasure for money paid. The commercialization of sport can, of course, be a way of seeing that the quality and abundance of playing

are increased; but it can and often does simply pervert sport into just another profitable pleasure industry. Many things give pleasure. Some of them can be bought. The play-world is not one of them. Over-commercialization of sport disillusions the spectator and risks defeating the objectives of commercialization.

The play-world in general offers itself to anyone who wishes to enter it, either as participant or as spectator. But to receive the gift of play he must take up the values of the game as important in and for themselves. He may get angry with "his" team when it plays badly and boast of it when it plays well; but he will not view the players simply as objects employed to give him a pleasurable spectacle. This is a purely objectivist viewpoint and a form of reductionism. It is easy for a spectator to drift into this attitude, because his relation to the game is only partial. He bears no responsibility, and he lives the risks and thrills, defeats and victories in a moving but not a completely involved way. The player is committed with his body and plunges in as one participant; the spectator participates as the whole team, but indirectly. Nevertheless, play calls for and can achieve a vantage point which undercuts the distinction of the purely subjective and the purely objective, in which I am here and they are there. The fan enjoys a special complicity with his team and easily transfers the symbolic value of the victory to himself and his group. He feels himself in some sense one with the participants of the game. What unites them is the particular form of the play-world, and the importance of its objectives and values.

In sum, then, sport can nourish the spirit of objectivity, for it contains a native generosity with which it seeks excellence of form and action in obedience to conventional rules and submits freely to the award of victory or defeat according to those rules. In so doing, sport manifests a distinctive mode of human life, combining creative freedom with disciplined order for the sake of skilled competition and earned victory. In the engagement the player must encounter his opponent not as an enemy in war but as one whose excellence challenges him and makes possible his own best performance. Players and spectators discover in a new dimension the significance of competitors, team and fans. The sharp difference of subject and object is bridged by the common context and objectives. A fan may surprise himself applauding an exceptionally fine play against his own team, or at least unhappily admiring it. At a race-meet fans from several schools spontaneously urge on the front runner who seems able to beat the existing record, even though he will beat their own runners. It is a victory of man against time and space and himself. Of course, the spectator can be treated as one who needs bread and circuses, but wiser sports managers will try to transform an appetite for constantly renewed sensations into an experience of community. The radical breaking-down of more traditional ties has seen the rise of massive spectator sports. Is it not possible that the attraction of sport for non-players lies in the invitation to experience freedom, meaning and excellence in the context of a free community of individuals bound together by a common appreciation for the values of the game? In that experience of free community men discover new possibilities of human excellence and reach out to recover a fuller meaning of themselves.

1. For example, G. Marcel, *The Mystery of Being* (Gifford Lectures, 1949–50), Regnery, Chicago, 2 vols., n.d.
2. See Eugen Fink, *Spiel als Weltsymbol*, Kohlhammer, Stuttgart, 1960.
3. *Homo Ludens: a study of the play element in culture,* (1944), Beacon, Boston, 1955, p. 36. See also Fink, *op. cit.,* pp. 66 ff.
4. Huizinga, *op. cit.,* p. 4.

The Elements of Sport

BERNARD SUITS

I would like to advance the thesis that the elements of sport are essentially—although perhaps not totally—the same as the elements of game. I shall first propose an account of the elements of game-playing, then comment on the relation of game to sport, and finally suggest that the resulting view of sport has an important bearing on the question as to whether sport is or is not serious.

The Elements of Game

Since games are goal-directed activities which involve choice, ends and means are two of the elements of games. But in addition to being means-end oriented activities, games are also rule-governed activities, so that rules are a third element. And since, as we shall see, the rules of games make up a rather special kind of rule, it will be necessary to take account of one more element, namely, the attitudes of game-players *qua* game-players. I add "*qua* game-players" because I do not mean what might happen to be the attitude of this or that game player under these or those conditions (e.g., the hope of winning a cash prize or the satisfaction of exhibiting physical prowess to an admiring audience), but the attitude without which it is not possible to play a game. Let us call this attitude, of which more presently,

Reprinted from Robert Osterhoudt, editor, *The Philosophy of Sport: A Collection of Essays* (pp. 48–64), 1973. Courtesy of Charles C Thomas, Publisher, Springfield, Illinois.

the *lusory* (from the Latin *ludus*, game) attitude.

My task will be to persuade you that what I have called the lusory attitude is the element which unifies the other elements into a single formula which successfully states the necessary and sufficient conditions for any activity to be an instance of game-playing. I propose, then, that the elements of game are (1) the goal, (2) means for achieving the goal, (3) rules, and (4) lusory attitude. I shall briefly discuss each of these in order.

The Goal

We should notice first of all that there are three distinguishable goals involved in game-playing. Thus, if we were to ask a long distance runner his purpose in entering a race, he might say any one or all of three things, each of which would be accurate, appropriate, and consistent with the other two. He might reply (1) that his purpose is to participate in a long distance race, or (2) that his purpose is to win the race, or (3) that his purpose is to cross the finish line ahead of the other contestants. It should be noted that these responses are not merely three different formulations of one and the same purpose. Thus, winning a race is not the same thing as crossing a finish line ahead of the other contestants, since it is possible to do the latter unfairly by, for example, cutting across the infield. Nor is participating in the race the same as either of these, since the contestant, while fully participating, may simply fail to cross the finish line first, either by fair means or foul. That there must be this triplet of goals in games will be accounted for by the way in which lusory attitude

39

is related to rules and means. For the moment, however, it will be desirable to select just one of the three kinds of goal for consideration, namely, the kind illustrated in the present example by crossing the finish line ahead of the other contestants. This goal is literally the *simplest* of the three goals, since each of the other goals presupposes it, whereas it does not presuppose either of the other two. This goal, therefore, has the best claim to be regarded as an elementary component of game-playing. The others, since they are compounded components, can be defined only after the disclosure of additional elements.

The kind of goal at issue, then, is the kind illustrated by crossing a finish line first (but not necessarily fairly), having x number of tricks piled up before you on a bridge table (but not necessarily as a consequence of playing bridge), or getting a golf ball into a cup (but not necessarily by using a golf club). This kind of goal may be described generally as *a specific achievable state of affairs*. This description is, I believe, no more and no less than is required. By omitting to say *how* the state of affairs in question is to be brought about, it avoids confusion between this goal and the goal of winning. And because any achievable state of affairs whatever could, with sufficient ingenuity, be made the goal of a game, the description does not include too much. I suggest that this kind of goal be called the *pre-lusory* goal of a game, because it can be described before, or independently of, any game of which it may be, or come to be, a part. In contrast, the goal of winning can be described only in terms of the game in which it figures, and winning may accordingly be called the *lusory* goal of a game. (It is tempting to call what I have called the pre-lusory goal the goal *in* a game and the lusory goal the goal *of* a game, but the practice of philosophers like J. L. Austin has, I believe, sufficiently illustrated the hazards of trying to make prepositions carry a load of meaning which can much better be borne by adjectives and nouns.) Finally, the goal of participating in the game is not, strictly speaking, a part of the game at all. It is simply one of the goals

that people have, such as wealth, glory, or security. As such it may be called a lusory goal, but a lusory goal of life rather than of games.

Means

Just as we saw that reference to the goal of game-playing was susceptible of three different (but proper and consistent) interpretations, so we shall find that the means in games can refer to more than one kind of thing; two, in fact, depending upon whether we wish to refer to means for winning the game or for achieving the pre-lusory goal. Thus, an extremely effective way to achieve the pre-lusory goal in a boxing match—viz., the state of affairs consisting in your opponent being *down* for the count of ten—is to shoot him through the head, but this is obviously not a means to winning the match. In games, of course, we are interested only in means which are permitted for winning, and we are now in a position to define that class of means, which we may call *lusory* means. Lusory means are means which are permitted (are legal or legitimate) in the attempt to achieve pre-lusory goals. Thus a soccer player may use foot or head, but not hand, in his efforts to achieve that state of affairs wherein the ball is in the goal. And a player who does not confine himself to lusory means may not be said to win, even if he achieves the pre-lusory goal. But achievement of the lusory goal, winning, requires that the player confine himself to lusory means, so that confinement to lusory means is a necessary (but of course not a sufficient) condition for winning.

It should be noticed that we have been able to distinguish lusory from, if you will, illusory means only by assuming without analysis one of the elements necessary in making the distinction. We have defined lusory means as means which are *permitted* without examining the nature of that permission. This omission will be repaired directly by taking up the question of rules. But we may provisionally acknowledge the following definition: *lusory means,* means permitted in seeking pre-lusory goals.

Rules

As with goals and means, two kinds of rules figure in games, one kind associated with pre-lusory goals, the other with lusory goals. The rules of a game are, in effect, proscriptions of certain means useful in achieving pre-lusory goals. Thus, it is useful but proscribed to trip a competitor in a foot race. This kind of rule may be called constitutive of the game, since such rules together with specification of the pre-lusory goal set out all the conditions which must be met in playing the game (though not, of course, in playing the game skillfully). Let us call such rules *constitutive* rules. The other kind of rule operates, so to speak, *within* the area circumscribed by constitutive rules, and this kind of rule may be called a rule of skill. Examples are the familiar injunctions to keep your eye on the ball, to refrain from trumping your partner's ace, and the like. To break a rule of skill is usually to fail, at least to that extent, to play the game well, but to break a constitutive rule is to fail to play the game at all. (There is a third kind of rule in games which appears to be unlike either of these. This is the kind of rule for which there is a fixed penalty, such that violating the rule is neither to fail to play the game nor [necessarily] to fail to play the game well, since it is sometimes tactically correct to incur such a penalty [e.g., in hockey] for the sake of the advantage gained. But these rules and the lusory consequences of their violation are established by the constitutive rules, and are simply extensions of them.)

Having made the distinction between constitutive rules and rules of skill, I propose to ignore the latter, since my purpose is to define not well-played games, but games. It is, then, what I have called constitutive rules which determine the kind and range of means which will be permitted in seeking to achieve the pre-lusory goal.

What is the nature of the restrictions which constitutive rules impose on the means for reaching a pre-lusory goal? The effect of constitutive rules is to place obstacles in the path leading to a pre-lusory goal. I invite the reader to think of any game

at random. Now identify the pre-lusory goal, being careful to remember that the pre-lusory goal is simply any specific achievable state of affairs. I think you will agree that the simplest, easiest, and most direct approach to achieving such a goal is always ruled out in favour of a more complex, more difficult, and more indirect approach. Thus it is not uncommon for players of a new and difficult game to agree among themselves to *ease up* on the rules, that is, to allow themselves a greater degree of latitude than the official rules permit. This means removing some of the obstacles or, in terms of means, permitting certain means which the rules do not really permit. But if no means whatever are ruled out, then the game ceases to exist. Thus, we may think of the gamewright, when he invents games, as attempting to draw a line between permitted and prohibited means to a given end. If he draws this line too loosely there is danger of the game becoming too easy, and if he draws it with utter laxity the game simply falls apart. On the other hand, he must not draw the line too tight or, instead of falling apart, the game will be squeezed out of existence. For example, imagine a game where the pre-lusory goal is to cross a finish line, with an attendant rule that the player must not leave the track in his attempt to do so. Then imagine that there is a second rule which requires that the finish line be located some distance from the track.

We may define constitutive rules as rules which prohibit use of the most efficient means for reaching a pre-lusory goal.

Lusory Attitude

The attitude of the game-player must be an element in game-playing because there has to be an explanation of that curious state of affairs wherein one adopts rules which require him to employ worse rather than better means for reaching an end. Normally the acceptance of prohibitory rules is justified on the grounds that the means ruled out, although they are more efficient than the permitted means, have further undesirable consequences from the viewpoint of the agent involved. Thus, although the use of nuclear weapons is more efficient than is the use of conventional weapons in winning battles, the view still happily persists among nations that the additional consequences of nuclear assault are sufficient to rule it out. This kind of thing, of course, happens all the time, from the realm of international strategy to the common events of everyday life; thus one decisive way to remove a toothache is to cut your head off, but most people find good reason to rule out such highly efficient means. But in games, although more efficient means are—and must be—ruled out, the reason for doing so is quite different from the reasons for avoiding nuclear weaponry and self-decapitation. Foot racers do not refrain from cutting across the infield because the infield holds dangers for them, as would be the case if, for example, infields were frequently sown with land mines. Cutting across the infield is shunned solely because there is a rule against it. But in ordinary life this is usually—and rightly—regarded as the worst possible kind of justification one could give for avoiding a course of action. The justification for a prohibited course of action that there is simply a rule against it may be called the *bureaucratic* justification; that is, no justification at all.

But aside from bureaucratic practice, in anything but a game the gratuitous introduction of unnecessary obstacles to the achievement of an end is regarded as a decidedly irrational thing to do, whereas in games it appears to be an absolutely essential thing to do. This fact about games has led some observers to conclude that there is something inherently absurd about games, or that games must involve a fundamental paradox. (1) This kind of view seems to me to be mistaken. (2) The mistake consists in applying the same standard to games that is applied to means-end activities which are not games. If playing a game is regarded as not essentially different from going to the office or writing a cheque, then there is certainly something absurd, or paradoxical, or simply stupid about game-playing.

But games are, I believe, essentially different from the ordinary activities of life, as perhaps the following exchange between Smith and Jones will illustrate. Smith knows nothing of games, but he does know that he wants to travel from A to C, and he also knows that making the trip by way of B is the most efficient means for getting to his destination. He is then told authoritatively that he may *not* go by way of B. "Why not," he asks, "are there dragons at B?" "No," is the reply. "B is perfectly safe in every respect. It is just that there is a rule against going to B if you are on your way to C." "Very well," grumbles Smith, "if you insist. But if I have to go from A to C very often I shall certainly try very hard to get that rule revoked." True to his word, Smith approaches Jones, who is also setting out for C from A. He asks Jones to sign a petition requesting the revocation of the rule which forbids travellers from A to C to go through B. Jones replies that he is very much opposed to revoking the rule, which very much puzzles Smith.

Smith. But if you want to get to C, why on earth do you support a rule which prevents your taking the fastest and most convenient route?

Jones. Ah, but you see I have no particular interest in being at C. *That* is not my goal, except in a subordinate way. My overriding goal is more complex. It is "to get from A to C without going through B." And I can't very well achieve that goal if I go through B, can I?

Smith. But why do you want to do that?

Jones. I want to do it before Robinson does, you see?

Smith. No, I don't. That explains nothing. Why should Robinson, whoever he may be, want to do it? I presume you will tell me that he, like you, has only a subordinate interest in being at C at all.

Jones. That is so.

Smith. Well, if neither of you wants, really, to be at C, then what possible difference can

Jones. Let me ask you a question. Why do you want to get to C?

Smith. Because there is a good concert there, and I want to hear it.

Jones. Why?

Smith. Because I like concerts, of course. Isn't that a good reason?

Jones. It's one of the best there is. And I like, among other things, trying to get from A to C without going through B before Robinson does.

Smith. Well, *I* don't. So why should they tell me I can't go through B?

Jones. Oh, I see. They must have thought you were in the race.

Smith. The what?

I believe that we are now in a position to define *lusory attitude:* the knowing acceptance of constitutive rules just so the activity made possible by such acceptance can occur.

Summary

The elements may now be assembled into the following definition. To play a game is to attempt to achieve a specific state of affairs (*pre-lusory goal*), using only means permitted by rules (*lusory means*), where the rules prohibit use of more efficient in favor of less efficient means (*constitutive rules*), and where such rules are accepted just because they make possible such activity (*lusory attitude*). I also offer the following only approximately accurate, but more pithy, version of the above definition: Playing a game is the voluntary attempt to overcome unnecessary obstacles.

Games and Sport

As I indicated at the outset, I believe that sports are essentially games. What I mean by this is that the difference between sports and other games is

much smaller than the difference between humans and other vertebrates. That is to say, sport is not a species within the genus *game*. The distinguishing characteristics of sport are more peripheral, more arbitrary, and more contingent than are the differences required to define a species.

I would like to submit for consideration four requirements which, if they are met by any given game, are sufficient to denominate that game a sport. They are: (1) that the game be a game of skill, (2) that the skill be physical, (3) that the game have a wide following, and (4) that the following achieve a certain level of stability. If I can persuade you that these features or something very much like them are at least the *kind* of differentiating marks we are seeking, I will be satisfied. I have no theory to support the list, except the theory that the features are more or less arbitrary, since they are simply facts about sport. Finally, I have little to say about them aside from presenting them, except as regards the question of skill, which I am interested in taking up on its own account.

Skill in Games

One may agree with my account of what it is to play a game and still find unanswered the rather pressing question why anyone would want to do such a thing (aside from professionals who do so for money and prestige). Smith was no doubt puzzled about this question even after Jones' explanation. Let me propose the following general answer. People play games so that they can realize in themselves capacities not realizable (or not readily so) in the pursuit of their ordinary activities. For example, some people enjoy running competitively, but the opportunities for this are severely limited in ordinary life. One can run for a bus, but even this small range of operations is further limited by the fact that one does not always have the good fortune to arrive tardily at a bus stop. One can, of course, intentionally allow less than enough time for getting punctually to the point of departure, in the hope that a race with the time table will then be necessary. But such a move is precisely to create a game where there was no game before, by virtue of the constitutive rule requiring you to leave your home or office late. Some kinds of games—such as racing games—have this rather obvious affinity with actions performed aside from games. But most games do not have such a clear counterpart in ordinary life. Ball games which are at all elaborate have affinities with ordinary life only piecemeal; in life, too, one throws and runs and strikes objects, but there is nothing in life which much resembles baseball or football or golf *in toto*. Board games provide similar examples of the hiatus between games taken as wholes and the kinds of structured activities which characterize the rest of life. Thus, with the invention of games far removed from the pursuits of ordinary life, quite new capacities emerge, and hitherto unknown skills are developed. A good golf swing is simply useless in any other human pursuit. And despite the literary mythology which frequently represents superior military and political strategists as being (it is almost presumed to go without saying) master chess players as well, there is as much similarity between those two skills as there is between the skills of golf and wood chopping. Purely topological problems are just vastly different from political and military problems. So people play games not only because ordinary life does not provide enough opportunities for doing such and such, but also (and more interestingly) because ordinary life does not provide any opportunities at all for doing such and such.

Games are *new* things to do, and they are new things to do because they require the overcoming of (by ordinary standards) *unnecessary* obstacles, and in ordinary life an unnecessary obstacle is simply a contradiction in terms.

Although I believe, as I have said, that people play games in order to realize capacities not otherwise realizable (or not readily realizable), and although in most games these capacities are, or intimately involve, specific skills, there are certain activities called games which almost conform to my definition but which do not involve skill.

I mean games of chance; that is, games of *pure* chance. Draw poker is not such a game, nor, perhaps, is standard roulette (perhaps a debatable point), but show-down is, and so is Russian roulette. These games do not involve the capacity to exercise a specific skill because no skill is required to play them. Instead of skills, what is put into operation by such games is, I suggest, hope and fear. Bored people are deficient in these feelings, it seems safe to say, since if they were not they would not be bored. But hope and fear can be artificially induced by games of pure chance. (They also appear in games of skill, to be sure, but people to whom games of chance especially appeal are too bored to learn new skills.) What games of chance provide for their players may be described in almost the same words that Jan Narveson has used to describe paranoia: a false sense of insecurity. However, for games of chance the word *false* should be replaced by the word *invented,* for there is nothing false about the capacities which games bring forth, just something new.

All sports appear to be games of skill rather than games of chance. I suggest that the reason for this is that a major requirement in sports, for participants and spectators alike, is that what the participants do must be admirable in some respect. The exercise of virtually any skill—even the skills involved in goldfish swallowing or flag pole sitting—will elicit *some* degree of admiration. But the spectacle of a person sweating in hope and fear as the chamber slowly turns in the revolver evokes not admiration but morbid fascination or clinical interest.

Physical Skill

It is not difficult to draw a line between games which require physical skill and games which do not. It is not necessary first to decide very grave metaphysical issues, such as the relation between mind and body. It is a plain fact that how chess pieces are moved has nothing whatever to do with manual dexterity or any other bodily skill. One can play chess, bridge, and any number of other games solely by issuing verbal commands, as is the case when chess is played by mail. "Physical games" designates a quite definite class of objects, and the term "sport" is confined to this class (though it is not necessarily coterminous with it). The issue is thus wholly terminological; that is, the question "Why do sports have to involve physical skills?" is not a well formulated question. The question should be, "What kind of skill do we find in the class of activities we call sport?" And the answer is "Physical skill." Thus, chess and bridge appear to have all the features requisite for something to qualify as a sport, except that they are not games of physical skill. They do involve skill, and of a high order; they have a wide following and their popularity is of sufficiently long standing so that each of them may be characterized as an institution rather than a mere craze. Each can boast international tournaments, a body of experts, teachers, coaches—all the attendant roles and institutions characteristic of the most well-established sports. It is just that physical skill is not involved.

A Wide Following

I have perfected the following game originally created by Kierkegaard. A high ranking official of my university has the constitutional peculiarity that when angry his anger is manifested solely by the appearance of a bead of perspiration at the centre of his forehead which then rolls slowly down his nose, clings for an instant to its tip, and finally falls. If the official's ire continues or recurs, the same steps are repeated. Whenever I have a conference with him I adopt as a pre-lusory goal that state of affairs wherein three separate beads of perspiration shall have progressed through their appointed stages inside of fifteen minutes. And I adopt the constitutive rule that I will refrain from employing as a means to this goal either threats of violence against the person of the official or aspersions on his personal and professional reputation. Although this is, I flatter myself, a pretty good game, I readily admit that it is not a sport.

It is too private and too personal to qualify for that status. Imagine my being asked by a colleague in the Faculty of Physical Education what sports I participate in, and my responding that I am very keen on Sweat-Bead.

Still, though Sweat-Bead is not now a sport, it could conceivably become one. If there were a great many people who shared the constitutional peculiarity of my official, and if there were a great many people equipped with the kind of sadism to which this game appeals, and if the rules were clearly laid out and published, and if there were to grow up a body of experts whose concern it was to improve the game and its players, then Sweat-Bead would become a sport. But short of these much to be hoped for developments I must accept the reality that it is simply a highly idiosyncratic game.

Stability

That a game is one of physical skill and that it is very popular is not quite enough to qualify it as a sport. Hula-Hoop, in its hey-day, met these requirements but it would be proper to call Hula-Hoop a craze rather than a sport. The popular following which attends sports must have a stability which is more than mere persistence through time. Even if Hula-Hoop had lasted for fifty years it would still be a craze, only a very tiresome craze.

What is required in addition to longevity is the birth and flowering of a number of attendant roles and institutions which serve a number of functions ancillary to a sufficiently popular game of physical skill. The most important of these functions appear to be the following: teaching and training, coaching, research and development (Can the sport be improved by making such and such changes?), criticism (sports pundits), and archivism (the compilation and preservation of individual performances and their statistical treatment). Not all sports, of course, require all of these ancillary functions in order to be accepted as sports, but at least some of them will be associated to some degree with every game worthy to be called a sport.

Sport and Seriousness

The conventional wisdom about fun and games which, with brief and infrequent counter-tendencies, has prevailed from classical antiquity to the very recent past is well expressed by the following observation of Aristotle: ". . . to exert oneself and work for the sake of playing seems silly and utterly childish. But to play in order that one may exert oneself seems right." Play, games, and sport are seen, on this view, as subordinate to other ends, so that they may be taken seriously only if the ends to which they are subordinate are taken seriously. Thus, sports are regarded as serious insofar as they promote, for example, health, which is accepted as a serious matter; but sport unjustified by some such serious purpose is just frivolity. In a "work" ethic, work is the serious pursuit which gives play (and indeed health) what derivative seriousness it possesses. But in a leisure ethic, of the kind which much of the world appears now to be assuming, these old priorities are rapidly changing. For a person in whom the Protestant ethic is quite firmly established it is difficult, if not impossible, to ask the question, "To what further interests is work itself subordinate?" and in times and societies where human and material resources are exceedingly scarce it is perhaps as well for the survival of the human race that such questions are not asked. For under conditions where unremitting labor is necessary for the bare preservation of life, the answer to the question "What are we working for?" is "Just to live." And since the life whose preservation requires continuous toil is just that toil itself, the toiler might well wonder whether the game is worth the candle.

But in a leisure ethic we have not only the leisure to ask why we are working, but the fact of leisure itself provides us with an answer which is not too bleak to bear. The industrial unionist of today who makes a contract demand for shorter working hours is not prompted to do this by Aristotelian considerations. He does not want more time for fishing, bowling, the ball park, or television so

that, renewed and refreshed, he can increase his output on the assembly line on Monday. (In any case, that output will also be fixed by the new contract, and cannot be increased.) The attitude of the contemporary worker about work may be expressed as the exact inversion of Aristotle's dictum: "To play so that one may work seems silly and utterly childish; but to work in order that one may play seems right."

I do not think it is too great an overstatement to say that whereas for the Puritan it was work which gave play (as, e.g., exercise) what derivative seriousness it was accorded, it is now play—or at least leisure activities—which gives work a derivative seriousness. Another way to put this is to acknowledge that work is good because it provides us with leisure as well as the means to enjoy leisure. Work is good chiefly because it is *good for* something much better. The things for which it is finally good are good in themselves. They are intrinsic goods. This is not, as a general view, at all novel. It, too, goes back to Aristotle. The only difference in Aristotle's view (and in the view of many others who are in this respect like him) is that for him just a very few things count as intrinsically good, things like virtue and metaphysics. Partisans of this kind have typically managed to get a kind of monopoly on the notion of intrinsic good and have tried, with some success, to persuade the rest of us that only such and such pursuits were worthy of the name. Sometimes it has been holiness, sometimes art, sometimes science, sometimes love. But it seems perfectly clear that any number of things can be intrinsic goods to someone, depending upon his interests, abilities, and other resources, from philately to philosophy (including work itself, if you happen to be Paul Goodman). This view has quite wide, even if tacit, acceptance, I believe, outside of churches and universities.

The new ethic, then, is not only one of greatly increased leisure, it is also one of pluralism with respect to the goods we are permitted to seek in the new time available. It has been some time since our sabbaths were confined to theological self-improvement with the aid of the family bible, of course, but recent changes in our views of leisure activity are just as striking as was our emergence from puritanism. Thus, the view no longer prevails (as it did in the quite recent past) that although leisure was a good thing it was wasted if one did not devote most of it to the pursuit of Culture with a capital C. Today people with the most impeccable cultural credentials may without impropriety savour jazz (even rock) and motor racing.

Although we recognize a class of things which are serious just because they are intrinsically worthwhile, there seems some reason to believe that sports (and games in general) cannot be among these things. It is as though there were something built into the very structure of games which rendered them non-serious. This view is conveyed by the expression, ''Of course, such and such is just a game,'' as though there were something inherently trifling about games. And by the same token, if we find that someone takes a sport or some other game with extraordinary seriousness, we are inclined to say that the pursuit in question has ceased to be a game for him.

This view, though incorrect, may be made quite plausible, I believe, by the following example. Consider The Case of the Dedicated Driver. Mario Stewart (the dedicated driver in question) is a favoured entrant in the motor car race of the century at Malaise. And in the Malaise race there is a rule which forbids a vehicle to leave the track on pain of disqualification. At a dramatic point in the race a child crawls out upon the track directly in the path of Mario's car. The only way to avoid running over the child is to leave the track and suffer disqualification. Mario runs over the child and completes the race.

One is inclined to say that for Mario motor racing is not a sport at all (and certainly not a game!), but a kind of madness. Games (and sports) require a limitation on the means their players may employ, but Mario is obviously the kind of driver who would do anything to win the race. By his insane refusal to stay within proper limits he is no longer playing a game at all. He has destroyed the game.

I submit, however, that we now know what it

takes to destroy a game, and that the behaviour of Mario is not what it takes. If Mario had cut across the infield in his efforts to get ahead of the other drivers, or if he had earlier violated a rule governing engine capacity in the construction of his vehicle, then his behaviour would cease to be game-playing, for he would have broken a constitutive rule. It is thus true to say that there is a limitation imposed in games which is not imposed in other activities, and it is also true that the limitation has to do with the means one can legitimately employ. Hence the plausibility of concluding that Mario was not playing a game, since there appeared to be absolutely no means he would not adopt. But it will be recalled that we earlier discovered that more than one kind of goal is associated with games, and more than one kind of means. The plausibility of the claim that racing for Mario had ceased to be a game rests on a confusion between two of these goals. It is perfectly correct to say that not any means whatever may be used to achieve a *pre-lusory* goal, but this limitation in no way entails a quite different kind of limitation, namely, a limitation on the means for *playing* the game (i.e., attempting to achieve what I earlier called the lusory goal of life).

The point of the story, of course, is not that Mario did a terrible thing, but that it is possible to make a game or a sport the over-riding concern of one's life without falling into some kind of paradox. That extreme dedication to a pursuit should somehow destroy the pursuit would be the real paradox. But that a person will do anything to continue playing a game does not destroy the game, even though it may destroy the person. So saying to Mario that motor racing is just a game is very much like saying to the Pope that Catholicism is just religion, to Beethoven that the quartets are just music, or to Muhammad Ali that boxing is just a sport.

I therefore conclude that sports are precisely like the other interests which occur prominently as leisure activities. They are a type of intrinsic good which, along with many others, make up the class of goals to which we ascribe that primary seriousness which provides such things as factories,

armies, and governments with the derivative seriousness to which they are entitled.

Author's Note.   The section of the paper titled *The Elements
of Game* is a restatement of the substance of the thesis advanced
in "What Is a Game?"[3] However, the language used here is
different from the language of that version, and the definition
of game-playing that I propose has been somewhat altered. The
strategies of the two versions also differ. In "What Is a Game?"
I attempted to produce an adequate definition by successively
modifying a series of proposed definitions. Here, assuming
the adequacy of that definition, I explain and illustrate the elements of game-playing which the definition designates. I should
also note that some of the examples used in the present paper
were originally used in "What Is a Game?"

Bibliography

1. Kolnai, A.: "Games and Aims," *Proceedings of the Aristotelian Society* (1966).
2. Suits, Bernard: "Games and Paradox,"
   Philosophy of Science (1969).
3. Suits, Bernard: "What Is a Game?"
   Philosophy of Science (1967).

A Critique of Mr. Suits' Definition of Game Playing

FRANK McBRIDE

In his book, *The Grasshopper: Games, Life and Utopia* (4), Bernard Suits evolves a unitary definition of "game playing." He has, as he intimates in the Preface, taken Wittgenstein's admonishment to "*look* and *see*" whether there is anything common (to all games) seriously: to have looked, that is, to have seen, and to have found that *game playing* (if not games) does have a common set of characteristics.

To play a game is:

(1) to attempt to achieve a specific state of affairs (prelusory goal)[1]

(2) using only means permitted by the rules (lusory means)

(3) where the rules prohibit use of more efficient in favour of less efficient means (constitutive rules) and

(4) where the rules are accepted just because they make possible such activity (lusory attitude).

(4: p. 41, numbering added)

For those who have struggled with this problem (more generally, the problem of universals),[2] the demands on such a definition are well known; they, nevertheless, bear repeating. Not only must such a definition meet the tests for narrowness and broadness (an extremely difficult matter when dealing with a general term), but it also must avoid the pitfalls of internal and borderline vagueness

and ambiguity, internal inconsistency, and, of course, the vicious circularity almost inherent in a recursive definition. Notwithstanding the severity of these tests, I must say that Mr. Suits has been remarkably successful in this undertaking, far beyond my expectations. As a result of his efforts, I now believe, for example, that both the concepts of "game playing" and of "games" are much less general than I previously thought. I also believe, although I cannot say for certain, that *the proposed definition successfully defines a large class of the game playing universe!* This I find remarkable.

If there are those who view what I have just said as the capitulation statement of a reformed Wittgensteinian, Mr. Suits will not be among them. For, what I have in mind and what he had in mind are, so to speak, horses of different colors. What I have in mind is a "large class of cases." What he had in mind was *all* cases: "a single formula which successfully states the necessary and sufficient conditions for any activity to be an instance of game playing" (4: p. 35). The strength of this claim exposes the definition to even a single, viable counterexample of narrowness or broadness. In what follows I shall take up the challenge to present such a case. I hope that my efforts may also represent a suitable refutation of my reformation.

Reprinted from *Journal of the Philosophy of Sport*, VI, (1979), pp. 59–65. Copyright 1979 by the Philosophic Society for the Study of Sport. Reprinted by permission.

I

The Test of Narrowness

In a memorable account of one of his experiences with Wittgenstein, Norman Malcolm recalls:

> After about two hours of reading or discussion, we would go for a walk and then have tea at Lyons, or in the restaurant above the Regal cinema. Sometimes he came to my house in Searle Street for supper. Once after supper, Wittgenstein, my wife and I went for a walk on Midsummer Common. We talked about the movements of the bodies of the solar system. It occurred to Wittgenstein that the three of us should represent the movements of the sun, earth and moon, relative to one another. My wife was the sun and maintained a steady pace across the meadow; I was the earth and circled her at a trot. Wittgenstein took the most strenuous part of all, the moon, and ran around me while I circled my wife. Wittgenstein entered into this game with great enthusiasm and seriousness, shouting instructions at us as he ran. He became quite breathless and dizzy with exhaustion. (2: pp. 51–52)

Our first task, without reference to the definition, is to decide whether or not this is an account of a game. It seems to me to be a game. Malcolm calls it a "game." In point of fact it seems to be *par excellence* an example of what Suits calls an "open game." "There appear to be what I should be inclined to call *open games*. . . . games which have no inherent goal whose achievement ends the game: crossing a finish line, mating a king, and so on. Games which do have such goals we may call *closed games*" (4: p. 133). At another point he distinguishes open games from closed games by the former's being cooperative ventures and the latter's being competitive ventures. There is, also,

no question that the definition of game playing is intended to account for open games as well as for closed games (4: p. 137).

We must now take a look at this game of "Sun, Earth and Moon" to see whether or not such activity fits the definition of game playing put forward. What we find, I think, will be somewhat perplexing. Taking the criteria of the definition in order, there appear to be: (1) no distinguishable prelusory goal; (2) no specification of means whatsoever; (3) no constitutive rules prohibiting the use of more over less efficient means; and (4) no choice as to why the rules are accepted, just the choice to play or not to play.

With this I must pause for a moment to reflect. Can it be that the definition fails to fit on all four counts? If my analysis is correct the disjunction seems clear: either playing SEM (as I shall abbreviate it) is game playing and the definition is faulty, *or* the definition is valid and playing SEM is not game playing. What I would rather say, at the cost of repeating myself, is that the definition is fine for a very large class of game playing cases, but that it is not sufficient for all cases. However, let us retrace our steps to the game playing itself, and the criteria of the definition.

Try as I will, I seem unable to find a prelusory goal. I find only the lusory goal of representing the movements of the sun, earth, and moon in relationship to each other. Be that as it may, let us assume that I have missed it, that there is a prelusory goal or that the goal which I have identified is prelusory. What will we say about criterion #2, "using only means permitted by the rules (lusory means)?" I can only repeat what I said earlier: there appears to be no specification of means whatsoever.

Perhaps this will all unravel if we turn to criterion #3: "where the rules prohibit use of more efficient over less efficient means (constitutive rules)." Here we encounter what may be an oversight. The constitutive rules of game playing characteristically *define the lusory goal,* not just (if at all) the lusory means. For example, in chess the constitutive rules of the game stipulate *what shall count* as having immobilized the king, as well as the permissible means. We begin with a conventional concept of immobilization (the state of affairs referred to as the prelusory goal), then codify that concept with the constitutive rules of the game, i.e., we add on such conditions as "may not move into check."[3] The unusual thing about SEM is that neither form of constitutive rule seems to fit very well. The only apparent constitutive rule is the rule requiring the players to represent the movements of the sun, earth, and moon, and that rule (or these rules, if you prefer) neither codifies the sought after state of affairs nor restricts the means for seeking that state of affairs. A rejoinder might be anticipated at this point, e.g., "But there is an implied restriction of means, i.e., seeking to achieve the sought after state of affairs *on foot.* It would be more efficient, at least for the moon person, to go by motorscooter (perhaps a handy one that Wittgenstein had placed in the nearby bushes that morning in anticipation of the game)." But this won't do! I do not think that any one of what I have come to call "Bernard's Utopian Condition Devices" (ladders, catapults, escalators, and homing propellant devices) will be sufficient to show that going by foot is a restriction of means. One could, for example, play the game in the air, on land, or in the sea; by plane, on horseback, or by boat; or with any combination of these media. To further complicate the efficiency of means question, neither the size of the orbits nor the speed factors are stipulated. It is merely a general relation or representation that is called for. Besides, one could still play the game in the most austere setting imaginable, for example, at the North Pole with no other means available than foot power. Another way to say it is that one can play a game, at least many games, with *the most efficient available means.*

A final comment on criterion #3 is needed. On Mr. Suits' (4: p. 54) own grounds the concepts of efficiency and inefficiency are vacuous in the absence of a limited resource. The question comes to mind: What is the limited resource of SEM? What is it that we are forbidden to use more of

rather than less of? I have been unable to find such a resource.

Finally, to complete the serial analysis, let us look at criterion #4, "where the rules are accepted just because they make possible such activity (lusory attitude)." The kind of rules referred to here are, I think, constitutive rules restricting the means, i.e., the rules mentioned in criterion #3. *If there are no such rules,* as I have argued, *then there could be no such attitude.* More simply, it seems to me, one either chooses to play or not to play.

What I have attempted to show is that SEM fails to fit the definition in all four respects. What I needed to show, to establish the claim of narrowness, was that SEM failed to fit the definition in at least some respect.

II

The Test of Broadness

I take the following three claims to be true:

A. Some games are sports.
B. Some games are not sports.
C. Some sports are not games.

Clear-cut examples of each category abound: of A, baseball; of B, bridge; of C, fishing. Borderline cases can also be found, such as billiards and bowling. If one were to query a bystander—not a philosopher of sport—for an explanation of this juncture and disjuncture the reply might be something like, "Well, sports involve some sort of physical test. Some games involve this element and some don't"—an adequate response from a bystander, but not from a philosopher of sport. It would not be difficult to point out the inadequacies of the response (which I shall not do here). What is difficult is for anyone, philosopher or nonphilosopher, to give an adequate explanation of these phenomena. Among other things, such a response would require a unitary definition of both sport and games. Upon hearing that Mr. Suits had succeeded in defining game playing, one of my first responses was to think, "Well, at least half of the job is done."

Curiously, what I find in scrutinizing the situation is that the distinction between games and sport is, if anything, less discernible now than it was before. Before, I would have been quite willing, despite the lack of unitary definitions, to have claimed that activities such as high jumping, foot racing, and mountain climbing were sports but not games. Now, I have been told, at least indirectly, that these are examples *par excellence* of game playing. I need not argue here *how these activities fit the criteria of game playing;* Mr. Suits has done so admirably. What I do want to argue is that *they are not examples of game playing* (playing yes, but not game playing). To put the matter more succinctly, with reference to the issue of broadness, what I am saying is that high jumping, foot racing, and mountain climbing are not ordinarily thought of as games and yet they fit the criteria of the definition in all respects. This is, I think, precisely what is meant by saying a definition is too broad. Curious, is it not?

I shall pursue the matter somewhat further, through the conditions of the definition, with an example of my own choosing: Marathoning. Surely, to run a marathon is not to play a game. It is not even, for the vast majority, a race. For many, it is more of a test of their conditioning, or even a festive occasion to meet old friends and to enjoy the countryside and the townsfolk along the route. For some, it is more of an annual ritual than anything else. Whatever the motive or intent, there is usually, perhaps necessarily, a limited resource involved. For most, it is time, but for many it is glycogen, coolant, muscle endurance, or all three of these, i.e., the things needed just to get from A to C via B. Whichever, the one thing these marathoners share is *the conditions of Mr. Suits' definition:* (1) *prelusory goal:* to get from point A to point C, e.g., from Hopkinton to

Boston; (2) *lusory means:* those permitted by the rules; (3) *constitutive rules* (prohibiting more over less efficient means), e.g., by foot via route B, through Wellesley Hills. (It would of course be more efficient to take the Press Bus or to accompany Howard Cosell by helicopter to the roof of the Prudential Center.)[4] (4) *lusory attitude:* acceptance of the inconvenience of having to run the entire way, hills and all, on foot (by the rules, that is) just because it makes the activity possible. The other thing these marathoners share is not being examples of game players. I do not think this latter claim requires an argument; it would be counter-intuitive, I think, to claim that Marathoning is game playing. The burden of proof, so to speak, falls on the inclusion claimant. Surely, if I had introduced Dueling and Debating as counter-examples (which I have not, and will not),[5] I would not be expected to show that these activities are not ordinarily thought of as game playing. The fact that Marathoning is, ordinarily, regarded as a sport does not make it a game.

III

Thus far my critique of Mr. Suits' definition of game playing has been limited to considerations of narrowness and broadness. The thrust has been to provide viable counterexamples. With respect to narrowness, I presented one counterexample from one category of games. For the broadness argument, I mentioned several examples, all from the related category of sport. Several further questions come to mind regarding the issues of narrowness and broadness. I will not attempt to answer these questions here; I merely wish to raise them and to offer a few comments or conjectures about them.

An intriguing question is whether or not other open games (other than SEM) present similar problems. This is another way of re-issuing the question that the Grasshopper and Skepticus supposedly laid to rest, namely, whether or not the original definition will accommodate open games. In retrospect, I think that the root problem with some of these games is the difficulty in making the prelusory-lusory goal distinction. The other problems (lack of a limited resource and no apparent restriction of means) may, at least in part, emanate from this characteristic. There is another problem, an ambiguity of the concept of means, that complicates the analysis of both open and closed game playing situations. To illustrate, in the "Getting from A to C via B" case, there is both *a route* means (via B) and *a conveyance* means (by foot, or whatever) (4: pp. 39–40). The definition does not make it altogether clear whether we should regard one or the other or both as *the* less efficient means. In some games there may be only one kind of means; and in some games one kind of means may be stipulated and the other left open. At any rate, in summary, I think there are sufficient grounds for Skepticus to reopen the argument with respect to open games.

A second question relevant to the issue of narrowness is whether or not the definition applies to all closed game situations. While I believe the definition fits the vast majority of these, I have a notion there may be problems with some. Prime candidates for the trouble here are the so-called guessing games. The trouble begins right at the beginning, i.e., in the determination of the sought after state of affairs. Some of these games have both a deceiver and a deceivee. The sought after state of affairs of the deceiver is not the sought after state of affairs of the deceivee. (Mr. Suits might describe this as "a two player, two role *non-reciprocating* system involving two radically different sought after states of affairs.") The question is whether or not the definition, *as stated,* can accommodate such antagonistic goals.

Another problem relates to the restricted means criterion. Either player, or both, may be encouraged to use the most efficient available means (in one sense or the other) to carry out their goal. This problem may be linked in once again to the apparent lack of a limited resource.

All three of these problems also accompany what I call the "negative goal" game situations, for example, "Step On a Crack and You'll Break Your Mother's Back." In games of this sort, the player(s) attempt to avoid rather than to achieve a certain state of affairs. Despite the logical similarity, I believe there are some attendant troublesome twists. At any rate, at least part of what I want to say here is that until the definition has been tested against all of these aberrant case types we will not be able to say that it applies to all game playing.[6,7]

The unanswered question with respect to broadness is whether or not there are viable non-sport counterexamples. Dueling and debating (the aforementioned candidates) present an interesting initial venture in the search. Both of these conform nicely to the first three criteria of the definition. The applicability of criterion (4), however, is questionable: the purpose of both the dueler and the debater would seem to be something more substantive than the required "just because they make possible the activity." Be that as it may, I suspect that if there are non-sport counterexamples of broadness they will be long on ritual and short on substance.

To conclude, I should add that I have not dealt directly with the overall concept vagueness and ambiguity questions, both of which are linked to the question of fixed meaning, nor have I treated explicitly the question of internal consistency. I should also add that, despite the criticism I have offered, I still find it remarkable to have developed a definition that encompasses so much of the game playing universe.

Notes

1. From the Latin *ludus,* game.
2. For an enlightening discussion of the problem and Wittgenstein's approach to its solution, see Renford Bambrough, "Universals and Family Resemblances" (1).

3. One could hardly be more explicit about the matter than the following: ''We may therefore define constitutive rules as rules which prohibit use of the most efficient means for reaching a prelusory goal'' (4: p. 38).

4. There is also, by the way, a constitutive rule defining what counts as winning a marathon.

5. George Pitcher (3: p. 220) mentions these activities as possible broadness counter-examples. (While the first three criteria seem to fit, there is some question about whether the attitude of the duelist and the debator is lusory.)

6. For starters, we might consult the varied collection of 350 games from all over the world assembled by Iris Vinton (5).

7. A tangential question is whether or not the integrity of the open-closed game dichotomy can be maintained.

Bibliography

1. Bambrough, Renford. ''Universals and Family Resemblances.'' *Proceedings of the Aristotelian Society, LXI* (1960–61), 207–222.

2. Malcolm, Norman. *Ludwig Wittgenstein, A Memoir.* London: Oxford University Press, 1967.

3. Pitcher, George. *The Philosophy of Wittgenstein.* Englewood Cliffs, N.J.: Prentice-Hall, Inc., 1964.

4. Suits, Bernard. *The Grasshopper: Games, Life and Utopia.* Toronto: University of Toronto Press, 1978.

5. Vinton, Iris. *The Folkways Omnibus of Children's Games.* Harrisburg, Pa.: The Stackpole Company, 1970.

On McBride on the Definition of Games

BERNARD SUITS

Reply to McBride

As a Wittgensteinian who is disposed seriously to participate in the process of definition testing, McBride is, if not a downright contradiction in terms, then at least a decidedly anomalous individual. For most Wittgensteinians are *a priorists* when it comes to definitions, being quite certain beforehand that any attempt to formulate one is an entirely futile undertaking. So McBride's astonishment at finding that my definition captures a large class of games is no greater than my astonishment at McBride's finding that it does. And though he assures us that he is not a reformed Wittgensteinian, there is good reason to anticipate such a change in his future. For in granting that my definition has captured a large class of games, he is also granting that the list of nine games Wittgenstein presents in *Philosophical Investigations*— as demonstrating decisively the lack of commonality among things called games—contains eight games that my definition captures. In short, McBride acknowledges that in Wittgenstein's paradigmatic anti-definitional example, the master is nearly ninety per cent wrong.

Indeed McBride, in his largely lucid exposition

and questioning of my definition (save for certain exceptions to be noted in due course), does not sound like a Wittgensteinian most of the time. For one does not have to be a Wittgensteinian in order to ask the questions McBride asks; probably one *cannot* be a Wittgensteinian and still ask them. Throughout his remarks McBride sounds a good deal more like Socrates than he does like Ludwig.

The burden of McBride's critique consists in his advancing what purport to be two decisive counter-examples to the definition of games I propose. The existence of certain racing events, he argues, shows that my definition is too broad, for such events, while conforming in every respect to my definition, are not thought of as games. And on the other side, he contends that the definition is too narrow on the ground that it excludes a game once played by Wittgenstein. I shall argue that McBride is answerable on both counts, beginning with races.

The Fool on the Hill

In denying that races (and in general track events) are games, McBride uses as his specific counter-example the Boston Marathon. But the way in which he presents this example needs some cleaning up before it can serve his purpose. He writes that he is not even sure that "Marathoning" (McBride's expression, not mine) is a race, since for many of the entrants it may be just a pleasant outing in the country, or the like (1: p. 63). But

Excerpt reprinted from "McBride and Paddick on *The Grasshopper*", *Journal of the Philosophy of Sport*, VIII, (1981), pp. 70–78. Copyright 1982 by the Philosophic Society for the Study of Sport. Reprinted by permission.

what is the relevance of this observation? If for some entrants the event is not even a race, then I would hardly want to claim that it was, for those entrants, a game either. In any case, when McBride gets down to showing that the event conforms to my definition (which is, after all, the whole point of his criticism here), he analyzes it as a race, not as a pleasant outing. And now to my reply.

In constructing my definition I began with certain activities which are indisputably games—what might be called hard core games: if the members of such a group are not games, then nothing is. In this group I included bridge, baseball, golf, hockey, chess, Monopoly—things everyone calls games. I have no doubt that McBride would include such games in the class that he agrees my definition captures. But he balks at my inclusion of races within that class because races, while they do conform to my definition, are not called (or thought of as) games. Superficially this looks like a perfect counter-example, and it would be if my definition purported to define all (and only) uses of the word "game." But it does not. The definition is intended to give an account not of all uses of the word "game," but an account of what games are, a task neither totally independent of usage nor totally dominated by it. The criticism thus misses, or at least it falls short of, its mark. For I submit that when some activity or enterprise not initially included in the hard core group (e.g., because it is not called a game) is seen, upon examination, to conform to the group's definition, then there exists a good *prima facie* reason for granting that that activity or enterprise *is* a game, despite the fact that it is not called one. It seems to me that now the burden of proof shifts to the critic, and that he must show cause why that additional activity should *not* be acknowledged to be a game. And this showing cause must, I suggest, consist in his identifying a property of the additional activity which is sufficient to include it in a class different from, and exclusive of, the class my definition picks out. Now the required property, I further suggest, cannot be simply the property of being *called* something else, because

that is not a feature of the thing but of our language about things, and one of the chief purposes of definition is to correct, or at least to make more exact, our referential language.

I believe that the general principle here at issue can be made quite convincing by the following example. Let us identify the following class of activities: watching things dip. This class includes watching the boat dip against the background of the horizon, watching dancers dip against the background of the ball room, watching a dipper dip through the water in the bucket, and so on. Now I want to include one additional item in this class: watching the earth dip—which anyone can do by facing east at dawn on a clear day. But we find that this activity is never called, nor is it customarily thought of, as watching the earth dip. It is always called, and almost always thought of, as watching the sun rise. So very often we call things by the wrong names because of culture lag: our ancestors, who formed this part of our language, thought the sun moved. It is true, of course, that we also call things by the wrong names not because of culture lag but simply because it is more useful to call then by the wrong names: since it *looks* as though the sun is rising, we are calling attention to a common experience by using the expression "sunrise." I am not, accordingly, calling for a reform of our language. I am not recommending, for example, that we begin saying things like "That was a beautiful earth-dip this morning." For even astronomers use the expression "the sun is rising" while knowing full well that it is really the earth that is revolving. And the fool on the hill sees the sun going down, but the eyes in his head see the world spinning round. So I am not particularly suggesting that races of the kind under consideration be called games; just that, in the absence of some further distinguishing property, they be acknowledged, upon reflection, to *be* games.

The Malcolms in the Field

The issue here is a putative game which McBride introduces by quoting Norman Malcolm's account of it as played by himself, Mrs. Malcolm, and Wittgenstein: Mrs. Malcolm, representing the sun, walked across a meadow while Norman as the earth trotted around her, and at the same time Wittgenstein as the moon sped around Norman. For short, McBride (1: p. 60) calls this enterprise SEM, for Sun, Earth, and Moon. McBride claims that since SEM is a game but does not conform to my definition, my definition of games is shown to be too narrow.

Let me preface the body of my reply to McBride on this point by putting some preliminary questions to him. Mr. McBride, in proposing counter-examples to my definition, how do you know whether you have got hold of a game example or of a non-game example? Is it enough for something to count as an example of a game that someone has called it a game, even if it is only Norman Malcolm who has done so? And is it enough for something to count as an example of a non-game that no one has called it a game? And if no one, not even Norman Malcolm, had called SEM a game (but, say, a pastime instead), would you still count it as an example of a game? These are not idle or rhetorical questions, but serious inquiries from one worker in the Socratic vineyard to another.

In maintaining that my definition does not capture SEM, McBride (1: p. 60) claims that SEM contains ''(1) no distinguishable prelusory goal; (2) no specification of means whatever; (3) no constitutive rules prohibiting the use of more over less efficient means; (4) no choice as to why the rules are accepted, just the choice to play or not to play.'' Now, the fact that McBride didn't find any of these things in SEM is not conclusive proof that they are not there to be found. With care and patience, let us see if we can succeed where he has failed.

Putting aside SEM for just a moment, follow along with me, if you will, while I invent a game. First I set myself a goal: to be running around some object. Now, I can make this more easy or more difficult for myself. In as much as my rate of speed and my endurance are limited resources, I can make the enterprise more difficult by running around a moving rather than a stationary object, and so I set up the situation in that way. Now, there appear quite clearly to be two means at my disposal for circling the object: (a) by regulating its velocity, or (b) by regulating my own. I adopt the means-limiting constitutive rule: Do not decrease the velocity of the object (or do not decrease it below a certain level, or at least do not decrease it to zero—depending on how great I want the challenge to be). And my reason for adopting that rule is just so that I can be engaging in the activity constituted by its adoption (and not for some further purpose, e.g., so that I can observe all sides of a runner moving at a certain velocity—something a trainer of athletes might conceivably, even if implausibly, want to do on some occasion).

I submit that the above is a game according to my definition of games. (I have formulated it as an open game, but I could equally well have made it a closed game by setting up a slightly different prelusory goal, e.g., circling the object five times.) Though the foregoing is, I am satisfied, a game, it is not SEM. So let us ask what SEM adds to the game I have described. It might at first be thought that SEM adds nothing more to the game than some non-essential ornamentation, like the coloured head-bands some tennis players now wear. But there is a bit more to it than that. Notice first that the game I have described—let us call it CMO for Circle a Moving Object—is at most a two-person game (I say ''at most'' because the player of CMO could be moving around objects other than persons—streetcars, for example): one person to run and another person to run around the first. So SEM differs from CMO by adding a third participant and also, of course, by giving each an astronomical role to perform.

Now, keeping CMO at the back of our minds, let us observe the following game of SEM in progress. The Malcolms are performing their roles of sun and earth effortlessly and well, but Ludwig is red in the face, panting, and beginning to stumble. Seeing this, Mrs. Malcolm calls out, ''Norman, let us stand still for a bit, so that Ludwig can get around you next time without killing himself.'' But Ludwig calls back, ''Don't you dare stop, Norman, that would ruin the game.'' There are, I suggest, two different reasons Ludwig might have for declining Mrs. Malcolm's humanitarian proposal. (1) If SEM is just ornamented CMO, his reason would be that to accept this easing of the situation would be to break a constitutive rule of the game. But, (2) if SEM is not CMO, but just a depiction of the relative movements of the sun, earth, and moon, then his reason for declining the offer would be that the heavenly bodies do not stop in their courses. In one case, Norman's stopping would be to cheat (or at least to commit an infraction) in a game; in the other case, it would be to misrepresent the solar system. Well, then, which is SEM—the game of CMO or the production of a planetary model? It could be either one of these things, I shall argue, depending upon the motives of the participants.

(1) In considering the possibility that SEM is essentially CMO, there appears to be an initial difficulty. If we hold that the third player required by SEM (but not by CMO), as well as the astronomical roles assumed by the players, are irrelevant bits of ornamentation—and thus just excess baggage—we weaken our claim that SEM could be *essentially* CMO. But I think that the theatrical elements of SEM—the characters and plot, as it were—are quite intimately related to the strictly game features of CMO, in the following way. CMO can, of course, be played by making the unenforced decision not to retard or stop the object being circled, just as honest golfers tally all their strokes even when no one is watching them. But by imbedding CMO in SEM (or by constructing SEM as a setting for CMO), the abstract prohibition against stopping the O in CMO is given dramatic embodiment: to cheat (or to commit an infraction) is at the same time to destroy the model in terms of which the game is expressed and the game's cardinal rule dramatically enforced. This is a very different kettle of fish from mere ornamentation. If we move from coloured headbands to the representational features of chessmen, we are moving away from mere ornamentation and toward that intimate relation which exists between the astronomical features of SEM and the abstract

features of CMO, but we are not moving very far in that direction. That the clergy is represented in chess as always moving obliquely is, to be sure, amusing on its own account, but the real-life counterpart of no chess piece has the direct impact on chess that the movements of sun, earth, and moon have on SEM-as-CMO.

A final word on the possibility that SEM is essentially CMO is in order before turning to the possibility that it is essentially something else. It might reasonably be said that if SEM is the kind of game I have described, then it is a somewhat unusual game, for of the three participants only two are playing (Mrs. Malcolm is not making CMO moves), and Norman and Ludwig appear to be playing slightly different, though intimately related, games (in very much the way that two engaged gears are intimately related). That is so. SEM is, in terms I used in *The Grasshopper* to describe the behaviour of Porphyryo Sneak and Bartholomew Drag, a three-person two-player game. It is even possible that SEM as played by the Malcolms and Wittgenstein was a three-person *one*-player game, where Ludwig alone was playing CMO while the Malcolms functioned as little more than a piece of playground equipment, namely, a two-geared machine for producing a suitable moving object. This possibility receives some support from Malcolm's concluding remark in describing the enterprise: "Wittgenstein entered into this game with great enthusiasm and seriousness, shouting instructions to us as he ran. He became quite breathless and dizzy with exhaustion" (1: p. 60).[1] As a three-person one-player game the relation between SEM and CMO takes on a somewhat sinister aspect, does it not? I, at any rate, cannot avoid the feeling that in suggesting SEM to the Malcolms, Wittgenstein had conned them into constructing a planetarium just so he could be playing CMO.

(2) Let us now consider the possibility that SEM is not a dramatic vehicle for playing CMO, but a forthright attempt to construct a model of part of the solar system out of the motions of three human bodies. At once everything changes. For now the extra effort required to circle a moving

in contrast to a stationary object is regarded not as the focusing challenge of the entire enterprise (as it is in SEM-as-CMO), but simply as the most difficult and bothersome part of constructing this particular model. And here the following kinds of tactics would be reasonable ones to employ, whereas in SEM-as-CMO they would be just the ones to avoid: slowing down the rates of sun and earth so that earth and moon could perform their orbitings more effectively, assigning the person with greatest endurance to the moon role (the moon does not wheeze or falter), and so on.

The difference between the two interpretations of SEM that I have suggested can be summarized by imagining Wittgenstein putting to himself the following question: "Am I running around Norman in order to be producing a planetary model, or am I producing a planetary model in order to be running around Norman?" And if one is inclined to answer "Both," that does not affect the point I shall presently make (though I believe it raises difficulties of its own), which is that there still are two possible interpretations of SEM, and that one of them warrants calling SEM a game and the other does not.

If McBride had analyzed SEM as essentially a case of adroitly theatricalized CMO, I would, of course, agree with him that SEM ought to be called (and thought of) as a game. But if McBride were to agree that he was justified in calling SEM a game for *that* reason, then SEM would not be a damaging counter-example to my definition, since SEM as CMO *does* conform to the definition. So I shall assume that McBride would think that SEM is a game even when it is undertaken as straightforward model construction. What reason would McBride have for thinking this? I suspect the answer is that McBride is inclined to call SEM a game solely because it was undertaken, in Malcolm's account of it, as a leisure-time pursuit. He calls it a game, if my suspicion is correct, because of the social context in which it occurred, and not because of anything it inherently is. For it is clear that SEM would not be called (or thought of as) a game even by McBride if it were performed by a group of astronomers who wished to

exhibit to view the workings of the solar system but lacked any equipment for doing so except their own bodies. For the madcap Malcolms and their illustrious companion, in contrast, the setting for their performing SEM was not work-time but play-time. So they think of themselves as playing a game while the astronomers would think of themselves as activating a planetarium. But surely SEM ought to be called a game for *this* reason, only if *all* pastimes ought to be called games (dancing a jig, singing a song, building a snowman). Perhaps this is *not* why McBride wants to call SEM a game. If it is not, then I would like him to ask himself why he does want to call it a game, and if he should come up with an interesting answer I would be pleased to have him report back.

In presenting SEM as a counter-example, McBride claimed (a) that it was a game, and (b) that it was not encompassed by my definition. But the foregoing analysis appears to show that SEM cannot meet both these requirements. If it is interpreted as a game, it fails to meet requirement (b), and if it is so interpreted that it is not encompassed by my definition, it fails requirement (a). Therefore, pending a third interpretation of SEM that meets both requirements, I conclude that the counter-example fails.

The Fliers in the Ointment

The third and concluding section of McBride's discussion consists very largely in his taking a number of fliers (that is, drawing a number of bows at a venture) in hope of hitting something. Such fliers are not really criticisms—if a criticism is something that can sensibly be responded to—but what I am inclined to call "wonderments." To let loose a wonderment in discussion is to mention something about your opponent's position which might (but equally well might not) entail a weakness in that position, and then to leave the matter there. Here is a non-philosophical example of using a wonderment in this way:

"Where are you off to, then?"

"I'm going to meet John in the common room."

"I wonder if he'll be there."

"What makes you think he won't be there?"

"I *don't* think he won't be there."

"Well, do you have some reason for thinking he *might* not be there?"

"Not particularly."

"You haven't heard that he has fallen ill or been called away or detained somewhere else?"

"No, certainly not, though any one of those things is surely possible."

"No doubt one can wonder about every bloody thing that comes up, but in the absence of any relevant data pro or con, such wondering is surely idle."

"I wonder if that's always the case."

"Do you have some evidence that it is not always the case?"

"No, I was just wondering."

The insidious thing about wonderments in philosophical discussion is that they can easily be mistaken for genuine criticisms, and once that mistake has been made the respondent to a wonderment finds himself doing a decidedly odd thing. For in order to respond to a wonderment it is necessary to render it non-vacuous, and so the respondent in the common room episode was easily seduced into suggesting to his tormentor a number of possible circumstances which might give some point to the blank wonderment as initially expressed. Was the wonderer suggesting that John had fallen ill, been called away, detained? Thus the wonderment ploy, when it works, requires the respondent not only to answer an objection, but also to formulate the very objection he must answer, and thus to do all of the "critic's" work for him.

McBride (1: p. 68) is, in effect, merely wondering about the following points: (1) whether the fact that games are likely to permit multiple means raises any problems for the definition; (2) whether games where the players have different goals have any impact on the definition; (3) whether there can be games where the players are expected to play with unlimited efficiency. (Re-reading Chapter Eight might help McBride here, though to say so is to begin to slide into the trap of trying to formulate McBride's objection for him). (4) McBride

begins to raise a non-vacuous issue with his question about negative goals, but instead of pursuing the issue he lets it peter out in a wonderment. He asks whether games like Step on a Crack and Break Your Mother's Back (we will call it SCBYMB) require the player to avoid rather than to achieve some state of affairs. If so, such games would appear to discredit the definition, which represents games solely as efforts to *achieve* some state of affairs. But, having raised the issue, McBride (1: p. 64) does not pursue it, but simply wonders about it: "Despite the logical similarity I believe there are some attendant troublesome twists." Period. Nevertheless, I shall be sporting in this case and deal with SCBYMB. If that game has the negative goal of not stepping on a crack, then the game can be played (and won) by never going outside your broadloomed abode, or by always going about in a wheelchair. So there must be something wrong with saying that the game requires its players to avoid rather than to achieve something, and then just leaving the matter there. In fact, SCBYMB requires its players to achieve that state of affairs consisting in (1) walking, (2) on a surface that contains some cracks, (3) without stepping on any of them. This is, of course, a positive goal; the fact that it involves a prohibition does not make the goal negative, any more than the off-sides rule in North American football means that football players are trying to avoid *rather than* to achieve something.

Finally (5), toward the close of his critique, McBride (1: p. 64f) hauls off and lets fly a kind of capping wonderment which may not at first be recognized as such, because it is wrapped up in another debating technique, the Disingenuous Disclaimer Ploy: "I should add that I have not dealt directly with the overall concept vagueness and ambiguity questions, both of which are linked to the question of fixed meaning, nor have I treated explicitly the question of internal consistency." McBride is here inviting the reader to wonder about three (or possibly four) distinct sources of possible difficulty without giving the slightest hint as to why they should be so regarded. Compare prosecuting counsel concluding his summation to the jury: "Finally, the Crown takes due note of the fact that twenty witnesses have attested to the good character of the accused, and let me candidly admit that I have simply not dealt with the possibility that, unknown to those witnesses, accused is in fact a wife-beater, a perjurer, and a drunkard." A final comment on McBride's disclaimer. If he has not, in fact, satisfied himself as to the definition's adequacy with respect to the three or four conditions he mentions, how on earth can he believe that the definition captures a large class of games, or indeed anything at all?

The Dregs in the Cup

Four mini-issues raised by McBride deserve comment: (1) McBride (1: p. 59) refers to my definition of games as a "recursive" definition. It isn't. (2) He questions (1: p. 64) the presence of lusory attitude in the cases of dueling and debating. My reply is that honest duels (that is, duels which are not merely set-ups or charades played out to meet the technical demands of a code of honour) are games and so involve lusory attitude. Chapter Thirteen discusses this kind of issue at length. Debating, I should think, is not a game, but a member of that class of inherently *judged* events (as opposed to refereed events) which also includes diving and band competitions, as well as pie baking and beauty contests. (I here repudiate the view I once expressed—though not in *The Grasshopper*—that all sports are simply athletic *games* institutionalized in certain ways.) (3) McBride (1: p. 62) complains that my account of games has left more blurred than it was before the line between sports and games. Surely not. It is just that, if my definition is accepted, more sports are games than McBride would have thought, and that in general there are more games in heaven and earth than McBride has dreamt of in his philosophy. Fewer, too. (4) Finally, I return, as McBride (1: p. 65) does in his last sentence, to the "remarkable" fact that my definition has encompassed "so much of the game playing universe." This is remarkable to Wittgensteinians only because they have, remarkably, failed to notice that ordinary language has a strong essentialist bent. To a considerable extent, that is what makes it possible for ordinary people to communicate with one another.

Notes

1. This possibility is lent further support by noticing that the planetary model which emerges in the process of performing SEM is inaccurate in two interesting respects: (1) Surely Mrs. Malcolm as Sun ought to be stationary rather than mobile in the heliocentric model that SEM is clearly meant to be. (2) Norman as Earth ought to be spinning at the same time that he is orbiting Mrs. Malcolm as Sun. But if Sun and Earth are *not* primarily astronomical representations but, taken together, primarily a device for producing an object moving at a desired rate of speed, these anomalies are explained. (1) Sun's moving demands a velocity in Earth's orbit greater than would be the case if Sun were stationary, and this in turn produces a greater challenge for Moon. (2) Since it is no more of a challenge to circle a spinning object than it is to circle a non-spinning object, Earth is not required to revolve on its axis in what need be, after all, only an approximately accurate planetary model—just accurate enough to facilitate the playing of CMO.

Bibliography

1. McBride, Frank, "A Critique of Mr. Suits' Definition of Game Playing." *Journal of the Philosophy of Sport.* 6 (1979), 59–65.
2. Suits, Bernard, *The Grasshopper: Games, Life and Utopia.* Toronto: University of Toronto Press, 1978.

The Ethos of Games

FRED D'AGOSTINO

This paper is concerned with games of the ordinary kind such as cricket, baseball, soccer, hockey, and basketball, and not with practices (speaking, behaving morally, etc.), which may or may not be games, or which may be games only in some metaphorical sense.[1] What I say may, however, have some bearing on our understanding of such practices.

My aim is to show that it is important to recognize that any particular game has an ethos as well as a set of formal rules. By the ethos of a game I mean those conventions determining how the formal rules of that game are applied in concrete circumstances.

I will consider a widely canvassed account of games that does not recognize the importance of the ethos of a game, show that this account is irreparably defective in various ways, and show that an account of games which recognizes that every game has an ethos is not defective in these ways and has other advantages as well.

Formalism

I use the term "formalism" to refer to an account of games according to which various game-derivative notions are defined solely in terms of the formal rules of a game. According to formalism, then, for a particular game G:

1. 'is playing G' MEANS 'is following the formal rules of G'. "To engage in a practice . . . means to follow the appropriate rules." (8: p. 26)

2. 'is action in G' MEANS 'is action in accordance with the formal rules of G'. "Action breaking a rule will be ineffectual or impossible within the rule-context, or it will be judged not in that context at all." (5: p. 270)

3. 'is an instance of G' MEANS 'is activity in accordance with the formal rules of G'. "If an instance of behavior does not fulfill the rules of a game . . . [we] discount the behavior as an instance of playing the game." (3: p. 73)

4. 'wins G' MEANS 'succeeds by means of activity in accordance with the formal rules of G'. "One cannot (really) win the game unless he plays it, and one cannot (really) play the game unless he obeys the rules of the game." (10: p. 150)

As stated, formalism is a very strong thesis. We shall see just how strong in the next section. I do not define formalism in this way in order to set up a straw man, however; I have in fact at least three reasons for defining formalism in this way: (a) formalism informs many philosophically standard accounts of games; (b) those philosophers who have recognized that formalism is, as I will argue, overly strong have by and large done so in the context of otherwise formalistic discussions of games;[2] (c) formalism has a valid kernel or core; it does help illuminate certain aspects of games. I will consider this third point in the next section.

Reprinted from *Journal of the Philosophy of Sport,* VIII, (1981), pp. 7–18. Copyright 1982 by the Philosophic Society for the Study of Sport. Reprinted by permission.

Proformalistic Considerations

One can have various personal ends in view when playing a particular game. But whatever these ends, one thing is clear: One's means for achieving these ends are importantly limited in ways they would not be in a more purely "technical" exercise. If one chooses to realize some end by playing a particular game, then there are some means to that end which one cannot appropriately employ. It is quite natural to suppose that the rules of the game determine the limits on the means which can be employed in playing that game to achieve some particular end. Black (1: p. 124) put this point as follows: "Games of skill are played for the sake of winning *according to the rules* (if all you wanted was a touchdown, why not shoot the opposing team?)." Here, then, is part of the appeal of formalism when it is formulated as a strong thesis. If 'is playing G' MEANS 'is following the formal rules of G', then we can explain why participants in a game employ only limited means (and means limited only in particular ways) to achieve whatever ends they may have in view. The explanation is as follows. It is a consequence of formalism that 'to achieve an end by playing G' MEANS 'to achieve an end by following the rules of G'. But the behavior of one who follows such rules is limited by them in particular ways.

Formalism also has a ready and plausible explanation for another important and undoubted fact about games. When someone refuses to submit to authoritative official decisions about the conduct of some game G, he or she will, in the ordinary course of events, be banished from the field of play or be held to have forfeited the game (or both). Here is another part of the appeal of formalism. When it is formulated as a strong thesis, we can explain why participants in a game who refuse to submit to authoritative official decisions are banished from the field of play. The explanation is this. According to formalism, 'is playing G' MEANS 'is following the formal rules of G'. But

authoritative official decisions about the conduct of G invoke the formal rules of G. Following these rules thus entails being willing to submit to such decisions. From this, it in turn follows that a necessary condition for the truth of 'x is playing G' is that x be willing to submit to authoritative decisions invoking the rules of G.' It is a consequence of formalism, then, that 'is unwilling to submit to authoritative decisions about G' MEANS 'is unwilling to play G'. But it is natural to banish from the field of play persons who are unwilling to behave as players.

Formalism as I have formulated it is not a straw man, then, at least partly because it does have explanatory power with respect to some important features of games. This is the appealing side of formalism. I consider its unappealing side in the next section.

Antiformalist Considerations

At least two telling points against a formalist account of games exist.

1. If 'is playing G' MEANS (as it does according to formalism) 'is following the formal rules of G' then a formalist account of games effaces the distinction in ordinary language between playing and playing fairly (i.e., according to the rules). Against formalism, we might maintain, with Quinn (7: p. 80), that "it seems more reasonable to say that the cheater is not playing fairly than that he is not playing at all." Furthermore, one need not regard ordinary language as authoritative to find this distinction an important and useful one. It is useful, for instance, in explanatory contexts. Why was x penalized? It seems right to say that x was penalized because he or she was not playing fairly. It does not seem right to say that x was penalized because he or she was not playing at all. If this individual was not playing at all, then what is the *point* of penalizing him?

2. According to formalism, 'x is an instance of G' MEANS 'x is activity in accordance with

the formal rules of G'. But in this case, formalists are driven to a kind of Platonism about games. For them, games are ideal types; they are only very imperfectly realized in their alleged instances. Certainly, any instance of G in which any rule of G is violated is not, on this account, really an instance of G.

Two points need to be made about the Platonistic implications of a formalist account of games. First, we have no reason to believe that formalists intended their account of games to be an account only of "ideal" games that are very imperfectly realized by the games people actually play. If they did have some such intention, then what is the point of their occasional ad hoc remarks about the excessive strength of formalism? Presumably, formalism could be excessively strong only if it were intended as an account of "real" games. Second, it is, in any event, not clear that Platonism about games is as innocuous as is Platonism in the natural or social sciences. When a scientist constructs an ideal type model of an actual physical or social system, the construction is justified to the extent that the behavior of the real system approximates that of the ideal system more and more closely as certain limiting conditions are approximated. And, if formalism is correct, this suggests that a "real" game should approximate its ideal type (in which no rule-violating behavior occurs) as its players become more and more skillful. But this, of course, is not the case. Although it may be true that more skillful players *unintentionally* engage in rule-violating behavior less frequently than less skillful players, it certainly need not be true that "real" games between more skillful players approximate more closely to their ideal types than do "real" games between less skillful players. More skillful players may intentionally engage in rule-violating behavior *more* frequently than less skillful players. (As we shall see, this depends on the ethos of the "real" game which they are engaged in playing.)

Of these anti-formalist considerations, this latter is, I think, the more telling. In the next two sec-

tions, I will construct a defense for formalism against this point, and subsequently, I will show why this defense fails.

The Problem of Platonism

Formalism entails that no activity is an instance of some particular game G if any rule of G is violated during that activity. This, in turn, entails that formalism provides what I have called a Platonistic account of games: if a rule of G is violated during an alleged instance of G, then this alleged instance is not in fact a genuine instance of G. This consequence of formalism can, however, apparently be avoided by interpreting the rules of a game in a particular way.

We might propose, then, that the rules of a game G are all conditional in form—that is, that they have one of a number of normal forms such as

R_m: if x performs action a, then x makes move m in G; or

R_p: if x performs action b, then x is subject to *penalty p*.

I call this proposal the regimentation thesis, since it embodies the claim that the forms of the rules of a game can be regimented in a particular way.

Now, if all of the rules of G have some such forms as R_m and R_p and, in particular, if none of the rules of G has the form

R_v: action b is prohibited in G,

it then follows that no rule of G can be violated. For instance, x does not violate a rule of the form R_p if he or she performs the action b. A rule of this form, unlike a rule of the form R_v, does not prohibit the performance of action b, and so is not violated if some player does perform this action.[4]

The regimentation thesis, then, provides a solution for the problem of Platonism. If the regimentation thesis is accepted, formalism does not entail a Platonistic account of games. This is so because formalism does entail Platonism only if it is possible to violate the rules of a game. But it is precisely this possibility which the regimentation thesis rules out. Any activity which positively instantiates the rules of G will, on this account, count as a genuine instance of G.

Before saying why this solution does not really rescue formalism from all of its difficulties, it may be appropriate to consider the status of the regimentation thesis. This thesis is not an empirical one. It is not a claim about the forms of rules of games as these are actually recorded in official rulebooks. It is, rather, a proposal of a kind rather similar to Quine's (6: §33) proposal about the regimentation of ordinary language. According to the regimentation thesis, we can better understand the nature of games by treating their rules as if they did in fact conform to the standard normal forms R_m and R_p. This proposal is incorrect, however, as I will show in the next section.

Against the Regimentation Thesis

There is at least one good reason for rejecting the regimentation thesis and, with it, the possibility of defending formalism in the way previously outlined. We would normally be inclined to say, and it is explanatorily useful to be able to say, that a penalty in G is invoked because some rule of G has been violated. The *point* of penalties in G is to punish violations of the rules of G. But the regimentation thesis rules out the possibility of describing the point of penalties in this way. If the regimentation thesis is correct, then the rules of some game cannot be violated and, a fortiori, we cannot say that penalties in G have been imposed because the rules of G have been violated. To preserve a quite sensible account of penalties, then, we must reject the regimentation thesis and, with it, the possibility of avoiding the Platonistic implications of formalism.

Of course, the recommended account of penalties is that suggested by our ordinary intuitions

about games. Rejecting these intuitions, the formalist might offer something like the following alternative account of the point of penalties. A regimented rule of the form R_p of G specifies a kind of behavior b and a kind of penalty p which is to be invoked when b is performed in G. The penalty p is invoked against b, then, because invoking p is, according to the rule of the form R_p, the appropriate official response to b.

Ordinary intuitions aside, why is this account of penalties less satisfactory than that supported by these intuitions? This alternative account of penalties suggests that the only rational motive a participant in G might have for refraining from b is that engaging in such behavior is likely to be technically inefficient since it is likely to be penalized. But, surely, participants in G often refrain from b, not for reasons of technical efficiency, but because they believe that engaging in b is, by and large, inappropriate in the context of G. It is the inappropriateness, rather than the technical inefficiency of penalty-liable behavior which this alternative account of penalties fails to capture. The standard account, on the other hand, has a ready explanation for this fact. On this account, penalty-liable behavior is inappropriate because it is prohibited. Thus, ordinary intuitions aside, the formalist account of penalties is less satisfactory than the standard account.

Invoking the regimentation thesis rids formalism of its Platonistic implications only at the cost of exacerbating the problem of penalties. In the next section, I will construct a defense of formalism which takes the problem of penalties as a central concern. Subsequently, I will show why this defense of formalism also fails.

The Problem of Penalties

With or without the regimentation thesis, formalism cannot satisfactorily explain the nature of penalties. We can apparently solve this problem, however, by distinguishing two different kinds of rules of games.

We might propose that each rule of G is either a constitutive rule or a regulative rule, but not both constitutive and regulative. We might further propose: (a) that only the constitutive rules of G define various G-derivative notions ('is playing G', 'is an instance of G', etc.), and (b) that all the penalty-invoking rules of G are regulative rules and have the normal form R_v. (On this account, every penalty-invoking rule of G is regulative, but not constitutive. For instance, the rule in football prohibiting ''clipping'' is, on this account, a regulative but not a constitutive rule of football.)[5] I call this proposal the dichotomization thesis, because it embodies the claim that the set of rules of G can be dichotomized unequivocally into two subsets; namely, the subset consisting of the constitutive rules of G and the subset consisting of the regulative rules of G.

The dichotomization thesis provides a plausible solution for the problem of penalties. If x performs some action b prohibited by some regulative rule of G, then x ipso facto violates that rule, and this is the reason why x is penalized for performing that action. In short, if we interpret formalism in terms of the dichotomization thesis, then no problem of penalties is posed for formalism.

But since, on this account, only the constitutive rules of G define various G-derivative notions, the dichotomization thesis also apparently provides a solution for the problem of Platonism. If we say that 'is an instance of G' MEANS 'is activity in accordance with the *constitutive* rules of G', then only those alleged instances of G in which the constitutive rules of G are violated would fail to be genuine instances of G. Since, on this account, the regulative rules of G do not define G, the many candidate-instances of G in which only regulative rules of G are violated are, as commonsense dictates, genuine instances of G. In short, if we interpret formalism in terms of the dichotomization thesis, then formalism apparently has no Platonistic implications.

Before saying why this solution does not really rescue formalism from its various difficulties, it may be appropriate to consider the status of the dichotomization thesis. Like the regimentation the-

sis, the dichotomization thesis is a proposal, rather than an empirical claim. According to the dichotomization thesis, it is possible to treat the rules of a game as if each rule were unequivocally either constitutive or regulative, but not both, and to do so without conceptual or explanatory loss. In the next section, I will show that this proposal is, in fact, incorrect.

Against the Dichotomization Thesis

There are two related reasons for supposing that formalism, as interpreted by the dichotomization thesis, does not provide a satisfactory account of games.

1. According to the dichotomization thesis, all of the penalty-invoking rules of a game G are regulative, not constitutive rules of G. As such, the penalty-invoking rules of G do not define G or the various G-derivative notions.

Consider, then, a regulative rule r of G, and the game G', which differs from G only in that r is not a (constitutive or regulative) rule of G'. Because r does not define G, the games G and G' are, according to formalism, the same game. For some choices of r, our intuitions about G and G' will probably confirm this alleged identity. But for other choices, our intuitions are likely to be radically at variance with this alleged identity. For instance, let G be soccer, and let r be the rule prohibiting ''handball.'' Is G' here the ''same'' game as G? It seems clear that this identity fails to obtain in this case. (There is probably a continuum of cases in this regard.) Of course, we could avoid this conclusion by defining a game G in terms both of its constitutive and some of its regulative rules. But this account would again have Platonistic implications.

The dichotomization thesis and formalism together entail that G and G' are the same game just when they have the same constitutive rules, whatever their respective regulative rules might be. This claim is, in certain cases, refuted by compelling commonsense intuitions about the "identity of games." Thus, the dichotomization thesis cannot provide a satisfactory interpretation for the formalist account of games.

2. The argument just presented in effect establishes, contrary to the dichotomization thesis, that the distinction between constitutive and regulative rules is (for games at least) somewhat arbitrary. A rule which is regulative from the formal point of view (a penalty-invoking rule of the form R_v) may be constitutive from the intuitive point of view.[6] But, in fact, even if this dichotomy were not arbitrary in this way, it could be drawn only in a way which reduces, but does not entirely eliminate, the Platonistic implications of a formalist account of games.

Among the constitutive rules of G will be rules that define various moves in G and their effects, e.g., rules of the form

R_s: if x performs action a in G, then x scores in G.

Among the regulative rules of G will be rules which prohibit actions in G and specify the sanctions to be applied if such actions are performed in G, e.g., rules of the form R_v.

Let us now consider a player x of G who performs the action a referred to in a rule of the form R_s. Does this fact suffice to determine that x has scored in G? It does not, since, in performing a, x might also have performed the action b which is referred to in and prohibited by a rule of the form R_v. Because x violated this regulative rule by performing the action b, the fact that he or she also performed the action a does not suffice to qualify this individual as scoring in G. Consequently, we might say, in this case, that rules of the form R_s implicitly refer to rules of the form R_v, and thus ought to be construed as having the normal form

R_s*: if x performs action a in G, without at the same time performing any action prohibited by any regulative rule of G, then x scores in G.

We can now see that interpreting formalism in terms of the dichotomization thesis reduces, but does not eliminate, the Platonistic implications of formalism. I take these points in turn.

a. Even if the constitutive rules of G have some such normal form as R_s*, activities in which the regulative rules of G are violated may still count as genuine instances of G. For rules of this form are conditional and thus cannot be violated by players even when these players violate the regulative rules to which these constitutive rules implicitly refer. The player x does not violate a rule of the form R_s* when he or she performs the action b prohibited by some regulative rule of the form R_v. Of course, in the normal course of events, neither will x be adjudged to have scored in G, even though he or she may also have performed the action a referred to in a rule of the form R_s*. If we interpret formalism in terms of the dichotomization thesis, then at least some of its Platonistic implications can be avoided.

b. However, interpreting formalism in terms of the dichotomization thesis does not suffice to eliminate all of its Platonistic implications. We can see this as follows. According to the dichotomization thesis, only the constitutive rules of G define various G-derivative notions. We have seen that the dichotomization thesis must be modified slightly to take account of the fact that the constitutive rules of G implicitly refer to the regulative rules of G. Consider now an alleged instance of G in which the player x performs the action a referred to in a rule of the form R_s*; at the same time performs the action b referred to in a regulative rule of the form R_v; and, finally, is judged by game officials to have scored in G. Is this alleged instance of G a genuine instance of G?

From an intuitive point of view, the answer to this question depends on the reason why game officials (incorrectly) credited x as scoring. Some reasons—the officials were bribed by x—would clearly disqualify this alleged instance of G as a genuine instance of G. But other reasons—honestly mistaken judgment—would just as clearly not disqualify this alleged instance of G as a genuine instance of G. Game officials do (often) make honest mistakes, but this fact does not, from an intuitive point of view, disqualify as game action activity in which such mistakes are made.

From the formalist point of view, however, the reason for mistaken official judgment is irrelevant. If the constitutive rules of G define the G-derivative notion 'is an instance of G', and if these rules have some such normal form as R_s* above, then an official who mistakenly applies such rules engages in behavior not in accordance with them, and any activity in which such mistakes occur is thus ipso facto not a genuine instance of G. In short, interpreting formalism in terms of the dichotomization thesis does not suffice to eliminate its Platonistic implications.

We cannot, then, rescue formalism from its various difficulties by interpreting it in terms of the dichotomization thesis. An account of games other than that offered by formalism is required. In the next section, I will offer such an account.

The Ethos of Games

To see why formalism fails as an adequate account of games, consider, for instance, the game of basketball. (A very similar story could be told about football, hockey, and many other games.)

According to the formal rules of basketball, basketball is a ''noncontact'' sport: in general, physical contact between players is prohibited by the rules of basketball. But any game of American professional basketball is filled with (one might almost say consists of) incidents in which players (accidentally or deliberately) make contact with one another.[7] Of course, only some of these incidents are observed by game officials. But only some even of these observed incidents actually result in the invocation of penalties. Why is this so? This is so because the players and game officials have, in effect, conspired to ignore certain of the rules of basketball, at least in certain situations, in order to promote certain interests, which they share, for instance, with team owners and spectators—e.g., to make the game more exciting

than it would be if the rules were more strictly enforced.

Of course, when I say that the players and officials (in effect) conspire to ignore certain rules in certain situations, I do not mean to suggest that these particular rules cease to have any possible bearing on the conduct of the game. The formal rules of basketball specify sanctions which can be invoked, even though they are often ignored. Furthermore, a game in which certain kinds of foul moves are regularly ignored need not degenerate into anarchy, since there is, implicit in the ways in which basketball games are played and officiated, an unofficial *system* of conventions which determines how the official rules of the game will be applied in various concrete circumstances. Foul moves which deviate, not from the formal rules per se, but from the formal rules as these are interpreted in terms of a particular set of implicit conventions will, in fact, be penalized if detected. This, then, is the answer to Black's rhetorical question: ''Why not shoot the opposing team?'' Furthermore, this implicit set of conventions for interpreting the formal rules of basketball can be inferred by players from their own experience, and they can thus learn what sorts of formally prohibited behavior are, in some sense, ''acceptable.'' To determine the conventions which guide game officials in their application of the formal rules of a game, it does not suffice simply to consult the formal rules of that game: One must make this determination empirically, by investigating the actual practices which these conventions sanction.

In short, the unofficial, implicit, empirically determinable conventions which govern official interpretations of the formal rules of basketball constitute the ethos of American professional basketball.

The ethos of a game in effect provides the basis for making two distinctions where the formal rules of that game provide the basis for making only one such distinction. Thus, the formal rules of a game distinguish between behavior which is permissible (in that game) and behavior which is impermissible. On a formalist account of games, this distinction is interpreted as a distinction between behavior that is part of the game and behavior that is not part of the game at all. But the ethos of a game distinguishes between behavior that is permissible, behavior that is impermissible but acceptable, and behavior that is unacceptable. Permissible behavior is, on this nonformalist account of games, either in accordance with the formal rules of a game or violates those rules only in a way which, according to the ethos of that game, does not require the invocation of penalties. Impermissible but acceptable behavior, on this account, violates the rules of the game in a way which, according to the ethos of that game, does require the invocation of penalties. And unacceptable behavior violates the rules of the game in a way which, according to the ethos of that game, disqualifies its perpetrator as a player of that game. According to this nonformalist account of games, only such unacceptable behavior is not game-behavior; only a player engaging in such behavior ipso facto ceases to be a player. (The ethos of a game also distinguishes between those mistaken official judgments which are acceptable, and those which are unacceptable. This answers the point raised in the penultimate paragraph of the last section.)

I have suggested that our speculations about basketball would help us to see why formalism fails as an adequate account of games. Formalism fails, then, because its advocates ignore the role which the ethos of a game plays in defining various game-derivative notions. The ethos of a game G is that set of conventions which determines how the rules of G are to be applied in concrete circumstances. The ethos of G should thus figure in the definition of various game-derivative notions in the following way. Where, according to formalism, 'is an instance of G' MEANS 'is activity in accordance with the formal rules of G', our nonformalist account suggests that 'is an instance of G' should be understood as meaning 'is activity in accordance with the formal rules of G as these are interpreted by the ethos of G'. (This same transformation can be carried out for the other game-derivative notions.)

Why is such a nonformalist, ethos-incorporating account of games superior to the formalist account? First, the nonformalist account does not entail a Platonistic interpretation of games. Any alleged instance of some game G is, according to our nonformalist account, a genuine instance of G so long as it is activity within the limits jointly defined by the formal rules of G and the ethos of G—i.e., so long as it is ''acceptable'' activity in the sense already specified. According to formalism, however, activity within these limits which is not strictly in accordance with the formal rules of G will not count as a genuine instance of G. Formalism is Platonistic, in short, precisely because its advocates have failed to recognize the importance of the ethos of games.

Second, the problem of penalties has a trivial solution once we recognize the importance of the ethos of games. On the ethos-ignoring, formalist account of games, penalty-invoking rules have the normal form of prohibitions—i.e., have the normal form R_v. When a prohibited action is performed, a penalty is invoked because the rule prohibiting such an action has been violated. As we have seen, the formalist can offer such an account of penalties only at the cost of accepting a Platonistic interpretation of games. But an account of games that recognizes the importance of the ethos of games pays no such price. Penalties are invoked, on this nonformalist account, when rules prohibiting certain actions are violated in a way which, according to the ethos of the game, requires the invocation of a penalty. But action of this kind is, generally, action within the limits jointly defined (as ''acceptable'' if impermissible) by the rules and the ethos of the game in question. Those who engage in rule-violating behavior therefore only rarely ipso factor cease to be players on this non-formalist account.

Third, an account of games which recognizes the importance of the ethos of games explains a number of facts and intuitions about games which must remain puzzling on a formalist account.

a. Most habitual spectators would find a game of basketball in which no rule-prohibited actions were performed an extremely strange game of basketball. But such a game is, from the formalist point of view, an ideal game of basketball. We can explain the perceived "strangeness" of such a game only when we take into account the prevailing ethos of basketball, according to which all sorts of rule-violating behavior is, in fact, "acceptable."

b. Game officials sometimes deliberately ignore a foul move in the explicit interest of promoting some good (the continuity of play, an advantage gained by the opponents of the rule-violators, etc.). Such official action is, from the formalist point of view, (generally) inexplicable. We can account for such action only when we take into consideration the role played by the ethos of a game in determining how the rules of the game are applied. (Some games such as soccer, of course, incorporate a formal rule that permits game officials to ignore rule-violating behavior in order to "play the advantage." In such cases, the formalist account of games is, in this particular, on a par with the nonformalist account. For such games, we might say that part of the ethos of the game has been assimilated to its formal rules. But this situation by no means pertains to all games. And where it does not pertain—as in basketball— only an account of games which recognizes the importance of the ethos of a game will suffice.)

To all this, the formalist could, of course, reply that what I have called the ethos of a game is, in fact, (an unwritten) part of what he or she calls the formal rules of that game. This reply, however, is entirely ad hoc, since as far as I can tell, formalists have never even noticed that a game has an ethos, let alone suggested that this ethos forms a part of the rules of that game. In any event, my point is not that formalism cannot be salvaged as an account of games. It is, rather, that if formalism is to be salvaged, it must be supplemented, one way or another, by an account of the ethos of games.

Conclusion

I have here considered the standard formalist account of games, according to which various game-derivative notions are to be defined solely in terms of the formal rules of games. I have argued that this account of games is defective because it has Platonistic implications and because it fails to provide a satisfactory account of the function of penalties in games. I have suggested that formalism is defective because its advocates ignore the role of the ethos of a game in defining that game. The ethos of a game is that set of unofficial, implicit conventions which determine how the rules of that game are to be applied in concrete circumstances. On the nonformalist account of games recommended here, game-derivative notions are defined jointly in terms of the formal rules and the ethos of a game. I have shown that this nonformalist, ethos-incorporation account of games does not have Platonistic implications and does explicate the point of penalties. I have also shown that such an account explains certain facts and intuitions about games which must remain puzzling on any formalist account.

Notes

1. My particular thanks to Howard Burdick for his very helpful comments on a previous version of this paper. Thanks also to Jack Smart and Chris Mortensen.
2. In the context of an otherwise formalistic discussion of games, Black (1: p. 123) makes the literally parenthetical remark: "But of course occasional failure to observe the rules is not ground for disqualification as a player." I agree with this remark, but it is surely ad hoc in the context of Black's claim that "a man who failed to 'heed' the rules of chess *would not count* as playing the game." Of course, in Black's view, "heeding" does not entail "observing." There is no logical inconsistency here. What there is is a puzzle: How much "observing" is entailed by the "heeding" requirement? Black, too, finds this puzzling. He says that the "heeding" requirement "seems to imply also at least conformity

with the rules *on the whole.*'' But puzzlement is not illumination, and without illumination, Black's remarks remain ad hoc and unmotivated by anything more systematic than his quite correct intuitions about games.

3. I claim that this condition for the truth of '*x* is playing *G*' is, contra formalism, the maximal necessary condition. I can here only sketch an argument to this effect. For the pruposes of this sketch, I will take it as given that Quinn (7: p. 80) has established that '*x* follows the rules of *G*' is too strong a necessary condition. Quinn himself suggests (p. 79) that ''being able to follow the rules of a practice is surely a necessary condition for engaging in that practice.'' But this condition is also too strong. Being able to follow the rules of a game entails knowing those rules. But many games have quite recondite rules which are known to few of the persons we would normally (and rightly) regard as players of those games. Because such players do not know these (recondite) rules, they are not able to follow them. Being able to follow the rules of a game cannot, then, be a necessary condition for being a player of that game. Being willing to submit to authoritative decisions about even such recondite rules is, however, an unexceptionable necessary condition for being a player. It is, I think, the maximal such necessary condition which can be formulated in a precise way.

4. I developed the regimentation thesis on the basis of a (literally) parenthetical remark by Ganz (3: p. 94): ''One doesn't necessarily violate a rule by committing a foul; instead one's behavior might fall under a rule by so doing.''

5. My formulation of the dichotomization thesis depends on a distinction drawn by Hart (4: p. 9) between ''those rules of a game which veto certain types of conduct under penalty . . . and those which specify what must be done to score or to win.'' See also Searle (9: §2.6).

6. My claim that the constitutive/regulative dichotomy is arbitrary may be anticipated by Black (1: pp. 123–124) and by Cherry (2: pp. 311–313).

7. According to the *Boston Globe,* the final quarter of the sixth playoff game between Boston and Philadelphia in 1981 ''ticked down to a final quarter just bulging with karate chops, goal-line stands and cross-body blocks, pro basketball played according to NFL rules. . . . Typical was a Bird follow-up basket that featured at least six different fouls on the play—but no calls—and five bodies sprawled across the court.''

Bibliography

1. Black, Max. *Model and Metaphors.* Ithaca, NY: Cornell University Press, 1962.
2. Cherry, Christopher. ''Regulative and Constitutive Rules.'' *Philosophical Quarterly,* 23 (1973), 301–315.
3. Ganz, Joan. *Rules.* The Hague: Mouton, 1971.
4. Hart, H.L.A. *The Concept of Law.* Oxford: Clarendon Press, 1961.
5. Olshewsky, Thomas. ''On the Notion of a Rule.'' *Philosophia,* 6 (1976), 267–287.
6. Quine, W.V.O. *Word and Object.* Cambridge, MA: M.I.T. Press, 1960.
7. Quinn, Michael. ''Practice-Defining Rules.'' *Ethics,* 86 (1975), 76–86.
8. Rawls, John. ''Two Concepts of Rules.'' *Philosophical Review,* 64 (1955), 3–32.
9. Searle, John. *Speech Acts.* Cambridge: Cambridge University Press, 1969.
10. Suits, Bernard. ''What is a Game?'' *Philosophy of Science,* 34 (1967), 148–156.

Bibliography for the Nature of Sport, Play, and Game

Avedon, Elliot M., & Sutton-Smith, Brian. *The Study of Games*. New York: John Wiley & Sons, 1971.

Banham, Charles. "Man at Play." *Contemporary Review,* 207 (August, 1965), 61-64.

Best, David. *Philosophy and Human Movement*. London: George Allen and Unwin, 1978.

Blummenfield, Walter. "Observations Concerning the Phenomenon and Origin of Play." *Philosophy and Phenomenological Research,* I (June, 1941), 470-478.

Bowen, Wilbur P., & Mitchell, Elmer D. *The Theory of Organized Play*. New York: A.S. Barnes, 1927.

Brooks, J.D., & Whiting, H.T.A. *Human Movement: A Field of Study*. Lafayette, IN: Bart Publishers, 1973.

Browne, Evelyn. "An Ethological Theory of Play." *Journal of Health, Physical Education, and Recreation,* 39 (September, 1968), 36-39.

Burke, Richard. "'Work' and 'Play'." *Ethics, 82* (1971), 33-47.

Caillois, Roger. "Unity of Play; Diversity of Games." *Diogenes,* 19 (Fall, 1957), 92-121.

Caillois, Roger. "Play and the Sacred." In *Man and the Sacred*. Translated by Meyer Barash. Glencoe, IL: Free Press of Glencoe, 1959.

Caillois, Roger. *Man, Play, and Games*. Translated by Meyer Barash. New York: Free Press of Glencoe, 1961.

Champlin, Nathaniel. "Are Sports Methodic?" *The Journal of the Philosophy of Sport,* IV (Fall, 1977), 104-116.

Chase, Stuart. "Play." In *Whither Mankind*. Edited by Charles A. Beard. New York: Longmans, Green and Company, 1928.

Claeys, Urbain. "Evolution of the Concept of Sport and the Participation/Nonparticipation Phenomenon." *Sociology of Sport Journal,* 2 (September, 1985), 233-239.

Cox, Harvey. *The Feast of Fools: A Theological Essay on Festivity and Fantasy*. Cambridge: Harvard University Press, 1969.

Dearden, R.F. "The Concept of Play." In *The Concept of Education*. Edited by R.S. Peters. London: Routledge & Kegan Paul, 1967.

Ehrmann, Jacques. "Homo Ludens Revisited." In *Game, Play, Literature*. Edited by Jacques Ehrmann. Boston: Beacon Press, 1971.

Fogelin, Robert J. "Sport: The Diversity of the Concept." In *Sport and the Body: A Philosophical Symposium*. Edited by Ellen W. Gerber. Philadelphia: Lea & Febiger, 1972.

Fox, Larry. "A Linguistic Analysis of the Concept 'Health' in Sport." *Journal of the Philosophy of Sport,* II (September, 1975), 31-35.

Giddens, A. "Notes on the Concept of Play and

Leisure.'' *Sociological Review,* 12 (March, 1964), 73-89.

Graves, H. ''A Philosophy of Sport.'' *Contemporary Review,* LXXVII (December, 1900), 877-893.

Grazia, Sebastion De. *Of Time, Work, and Leisure.* New York: Twentieth Century Fund, 1962.

Groos, Karl. *The Play of Man.* New York: D. Appleton, 1901.

Gulick, Luther Halsey. ''Psychological, Pedagogical, and Religious Aspects of Group Games.'' *Pedagogical Seminary* (now *Journal of Genetic Psychology*), 6 (1899), 135-151.

Gulick, Luther Halsey. *A Philosophy of Play.* New York: Charles Scribner's Sons, 1920.

Hinman, Lawrence. ''On Work and Play: Overcoming a Dichotomy.'' *Man and World,* 8 (1975), 327-346.

Huizinga, Johan. *Homo Ludens.* London: Routledge & Kegan Paul, 1950.

Hyland, Drew A. *The Question of Play.* Lanham, MD: University Press of America, 1984.

Jeu, Bernard. ''What Is Sport?'' *Diogenes,* 80 (1972), 150-163.

Jolivet, Regis. ''Work, Play, Contemplation.'' Translated by Sister M. Delphone. *Philosophy Today,* V (Summer, 1961), 114-120.

Kaplan, Max. *Leisure in America: A Social Inquiry.* New York: John Wiley & Sons, 1960.

Keating, James W. ''Sportsmanship as a Moral Category.'' *Ethics,* LXXV (October, 1964), 25-35.

Keating, James W. ''The Urgent Need for Definitions and Distinctions.'' *Physical Educator,* 28 (March, 1971), 41-42.

Kleinman, Seymour. ''Toward a Non-Theory of Sport.'' *Quest,* 10 (May, 1968), 29-34.

Krug, Orvis. ''The Philosophical Relationship Between Physical Education and Athletics.'' Unpublished doctoral dissertation, New York University.

Loy, John, Jr. ''The Nature of Sport: A Defini-

tional Effort.'' *Quest,* 10 (May, 1968), 1-15.

Manser, Anthony. ''Games and Family Resemblances.'' *Philosophy,* XVII (July, 1967), 210-255.

McBride, Frank. ''Toward a Non-Definition of Sport.'' *Journal of the Philosophy of Sport,* II (September, 1975), 4-11.

Meier, Klaus V. ''On the Inadequacies of Sociological Definitions of Sport.'' *International Review of Sport Sociology,* XVI (1981), 79-102.

Melvin, Bruce L. ''Play, Recreation and Leisure Time.'' *Proceedings of the Sixty-Third Annual Meeting of the College Physical Education Association.* Washington, DC, 1960.

Metheny, Eleanor. ''This 'Thing' Called Sport.'' *Journal of Health, Physical Education, and Recreation,* 40 (March, 1969), 59-60.

Miller, David L. *Gods and Games: Toward a Theology of Play.* New York: World Publishing Company, 1970.

Morgan, William J. ''Some Aristotelian Notes on the Attempt to Define Sport.'' *Journal of the Philosophy of Sport,* IV (September, 1977), 15-35.

Neale, Robert E. *In Praise of Play.* New York: Harper & Row, 1969.

Osterhoudt, Robert G. (Ed.). *The Philosophy of Sport.* Springfield, IL: Charles C Thomas, 1973.

Osterhoudt, Robert. *An Introduction to the Philosophy of Physical Education and Sport.* Champaign, IL: Stipes, 1977.

Paddick, Robert Joseph. ''The Nature of a Field of Knowledge in Physical Education.'' Unpublished master's thesis, University of Alberta, Canada, 1967.

Paddick, Robert J. ''What Makes Physical Activity Physical?'' *Journal of the Philosophy of Sport,* II (September, 1975), 12-22.

Patrick, G.T.W. ''The Play of a Nation.'' *Scientific Monthly,* 13 (October, 1921), 350-362.

Petrie, Brian Malcom. ''Physical Activity, Games,

and Sport: A System of Classification and an Investigation of Social Influences Among Students of Michigan State University." Unpublished doctoral dissertation, Michigan State University, 1970.

Potter, Stephen. *The Theory and Practice of Gamesmanship.* New York: Bantam Books, 1965.

Reddiford, Gordon. "Constitutions, Institutions, and Games." *Journal of the Philosophy of Sport,* XII (1985), 41-51.

Renick, Jobyann. "The Structure of Games." *Journal of Human Movement Studies,* 3 (1977), 193-206.

Renshaw, Peter. "The Nature of Human Movement Studies and Its Relationship With Physical Education." *Quest,* 20 (June, 1973), 79-86.

Roberts, John M., Arth, Malcom J., & Bush, Robert R. "Games in Culture." *American Anthropologist,* 61 (August, 1959), 597-605.

Rossi, Ernest Lawrence. "Game and Growth: Two Dimensions of Our Psychotherapeutic Zeitgeist." *Journal of Humanistic Psychology,* 7 (Fall, 1967), 139-154.

Roszak, Theodore. "Forbidden Games." In *Sport in the Socio-Cultural Process.* Edited by M. Marie Hart. Dubuque, IA: Wm. C. Brown, 1972.

Sapora, Allen V., & Mitchell, Elmer D. *The Theory of Play and Recreation* (3rd ed.). New York: Ronald Press, 1948.

Slusher, Howard S. *Man, Sport and Existence.* Philadelphia: Lea & Febiger, 1967.

Steinbeck, John. "Then My Arm Glassed Up." *Sports Illustrated,* 23 (December 20, 1965), 94-102.

Stone, Gregory P. "Some Meanings of American Sport: An Extended View." In *Aspects of Contemporary Sport Sociology: Proceedings of C.I.C. Symposium on the Sociology of Sport.* Edited by Gerald S. Kenyon. Chicago, IL: The Athletic Institute, 1969.

Stone, Gregory P. "Some Meanings of American Sport." In *Sport and American Society.* Edited by George H. Sage. Reading, MA: Addison-Wesley, 1970.

Suits, Bernard. "What Is a Game." *Philosophy of Science,* 34 (June, 1967), 148-156.

Suits, Bernard. "The Elements of Sport." In *The Philosophy of Sport: A Collection of Original Essays.* Edited by Robert G. Osterhoudt. Springfield, IL: Charles C Thomas, 1973.

Suits, Bernard. "Words on Play." *Journal of the Philosophy of Sport,* IV (September, 1977), 117-131.

Suits, Bernard. "Sticky Wickedness: Games and Morality." *Dialogue* (Canada) 21, (December, 1982), 755-760.

Sutton-Smith, Brian. "A Formal Analysis of Game Meaning." *Western Folklore,* XVIII (January, 1959), 13-24.

Tangen, J.O. "Defining Sport: A Pragmatic-Contextual Approach." *International Journal of Physical Education,* 22 (1985), 17-25.

Thomas, Duane. "Sport: The Conceptual Enigma." *Journal of the Philosophy of Sport,* III (September, 1976), 35-41.

VanderZwagg, Harold J. "Sport: Existential or Essential?" *Quest,* 19 (May, 1969), 47-56.

VanderZwagg, Harold J. "Sports Concepts." *Journal of Health, Physical Education, and Recreation,* 41 (March, 1970), 35-36.

VanderZwagg, Harold J. *Toward a Philosophy of Sport.* Reading, MA: Addison-Wesley, 1972.

Vernes, Jean-Rene. "The Element of Time in Competitive Games." Translated by Victor A. Velen. *Diogenes,* 50 (September, 1965), 25-42.

Weiss, Paul. "Records and the Man." *Philosophic Exchange,* 1 (Summer, 1972), 89-97.

Part II

Sport and Embodiment

Before an extended philosophical investigation can be conducted into other metaphysical concerns about human participation in sport and play, it is necessary to analyze and to attempt to comprehend man's embodied nature. However, such an undertaking is neither a brief nor an uncomplicated venture. For instance, even thinkers who espouse that humans are unified beings or integrated wholes often resort to the utilization of dualistic terminology. Thus one often reads claims that man is composed of mind, body, and spirit, or that there are rather discrete physical and mental aspects of a human's functioning. For example, early physical educators, such as Luther Gulick and Jesse Feiring William, often assumed their role to be the fostering of bodily development to parallel the mental development occurring in academic classes.

Beliefs of this nature are often reflective of the acceptance of metaphysical ideas advanced by various philosophers who have wrestled specifically with the task of delineating the relationship existent among body, mind, and soul. Further, as will become very evident in this section, even a cursory glance at the history of philosophical ideas clearly attests that the important task of elucidating and resolving the problem of the interdependence of mind and body presents a plethora of intriguing and intricate difficulties. The question of assessing the relative importance or value of each component or dimension is, of course, inherent to the problem. Philosophic speculations contain numerous instances of those who either accord the greatest importance to the soul or who contend that the mind is the essential quality of humanness; few philosophers indeed have asserted that the body has the greatest value, although several noteworthy empiricists did challenge the earlier dominance of idealistic rationalism by attempting to establish its importance to the person's ability to know.

Despite the fact that an extensive exploration of all facets of the mind-body problem is clearly precluded herein, the essays contained in this section do provide at least an introductory exposure to selected influential philosophic analyses of human corporeality, ranging from the rationalistic positions espoused by Plato and Descartes to contemporary phenomenological expositions of the *lived-body*.

Because it is rather obvious that, in general, the dualistic conception of man still prevails in Western theories of epistemology, behavior, education, and, of course, human movement forms such as sport and play, it is useful to begin with a perusal of the seminal philosophic position championed by Plato. The brief excerpt from Plato's *Phaedo* clearly demonstrates that he forwards a position that radically separates the body and the soul (here to be understood in a broad connotation incorporating spirit or mind or the enduring essential quality of the individual), as well as denigrates the kinds of information and knowledge available through the senses. In point of fact, Plato's attitude towards the body is quite negative; this position is derived from his view that struggles with bodily demands and passions are detrimental to the achievement of harmony and moderation, as well as, of course, the attainment of true knowledge. It is necessary to note, however, that his negative opinions concerning the body should not automatically be equated or confused with his more positive approach to play and sport, a position delineated in both the *Laws* and the *Republic;* for further analyses of this aspect of Plato's writings, and its influence on the development of physical education of sport, see Fairs (1968), Kleinman (1970), Hyland (1977) and Dombrowski (1979). Be that as it may, Plato's negative perception of corporeality has been both profound and enduringly influential.

A rapid leap of roughly 2,000 years leads to consideration of an excerpt from Descartes' important *Meditations on First Philosophy.* This work provides, at first glance, a restatement of Plato's dualistic structure in a somewhat different guise. However, Descartes' categorical delineation of the inherent and necessary differences in kind between the physical, extended body and the immaterial, unextended mind is more extreme. Indeed, Descartes' radical bifurcation of these two entities has provided philosophy, and for that matter science as well, with a conception of man with which they have struggled for more than three centuries.

Cartesian dualism has not only spawned such dependents as the branch of inquiry known as the *philosophy of mind,* rigorous mechanistic physiological disciplines exploring the body-machine, and contemporary forms of radical behaviorism, but also markedly influenced certain significant modern philosophical inquiries into sport. The selection from Weiss' book presents clear echoes of Descartes' formulations. Once again, man is divided into two diverse substances, an extended body and an unextended mind, linked in a rather imprecise manner by the emotions. In addition, a hierarchical position is forwarded in which the superior mind directs, controls, disciplines, and, in effect, conquers the inferior body.

Despite this state of affairs, there is a noteworthy alternative. The most interesting and productive contemporary approaches to the study of embodiment are those to be found within the writings of several modern phenomenologists. These philosophers have broken away completely from the dualistic Cartesian structure to present a substantively different conception of man; namely, the view of man as an incarnate subject, a unity not a union of two discrete components. The body is the primary self, man's mode of being in the world; it is not an instrument of the mind or simply a vehicle for directed sensation. The study of the body-subject, thus, focuses upon man as a necessarily incarnate consciousness concerned with his continual unfolding in the world. The two short excerpts from the works of Sartre and Marcel both provide illuminating comments on the differences between the body treated as object and the body treated as self. In addition, Schrag's essay discusses the general parameters of the phenomenologists' approach to a consideration of the body.

Meier's article provides a culminating synthesis of some of the previously described material, in addition to presenting an extended exploration of Merleau-Ponty's seminal and enlightened phenomenological investigation of man's insertion into, and centering in, the world through the expressive body. Meier concludes his study by asserting that if the radical shift from Cartesian to phenomenological conceptions of the nature of man is acknowledged and accepted, then the distinctive potentialities of man's engagement in sport—including the full range of dynamic, lived experiences available therein—may be vigorously and philosophically profitably explored.

Curiously enough, those who have been interested in sport and physical education have shown little enthusiasm for fully understanding the nature of embodiment. They have focused their attention predominantly, if not exclusively, upon the body as object; consequently, they have concentrated solely upon the treadmill image of sport, centering upon the attainment and development of physical strength, motor skills, and technical efficiency. In such a mechanistic and often deprecatory environment, the body is restrained, trimmed, trained, and otherwise devivified. As previously indicated, however, phenomenologists champion a different conception that permits a more legitimate and fruitful analysis to occur of the dynamic and expressive components of human participation in sport.

Two additional essays, both of a very different nature than those previously discussed, complete this section. De Wachter's perceptive analysis of the logic of contemporary somatic culture, which deliberately employs the athletic body as a social symbol of healthy existence, representing not only status and gender identification, but also youthfulness and strength, is an article well worthy of perusal. Finally, Lingis' intriguing socio-philosophical discussion of bodybuilders, the resentment often felt and expressed against them, the curious paradox of massive musculature cultivated in an age when technological advancements in both industry and warfare make it superfluous, and other reflections on the cultural evolution of our bodies, offers numerous provocative insights.

Numerous other books and articles have been published in the general area of the philosophy of the body. Spicker's (1970) collection of readings still merits consultation, as do articles by Beets, Kwant, and Zaner contained within a special issue of *Humanitias* (Spring, 1966) devoted entirely to reflections on ''The Human Body.'' Sarano's (1966) book on the meanings of the body is most illuminating and still highly recommended.

To turn to phenomenological analyses of the body, it is necessary to commence with Zaner's (1964) comprehensive and influential work in the area. Other noteworthy studies investigating the ''radical reality'' of the human body and other aspects of the topic under discussion include Hengstenberg (1963), Gerber (1964), Jonas (1965), Kwant (1966), Zaner (1966), and Waelhens (1967). In addition, books on existential phenomenology in general, such as those authored by Luijpen (1960) and Schrag (1969), often include one or more chapters on the body or the experience of embodiment.

Some of the more significant analytic writings concerned with the body or the mind-body problem include Feigl, Maxwell, and Seriven (1958); Kohler (1961), McDougall (1961), Long (1964), Schaffer (1965, 1966), and Van Peursen (1966).

Studies that investigate the body specifically in the dynamic environment of sport include Belaief's (1977) essay, which characterizes sport as a positive bodily confrontation with the demonic; Meier's (1975) article, which develops further implications of Merleau-Ponty's conception of the body for sport; and Hammer's (1973) paper, which views sport as a bodily expression of the ego. Also of additional interest here are pieces by Van Den Berg (1962), Beets (1964, 1966), and Wenkart (1963, 1967). Several more contemporary essays discuss the concepts of body awareness and the experience of the passionate body available in various sport forms, particularly such activities as gymnastics (Fahey, 1977; Johns, 1985; Ravizza, 1977, 1983).

Access to Eastern philosophical reflections on the topic at hand may be gained from articles by Abe (1977, 1983) as well as from Kleinman's (1986) recent anthology, which contains several short essays commenting on the mind-body problem and differences between Eastern and Western conceptions of, and orientations toward, the body. Hoberman's (1981) study of the body as a political and ideological variable opens new directions of investigation. O'Neil (1964) and Krawezyk (1984) also present some interesting perspectives on social and cultural anthropology.

Finally, the question of woman as a body—that is, the question of whether or not unique epistemological or metaphysical insights are forthcoming from or elicited by differences in gender—has only recently received extensive philosophical consideration. In addition to the works included in the section on ethics dealing with women and sport, it is most worthwhile to consult Yonge's (1976) discussion of images of masculine and feminine movement; Young's (1980) phenomenological analysis of feminine body comportment, mobility, and spatiality; and Spelman's (1982) survey of ancient and contemporary views of women as bodies.

Most assuredly, there is more to be said about the importance of the philosophy of the body. However, it should be obvious that understanding the implications of the question of embodiment is a necessary precursor to the philosophic investigation of participation in sport as an individually meaningful and significant venture. The next section of this book addresses these issues.

The Separation of Body and Soul

PLATO

Do we believe death to be anything?

We do, replied Simmias.

And do we not believe it to be the separation of the soul from the body? Does not death mean that the body comes to exist by itself, separated from the soul, and that the soul exists by herself, separated from the body? What is death but that?

It is that, he said.

Now consider, my good friend, if you and I are agreed on another point which I think will help us to understand the question better. Do you think that a philosopher will care very much about what are called pleasures, such as the pleasures of eating and drinking?

Certainly not, Socrates, said Simmias.

Or about the pleasures of sexual passion?

Indeed, no.

And, do you think that he holds the remaining cares of the body in high esteem? Will he think much of getting fine clothes, and sandals, and other bodily adornments, or will he despise them, except so far as he is absolutely forced to meddle with them?

The real philosopher, I think, will despise them, he replied.

In short, said he, you think that his studies are not concerned with the body? He stands aloof from it, as far as he can, and turns toward the soul?

Reprinted with permission of Macmillan Publishing Company from Plato, *Phaedo*, translated by F.J. Church. Copyright © 1985 by Macmillan Publishing Company. Copyright 1951.

I do.

Well, then, in these matters, first, is it clear that the philosopher releases his soul from communion with the body, so far as he can, beyond all other men?

It is.

And does not the world think, Simmias, if a man has no pleasure in such things, and does not take his share in them, his life is not worth living? Do not they hold that he who thinks nothing of bodily pleasures is almost as good as dead?

Indeed you are right.

But what about the actual acquisition of wisdom? If the body is taken as a companion in the search for wisdom, is it a hindrance or not? For example, do sight and hearing convey any real truth to men? Are not the very poets forever telling us that we neither hear nor see anything accurately? But if these senses of the body are not accurate or clear, the others will hardly be so, for they are all less perfect than these, are they not?

Yes, I think so, certainly, he said.

Then when does the soul attain truth? he asked. We see that, as often as she seeks to investigate anything in company with the body, the body leads her astray.

True.

Is it not by reasoning, if at all, that any real truth becomes manifest to her?

Yes.

And she reasons best, I suppose, when none of the senses, whether hearing, or sight, or pain, or pleasure, harasses her; when she has dismissed the body, and released herself as far as she can from all intercourse or contact with it, and so, coming to be as much alone with herself as is possible, strives after real truth.

That is so.

And here too the soul of the philosopher very greatly despises the body, and flies from it, and seeks to be alone by herself, does she not?

Clearly.

And what do you say to the next point, Simmias? Do we say that there is such a thing as absolute justice, or not?

Indeed we do.

And absolute beauty, and absolute good?

Of course.

Have you ever seen any of them with your eyes?

Indeed I have not, he replied.

Did you ever grasp them with any bodily sense? I am speaking of all absolutes, whether size, or health, or strength; in a word, of the essence of real being of everything. Is the very truth of things contemplated by the body? Is it not rather the case that the man who prepares himself most carefully to apprehend by his intellect the essence of each thing which he examines will come nearest to the knowledge of it?

Certainly.

And will not a man attain to this pure thought most completely if he goes to each thing, as far as he can, with his mind alone, taking neither sight nor any other sense along with his reason in the process of thought, to be an encumbrance? In every case he will pursue pure and absolute being, with his pure intellect alone. He will be set free as far as possible from the eye and the ear and, in short, from the whole body, because intercourse with the body troubles the soul, and hinders her from gaining truth and wisdom. Is it not he who will attain the knowledge of real being, if any man will?

Your words are admirably true, Socrates, said Simmias.

• •

Let us assume then, he said, if you will, that there are two kinds of existence, the one visible, the other invisible.

Yes, he said.

And the invisible is unchanging, while the visible is always changing.

Yes, he said again.

Are not we men made up of body and soul?

There is nothing else, he replied.

And which of these kinds of existence should we say that the body is most like, and most akin to?

The visible, he replied; that is quite obvious.

And the soul? Is that visible or invisible?

It is visible to man, Socrates, he said.

But we mean by visible and invisible, visible and invisible to man; do we not?

Yes; that is what we mean.

Then what do we say of the soul? Is it visible or not visible?

It is not visible.

Then is it invisible?

Yes.

Then the soul is more like the invisible than the body; and the body is like the visible.

That is necessarily so, Socrates.

Have we not also said that, when the soul employs the body in any inquiry, and makes use of sight, or hearing, or any other sense—for inquiry with the body means inquiry with the senses— she is dragged away by it to the things which never remain the same, and wanders about blindly, and becomes confused and dizzy, like a drunken man, from dealing with things that are ever changing?

Certainly.

But when she investigates any question by herself, she goes away to the pure, and eternal, and immortal, and unchangeable, to which she is akin, and so she comes to be ever with it, as soon as she is by herself, and can be so; and then she rests from her wanderings and dwells with it unchangingly; for she is dealing with what is unchanging. And is not this state of the soul called wisdom?

Indeed, Socrates, you speak well and truly, he replied.

Which kind of existence do you think from our former and our present arguments that the soul is more like and more akin to?

I think, Socrates, he replied, that after this inquiry the very dullest man would agree that the soul is infinitely more like the unchangeable than the changeable.

And the body?

That is like the changeable.

Consider the matter in yet another way. When the soul and the body are united, nature ordains the one to be a slave and to be ruled, and the other to be master and to rule. Tell me once again, which do you think is like the divine, and which is like the mortal? Do you not think that the divine naturally rules and has authority, and that the mortal naturally is ruled and is a slave?

I do.

Then which is the soul like?

That is quite plain, Socrates. The soul is like the divine, and the body is like the mortal.

Now tell me, Cebes, is the result of all that we have said that the soul is most like the divine, and the immortal, and the intelligible, and the uniform, and the indissoluble, and the unchangeable; while the body is most like the human, and the mortal, and the unintelligible, and the multiform, and the dissoluble, and the changeable? Have we any other argument to show that this is not so, my dear Cebes?

We have not.

The Real Distinction Between the Mind and Body of Man

RENÉ DESCARTES

First, since I know that all the things I conceive clearly and distinctly can be produced by God exactly as I conceive them, it is sufficient that I can clearly and distinctly conceive one thing apart from another to be certain that the one is distinct or different from the other. For they can be made to exist separately, at least by the omnipotence of God, and we are obliged to consider them different no matter what power produces this separation. From the very fact that I know with certainty that I exist, and that I find that absolutely nothing else belongs necessarily to my nature or essence except that I am a thinking being, I readily conclude that my essence consists solely in being a body which thinks or a substance whose whole essence or nature is only to think. And although perhaps, or rather certainly, as I will soon show, I have a body with which I am very closely united, nevertheless, since on the one hand I have a clear and distinct idea of myself in so far as I am only a thinking and not an extended being, and since on the other hand I have a distinct idea of body in so far as it is only an extended being which does not think, it is certain that this ''I''—that is to say, my soul, by virtue of which I am what I am—is entirely and truly distinct from my body and that it can be or exist without it.

Furthermore, I find in myself various faculties of thinking which each have their own particular characteristics and are distinct from myself. For example, I find in myself the faculties of imagination and of perception, without which I might no doubt conceive of myself, clearly and distinctly, as a whole being; but I could not, conversely, conceive of those faculties without me, that is to say, without an intelligent substance to which they are attached or in which they inhere. For in our notion of them or, to use the scholastic vocabulary, in their formal concept, they embrace some type of intellection. From all this I reach the conception that these faculties are distinct from me as shapes, movements, and other modes or accidents of objects are distinct from the very objects that sustain them.

I also recognize in myself some other faculties, such as the power of changing location, of assuming various postures, and other similar ones; which cannot be conceived without some substance in which they inhere, any more than the preceding ones, and which therefore cannot exist without such a substance. But it is quite evident that these faculties, if it is true that they exist, must inhere in some corporeal or extended substance, and not in an intelligent substance, since their clear and distinct concept does actually involve some sort of extension, but no sort of intelligence whatsoever. Furthermore, I cannot doubt that there is in me a certain passive faculty of perceiving, that is, of receiving and recognizing the ideas of sensible objects; but it would be valueless to me, and I could in no way use it if there were not also in me, or in something else, another active faculty capable of forming and producing these ideas. But this active faculty cannot be in me, in so far as I am a thinking being, since it does not at all presuppose my intelligence and also since those ideas often occur to me without my contributing to them in any way, and even frequently against my will. Thus it must necessarily exist in some substance different from myself, in which all the reality that exists objectively in the ideas produced by this faculty is formally or eminently contained, as I have said before. This substance is either a body—that is, a corporeal nature—in which is formally and actually contained all that which is contained objectively and by representation in these ideas; or else it is God himself, or some other creation more noble than the body, in which all this is eminently contained.

• •

To begin this examination, I first take notice here that there is a great difference between the mind and the body, in that the body, from its nature, is always divisible and the mind is completely indivisible. For in reality, when I consider the mind—that is, when I consider myself in so far as I am only a thinking being—I cannot distinguish any parts, but I recognize and conceive very clearly that I am a thing which is absolutely unitary and entire. And although the whole mind seems to be united with the whole body, nevertheless when a foot or an arm or some other part of the body is amputated, I recognize quite well that nothing has been lost to my mind on that account. Nor can the faculties of willing, perceiving, understanding, and so forth be any more properly called parts of the mind, for it is one and the same mind which as a complete unit wills, perceives, and understands, and so forth. But just the contrary is the case with corporeal or extended objects, for I cannot imagine any, however small they might be, which my mind does not very easily divide into several parts, and I consequently recognize these objects to be

divisible. This alone would suffice to show me that the mind or soul of man is altogether different from the body, if I did not already know it sufficiently well for other reasons.

I also take notice that the mind does not receive impressions from all parts of the body directly, but only from the brain, or perhaps even from one of its smallest parts—the one, namely, where the senses in common have their seat. This makes the mind feel the same thing whenever it is in the same condition, even though the other parts of the body can be differently arranged, as is proved by an infinity of experiments which it is not necessary to describe here.

I furthermore notice that the nature of the body is such that no one of its parts can be moved by another part some little distance away without its being possible for it to be moved in the same way by any one of the intermediate parts, even when the more distant part does not act. For example, in the cord A B C D which is thoroughly stretched, if we pull and move the last part D, the first part A will not be moved in any different manner from that in which it could also be moved if we pulled one of the middle parts B or C, while the last part D remained motionless. And in the same way, when I feel pain in my foot, physics teaches me that this sensation is communicated by means of nerves distributed through the foot. When these nerves are pulled in the foot, being stretched like cords from there to the brain, they likewise pull at the same time the internal part of the brain from which they come and where they terminate, and there produce a certain movement which nature has arranged to make my mind feel pain as though that pain were in my foot. But because these nerves must pass through the leg, the thigh, the loins, the back, and neck, in order to extend from the foot to the brain, it can happen that even when the nerve endings in the foot are not stimulated, but only some of the intermediate parts located in the loins or the neck, precisely the same movements are nevertheless produced in the brain that could be produced there by a wound received in the foot, as a result of which it necessarily follows that the mind feels the same pain in the foot as though the foot had been wounded. And we must make the same judgment about all our other sense perceptions.

Finally, I notice that since each one of the movements that occurs in the part of the brain from which the mind receives impressions directly can only produce in the mind a single sensation, we cannot desire or imagine any better arrangement than that this movement should cause the mind to feel that sensation, of all sensations the movement is capable of causing, which is most effectively and frequently useful for the preservation of the human body when it is in full health. But experience shows us that all the sensations which nature has given us are such as I have just stated, and therefore there is nothing in their nature which does not show the power and the goodness of the God who has produced them.

Thus, for example, when the nerves of the foot are stimulated violently and more than is usual, their movement, passing through the marrow of the backbone up to the interior of the brain, produces there an impression upon the mind which makes the mind feel something—namely, pain as though in the foot—by which the mind is warned and stimulated to do whatever it can to remove the cause, taking it to be very dangerous and harmful to the foot.

It is true that God could establish the nature of man in such a way that this same brain event would make the mind feel something quite different; for example, it might cause the movement to be felt as though it were in the brain, or in the foot, or else in some other intermediate location between the foot and the brain, or finally it might produce any other feeling that can exist; but none of those would have contributed so well to the preservation of the body as that which it does produce.

In the same way, when we need to drink, there results a certain dryness in the throat which affects its nerves and, by means of them, the interior of the brain. This brain event makes the mind feel the sensation of thirst, because under those conditions there is nothing more useful to us than to know that we need to drink for the conservation of our health. And similar reasoning applies to other sensations.

From this it is entirely manifest that, despite the supreme goodness of God, the nature of man, in so far as he is composed of mind and body, cannot escape being sometimes faulty and deceptive. For if there is some cause which produces, not in the foot, but in some other part of the nerve which is stretched from the foot to the brain, or even in the brain itself, the same effect which ordinarily occurs when the foot is injured, we will feel pain as though it were in the foot, and we will naturally be deceived by the sensation. The reason for this is that the same brain event can cause only a single sensation in the mind; and this sensation being much more frequently produced by a cause which wounds the foot than by another acting in a different location, it is much more reasonable that it should always convey to the mind a pain in the foot rather than one in any other part of the body. And if it happens that sometimes the dryness of the throat does not come in the usual manner from the fact that drinking is necessary for the health of the body, but from some quite contrary cause, as in the case of those afflicted with dropsy, nevertheless it is much better that we should be deceived in that instance than if, on the contrary, we were always deceived when the body was in health; and similarly for the other sensations.

And certainly this consideration is very useful to me, not only so that I can recognize all the errors to which my nature is subject, but also so that I may avoid them or correct them more easily. For knowing that each of my senses conveys truth to me more often than falsehood concerning whatever is useful or harmful to the body, and being almost always able to use several of them to examine the same object, and being in addition able to use my memory to bind and join together present information with what is past, and being able to use my understanding, which has already discovered all the causes of my errors, I should no longer fear to encounter falsity in the objects which are most commonly represented to me by my senses.

And I should reject all the doubts of these last few days as exaggerated and ridiculous, particularly that very general uncertainty about sleep, which I could not distinguish from waking life. For now I find in them a very notable difference, in that our memory can never bind and join our dreams together one with another and all with the course of our lives, as it habitually joins together what happens to us when we are awake. And so, in effect, if someone suddenly appeared to me when I was awake and afterward disappeared in the same way, as do images that I see in my sleep, so that I could not determine where he came from or where he went, it would not be without reason that I would consider it a ghost or a phantom produced in my brain and similar to those produced there when I sleep, rather than truly a man.

But when I perceive objects in such a way that I distinctly recognize both the place from which they come and the place where they are, as well as the time when they appear to me; and when, without any hiatus, I can relate my perception of them with all the rest of my life, I am entirely certain that I perceive them wakefully and not in sleep. And I should not in any way doubt the truth of these things if, having made use of all my senses, my memory, and my understanding, to examine them, nothing is reported to me by any of them which is inconsistent with what is reported by the others. For, from the fact that God is not a deceiver, it necessarily follows that in this manner I am not deceived.

But because the exigencies of action frequently oblige us to make decisions and do not always allow us the leisure to examine these things with sufficient care, we must admit that human life is very often subject to error in particular matters; and we must in the end recognize the infirmity and weakness of our nature.

The Challenge of the Body

PAUL WEISS

We men live bodily here and now. This is as true of the most ecstatic of us as it is of the most flat-footed and mundane. No matter what we contemplate or how passive we make ourselves be, we continue to function in a plurality of bodily ways. Whatever our mental state, throughout our lives our hearts beat, our blood courses through our arteries, our lungs expand and contract. Our bodies grow and decay unsupervised, and, in that sense, uncontrolled. Only a man intoxicated with a Cartesian, or similar, idea that he is to be identified with his mind will deny that he is a body too.

Some, with the brilliant Merleau-Ponty, think that man's body is unique, not to be compared with the bodies of other living beings. Most men, instead, follow Darwin and view the human body as a minor variant on the kind of body that primates have. Today a number are reviving La Mettrie's idea that the human body is only a machine. They, and sometimes some of the others, occasionally claim that a man is nothing more than a body. Since they have at least mind enough to think there is nothing more than a body, I have no mind to follow them. The body is, of course, a precondition for the exercise of some, and perhaps even all, mental functions. This fact is sufficient to make it desirable to cultivate the body, and to consider the body seriously in any attempt at understanding the nature of man, without requiring us to suppose a man is only a body.

Everyone lives at least part of the time as a body. Occasionally our minds are idle, sometimes we sleep; we can spend much time in just eating and drinking. Though no one is merely a body, every one of us can be lost in his body for a time. Sooner or later, however, the minds in most of us awaken and we stray to the edges of reflection.

Even a dedicated sybarite has flashes of self-consciousness. Like the rest of us, he sometimes remembers and expects. He, too, looks to what lies beyond the here and now, and even beyond the whole world of bodily experience, to take account of ideals, if only to dismiss them. And sometimes, with poets and religious men, he deliberately detaches himself from his body and tries for a while to have a nonbodily career, occupied with fancies, myths, and transmundane beings.

He who gives himself to the life of the mind acknowledges as limits only what, if anything, is found to be beyond the reach of thought. But no one can totally identify himself with his mind. Bodily demands are imperious; the body's presence intrudes on consciousness. A man may escape the thrall of his body for a while, crush his desires, or focus on what is eternal, but sooner or later his body will show that it will not be gainsaid. It has needs and makes demands which must be met.

The life of thought proceeds at a different pace and pursues a different set of ends than that which concerns the life of the body. Each exhibits in a special shape what man can possibly be and do. Neither is replaceable, though the full use of either at a given time precludes the full use of the other; a career devoted to one alone is possible to only half a man.

Reprinted from *Sport: A Philosophic Inquiry* by Paul Weiss, 1969, Carbondale, Illinois: Southern Illinois University Press. Copyright 1969 by Southern Illinois University Press. Reprinted by permission.

The body is voluminous, spread out in space. Through it we express tendencies, appetites, impulses, reactions, and responses. The mind, in contrast, is a tissue of implications, beliefs, hopes, anticipations, and doubts. It has no size, and cannot, therefore, be identified with a brain. But the two, body and mind, are not distinct substances, closed off from one another. They are linked by the emotions.

Emotions are at once bodily and mental, inchoate unifications of mind and body. A controlled expression of the emotions drains them of their confusion at the same time that it intensifies the unity which they provide for the mind and the body. That is why emotions should not be allowed to come forth unchecked and unguided. Because art and sport involve a controlled expression of emotions, making it possible for minds and bodies to be harmonized clearly and intensely, they offer excellent agencies for unifying man.

Never in full possession of their bodies, men are always more than they bodily reveal themselves to be. Their bodies can only partly reflect what they are; the fullest bodily life exhibits them as less than they can be and less than they ought to be. This remains true even when the mind is put at the service of the body. A more independent and freer exercise of the mind is desirable, for the controlled expression of the emotions is then given a greater role, thereby making possible the production of a more complete man.

These remarks summarize a vast literature, bypass discussions centuries old, and hide perhaps as much as they make evident. Our minds are mysteries. The interplay of mind with body is more a matter of supposition and speculation than of solid fact, unimpeachably evidenced. But if we stop here to make sure that all will be persuaded about that which all believe, we will lose our chosen topic. This is not the place to give full attention to the nature of the mind or the emotions, and the way they can and should relate to one another or to the body. Perhaps, though, enough has been said to make what follows not be as dogmatic as it may at first sound.

At the very beginning of life the mind's course is determined by what the body does and what it encounters. Soon the imagination, aided by language, the consciousness of error, self-awareness, and the unsatisfactoriness of what is available, begins to operate. The mind then turns, sometimes hesitantly but occasionally boldly, to topics which may have little relevance to what the body then needs, to what it may encounter, or to the ends it should serve.

One cannot live a life solely of the mind for very long. Its exercise is brought suddenly to a halt when the unsupervised body becomes mired in difficulty. To restrain, redirect, and protect the body, the mind must be forced back into the service of that body. But now it need no longer wait on bodily prompting. By itself it has learned a good deal about ideals, abstract categories, and logical consequences. Some of that knowledge it can now use to point the way the body ought to go. A mathematical notion will help clarify how this is done.

Mathematicians speak of a "vector" as a quantity having a direction and magnitude. The term has been adapted by astronomers and biologists for more special uses. I follow their lead and treat the bodily relevant mind as a vector, reaching from the present toward a future prospect. Normally that mind terminates at a bodily pertinent prospect, an objective for the body to be realized in subsequent bodily action. The mind in this way provides the body with a controlling future.

Far down in the scale of living beings, bodies are comparatively simple, but they still thrust vectorially, albeit not consciously, toward the future. What they do is triggered in good part by occurrences that are relevant to their welfare. As we go up the scale the bodies become more and more complex, and some impulses arise without any bearing on external occurrences. And some of the occurrences that elicit responses may do so at the wrong time and in the wrong way, leading the individual into disaster and maybe death.

Were there any completely unsupervised, complex bodies their health would be most precarious and their life span very short. Fortunately, the higher organisms embody an intelligence, at service to their bodies. Without effort, though, none embodies as much intelligence as it can.

The human body, like all others, on one side is part of an external world. It too is to be understood in terms of what the world offers and insists upon. To be fully a master of its body, a being must make it act in consonance with what that body not only tends to, but what it should, do. This is an accomplishment possible only to men. Only they can envisage what is really good for the body to be and to produce. Only men can impose minds on bodies. Those minds have many grades and functions, running from attention to commitment. Man uses his mind to dictate what the body is to do.

Literally, "attention" means "a stretching out" (of the mind). Since this implies a consciousness, he who is attentive evidently has a vectoral, conscious mind. By directing itself at bodily relevant prospects, that mind makes certain places and objects into attended referents for that body. Desire, intention, and commitment, as we shall see, build on this base.

The athlete comes to accept his body as himself. This requires him to give up, for the time being, any attempt to allow his mind to dwell on objectives that are not germane to what his body is, what it needs, and what it can or ought to do. But that to which he consciously attends is not always that which his body is prepared to realize. It becomes a prepared body only after he has learned how to make it function in accord with what he has in mind. Normally, he does this by habituating his body to go through a series of acts which, he has learned, will eventuate in the realization of the prospect to which he attends. Training—of which therapy is a special instance— is the art of correcting a disequilibrium between mind and body either by altering the vector, or, more usually, by adjusting the way in which the body functions until the body follows the route that the vector provides.

To function properly as a body, it is necessary for the athlete to correct the vectorial thrust, or to alter the body so that it realizes the prospect at which the vector terminates. Correction of the vectorial thrust is one with a change in attitude and aim, themselves presupposing some change in what the mind does. Alteration of the body demands a change in the bodily organization and activity. Both changes are involved at the very beginning of the process of making an athlete. To ignore the need to undergo these changes is to remain with a disaccord of body and mind, of present and future. It is to allow the body to react to what occurs, or to allow the mind to follow its own bent, without regard for what the body is to do. Most of us exhibit the disaccord too frequently in the first of these ways. It is a characteristic defect of the intellectual; in his occupation with the life of thought, he leaves his body insufficiently supervised and directed.

The correction of the direction of the vectorial thrust is promoted by the awareness of the inadequacy of a project, an appreciation of other goals, and a temptation to change. Men usually make this correction after listening to authorities. Coaches, teachers, and models help them to change their course so that they have an object of attention which they will bodily realize.

• •

A training program's central purpose is to make men well trained. By making them go through various moves and acts many times its aim is to get their bodies to function in accord with what those bodies are expected to do. Training helps them to be their bodies, to accept their bodies as themselves. It makes those bodies habituated in the performance of moves and acts while enabling them to function harmoniously and efficiently, and thereby be in a position to realize the projects at which the vectorial minds terminate.

Some men do not train. Their bodies proceed from beginning to end, often without needing to be redirected in the course of it. Eventually, it is hoped, he who trains by mastering distinct moves will reach this state too, though it is a question whether he will then ever do more than blur the checking points that his moves provided.

• •

No one is completely ripened, incapable of being improved through training. Whether young or old, all must learn not to yield to the body, not to allow its reactions and responses to determine what will be done. The body is to be accepted, but only as subject to conditions which make it function in ways and to a degree that it would not were it left to itself. He who refuses to do this is self-indulgent, almost at the opposite pole from the self-disciplined and controlled athlete. Men do not play well persistently unless they are well trained.

A man who is content to be successful in the perpetual adventure of withstanding or overcoming the world he encounters is hard to distinguish from a well-functioning animal. A man should do more. He should use his mind to quicken and guide his body. He should make his body a locus of rights and duties, and a source of acts, desirable and effective. Only if he so structures and directs this body will he have a body that is used and not merely worked upon by what is external to it. Only he who expresses his emotions through such a possessed and structured body can become well-unified and not be undone by what he feels.

Most men, a good portion of the time, are in control of their bodies. What they do part of the time, without much thought or concentration, the athlete does both persistently and purposively. It is tempting, therefore, to say that for the athlete the body has an exclusive role, in contrast with the intellectual for whom it serves only as a place in which, and perhaps as an avenue through which, he expresses what he has independently discovered. But no athlete lives entirely in his body, any more than a thinker has only thoughts that are entirely unrelated to what is going on somewhere in the physical world.

Athlete and thinker differ in the attention they give to improving their bodies and their bodies' performance. The former, but not the latter, pushes himself toward the state where he so accepts his body that he cannot, without difficulty, distinguish himself from it. Mind and body are united by both. In neither case are mind and body related as are hand and glove. Their connection is more like that of fingers to one another. They presuppose a self just as the fingers presuppose a hand.

• •

An athlete makes use of his good condition to vitalize moves and acts under restrictive rules, both in practice sessions and in actual contests and games. He prepares himself primarily to be ready to discover in the course of a genuine struggle how good he is in comparison with others. Until he meets that test, although he is fulfilled as well-trained, he is still unfulfilled as an athlete.

The good coach makes a preparation be more than an exercise and less than a game. He understands that the body offers a challenge to one who would achieve excellence through bodily acts, and that it must be structured, habituated, and controlled by the object of a vectorial mind. This makes it possible for him to see to it that his athletes are in fine condition, and that this condition enables them to perform well. No preparation can, of course, guarantee a fine performance. The circumstances may be untoward, or the athlete may be out of sorts at the time.

The art of training and coaching is the satisfying and dissatisfying of athletes at one and the same time. It is also part of the art of making men. That art comes to completion when the athlete makes himself be not merely a fine body, but a body in rule-governed, well-controlled action. Athletics is mind displayed in a body well made, set in particular situations, involved in struggles, and performing in games.

Embodiment, Sport, and Meaning

KLAUS V. MEIER

As even a cursory glance at the history of philosophy attests, the significant task of elucidating and resolving the problem of the interdependence of mind and body presents a plethora of intriguing and intricate difficulties. Indeed, David Hume (6: pp. 76–77) asserted that there is no "principle in all nature more mysterious than the union of soul with body, by which a supposed spiritual substance acquires such an influence over a material one that the most refined thought is able to actuate the grossest matter."

The recent literature in the philosophy of sport has addressed itself, in part, to anthropological inquiries investigating the nature and structure of man. Specifically, the question of the relationship of mind and body and its applicability to, or manifestation in, sport has been actively pursued (1; 7; 12; 17; 22: pp. 33–42; 24: pp. 37–57). Unfortunately, philosophical research efforts concerned with the problem of embodiment and sport have often produced expositions replete with imprecise statements, contestable assertions and, at times, unsupported or simply erroneous conclusions. Thus, it appears appropriate to investigate anew the basis of contemporary perceptions of the ontological structure of man and, subsequently, to clarify some of the essential components of man's engagement in sport in relation to the formulated parameters.

The systematic theory of the relationship between the human body and the human mind developed by René Descartes provided philosophy with a conception of man with which it has struggled for more than three centuries. It is, therefore, necessary to scrutinize, in a limited manner, the labours and achievements of this renowned philosopher. Following the investigation of Descartes, the phenomenological anthropology of Maurice Merleau-Ponty will be delineated, including his significant criticism of Cartesian and ensuing mechanistic anthropologies, to provide a contemporary philosophical alternative for the resolution of the mind-body problem. Finally, the significance of the radical shift in the characterization of the nature of man will be analyzed specifically in relation to man's engagement in sport. At this stage it will be necessary to criticize certain philosophy of sport expositions deemed to be inadequate in light of the analysis conducted within this study and, also, to provide an orientation perceived to be more efficacious.

I

Descartes sought to develop a foundation for science that would avoid the presuppositions and inadequacies of Scholasticism and possess the rigorous certainty of mathematics. He contended that only through an extension of mathematical procedures to the investigation of things in the natural world could clear, certain, and final knowledge be attained.

Following careful and extensive deliberations utilizing, among other procedures and techniques, the process of "radical doubt" and the doctrine of "clear and distinct ideas," Descartes concluded that man is composed of two distinct substances— body and mind (or soul, to utilize Descartes' term) —the essential attributes of which differ radically. The body is viewed as an unthinking, extended, material substance; the mind is a thinking, unextended, immaterial substance. The body is an unconscious machine, as mechanical as a watch (3: p. 116), conforming to the unwavering and rigid laws of nature; the mind (the true "essence" of man) is a conscious and free substance possessing no qualities of extension and, therefore, not susceptible to, or dominated by, the mechanical laws of nature. The two substances are thus perceived to be totally distinct and independent.

The postulation of such an extreme bifurcation of mind and body, of course, elicits immediate difficulties. Despite the apparent impossibility of any interaction between two such dissimilar, demarcated, and mutually exclusive substances, open reflection on lived human experiences indicates that perhaps the distinction is not absolute. Although occasional, specific human activities may be performed unconsciously and mechanically, through reflex action for example, selected components of conscious perception and awareness, such as sensations of pain and sound, appetites of hunger and thirst, and the elicitation of emotions and passions, challenge significantly the dualistic structure through the implication of an intimate union between mind and body. Numerous other occasions attesting to, at least, a "quasi-substantial" union of the mind and body may be readily forwarded. In some sense, for example, it is surely legitimate to assert that the mind possesses the ability to suppress or re-direct sensual appetites. Also, particular mental states such as excitement or ela-

tion appear to manifest noticeable changes in the cardio-respiratory system and in the degree of intensity of the performance of physical activities.

Descartes, of course, was cognizant of experiences of the aforementioned nature; in the "Sixth Meditation" he claimed that they were the result of "certain confused modes of thought which are produced by the union and apparent intermingling of mind and body" (3: p. 192). To explain consciously directed or volitional action, Descartes acknowledged further that the body deviates from its mechanical procedures of performance at "the direction of the will," which in turn depends on the mind (3: p. 195). Such occurrences can only be intelligibly comprehended through the acknowledgment of some form of structural intercourse or unity of composition.

The admission that the mind consciously influences the motions of the body, and conversely is affected by its physiological states or activities, clearly demonstrates the basic difficulty of Cartesian dualism: namely, how can an extended, material substance be influenced by a spiritual substance that has no extension and, therefore, no spatial location for interaction? In other words, how can radically distinct substances form a substantial union?

In an attempt to respond to this difficulty, Descartes stated that the mind is indeed connected to the body, however, the nature of this interaction is, at the very least, obfuscated. Attuned to the necessity for the explication of mind-body interaction and fully aware of the constraints of his ontological edifice, Descartes couched his response in such nonspecific and imprecise terms as "occasion" or "spontaneous occurrence." Nonetheless, despite the utilization of, at times, deft linguistic manipulations, the essential difficulty remained unshaken.

Descartes attempted to solve the problem by asserting that the interaction of the mind and body is limited to one central location. Although the soul radiates throughout and "is in each member of the body," it exercises its functions most particularly in one specific part—the pineal gland, the apparent convergent or terminal of all nerve systems, situated in the midst of the brain (3: pp. 293, 345). Through its diverse manipulations in the pineal gland, the soul was postulated to regulate and thrust forth "animal spirits" (subtle and exquisitely refined parts of the blood, flowing to and from the brain through the arteries and nerves almost like "air or wind"), to direct the movements of the body's limbs (3: p. 333).

The choice of the pineal gland as the locus of the elusive connection and incarnation of the substantial union of body and mind, wherein the mind can exercise control of the body's movements and conversely be affected by the "animal spirits" agitated by physiological change, was certainly ingenuous, if not accurate. However, it was also "regarded as signally unfortunate" (5: p. 144) even in Descartes' own day. The reason for this reaction, of course, was that the introduction of "animal spirits," even of a highly rarified and special nature, was simply a matter of procrastination. The frustrating question of how there can be interaction between a substance that is purely spiritual and a substance that is purely material remained to be answered. The pineal gland, rather than providing a solution, appears to be simply an attempt at a "metaphysical tour de force."

Nonetheless, the influence of Descartes' philosophy was enormous. Enamoured by the thrust, mode, and content of Descartes' writings on the nature of man, a significant number of his contemporaries and followers forwarded many concepts and theories based largely on his work. The ideal of a purely mechanistic doctrine of physiology, with its view of the 'body-machine' working under the strict dictates of mechanical laws, was accorded considerable support in the European scientific community and has guided scientists since the seventeenth century.

The influence of mechanistic physiology on the contemporary understanding of man in sport is vast and will be discussed shortly; however, it is first necessary to delineate briefly a substantively different conception of the nature of man.

II

The problem of relating mind and body in the manner attempted by Descartes may be artificially created. It is extremely difficult, if not logically precluded, to meaningfully synthesize two elements or substances which are asserted to be of such radically diverse, distinct, and discontinuous natures into one functioning, complex entity. However, the attempt itself to promulgate a conception of man rent thusly asunder may be the source of fundamental error. If the postulated bifurcation is perceived to be the major dilemma, the problem may be approached in an entirely different manner. Rather than forwarding and championing an inherent dualistic conception, a monistic approach which accounts for both consciousness and embodiment may be noticeably more productive.

Maurice Merleau-Ponty (13; 14; 15; 16) dedicated his abbreviated philosophic career, to a considerable extent, to resolving the Cartesian problem of how man can experience himself as incarnate through a rigorous and adroit phenomenological analysis of man's 'being-in-the-world' and the nature of his corporeality.

Existential phenomenology in general, and the works of Merleau-Ponty specifically, are based on the tenet that "the most decisive trait of human consciousness, coloring all its manifestations, is that it is an *embodied* consciousness" (11: p. 10). Existence furnishes the point of departure. Man's contingencies, his finiteness, and his 'being-in-the-world' as a subject are, thus, perceived as the starting points. Consequently, the Cartesian categories are opposed as presupposing too little and offering misdirection.

Man is viewed as an incarnate subject, a unity not union of physical, biological, and psychological events all participating in dialectical relationships. The motions and activities of the 'lived-body' are not distinct from consciousness; rather, consciousness is deeply embodied in them. Merleau-Ponty perceived man as a 'body-subject' or incarnate consciousness—a being in the world concerned with his unfolding in the world. The existence of a disembodied, separate, or distinct mind is emphatically denied. For him, body and mind are simply limiting notions of the 'body-subject' which is a single entity or reality neither simply mental nor merely corporeal, but both, simultaneously.

Any delineation depicting man as being solely an intellectual interiority (the mind), or the simple seat of sensations (the extended body), or even a union of these types of being is rejected. Phenomenologists repeatedly assert that the human body is not a mere thing or object subject to the inclinations of the mind, rather, it is a subject in itself, deriving its subjectivity from itself. "To say that the soul acts on the body is wrongly to suppose a univocal notion of the body and to add to it a second force which accounts for the rational significance of certain conducts" (13: p. 202).

Similarly to Gabriel Marcel, Merleau-Ponty raised significant questions concerning the appropriateness of such statements as "I have a body" or "I use my body." He emphasized the peculiarity and inappropriateness of conceiving of one's body as an object or implement. "The body is more than a commodious instrument that I could do without: my body is myself, the man who I am" (20: p. 49). The manner in which man lives his body from the inside presents a sharply different perception than the objective body which is externally observed through the delimited scope of the anatomical and physiological sciences. The 'lived-body' is not an object which man possesses, rather it *is* man and man *is* his body. Man's mode of insertion into the world is the body; it is his foundation in existence. It is "the constantly moving and constantly irrevocable manner in which I insert myself in reality" (23: p. 164). Therefore, it may be seen that "being a body" is a radically

different characterization than "having a body" or "using a body."

However, there is a specific sense in which man does indeed "use" his body as an instrument, but certainly not in the same sense as he uses, for example, a hammer or a chair (26: p. 81). Since consciousness and the body may be described as inexorably inseparable—that is, consciousness is primordially embodied in the world—the body is man's means of perception of, and action upon, objects and the world. The body is not simply another object in the world, rather it is "an anchorage in the world"; it is man's mode of communication and interaction with it.

Thus, the rigid Cartesian structure of the mind-subject as a totally distinct and superior substance somehow controlling the inferior body-object is perceived to be erroneous and replaced by a structure deemed more appropriate.

It must be noted at this point that the investigation of an incarnate consciousness, projecting itself in the world and fully immersed in its perceptions and experiences, necessarily elicits ambiguity. No longer can the account of man and reality be delineated with total lucidity.

I have no means of knowing the human body other than that of living it, which means taking up on my own account the drama which is being played out in it, and losing myself in it. I am my body, at least wholly to the extent that I possess experience, and yet at the same time my body is as it were a "natural" subject, a provisional sketch of my total being. Thus experience of one's own body runs counter to the reflective procedure which detaches subject and object from each other, and which gives us only the thought about the body, or the body as an idea, and not the experience of the body or the body in reality (14: pp. 198–99).

Ambiguity, rather than lucidity, is an integral component of the manifestation and essence of human existence. The numerous, diverse perceptions and meanings of embodiment; the lived experience of "the chiaroscuro of the body" (10: p. 46); and the open dialogue with the sensible world—are precisely the occurrences which must be investigated and not rejected because they violate arbitrary Cartesian doctrines of "clear and distinct" ideas. Human existence, due to the distinct nature of incarnate consciousness, is obfuscated and, therefore, ambiguity arising in its investigation is simply an indication that the analysis has not departed from reality or succumbed to artificial distortion or inappropriate reduction.

An analysis of man's incarnation reveals that man is an opaque and partially concealed 'body-subject' without clear and precise points of demarcation for the various aspects of his being; he is a unity of physical, biological, and psychological relationships necessarily interrelated and only meaningfully investigated when analyzed as a whole.

Man's 'being-in-the-world' is given a viewpoint only through his body. The body is "the seat or rather the very actuality of the phenomenon of expression" (14: p. 235); it is the locus of a dialectical relationship with the world and the fabric into which all objects are woven; and, finally, it is the center of openness, intentionality, and meaning-producing acts.

> The body is our general medium for having a world. Sometimes it is restricted to the actions necessary for the conservation of life, and accordingly it posits around us a biological world; at other times, elaborating upon these primary actions and moving from their literal to a figurative meaning, it manifests through them a core of new significance: this is true of motor habits such as dancing and sport. Sometimes, finally, the meaning aimed at cannot be achieved by the body's natural means; it must then build itself an instrument, and it projects thereby around itself a cultural world (14: p. 146).

Through his corporeality man is provided with a foundation in, and is open to, the world. Mean-

ing arises, is created, and is constituted by the interaction of the 'body-subject' and the world through the body's power of expression. Man, dwelling in a world of fluctuating perspectives, possesses the possibility of unfolding diverse projects of personal import—in the laugh of a child, a gesture of a hand, the work of an artist, or the movement of an athlete, meaning is manifested.

Thus, in summary, the phenomenological analysis of man depicts him in a radically different manner than the inadequate and deceptive Cartesian dualistic structure which "portrays man as ontologically schizophrenic" (4: p. 156). Rather than stripping him of his existential character and delineating him as composed of two diverse and discrete substances, man is characterized as embodied consciousness—the distinction between the subjective and objective poles is blurred in the experience of the lived, meaning-bestowing body. Man is acknowledged as an open and engaged being dwelling in the world, capable of developing personal meaning in the process of actively manifesting himself.

III

It would appear to be most logical to assume that, of the multitudinous realms of human enterprise, the particular areas of the philosophy of sport and theories of physical education would be the most enlightened in regard to the nature of man's corporeality and, therefore, predisposed to advocate and to actively support an image of man consummate with the phenomenological analysis of the 'lived-body'.

However, such an assumption would be most imprudent. The philosophy of sport is replete, both in theory and practice, with implicit and explicit restatements and affirmations of Cartesian dualism, despite occasional assertions to the contrary. The flight to the respectability and acceptability of the natural scientific framework and the appropriation of stimulus-response and behaviouristic schema are much in evidence, with the ensuing result that man's incarnate being is more often objectified and reduced, than expressed or celebrated.

Paul Weiss (24), for example, in one of the first two philosophical treatises to investigate sport in considerable detail, stated that the fundamental task facing the athlete is that of eliminating the dissonance and disequilibrium between mind and body by struggling toward unification and harmony. According to Weiss (24: pp. 221, 218, 41), although he "starts with a separated mind and body," "the athlete becomes one with his body through practice," and "comes to accept the body as himself."

A very brief delineation of Weiss' conception of man will clarify the preceding statements and those which follow. In a manner similar to Descartes, Weiss divided man into two diverse substances—an extended, "voluminous" body characterized by "tendencies, appetites, impulses, reactions, and responses" and an unextended, immaterial mind, "a tissue of implications, beliefs, hopes, anticipations, and doubts." He asserted further that the two substances are linked by the emotions which are at once "bodily and mental, inchoate unifications of mind and body" (24: p. 38).

Much akin to Descartes' supposition of the pineal gland as the locus of the interaction between mind and body, recourse to the emotions (the nature of which remains largely unspecified), elicits and amplifies, rather than diminishes difficulties. Weiss stated further that the emotions require control, and to supply this regulating force he professed the existence of a "self" (24: p. 54). Unfortunately, he declined the opportunity to elaborate and clarify the intriguing distinctions and relationships among mind, body, emotions and self. The inevitable result is a rather bewildering and confusing portrait of man in general and the athlete in particular.

Of specific interest to the present discussion is Weiss' extensive and active support of a hierarchical, dualistic conception of man. He strongly and repeatedly emphasized the power of mind over

body throughout his analysis of the athlete and his body. Weiss (24: pp. 41, 46) declared that an athlete, on his journey toward the attainment of excellence in sport, engages in a rigorous training program designed "to correct" or "to alter the body" by means of "adjusting the way in which the body functions," until it proceeds in accord with the mind's expectations; "man uses his mind to dictate what the body is to do."

> Whether young or old, all must learn not to yield to the body, not to allow its reactions and responses to determine what will be done. The body is to be accepted, but only as subject to conditions which make it function in ways and to a degree that it would not were it left to itself (24: pp. 53–54).

The dualistic structure immediately evident in the preceding statements is reinforced continuously in Weiss' analysis: the mind uses, alters, directs, controls, restrains, restructures, disciplines and conquers the body (24: pp. 40, 217). The precise and pointed terminology clearly demonstrates that, for Weiss, the athlete utilizes the body as an object; he must subdue and control his corporeal aspects. This orientation obviously depicts the athlete as "possessing" a body rather than fully "being" a body.

In much of modern sport theory and practice, the human body is completely reified and reduced to the status of an object to be altered and manipulated or an obstacle to be surmounted. To utilize Sarano's (20: p. 63) suggestive metaphor, the body is often perceived as an entity which "must be bridled as a restive mount." Thus, in preparation for athletic endeavours the body is drilled, trimmed, strengthened, quickened and otherwise trained to improve its fitness and functioning and often handled as an instrument or utensil to be appropriately directed and mastered.

In accord with such an orientation, the anatomical, kinesiological, bio-mechanical, and physiological sciences are intensely and tenaciously pursued and granted almost exclusive sanction to scrutinize, analyze, and manipulate man's corporeal nature and his participation in sport. As a result, the athlete is often regarded as "capable of being completely understood by means of stimulus-response conditioning, laws of learning, transfer of training, and neurological brain wave analysis" (9: p. 176).

However, as the phenomenology of the body demonstrated, objective approaches are inadequate and inappropriate to fully comprehend the nature of man's embodied being. The 'body-subject' not only is sensed, but also does the sensing. The body perceived totally as an object is, in a legitimate sense, drained of its humanity; it is a dead body devoid of its vivifying, expressive and intentional abilities and qualities.

The rejection of Cartesian concepts and dichotomies permits man to rescue the objectified, maligned, and mistreated body to attain an increasing awareness of the depth and richness of his 'lived-body' and to approach it as a diverse and dynamic reality. Rather than continued repetition and support of discrete, hierarchical notions of mind-body interaction, it appears to be substantially more fruitful to transcend such limiting orientations. If reductive approaches are altered and mental-physical polarities are eliminated, it is possible to accord the physical attributes of man due respect as integral facets of his nature and, subsequently, to rejoice in the total aspects of the conscious body. Consequently, instead of perceiving human action as depersonalized movement largely, if not totally, comprehensible through external quantification, the unfortunate manner in which much of sport is currently viewed, such activities may be openly apprehended as configurations inscribed with shapes and qualities expressive of the texture of the being of the participant.

Man is anchored and centered in the world through his body which provides him with an oriented focus for action and projection. "Nothing is more expressive than the human body, our hands and fingers, our dancing feet, our eyes, our voice in joy and sorrow" (17: p. 114). It is through the power and gestures of the 'lived-body', fully and openly engaged in dialogue with the world, that man discloses, establishes, and broadens the personal meanings of his existence. Moments of "intense realness" available in sport provide opportunities for the unfolding of new insights and the restructuring of previous perceptions. During instances of total immersion and dynamic individuation man unfolds his powers, becomes aware of his capabilities and his limitations, develops forms of self-expression, and affirms himself.

In addition, it should also be noted that "the body is the vehicle of an indefinite number of symbolic systems" (16: p. 9). Consequently, sport, as a vibrant form of human endeavor capable of manifesting and transmitting affective states and meanings, may be viewed both as a symbolic medium and as a potentially artistic enterprise capable of releasing and celebrating the creative subjectivity of the participant.

Thus, it may be seen that the open and aware athlete apprehends and experiences his body neither solely as an object or an instrument to be manipulated nor externally as others view him, but rather, as a multi-faceted being totally, uniquely, and indelibly an embodied consciousness. The comportment of the body is the manner in which man exists for himself and sport permits him to attain acute insight into the depth and mettle of his existence. Further, sport affords the athlete the opportunity not only to become aware of his incarnation, but it also "multiplies, extends, consolidates, and confirms this insertion" (20: p. 154), through engagement in the world in the form of projects which express his individual being.

In conclusion, it may be asserted that if the radical philosophical shift from Cartesian to phenomenological conceptions of the nature of man is acknowledged and accepted, the distinctive potentialities of man's participation in sport may be vigorously and profitably explored. Rather than concentrating solely on the objectified, treadmill image of sport, predominantly centered upon the development and attainment of physical strength, motor skills, and technical efficiency, it appears to be legitimate, fruitful, and imperative to focus upon the full range of dynamic, lived experiences available therein.

Through free, creative, and meaning-bestowing movement experiences, man becomes cognizant of the limits and potentials of his existence. His actions in sport represent, express, and affirm his capabilities, intentionality and mode of being. In short, sport may be characterized and extolled as the celebration of man as an open and expressive embodied being.

Bibliography

1. Abe, Shinobu. "Interdependence of Body and Mind as Related to Sport and Physical Education." Essay presented at the Annual Meeting of the Philosophic Society for the Study of Sport at the University of Western Ontario, London, Canada, November 16, 1974.

2. Barral, Mary Rose. *Merleau-Ponty: The Role of the Body Subject in Interpersonal Relations.* Pittsburgh: Duquesne University Press, 1965.

3. Descartes, René. *The Philosophical Works of Descartes. Vol. One.* Translated and edited by E.S. Haldane and G.R.T. Ross. Cambridge, England: Cambridge University Press, 1967.

4. Dillon, M.C. "Sartre on the Phenomenal Body and Merleau-Ponty's Critique." *Journal of the British Society for Phenomenology, 5* (1974), 144–158.

5. Hocking, William Earnest. *Types of Philosophy. Third Edition.* New York: Charles Scribner's Sons, 1959.

6. Hume, David. *An Inquiry Concerning Human Understanding.* Edited by Charles W. Hendel. New York: The Liberal Arts Press, 1955.

7. Kaelin, Eugene F. "Being in the Body." *Sport and the Body: A Philosophical Symposium.* Edited by Ellen Gerber. Philadelphia: Lea and Febiger, 1972.

8. Kapp, R.O. "Living and Lifeless Machines." *British Journal of the Philosophy of Science, 5* (1954), 91–103.

9. Kleinman, Seymour. "The Significance of Human Movement: A Phenomenological Approach." *Sport and the Body: A Philosophical Symposium.* Edited by Ellen Gerber. Philadelphia: Lea and Febiger, 1972.

10. Kwant, Remy. *The Phenomenological Philosophy of Merleau-Ponty.* Pittsburgh: Duquesne University Press, 1963.

11. Lawrence, N. and O'Connor, D. (Eds.). *Readings in Existential Phenomenology.* Englewood Cliffs, New Jersey: Prentice-Hall, 1967.

12. Meier, Klaus V. "The Pineal Gland, 'Mu', and the 'Body-Subject': Critical Reflections on the Interdependence of Mind and Body." Paper presented at the Annual Meeting of the Philosophic Society for the Study of Sport at the University of Western Ontario, London, Canada, November 16, 1974.

13. Merleau-Ponty, Maurice. *The Structure of Behaviour.* Translated by A.L. Fisher. Boston: Beacon Press, 1963.

14. _____. *The Phenomenology of Perception.* Translated by Colin Smith. London: Routledge and Kegan Paul, 1962.

15. _____. *The Primacy of Perception and Other Essays.* Edited by James M. Edie. Northwestern University Press, 1969.

16. _____. *Themes from the Lectures at the College de France 1952-1960.* Translated by John O'Neill. Evanston, Illinois: Northwestern University Press, 1970.

17. O'Neill, John. "The Spectacle of the Body." *Journal of the Philosophy of Sport, 1* (1974), 110–122.

18. Pirenne, M.H. "Descartes and the Body-Mind Problem in Physiology." *British Journal of the Philosophy of Science, 1* (1950), 43–59.

19. Ryle, Gilbert. *The Concept of Mind.*

Harmondsworth, England: Penguin Books Ltd., 1966.

20. Sarano, Jacques. *The Meaning of the Body.* Translated by James H. Farley. Philadelphia: The Westminster Press, 1966.

21. Schrag, Cavlin O. "The Lived Body as a Phenomenological Datum." *Sport and the Body: A Philosophical Symposium.* Edited by Ellen Gerber. Philadelphia: Lea and Febiger, 1972.

22. Slusher, Howard S. *Man, Sport and Existence.* Philadelphia: Lea and Febiger, 1967.

23. de Waelhens, Alphonse. "The Phenomenology of the Body." *Readings in Existential Phenomenology.* Edited by N. Lawrence and D. O'Conner. Englewood Cliffs, New Jersey: Prentice-Hall, 1967.

24. Weiss, Paul. *Sport: A Philosophic Inquiry.* Carbondale, Illinois: Southern Illinois University Press, 1969.

25. Zaner, Richard M. *The Problem of Embodiment: Some Contributions to a Phenomenology of the Body.* The Hague: Martinus Nijhoff, 1964.

26. _____. "The Radical Reality of the Human Body." *Humanitas,* 2 (1966), 73–87.

The Body

JEAN-PAUL SARTRE

The problem of the body and its relations with consciousness is often obscured by the fact that while the body is from the start posited as a certain *thing* having its own laws and capable of being defined from outside, consciousness is then reached by the type of inner intuition which is peculiar to it. Actually if after grasping "my" consciousness in its absolute interiority and by a series of reflective acts, I then seek to unite it with a certain living object composed of a nervous system, a brain, glands, digestive, respiratory, and circulatory organs whose very matter is capable of being analyzed chemically into atoms of hydrogen, carbon, nitrogen, phosphorus, etc., then I am going to encounter insurmountable difficulties. But these difficulties all stem from the fact that I try to unite my consciousness not with *my* body but with the body *of others*. In fact the body which I have just described is not *my* body such as it is *for* me. I have never seen and never shall see my brain nor my endocrine glands. But because I who am a man have seen the cadavers of men dissected, because I have read articles on physiology, I conclude that my body is constituted exactly like all those which have been shown to me on the dissection table or of which I have seen colored drawings in books. Of course the physicians who have taken care of me, the surgeons who have operated on me, have been able to have direct experience with

the body which I myself do not know. I do not disagree with them, I do not claim that I lack a brain, a heart, or a stomach. But it is most important to choose the *order* of our bits of knowledge. So far as the physicians have had any experience with my body, it was with my body *in the midst of the world* and as it is for others. My body as it is *for me* does not appear to me in the midst of the world. Of course during a radioscopy I was able to see the picture of my vertebrae on a screen, but I was outside in the midst of the world. I was apprehending a wholly constituted object as a *this* among other *thises,* and it was only by a reasoning process that I referred it back to being *mine;* it was much more my *property* than my being.

It is true that I see and touch my legs and my hands. Moreover nothing prevents me from imagining an arrangement of the sense organs such that a living being could see one of his eyes while the eye which was seen was directing its glance upon the world. But it is to be noted that in this case again I am the *Other* in relation to my eye. I apprehend it as a sense organ constituted in the world in a particular way, but I can not "see the seeing"; that is, I can not apprehend it in the process of revealing an aspect of the world to me. Either it is a thing among other things, or else it is that by which things are revealed to me. But it can not be both at the same time. Similarly I see my hand touching objects, but do not *know* it in its act of touching them. This is the fundamental reason why that famous "sensation of effort" of Maine de Biran does not really exist. For my hand reveals to me the resistance of objects, their

Reprinted by permission of Philosophical Library, Inc. from *Being and Nothingness* by Jean-Paul Sartre, translated by Hazel E. Barnes, © Copyright, 1956, by Philosophical Library, Inc., New York.

hardness or softness, but not *itself*. Thus I see my hand only in the way that I see this inkwell. I unfold a distance between it and me, and this distance comes to integrate itself in the distances which I establish among all the objects of the world. When a doctor takes my wounded leg and looks at it while I, half raised up on my bed, watch him do it, there is no essential difference between the visual perception which I have of the doctor's body and that which I have of my own leg. Better yet, they are distinguished only as different structures of a single global perception; there is no essential difference between the doctor's perception of my leg and my own present perception of it. Of course when I touch my leg with my finger, I realize that my leg is touched. But this phenomenon of double sensation is not essential: cold, a shot of morphine, can make it disappear. This shows that we are dealing with two essentially different orders of reality. To touch and to be touched, to feel that one is touching and to feel that one is touched—these are two species of phenomena which it is useless to try to reunite by the term "double sensation." In fact they are radically distinct, and they exist on two incommunicable levels. Moreover when I touch my leg or when I see it, I surpass it toward my own possibilities. It is, for example, in order to pull on my trousers or to change a dressing on my wound. Of course I can at the same time arrange my leg in such a way that I can more conveniently "work" on it. But this does not change the fact that I transcend it toward the pure possibility of "curing myself" and that consequently I am present to it without its *being me* and without my *being it*. What I cause to exist here is the *thing* "leg;" it is not the leg as the *possibility which I am* of walking, running, or of playing football.

Thus to the extent that my body indicates my possibilities in the world, seeing my body or touching it is to transform these possibilities of mine into dead-possibilities. This metamorphosis must necessarily involve a complete *thisness* with regard to the body as a living possibility of running, of dancing, etc. Of course, the discovery of

my body as an object is indeed a revelation of its being. But the being which is thus revealed to me is its *being-for-others*. That this confusion may lead to absurdities can be clearly seen in connection with the famous problem of "inverted vision." We know the question posed by the physiologists: "How can we set upright the objects which are painted upside down on our retina?" We know as well the answer of the philosophers: "There is no problem. An object is upright or inverted in relation to the rest of the universe. To perceive the whole universe inverted means nothing, for it would have to be inverted in relation to something." But what particularly interests us is the origin of this false problem. It is the fact that people have wanted to link *my* consciousness of objects to the body of the Other. Here are the candle, the crystalline lens, the inverted image on the screen of the retina. But to be exact, the retina enters here into a physical system; it is a *screen* and only that; the crystalline lens is a *lens* and only a lens; both are homogeneous in their being with the candle which completes the system. Therefore we have deliberately chosen the physical point of view—i.e., the point of view of the outside, of exteriority—in order to study the problem of vision; we have considered a dead eye in the midst of the visible world in order to account for the visibility of this world. Consequently, how can we be surprised later when consciousness, which is absolute interiority, refuses to allow itself to be bound to this object? The relations which I establish between the Other's body and the external object are *really* existing relations, but they have for their being the being of the for-others; they suppose a center of intra-mundane flow in which knowledge is a *magic* property of space, "action at a distance." From the start they are placed in the perspective of the Other-as-object.

If then we wish to reflect on the nature of the body, it is necessary to establish an order of our reflections which conforms to the order of being: we can not continue to confuse the ontological levels, and we must in succession examine the body first as being-for-itself and then as being-for-others. And in order to avoid such absurdities as "inverted vision," we must keep constantly in mind the idea that since these two aspects of the body are on different and incommunicable levels of being, they can not be reduced to one another.

Being-for-itself must be wholly body and it must be wholly consciousness; it can not be *united* with a body. Similarly being-for-others is wholly body; there are no "psychic phenomena" there to be united with the body. There is nothing *behind* the body. But the body is wholly "psychic."

If I Am My Body

GABRIEL MARCEL

October 24th, 1920

I am not at all sure about the soundness of the observations I made yesterday. This is the point I thought I had reached: if *I am my body* only means "my body is an object of actual interest for me" we have nothing that can confer on my body a real priority in relation to other objects. This is not so if "my body" is regarded as the necessary condition for an object to become a datum for my attention. But in that case the attention which is brought to bear on my body presupposes the exercise of this mediating element which itself falls outside the realm of the knowable. Only by an arbitrary step of the mind as in *(b)* can I identify the body-as-object with the body-as-mediator.

But what are we to think of the idea of a primary instrument of the attention (whether or not it coincides with what I habitually call my body)? From what I pointed out yesterday it emerges that no idea of a mediating principle by which the attention can be exercised is possible for me. But is that which can in no way be an object for me by that very fact incapable of being an object for anyone? Can we not conceive a type of organic structure and optics of the intellect that are different from ours so that from their standpoint the problem would collapse?

We must first of all delve deeper into the nature of the instrumental relation. Fundamentally it seems to me that every instrument is a means of extending or of strengthening a "power" that

we possess. This is just as true as regards a spade as regards a microphone. To say that these powers themselves are instruments would be merely playing with words; for we would need to determine what these powers themselves really prolong. There must always be some community of nature between the instrument and the instrumentalist. But if I look on my body as my instrument am I not yielding to a sort of unconscious illusion by which I give back to the soul the very powers which are merely prolonged by the mechanical dispositions to which I have reduced my body? It must be noted, moreover, that if I deny that the body is entirely thinkable, I am contesting that it can be treated as an instrument, since an instrument is essentially that of which an idea is possible, indeed that which is only possible through this idea of it.

Under such conditions the initial question changes its appearance. When I insisted on the necessity of a mediation for the attention to be concentrated on any object, had I not the impression that I was speaking of an instrument? And on the other hand when I said that, strictly speaking, I could not form an idea of that mediation, was I not implicitly denying that it was an instrument? I appear to be involved in a whole network of contradictions. All this should be taken up in detail.

If I think of my body as instrument I thereby attribute to the soul, whose tool it is, the potentialities which are actualised by means of this instrument. Nor is that all. I furthermore convert the soul into a body and in that way become involved in regression without end. To suppose on the other hand that I can become anything whatever, that is to say, that I can identify myself with anything whatever, by the minimum act of attention implied by an elementary sensation without the intervention of *any mediation whatsoever,* is to undermine the very foundations of spiritual life and pulverise the mind into purely successive acts. But I can no longer conceive this mediation as being of an instrumental order. I will therefore call it "sympathetic mediation." Is the idea of such mediation possible for an intelligence that is different from ours? Once again we need to make a roundabout approach. Instrumental mediation and sympathetic mediation seem to be bound up together and even unthinkable apart. But what exactly does their bond imply?

All that I can say from the standpoint which I have so far attained is that telepathy, for example, is doubtless only a particular case of a general mode of mediation which is alone capable of making instrumental mediation possible. But obviously we will not get an inch nearer the solution of the problem I have stated by interposing an unknown occult body between spiritual activity and the visible body. Moreover, the expression "spiritual activity" does not satisfy me. Things must be considered on a higher level. To say that the attention cannot be exercised directly on an object is to refuse to regard the attention as an independent reality. Could we not say that attention is always attention to self and inversely that there is only self where there is attention? Besides it is quite clear that to pay attention to something is always to pay attention to oneself as a feeling being. Yet we need to grasp that this *self* still *falls short* of all objectivity. Here we come back to the criticism that I made earlier of formalistic doctrine of the ego (as object that has nothing objective about it, that is neither a *what* nor a *who*).

I am unable to appear to myself otherwise than as an attentive activity bound up with a certain *"this"* on which it is exercised and without which it would not be itself. But have I not said that no idea of this *"this"* is possible? Whereas must it not at every moment be a given *such,* that is to say, must it not be determined? (I would not like to insist here on the problem regarding time that we will come up against soon enough.) The *this* of which I am speaking is not an object, but the absolute condition for any object whatever to be given to me as datum. I wonder whether I would be betraying the thought I am trying to "bring to birth" at this moment if I said that there is no attention save where there is at the same time a certain fundamental way of feeling that cannot in any way be converted into an object, that is in no way reduced to the Kantian *I think* (since this is not a universal form) and without which the personality is annihilated. To sum up, this fundamental sensation is confounded with attention to self (the self being no more than absolute immediacy treated as mediation).

But we must grasp clearly that this *Urgefühl* can in no way be felt, precisely because it is fundamental. For it could only be so in function of other sensations—but by that very fact it would lose its priority. But is it not conceivable that for other beings placed on another plane, this fundamental quality can on the contrary be felt? . . .

When I re-read the bulk of the foregoing reflections I think I can see a "hole" in my argument. Can I not be reproached for having taken as a sort of self-evident postulate that this fundamental quality cannot be identified with my body? Whereas I am really unable to identify the object and the condition of objectivisation.

Nor are we at the end of our difficulties. If my body is not to be identified with this mediating quality, how does it happen that my body appears to me as being *more* than an object amongst other objects? I think the answer is that for sympathetic mediation to take place, there must also be instrumental mediation. Hence, for there to be a medium there must also be a knowable instrument —i.e., a body.

The kind of antinomy involved in all this is essentially bound up with the very nature of personal life, because were all instrumental mediation lacking, we would be in the realm of pure diversity, of that which cannot be grasped.

The Lived Body as a Phenomenological Datum

CALVIN O. SCHRAG

Phenomenology, as a methodological principle, designates a disciplined attempt at a descriptive analysis and interpretive explication of the data of immediate experience. Husserl's formula *Zu den Sachen Selbst!* has become normative for all phenomenological enquiry. Heidegger, Scheler, Sartre, Merleau-Ponty, and others, have taken over Husserl's formula and applied it to various regions of man's lived experience. The differences among the phenomenologists are due primarily to variegated applications of the phenomenological method rather than to disputes concerning the nature of the phenomenological principle itself. My present task is not that of a historical examination of the similarities and differences between the different phenomenologists. Such an undertaking would indeed be helpful toward a further clarification of what is meant by phenomenology as a philosophical method, but the pursuit of this task would lead us too far afield. The specific purpose of this essay is that of developing a phenomenological analysis of the lived body. The phrase "the lived body" denotes a structure of human subjectivity. It indicates the experience of my body as it is disclosed to me in my immediate involvements and concerns. Sartre, Marcel, and Merleau-Ponty have given studied attention to the phenomenon of the lived body; but their descriptions are often

fragmentary and singularly impoverished on rather decisive issues. Heidegger, on the other hand, has virtually nothing to say about the body. His *Dasein* appears to be a disembodied *Existenz* who moves about in his world of care in an abstracted unawareness of his bodily engagements and orientations. As Hegel, in his *Science of Logic,* had viciously abstracted reason from its context in man's lived historical existence, so it would seem that Heidegger comes perilously close to abstracting *Existenz* from its concrete bodily involvement. What is sorely needed as a corrective to the Heideggerian's neglect of the body is another Feuerbach to call us to an awareness of the bodily dimension of human existence, and another Nietzsche to remind us that life is lost in the moment that man no longer remains faithful to the earth.

In the following discussion I will seek to analyze and describe the datum of the lived body as it evinces a fourfold expression: (1) the lived body as self-referential, (2) the lived body in reference to other, (3) the lived body and human space, and (4) the lived body and human time.

I. The Lived Body as Self-Referential

I experience my body as uniquely and peculiarly my own. My body is so intimately related to what

Reprinted from *The Modern Schoolman,* XXXIX, (March, 1962), pp. 203–218. Copyright 1962 by *The Modern Schoolman.* Reprinted by permission.

and who I am that the experience of selfness is indissolubly linked with the existential projects which radiate from my body as it is actually lived. My body is immediately experienced and initially disclosed as my concrete mode of orientation in a world of practical and personal concerns. The phenomenon in question is *my* body as *concretely lived.* The body as immediately apprehended is not a corporeal substance which is in some way attached to, or united with, another substance, variously called in the tradition a ''soul,'' ''mind,'' or ''self.'' The body thus conceptualized is a later abstraction and objectivization, which is phenomenologically eviscerated and epistemologically problematic. I experience my body first as a complex of life-movements which are indistinguishable from my experience of selfness. My primordial experience is one of engagement in a world of concrete projects—projects which receive their significance through my body as the locus of concern. The distinctions between soul and body, or mind and body, as they have been formulated in the tradition (particularly by Descartes), are reified and objectivized distinctions, foreign to man's experience as it is immediately lived. Thus, the body as *concretely lived* must be consistently contrasted with the body as *objectively known.* The body as objectively known is a proper datum to be sure, but it is a scientific datum for the investigations of the anatomical and physiological sciences. The body as objectively known is a corporeal entity, properly defined as a complex of brain waves, neural pathways, endocrinal discharges, and muscular fibers. This is the body as it exists for the physiologist and the physician. But this is not the body which I experience in my lived concreteness and which I apprehend as being indelibly and uniquely my own. The body as an item for the special sciences, in which all data necessarily are objectivized, is an abstracted and general body which applies to everyone but characterizes no one in particular. It becomes a body conceptualized in its objectivized mode of being-for-another. No one can ''know'' his pituitary gland or his cerebral cortex as it is known objectively by the brain surgeon.

To be sure, I can infer from my knowledge of cadavers that I have the same anatomical structures and the same physiological functions as have other bodies; but this is a level of knowledge in abstraction from the experience of my body as concretely lived.

The lived body, I have suggested, signifies a mode of orientation rather than a conceptualized entity. This mode of orientation is part and parcel of man's preobjective world. Merleau-Ponty has made the notion of a preobjective world central not only to his phenomenology of perception, but to his philosophy as such.[1] Being in the world, as a primordial experience, is a global structure of interrelating practical projects and not a conceptualization of a world schematized through the objectivizing categories of substance, quantity, and abstract quality. The world is initially disclosed as an instrumental world in which tools are accessible for the realization of my practical concerns, and a social world in which I already find myself concretely related to other selves. A putty knife, in the primitive and subjective experience of my world, is a utensil with which I seal the window pane to keep out the wintry draft. The putty knife *as object,* although still the same putty knife, is a thematized and conceptualized entity to which I attach certain abstract qualities of weight, shape, and solidity. The former movement discloses my preobjective world; the latter is a construction of my objective world. Now it is in this preobjective world that the lived body makes its appearance. Preobjectively understood, the lived body is always related to an environment and social horizon, but in this relational complex it always appears as that which refers to itself as the locus of this relatedness. The lived body is self-referential.

It is through the orientation of my lived body that the personal meanings of my preobjective being in the world are disclosed, established, and broadened. The hand plays a privileged role in this disclosure and creation of meanings in my world orientations. It is through the use of my hand that I project meanings by pointing and touching, by writing and counting, by striking and stroking, by giving and taking. It is through the use of the hand that I create new worlds and refashion the old. The hand makes man a creator. Clocks and microscopes are works of the hand which express man's creativity and his power over the given. The lived body creates meanings by refashioning that which is simply given. Man becomes a maker of tools and a creator of values through the use of his hand. So also it is through the use of my hand that the personal meanings in my relations with others are established and expressed. In the handshake and in the gesture, complexes of meaning are at once created and revealed. Karl Jaspers in his illuminating discussion of the hand in *Von der Wahrheit* has concretely defined man as that being who makes use of his hands. Man is *homo faber* as well as *homo sapiens*. It is this existential quality which differentiates man from the animal. An animal is bound to its environment and must accommodate itself to it; man modifies his environment through the use of his hand, which determines the application and use of his thought. One of the fateful errors of philosophy, continues Jaspers, is the vicious separation of doing and thinking. All activity involving the use of the hand already discloses thought as inextricably intertwined with the activity, and it is through the activities of the hand (*Handtätigkeiten*) that the activities of thought (*Denktätigkeiten*) are explicated.[2] The body in its lived concreteness expresses a concomitant upsurge of thought and activity through which I both grasp and shape the meaning of my incarnated being-in-the-world.

The self-referential quality of the lived body is most directly disclosed in my experience of my body as that which individualizes me. The body confers upon me my existential identity. The tradition was right in viewing the body as a principle of individuation but erred in objectivizing the individuating principle as an abstract *materia signata quantitate* which individuates the particular by somehow uniting with form. Particularly in the Aristotelian tradition does individuation remain abstract and objective, with the result that individuation never *individualizes*. Only when I apprehend

my body in the particularity of its lived concreteness is it disclosed as a factor of individuation. The body individuates me in that it signifies the projects which are peculiarly my own—my hand grasping the pen with which I write, my head nodding to the person with whom I converse, my anticipation of the death which I alone must die. Sartre has clearly expressed this notion in stating that the body "represents the individualization of my engagement in the world."[3] I apprehend myself as being marked off from other selves, and from objects and things, in the moment that I apprehend my lived body in its concrete involvements, referring to projects that are peculiarly and uniquely my own.

The lived body is not a *something,* objective and external to the self, which when attached to the self individuates it and marks it off from other selves. This external view of the body transforms it into an objectively conceptualized material substance. But on the level of the preobjective experience of the body as mine no such material substance can be found. Marcel elucidates this when he writes: "In the fact of *my body* there is something which transcends what can be called its materiality, something which cannot be reduced to any of its objective qualities."[4] Further clarification on the distinction between the objective and the preobjective understanding of the body is forthcoming in Marcel's distinction between "having" and "being." Viewed as an objective determinant of individuation, the body is understood as something that the self *has*. The self has a body analogous to the way in which the courthouse has a goldplated dome. The body, in such a view, is adventitious or external to the self. On the other hand, the body preobjectively understood as the *lived body* is not something which I *have;* rather it signifies who I *am*. *I am my body* or *I exist as body*. Immediate experience testifies to the fact that the body is not something which I possess and consequently use in one way or another as an instrument or a utensil. As formulated by Marcel: "I do not *make use of* my body, I *am* my body. In other words, there is something in me that denies the implication that is to be found in the purely instrumentalist notion of the body that my body is external to myself."[5] I am not related to my body in an external way. It is not a possession which I have and use. The lived body makes use of instruments and utensils in its world orientations, but the body is not itself an instrument. The body is myself in my lived concreteness. It is *who I am,* and indicates the *manner in which I am.* The lived body refers to my personal manner of existing, and the meanings attached to this manner of existing, in a world in which I experience presence.

II. The Lived Body in Reference to Others

My body is lived in an existential immediacy and is apprehended as uniquely my own. But my body is also lived in such a manner that it is apprehended by the other. The lived body is not an isolated phenomenon. It is intentionally related to a world—a world which emerges in one's pre-objective experience as a phenomenon in which various regions of concern are manifested. A most fundamental region of concern in one's primordial experience of being in the world is the region of interacting and interdependent selves. I apprehend my body in a communal context in which other selves are disclosed as already being there. This communal context adds another aspect to the experience of my body in its lived concreteness. A phenomenological analysis and description of this communal aspect will disclose a structure of experience in which there are two separable moments of awareness—the body of the other as known by me and the reapprehension of my body as known by the other. The experience of my body as mine is always coextensive with my experience of the body of the other and the consequent reappraisal of myself as existing in the world of the other. These two moments of consciousness can and must be separated for purposes of analysis, but it must

not be forgotten that in man's immediate experience they are simultaneously given. The post-analytic fallacy, in which there is a reification and separation of analyzed components read out of a situation of prior relatedness, must be judiciously avoided. The engagements of the lived body always proceed within a self-other correlation. I seek to realize the projects of my lived body through a continuing encounter with the body of the other. The other is disclosed as part of my situation. His body is a factor in my world. It arises in my world either as an obstacle to be overcome (a coefficient of adversity, as Sartre would say), or as an instrument which I can use (coefficient of utility), or as an occasion for authentic communication and mutual fulfillment (the possibility of the latter would seem to be denied by Sartre). In any case, I must reckon with the incarnated other. I must assume some kind of existential attitude toward him.

After being thrust into the presence of the other I seek to apprehend his lived body as I seek to apprehend my own. Now what kind of knowledge is rendered possible through my encounter with the other? Quite clearly, I can never "know" the body of the other as he lives it. The interior of the projects of the other never becomes fully transparent to me. The movements of his body and the projects which they intend are always in some sense clothed with opaqueness and mystery. To be sure, I can describe empirically some of the obvious characteristics relative to his pigmentation, bone structure, eye color, texture of the hair, and the like; but in the specification of all these empirical determinants one can hardly attest that the lived body of the other has been comprehended. There is, however, a reality element which is disclosed in my encounter with the lived body of the other. His body is revealed as a unity of life movements which expresses a world orientation of its own. The body of the other constitutes *his* project of being in the world. I cannot penetrate this project as lived by the other, but I can apprehend and describe the project as it exists for me. In this apprehension I always apprehend a totality. Sartre makes this point when he says that the body of the other ''appears within the limits of the situation as a synthetic totality of life and action.''[6] There is the simple corporeal unity of arms, legs, thorax, and head disclosed as a living complex. We never experience the arm or the foot or the eyes of the other in isolation. To experience them thus would be to experience them as lifeless appendages or parts of a material composite but not as expressions of a living unity. We perceive the other as kicking his leg, raising his arm, squinting his eyes. In each of these perceptions a project or a complex of products of the other as a living whole becomes apparent. We find a negative testimony of this *Gestalt* character in the perceptual shock which occurs when one sees staring eyes which are not localized in a head, or fingers severed from a hand. Sartre in *Being and Nothingness* reminds us of the horror which we feel when we see an arm which looks as if it did not belong to any body, and perceive a hand (when the arm is concealed) crawling like a spider up the side of a doorway.[7] All these instances point to a structural life-unity which characterizes the lived body of the other as it is apprehended by me.

In my encounter with the lived body of the other there is thus the structural moment of the other as known by me. But equally a part of the situation of encounter is the structural moment of the reapprehension of my lived body as known by the other. When I emerge in the world I find that I am already looked at. My body is perceived by the other and exists for the other. The other, in formulating and executing his projects, sucks me into the orbit of his concerns and transforms me into an item for his world. I then reapprehend myself in the mode of being apprehended by the other. I become aware that the other has a certain image of my lived body and makes an appraisal of it, either tacit or explicit. I can take over this image and appraisal made by the other and seek to shape my life in accordance with them. I can also reject the formulated images and appraisals, and seek means of changing them or seek to affirm my individuality and my freedom in spite of

them. In any case, whatever my particular response may be, my life and action are defined in reference to the other. The other is inescapable. He constitutes an irreducible element in my world orientations. He is responsible for my situation being one in which I stand before the other—in fear, anger, shame, and love. It is only in the presence of the other that I can experience these existential moods. These are revelatory moods, in the guise of preobjective intentional disclosures, which reveal my lived body as a body viewed and appraised by the other.

We have seen that the lived body in reference to the other involves at the same time an apprehension of the other and a being apprehended by the other. This structure of intersubjectivity or being with the other exhibits two possible existential qualifications—alienation and communication. I alienate myself from the other either by objectivizing his lived body and thus transforming it into an object or a thing, or by apprehending it solely as an instrument which I can use and manipulate for my own private ends. I thus deprive his lived body of its life quality—that is, its unique existential freedom—by dissolving his world of projects. Indeed, I seek to remove the other as lived body by transforming him into material for my self-actualization. But this can never fully succeed because I confront resistance through the counter projects of the other. I do not constitute the other; I encounter him. And in my encounter with the other I not only apprehend the other, but I experience myself as apprehended by the other. The other seeks to absorb me into his world of projects and divest me of my subjectivity, just as I seek to render him into an item for my projects. Alienation is the dialectical movement of perceiving and being perceived, acting and being acted upon, using and being used. Sartre has formulated an engaging elucidation of this dialectical movement in his chapter ''The Look'' in *Being and Nothingness*. The other decentralizes my world through his look and divests me of my freedom by transforming me into a ''being as object'' or a ''being as seen by another.'' The ''fall'' of man for Sartre comes about through the emergence of the other.[8] Sartre's dialectical analysis and description of the resistance of the other in the movement of alienation or estrangement seems to draw heavily from the insights of Hegel's teaching on the "unhappy consciousness" and the master-servant polarity. The master, which is self-consciousness striving for purity, actualizes himself by transforming the other into a servant. The master exercises his power over his servant by demanding various services. Thus the servant is dependent upon the master. But in the moment that the servant becomes conscious of himself as servant he drives toward independence and elevates himself above the status of a servant. Only through the servant can the master enjoy the services which are provided. The master now becomes dependent upon the servant. This is the structure of dialectical movement toward the unhappy or alienated consciousness.

All the movements of the lived body in its intersubjective field express various forms of alienation or estrangement. There is, however, another existential quality, equally important, which defines the relations of selves. This is the drive toward communion. It is on this point that Sartre's analysis remains singularly impoverished. Alienation, for Sartre, plays the trump card. Jaspers, Marcel, and Merleau-Ponty, on the other hand, have made the theme of communion central to their philosophies and thus established a counter-thrust to the alienating egocentrism of Sartre's existentialism. Marcel has formulated a doctrine of intersubjectivity in which the other can be encountered as a nonobjectivized presence. Communion is made possible only when the other is acknowledged as a subject with whom I experience a copresence in such a manner that our individual freedoms are mutually acknowledged. Communion involves communication. If I am to exist in communion with the other I must be able to communicate the meanings which are disclosed in the projects of my immediate concerns. The lived body plays a significant role in this communication of meanings. The projects of my lived body are intrinsically communicative. My lived body is an *act of communication*. This is to say more than to say that the body is simply a vehicle of communication. To speak of the body as a vehicle is already to externalize it and make it adventitious to the communication process itself. Merleau-Ponty has described the body as "expression and speech" in one of the chapters in his book *Phénoménologie de la perception*.[9] I convey meanings to the other through the gestures and movements which constitute my body as a living synthetic unity. The smile and the frown, the wink and the stare, the caress and the kiss, the handshake and the slap, are all modes of speech which disclose meanings in the world of my concrete lived experience. Merleau-Ponty elucidates this point when he refers to speech as a gesture which intends or signifies a world ("la parole est un geste et sa signification un monde").[10] Speech is a mode of orientation through which one discloses to others the world of one's projects. The gesture-complex of the lived body is an example of speech thus understood. Ordinary language gives clear evidence of such an apprehension of the lived body: "he speaks with his hands"; "her eyes reveal her inmost feelings;" "he uses the language of love." All these phrases bear testimony to a lived body as expression and speech. Any phenomenology of experience, which seeks to remain true to the data as they show themselves, will need to give disciplined attention to this form of communication.

III. The Lived Body and Human Space

Spatiality is an existential quality of the lived body. The concept of space, in both the history of philosophy and the history of science, has fallen heir (or victim) to widely differing interpretations. Some have argued that space is infinite; others have argued that it is finite. Some have maintained it is absolute; others have maintained that it is relative. Some have asserted that it is to be identified with matter; others have persuasively denied its materiality. It becomes evident upon investigation that such arguments pro and con presuppose space to be some kind of externally observable entity or state which can be objectively defined. It may indeed be that Kant has demonstrated in his transcendental dialectic once and for all that space as a unifying condition in one's objective view of the cosmos remains for ever unknowable. In any case, the spatiality which qualifies the lived body is not an objective space. It is *human space,* or what Merleau-Ponty has appropriately called "espace orienté." The space in which I live and in which I apprehend my lived body is articulated in and through my practical and personal projects, and as such must be consistently contrasted with the quantitative and measurable space which defines my objective world as an extensive continuum. Mathematical space, as an instance of quantifiable space, is properly defined as an abstract extensive continuum constituting a region of points. Whether this space is Euclidean or non-Euclidean, three-dimensional or multi-dimensional, is at this point irrelevant. The point which is relevant is that mathematical space is isotropic—that is, all the dimensions have the same value—and it is precisely this which makes it measurable in terms of spatial co-ordinates. Human or oriented space, which qualifies the lived body, is what Henri Ellenberger has called "anisotropic," having dimensions of different specific values and thus being contrasted with the abstract space of mathematics. The dimensions (or what might preferably be called "directions") of oriented space take on different values relative to the situation in which the lived body actualizes its projects. Merleau-Ponty has contributed the distinction between "spatiality of position" (*spatialité de position*) and "spatiality of situations" (*spatialité de situation*). The former characterizes the abstract space of mathematics, the latter the concrete oriented space of the lived body.[11]

Human space has three directional axes. The primary axis is the horizontal axis of front and back, or before and behind. In this primary axis

the existentially proximate direction is that of frontward or forward. For the most part I spatialize my world in a forward direction. I face the table on which I write; I face the mountain which I must surmount; I face the person to whom I speak. In each of these projects an existential distance is already disclosed. The table is near when it is accessible for the writing of my book; it is too far away when it makes difficult the task of writing, producing a coefficient of adversity. Utensils become most readily accessible on the horizontal axis of front and back; and the concrete movements of my body, such as actualizing a project by walking, proceed for the most part on this axis. But there is also the directional axis of right and left. The hammer with which I pound the tack is to my left. Its place in my field of concerns is not some abstract locus geometrically defined relative to an extensive continuum of points, but rather that place where it belongs so as to be accessible for the realization of my project. It is near when it is in its right place—within reach—and thus can be spatially distinguished from other utensils, which, although metrically nearer, are existentially remote from the lived body. For example, at the same time that I reach for the hammer there may be a garden spade to my right which is six inches closer to me than the hammer. But the garden spade, in the context of my situation, remains exterior to my projects and thus existentially remote. Human space, and the value of its directions, vary with the situation. Human space is anisotropic. It is indissolubly linked with the projects of human concern. A proper phenomenological use of language, therefore, would refer to the body not as something which is *in* space but rather as a field of concern which *lives* its space.

The third directional axis is the vertical axis of up and down. I also live my space in the upward and downward direction. In standing up and sitting down, in raising and lowering my arm, in perceiving what is above and what is below, I express a concrete movement along this vertical axis. These various directional axes disclose themselves through the concrete movements of the lived body.

The task of phenomenology is that of describing the phenomena as they show or disclose themselves. Hence any phenomenology which seeks to return to the data of immediate experience must pay due attention to the reality of human or oriented space. Ellenberger states the case clearly when he writes: "We know that the horizon and the celestial dome are not scientific concepts; but for our daily experience and for phenomenology, they are very important entities."[12]

IV. The Lived Body and Human Time

Phenomenology discloses not only the spatiality of the lived body but also its temporality. These two phenomena are disclosed simultaneously in the fundamental project of the body as a living synthetic unity. The concrete movements of the body always occur within a correlated complex of lived space and lived time. My body is immediately and preobjectively revealed as coming from a past and moving into a future. Just as there is a spatial directionality, so also there is a temporal directionality. I will describe this temporal directionality in terms of a retentional protentional axis (categories already used by Husserl). The lived body is qualified by its past, indicating a retentional mode. My lived body is constituted by that which I have been. Hence my body *is* its past. To speak of the body as *having* a past is to externalize the past and violently abstract the body from its concrete temporalization. The past which qualifies the lived body is never left behind so long as the body exists. My past projects and the environmental and social complex in which these projects were defined are continuing determinants of my lived body. To be sure, my environmental and social world are no longer objectively present, but they remain *subjectively real*. The past is still a living reality, and it is lost in the moment that it is objectivized as a series of discrete nows which have somehow "passed by" and become divested of reality. The

lived body is not an objectivized instant within an objectively measured time. The categories of quantitative or objectively measured time are inapplicable to the lived time of human experience. Human time is qualitatively unique. Quantitative time is an abstracted and objectivized time, which transforms the temporal unity into an infinite succession of nows correlated with geometrical points. Quantitative time co-ordinates time and space by postulating an abstract spatio-temporal continuum. Human time, or the time of immediate experience, remains concealed so long as time is understood as a succession of abstracted nows which precede each other in an objective order of coming to be and passing away. Quantitative time severs the past from the future and both from the present. Human time has a past which is still present and a future which is already present. The directions of time are integrated in a synthetic unity of the body as concretely lived. Only for the anatomical biologist and the physiologist does the body become a lifeless objective which somehow rests within an order of objective time. The lived body has time within itself. It does not *occur in time;* it *exists as time.* All of its projects or orientations are permeated with temporality. This temporality has both a retentional and a protentional direction. The lived body is temporalized retentionally in that at every moment it is a synthetic unity of its past projects, which includes its past environmental and social influences. This is what Heidegger and Sartre have called the *facticity* of human existence; that is, existence as qualified by pastness. But human existence is also qualified by futurity. The lived body is temporalized protentionally as well as retentionally. It is this protentional directionality which constantly reopens my past and keeps it from being solidified into a series of objectivized nows. It rescues my past from the determinism of an empirical necessity. In any given moment I can remember my past lived body as a burden—as an occasion for regret or remorse.[13] But this past, for human time, is not irrevocably closed or finally fixed. It can be translated into an existential possibility through the acknowledgment of futurity. The past can be retrieved and changed through the adoption of a new attitude toward it. That which weighs upon me as a burden can be transformed into a burden to be overcome—into a creative possibility. The memory of my lived body as a body whose projects have been limited by a withered arm can be translated into a future possibility of reappraisal.

The phenomenon of the lived body thus shows itself in immediate experience as a body qualified by temporality—qualified retentionally in that it is a body which has already become that which it is, defined by itself, its environment and other selves; but also it is qualified protentionally in that it is a body which has not yet lived out its projects. It is protended into a future and confronted with the task of appraising the meaning of its past as this past is translated into possibility. In this protential directionality a final limit to the projects of the lived body is disclosed. This limit is death or the total dissolution of my being in the world. The unity of the lived body as a synthetic whole is achieved only when this final limit is interiorized and taken up in the present projects of the existing subject. Heidegger has elucidated this in his existential concept of *Sein-zum-Tode,* which means that death is a mode of existence qualifying man's being as soon as he is and so long as he is. (However, it is not clear in what sense death, in the Heideggerian analysis, has a bodily reference.) Death is not simply an empirical factuality apprehended only in the instant. This would comically place death outside experience insofar as when it would occur the lived body would no longer be there. Death is a mode of existence which involves the task of assuming some kind of existential attitude toward one's final limit. Death can become the occasion for cowardly retreat, poetic melancholy, martyrdom or dying for a cause, or resolute and courageous acceptance of it as the irrevocable limit of existence. The final meaning of the lived body as a synthetic unity of past and future is thus achieved in the taking over of one's death as the final possibility of the body. Death itself is interiorized and translated into subjectivity.

Notes

1. See particularly *Phénoménologie de la perception* (Paris: Gallimard, 1945), Part I, "Le Monde Perçu," and Part II, "L'Etre-pour-soi et l'être-au-monde." Also pertinent to the topic is his book *La Structure du comportement* (Paris: Presses Universitaires, 1953), especially Chap. 3: "L'Ordre physique, l'ordre vital, l'ordre humain." Gabriel Marcel points to the same phenomenon when he speaks of the world being initially presented as a confused and global experience: "What is given to me beyond all possible doubt is the confused and global experience of the world inasmuch as it is existent" (*Metaphysical Journal* [Chicago: Henry Regnery Co., 1952], p. 322).

2. "Wie sehr alles Tun mit der Hand schon ein Denken in sich schliesst, ist daran zu bemerken, dass Denktätigkeiten durch Handtätigkeiten ausgedrückt werden" (*Von der Wahrheit* [München: Piper, 1947], p. 329).

3. Sartre, *Being and Nothingness,* trans. Hazel Barnes (New York, Philosophical Lib.), p. 310.

4. Marcel, *Metaphysical Journal,* p. 315.

5. *Ibid.,* p. 333.

6. *Being and Nothingness,* p. 346.

7. *Ibid.*

8. *Ibid.,* p. 263. Cf. p. 267: "Thus being-seen constitutes me as a defenseless being for a freedom which is not my freedom. It is in this sense that we can consider ourselves as 'slaves' insofar as we appear to the Other. But this slavery is not a historical result—capable of being surmounted—of a *life* in the abstract form of consciousness. I am a slave to the degree that my being is dependent at the center of a freedom which is not mine and which is the very condition of my being."

9. See Part I, Chap. 6: "Le Corps comme expression et la parole."

10. *Phénoménologie de la perception,* p. 214.

11. *Ibid.,* p. 116.

12. R. May, E. Angel, and H. Ellenberger (eds.), *Existence: A New Dimension in Psychiatry and Psychology* (New York: Basic Books, 1958), p. 110. It is interesting to note that Ludwig Binswanger has made extended use of the phenomenological concept of oriented space in his existential psychotherapy. In its psychological expression oriented space becomes what he calls "attuned space" (*gestimmter Raum*), space conditioned by one's emotions and feelings. Space thus becomes allied with a psychological mood. One's mood determines space as being full or empty, expanding or constricting. For example, love is "space-binding" in that it produces a feeling of nearness to the beloved, even though the metrical distance may be great. Happiness expands attuned space, sorrow constricts it, and despair makes it empty (*ibid.,* pp. 110 ff.).

13. Minkowski has differentiated regret and remorse in terms of different retentional values. The zone of remorse is the zone of the immediate past. The zone of the regretted is the zone of the mediate past. Finally, there is the zone of the obsolete which corresponds to the remote past. See his book *Le Temps vécu* (Paris: D'Artre, 1933).

The Symbolism of the Healthy Body: A Philosophical Analysis of the Sportive Imagery of Health

FRANS DE WACHTER

The philosophy of medicine has made substantial analyses of the concept of health, but it has never investigated its relationship with sports (e.g., 5; 19). Obviously, the relationships are manifold and depend on the different definitions given to the ambiguous concept of "health." An excellent introductory analysis was made several years ago by Fox (6), who differentiated correctly between a privative definition of health as the absence of pathology, and a positive meaning as fitness for activities. Obviously in both cases, sports, or training for sports, has an important function. Not only can they prevent morphological and physiological disorders, but they can also, if properly conducted, contribute to overall fitness, to the optimum development of strength (both muscular and cardiovascular), and to flexibility and endurance, so that the body becomes the best it can be and performs to its potential. In this kind of approach, the relationship is viewed as instrumental: to what

extent are sports good for your health? This is an empirical question, to be settled by sports medicine. Sophisticated results have been obtained in the last decade and are slowly trickling down to the everyday amateur and ordinary citizen.

In this paper, however, I shall concentrate on a noninstrumental, representational type of relationship. In our civilization, bodily health is often represented by the "athletic body." This body is not merely healthy, it also functions as a social symbol of a healthy existence. Data to support this position are available from sport sociologists who have studied the ways in which sport can socially demonstrate not only social status and masculinity, but also youthfulness, strength, and health (e.g., 16). The use of the athletic body in advertisements is perhaps the most striking example. We are reminded of the famous *Encyclopédie Française*. Its volume on health, edited by the world-famous surgeon, Dr. Leriche, has the picture of a shot-putter on its title page. Why? Why not a Kazakhstan farmer, a monk, or a professor in philosophy, whose health might be

Reprinted from *Journal of the Philosophy of Sport*, XI, (1984), pp. 56–62. Copyright 1985 by the Philosophic Society for the Study of Sport. Reprinted by permission.

as good or better than the athlete's, and who has a longer life expectancy than the average athlete?

The answer must start with a definition of "social symbol." The word is used here in the same way as when we call Marilyn Monroe a sex symbol or a sheik a symbol of wealth. Symbol here means a sign that refers to the object it denotes, not only by having factual connections with it (Peirce's indexical sign), not just by sheer convention (Peirce's restricted definition of symbol), but by the fact that it exhibits socially dominant features or attributes of the denotatum. Not all rich people are symbols of wealth. A sheik *is not* just very rich; he exhibits, by his demonstrative over-consumption, a special property of wealth, namely to be in a position to buy every conceivable thing. The reason why specific features become so dominant that they trigger the symbolic function is due to the particular ideology of a culture. Semiotically speaking, a culture is a capacity shared by a whole group to recognize, interpret, and produce signs in a similar way. It is a coherent system of semiotic habits.

This coherence is based on common presuppositions on the basis of which a shared sign production and sign recognition is possible. So our question finally is: What common presuppositions exist in modern society that could explain why health is represented not by a monk or a professor, but by a shot-putter? I shall offer two explanatory hypotheses, starting from two important developments in the common cultural understanding of health: First, a static conception of health has been replaced by a dynamic one; and second, an instrumental conception has been superseded by a representational one.

A Dynamic Conception of Health

Traditional definitions of positive health (fitness for activities) share a homeostatic viewpoint. In this view, a healthy organism is one that is adapted to the normal requirements of the life situation. It is in equilibrium with the environment and is capable of ordered behavior, so that it can respond by appropriate reactions. On the basis of such a definition, of course, the athletic image of health cannot be understood. Soft physical education will do: If I live the life of a philosopher, only a minimum level of fitness is required to survive in a technical world. Why not philosophers instead of sportsmen on advertisements for health food? Moreover, the definition is wrong. As is demonstrated by the French physician and philosopher, Canguilhem (3), even in disease the patient builds up a new equilibrium with his or her environment by creating new physiological constants (blood pressure, etc.) and new behavioral constants to cope with the new situation. A neuro-vegetative disturbance will lead me to take my vacations at the seaside and not in the mountains. And hemophilia is insignificant as long as a trauma does not occur. The unfit person does not lack order or equilibrium. He/she does function well, but only in a given, narrow environment. He or she lacks the ability to transcend the norm that defines the momentary normal—the ability to tolerate infractions of the habitual norm and to institute new norms for new situations.

Finally, the homeostatic concept no longer corresponds to the Weltanschauung of modern man or woman. In the traditional culture, life was considered a tendency to conserve and to survive. Fitness used to mean the ability to walk up a flight of stairs without puffing, or the ability to do one's job. Modern man or woman considers life as a tendency to expand, has a more dynamic relationship with his/her *Umwelt,* and feels in good health when he/she can explore new environments, exhibit creative and bold generosity, and respond to new and higher demands. This attitude is reflected not only in Canguilhem's definition of health as normative normality, but also in the definition given by Parsons (15, italics added): "A capacity to maintain a favorable, self-regulated state, which is a prerequisite of the effective performance of an *indefinitely wide range* of functions both with-

in the system and in relation to its environment.''
It is precisely this indefinitely wide range of performances that is exhibited by the athletic body.
This body pushes back the frontiers of corporeal
existence, responds to new challenges, lives up to
its limits, and establishes new vital norms—even
up to a level that could damage it. Coubertin (4)
exclaimed: ''O sports, you are audacity! What
good is there in muscles, what good in skill and
strength, if it is not for daring?'' In modern
society, sport is a symbol of health because there
is a sportive conception of health, and even of life
in general, as is reflected in the vitalistic views
of Ortega or Novak.

A Representational Conception of Health

Our second explanation starts from the idea that
an instrumental concept of health has been superseded by a representational one. Positive health,
or fitness, has become more than an instrument
for survival, more than a biological imperative.
It has become even more than a prerequisite for
a dynamic existence. It has become a social imperative: It represents prestige, social election, and
social differentiation. It is, of course, common in
medical sociology to say that views of health and
health behavior differ in the various strata of
society. A classical hypothesis is the following:
In a social group that is economically dependent
on physical labor, the body is primarily experienced as an economic function and will not
be an object of reflective attention, care, or culture. Somatic culture will become more explicit
as this economic function decreases (2). Since this
economic function is class-related, somatic culture
(including concern for fitness or participation in
sports) is class-related also and may function as
display of social status: a fact well known in sport
sociology (e.g., 9; 17).

However, social differentiation means more
than just the status symbolism that sociology has

been talking about since Veblen. It could also
mean a differentiation between people as such,
which brings us to the position of Baudrillard (1).
Humankind has entered a civilization of signs. The
objects consumed are taken up in their sign form,
their meaning derived from their position in a system of differentiations, from the way in which they
differ from, and relate to, other signs. Consumption is not only a functional activity; it is also a
semiotic activity of sign production by which I can
differentiate myself from others.

Keeping this in mind, it is possible to abstract
from Baudrillard's structuralist terminology and
give our own examples that are relevant for somatic culture. In fashion, for instance, the length
of the skirt changes every year. The meaning of
this is not related to the functional satisfaction of
needs. Nor does it have anything to do with the
climate growing colder, with the price of textiles,
with varying moral permissiveness, or with changing ideas of elegance. It just refers to being different. The body itself has become a system of
differentiation. Decades ago, women did not have
a body. They had a figure, and this figure was like
a hanger for clothes. Nowadays, the female body
has become fashion. The body has become its own
garment. The fashion is called fitness; the mannequin is Jane Fonda. This body is a status symbol
par excellence, and it expresses precisely the same
thing as did the corset of the Victorian age—
namely that the owner is free from labor and has
been socially elected to devote herself to higher
activities. But it is more than just a class symbol
in Veblen's sense. Somatic culture also differentiates people as such. It constitutes identity.

In a way, all activities are representational sign
activities because through them I construct a social
image of myself, which is constitutive for my identity. This idea is brilliantly developed by Goffman
(8) and just as brilliantly applied to sport activities by Gebauer (7). However, they do not clarify
sufficiently the specific importance of corporeal
activities in this construction. The following
hypothesis could be suggested: As natural objects,
all bodies are more or less alike, equally subject

to the same laws and equally determined by the same mechanisms; that is, they are the bodies of the textbooks of anatomy and physiology. But by transforming this anonymous natural object into a cultural creation, man appropriates his body and makes it into his *own* body. Primitive body painting, modern fashion, makeup, and fitness fads all affirm self-identity on the very corporeal level where man tends to be identical with others.

It is precisely here that the athletic body enters the scene. Of course, the fitness of the athletic body is not only intended as display, it is also designed for action. And for this reason it exhibits the quest for self-identity through differentiation in a very eminent way. Because, as Lenk (13; 14) rightly noted, distinctiveness can only fully be engendered and documented by action, not by mere reception and consumption. The athletic body is not only on display, it is at work. In its performance, it demonstrates man's or woman's command of self. In competitive activity it enters a permanent, sophisticated system of hierarchical classification and differentiation. If fitness is a representation of self-identity through distinctiveness, the athletic body is its perfect image because it exhibits this feature in a special way, namely, on the level of performance.

The Logic of Somatic Culture

So far, I have shown that the athletic body can function as a true social symbol of health and fitness because it exhibits two special features: It is a dynamic relation with the *Umwelt,* and it represents self-identity through differentiation. Both features can be understood now within the logic of somatic culture in general. There is some truth in the old Cartesian mind-body dualism; corporeal experience *is* a profoundly alienating experience of duality. In growing bald, or ugly, or old, or sick, I live my immersion in nature. Nature mercilessly goes its own way, contradicting my human dream of self-mastery, autonomy, and subjectivity. Fitness represents this dream. The dream of dynamic freedom—where I can push

back all frontiers—is the utopia of absolute health, which is the dream of infinity or the denial of finitude and death (comp. 12). The dream of differentiation and self-identity is the dream of realized subjectivity and self-command, which is the dream of being the *causa sui* or the unmoved mover, the dream of being like unto God. The athletic body fascinates because it represents this dream in the very realm where it is utterly impossible, the realm of finite corporality.

I would now venture a rather surprising conclusion, namely that in somatic culture the glorification of the athletic body fulfills the same function as sexual taboos. Such taboos are likely to represent the same denial of finitude and naturality. This idea could be supported by recent studies on taboos (e.g., 20). Let me simply substantiate it by a text of St. Augustine. In his *City of God* (XIV, 23–24), he raises the question whether, if sexual desire is sinful, procreation would have taken place in Paradise if there had been no original sin. The question is as amusing as the answer is instructive. In a rather hysterical way, Augustine viewed all sexual desire as bad in itself. But why? His main concern seemed to be the erection. Because there the body is set in motion not by a rational act of will, but by lust, by the stimuli and spurs of nature. In Paradise the situation would have been different. Even in our sinful world, he said, we generally command our body. We can set our hands and feet in motion to do the things that are theirs to do. Some people have even acquired great dexterity, so that their bodies are under the control of their wills. So, he concluded, what is there to keep us from believing that human members (i.e., the male organ) may have obeyed the human will without lust, for the procreation of offspring: "the organ created for this work would have sown its seed upon the field of generation, as the hand does now upon the earth." The hand of the farmer, indeed, makes a movement that is under the complete control of the farmer's rational will.

Most interpretations of taboos view them as mechanisms that are designed to safeguard ethical values, such as social bonds or unions, against the whims of the self. Augustine's text leads us to look beyond this level of social utility. His story shows clearly that traditional taboos on sexuality are ultimately based on the desire for self-control or autonomy, and on the denial of our heteronomy or naturality. The sexual domain is by definition the domain where I am plunged into nature: The act can only be achieved when I give up my self-constraint, when I let myself go, when I give myself away. Complete control would imply impotence. The other extreme in Augustine's story are the people with great corporeal dexterity. They show us that even the human dimension that is the closest to nature, corporality, can be brought under control. He presented some curious examples: people who can wriggle their ears or move their scalp. If he were alive now, he would surely have mentioned athletes who can perform completely calculated or rational movements. They fit perfectly into his scheme: "In workers in all kinds of physical tasks, a natural capacity that is too weak and slow is fitted for its employment by the application of great dexterity and effort. . . . The body serves certain people beyond the ordinary limits of nature in many kinds of movements, although they are living in perishable flesh."

It is clear that such glorification of the sophisticated movements of the fit body has the same function as his previous taboo on sexuality. To put it more generally, in somatic culture the transcendence of human heteronomy is achieved either by the denial of the dimension where this heteronomy is definitional or by displaying autonomy in that very field of corporeal existence. Dust thou art and unto dust thou shalt return. Somatic culture permanently denies this truth by the symbolic creation of a bodily world of freedom and differentiation (comp. 20). Of this world, the athletic body is the perfect image. If it is a dream, it is the dream that my body is mine.

Concluding Remarks

Utopias are fruitful as long as we realize they are utopias. Otherwise, the utopia of the perfect athletic body might turn into a Promethean myth (cf.

13) containing its own punishment. The first utopia mentioned, fitness as a dynamic project of infinity, would have perverse consequences if it were not balanced by the acceptance of finitude. Fitness can never mean fitness for anything and everything. The ultimate question is, fit for what? There are limits to what we can and may endeavor, finally of an ethical nature, based on the human condition. Weiss (21) rightly introduced ethical categories in his definition of health: The fully healthy man does justice to himself. Without such an acceptance, the picture looms of athletes who, in a paradoxical way, damage their health for the sake of fitness. This is Nietzsche's paradox, when he claimed that sickness is a higher, greater kind of health, because it stimulates dynamic and creative existence (for a survey of all his texts on this topic, see 18).

Further, there is also the picture of those ex-athletes who, spoiled by a golden myth of eternal youth and dynamic hyper-activism, can never assimilate their being thrown back into the world of finitude and aging. Such pictures could be avoided if the culture would present the athletic body not only as a symbol of infinite dynamism, but also as a symbol of finitude. Sports in fact not only push back frontiers, they also enable the human to discover the limitations of his or her finite being (cf. 11).

The second utopia, fitness as representing self-identity through differentiation, could be self-defeating as well. In the dream of rational control over corporeal existence, the picture looms of growing medicalization and technology to such an extent that the body is controlled, not by nature this time, but by our own inventions. In this case, the alienating power of nature over my body is not abolished but simply replaced by another power. And this power is not only technical, it also requires the infrastructure of an entire social, economic, and political system. This is Heinilä's (10) nightmare of totalization. Have we already come to the time when the athletic body no longer represents dynamism and differentiation, freedom and subjectivity, but instead has become the image of totalitarian uniformity, of man's power over man?

Bibliography

1. Baudrillard, J. (1970). *La Societé de Consommation.* Paris: Gallimard.
2. Boltanski, L. (1971). "Les Usages Sociaux du Corps." *Annales. Economies Sociétés Civilisations,* 26, 205–233.
3. Canguilhem, G. (1943). *Le Normal et le Pathologique.* Paris: P.U.F.
4. Coubertin, P. (1967). *L'idée Olympique: Discours et Essais.* Schorndorf: Hofmann.
5. Engelhardt, H.T. (1975). "The Concepts of Health and Disease." In *Evaluation and Explanation in the Biomedical Sciences.* Edited by H.T. Engelhardt and S.F. Spicker. Dordrecht: Reidel.
6. Fox, L. (1975). "A Linguistic Analysis of the Concept 'Health' in Sport." *Journal of the Philosophy of Sport,* 2, 31–35.
7. Gebauer, G. (1973). " 'Leistung' als Aktion und Präsentation." In *Philosophie des Sports.* Edited by H. Lenk, S. Moser and E. Beyer. Schorndorf: Hofmann.
8. Goffman, E. (1959). *The Presentation of Self in Everyday Life.* Harmondsworth: Penguin.
9. Gruneau, R.S. (1975). "Sport, Social Differentiation and Social Inequality." In *Sport and Social Order: Contributions to the Sociology of Sport.* Edited by D.W. Ball and J.W. Loy, Reading, MA: Addison-Wesley.
10. Heinilä, K. (1982). *The Totalization Process in International Sport.* Jyväskylä: University of Jyväskylä.
11. Jeu, B. (1975). *Le Sport, la Mort, la Violence.* Paris: Editions Universitaires.
12. Kohler, O. (1978). "Die Utopie der Absoluten Gesundheit." In *Krankheit, Heilkunst, Heilung.* Edited by H. Schipperges e.a. Freiburg - München: Alber.
13. Lenk, H. (1979). *Social Philosophy of Athletics.* Champaign, IL: Stipes.
14. Lenk, H. (1982). "Tasks of the Philosophy of Sport: Between Publicity and Anthropology." *Journal of the Philosophy of Sport,* 9, 94–106.
15. Parsons, T. (1978). "Health and Disease: A Sociological and Action Perspective." *The Encyclopedia of Bioethics. Volume 2.* Edited by W.T. Reich. New York: Free Press; London: Collier McMillan.
16. Pfister, G. (in press). "Sport and Image." In *Proceedings of the Congress on Sport and International Understanding.* Edited by M. Ilmarinen. Helsinki.
17. Renson, R. (1976). "Social Status Symbolism of Sport Stratification." *Hermes,* 10, 433–443.
18. Schipperges, H. (1975). *Am Leitfaden des Leibes: Zur Anthropologie und Therapeutik Friedrich Nietzsches,* Stuttgart: Klett.
19. Schipperges, H. (1984). *Die Vernunft des Leibes: Der Wandel der Begriffe Gesundheit und Krankheit seit der Aufklärung.* Graz - Wien - Koln: Styria.
20. Vandekerkhove, L. (1982). *Gemaakt van As. Lichaam en Norm in de Westerse Kultuur.* Tielt-Bussum: Lannoo.
21. Weiss, P. (1969). *Sport: A Philosophic Inquiry.* Carbondale: Southern Illinois University Press; London - Amsterdam: Feffer & Simons.

Orchids and Muscles

ALPHONSO LINGIS

The Body Builders

A cult, certainly, rather than an enterprise—that of *mens sana in corpore sano*—that culture can know and integrate. A cult that has its clandestine repairs, its passwords, its initiations, its legends, its rituals, its undeciphered codes. The alerted eye can spot them in the crowds, not, like punks, by the tribal garb and arcane jewelry, but rather by the way neither work nor leisure garb fits their bodies, by the strained fabrics, the pulled seams. If they wear jewelry, they most often do not wear them as embellishments or citations, but as amulets. Sportswear and beachwear, designer conceived for voyeurist eroticism, pulled tight over their loins like chastity belts. In the bus stations and sidewalks, in the midst of the streams of the busy and the preoccupied, space warps and strains about them, as though lacking the gravity these sprung arms and plowshare thighs are made to furrow. The civilized head that looks at them is deviated; it wonders not where they are going, but where you can get with them.

The erotic eye, that which scouts the erotogenic terrain in the body of another—not the rolling surfaces of taut cutaneous membrane, but the spongy zone of susceptibility just beneath and the mucous membrane of orifices—is disconcerted to run into packed thongs of drawn muscle. Not muscle that answers to the ungendered resistance of

Reprinted from *Journal of the Philosophy of Sport,* XIII, (1986), pp. 15–28. Copyright 1987 by the Philosophic Society for the Study of Sport. Reprinted by permission.

tools and implements, but specifically male and specifically female muscle alignments. One cannot resist feeling the very hardness of these muscles to be the badgering of the glands of lust. Whole anatomies pumped like priapic erections, contracting poses and shifting with held violence from one pose to the next with the vaginal contractions of labor pains. Flaunting in the nose of an antiseptic consumer public leathery rutting odors, gleaming with oils that deviate the hold the inspecting eye fixes on these bodies into the sliding suctions of octopus eros.

Their codes are undeciphered; one does not understand the programming, or the decision process that assigns them their hours in cellars full of iron millstones and rudimentary machines. The process that elaborates, selects, and distributes the programming is not in the control rooms of culture nor even in the science of coaches and trainers; it is rigged up in their own taciturn and superstitious skulls. The unguarded, unwary eyes with which they walk in the frenetic halls of stock exchanges or in the night of urban jungles do not seem practiced in the predatory uses of the sense organs perfected by the millenia of hunters whose genes we inherit; and, unlike the surveillance a miller maintains on the ox or the waterwheel that turns the millstone, their eyes unfocused on their unrotating wheels of iron seem rather to watch the inward spread of monotonous fatigue and seeping pain. Their arms that handle but poles without fulcrum and wheels that grind nothing are uneconomic, detaching or transforming nothing from the raw or recycled materials of nature and industry. In their handshake we feel no understanding; we feel an indextrous hand that is not held to the equipment of our culture. Like kundalini yogis forcing the semen flow back upstream and upward, they detach the few implements they use from the instrumental complex of civilization, detaching themselves from these very implements even as they fit themselves into them, forcing the power and the mass back upstream, from clenched fist toward drummed vortex of the solar plexus.

The Civilizing of the Body

Natural evolution elaborated the neurological and physiological potentials in the human primate that made culture—implements, language, social institutions—possible. But Homo sapiens is a domesticated species, whose nature is civilized. What has civilization done to the biological nature of this primate? Paleontologist Leroi-Gourhan (4) distinguishes four stages in the technological history of our species that have decisively evolved our biological nature. The first stage is that of the use of tools—cutters, choppers, and grinders. The baboons, as all earthbound mammals, advance into the world snout-first; it is with their teeth that they maneuver their way. The human primate puts chipped stones in his front legs to cut, to chop, and to grind. He exteriorizes the functions of his teeth and powers them with what now become hands. He transforms himself biologically into an upright animal feeling his way with his hands, lifting his eyes to survey the distances. At the same time the senses of his nose and the power of his teeth begin their atrophy. The exteriorized teeth, the chipped stones, still have to be maneuvered with muscle power.

The next species-decisive stage will be the harnessing of exterior motor power, that of animals, water, and wind, to drive his implements for him. The primacy of the sense of the vision that sur-

veys will be definitively enhanced—even in his sexuality, Freud hypostasized, now unseasonal, for not primarily excited by menstrual odors but by the visually exposed genitals of the upright ape. At the same time his hide thins into skin and his muscles begin their atrophy. But the wind, water, and draft animals that operate his implements—instead of his own hands—still require his surveillance. The next species-decisive stage will be the invention of machines—contrivances that start and stop, control, and, more and more, correct their operations.

This stage begins with the invention of the mechanical clock. Its new virtue, by comparison with the hourglass and clepsedra, is that it recycles itself, and can trigger other movements. The first clockmakers of Europe immediately set out to construct clocks that filled towers and, as they struck the hour, opened doors from which the three kings and the four horsemen of the apocalypse advanced and gesticulated, while the cathedral clarion tolled above without a bell-ringer. Mechanisms now liberate humans from their surveillance—and the attention span of machine-age humans begins its atrophy. Television viewers, their fingers on channel-change knobs, today look with incomprehension at Guatemalan Indians whose attention may be held on the patterns of a loom for hours on end. Still, the surveillance mechanisms have to be programmed by the neurological circuitry of the human brain.

Today our technological civilization has entered into a cybernetics revolution—which is also a new stage of our biological evolution. Computers henceforth assemble and evaluate the data, and make the decisions. The faculty of memory, reason, and decision evolved in our nature through the history of our civilization now begins its atrophy. The film *The Terminator* is set a generation from now, when the master computers deciding the racing of the military–industrial complex now determine the use of all resources and of the human species. A band of guerrilla resistors, led by John O'Connor, is waging operations of sabotage against the cybernetic police. The master computers select the Terminator (Arnold Schwarzenegger) to be time-projected back into the 20th century with a mission to terminate the life of Sarah O'Connor, John O'Connor's mother, and thus ensure that the guerrilla leader will never be born. The human species has, with the next evolution of its technological civilization, undergone regression back into manpower, and the film plots its retrogressive abortion as a biological species endowed with initiative.

This film is in fact no science fiction fantasy; today the stockpiling of weapons of extinction is the most important sector of our industry, and its exponential advance is already programmed by internal feedback circuitry. This 40-year-old industry has already stockpiled nuclear weapons enough to detonate a Hiroshima-size thermonuclear bomb over a city of our civilization every day for the next 3,500 years. The equivalent of the annual production of the poorest fifth of toiling humankind is now devoted to weapons—the total productive energy of one human being employed to fabricate weapons to exterminate the other four. Certainly not our fellow citizens, but not their political leaders either, are in control of the military industry; our Secretary of Defense awaits the data electronically satellite-espionaged from the Soviet Union to be processed by the Pentagon computers, and they will make the decisions as to what new weapons our technology must fabricate; the Soviet Presidium similarly only relays the decisions.

We have already evolved into pure spectators, the mouse folk Kafka imagined, with huge eyes feeding into massive brains, floating in the air, with minuscule, atrophied limbs dangling. Or rather, our sight disconnected from any decision or motor functions, its content determined by the image industry programming, hoisted into the space of visibility on the massive trunks of cybernetic forests—our bulbous and succulent organisms biologically evolving, Leroi-Gourhan says, into orchids. Organisms with atrophied trunks and limbs, parasitically clinging on the rising trunks

that shut out the sun, flowering their huge showy sex organs, awaiting the bees for their orgasmic unions. But is not the glorification of our primary and secondary sexual splendors—the orchid-woman flowering against the hood of the Mercedes, the orchid-man flowering under the sky-diver parachute—also destined to lose their biological relevance and atrophy, in the measure that the flickering computer chips of biological engineering, and not our physiological ostentations, will decide which genes will be reproduced?

Every great epoch of culture, Nietzsche wrote, is not only an epoch in humankind's cultivating of nature—transforming of nature's resources in accordance with its own idea—it is also an epoch in the history of humankind's cultivation of its own nature—transforming its own nature in accordance with its ideal. Every great culture, marked by distinctive intellectual, artistic, and moral productions, has also set up a distinctive icon of bodily perfection. The physical ideal of the yogi, the lion-maned moran of the African savannah, of the serpent-plumed Mayas, of the Olympians of the age of Pericles, of the samurai, of the baris knights of Bali—each great center of culture has set up the corrals, perfected the breeding and training methods, ordered the subjugations and the testings for its own body ideal. In the new institutions specific to modern western society—barracks, factories, public schools, prisons, hospitals, asylums—Foucault identified the specifically modern ideal of the *disciplined body*.

All these ideal bodies have now become obsolete. Yukio Mishima (5) remarked on the anomaly of the cult of body building (it appeared in Japan only after the defeat of the Second World War—the last samurai fantasy) that it is pointless in a Japan where massive musculature is without employ in high-tech industry and in a nation whose constitution forbids any remilitarization. It is, indeed, irrelevant across our planet without such constitutions, where the next war will be won or lost (more exactly, reciprocally lost) by fingers pushing buttons, and where in the hour it will last there will be no occasion for ingenious strategic plans, skillful tactics, heroic feats of endurance, or nonparticipation.

The Cause, the Adventure, the Corrida

There is a pervasive resentment of the exhibitionism of body builders. It is not a resentment of physical exhibitionism; human nature in our epoch is cultivated especially by means of the glorification of athletes, female nudity, and feats of physical bravado.

A cause wins with the athlete—the school, the French nationalized automotive industry, the nation state, the free market world. In the team instincts of football players, the tailgaters read the name of a brand of beer that is on their own gregarious chests too; in the personal engineering of mountain climbers, the telespectators read the name of a multinational corporation in which they are programmed stockholders; in the single-mindedness of boxers they read the ruling finality of one of those multicorporation consortiums with a world market in view called nations. The bodies of athletes are causes. They are also feedback loops in the marketing industry. Achievement comes from the computer-revealed genetic potential, individually computerized diet and training, drugs and publicity and marketing. The purely abstract, formal, numerical, causes of their competitions feed into the causes of the rising and falling stocks of multinational enterprises.

At Penn State, Ken Graves attends a bodybuilding meet at the local high school; he reports that not even the high school kids were there, only the body builders, their siblings, and their spouses. The amateurs Ken Graves is interested in have no patrons, and train and go to exhibitions at their own expense, which the trophy the top one of the class will receive will not reimburse; even the world-class professionals can earn extra dividends as ad layout models only for barbell companies

and vitamin supplement products bought by the other body builders.

Ken Grave's camera encounters them pumping and oiling themselves in the dilapidated movie theaters of small towns, in locker rooms covered with graffiti and in classrooms whose blackboards are covered with musical scales and high school geometry formulas. Indeed the public imagination depicts them as fixated adolescents in high school locker rooms after hours. In the absence of a public cause before them and before us, the public mind can only rummage around for psychological causes producing these cases—distorted father figure, antisocial underworld instincts sublimated by fear of the police, fixated libidinal compulsions. One sees them narcissistically pumping themselves into ostentatious sex symbols—but symbols the sexually liberated public recognizes as the obsolete figure of virile protector, who was also phallocrat and wife beater. When the mind finds itself seduced to look where there is no cause written, it turns away in resentment.

What is she trying to prove, that women who has gotten herself hung up on a centimeter here and a centimeter there on her calves and neck? The image industry of our time instead glorifies the exhibitionism of the unathletic female, but not male, body. The nudity of the male athlete is a locker room nudity before or after the competition, just the time to buy or sell a Marlboro. The nudity of the male nonathlete is that justified baring of the arms to operate machinery, baring of the legs for speed, stripping for underwater welding. The precision tooling gives the male body seriousness and seemliness; the axis of bravery can give it nobility. Without the gearing-into the tool—or without a vision of bravery at grips with death—the unathletic male nudity is ridiculous.

But the female anatomy verges on the ridiculous too, as our advertising, our high art, and our pornography know; it has to be relayed with stage props—be they reduced to the minimum, as in Nô theater, to high-heeled shoes, a garter, atmosphere spread with vaseline on the camera lens, or, as Marilyn Monroe said, perfume. With the props the female anatomy is exhibited in a theater where acts, be that of lying there indolent and fatuous, have consequences and weave a plot. The theater of adventure is a space maintained alongside the politico–economic fields of our enterprises.

Maleness is exhibited in an enterprise, where the causes that produce results are also the causes of our industrious and mercantile zones; femaleness is denuded in a theater, where the causes are aleatory and the chain of consequences an adventure. Secretively, clouded with gauzy sunlight, or brazenly, in front of a cast-off nurse's uniform, the female nudity is a cause in the plot of an adventure that justifies it. The voyeur, crouched behind his telescope lined up with the windows of the building opposite, or crouched before his videoscreen, thinks not of blueprints, data, and will power, but dreams of luck and white magic, believes the chemistry of alchemical legends, the chance encounters by which an ineluctable destiny in the time of horoscopes is deciphered. He fiercely resents those women who, rebuilding their bodies out of muscle, are ruining the anatomy of the central character required for the theater of adventure.

But what about the corrida? No woman spread-eagled in a stripshow is as brazenly exhibited as the matador in the corrida. His body and his blood are exalted in a monstrance of scarlet velvets, spun-silver lace, and jewels over against the black fury of the bull. Insolence flaunts his torso, contempt splays his thighs, flash-fires of foolhardy intelligence crackle across his tensed and cynical posturings, his testicles and penis jeweled in the codpiece and provocatively exposed to the lusts of the crowds. It is, Hemingway (3) says, not gladiatorial spectacle, but tragic theater. It also became this only in our time. Only a century ago did the corrida change from being an activity of aristocrats for the sake of killing bulls into a theater for the extreme glorification of the torero, whose splendor blazes not in the ecstatic love of killing (the love of killing, and consequently the gift for it, Hemingway reports, all but obsolete in the legendary matadors of our time), but in the sover-

eign power to lead the raging horns of the doomed bull to his own brandished torso and to a torrent of blood and death at his feet.

Hemingway misleads us to think of it not as Roman gladiatorial spectacle but Greek tragic theater. Greek tragic theater is not a theater for the exhibition of deeds, but for the ineluctable revelation of a concealed truth. The death of the hero is decided by a destiny that the spectators are induced to grasp with a higher intelligence, which the insertion of the individual into a cosmic order or providence or political cause made possible. In the corrida it is not the death of the torero but that of the bull that is plotted, in the third act, within 15 minutes of the opening of the gates. The facts are that all the toreros do get gored, but most die of syphilis or tuberculosis. The death present in this Black Mass is not a sacrificial death; it is not the Orphic death of a god by which his power will pass into the cosmic order; it is not the intelligible exposition of death in nature where the dying of one organism is its redistribution into others; it is not a cultural death where a dynasty, an age, a revolution triumphs through or perishes with the death of the tragic hero.

Here there is not a solitary life that confronts its place in a revolution, a kingdom of God, or the cosmic order; there is an animality in which nothing is visible but a condensation of the ferocity of nature, a single-minded and brave, unretreating rage that drives the bull to his death, but which has made of the organization of life in him the most powerful in nature. The corrida then is not a theater with a plot of interactions to be intelligibly grasped, nor a truth to be deduced from events, nor a confused spectacle to be understood in narrative order, with beginning, middle, and end; it is a ritual of atavist nature, in the time of repetition, the time of In the Beginning.

What is true is that it is the inner force that calls forth death that here is revealed as what the male body is made of. This force is the dark blood of nobility that swells the phallic anatomy. All the minor arts of costume and jewelry, or choreographed mannerisms and manicuring, all the flattering cultivation of patronage and the priming of critics with gifts, which would make an athlete fall to the ridiculous, do not tarnish but set off the dark light of nobility in his exposed carnality. The ritual of the torero is made of precise and complex and instantaneously discharged intelligence, to be sure, and neurological precision, and the impeccable taste breeding and not training can produce, and the unwavering force of valor. All this visibly is inscribed on, is sustained by, or produces an epiphany of arrogant and fateful phallic sexuality. It is virility erected in splendor at the brink of raging death.

What our culture's mind can understand is a *virile body*, a body whereby virility is virtue, the primary virtue of courage. Socrates at his trial, at which the virtue or aberrancy of his pedagogical enterprise was to be defended, instead spoke of his courage in battle, which all his fellow citizens knew. Aristotle was to explain further, when in the *Nicomachean Ethics* (1) he put courage first in the list of virtues, that courage is the transcendental virtue, the condition for the possibility of all the others; without courage neither honesty nor magnanimity nor service nor even wit in conversation are possible.

But all courage, the courage to endure physical pain as well as the courage required to make decisions, is but a ramification of the courage in the face of death. It is through the power to hold one's own posture as the ground gives way beneath one that every power to take a stand is derived. Is it not the dim sense that all the causes and works of civilization are so many ideals or idols set up to defy death, that the virtues of laborers and of athletes, inasmuch as they are ways of holding firm when pain assaults and when the support of the others gives way, are derivative of the power to withstand the confrontation with death, that saves us from seeing a ridiculous anatomy under the glory we flood on their bodies? Is not the corrida a ritual in which this dim intuition is maintained in the midst of our laborious culture that produces only comfort and security?

There is then perhaps in our resentment of them

a dim sense that the cult of the body builders desecrates the ritual structure with which we maintain dignity in and conjure ridicule from our physical nature. The public does not see in body builders ferocious and destructive brutes that offend its sacralization of civilization—they are known to use their massive power as guardians of bourgeois property, taking jobs, typically, as night watchmen and bouncers in night clubs where the rich idle, and are suspected of being steroid-pumped eunuchs from whom the debutants have nothing to fear. But the resentment senses in them a virility insulated from death. Years of training that lead to no corrida, only to the footlights of a high school stage.

Rather than a brave contest with death, a sentimental fantasy of immortality on glossy photographs, fetishized into the metal figures of trophies. The duelling scars obligatory in German university students of the last century confirmed the nobility of their caste; the steel of the bodybuilder's equipment is nothing but inertia, exorcised of the death that forged the saber. There is a feeling at large that the musculature gained in work and in rule-governed contests, the bodies of construction workers, deep-sea divers, and boxers, is virile and virtuous; the musculature built in the rituals of the body-builder's cult grotesque.

The hands of the body builders do not contend with the inertia of implements or weapons, but rise to unfold in the sunlight or fold to frame their great swollen bosoms; beneath their wasp waists their legs pirouette; Arnold Schwarzenegger studied in a ballet studio how to walk with the grace of a prima donna. The discomfort so voiced today before the new breed of women body builders makes rise to the surface the vision of the hermaphrodite that one meant when one called the excessive anatomy of the male body builders grotesque. Psychoanalyst Julia Kristeva, after viewing the film *Commando,* spoke of how explicit this has now become, Arnold Schwarzenegger in happy domesticity, tender, caring, feeding his child—no mention of a woman that would have given birth to this child or of what had become of her. The body builder does not only stand in phallic hardness; he or she also moves rhythmically with the tensed violence of labor pains.

Is it not true that this body is not ennobled with the contention of power with death within it because it is oriented in the other direction—toward the fatality of genetic potential it is grappling with, toward birth? Bringing the dead weight of the steel within his/her muscles, the body builder brings himself/herself ever closer to that limit determined by birth. One's genes harbor another death, an inner death; as soon as we are born we are old enough to die, says an ancient wisdom. In pushing back to the genetic coding of the genus, one pushes one's way to the death sentence written in the individual by the immortality of the genetic formula.

The living organism, Freud taught, discharges its forces to ward off the death exterior to it only in order to seek its own death, its own advance to the death that is its own. The courage that forces one into this internal death, this death that is one's own, is the very courage with which one is born. Freud was only thinking that every living organism has a life span that is indistinguishable from its definition as a species, even though its life forces are so many resistances to the death-dealing blows that fall upon it from without; the sequoias are not killed by the lightning that strikes them every year and burns our their cores; the seed was programmed to live for 2,000 years, and then to die.

But the body builder tears down, muscle system by muscle system, all the strength in his/her fibers and cells against the death of the steel, and he/she knows that the hard will that takes him/her all the way to the limits of his/her exhaustion is the very movement by which power, and new, greater, power is born. His/her work, and feats, are nothing but labor pains; and he/she knows what is genetically coded to be born in him/her only in knowing the time and the effort it takes to leave all his/her force on the dead inertia of the steel. There is then in the force with which the body builder assumes all that is and could have

been born in him/her also a courage and a splendor—even if, viewed from the outside, it appears as the monstrous excrescence of maternity in the virile figure of power.

The Surfacing of Splendor

Monstrous—that is, not only the anomalous and the gigantic, but the ostentatious (monster, *monstrare*). This anomalous, gigantic, and ostentatious figure would be the way the cult overcomes derision before the evolution of the human anatomy reduced to nature. Is not the conviction that our anatomy, ridiculous by nature, has to serve as the material for art coextensive with all civilization?

The civilization our species has launched and pursued to relay its evolution appears in nature not only as the exteriorization of the powers in our organs but also as the exteriorization of the splendors in the periodicity of our impulses. Leroi-Gourhan (4) divines that the first art is the most inward—an artistry done on one's visceral core in the yoga of Mohenjdodaro and Harappa 4,000 years ago, an artistry that condensed chant or invocation into a mantra which is sounded only inwardly, which concentrated the periodic motility of the body into the scanned rhythms of the circulation of air and blood and semen. The compulsion for ordering the circulation of men and goods in outer, public space, which Freud found contemporary with the first beginnings of civilization, and which he attributed to the compulsion of the principle of economy, we would rather see to be an exteriorization of the sense of inner rhythm and circulation that were the materials for the first artistry our species worked on its own nature. The first artists worked, Nietzsche said, with the noblest clay and oil, the artist's own flesh and blood.

The epochs of the splendors of civilization appear to Leroi-Gourhan (4) to be epochs of the progressive exteriorization of this inwardly working artistic compulsion. Thus the art of body movement and vocalization, dance and song, would issue from the older visceral artistry of the yogis. Glorification of the body surfaces exposed to view comes out of the distant epochs where dance and song were the media for our species's self-glorification; making of the body surfaces a collage of bird-of-paradise plumes and boars's tusks, or a cuneiform tablet of tattooings and scarifications is an artistry that arises in a culture of festivity and chant.

A next stage of exteriorization is that of the architectonic splendors of Babylonian, Athenian, Mayan, Ottoman, and Gothic culture, which honored as major artists those who frame the construction and urban layout that houses human movements. The art exteriorized on surface effects—in the age when those who are preeminently called artists were painters—, the "humanist" art of the European Renaissance and subsequent modern period of painting, was in fact an artistry worked on the exterior spectacle as blocked off and framed into a perspective by the human eye.

Now the buildings that humankind's earlier artistry had surrounded them with serve as the points of departure for an artist's eye that orders into splendor the views from the balconies and the towers. Our contemporary art now extends itself beyond the perspective spread out before the human sense organs to the spaces reached for by the mind and by its electronic relays—to microcosmic and macrocosmic exteriority. Contemporary art is conceptual, framing the designs of microchemistry and astronomy; contemporary music captures the songs of the whales and those of the earth's magnetic field.

The meaning and the origin of the drive productive of splendor seemed to Freud as enigmatic as it seemed certainly coextensive with the defensive and utilitarian drives that transform nature and transform our nature. Living things are not only equipped with organs to perceive what is exterior; they are also equipped with organs designed to be perceived. Splendor, if created by the chance coincidence of random events in a canyon in a desert, in a sunset over equatorial waters, is also an organic production of living things.

This was the thesis of Adolph Portman (7), who argued that the patterns of animal body surfaces have their own intelligibility. The morphology of the inner, functional body, the form and the arrangement of the skeleton, of the respiratory, circulatory, digestive, and reproductive organs, and of the prehensile and locomotive organs, does not make intelligible the always regular and often intricate and ostentatious patterns of the body surfaces and extremities. These have to be understood, he argues, as organs-to-be-seen, whose designs and colors become intelligible only when we correlate them with the specific powers of the witness-organs for which they are contrived. The inwardly coiling horns of the mountain sheep and the hairless, protuberant buttocks of the baboons are, he says, organs as closely fitted to the eyes and lips of the spectator as the jaws and hoofs are fitted to the terrain and the specific foods of the species.

In the human primate, a distinctive reflexive circuit was set up with the evolution of the hand. The human species began by putting the cutter, chopper, and grinder functions of the jaws into its hands. The front legs no longer serve to drive the jaws to make contact with the world; they rise from the ground and conduct samplings of the world to the head. The human animal now acquires a face. Its muscular configurations no longer react immediately to the front line of contact with external nature, but turns to its own hands. A smile and an apprehensive grimace now become possible—movements that are *expressive,* that is, that address a sample, a representative of the independent exterior held in the hand—and, soon, held with a mental grasp before an inner eye, an animal that faces another considers representations it has apprehended. Its manual musculature becomes not prehensile only but also expressive; the hands position their take for an appraising eye. They address themselves also to the eyes of another animal that has acquired a face; they speak. Little by little our whole musculature has learned to speak. The throat muscles designed for devouring and for expelling substances and the body's own biles and rages now learns from the hands how to shape the samples and representatives of the outside, how to exteriorize the comprehensive expressions the hands first learned to make. The whole torso becomes organs-to-be-seen, the abdomen struts and cowers, the legs and thighs acquire humility and pride, the shoulders and back, turned from the face-to-face circuit, sway with resentment and defiance.

Unlike the birds-of-paradise and the mountain sheep and the baboons, the human species did not develop distinctive organs-to-be-apprehended in addition to its organs-for-apprehending. Its hair, become functionally obsolete, is in an advanced state of disappearance; it has not deviated into a patterned pelt. Its teeth, whose functions were exteriorized onto tools, are in an advanced state of atrophy, and have not deviated into coiling tusks to make impressive the face. With the upright posture, Freud assumed, the primate genitals are permanently exhibited to the frontal view of another, and, Freud assumed, this has led to the primacy of the eyes over the nose as the chief organ for sexual stimulation, to the end of a rutting season, and the unseasonableness of human libido. But the human genitals remain organs fitted for contact, and have not become expressive organs. To be sure, the human species has contrived snares for the eye—penis sheaths, cache-sexes, pendants hung over the breasts—but these are exterior to its own genitalia, which remain glandular, orifices of the inner, functional body.

What has happened is that it is the human muscular system that has taken on the second, expressive, role for which the other animals have evolved distinctive organs-to-be-seen. The human muscular system is not only the scaffolding that positions and turns the sense organs, the organs-for-apprehending; the vectors and surges of motor energy illuminate the muscular network itself and make its mesh and mounds snares for the eye. On human bodies muscle frettings are their peacock tails, curls worked on the lips their crests, biceps and pectorals their coiled horns, finger waverings their lustrous pelt.

But civilization, in that epoch when the hunter-gatherers mutated into self-domesticated animals, altered the human muscular system. As it exteri-

orized motor efficacy from the human muscles to the animal, wind, water, and steam power that relayed them, it exteriorized the ostensive functioning of muscles into masks, talismans, and costume.

To be sure, this exteriorization has not yet become complete and definitive; there still floats in civilization an imagination that feeds on muscles. Indeed the imagination, that unpenetrating, superficial vision, vision of surfaces without depth, is a *faculty of the muscles.* Mishima spoke of the *displacement* of his sense of himself when, an intellectual, he committed himself to body building; there is a specific sense of one's identity that rises out of the visceral or cerebral depths to find itself henceforth in the contours one's substance spreads out to the sun. This self, spread in the tensions of the musculature, doubles them up as imagination, inhabiting and fascinated with forms, patterns, surfaces, a fascination anchored in the image one's self forms. And muscles are not exposed without doubling up their surfaces before the imagination of another. It is the first effect of their reality; their contours excite the imagination before they displace resistances.

That the visceral system does not have such an effect can seem puzzling. The awareness of the content of fluids in us of the saline and mineral composition of ocean water, the inner gulf streams, currents, and tides, the coral reefs, channels lined with tentacled anemones, and floating plankton within does not double up our sense of ourselves with a vision of the oceans from which, tide pools now enclosed in a porous sack of skin, our muscles have carried us. In fact the imagination is not divinatory and does not penetrate the deep; it is a surface sense, its mirages mirroring superficial mappings of the terrain, excited by the contours of muscles. And our muscles, becoming more and more obsolete in mechanized industry and automated war, become the more designed for the faculty of imagination.

In the obsolescence of an epic imagination does there not spread now only a topical erotic imagination? The Marlboro man, a torso hardened, according to the legend, by riding the range, is perhaps a torso riding the range in order to be hardened into a Marlboro model. The editorial writers of *Playboy* and *Playgirl* declare that the anatomies they exhibit have been fashioned by Olympic nautical training and ocean sailing; but swimming, sailing, bicycling (on stationary machines before mirrors), and workouts on Universal equipment are perhaps designed to produce the play musculature. Is the human muscle sheath, strapped to machines, monitored by cardiovascular and fat ratio dials, turning into the showy carnal corollas and petals of human orchids?

This evolutionary destiny is unclear; the future is complicated by the existence of the cults. In them the body substance is turned into muscle everywhere, the glands of the abdomen and its coiled membranes into muscles that can parry the blows of a fist, the atrophied mammary glands of males into matrices of trust and power, the chords of the neck are not neglected, nor the threads pulling the fingers. But they use the most elementary bars and weights; to this day no world-class body builder has trained on the Nautilus machinery scientific intelligence has designed for them. These are atavist bodies, halted before the age of the self-domestication of the hunter–gatherer. We found no real difference between the scene in Gold's Gym and on the banks of the Ganges, where the origins of every method to divinize the mind with every possible cosmological system but also every method to divinize the body with sublunary power can be traced back to, and where we saw, in 1980, young men making the prostrations before the idols of the Aryan ape-god Hanuman which we term push-ups and calisthenics, and, while intoning mantras, lifting before him rocks and pairs of millstones fixed on poles. Cults where we see not body mechanisms made on machines, but primogenitor bodies made of *the elemental*— the weight of the terrestrial, and rivers, and sun.

The body builder's implements do not relay the passage of his/her own body force outward. He/she confronts the steel, the opaque, inert mineralization of death, with all his/her animate power, in what is not a contest but a process of symbiosis or synthanatosis. He/she tears down his/her muscles on steel, exhausting all his/her force on it, and when muscle failure has been reached, receives from the metal its properties. His/her biceps become tempered flails, his pectorals, that is, his mammaries, his femaleness, become gearing, the membrane of his/her abdomen a sheet of corrugated steel, his/her knuckles themselves brass. The luster of his/her muscle contours acquire for the eye the opaque impenetrability of metal. At the same time in the repetitions, the contractions and flexions, the body builder internalizes into channels of surging power the fluidity of the sweat and the oils, the vaporous currents of steam, showers, surf, and sunlight. The power that holds him/her upright is no longer that of a post before equipment civilization has erected. Tide pools of the maternal ocean enclosed in a porous sack of skin carried up to dry land by developing muscles, they stand erect now with the form that a fountain maintains by the incessant upsurge and fall of streams of power.

The body builder senses his/her identity on the bronzed, metalized luster of the beams of musculature exposed to the sun; it is on the sweat sheets across this hard skin and the surface gleam of the sun, and on the surfaces of mirrors displaying the oiled definition that he/she now seeks himself/herself. Existence, for the self, no longer means inwardness, visceral or cerebral involution, but exposure. This self is a movement to extend itself across contours and forms, and not to maintain a point of view, a repair in space. As the ego surfaces, distends and exposes itself, it depersonalizes. The steel does not only transfer its own properties into the living tissue that has exhausted its own force on it; its homogeneity drives out the principles of individuality in the bodies that devote themselves to it. It does away with the eccentricities—the dry and irritable skin, the concave faint-hearted chest, the indolent stomach, the furtive hand, the shifting eye—by which movements of retreat set up the as-for-me of individuality and leave their marks on the body. On his/her contours the body builder watches emerging not the eccentricities his tastes and vices leave in his carnal substance, but the lines of force of the generic *human animal.*

How little the rest of us see of our bodies! Our genitals we conceal, even from ourselves, judging them, with Leonardo da Vinci, of an irremediable ugliness; our visceral and glandular depths, the inner coral reefs and pulsating channels of antennas and gyrating polyps, our very imagination blinds itself to. Our musculature we attend to with a clinician's or mechanic's inspection. The drive to visibility, to high-noon exposure, is so alien to us that it has to be driven into our substance by the steel. Ken Graves speaks of the watchmaker eye body builders have for the individual components. They do not, like the rest of us, see a charm or a brutality; their eye is specialized for details, trained in instant measurings, intolerant of dissymmetries. As they wait in the wings for the decisions of the judges, the contestants line up, he says, in almost exactly the order the judges will have placed them. As though it is not the individual eye permanently fixed in a point of view and a perspective that sees, but the impersonal eye of a species in evolution appraising its organs and limbs for an advance whose duration and direction are unknown.

Body builders look at one another, and each at himself/herself, also with an alchemist's eye full of chemical formulas, protein supplementations, quack remedies inspired by analogies, and drugs made in biochemical laboratories. They know their muscle substance with a cellular and not general and conceptually formulated knowledge, with a knowledge that thinks in the pain of cells being stretched and elongated, being torn down, a knowledge that does not preside over but yet somehow accompanies the invisible movements of the millions of antibodies within that are the real cause of and reality of the separateness of our bodies.

One does not know what role evolution will find for these prodigies of musculature—or, rather,

what evolution their artistry is contriving for the species. No one, Nietzsche wrote, is more readily corrupted than artists. Their souls, their taste, can be bought by venal priests of pagan religions, by the big investors in the image industry, by the master computers of the racing military–industrial complex, and by their own followers and flatterers. Today the names of the body builders whose names are known are the names of so many industries, auxiliary epicycles in the wheels of the planetary machinery.

But the imagination that feeds of muscles imagines something else—imagines that the deviation their cult makes from the path of civilization might be carried further. Civilization destined the self-driving power of human bodies to be transferred into tools, and then to be transferred out of human muscles into draft animals, wind, water, steam, atomic fission. The body builders at this late date reverse the movement, disconnect from the tools, having interiorized their elemental properties, and make of musculature a splendor. Civilization destined the powers of surveillance in human sense organs to be directed on the motor force now exteriorized in draft animals, windmills and waterwheels, electric and atomic-fission generators, and then to be transferred out of human sense organs into automatic and feedback mechanisms. Can we imagine at some future date the eyes, the touch, the heart disconnecting from the machinery that feeds in the images and the information, and swelling and glowing with their own resplendence? Civilization evolved the faculty of memory, reason, and decision, and destined it to program the electronic sensors and feedback mechanisms that make the human sense organs obsolete. Can we imagine at some future date the faculty of memory, reason, and decision disconnecting from the computers it now serves, ceasing to be but an organ-for-apprehending, and, swollen with its own wonders, become an organ-to-be-apprehended, orchid rising from the visceral and cerebral depths of the cybernetic forest with its own power, rising into the sun?

Bibliography

1. Aristotle. *Nicomachean Ethics.* Translated by Martin Ostwald. Indianapolis: Bobbs-Merrill, 1962.
2. Freud, Sigmund. *Civilization and its Discontents.* Translated by James Strachey. New York: Norton, 1962.
3. Hemingway, Ernest. *Death in the Afternoon.* New York: Scribner, 1960.
4. Leroi-Gourhan, André. *Le geste et la parole* (2 vols.). Paris: A. Michel, 1964-65.
5. Mishima, Yukio. *Sun and Steel.* Translated by J. Bester. New York: Grove Press, 1970.
6. Nietzsche, Friedrich. *On the Genealogy of Morals.* Translated by W. Kaufmann. New York: Vintage, 1969.
7. Portmann, Adolf. *Animal Forms and Patterns.* Translated by Hella Czech. New York: Shocken Books, 1967.

Bibliography for Sport and Embodiment

Abe, Shinobu. "Interdependence of Body and Mind as Related to Physical Education and Sport." In *The Philosophy of Physical Education* (6th ed.). Tokyo: Shoyo-Shoin, 1977.

Abe, Shinobu. "Sport From a Viewpoint of Sensibility." In *Topical Problems of Sport Philosophy*. Edited by H. Lenk. Köln, Germany: Bundesinstitut für Sportwissenschaft, 1983.

Aristotle. "De Anima." Translated by J.A. Smith. In *Introduction to Aristotle*. Edited by Richard McKeon. New York: Random House, The Modern Library, 1947.

Bandy, Susan. "A Humanistic Interpretation of the Mind-Body Problem in Western Thought." In *Mind and Body: East Meets West*. Edited by Seymour Kleinman. Champaign, IL: Human Kinetics, 1986.

Barral, Mary Rose. "Merleau-Ponty: The Role of the Body in Interpersonal Relations." Unpublished doctoral dissertation, Fordham University, 1963.

Bazzara, Carmelo. "The Body's Role in the Philosophy of the Renaissance Man." In *Mind and Body: East Meets West*. Edited by Seymour Kleinman. Champaign, IL: Human Kinetics, 1986.

Beets, N. "The Experience of the Body in Sport." In *International Research in Sport and Physical Education*. Edited by E. Jokl and E. Simon. Springfield, IL: Charles C Thomas, 1964.

Beets, N. "Historical Actuality and Bodily Experience." *Humanitas*, 2 (Spring, 1966), 15-28.

Belaief, Lynn. "Meanings of the Body." *Journal of the Philosophy of Sport*, IV (1977), 50-68.

Bennett, Lorraine A. "Reification of the Human Body in Ancient Greece: A Metabolic Investigation." Unpublished doctoral dissertation, University of Oregon, 1976.

Broekhoff, Jan. "Physical Education and the Reification of the Human Body." *Gymnasion*, 9 (Summer, 1972), 4-11.

Conry, Barbara J. "An Existential Phenomenological View of the Lived Body." Unpublished doctoral dissertation, Ohio State University, 1974.

Cornman, James W. "The Identity of Mind and Body." *Journal of Philosophy*, 54 (1962), 486-492.

Dombrowski, Daniel E. "Plato and Athletics." *Journal of the Philosophy of Sport*, VI (1979), 29-38.

Doud, Robert E. "Sensibility in Rahner and Merleau-Ponty." *The Thomist*, 44 (1980), 372-389.

Duhrssen, Alfred. "The Self and the Body." *Review of Metaphysics*, 10 (September, 1956), 28-34.

Fahey, Brian. "The Passionate Body." In *Being Human in Sport*. Edited by Dorothy J. Allen and Brian Fahey. Philadelphia: Lea & Febiger, 1977.

Fairs, John R. "The Influence of Plato and Platonism on the Development of Physical Education in Western Culture." *Quest,* 9 (December, 1968), 14-23.

Feezell, Randolph M. "Sport: Pursuit of Bodily Excellence of Play—An Examination of Paul Weiss's Account of Sport." *The Modern Schoolman,* 58 (1981), 257-270.

Feigl, H., Maxwell, G., & Scriven, M. (Eds.). *Concepts, Theories and the Mind-Body Problem. Minnesota Studies in the Philosophy of Science, Vol. 2.* Minneapolis: University of Minnesota Press, 1958.

Fetters, Janis Lynn. "The Body Beautiful: Beyond Stereotypes." *Journal of Health, Physical Education, Recreation and Dance,* 53 (1982), 31-32.

Fraleigh, Warren. "A Christian Concept of the Body-Soul Relation." In *Sport and the Body: A Philosophical Symposium.* Edited by Ellen W. Gerber. Philadelphia: Lea & Febiger, 1972.

Gerber, Rudolph J. "Marcel's Phenomenology of the Human Body." *International Philosophical Quarterly,* 4 (1964), 443-463.

Hammer, J. "Bodily Experience of the Ego in Sports." In *Sport in the Modern World—Chances and Problems.* Edited by Ommo Grupe, Dietrich Kurz, and Johannes Teipel. New York: Springer-Verlag, 1973.

Hengstenberg, Hans-Eduard. "Phenomenology and Metaphysics of the Human Body." *International Philosophical Quarterly,* 3 (1963), 165-200.

Hissinson, T.W. "Saints and Their Bodies." In *The American Sporting Experience: A Historical Anthology of Sport in America.* Edited by Steven A. Riess. West Point, NY: Leisure Press, 1984.

Hoberman, John M. "The Body as an Ideological Variable: Sportive Imagery of Leadership and the State." *Man and World,* 14 (1981), 309-330.

Holbrook, Leona. "A Teleological Concept of the Physical Qualities of Man." *Quest,* 1 (December, 1963), 13-17.

Hyland, Drew A. " 'And That Is the Best Part of Us': Human Beings and Play." *Journal of the Philosophy of Sport,* IV (1977), 36–49.

Johns, David. "Body Awareness and the Gymnastic Movement." *Phenomenology and Pedagogy,* 3 (1985), 116-125.

Jokl, Ernst. "Brain, Mind and Movement." In *Topical Problems of Sport Philosophy.* Edited by H. Lenk. Köln: Bundesinstitut für Sportswissenschaft, 1983.

Jonas, Hans. "Life, Death, and the Body in the Theory of Being." *Review of Metaphysics,* 19 (September, 1965), 3-23.

Kaelin, Eugene F. "Being in the Body." In *Sport and the Body: A Philosophical Symposium.* Edited by Ellen W. Gerber and William J. Morgan. Philadelphia: Lea & Febiger, 1979.

Keen, Sam. "Sing the Body Electric." *Psychology Today,* 4 (October, 1970), 56-58, 88.

Keen, Sam. "We Do Not Have Bodies, We Are Our Bodies." *Psychology Today,* 7 (September, 1973), 65-73, 98.

Kelly, Darlene Alice. "Phenomena of the Self Experienced Body." Unpublished doctoral dissertation, University of Southern California, 1970.

Kleinman, Seymour. "The Significance of Human Movement: A Phenomenological Approach." In *Sport and the Body: A Philosophical Symposium.* Edited by Ellen W. Gerber and William J. Morgan. Philadelphia: Lea & Febiger, 1979.

Kleinman, Seymour. "Will the Real Plato Stand Up?" *Quest,* 14 (June, 1970), 73-75.

Kleinman, Seymour. (Ed.). *Mind and Body: East Meets West.* Champaign, IL: Human Kinetics, 1986.

Kohler, Wolfgang. "The Mind-Body Problem." In *Dimensions of Mind.* Edited by Sidney Hook. New York: Collier Books, 1961.

Koizumi, Tetsunori. "The Importance of Being

Stationary: Zen, Relativity, and the Aesthetics of No-Action." In *Mind and Body: East Meets West*. Edited by Seymour Kleinman. Champaign, IL: Human Kinetics, 1986.

Krawezyk, Zbigniew. "The Ontology of the Body: A Study in Philosophical and Cultural Anthropology." *Dialectics and Humanism, The Polish Philosophical Quarterly*, 11 (1984), 59-74.

Kwant, Remy. "The Human Body as the Self-Awareness of Being." *Humanitas*, 2 (Spring, 1966), 43-62.

Linde, O.D. "The Puritan Concept of the Body." Unpublished master's thesis, Temple University, Philadelphia, PA, 1981.

Long, Douglas C. "The Philosophical Concept of a Human Body." *Philosophical Review*, 73 (1964), 321-337.

Luijpen, William A. "The Body as Intermediary." In *Existential Phenomenology*. Pittsburgh: Duquesne University Press, 1960.

Marcel, Gabriel. *Metaphysical Journal*. Translated by Bernard Wall. Chicago: Henry Regnery, 1952.

McDougall, William. *Body and Mind*. Boston: Beacon Press, 1961.

Meier, Klaus V. "Cartesian and Phenomenological Anthropology: The Radical Shift and Its Meaning for Sport." *Journal of the Philosophy of Sport*, II (1975), 51-73.

Meier, Klaus V. "The Pineal Gland, 'Mu', and the 'Body Subject': Critical Reflections on the Interdependence of Mind and Body." In *The Philosophy of Physical Education* (6th ed.). Edited by Shinobu Abe. Tokyo: Shoyo-Shoin, 1977.

Nietzsche, Friedrich. "The Despisers of the Body." In *Thus Spake Zarathustra*. Translated by R.J. Hollingdale. Harmondsworth, England: Penguin, 1967.

O'Neil, John. "The Spectacle of the Body." *Journal of the Philosophy of Sport*, I (1974), 110-122.

Osterhoudt, Robert G. "Prolegomenon to a Philosophical Anthropology of Sport." *Philosophy in Context*, 9 (1979), 95-101.

Osterhoudt, Robert G. "The Mind-Body Problem in World Intellectual History: The Case of Sport in Personalistic Monotheism." In *Physical Education and Sport in the Jewish History and Culture* (3rd ed.). Edited by U. Simiril. Natanya, Israel: Wingate Institute for Physical Education & Sport, 1981.

Osterhoudt, Robert G. "Empiricistic Dualism: The Paradoxical Basis/Nemeses of Modern Physical Education." *Quest*, 36 (1984), 61-65.

Ravizza, Kenneth. "The Body Unaware." In *Being Human in Sport*. Edited by Dorothy J. Allen and Brian Fahey. Philadelphia: Lea & Febiger, 1977.

Ravizza, Kenneth. "There Is a Silence That Surrounds Me: The Lived-Body Experience in Gymnastics and Hatha Yoga." In *Topical Problems of Sport Philosophy*. Edited by H. Lenk. Köln: Bundesinstitut für Sportswissenschaft, 1983.

Ross, Saul. "Cartesian Dualism and Physical Education: Epistemological Incompatibility." In *Mind and Body: East Meets West*. Edited by Seymour Kleinman. Champaign, IL: Human Kinetics, 1986.

Sarano, Jacques. *The Meaning of the Body*. Translated by James H. Farley. Philadelphia: Westminster Press, 1966.

Schrag, Calvin O. "The Embodied Experiencer." In *Experience and Being: Prolegomena to a Future Ontology*. Evanston, IL: Northwestern University Press, 1969.

Shaffer, Jerome A. "Recent Work on the Mind-Body Problem." *American Philosophical Quarterly*, 2 (April, 1965), 81-104.

Shaffer, Jerome A. "Persons and Their Bodies." *Philosophical Review*, 25 (January, 1966), 59-77.

Shvartz, Esar. "Nietzsche: A Philosopher of Fitness." *Quest*, 8 (May, 1967), 83-89.

Spelman, Elizibeth V. "Women as Body: Ancient and Contemporary Views." *Feminist Studies,* 8 (1982), 109-132.

Spicker, Stuart F. (Ed.). *The Philosophy of the Body.* Chicago: Quadrangle Books, 1970.

Staley, Steward C. "The Body-Soul Concept." In *The Curriculum in Sports (Physical Education).* Champaign, IL: Stipes, 1940.

Van Den Berg, J.H. "The Human Body and the Significance of Human Movement." *Philosophy and Phenomenological Research,* 13 (1952), 159-183.

Van Peursen, C.A. *Body, Soul, Spirit: A Survey of the Body-Mind Problem.* Translated by Hubert H. Hoskins. London: Oxford University Press, 1966.

Waelhens, Alphonse de. "The Phenomenology of the Body." Translated by Mary Ellen and N. Lawrence. In *Readings in Existential Phenomenology.* Edited by Nathaniel Lawrence and Daniel O'Connor. Englewood Cliffs, NJ: Prentice-Hall, 1967.

Weiss, Paul. *Nature and Man.* New York: Henry Holt, 1947.

Weiss, Paul. *Sport: A Philosophic Inquiry.* Carbondale, IL: Southern Illinois University Press, 1969.

Wenkart, Simon. "The Meaning of Sports for Contemporary Man." *Journal of Existential Psychiatry,* 3 (1963), 397-404.

Wenkart, Simon. "Sports and Contemporary Man." In *Motivations in Play, Games and Sports.* Edited by Ralph Slovenko and James A. Knight, Springfield, IL: Charles C Thomas, 1967.

Yonge, George D. "A Dynamic Image of Masculine and of Feminine Movement." *Journal of Phenomenological Psychology,* 6 (1976), 199-208.

Young, Iris M. "Throwing Like a Girl: A Phenomenology of Feminine Body Comportment, Mobility, and Spatiality." *Human Studies,* 3 (1980), 137-156.

Zaner, Richard M. *The Problem of Embodiment: Some Contributions to a Phenomenology of the Body.* Dordrecht, Holland: Martinus Nijhoff, 1964.

Zaner, Richard M. "The Radical Reality of the Human Body." *Humanitas,* 2 (Spring, 1966), 73-87.

Part III

Sport, Play, and Metaphysics

Concerns about the ultimate nature of reality—that is, the fundamental constitution or underlying essence of things, or even 'being' as such—are the main foci of the branch of philosophy known as *metaphysics*. Although other forms of investigation also deal with specific aspects of the structure of reality, metaphysics does not, for example, employ the discretely segmented and purposely fragmented perspective of the various branches of the natural or social sciences. Rather, it pursues its inquiry in more breadth, at a higher level of generality, and with the intent of obtaining knowledge of a more synoptic nature.

Be that as it may, and despite the fact that there are at least three traditional areas subsumed within the realm of metaphysics, this section will not address matters of cosmology or theology; instead, it will deliberately focus solely upon ontological questions. At the risk of oversimplification, *ontology* is herein utilized to indicate the investigation of reality from the standpoint of human existence. More specifically, whereas the previous portion of this volume discussed metaphysical aspects of the nature of man and embodiment, the readings included in this section all address the ontological status of human participation in sport and play, as well as the meaningful experiences derived therefrom.

One of the classic and most seminal works in the area is Fink's "The Ontology of Play." The basic thesis advanced in this essay is that play is a fundamental, irreducible mode of human existence, which, to be experienced fully in all of its richness, presupposes a certain self-conscious awareness of what it means to be a human being actively sojourning in the world. Burke argues for a point intermediary between those who view play as trivial and childish and those who claim that only play can complete our humanity. He argues that play should be acknowledged and revered for the same reasons that art and science are important, namely, as freely constructed and important worlds of symbolic meaning.

The selection extracted from Sartre's magnum opus *Being and Nothingness* presents one of the most provocative accounts of play to be found in the literature. In the full work, Sartre's discussion of play is preceded by a lengthy analysis that argues that virtually all human strivings (e.g., work, art, science) can be reduced to the general category of desire known as 'having'; in other words, the self's basic relation to objects or things as one in which the former seeks to use, possess, appropriate, or dominate the latter. Yet, according to Sartre, there remains one human enterprise that apparently cannot be subsumed under this possessive relationship—namely, play. The goal of play is not to possess, but to provide expressive outlets for the participant's unique subjectivity. However, Sartre argues that, on closer inspection, even play discloses itself to be at bottom possessive towards the world of things.

Esposito, proceeding along a somewhat similar path, argues that the core experience of play—that which makes playing sports or games so prevalent and desirable—is the confrontation with possibilities. That is, play activities are viewed as contrived human activities specifically structured in such a manner that the player is purposively confronted with a variety of possibilities in the form of obstacles or challenges to be overcome. In the next essay, Algozin extends this theme by contending that the fascination with sport can be traced ultimately to human yearning for *unalienated action*. Whereas most everyday activities are of the alienated variety, Algozin argues that the sport experience clearly provides opportunities for the identification and fulfillment of tangible goals in a much different environment, thereby qualifying as a form of unalienated activity.

In the final essay of this section, Meier presents an extended, deliberately provocative apology for, and appreciation of, play which argues that—contrary to the current high adulation assigned to the ideology of prudent utilitarianism and economic instrumentality, characterized by the permeation, acceptance, and avid glorification of the spirit of work—play is located at the center of life, not relegated to its distant perimeter. Following a lengthy discussion of the specific nature of the stance of play (that is, the play mode of comportment in the world), as well as comments on its interrelationships with theology and aesthetic theory, Meier concludes by celebrating the vibrant possibilities inherent to open and aware participation therein. He contends that play provides numerous opportunities to luxuriate in the intense, fully-lived release, if not explosion, of subjectivity. Thus, the prize of play is perceived to be play itself.

Those interested in a further study of play and sport from the metaphysical perspective will readily find extensive additional reading material that explores the nature and significance of sport and play in terms of various elements of the human condition. Consequently, such themes or topics as finitude, time, space, freedom, and authentic and inauthentic existence are all viable and represented areas of inquiry.

For further comments on and analyses of Sartre's imputation of an appropriative element in play, see the essays by Netzky (1974), Keating (1978), and Fell (1979). Wilkes (1982) provides a detailed critical analysis of these three commentaries in addition to an informative reanalysis of Sartre's original position. Hinman (1974) interprets Nietzsche's musings on man and the world from the standpoint of play. Erhmann (1971), Axelos (1971), and most importantly Krell (1972) all offer comments on Fink's position. Feezell (1981, 1984) offers further reflections on play and freedom; Roochnik (1975) and Hyland (1980, 1984a) view play as a stance people assume toward various activities, namely, one of *responsive openness;* and finally Reizler (1941) discusses the sport experience from the perspective of the participant's attitude.

Attempts to reflect on or analyze the meaningfulness of engagement in sports have been rather numerous. Metheny's (1967, 1968) systematic examination of the meaning of sport, dance, and exercise still warrants reading. Gebauer (1973) and Franke (1973) both offer characterizations of sport as a reconstructed world with its own peculiar system of signs as well as meaning context. Other sources addressing the topic include Arnold (1979), Weiss (1969), Bouet (1973, 1968), many of the readings contained in Slovenko and Knight (1967), as well as essays by Santayana (1894), Doherty (1964), and Progen (1979).

Morgan (1976a, 1978a, 1978b) and Vernes (1965) both provide accounts of sport based upon its temporal orientations. White (1975) examines the constitutive elements of the so-called great moments in sport, whereas Welter (1978) discusses *complete moments* to be found therein. And Garret (1976) provides an interesting description of the perspective and articulation of the sport of baseball.

DeSensi (1980) explores Buber's thoughts on human relationships in connection with sports participation, whereas Meier (1976) analyzes two specific forms of interpersonal communication, namely, the *kinship of the rope* and the *loving struggle,* as evidenced within the sport of mountain climbing. Slusher (1969),

Fraleigh (1973a, 1973c), and Coutts (1968) all investigate the different forms of freedom available in sport. Several dissertations employing a phenomenological perspective on various aspects of the human condition experienced in sport, including those by Thomson (1967), Stone (1970), Harper (1971), and Kretchmar (1971), make significant contributions. Herzog's (1953) informative participant description of the physical dangers, as well as the rewards, to be found in mountain climbing introduces the encounter with personal finitude in sport in a most dramatic and accessible fashion; Wyschogrod (1973), in turn, offers more general philosophical reflections on risk sports and death. Finally, Meier (1975), subsequent to an analysis of the nature of authentic existence as delineated in the writings of Heidegger and Jaspers, provides an extensive investigation of the potential for the manifestation of this state of being in sport.

Although not specifically addressed in this section, the literature available in one related area of metaphysics merits brief mention at this point; namely, scholarly reflections on the religious significance of play and sport. Huizinga (1950) provides early preliminary comments on the matter. Rahner (1967), Neale (1967), and Miller (1970) all forward extensive and highly original comments concerning play and theology, whereas DeCaluwe (1979) contributes a comprehensive and enlightening study of their works. Moltmann (1972) and Cox (1969, 1973) also address the topic of the theology of play at length. Morgan (1973) discusses additional aspects of sport as a religious experience. Keen (1970) extolls a playful, dancing god, and Novak (1976) argues that sport qualifies as a natural religion. Finally, and from a different perspective altogether, Hoffman (1976) delineates the shortcomings of any attempts to integrate Christian theology specifically with athletics or sport.

The Ontology of Play

EUGEN FINK

In an age characterized by the noise of the machine, the role of play, in the structure of human life becomes more and more apparent. Not only the expert analysts of civilization, educators and specialists in anthropology as well are agreed on this point. Modern man himself has become aware of the importance of play. Contemporary literature and the passionate interest in games and sports are evidence enough. For modern man play is a vital-impulse with its own value and sphere of activity, participated in for its own sake. It is a kind of reward for the unpleasantness that goes with material progress in modern technocracy. It is also seen as a means of rejuvenating one's inner vitality, a return to the morning freshness of life at its origin, to the source of one's creative powers. In human history there have certainly been times a good deal more gay, more relaxed, more given to play than our own; when there was more play, when men had more leisure and were more familiar with the Muses. However, no other age has had so many possibilities and occasions for play. Never has there been such a systematic exploitation of life on a grand scale. Playfields and stadiums are in the original plans of cities. Games in vogue in different countries are brought to international competitions. Playing materials are mass-produced. But it is still in question whether our

age has reached a deep understanding of the nature of play. Can we evaluate the many meanings of the term or thoroughly penetrate the aspect of being in the phenomenon-play? Do we know what constitutes play and specifies it from the philosophic point of view?

We want to consider that strange and very particular mode of being that characterizes the play of man, to conceptualize the elements that make up its being and give rough draft of the speculative concept of play. To some this subject may seem dry and abstract. We would surely prefer something of the very atmosphere of play with a lightness of touch in treating the subject, stressing its creative fullness, its overflowing richness and its inexhaustible attraction. A brilliant essay could be written, a game with the reader discovering the hidden sense of words and ideas through the surprise effect of a play on words; something pertaining to a literary *genre* rather than a treatise on play. In using a serious approach there is the feeling of betraying the very nature of play. Philosophy, as with Plato, has made contributions poetic-wise in the domain of speculative thought. A consideration of play in the same vein might achieve the same end, since the subject itself is provocative of a sublime play of the spirit. But such a treatment demands something of the Attic wit. Our consideration, therefore, will be simple, with no pretence to poetry. It will be in three parts: a preliminary characterization of the phenomenon-play; the analysis of its structure; the relation of play and being.

Reprinted from *Philosophy Today,* 4, (Summer, 1960), pp. 95–110. Copyright 1960 by *Philosophy Today,* Carthagena Station, Celina, Ohio 45822. Reprinted by permission.

I

Play is a vital fact which each of us knows subjectively. Everyone has taken part in play and can speak of it from experience. It is hardly necessary to make it the subject of scientific research to discover it and to disengage it from other phenomena. Play is universally known. Each of us understands it in its many forms. Our experience is all the evidence we need. Each of us has been a player. Moreover, familiarity with play is more than individual. It is a public act in which all can participate. Play is an accepted and ever recurring fact of the social world. We live through abandon[ing] ourselves to it, we recognize it as an ever possible act. Through play we find ourselves no longer imprisoned and isolated on our own individuality. In play we are assured of a social contact of particular intensity. All play, even that which seems to turn in upon oneself, such as that of the solitary child, has a social dimension. The fact that we actually live ourselves into the act of play, approaching it as something interior to ourselves, makes man as the subject of the attribute-play. However does man alone play? Can we say that animals play, the vitality of each living creature expressing itself exteriorly in a sort of joy of living? Biology, it is true, presents us with some interesting cases of animal behavior which occasionally resemble the play of human beings. It would be a mistake, however, to consider these on the same plane in terms of constituent elements, as if surface resemblance presupposes identity in mode of being. We can certainly formulate a biological concept of behavior in play which would link man and animal from the point of view of animality. But this would say nothing about the mode of being behind the exterior manifestations which resemble each other. We cannot proceed with the discussion from this point of view until the question of the ontological mode of being of man and animal is clarified. In our opinion human play possesses a meaning and exclusiveness of its own. Only a halting metaphor can be used to apply it to the case of either animals or the ancient gods. In the final analysis, what is important is the way in which the term "play" is applied, the fullness of meaning attributed to it, its delimitation in terms of reference, the conceptual penetration we give it.

We propose the question of human play, beginning with the fact such as moments of play, we are freed by it, we understand it in our daily experience. Play does not enter into our lives as simply as vegetative processes. It is always a process that has a meaning, a lived experience. All our life consists in enjoying this act (which does not require reflexive consciousness). Generally, if we give ourselves over to play, we are far from reflection. And yet, all play presupposes the awareness of our own activity. There is a current and rather pedestrian view of play, a sort of vulgar interpretation: that play is nothing more than a phenomenon on the margin of human life, a peripheral fact, an occasional sort of thing. The more important moments of our existence lie elsewhere. We consistently hear it opposed to the serious occupations of life that are filled with a sense of responsibility; it is referred to as "recreation," "relaxation," and "diversion." It is claimed that life finds its fulfillment in the difficult pursuit of knowledge, in moral excellence or a professional attitude of mind, in prestige, in dignity and honor, in power, prosperity and similar goals. Play, on the other hand, seems to be like an occasional break, a pause that highlights the more genuine and serious aspects of life, like a dream opposed to being awake. From time to time, it is argued, man should slip from under the yoke of slavery, free himself from the shame of always starting over, lift the weight of the daily grind, quit watching the clock—for a more leisurely pace, perhaps even squandering time. In the economy of life "tension" alternates with "relaxation," business with leisure. We prescribe for ourselves "weeks of hard work" and "holidays for merry-making." Thus play seems to have a legitimate but quite restricted place in the vital rhythm man has set himself. Play is an *ergänzung,* a supplementary thing, a recreative pause, a surcease from burdens, a ray of light over the darker and severe landscape of life. By force of habit we limit play by contrasting it to the seriousness of life, to an attitude of moral commitment, to work—to all the prosaic things of reality. We identify it with frolic, with flight toward the regions of imagination, away from the hard realities of life to dreams and utopia. It exists just to keep man from succumbing to the modern world of work, from forgetting how to laugh amid moral rigorism, from becoming the prisoner to duty. Analysts of civilization recommend play to ward off disasters. It takes on a therapeutic value against the ills of the soul. But the question is, how does such advice understand the very nature of play? As a peripheral phenomenon in contrast to the serious? Can we never look at it except in terms of work, of a drive against odds? Is there not within us a little of that divine detachment of spirit, of the joyous buoyancy of play that joins us to the "birds of the air" and the "lilies of the field?" Is play only for preventing psychic disorders that trouble men in the modern world? As long as we accept such implications, "play and work," "play and the realities of life," play cannot be thought of in its proper sense and in its true ontological dimensions. It remains in the shadow of phenomena seemingly opposed to it, which obscure and deform it. It is considered as the non-serious, the non-obligatory, the non-authentic, as mere idleness. It is precisely by the very way in which its salutary effects are praised that we prove our estimation of it as a marginal phenomena, a peripheral counterbalance or as a sort of ingredient adding flavor to the insipidity of our existence.

It is even doubtful that such a view gives an adequate understanding of play as phenomenon. It is true that the behavior of adults shows less and less of the grace natural to play. Too often their games are nothing more than an organized escape from boredom. An adult seldom plays naturally. But for a child, play is the undisturbed center of existence. It is the very stuff of child-life. As age forces him to leave this center, the rude storms of life get the upper hand. Duty, care and work use up the vital energies of the adolescent. As the serious side of life asserts itself, the importance of play diminishes. We usually consider how we can educate the child to pass smoothly from a being who plays into one that works. We present work to the child under the aspect of play, as a methodical and disciplinary game where the burden becomes unnoticeably heavier little by little. The point is to keep a maximum of spontaneity, imagination and initiative as in play, to create a kind of joy in work. This well-known pedagogical experience is based on the general conviction that while play is inherent in man, especially during childhood, it occupies a less conspicuous place with the advancement of age. The play of the child shows more freely certain traits characteristic of human play. It is more ingenuous, less equivocal and dissimulating than the play of adults. The child knows little about the seduction of masquerading. It plays in all innocence. But how much hidden play is disguised in the serious affairs of the adult world, in honors, social conventions; how much hidden drama in the meeting of lovers. Everything considered, perhaps we would not want to say that ideal play is that of the child. The adult can also play, but in a different way that is more furtive, more masked. If we take our notion of play from the world of the child alone, we misunderstand its nature, fall into equivocation. In fact, the domain of play extends from the little girl's playing with a doll to the tragedy. Play is not only a peripheral manifestation of human life, it is not a contingent phenomenon that emerges upon occasion. In essence, it comes under the ontological dispositions of human existence. It is a fundamentally existential phenomenon. It is not derived from any other manifestation of life. To oppose play to any other phenomenon is to risk misunderstanding it. On the other hand, we must recognize that the fundamental phenomena which are decisive in human existence are all interlaced and intertwined. They never appear isolated or juxtaposed against one another. They interpenetrate, interinfluence. Each has a hold over the whole of man. To throw light upon the reciprocal influence of the moments of existence, the tensions and harmonies, is the task of an anthropology not limited to the description of biological, psychic and intellectual facts, but which penetrates by intuition the paradoxes of lived existence.

Man, at every stage of existence, is marked by the all-pervasive proximity of death, inescapable. And in so far as he has a body and sensitive life, he is affected by his relations to the earth which both resists him and yields its riches. The same is true of domination and love, all his dealings with his fellowmen. In his essence man is mortal; by nature he works, he struggles, and by the same count, he plays. Death, work, domination, love and play, these are the elements of the patterns which we find in human existence, so enigmatic and ambiguous. And if Schiller says, ". . . A man is whole only when he plays," it is also true to say that he is whole only when he works, struggles, opposes death and loves. We cannot draw up principles for an interpretation of human existence without referring to these fundamental phenomena. It will be sufficient to say in passing, though, that all of them are manifested in changing, enigmatically and ambiguous ways. The principal reason is that man is exposed and abandoned and at the same time watched over and protected. He is not completely carried along by instinct like the animal, nor is he as free as the immaterial angel. His is a freedom in the midst of a nature which binds him to an obscure tendency which permeates his being. And he simply integrates it into his knowledge of his own existence. On the other hand, free acts completely control his life. Because of this mingling of self-expression and repression, his existence is a continual tension within the self. We live within ourselves constantly preoccupied with ourselves. Only the vital being, of whom it can be said that "into his being he goes with his own being," can die, work, struggle, love and play. Only such a being is in touch with surrounding reality and the total environment—the world. To be related to self, to understand being and to reveal oneself to the world, this triple moment is known perhaps less easily in play than in the other fundamental phenomena of human existence.

But that is why play exists. It is act in its spontaneity, acting in its very activity, the living impulse. Play is life that moves within its own orbit. However, the moving forces of play do not coincide with the other forces of human life. For in all action other than play—whether it be the simple "praxis" which has its end in itself or the production of the artist (*poiesis*) where the end is the work—there is essentially implied a tendency toward the end of man, toward beatitude, toward *Eudaimonia.* We are busy finding the virtuous path to the fullness of life. For us life is a "task." Consequently, at no moment can we be said to have a place of rest. We are aware of the fact that we are "travelers." The violence of our vital project constantly lifts us out of the established moment to carry us toward a life of virtue and happiness. Thus we are compelled to attain *Eudaimonia,* though we are not in agreement as to what it is. We are not only moved by aspirations that uplift us, we are not at rest until we can give the one and only "interpretation" of this happiness. It is one of the paradoxes of human existence that in the incessant pursuit of *Eudaimonia* we never attain it; we cannot be happy in the sense of perfect achievement in this life. While we breathe, our life is caught in a vertiginous cascade. We are carried forward by the desire to perfect and complete our fragmentary being. We live in terms of the future. We experience the present moment as a preparation, as a stage, as a passing phase. This strange "futurism" of man's life is bound up with his fundamental character. We are not a simple fact like plants and animals. We force ourselves to find a "meaning" in our existence. We must understand the reason for our life on earth. It is a demon-like urge which drives man to search for an interpretation of his earthly journey, a passion of the soul. Something within makes man search for the source of his grandeur as well as his misery. No other creature is troubled in his very being by the question of the mysterious meaning of his existence. The animal cannot and God has no need to ask the question. All human response to the question of the meaning of life means that man has an end which will finally be attained. With most men the position is not explicit, but their conduct is directed by the basic idea which they form of the "supreme good." The different ends which permeate our daily life are ordered in terms of a principle which harmonized their oppositions and indicates the final end. Particular ends are linked to what the community considers the absolute end of man.

Within this architectonic ordering of ends all human work is carried on. The serious side of life is developed, authentic attitudes are produced and confirmed. But the tragic element in man's situation is that he cannot guarantee in any absolute sense his final end by his own efforts. When the major question of his existence is brought up, he gropes in the night unless a superhuman power comes to his aid. That is why the confusion of Babel reigns among men as soon as we ask what can be the true end, the destination, the true happiness of human nature. This is also why unrest, anxiety and uncertainties are characteristic of human life.

But play fits into this situation in a way quite different from any other human activity. It stands out in remarkable relief to all that characterizes life teleologically. It cannot be expressed in terms of the architectonic complex of ends. It does not fall under the final end as do other actions. Its activity is not disturbed by the fundamental uncertainties which we take into account in interpreting happiness. If we compare play to the rest of life with its impetuous dynamism, its provoking orientation toward the future, play appears as a serene "presence" with a meaning sufficient to itself. It is like an oasis of happiness found in the desert of our questing, which in itself recalls the punishment of Tantalus. Play enraptures us. During play we are momentarily freed from the daily grind and, as it were, magically transported to another planet where life seems more light, more carefree, more happy. We often hear that play is a gratuitous activity, without finality. This is not exactly the case. Considered as a whole, play is determined by an internal end and we will discover in its different stages the particular ends which form

a whole. However, the immanent end of play is not directed as that of the other activities of man toward the supreme end. The activity of play has only internal finalities which do not transcend it. This brings to mind that particular form of play that is seen in terms of its physical attraction: military formation. For the sake of our well being, play is here found in an adulterated form, an activity in view of an end other than its own. Play is here in terms of ends extraneous to its nature and it is not easy to see just how much value comes from it as play. It is precisely because play in an unadulterated form is self-sufficient that it possesses a complete and firmly established meaning which makes it possible for man to find in it an asylum in time where time itself is no longer that torrent which carries us forward. It is rather a respite with a spark of eternity in it. It is apparently the child, therefore, who plays best. Again it is the child who knows that relation to time most intimately of which the poet Rilke speaks:

O childhood hours, behind whose
   make-believe
Was hid more than the past and before
   us lay
No future to contend. Though we dreamed,
   'tis true
Of growing up and were perhaps in haste to be
   well grown,
More was it for the love of being those
Who had no other merit than being grown.
While yet not hid from life, we tasted joy
Which gives repose and were suspended
   thence
In an interval between the universe and play,
   a place,
From all eternity, chosen for the pure event.
           (Rilke, *Duineser Elegien—*
                    Vierte Elegie)

For the adult, play is a strange oasis, a place of rest filled with dreaming along the relentless, pressing course of life. Play gives us a "presence." But it does not reach into the silent depths of the soul where we listen to the eternal breathing of the universe and contemplate pure images in the stream of passing things. Play is activity, creative force, and still it is near what is unchangeable and eternal. Play breaks the continuity of life's course, its coherence which determines the final end. It cuts across the groove in which life ordinarily runs. It sees things "at a distance." However, in seeming to subtract from the unified current of life, it sets up a relation in a meaningful manner: the representation which it gives of it. When, as is the custom, we do not restrict play by relating it to work, to reality, to the serious, to the authentic, we commit the fault of not placing it with the other phenomena of existence. For play is itself a fundamental phenomenon of existence, just as original and basic in itself as death, work and domination. Only it is not linked to the other fundamental phenomena in a common pursuit of the ultimate end. It confronts them, as has been pointed out, to use them representationally. We play with the serious, the authentic, the real. We play with work and struggle, love and death. We even play with play.

II

Let us look at the matter a little more closely. In making the initial step in understanding this valuable concept of play, we must examine the articulations and the structure of the whole of play just as it is.

We can indicate at first sight, as an essential element of play, that it is a passion of the soul. We can say that all man is and does is colored by either one or the other states of the soul—joy, sadness or the gray tone of indifference. Play, at least in its source, has the coloring of joy. Joy reigns in it as undisputed master at each moment, carrying it forward and giving it wings. As soon as the joy is gone, the action disappears. This does not mean that throughout the duration of play we must be gay and in good humor. The joy arising from play

is a singular pleasure, difficult to put your finger on. It does not resemble the pleasures of the senses in the relaxation of the body or the physical intoxication with speed. On the other hand, neither is it a purely spiritual delight, sheer intellectual joy. It is a joy rooted in a most special creative activity, open to many interpretations. It can include a profound sadness, a tragic suffering. It can embrace the most striking contraries. The pleasure which accompanies tragic action from one end to the other draws its power of ecstasy and emotion, mixed with terror and rapture, from the reign of the dreadful. The representation of horror is the source of the pleasure. Play transfigures even the mask of the Gorgon.

What is that strange pleasure which drastically mixes contraries, overlapping one with the other, leaving joy in the first place? However moved to tears we may be, we smile at the comedy and tragedy which are our life and which the play represents to us. Does the pleasure of play include the suffering and grief thus presented to us in this evocation because the action refers to past afflictions and time has softened them? Or is it that the turning back of the wheel of time alleviates the living bitterness, the sorrows formerly so real? By no means. In play we do not experience "real pain"—and, yet, the emotion of play gives rise to a strange type of pain which, actually but not really, moves us, seizes us, touches us, shakes us. The sorrow is only played, but even modified by play it is still a power that moves us. It has this capacity only because the delights of play include it. This delight is indispensable to the activity of play. We cannot compare it to other known forms of functional pleasure. It is true that we always feel a sense of well-being unrelated to any object whenever we do not submit our life passively but offer our being with spontaneous initiative, direct it in assuming responsibilities and mold it in creative processes. The creative quality of existence is in itself a "surge forward." But the fulfillment of play is accompanied by a pleasure which we cannot compare with the joys experienced in any other action or psychic urge. The pleasure in play is grounded not only in the element of creative spontaneity—it is also the ecstasy which accompanies our entry into any "universe," into the objective world. It is not only the pleasure experienced in playing, but a joyous attitude with regard to play as well.

A second step in studying the structure of play is to point out the meaning play establishes. Each type of play, as far as we can see, establishes a certain meaning. But purely physical movement, exercising arms and legs by repeating certain rhythms is not play in the strict sense of the word. It is simply confusing to call play such behavior as that of relaxing indulged in by young animals and children. These movements bring no meaning whatsoever to their author. We can speak of play only when the meaning of a specific end creatively accompanies such movements. Furthermore, in a particular game, we must distinguish between the intrinsic meaning of play—the meaningful bond between things, actions and played relations—and the external meaning, the meaning of play for those who initiate it and take part in it, as well as the meaning it is supposed to have for the spectators. It is evident that there are games which include spectators as spectators (such as games at the circus), and games which exclude them.

We might mention a third element in play: the community element. Play is a fundamental possibility of social life. To play is to play together, to play with others; it is a deep manifestation of human community. Play is not, as far as its structure is concerned, an individual and isolated action; it is open to our neighbor as partner. There is no point in underlining the fact that we often find solitary players playing alone at personal games, because the very meaning in play includes the possibility of other players. The solitary player is often playing with imaginary partners. The community of play does not necessarily require real persons present. It is enough for a real player to have a real game and not merely an imagined one.

Another essential element is that of the rule in play. Play is established by a commitment and bound to it; it is limited by whatever concerns the arbitrary modification of any action. It is not entirely free. There is no play without a commitment agreed upon and accepted. However, the rule of play is not a law; the commitment is not irrevocable. Even in the course of play, we can change the rule with the permission of partners. However, then the modified rule holds and fixes the course of what can be done by either. We all know the difference between traditional games where we adopt rules already formulated and the improvised games that are just made up. The community of play has to come to an agreement about the rules of the latter. We might expect these improvised games to be the most popular, since they leave the field open to imagination and permit the development and free reign of pure possibilities. But this is not necessarily the case. The act of being bound to a pre-established rule is often a positive experience with its own delights. This may seem strange, but it is explained by the fact that traditional games are often bound up with collective imagination, with self-commitments rooted in the deep primordial patterns of common experience. A number of children's games, which may seem naive, are in fact rudiments of certain magical practices of antiquity.

Each type of play demands equipment. Each of us knows about playthings, but it is still hard to define them. We do not have to enumerate all possible types, but we must know their nature or at least recognize that there is a problem. Playthings do not make up a definite world of their own, as is the case with things that are made. According to nature (in the larger sense of that which exists in itself), these are not artificial objects if man has not made them. It is only by his own work that man produces artificial things. He is the artisan (technités) of a human environment. He cultivates the earth, tames the animals, makes tools. A tool is an artificial thing that human work has formed. We can distinguish artificial things from natural things, but they are one and the same in being on the plane of the same universal reality which includes them all.

Though a plaything can be an artificial object,

it is not necessarily so. Just a piece of wood, a fallen branch, can function as a doll. The hammer, which, by its very form, is the will of man imposed on an assemblage of wood and iron, belongs just as the wood, the iron, and the man himself, to one and the same order of reality. It is not so with playthings. Seen from the exterior, that is from the point of view of those who do not play, it is evidently a fragmentary object of the real world. It is simply something that holds a child's attention. The doll is a product of the toy industry, it is a mannequin made up of material and a piece of wire or of plastic. We can buy it at a certain price; it is merchandise. But seen with the eyes of a little girl who plays, the doll is a child and the small girl is its mother. Perhaps it is not as though the child thought the doll were actually a living child, for she is not under a false impression nor apt to confuse the nature of things. She possesses, on the contrary, a simultaneous knowledge of the doll as such and its meaning in play. The child who plays lives in two worlds. What makes a thing a toy—gives the essence of toy—is something rather magical. It endows an everyday thing with a kind of mysterious being. It is then infinitely more than a simple means of amusement, more than a thing which one must put together and keep in hand. Human play has need of playthings. Above all, in his specifically human actions, man is not free to bypass things. He needs them. He cannot ignore the hammer in his work, the sword for conquest, the couch for love, the lyre if he be a poet, an altar for religion—and playthings for play.

Each plaything symbolizes the totality of real things. To play is to take an explanatory attitude toward being at all times. Reality is concentrated in the plaything in the form of a single thing. All play is an attempt to have the plaything yield to the vital energy of man so that he might test symbolically the totality of the resistance of being. But human play not only comes under the magical intimacy with playthings. We must look a little closer at the notion of the player, for we are in the presence of a very particular type of "schizophrenia,"

of the duality of man; which of course is not pathological. The player who engages in play performs a precise action in terms of the real world, quite recognizable. However, as to the meaning and intrinsic context of play he assumes a role. It then becomes necessary to distinguish between the real man who "plays" and the man charged with a role within the context of play. There is a real basis for saying that the player loses himself in his role. He lives his role with a very particular intensity and, for that reason, not in the manner of an hallucination where we cannot distinguish "reality" from "illusion." The player can renounce his role. Even at times he is necessarily engrossed, the consciousness of his double existence does not abandon him. He lives in two worlds, but not through distraction or want of concentration. The duality belongs to the very nature of play.

The structural elements we have thus listed are all present in the fundamental concept, "the world of play" (*Spiel welt*). All play is a magical creation in the world of play. It is here that the player assumes a role, that the community of play alternately distributes the roles, that the rules of play are imposed and that the plaything takes on meaning. The world of play is an imaginary sphere. It is a difficult problem, therefore, to clarify its essential structure. We play in the world which we call real, but in so doing, we create for ourselves another world, a mysterious one. This is not just nothing and still it is not something real either. In the world of play we act according to our role; but in this world imaginary persons live, as the "child" which takes on body and life, but which is nothing more than a doll or even a piece of wood in reality. In projecting a world of play, the player disguises himself as a creature of that "world," losing himself in the project, becoming that person whose role he has assumed and moving, for the present, in the midst of things and among partners who belong to such a world of play. Confusion might arise here for in imagination we think of things of the world of play in themselves as "realities" and even the distinction between reality and illusion can frequently be re-adjusted.

But it does not follow that the real things in our daily world are veiled or even masked by the superimposition of the world of play to the point that we no longer recognize them. This is not at all the case. The world of play does not interpose a wall between us and being that surrounds us. Strictly speaking, the world of play has neither place nor duration but operates in interior space and time proper to it. However when we play we use real time and have real space besides. But we do not pass by continuous transition from the space of the world of play to that we ordinarily occupy. The same holds for time. The strange interlacing of spheres of the world of reality and that of play cannot be explained by any other example known of spatial-temporal proximity. The world of play is not suspended in a domain of pure imagination. It always possesses a real theatre. However, it is never a real thing among other real things. But real objects are indispensable to it as props. This is to say that the imaginary character of the world of play cannot be reduced to purely subjective illusion, nor defined as fancy not affecting us except interiorly and unable to make its appearance in the world of real things.

We come now to the fundamental characteristics of play. Human play is a creation through the medium of pleasure of a world of imaginary activity. It is the singular joy of ''appearances'' *(Freud am Schein)*. Play is always characterized by an element of representation. This element determines its meaning. It then effects a transfiguration; life becomes peaceful. We are freed little by little, and we eventually discover that we have been redeemed from the weight of real life. Play lifts us from a situation of fact, from an imprisonment depressing by nature, and by means of fantasy helps us enjoy passing through a multitude of ''possibilities,'' without imposing on us the necessity of making a choice. In playing man lives out two extremes of existence. One puts man at the peak, gives him an almost unlimited power of creation, establishes a freedom that is impossible in reality. The player feels himself master of his own creations; play becomes a possibility

scarcely limited by human freedom. At the highest point in play freedom prevails. But we also find in play the contrary of freedom (a facet of being taken perhaps from the real world) which can bring about a sort of alienation from enchantment, even to the point of coming under the demoniacal power of the mask. Play can conceal the Appolonian clarity of free ipseitas as well as the Dionysian inebriation which accompanies a certain abandonment of human personality.

Man's relationship to the enigmatic ''appearances'' of the world of play, to the sphere of the imaginary, is ambiguous. Play is a phenomenon for which we cannot easily find adequate categories. It is perhaps a dialectic much concerned with not reducing paradoxes to a dead level, which would let us for that very reason experience the tantalizing ambiguity of dialectic. The great philosophers have insisted on the eminent meaning of play. If common sense does not recognize this it is because play means nothing more to it than a lack of seriousness and authenticity, because it sees in play only pointless activity. Hegel, however, said that in its indifference and extreme lack of seriousness, play is the unique and most sublime expression of true seriousness. And Nietzsche in *Ecce homo:* ''I do not know of any other method than play for facing the most important tasks.''

Can play be explained if it is not seen purely and simply as an anthropological phenomenon? Could it be that our consideration has gone beyond man? Does this mean that we must study the behavior of play as it involves other creatures also? The problem is really that of knowing whether or not we can understand play in its ontological structure without limiting it by paying attention to the sphere of the imagination. Whether play is something man alone can do is a question which remains open and depends on whether man the player is still bound to the human world or if he has entered a superhuman world.

From the beginning, play is a symbolic act of representation, in which human life interprets itself. The most ancient games are magical rites, the principal liturgical cultures of primitive man, expressing his being-in-the-world in which he represents his destiny, commemorates the events of birth and death, weddings, war, the chase and work. The manner of symbolic representation in magical games draws its elements from the simple world around men just as he draws upon the nebula world of the imagination. In primitive times, play was not practiced so much as an act in its pleasure-giving aspect as is the case for those isolated individuals or groups, who periodically detach themselves from the social group to inhabit their own little isle of passing happiness. Originally, play was the strongest unifying force. It found a community quite different, it is true, from that of the living and the dead, the governing and governed, and even from that based on the family. The community of play of primitive man included all the forms and structures of common life that we have enumerated and it called forth a reliving of all the elements of life. This reached its high point with the community keeping festival. The ancient feast was more than a popular form of rejoicing. It was reality itself—hoisted to the world of magic—the reality of human life in all its relations. It was a liturgical spectacle where man experienced the proximity of the gods, heroes, the dead, and where he found himself in the presence of all the beneficent and dreadful powers of the universe. Primitive play had deep contacts with religion. The community *en fête* included the spectators, the mysteries and epics; here the exploits and sufferings of the gods and man were passed in review. What was represented was nothing less than the whole universe.

III

In attempting to reduce the structure of play to a certain number of fundamental concepts, such as the climate of play, community of play, rule of play, plaything, and the world of play, we often used the word "imaginary." An equivalent of this word would be "appearing-to-be." However, in this term is concentrated a remarkable intellectual aporia, a dead end. We understand the term "appearing-to-be" in its strictest sense when it operates in concrete determined situations. But it is still a difficult and complicated matter to say precisely what we mean by it. The most important philosophic questions and considerations are involved in the most everyday things and words. The concept "appearing-to-be" is altogether as obscure and indefinable as that of "being." And the two concepts are related to each other in an intricate, perplexing and even inextricable manner; they interpenetrate and intermingle in their application. In thinking all this out we get further and further into the labyrinth of being.

With the question of the "appearing-to-be," in so far as it is related to the domain of human play, we ask a truly philosophic problem. Play is a "creative producing." Its effect, that is in the world of play, is exercised in the sphere of the "appearing-to-be," a field in which we can hardly expect consistency. The "appearing-to-be" of the world of play cannot be dismissed simply by calling it nothingness. We actually move within it when we play. We live in it at times, certainly, a life that is as free and fanciful as that of a dream, but sometimes we give ourselves over to it with genuine zeal. At times such an "appearing-to-be" has a presence and suggestive force more powerful and impressive than the everyday affairs which are quite banal in their very seriousness. What then is the imaginary? Where should we locate this strange "appearing-to-be," what is its condition? On the determination of that place and condition depends, in great part, the understanding of the ontological nature of play.

We are in a habit of speaking of "appearings-to-be" in various acceptations of the term. For example we think of the exterior appearance of things, of their superficial aspect, of their frontal aspect, and the like. That which "appears-to-be" pertains to what is represented as the shell pertains to the nut and as the substance to its manifestation. More often we speak of an "appearing-to-be'' as in the case of a subjective fallacious interpretation, of an erroneous opinion, of a confused representation. In this case, we who interpret reality poorly have within us a semblance of that which resides in the subject. But there is also a subjective ''appearing-to-be'' with a legitimate place within us. It is a product of the imagination and does not relate to the categories of truth and error as does the representation and objects represented. With these abstract distinctions we can formulate our question. Which ''appearing-to-be'' is in the world of play? The outer appearance of things? A fallacious representative? A phantasm produced within us? We cannot deny that in play as a whole imagination manifests itself and unfolds in a particular manner. However, is the world of play nothing more than a product of the imagination? We might find an easy way out by saying that the imaginary universe that is the world of play exists uniquely in the human imagination and cite accordingly the case of hallucination and individual imaginary occurrences which have been united into collective hallucination or ''intersubjective fantasy.'' To play, however, is always to use playthings. Anyone who considers the nature of a plaything will attest that play does not come into our life only in a purely interior manner, for it cannot escape being related to the objective exterior world. The world of play consists in both subjective elements of the imagination and objective ones or real ones. The imagination is known as the psychic power. We recognize the dream as such, as well as interior percepts and various imaginary contents. But what is the significance of the objective or real ''appearing-to-be''? It exists in the reality of curious things which, without doubt, are in themselves something of reality and yet contain an element of un-reality. This may seem both singular and astounding. However, this is commonly known, though we ordinarily do not speak of it in terms so involved and abstract. All that is needed is simply images presented objectively, as a poplar on the shore of a lake projecting its reflection over the mirroring surface of the water. The reflections themselves make up part of the whole of the optic phenomenon, which consists of real things and the light which envelops them. Things exposed to light project their shadows. The trees on the bank are reflected in the lake, a smooth and highly polished metal surface reflects the objects around it. What is reflected? As an image it is real; it is a real reproduction of a real tree, its source. But it is ''in'' (or ''as'') image that the tree is represented. It appears to be on the surface of the water, but in such a way that it springs from the medium of the reflection and is not there in reality. An ''appearing-to-be'' of that nature is a kind of being apart. As a constituent element of its reality it possesses a specifically unreal element. It resides on the surface of another being which is simply real. The reflection of the poplar does not hide the surface of the water which it covers and which serves it as a mirror. The reflections of the poplar are there as reflection, a real thing known in itself and an unreal poplar in the sphere of reflection. This may seem sophistic; however, this fact is in everyone's experience and easily distinguished, for it is of daily occurrence. The doctrine of being of Plato, which has profoundly influenced western philosophy, takes as a model at decisive moments in his elucidation, the notion of image in terms of shadow and reflection and thus interprets the structure of the universe.

There is more than a simple parallel between the real ''appearing-to-be'' (reflection and the like), and the work of play. The real ''appearing-to-be'' is by priority counted as a structural element in the world of play. To play is real behavior, which includes what we call a ''reflection,'' the attitudes which the world of play portions out according to the roles one takes in it. When all is taken together, the possibility that a man might construct a real ''appearing-to-be'' proper to a world of play depends, in a great measure, on the fact that such already exists in nature. Man not only knows how to make artificial objects generally, but he knows how to produce things which properly belong to an ''appearing-to-be-that-is.'' He projects imaginary worlds of play. The little girl raises the body of material composition, doll, to the sphere of her "living child" by an act of the imagination, and with it herself to the role of "mother." Real things are always involved in the world of play; but they take on the character of a real "appearing-to-be"; sometimes even they are related to a subjective "appearing-to-be" which comes from the human spirit. Play is a creation with limited possibilities in the magical world of appearances.

The problem of explaining how the real and unreal interlace in human play requires untiring effort. The ontological determination of play leads us into the chief questions of philosophy, to being and nothingness, to the "appearing-to-be" and becoming. We see that the expression, "the unreality of play," is both hasty and superficial, unless understood in terms of the enigmatic world of the imaginary. But we ask, what human and what cosmic meaning does the imaginary have? Is it a limited sphere in the midst of real things? Is the strange country of the unreal that exalted place where we call upon the presence of the "essences" of all things? In the magical reflection which operates in the world of play, it is not important which isolated object (for instance the plaything) becomes *symbol.* It represents another thing. Human play (even if we no longer recognize it as such after a while) is the symbolic action which puts us in the presence of the meaning of the world and of life.

The ontological problems which play poses for us do not exhaust the questions which have been brought up concerning the mode of being of the world of play and the symbolic value of playthings or of the action of play. In the history of thought, there have been those who have not only tried to conceive of the being of play, but also have dared an unheard of inversion of the process, concluding that the meaning of being springs from play. This is what I would call the speculative concept of play. In short, speculation is the characterization of the nature of being which takes for its point of departure the metaphorical consideration of a being. It is a conceptual formula of the essence

of the world developed from a model within that world. The philosophers have used and perhaps abused models of this kind: Thales, of water; Plato, of light; Hegel, of the spirit; and the like. But the clarifying force of these models does not depend on the arbitrary choice of each of these thinkers. It is important, above all, to know whether or not the whole of being can be found in reflection in a single isolated being. In the measure in which the cosmos reproduces itself metaphorically in something which makes up part of the world in terms of structure and imprint, a key-phenomenon of philosophy can be discovered from which a speculative formula of the world can be developed.

As far as that goes, the phenomenon of play is a manifestation distinguished by the fundamental character of symbolic representation. Could it be then that play is a spectacle which might represent the whole as in parable, producing a clarifying and speculative metaphor of the world? One philosopher has had the courage or rather the temerity to think so. At the dawn of European thought, Heraclitus had formulated the sentence: "The course of the world is a child who plays at moving his pawns—a kingship of childhood." (Frg. 52, Diels.) And about twenty-five centuries later in the history of thought, we find in Nietzsche: "Becoming and disappearing, constructing and destroying, without moral imputation, with an eternally childlike innocence, behold what is reserved in the world for the souls that play, those of the artist and the child." "The world is Zeus' play . . ." (*Die Philosophie im tragischen Zeitalter der Griechen.*)

The depth of such a concept has its danger and its power of seduction, for it impels one to an esthetic interpretation of the world. But the strange formula of the world through which the totality of being is viewed as a game could be made to bear out the fact that play is not an anodyne, a peripheral or even puerile phenomenon, that we mortals are oriented to play in a mysteriously fundamental sense, precisely because we can produce magically things that testify to our creative power and our glory. If the essence of the world were thought of as play, it would follow that man is the only being within the immensity of the universe who can understand the infinity of the whole and respond accordingly. This is nothing more than recovering for himself the sense of the infinite, that eludes him, that he might be able to reach to the source of his being.

The opening up of human existence to the abyss of being by means of play, to being as a whole, which is also a form of play, is a theme that has inspired the poet Rilke:

So long as you merely catch, what you
  yourself
Toss up—'tis only skill of a minor range.
Only when you suddenly catch the ball
Thrown by your eternal Companion of play
Against your center, in a perfect gesture,
In one of the arcs, traced against the great
  bridge of God
Does knowing how to seize it really count—

Not for yourself, but for the world. And if,
  perchance,
You had the force and courage to return it—
Why then, 'tis no miracle;
But if lacking the strength and courage,
  you still
Have thrown it, as the Year throws the birds,
The southward seeking birds to the Young
  Warmth
Of the land beyond the seas—then first
In such a feat do you really play the game.
Do not bother to throw again.
Be not disturbed. Out of your hands it springs
Like a Meteor and settles in its proper sphere.
(Translation of Fritz Klatt in *Rainer Maria Rilke,* p. 79.)

When philosophers and poets stress the power and meaning of play as a profound human reality, perhaps we should remember the words that warn us that we will not enter into the kingdom of heaven unless we become like little children.

Taking Play Seriously

RICHARD J. BURKE

At least since the Renaissance, our culture has been dominated by the idea of work. This idea takes various forms. One is the Puritan vocation or calling, generalized from the clergy of the Middle Ages; another is the capitalist pursuit of profit; still another is the industrial imperative to maximize efficiency and productivity. These can be combined, as they were throughout most of American history in "the Protestant ethic." But each can also exist without the others. In the medieval monastery there was vocation without capitalism or industrial productivity (although the beginnings of both have been traced there[1]); in the Italian nobility of the Renaissance there was capitalism without piety or industrialism; and in the Soviet Union today there is industrialism without piety or capitalism. These activities are quite different; but they are all pursued as means to an end, hence they involve some postponement of gratification even though they have also become ends in themselves for many.

We assume that man has always had to work almost constantly in order to survive, and pride ourselves on having lowered the average work week to about forty hours. It is a shock, therefore, when anthropologists tell us that on average, the adults in surviving hunting and gathering societies work only 3-5 hours per day![2] Still, we tend to answer questions about our identity by giving our occupation, and work is always taken seriously. Marx thought that human nature itself had been shaped through the changing forms of work.[3]

Reprinted from *Listening*, 16, (Winter, 1981), pp. 56–67. Copyright 1981 by *Listening*. Reprinted by permission.

Freud could even identify the work attitude in general with what he called the "reality principle," and with psychological maturity.[4]

Play, on the other hand, is thought of as childish and trivial activity, almost by definition. My *Encyclopedia Britannica* (1970) has no article on "Play" in general, but only one of "Play in Animals," in which the author explains that this behavior is characteristic of immature animals. (How about the animals closest to man—chimpanzees, dolphins, otters—which seem to spend most of their adult lives playing?) In contrast to Herbert Spencer's discredited theory that play is getting rid of "surplus energy," this author says, we now understand that it serves an important biological function: it develops the animal's sensory and motor skills so it can perform adult activities—feeding, fighting, mating—more effectively.[5] Jean Piaget's excellent analyses of types and levels of play are limited to showing how children's play prepares us for serious adult life.[6] A huge recent anthology of articles by psychologists about play, edited by Jerome Bruner and others, is entirely confined to this theme.[7]

But anyone who *looks* will see that adults in all cultures spend a lot of time playing, and watching others play, even in the narrowest sense of the word: games, sports, and leisure pastimes of all kinds. Is this just a holdover from childhood, or to keep our sensori-motor skills in fighting trim? Hardly. Anyone watching the Olympics, or even a weekend golfer lining up a putt, knows that this cannot be the whole story. We take these activities too seriously, devote too much time and energy to

159

them and derive too much satisfaction from them, for this sort of explanation to be plausible.

Play Is Serious

I want to briefly sketch the opposite theory, that the psychological structure of play is characteristic of the fullest development of human nature, so that it *cannot* be taken too seriously. This is an ancient idea, developed cogently by Friedrich Schiller in the 18th century,[8] but given classic formulation by Johan Huizinga in 1938 in his brilliant book *Homo Ludens*. He showed, at the very least, that there is an important ''play element'' in all the ''serious'' cultural activities of man: art, religion, science, politics, business, even warfare.

> The great archetypal activities of human society are all permeated with play from the start. Take language, for instance—. . . Behind every abstract expression there lies the boldest of metaphors, and every metaphor is a play upon words. Thus in giving expression to life man creates a second, poetic world alongside the world of nature.
>
> Or take myth. . . . In myth, primitive man seeks to account for the world of phenomena by grounding it in the Divine. . . . Or finally, let us take ritual. Primitive society performs its sacred rites, its sacrifices, consecrations and mysteries, all of which serve to guarantee the well-being of the world, in a spirit of pure play truly understood.
>
> Now in myth and ritual the great instinctive forces of civilized life have their origin: law and order, commerce and profit, craft and art, poetry, wisdom and science. All are rooted in the primaeval soil of play.[9]

Huizinga's argument has not received the attention it deserves from philosophers. In fact, there is no article on ''Play'' in the Collier-Macmillan *Encyclopedia of Philosophy,* and not a single listing in the Index. Huizinga is mentioned only once in the *Encyclopedia,* in connection with a different topic.

I will make use of some of Huizinga's ideas; but one need not agree with him that cultural activities are *essentially* forms of play in order to grant that the structural parallels are striking. Another thinker with a similar theory, also neglected by philosophers, is the French sociologist Roger Caillois, who distinguishes four basic types of play and correlates them with four types of culture.[10] Still another author, Jacques Ehrmann, criticizes both Huizinga and Caillois for not going far enough. After noting that they both define play in contrast to ''ordinary life'' or ''reality,'' he continues:

> It is legitimate to wonder by what right ''reality'' may be said to be *first,* existing prior to its components—play in this case . . .—and serving as their standard. How could ''reality'' serve as a *norm* and thereby guarantee *normality* even before having been tested and evaluated in and through its manifestations? For . . . there is no ''reality'' (ordinary or extraordinary!) outside of or prior to the manifestations of the culture that expresses it. (Italics in original.)[11]

Later in the same essay, Ehrmann makes his own position explicit:

> Each text contains in itself its own reality . . . Play, reality, culture, are synonymous and interchangeable. Nature does not exist prior to culture.[12]

A complete response to Ehrmann would take me too far into the arguments against idealism in epistemology and metaphysics, along the lines of G.E. Moore's ''A Defense of Common Sense'' (1923). I will simply assume in this essay that nature *does* exist prior to culture, although *ideas* about nature are of course elements of culture; and that play can be defined over against ''reality'' in some philosophically adequate sense of that term. In the same way, one may explore the world of Shakespeare without raising the issue of whether Shakespeare's world is *the* world. Prima facie, at least, play is a form of ''make-believe,'' even when the player is utterly absorbed in it.[13] I will develop this concept, then offer a common-sense argument that play is therefore not as fully serious as several other human activities, including work. I will make use of a distinction by Kurt Riezler between a playful *attitude* and the *object* with which this attitude is concerned.[14] Unlike Riezler, however, I will argue that since the object is not fully real but a symbolic creation, the attitude should not be fully serious.

First of all, every game, from football to chess and from hide-and-seek to poker, has rules. These rules not only define which moves are permitted and which are not, and which win and which lose, but what is to count as a move in the game. They thus define a subset of all the infinite possible things people can do as constituting a system, a "little world" or microcosm, in which each move has a meaning in relation to all the others. These rules are freely adopted by anyone who wants to play, and have been invented and refined by generations of players to make the resulting microcosm as interesting as possible.[15] I think this analysis applies even to solitary pastimes like bouncing a ball or "doodling" on the edge of a piece of paper. The rules of a game like football can be very complex, but the world they create is still far simpler than the real world, with its infinity of possible categories of behavior. Each game or sport picks out a few of these, stylizes them, and creates a relatively simple model of reality defined solely in these terms. This relative simplicity, with its corollary of unambiguous meanings and definite outcomes, may well be the basic reason for the appeal of all sorts of games.

Games are simpler than reality also by being limited in space and time. Often they are played on a field or court, with the line between microcosm and the rest of the world neatly drawn on the ground or marked on the board. The beginning and end of the game are clearly defined, creating a finite stretch of game time. Less organized forms of play have vaguer boundaries, but are still spatio-temporally limited in a way that life as a whole is not.[16]

Finally, the participation of players in a game is also necessarily limited, in that we do not play with our whole self, but only with that aspect of us which is relevant to the game-world as defined by the rules. A college football player puts plenty of energy into the game, but his grades in school, his love life, and a hundred other things about him are irrelevant when he steps onto the field. He may be totally committed to playing as well as he can, but objectively the player is a limited aspect of the person, a role.[17] It is this feature of play which makes it questionable whether a gambler who risks more than he can afford to lose is still "playing."

Now the arts and sciences share many of these same features. Here too we create symbolic worlds, simpler than the real one by virtue of selecting a certain problem, then responding to it in terms of a network of conventionally defined concepts and methods.[18] Is this only a superficial parallel, or does it reveal a deep spiritual or intellectual relationship?

The easiest case is the arts. Many people have pointed out that one "plays" music,[19] that dramatists write "plays" in which actors "play" roles, etc. If "play" is defined as free participation in a simplified microcosm modeled on a few selected features of life, and created for its intrinsic interest rather than for any utilitarian purpose, the arts are either forms of play or very much like play. Suzanne Langer's analysis of the "world" created by each artistic genre, and ultimately by each individual work within the genre, helps to make this comparison plausible.[20] In fact, the only real question here is why we use the word "work," as I just did, to refer to the products of artistic creation but not to those of playful activities. The answer lies in realizing that the terms "work" and "play," while often contrasted, are not really opposites. They refer to different *aspects* of an activity—"work" to its instrumental relation to other activities, and "play" to the free spirit in which it is carried on—so that the same activity can be both "work" and "play" from different points of view; and *parts* of play can be work, like practicing to be a better athlete or musician, and perfecting "teamwork."

There is a characteristic attitude associated with playful activities, and a different ("serious") attitude associated with work. Since one cannot have both attitudes at once, we generally assume that one cannot work and play at the same time. But since it is possible, even common, to be serious about play, and to be playful about one's work, the attitude characteristic of each must be only *part* of its nature. A professional athlete, actor or musician is "working" in the sense that he gets paid. His attitude may, however, still be the same as it was before he "turned pro," when he loved "playing" so much he got good enough to make a living at it. Certainly, the activity itself is still essentially the same. And the activity of amateurs may involve long hours of drudgery to perfect one's technique, and may require careful coordination of parts in a whole, both features of many kinds of work. Rather than struggling to decide whether a serious athlete, actor or musician is working *or* playing, it seems better to admit that these activities (and many others) are *both* working and playing in themselves, whatever the participant's attitude on a particular occasion (or at a particular moment!) may be.[21] If this argument is sound, the International Olympic Committee should stop making a distinction where there is characteristically no difference, and permit professional athletes to compete in the games.

It is a bit harder to see what the sciences have in common with play. While the arts involve imagination, and thus are free (like play) to transcend ordinary reality, it seems that science is tied to the explanation of whatever exists. Granted, a scientist can be creative in inventing hypotheses; but does he not differ from the philosopher and the poet in just this, that unlike them he must bear the burden of proof, must show that his hypotheses conform to the facts? There is certainly a kernel of truth in this assumption; but such commonsense realism about science has been problematic at least since Hume and Kant, and was dealt a serious blow by T.S. Kuhn's *The Structure of Scientific Revolutions*.[22] Kuhn showed that at any given time each branch of science is guided in its theorizing and research by a "paradigm" or basic model,

and that changes from one paradigm to another are brought about more by persuasion than by proof, so that science cannot be sharply distinguished from rhetoric. While Kuhn's position is still controversial, most philosophers today seem to agree that science is an activity of creative model-building in which the model can never be compared to nature directly, and is known to be a simplification which at best approximates to it.[23] Just as the rules of football, although complex, are simple compared to real life, so the equations of a scientific theory are always simpler than the process they attempt to portray. Can the scientist's state of mind be compared to that of the player or the artist? While they may sometimes be thinking of practical uses to which their discoveries may be put—in medicine, for example—it is typical for a scientist to be captivated by the intrinsic beauty and interest of the ideas themselves. Jacob Bronowski, in his BBC-TV series "The Ascent of Man," has beautifully captured this aesthetic character of science, and the lack of any fundamental distinction between science and art in this respect.[24]

If the psychological structure of adult play is similar to that of the arts and sciences, "education for leisure" becomes far less paradoxical than is commonly supposed. The creation of, and joyful participation in, simplified versions of life defined by a freely adopted set of rules begins to look less like a temporary respite from serious activity, and more like the characteristic human response to the world. The fact that some people play games or sports better than others, just as some are better artists or scientists than others, also becomes more significant. Playing is *not* something we all do by "instinct," but a form of behavior that must be learned, that is learned better by some than by others, and that presumably could be learned better by everyone if it were better taught. Play and games should be used in school not only as "simulations" of reality, so that students will be better prepared for their jobs in the "real world," but as valuable activities in their own right. The equation of the world of work with reality, and the "worlds" of play with childish fantasy, is philosophically naive.[25]

But Not Fully Serious

While the argument I have just summarized undoubtedly has merit, the conclusion that play can be as serious as any other human activity seems too strong. An adult who devotes himself primarily to playing games, or to being "number one" at some particular game, does seem to lack something. But the same can be said, for the reasons outlined above, of the arts and sciences. To take any of these for life itself attributes too much importance to the enjoyment of our own symbolic creations, and not enough to coping with reality in its intractable fullness. Granting that life can be made "meaningful" by interpreting it in terms of symbols—the world can be imagined as a "kingdom" (with "God" as the "king"), history as a "drama," a "contest," etc.—we must never forget that symbols are deliberate simplifications. Drawing on the same analysis of play as the enjoyment of a symbolic microcosm, I suggest that play should therefore *not* be taken with full seriousness. My argument will be analogous to the critique of "idolatry" by the ancient Hebrew prophets, and to the "seriousness and labor of the negative" in Hegel's *Phenomenology of Spirit*.

When a friend says, "Don't play games with me," what exactly does he mean?[26] He wants to be taken seriously. He wants to be reacted to in his own terms, not just as part of someone else's scenario, however clever and creative. Each of us constructs an interpretation of each of our acquaintances, and of humanity in general. We interact with people in terms of these interpretations, and usually this works fine. But when we know someone well, he expects our interpretation of him to be not only more accurate, but also *open* to his reality. We are not free to relate to him as we

please in the face of resistance. We have a moral obligation—perhaps this is even our most fundamental obligation—to be *responsive* to other people as they are in themselves, as opposed to our own mental reconstructions of them. Kant was making this point, I think, when he argued that morality concerns persons in themselves, while theoretical understanding is only of "phenomena" or "objects." Likewise, existentialists from Kierkegaard to Sartre have emphasized the need to respect the "otherness" of other people.

This idea may be generalized to include other animals and plants, in fact the whole of nature. The ecology movement has combined with increasing awareness of non-Western cultural attitudes to "raise our consciousness" about the narrowness of the Western exploitative relationship to nature. "Nature is like a great machine," said Descartes. His successors omitted the "like," and proceeded to find as many ways as possible to put that machine to work for us. Just as we should be open and responsive to the full reality of other people, so we should ideally be equally open and responsive to all of nature. From this perspective the medieval bestiaries, with their moral homilies on each species of animal—"the elephant and his wife represent Adam and Eve," "the ibex symbolizes learned men,"[27]—illustrate the same Western tendency to see in nature only what we ourselves have put there for our own purposes. Perhaps, as historian Lynn White, Jr. has argued, this tendency goes back to the Book of Genesis;[28] perhaps it is even universal. Still we must recognize it as a weakness, and struggle to overcome it.

If play, art, and science all involve the creation of simplified microcosms which at best approximate to reality, these reflections suggest that none of them should be taken with full seriousness. This idea is bound to seem strange: if the works of Michelangelo or Shakespeare or Einstein are not fully serious, what is? Surely not the pathetic attempts of the ordinary person to eke out a modest living. The paradox becomes more tolerable if we think of Michelangelo and Shakespeare and Einstein not as typical artists and scientists, but as rare exceptions. I suggest that their work is of great seriousness not quâ artists or scientists, but because each of them was responsive to the fullness of reality. This is what made them great. They *transcended* the activity of model-building, of "playing" with ideas even in Huizinga's extended sense, and let in some of the icy wind from the great world—the "macrocosm"—outside.

One may try to define "art" and "science" normatively, of course, so that "true art" always involves such transcendence and "true science" is always revolutionary.[29] But then most "artists" and "scientists" should really be called by other names. When Plato (or Socrates) first defined "true" being normatively, so that "true" humanity is an ideal that might never be exemplified, it was itself a great achievement of philosophical "transcendence"; but today it is only a rhetorical gambit, and of dubious value. We might as well admit that most practicing artists and scientists remain securely within the symbolic worlds that they and their colleagues have created, delighting in the discovery of ever new implications of their own ideas. This is the "play element" in the arts and sciences, and I do not mean to denigrate it. On the contrary, it *is* a characteristically human response to the world, and one which can call forth seemingly inexhaustible talent and ingenuity.

Riezler says that whenever the attitude of artists toward their work has been "merely playful," this indicates decay, a second-rate work, the end of a style. He says that a "real artist" recognizes an "unconditional obligation" to strive for a "mysterious something" in his work, to follow a "supreme lead" which is "not man-made" and which renders art "as earnest as religion to the religious man."[30] Such romanticism about art is not unfamiliar; but the weakness of the *argument* involved is that the same phrases *could* be used about playing sports, or indeed any other activity. (Also, some of the greatest art seems "merely playful": Bach's *Art of Fugue*, Sterne's *Tristram*

Shandy, Joyce's *Finnegans Wake* come to mind.) Granted that one's *attitude* toward art or science may well be "deadly serious," the question is whether this attitude is any more warranted by the nature of the activity than in the case of play. I am arguing that it is not.

How about other human activities? Is work, for example, intrinsically more serious than play? Yes and no. The *forms* of work vary widely from one culture to another, and are often as laden with symbolic significance as any art form. In this sense work too is a human creation, and gives rise to a "microcosm" of limited importance. But insofar as it is necessary for survival, it involves coping with the very real limitations and exigencies of the human condition. This is epitomized in the revealing phrase "making a living." It is what led Freud to associate work with the "reality principle." Perhaps human life would be less meaningful without some form of creative symbolism; but it would not exist at all without work. This simple tautology is often overlooked in our preoccupation with "the search for meaning." In this sense, and *only* in this sense, there is a residual seriousness about work that is found neither in play, nor in the arts and sciences. One can make a living as an artist or a scientist, of course, just as he can as a football or bridge player; but this is an accident of our culture, irrelevant to the intrinsic structure of the activities.

The same sort of distinction should be made with regard to other human activities, such as sex and war, which are often embedded in a rich web of symbolic significance, but which are at bottom matters of brute survival. Huizinga has a chapter on the "play element" in warfare, by which he means the element of ritual, of limiting conventions and stylized heroism, by which almost every culture (at least prior to the 20th century) has sought to distinguish the conflicts between men from the ruthless struggles of animals.[31] We need not enter the controversy among anthropologists about the nature of warfare, and whether it is really any different from those animal struggles. The point here is that man has always *thought* it was, and tried to make it as "cultural" as possible, including concocting ideological justifications for it. But to lose oneself entirely in the game or ritual aspect of war, as some outstanding military strategists have done (Genghis Khan? Napoleon?), is to lack due respect for the human misery involved. In that sense, it is to "play" at war; to not take life seriously enough.

There was no need for a chapter on "the play element in love" in Huizinga's book, since the poets have long made this theme familiar to everyone. What is perhaps more likely to be forgotten in this age of "the pill" is the absolute necessity of sex for the survival of the species, and the respect for the connection between love and procreation that this implies. Without love, sex is less "meaningful"; but without procreation we would not be here. There is thus a "residual seriousness" in sexuality that is not present in sentimental or romantic love.

Finally, what about religion? Man's playfulness has shown itself profusely in thousands of myths and rituals, in religious art and architecture, etc. Some religious traditions have encouraged this impulse more than others: Hinduism more than Theravada Buddhism, ancient Greek cults more than Roman, Catholicism more than Protestantism. Recently several American theologians have tried to revive the sense of devout playfulness in our Protestant, work-oriented culture.[32] But even the most austere Calvinist believes that human life is given meaning by the "drama" of sin and redemption in the Bible, from the Fall of Adam through the Death and Resurrection of Christ to the Last Judgment. From the perspective of this essay, this story is another of man's attempts to give form and structure to his life by interpreting it in familiar categories, inevitably simplifying and obscuring other insights—for example, those of Buddhism— in the process. Obviously this is highly controversial territory; but to commit oneself entirely to any one set of theological categories would seem to be "idolatry" in the Biblical sense: taking a

manmade symbol to be reality itself. In religion, where the concern is with whatever is ultimately or fundamentally real, it is especially important to keep our symbols distinct from what can never be exhaustively symbolized, but must be responded to. The great theologians have all emphasized this "transcendence";[33] but it tends to be forgotten by zealots and sectarians. If play is like art and science in creating and enjoying a symbolic microcosm, this applies to much of religion too. But central to religion is the insistence that reality always transcends our interpretations of it, and the demand that we respect that transcendence. It is this, and only this, that merits our total commitment. While there is an important "play element" in religion, it would be highly misleading to treat religion (as Huizinga seems to do) as a form of play, or even to regard play as essential to it. Some forms of mysticism (the so-called "via negativa") seem to be attempts to eliminate all vestiges of play from religion, including the play of ideas; and what remains may well be the most precious gift of religion to mankind.

A full discussion of the relation of play to art, science, work, love, and religion would obviously require a book, even many books. Some of these books have already been written, and among these Huizinga's *Homo Ludens* is a masterpiece. In combating our tendency to regard play as trivial and childish, however, he seems to have gone too far toward the opposite extreme; and Ehrmann goes even further. My purpose here has been to sketch the outlines of a more balanced treatment, based on reflective common sense. Play is *not* just letting off surplus energy, nor is it just preparation for mature functioning. It can be a fully adult activity, similar in psychological structure to art and science, and deserving of the same respect. It is one of the ways in which we "humanize" our lives and render them "meaningful." But it also lacks the ultimate seriousness of morality, work, war, and religion, each of which brings us up against the limits of our formidable symbolic powers, and forces us to deal as whole persons with reality.

Notes

1. L. Mumford, *The Myth of the Machine* (New York: Harcourt, Brace and World, 1967), pp. 263–72.

2. M. Sahlins, *Stone Age Economics* (New York: Aldine-Atherton, 1972), chap. I.

3. See especially "Private Property and Communism," in *Karl Marx: Early Writings*, trans. and ed., T.B. Bottomore (McGraw-Hill, 1963), pp. 152–67.

4. See D. Riesman, "The Themes of Work and Play in the Structure of Freud's Thought (1950)," reprinted in *Individualism Reconsidered* (Free Press of Glencoe, 1954), pp. 310–33.

5. *Encyclopedia Britannica*, Vol. 18, pp. 39–41.

6. *Play, Dreams, and Imitation in Childhood* (New York: Norton, 1951), Part 2.

7. J. Bruner, A. Jolly, K. Sylva, eds., *Play, Its Role in Development and Evolution* (New York: Basic Books, 1976).

8. *On the Aesthetic Education of Man*, trans. R. Shell (Yale University Press, 1954).

9. *Homo Ludens* (Boston: Beacon Press, 1950), pp. 4–5.

10. *Man, Play, and Games*, trans. M. Barash (New York: Free Press, 1961).

11. J. Ehrmann, "Homo Ludens Revisited," in *Game, Play, Literature* (Boston: Beacon Press, 1968), p. 33.

12. *Ibid.*, p. 56.

13. Huizinga, *op. cit.*, p. 13.

14. "Play and Seriousness," *Journal of Philosophy*, XXXVIII (Sept. 1941), p. 209.

15. On the evolution of flexible attitudes towards the rules of games, see J. Piaget, *The Moral Judgment of the Child*, trans. M. Gabain (New York: Free Press, 1965), Part I.

16. The last two paragraphs are based loosely on Huizinga, *op. cit.*, especially chap. I; the next paragraph, however, has a different emphasis from his. For more on the symbolic nature of play, see R. Grathoff, *The Structure of Social Inconsistencies* (The Hague: M. Nijhoff, 1970), chaps. 6–7.

17. I assume here that a person is more than any set of roles that he plays. This may seem questionable, especially in certain pathological cases: "multiple personality," etc. But even G.H. Mead, one of the founders of "role theory," showed in *Mind, Self and Society* (University of Chicago Press, 1934), pp. 173–78, that we must postulate an active agent—the "I"—interacting with and constituting all its systematic relationships with "significant others." I think some such analysis applies to all forms of human pathology as well, and has important implications for moral and legal issues in psychiatry; see T. Szasz, *The Myth of Mental Illness* (Dell Publishing Company, 1961), pp. 223–40.

18. My approach in the next few paragraphs derives broadly from Ernst Cassirer's "philosophy of symbolic forms."

19. In many languages, not just English; see Huizinga, *op. cit.*, chap. 2.

20. *Feeling and Form* (New York: Scribner's, 1953).

21. I have developed this argument more fully in " 'Work' and 'Play,' " *Ethics*, Vol. 81, no. 1 (October 1971), pp. 33–47.

22. University of Chicago Press, 1962. Compare also C. Turbayne, *The Myth of Metaphor* (University of South Carolina Press, 1962), published in the same year. But most of the credit should go to Hegel.

23. M. Polanyi, *Personal Knowledge* (University of Chicago Press, 1958); K. Popper, *Conjectures and Refutations* (New York: Basic Books, 1962); P. Feyerabend, *Against Method (Minnesota Studies in the Philosophy of Science IV*, 1970), etc.

24. J. Bronowski, *The Ascent of Man* (Little, Brown, and Company, 1973).

25. The classical ideal of "education for

leisure'' has been revived recently, on somewhat different philosophical grounds from the ones outlined here, by Thomas Green in *Work, Leisure and the American Schools* (New York: Random House, 1968).

26. I owe this example to Edgar Z. Friedenburg.

27. *The Bestiary,* trans. T.H. White (New York: Capricorn Books, 1954), pp. 27, 30.

28. ''The Historical Roots of Our Ecologic Crisis,'' *Science,* Vol. 155 (March 10, 1967), pp. 1203–07.

29. This is precisely Riezler's position, *op. cit.,* pp. 211–13.

30. *Ibid.,* p. 211.

31. *Op. cit.,* pp. 89–104.

32. E.g., Harvey Cox, *Feast of Fools* (Harvard University Press, 1969); Robert Neale, *In Praise of Play* (New York: Harper & Row, 1969); Sam Keen, *To a Dancing God* (New York: Harper and Row, 1970).

33. See Thomas Aquinas, Maimonides, Al-Ghazali, etc. Wilfred Cantwell-Smith has shown with scholarship and eloquence that therefore no one religious tradition can claim a monopoly of spiritual insight, in *The Meaning and End of Religion* (New York: Harper Torchbook, 1978).

Play and Sport

JEAN-PAUL SARTRE

There remains one type of activity which we willingly admit is entirely gratuitous; the activity of *play* and the "drives" which relate back to it. Can we discover an appropriative drive in sport? To be sure, it must be noted first that play as contrasted with the spirit of seriousness appears to be the least possessive attitude; it strips the real of its reality. The serious attitude involves starting from the world and attributing more reality to the world than to oneself; at the very least the serious man confers reality on himself to the degree to which he belongs to the world. It is not by chance that materialism is serious; it is not by chance that it is found at all times and places as the favorite doctrine of the revolutionary. This is because revolutionaries are serious. They come to know themselves first in terms of the world which oppresses them, and they wish to change this world. In this one respect they are in agreement with their ancient adversaries, the possessors, who also come to know themselves and appreciate themselves in terms of their position in the world. Thus all serious thought is thickened by the world; it coagulates; it is a dismissal of human reality in favor of the world. The serious man is "of the world" and has no resource in himself. He does not even imagine any longer the possibility of *getting out of* the world, for he has given to himself the type of existence of the rock, the consistency, the inertia, the opacity of being-in-the-midst-of-the-world. It is obvious that the seri-

ous man at bottom is hiding from himself the consciousness of his freedom; he is in *bad faith* and his bad faith aims at presenting himself to his own eyes as a consequence; everything is a consequence for him, and there is never any beginning. That is why he is so concerned with the consequences of his acts. Marx proposed the original dogma of the serious when he asserted the priority of object over subject. Man is serious when he takes himself for an object.

Play, like Kierkegaard's irony, releases subjectivity. What is play indeed if not an activity of which man is the first origin, for which man himself sets the rules, and which has no consequences except according to the rules posited? As soon as a man apprehends himself as free and wishes to use his freedom, a freedom, by the way, which could just as well be his anguish, then his activity is play. The first principle of play is man himself; through it he escapes his natural nature; he himself sets the value and rules for his acts and consents to play only according to the rules which he himself has established and defined. As a result, there is in a sense "little reality" in the world. It might appear then that when a man is playing, bent on discovering himself as free in his very action, he certainly could not be concerned with *possessing* a being in the world. His goal, which he aims at through sports or pantomime or games, is to attain himself as a certain being, precisely the being which is in question in his being.

The point of these remarks, however, is not to show us that in play the desire to *do* is irreducible. On the contrary we must conclude that the desire to do is here reduced to a certain desire to be. The

Reprinted by permission of Philosophical Library, Inc. from *Being and Nothingness* by Jean-Paul Sartre, translated by Hazel E. Barnes, © Copyright, 1956, by Philosophical Library, Inc., New York.

act is not its own goal for itself; neither does its explicit end represent its goal and its profound meaning; but the function of the act is to make manifest and to present to *itself* the absolute freedom which is the very being of the person. This particular type of project, which has freedom for its foundation and its goal, deserves a special study. It is radically different from all others in that it aims at a radically different type of being. It would be necessary to explain in full detail its relations with the project of being-God, which has appeared to us as the deep-seated structure of human reality. But such a study can not be made here; it belongs rather to an *Ethics* and it supposes that there has been a preliminary definition of nature and the role of purifying reflection (our descriptions have hitherto aimed only at *accessory* reflection); it supposes in addition taking a position which can be *moral* only in the face of values which haunt the For-itself. Nevertheless the fact remains that the desire to play is fundamentally the desire to be.

Thus the three categories "to be," "to do," and "to have" are reduced here as everywhere to two; "to do" is purely transitional. Ultimately a desire can be only the desire *to be* or the desire *to have*. On the other hand, it is seldom that play is pure of all appropriative tendency. I am passing over the desire of achieving a good performance or of beating a record which can act as a stimulant for the sportsman; I am not even speaking of the desire "to have" a handsome body and harmonious muscles, which springs from the desire of appropriating objectively to myself my own being-for-others. These desires do not always enter in and besides they are not fundamental. But there is always in sport an appropriative component. In reality sport is a free transformation of the worldly environment into the supporting element of the action. This fact makes it creative like art. The environment may be a field of snow, an Alpine slope. To see it is already to possess it. In itself it is already apprehended by sight as a symbol of being.[1] It represents pure exteriority, radical spatiality; its undifferentiation, its monotony, and its

whiteness manifest the absolute nudity of substance; it is the in-itself which is only in-itself, the being of the phenomenon, which being is manifested suddenly outside all phenomena. At the same time its *solid* immobility expresses the permanence and the objective resistance of the In-itself, its opacity and its impenetrability. Yet this first intuitive enjoyment can not suffice me. That pure in-itself, comparable to the absolute, intelligible plenum of Cartesian extension, fascinates me as the pure appearance of the not-me; What I wish precisely is that this in-itself might be a sort of emanation of myself while still remaining in itself. This is the meaning even of the snowmen and snowballs which children make; the goal is to "do something out of snow"; that is, to impose on it a form which adheres so deeply to the matter that the matter appears to exist for the sake of the form. But if I approach, if I want to establish an appropriative contact with the field of snow, everything is changed. Its scale of being is modified; it exists bit by bit instead of existing in vast spaces; stains, brush, and crevices come to individualize each square inch. At the same time its solidity melts into water. I sink into the snow up to my knees; if I pick some up with my hands, it turns to liquid in my fingers; it runs off; there is nothing left of it. The in-itself is transformed into nothingness. My dream of appropriating the snow vanishes at the same moment. Moreover *I do not know what to do* with this snow which I have just come to see close at hand. I can not get hold of the field; I can not even reconstitute it as that substantial total which offered itself to my eyes and which has abruptly, doubly collapsed.

To ski means not only to enable me to make rapid movements and to acquire a technical skill, nor is it merely to *play* by increasing according to my whim the speed or difficulties of the course; it is also to enable me to *possess* this field of snow. At present *I am doing something to it*. That means that by my very activity as a skier, I am changing the matter and meaning of the snow. From the fact that now in my course it appears to me as a slope to go down, it finds again a continuity and a unity which it had lost. It is at the moment connective tissue. It is included between two limiting terms; it unites the point of departure with the point of arrival. Since in the descent I do not consider it in itself, bit by bit, but am always fixing on a point to be reached beyond the position which I now occupy, it does not collapse into an infinity of individual details but is *traversed toward* the point which I assign myself. This traversal is not only an activity of movement; it is also and especially a synthetic activity of organization and connection; I spread the skiing field before me in the same way that the geometrician, according to Kant, can apprehend a straight line only by drawing one. Furthermore this organization is marginal and not focal; it is not for itself and in itself that the field of snow is unified; the goal, posited and clearly perceived, the object of my attention is the spot at the edge of the field where I shall arrive. The snowy space is massed underneath implicitly; its cohesion is that of the blank space understood in the interior of a circumference, for example, when I look at the black line of the circle without paying explicit attention to its surface. And precisely because I maintain it marginal, implicit, and understood, it adapts itself to me, I have it well in hand; I pass beyond it toward its end just as a man hanging a tapestry passes beyond the hammer which he uses, toward its end, which is to nail an arras on the wall.

No appropriation can be more complete than this instrumental appropriation; the synthetic activity of appropriation is here a technical activity of utilization. The upsurge of the snow is the matter of my act in the same way that the upswing of the hammer is the pure fulfillment of the hammering. At the same time I have chosen a certain point of view in order to apprehend this snowy slope: this point of view is a determined *speed,* which emanates from me, which I can increase or diminish as I like; through it the field traversed is constituted as a definite object, entirely distinct from what it would be at another speed. The speed organizes the ensembles at will; a specific object does or does not form a part of a particular group ac-

cording to whether I have or have not taken a particular speed. (Think, for example, of Provence seen ''on foot,'' ''by car,'' ''by train,'' ''by bicycle.'' It offers as many different aspects according to whether or not Béziers is one hour, a morning's trip, or two days distant from Narbonne: that is, according to whether Narbonne is isolated and posited for itself with its environs or whether it constitutes a coherent group with Béziers and Sète, for example. In this last case Narbonne's *relation to the sea* is directly accessible to intuition; in the other it is denied; it can form the object only of a pure concept.) It is I myself then who give form to the field of snow by the free speed which I give myself. But at the same time I am acting upon *my matter.* The speed is not limited to imposing a form on a matter given from the outside; it *creates* its matter. The snow, which sank under my weight when I walked, which melted into water when I tried to pick it up, solidifies suddenly under the action of my speed; it supports me. It is not that I have lost sight of its lightness, its non-substantiality, its perpetual evanescence. Quite the contrary. It is precisely that lightness, that evanescence, that secret liquidity which hold me up; that is, which condense and melt in order to support me. This is because I hold a special relation of appropriation with the snow: *sliding.* This relation we will study later in detail. But at the moment we can grasp its essential meaning. We think of sliding as remaining on the surface. This is inexact; to be sure, I only skim the surface, and this skimming in itself is worth a whole study. Nevertheless I realize a synthesis which has depth. I realize that the bed of snow organizes itself in its lowest depths in order to hold me up; the sliding is action *at a distance;* it assures my mastery over the material without my needing to plunge into that material and engulf myself in it in order to overcome it. To slide is the opposite of taking root. The root is already half assimilated into the earth which nourishes it; it is a living concretion of the earth; it can utilize the earth only by making itself earth; that is, by submitting itself, in a sense, to the matter which it wishes to utilize. Sliding, on the contrary, realizes a material unity in depth without penetrating farther than the surface; it is like the dreaded master who does not need to insist nor to raise his voice in order to be obeyed. An admirable picture of power. From this comes that famous advice: ''Slide, mortals, don't bear down!'' This does not mean ''Stay on the surface, don't go deeply into things,'' but on the contrary, ''Realize syntheses in depth without compromising yourself.''

Sliding is appropriation precisely because the synthesis of support realized by the speed is valid only for the slider and during the actual time when he is sliding. The solidity of the snow is effective only for me, is sensible only to me; it is a secret which the snow releases to me alone and which is already no longer true *behind my back.* Sliding realizes a strictly individual relation with matter, an historical relation; the matter reassembles itself and solidifies in order to hold me up, and it falls back exhausted and scattered behind me. Thus by my passage I have realized that which is unique *for me.* The ideal for sliding then is a sliding which does not leave any trace. It is sliding on water with a rowboat or motor boat or especially with water skis which, though recently invented, represent from this point of view the ideal limit of aquatic sports. Sliding on snow is already less perfect; there is a trace behind me by which I am compromised, however light it may be. Sliding on ice, which scratches the ice and finds a matter already organized, is very inferior, and if people continue to do it despite all this, it is for other reasons. Hence that slight disappointment which always seizes us when we see behind us the imprints which our skis have left on the snow. How much better it would be if the snow re-formed itself as we passed over it! Besides when we let ourselves slide down the slope, we are accustomed to the illusion of not making any mark; we ask the snow to behave like that water which secretly it is. Thus the sliding appears as identical with a continuous creation. The speed is comparable to consciousness and here symbolizes consciousness.[2] While it exists, it effects in the material the birth of a deep quality which lives only so long as the speed exists, a sort of reassembling which conquers its indifferent exteriority and which falls back like a blade of grass behind the moving slider. The informing unification and synthetic condensation of the field of snow, which masses itself into an instrumental organization, which is *utilized,* like the hammer or the anvil, and which docilely adapts itself to an action which understands it and fulfills it; a continued and creative action on the very matter of the snow; the solidification of the *snowy mass* by the sliding; the similarity of the snow to the water which gives support, docile and without memory, or to the naked body of the woman, which the caress leaves intact and troubled in its inmost depths—such is the action of the skier on the real. But at the same time the snow remains impenetrable and out of reach; in one sense the action of the skier only develops its *potentialities. The skier makes it produce* what it can produce; the homogeneous, solid matter releases for him a solidity and homogeneity only through the act of the sportsman, but this solidity and this homogeneity dwell as properties enclosed in the matter. This synthesis of self and not-self which the sportsman's action here realizes is expressed, as in the case of speculative knowledge and the work of art, by the affirmation of the right of the skier over the snow. It is *my* field of snow; I have traversed it a hundred times, a hundred times I have through my speed effected the birth of this force of condensation and support; it is *mine.*

To this aspect of appropriation through sport, there must be added another—a difficulty overcome. It is more generally understood, and we shall scarcely insist on it here. Before descending this snowy slope, I must climb up it. And this ascent has offered to me another aspect of the snow —resistance. I have realized this resistance through my fatigue, and I have been able to measure at each instant the progress of my victory. Here the snow is identical with *the Other,* and the common expressions ''to overcome,'' ''to conquer,'' ''to master,'' etc. indicate sufficiently that it is a matter of establishing between me and the snow the relation of master to slave. This aspect of appropriation which we find in the ascent, exists also in swimming, in an obstacle course, etc. The peak on which a flag is planted is a peak which has been *appropriated.* Thus a principal aspect of sport—and in particular of open air sports—is the conquest of these enormous masses of water, of earth, and of air, which seem *a priori* indomitable and unutilizable; and in each case it is a question of possessing not the element for itself, but the type of existence in-itself which is expressed by means of this element; it is the homogeneity of substance which we wish to possess in the form of snow; it is the impenetrability of the in-itself and its non-temporal permanence which we wish to appropriate in the form of the earth or of the rock, etc. Art, science, play are activities of appropriation, either wholly or in part, and what they want to appropriate beyond the concrete object of their quest is being itself, the absolute being of the in-itself.

Thus ontology teaches us that desire is originally a desire *of being* and that it is characterized as the free lack of being. But it teaches us also that desire is a relation with a concrete existent in the midst of the world and that this existent is conceived as a type of in-itself; it teaches us that the relation of the for-itself to this desired in-itself is appropriation. We are, then, in the presence of a double determination of desire: on the one hand, desire is determined as a desire to be a certain being, which is the *in-itself-for-itself* and whose existence is ideal; on the other hand, desire is determined in the vast majority of cases as a relation with a contingent and concrete in-itself which it has the project of appropriating.[3]

Notes

1. See section III.
2. We have seen in Part Three the relation of motion to the for-itself.
3. Except where there is simply a *desire to be*—the desire to be happy, to be strong, etc.

Play and Possibility

JOSEPH L. ESPOSITO

General accounts of game-playing have been advanced from various perspectives within the social sciences. From the sociological and psychological point of view, social play is regarded, in fact, as serious business—a primitive rehearsal for socialized activity (Huizinga), modeling behavior in children, sacred activity gone secular, etc. Caillois, for example, claims that "games and toys are historically the residues of culture."[1] Games re-enact cosmic and social dramas whose meanings have long been forgotten; the wish for heavenly conquest becomes the greasy pole; football, the titanic struggle between opposing forces over possession of the solar globe; kite-flying, the soul's quest to escape the body; hopscotch, the labyrinth; chess, the drama of medieval life; and monopoly, I would imagine, practice in how to get on in civil society.

The social function of games has also been the subject of considerable study. Correlations between culture and social structures have been sharpened by comparative studies of the degree of cheating allowed by cultures in their games. It has been claimed, for example, that it is characteristically Anglo-Saxon to have a game (golf) in which the possibilities of cheating are unlimited but in which the game immediately loses its point once the rules are violated. Social opportunity has been tied to the idea of being a "good sport"; sportsmanship and the premium it places on self-discipline are supposed to result from an upper-class which need no longer hope to achieve economic success. In these circumstances, playing with dignity becomes nearly everything; winning, not very much.

Social attitudes toward games of chance are supposed to reflect deep-seated commitments on the part of a society to a certain theory of history and the way rewards are distributed. In opposing lotteries, a society is supposed to be saying that it is not wise to look for success apart from intended and disciplined effort.

Such sociological accounts of games are, for the most part, informative and, sometimes, even enlightening. That there is some legitimacy to the approach can be seen simply by noting the connection between certain kinds of games and the audience they attract. In this limited sense, Caillois is correct in noting that "games discipline instincts and institutionalize them."[2]

There is also a large body of philosophically uninteresting material on games—primarily games involving athletic competition—which emphasizes the benefits of being educated physically. Fitness, readiness, good citizenship, the proper attitude—these are the rewards of sport, looked at from the psycho-developmental point of view.

In my view, however, in neither the sociological nor psychological approaches to game-playing is there anything like a treatment which explains what it is specifically in a game-playing situation which makes that form of human activity so prevalent. One reason for this, I think, is that not enough attention has been given to the players' point of view. In short, what has not been asked is what is in the game-situation which makes players want

Reprinted from *Philosophy Today,* XVIII, (Summer, 1974), pp. 137–146. Copyright 1974 by *Philosophy Today,* Carthagena Station, Celina, Ohio 45822. Reprinted by permission.

to engage themselves within it. All of the classification of the forms of play (for example, games of competition, chance, mimicry, vertigo) only tangentially touch upon what I shall characterize below as the common-root experience of all game-playing, an experience which any reflective participant recognizes as the essential point of game-playing, and which even the more unreflective participants can be made to see if probed in the proper manner.

Work is often contrasted to play, the implication being that play is an escape from the rigors of highly structured activity directed toward a practical goal. Work involves the routine; play is the special event. Work is serious; play is engaged in for fun. This is the view we would expect to be plausible to someone who is a part of an industrial culture. For the economic demands of that culture are such that a person can only play games after his work for the day or week has been completed. It could then easily become apparent in such a context that the essential point of game-playing must be relaxation, entertainment, or excitement. I suspect that there are people who take up one form of game-playing or another just for these reasons. Their behavior may be explained as one more of the indications of social imitation in mass society or as the result of successful recruitment by "leisure industry." However, they are not likely to take on interest in game-playing for any reason that would sustain such activity for very long. What would be lacking again is that root-experience I shall now attempt to characterize. In what follows I set out an element which appears to me characteristic of nearly all game-playing and then suggest in what way game-playing can be seen as a fundamentally integral human activity—one which may tie together and explain the plausibility of the other approaches.

Children have been noted to make up games out of the context of the moment. Rules are established, the "game" is played, and soon a verdict of success or failure is brought in. Then the "game" is finished, in many cases never repeated again. A child might decide that he "loses" if he steps on any of the cracks in the sidewalk pavement. A challenge is set up. And even if the stakes are pronounced as high ("Step on a crack—Break your mother's back!") no other sanction than the failure of staying off the crack itself is necessary for the playing of the game. In what could be called the "primal condition" of game-playing the child plays against himself. He sets up his own rules, assesses his performance against the rule-structured situation, and passes a verdict on himself. Beyond this the game can take on a social context. The children can compete against each other; they can make the game an occasion for hurling insults, strengthening allegiances, and so forth.

Analogously, game-playing in college and professional sports can take on a social meaning that may be charged with all sorts of emotional tensions, tensions which are, from the standpoint of the primal condition of play, really beside the point. Fan allegiance surely makes possible the use of athletics as a factor in achieving self-identity and self-awareness. For example, the growth of new major cities produced a corresponding growth in professional teams as a way these cities attempted to achieve in a short time an almost Hegelian-self-consciousness. But again, in none of this can we find the reasons games are played, even by professional athletes. True, a game would nowise be an object of such widespread interest unless it presented a challenge with which the fan wanted to associate himself. But his doing so may have nothing whatsoever to do with his appreciation, which may, in fact, be lacking, of what it is like to play the game itself. He may simply want a bit of the glory his own allegiance helps produce to rub off on himself. Those attracted to games because they present situations embodying the primal condition would play them even without an audience. The social effects of games are themselves socially determinate and, so, do not shed light, in my view, on the nature of game-playing. With respect to this social context of games, Caillois' remark that "games generally attain their goal only when they stimulate an echo of complicity,'' surely misrepresents the more important reasons games are played.[3] Games are created, not because of something that happens in the audience, but because of something the players themselves experience. Without such an experience, games would lose their point. Caillois' remark, indicative of most accounts of game-playing, fails to distinguish between the differing standpoints of player and audience.

The player of games, if reflective about what he is doing, realizes that even beyond the success of winning the game, there is the interest he takes in the very act of playing itself. It is this interest that is difficult to understand from the view of the spectator who sees the activity of play only as a means to realizing the object of the game. To the player, the game, if properly constructed, presents not so much a challenge—in the usual sense of the word—as an opportunity to experience possibility. Games, in other words, are contrived situations, the purpose of which is to heighten and bring into focus the interplay between possibility and actuality. Each form of play, if my view is correct, should contain within it a moment when possibility can be acutely felt by the player.

Plessner has argued that ''play is always playing with something that also plays with the player . . .''[4] This point is correct, at least, in characterizing games played with elastic objects. In this case, it is the player's interaction with an object difficult to control that establishes the moment of possibility: in golf and tennis it is the moment of impact of ball and club or racquet; in basketball it is the moment of impact of ball and rim; in football, the handoff, kick or pass; and in soccer, the kick. The unpredictable bounce of the ball then creates almost immediate new situations for interaction and so also new possibilities.

Plessner's remark also can be made to apply to games played with nature. Rock-climbing is sport and not simply healthy exercise because it contains a moment of possibility—the foothold or grasp on the rock which might give way without notice. In sport-fishing it is the strike of the fish at the lure or bait. (Sporting fish, such as trout or bluefish, are those which attack suddenly and often unpredictably.) When nature has occasion to play with us, as also in sailing, surfing, hunting, gliding, etc., then these activities go beyond mere leisure activity and become occasions of sportive play.

My characterization of play as an encounter with possibility, unlike Plessner's, also has application to games of imitation. The moment to be sought by the child or actor playing someone else is that moment when he really feels he has become that person. Actors certainly speak of this struggle to make the role come alive, and children sometimes seem to behave as if they are momentarily convinced they are someone else. It is the difficulty of affecting such a transition and the clear possibility of failure which make games of imitation such a challenge to the imitator himself.

To anyone who observes game-playing activity from a non-participant point of view, the player's experience of possibility goes unnoticed. To such a person the interest players take in games is often fanatical or silly. Why, he asks, should someone walk around hitting a ball, spend hours shooting baskets with a basketball, entice fish with objects at the end of a line, or climb a mountain ''because it is there?'' The player himself, so long as he remains addicted to the experience of possibility contained in the situations of the game he plays, is left unmoved by such a criticism. The actual physical activity of the game—running, walking, moving pieces on a board, etc.—is of secondary importance to the player. He thinks nothing of sitting in a chair for hours or running furiously; his goal is the confrontation with possibility created out of the rules and structures of the game and his performance within that structure.

Existentialist philosophers have argued that what is most characteristic of human existence is what I have called ''the experience of possibility.'' In such an experience they see the source of our understanding of temporality, value, guilt, love and death. ''Higher than actuality stands *possibility,*'' notes Heidegger in *Being and Time.*[5] In less cryptic terms this means that a large part of the meaning of human experience is derived from the structuring that experience is given in time. Ortega y Gasset characterized this capacity to see experience as an unfolding of interlocking events as man's essentially historical nature; for Heidegger, it results from man's being as *Dasein.*

Heidegger distinguishes the sense of "possibility" I am referring to here from "modal possibility." The latter is either what is logically possible or what is "merely" possible ("the contingency of something present-at-hand").[6] In either of these latter cases we judge something to be possible from an abstract standpoint. The former kind of possibility, however, is something more important to us: "Possibility, as an *existentiale,* does not signify a free-floating potentiality-for-Being in the sense of the 'liberty of indifference' (*libertas indifferentiae*). In every case *Dasein,* as essentially having a state-of-mind, has already got itself into definite possibilities. As the potentiality-for-Being which [it] *is,* it had let such possibilities pass by; it is constantly waiving the possibilities of its Being, or else it seizes upon them and makes mistakes. But this means that *Dasein* is Being-possible which has been delivered over to itself—*thrown possibility* through and through."[7]

What Heidegger seems to be saying is that not all of our possibilities are regarded with equal seriousness. Some possibilities we could entertain as courses of actions are "merely" possible; we have no actual concern to tie them into the fabric of our experience. Still others present occasions for momentous decisions—they become specifically *our* possibilities and so become the object of serious concern. Perhaps nothing is so important an object of seriousness than a lost possibility. No reality may be felt as intensely as the unreality of what was not but should have been. *Existentiale* possibilities, in short, must be ones in which we have a stake through concern; in other words, ones in which failure (making mistakes) is an issue for us.

In *Being and Time* Heidegger argues that the experience of possibility is something *Dasein* seeks to avoid. Such avoidance becomes another occasion in the life of *Dasein* when the ontic and onto-logical become reversed. *Dasein* simply denies that its possibilities are real possibilities for itself. In Heidegger's words, "This levelling off of *Dasein's* possibilities to what is proximally at its everyday disposal also results in a dimming down of the possible as such. The average everydayness of concern becomes blind to its possibilities, and tranquillizes itself with that which is merely 'actual.'"[8] This desire to become undiscriminating about possibilities to philosophers like Kierkegaard, Sartre and Berdyaev, among others, is supposed to result from the burden of our freedom to choose the possible. The stakes in life itself are too high for us, they argue. Bad faith, inauthentic existence, the false stance of objectivity, and "slavery" (Berdyaev) are the responses we make to this situation. The institutionalization of human experience in the form of culture and civilization is supposed to mitigate our feeling of uneasiness in the face of possibility. The basis for this burden of confronting possibilities in life is precisely supposed to be in the condition that nothing is literally repeated in life. Having a conception of life, as we do, we see those possibilities which are an issue for us as demanding a timely response. This means that regret and guilt become part of the stakes of choosing in life, notably the result of mistakes.

Life itself could probably be played as a game were it not for the fact that most of us feel that death is an untimely imposition on life and not its natural culmination. The possibility of having no further possibilities, to use Heidegger's expression, reads back into the decision we make in the process of living a meaning etched in anxiety and dread. Everydayness helps to sanitize the implications of death by announcing national and other social purposes which have a seeming durability personal life does not have. What is missing in life as a whole, however, is any clear, unambiguous sense of what the rules of conduct are or how success is to be gauged. Then also in life there is not a final summing up and resolution of the effort by the players themselves, something I think essential to game-playing.

To those who believe in a life beyond life, it

is possible to regard life as a single rule-governed episode, say, for example, the journey of a soul toward its salvation. Huizinga has noted this connection between the forms of play and the sacred forms of ritual and myth.[9] So also has Santayana.[10] In the game of salvation there can be winners and losers. And the importance theologians give to the fine points in a doctrinal controversy suggests that they hold the tenets of creeds with the same regard as rules of any games must be held by those who play the game.

Kierkegaard argued that it was in the ethical and religious attitudes that the experience of the possible was most threatening to us. Aesthetic and intellectual attitudes were adopted, in his view, precisely in order to avoid the former attitudes: "Ethically regarded, reality is higher than possibility. The ethical proposes to do away with the disinterestedness of the possible by making existence the infinite interest."[11] Morality requires that certain possibilities have a demand on us to be actualized. These are the possibilities which, Kierkegaard is saying, have a greater status than the merely possible or, at least, ought to have if we are to be moral beings. They are possibilities which are supposed to engender dread in us.

In religion the dread of freedom is characterized by Kierkegaard as the experience of the demoniacal. And overcoming the demoniacal through resolute faith is the affirmation of freedom. One of the ways the demoniacal appears—a way appropriate to the present discussion—is in the sudden: "In case the demoniacal were something somatic," Kierkegaard writes, "there never would be the sudden. When a fever, insanity, etc., come back again, one discovers at last a law, and this law in some degree annuls the sudden. But the sudden recognizes no law. It does not properly belong among natural phenomena but is . . . the expression of unfreedom."[12] It is not an accident, Kierkegaard observes, that Mephistopheles appears suddenly in dramatization of *Faust*. His actions must not be continuous and, therefore, understandable.

In the religious attitude, Kierkegaard suggests, we have an example of the desire to overcome the fear of the possible by affirming the victory achieved by the "knight of faith" over the demoniacal. Precisely the opposite account of religion has been given by Feuerbach: religion closes off freedom and the possibility through its reification of value into a heteronomous structure which then is grasped, even if with passionate conviction, only by means of an act of accepting faith. It becomes a game where more effort is given to interpreting the rules than in playing the game, with the effect that daily ritual diminishes and intellectualized creeds take precedence. Of course, Kierkegaard also attacked intellectualized religion, but to Feuerbach and, more recently, to Santayana, his emphases on internal resolve would give little opportunity for one to experience the encounter with the possible in a playful manner.[13] To Feuerbach and Santayana the use of symbol and ritual afforded the opportunity to act out "salvation," i.e., experience religious value, in concrete, sensuous terms. Kierkegaard noted that mime was sometimes capable of capturing the sudden.[14] He should have realized that it could be possible to overcome the sudden in the same fashion—through mimic forms of religious ritual, what are usually called religious "celebrations" today.

Sportive playing is not burdened with difficulties of the religious or ethical attitude. Religion attempts to schematize all of life and so takes on too much. Aside from monastics most of us do not play the game of salvation throughout the daily course of our lives. The secular game, on the other hand, is of more modest design. It takes place within spatial and temporal confines more fit for human comprehension. Even beyond this, however, its most ingenious feature is that it produces a genuine experience of the possible where there is really, from life's standpoint, nothing at stake. Here the player can have his cake and eat it too. Unlike the religious drama, which is a matter of life or death where ultimate consequences weigh so heavily on the players, the sportive player enjoys a situation where all the fascination of encountering the possible exists, but where he can also assure himself that it is only a game. William

James' observation that in certain cases faith in a fact can create that fact has application here. The player gives his total commitment to the game-situation created out of the rules, and in so doing he makes the possibilities of action within the game possibilities that are an issue for him.

Kierkegaard and other existentialists have enjoined us to face the possibilities in our daily lives courageously, even while telling us how burdensome that could be. "If I were to wish for anything," Kierkegaard wrote, "I should not wish for wealth and power, but for the passionate sense of the potential, for the eye which, ever young and ardent, sees the possible. Pleasure disappoints, possibility never. And what wine is so foaming, what so fragrant, what so intoxicating, as possibility!"[15] The possibilities in game-playing are such for the player that they do not disappoint him, at least, so long as the player makes the commitment to the game situation. Game-playing, then, might be seen as the opportunity to experience genuine, yet benign, possibilities outside the context of daily life. This notion can help tie together several of the more prevalent accounts of game-playing. For some players, interacting with the possibilities of sportive play can serve as a rehearsal for dealing with life's possibilities. For them it is true that sport builds character. For others, the orderliness and lack of ambiguity in game-playing makes this form of play an escape from practical living—hence, the view of sportive play as leisure activity.[16] In either case the game remains the circumstance in which the outcome of actions lies within the game itself. How the player integrates his activity as a player with the other forms of activity in which he is engaged will depend largely on the character of the player himself. However, such social consequences of game-playing, as noted earlier, which comprise a great deal of the study of play, really do not explain the essential purposes of play in the manner I have here attempted.

Eugen Fink and Howard Slusher have both advanced theories of play somewhat similar to the one I have given. Both contend, in the words of Fink, that play is "an essential element of man's ontological make up."[17] In general, however, they devote most of their effort to a description of *consequences* of the experience of the possible without emphasizing the centrality of the experience itself. Fink, for example, emphasizes the spontaneity of play and the experience of "human timelessness in time . . . a glimpse of eternity."[18] Pure spontaneity, as Dewey often noted, does not have in it the makings of a constructive experience. The goal of the player is not spontaneity itself, but rather the reward of alert action—that is, encountering and quickly controlling possible events. It is the player's timely reaction to desired or undesired possibilities that makes spontaneity an asset in play. He seeks the goal of spontaneous action—viz., a satisfying measure of himself against possible contingencies. The timelessness of play should actually be characterized as the timeliness of action in the play situation. Rather than a sense of timelessness, the player experiences the effects of time's passage in games where events usually occur suddenly, or can (as in chess).

Slusher's account of sportive play largely hinges on his view that in sport, particularly competitive sport, the player gets the opportunity to be purely a self engaged in the act of becoming—self-transcendence, to use Sartre's term. "To open oneself up, and, in the process, transcend the self is one potential contribution of sport," Slusher notes.[19] The body as object is transcended toward the body as pure activity; awareness of the other as co-player becomes transcended toward the awareness of coexistence of all players into a team, what Heidegger and Sartre characterize as the experience of "being-with."[20]

Sport, in my view, does make such forms of transcendence possible; *how* it does this has been the subject of my concern. It is precisely one's opening oneself to *possibilities* that produces the feeling of achievement or failure so essential to the awareness of having become something one was not at an earlier point. There is no opportunity for such mental, physical or social transcendence in games which are either too easy or too difficult, in games, in other words, in which the player overwhelms the possibilities of the game or the possibilities of the game overwhelm the player.

Bibliography

1. Roger Caillois, *Man, Play, and Games,* trans. Meyer Barash, Free Press, (New York, 1961), p. 58.
2. *Ibid.,* p. 55.
3. *Ibid.,* p. 39.
4. Helmuth Plessner, *Laughing and Crying,* trans. J.S. Churchill and M. Grene, Northwestern Univ. Press, (Evanston, 1970), p. 77.
5. Martin Heidegger, *Being and Time,* trans. John Macquarrie and Edward Robinson, Harper and Row (New York, 1962), p. 63 (H38).
6. *Ibid.,* p. 183 (H143).
7. *Ibid.,* p. 183 (H144).
8. *Ibid.,* p. 239 (H194–195).
9. Johan Huizinga, *Homo Ludens,* Beacon Press, (Boston, 1950), p. 26.
10. George Santayana, *The Sense of Beauty,* Dover, (New York, 1955), p. 18. Also Howard S. Slusher, *Man, Sport and Existence: A Critical Analysis,* Lea and Febiger, (Philadelphia, 1967), Ch. IV.
11. Soren Kierkegaard, ''The Subjective Thinker'' from *Concluding Unscientific Postscript* in *A Kierkegaard Anthology,* ed. Robert Bretall, Modern Library, (New York, 1946), p. 226.
12. Soren Kierkegaard, *The Concept of Dread,* trans. Walter Lowrie, Princeton Univ. Press, (Princeton, 1967), p. 116.
13. The Deer Park episode in the *Concluding Unscientific Postscript* indicates the seriousness with which Kierkegaard regarded daily life in the light of faith.
14. *The Concept of Dread,* p. 118.
15. ''Diapsalmata'' from *Either/Or* in *A Kierkegaard Anthology,* p. 35.
16. John Updike's *Rabbit Run* is one of a number of works whose theme is that of the ex-athlete disillusioned with life because of the ambiguity he finds in it.
17. Eugen Fink, ''The Oasis of Happiness: Toward an Ontology of Play,'' in *Game, Play, Literature,* ed. Jacques Ehrmann, Beacon Press, (Boston, 1968), p. 19.
18. Fink, p. 21.
19. Slusher, p. 11.
20. *Ibid.,* pp. 37 and 63ff.

Man and Sport

KEITH ALGOZIN

Paul Weiss answers his question about man's fascination with athletic events in terms of our concern for excellence: "Unlike other beings we men have the ability to appreciate the excellent. We desire to achieve it. We want to share in it." The athlete, consciously or not, desires to achieve bodily excellence, and spectators of the game participate in the athlete's achievement: "In the athlete all can catch a glimpse of what one might be were one also to operate at the limit of bodily capacity." "The athlete is matched here by the thinker, the artist, and the religious man. Without loss of their individuality they too instantiate man in splendid form, which the rest of us accept as an idealized portrait of ourselves. But the athlete shows us, as they do not, what we ideally are as bodies."

Weiss's account of the game seems to me to invite a still fuller characterization of what it is about this event that rivets men's attention and calls forth their passionate emotional involvement. In this paper I will begin by sketching Weiss's account of the game and then I will go on to suggest those ingredients which are perhaps implied in Weiss's account but which seem to me to deserve more explicit stress.

I

For Weiss the model of the athletic display of bodily excellence is the Olympic Games. Men and women of all nations have trained their bodies to challenge the resistances of space and time with the speed, endurance, strength, accuracy and coordination prescribed by the various particular sports. Each nation is a team of athletes, a single body whose members strain to function at the outermost limits of their specialized capacities. The nations contest in the Games for the prize of being judged by impartial witnesses to represent human bodily excellence. A particular sport is the rules which keep a particular contest fair and at the outermost limits of man's bodily capacity in a particular situation. It is also the historical record of man's bodily achievement under these trying conditions. Thus, all sports taken together may be said to represent the form of the human body, both the self-definition it has so far achieved and the rules by which this effort to define itself by outdoing itself is to continue. In the Games the contesting athletes instantiate this event of human bodily self-definition; they represent the human body challenging itself to surpass itself. The record-setting victor of the Game instantiates human bodily excellence on behalf of all nations: all stand united and completed in the public display of that bodily excellence which all have helped reveal, which all now know they cherish, and which all now vicariously share: "By representing us the athlete makes all of us be vicariously completed men. We cannot but be pleased by what such a representative man achieves." To be sure, the athlete cannot claim to represent the full nobility of human being; he represents only the bodily substrate of those higher, spiritual values which are instantiated in the spiritual leaders of civilized

Reprinted from *Philosophy Today*, (Fall, 1976), pp. 190–195. Copyright 1976 by *Philosophy Today*, Carthagena Station, Celina, Ohio 45822. Reprinted by permission.

mankind and whose enactment by all men would be the crowning unification of nations. For this reason men in pursuit of excellence need neither engage in athletics nor even enjoy the Games. But in the Games all men can find a facet of the perfection they seek as men, and one which reflects in its way their higher aspiration: "By participating in a public game with others, the athlete makes an intimately related whole with them. The more the players act together, despite competition, to produce a common game, the closer is the bond uniting them all. Athletes make more vital that harmonization of men which religious men suppose God's presence in the world entails."

I have tried here to suggest the philosophical scope of Weiss's theory of sport for this can serve as a measure of any attempt to contribute further to our philosophical understanding of the widespread fascination with athletic events. As Weiss suggests, a plausible philosophical account of this phenomenon must relate it to man's basic concern for fulfillment. Sport is philosophically relevant because it does in fact attract men of all times and cultures; the wide-spread attraction of sport is the philosopher's clue that there is operative here, in some fashion, the most basic tendency of human nature. And a genuinely philosophical account of sport must therefore clarify what this activity is and must be simply because it is a human activity reflective of human nature itself. It must tie sport into the whole round of human endeavor by means of some principle which relates sport to everything else that men strive to be and do. Now when Weiss views the game in this philosophical light he sees it as an instance of man's universal endeavor to discover and to be what he is. Better: for Weiss the game is but one instance of man actually being what he is, namely, the communal discovery of what he is. While those involved in the game are focusing upon bodily excellence, the philosopher sees that what binds all elements of the game into a whole and relates that whole to all other human endeavor is the event of communal self-revelation itself. Thus, sport is seen to reflect human nature itself, and such a vision is the goal

of a philosophical account. An alternative philosophical account of the game (which Weiss spars with throughout his book) highlights the factor of competition and the fanatical enthusiasm of those whose deepest concern is for the victory, not of impersonal human excellence, but of their own side over the other: sport as but one instance of men's basic concern to subjugate one another, a socially acceptable outlet for aggression, a training ground for war. Both of these accounts of sport agree that the game is an occasion for some specifically human fulfillment, and both can argue their case without appealing to what those who are involved in sport say they find fascinating about the game. For only one who sees the game in the light of the whole of human endeavor can judge what it is that is really going on here.

While I would agree that a philosophical account of the fascination of the game cannot rest its case upon a poll of sports enthusiasts, I discern in myself and others some agreement as to why the game is exciting, an agreement which rests upon a common experience which may at first seem trivial but which may urge us to reflect upon the fascination of the game from a yet broader perspective. This broader perspective would not so much settle the issue between these two rival views of sport as it would complement them both. It would abstract from their disagreement over what particular goal men seek by nature and focus attention upon the assumption they share, that man is primarily a being that seeks to enact goals. The common experience that persuades me to occupy this middle ground between these opposed theories of the game is simply that of the excitement that is engendered by a close contest. The suspense of a close contest grips and excites us, but what is remarkable about this excitement is its independence from our concern with either bodily excellence or subjugation: while it may heighten because the contest is between the world's best athletes, it may be present also during a close contest between the world's worst; and while it may heighten when we are committed to one side over the other, it can occur too when the contest is close and we do not really care who wins. In short, when we speak of a good game we are often referring neither to how it is being played nor to who is winning but simply to the fact that it is close.

Excitement over the closeness of the game stands somewhere between the enthusiasm of the biased fan and the enthusiasm of Weiss's impartial spectator of bodily excellence. This excitement refers, I believe, to something which is at the core of our fascination with the game but which both of these opposed views must treat as relatively accidental, namely, its vivid display of utterly effective action. Both of these views are prevented from appreciating fully men's fascination with athletic events because their attempt to explain sport in terms of one particular human goal as opposed to another leads them to neglect the display here of what all human beings, regardless of their particular goals and by virtue of their very situation as human beings, must find pleasing: "unalienated action," action which is both fully illuminated with knowledge of the difference between victory and defeat and utterly effective because reverberating for good or ill throughout its world. What game is played, what victory and defeat are taken to mean, may well be personally or culturally relative, but there remains—especially at the climax of the game—that which can be the object of universal fascination—the display of unalienated action. In the following remarks I will try to place our fascination with the close game in the context of our human aspiration for unalienated action.

II

We humans exist by nature beyond our animal issue of merely staying alive; we search for that proper way of life which connects our accidental being to the substance of the world. It is our privilege, apparently, to know that something is at stake in the world, that there is a difference between good and evil; and it is our despair not to know what this difference is, or, when we feel we know it, to be powerless to enact it. In the paralysis of doubt, indecision and powerlessness we are on the periphery of things, outside of the garden looking in, and aware of our nakedness. To be sure, we are always dressed up to some extent in our language, in the revelations uttered by generations of men upon discovering what we are to be and do in various situations. In a language the basic units of meaning are the model actions of good conquering evil which are our customs and institutions, and to live within a language is to be guided daily by such models. In the light of such a model we see everything in our situation as it really is: this or that resistance or assistance to the good we supremely value. And if, in addition, we have the power to enact these immediate, absolute, final judgments upon our situation, our action is unalienated: we trip the lever which effectively transforms our situation of unfulfillment into one of fulfillment. Here, in the midst of unalienated action (e.g., doing everything appropriate to romantic love, driving a car, managing affairs of state) we are on top of the world, moving spontaneously from within our immediate perception of challenges and tools, keeping alive that order of things to which we are committed. Yet in the midst of our daily lives we often find ourselves estranged: we sense that what we can effectively bring about in the world is ultimately worthless. This estrangement occurs when we find that our attempts to bring about what is supremely good are ineffective. It occurs too when we no longer know what it is supremely good to be, do, and bring about in the world, when, consequently, everything in our world, including ourselves, appears ambiguous because we do not know precisely what is really at stake in our lives. In either case our action is alienated for we suspect that what we are doing is trivial. And we experience here our human aspiration toward that action by which we would engage, as spontaneously and effectively as we drive our cars or eat our meals, in the issue that is ultimately at stake in our lives. In such unalienated action we would be shaping our lives in terms of that meaning which defines our relationship to the essence of the world; we would be god-like actors who effectively order our world to conform to our idea of its truth; we would ourselves be the model of being human in the world. It is against this background of our human aspiration for unalienated action that I believe we may best appreciate our fascination with the close game.

The game carries to completion that mastery of our situation which we all glimpse in our daily lives but which often eludes us. In this connection it should be stressed that the world of the game is a real world: the players, who are trying throughout to keep their victory alive, are not actors following a script but men responding on their own to the challenges of contingent events. Thus the game can be a microcosmic display of what we feel we ourselves are going through when we are keeping alive the bonds of a family, remaining faithful in crises to a friendship, meeting challenges of a profession. But the game is an unreal world: it rests upon the arbitrary two-dimensional decision that in this delimited setting we will be dedicated solely to this definition of victory. The result of this decision is a single context of action, horizontally delimited from beginning to end and ruled vertically throughout by a hierarchy of unquestioned values. Especially important here are the sharp, unequivocal definitions of victory and defeat and the elimination of all skeptical questioning as to whether such victory is supremely worth-while. When more important matters break in upon the game, trivializing it, its spell is broken. To enter the world of the game is to leave behind that dimension of ourselves which can doubt and belittle all values and is to live within a closed system of action whose every present moment is both fully illuminated by a well-defined supreme value and transparently related to every other moment in the whole. Precisely such a closed, translucent system is necessary if there is to be a display of unalienated action.

At every moment of the game the athlete is at the center of this translucent system, acting spontaneously from within his immediate apprehension of what everything in his world truly is and requires in the light of the whole. At his disposal are the supreme value he is to realize, the unambiguous facts of his situation, and his practiced capacity to counter obvious resistances with obvious tools. He is the picture of action flowing smoothly from final judgments and decisions of conscience in appropriate response to the changing situation. (This illusion of conscious judgment and decision is heightened by slow-motion reruns of his action coupled with commentary on what was presumably going through his mind.) The delightful opportunity this spectacle affords those who know the intricacies of the game should not be underestimated. We men crave to pass final judgments upon things and often enough we make fools of ourselves by doing so, but in the midst of the translucent game we are in that delightful situation of being able to estimate with some accuracy the ultimate worth of actions and of men.

Finally, in addition to being unalienated in the sense of being fully illuminated with the knowledge of victory and defeat, the athlete's action is unalienated in the sense of being decisively effective in settling the issue at stake in this world. What is at stake, what victory in the game means to us—whether the triumph of bodily excellence or of ourselves over the other—is not as important here as the fact that an entire world is seen to be at stake, suspended between equally possible alternative completions and awaiting the decisive action that will settle its fate. At the center of this world the athlete is performing at every moment—especially at the climax of the game when all see that either victory or defeat might be the last word about this world—that utterly effective, world-reverberating action which, so unlike our own futile stabbing about, decides the fate of the world. At this moment it is as though the athlete is an extension of ourselves: we stretch in suspense toward knowing the outcome of the world and find in him the decisive action that settles the issue. Thus our dislike of chance outcomes and ties, and thus too our effort to pin-point the turning-point of the game. Man is the being to whom it can appear that the world is at stake, and games are ultimately symbols of the serious religious business of world-transfiguration and salvation. This feature of any game permits us to imagine that even the most minor contest is a world championship with everything riding on its outcome. It permits too widespread hero-worship of the athlete who has been at the absolute center of things performing the paradigmatic heroic action.

But from this perspective on athletic events as symbolic of world-salvation we should not be led to identify fascination with the game with the will to escape the real world: the game as an illusory world, like that of drunkenness or drugs, where defeated man can have the meaning and power denied him in the real world. No doubt the game can serve as the occasion for escape from reality, but it can just as well serve to display and confirm the lives of those men who are creatively engaged in unalienated action in the important social and political dimensions of any culture.

Are we then to view the fascination with the game as essentially human self-worship: the game as the image of human self-salvation, man playing God? I think not. I have located our fascination with the athletic game at the intersection of our human suspense about the outcome of the world and our human aspiration toward the unalienated action which decides the issue. Suspense is a broad category of fundamentally human experience which occurs whenever we are in doubt about an outcome. And, of course, doubtful outcomes are of the very stuff of our lives. We are the being who can surround any beginning with the open space of many possible alternative endings. We are in suspense during a joke, a roll of the dice, a sentence, our inquiry into a crime or the universe, a prayer to God, and, in general, from one moment to the next. But in the midst of our suspense we look always to that decisive operation of the essence of our situation which we believe will properly complete what has begun, and even when we believe that this essence of things is no human action whatever we think that some way of properly being ourselves is essentially bound up with its operation: the dice player's superstitious rituals, the penitent's good deeds or properly prayerful attitude, the scientist's appropriate attitude of impartial openness to the truth, etc., etc. In short, in our suspense we look always to some unalienated agency which is the essential truth of the situation, and we feel that there is something we are to appropriately be or do, some unalienated action we are to perform, in order to be properly attuned to this essential truth of things. Whatever agency is thought to be operative in the universe, unalienated action is the primary human concern, and I have contended only that because the athletic game is a vivid, concretely physical display of unalienated action itself, it can be an object of fascination for all men. In closing it should be noted that we have gone no distance in resolving the issue between Paul Weiss and his opponent as to whether athletic competition is essentially men's dialogical revelation of bodily excellence or an instance of their will to power. The question, whether communication or tyranny is the unalienated action given to men to perform lies subsequent to the general fascination with unalienated action itself, which can draw both groups to the game.

An Affair of Flutes:
An Appreciation of Play

KLAUS V. MEIER

In this paper,[1] I wish to proclaim, to extol, to champion, and to celebrate the cause of frivolity, uselessness, unproductivity, inconsequentiality, nonachievement, gratuitousness, irrelevance, and irreverence. In short, I wish to offer an apology for, and an appreciation of, play.

I

The phenomenon of play has permeated all of human history; no civilization has ever been free of its influences. "In culture we find play as a given magnitude existing before culture itself existed, accompanying it and pervading it from the earliest beginnings" (20: p. 14) up to contemporary phases of civilization.

Despite the universality of play, serious and scholarly investigations of its basic nature, structure, and intricacies have produced a multitude of diverse, sometimes indiscriminate, and not occasionally antithetical characterizations, at times imbued with value connotations alternately condemning or exalting the enterprise. This state of affairs is not altogether unexpected given the application of and references to the concept in current usage:

"Play" is a term which has been applied to many of the affairs of nature, man and God. We speak of a piston rod playing in its cylinder, a fountain playing streams of water, the play of wind on fields of grain, and the play of otters who fashion slides out of mudbanks and slip on their backs into the water. We see ourselves as players of games and musical instruments, participants in love-play, and players of both ends against the middle. It has even been asserted that existence itself is the play of the gods and that to be in tune with these gods is to be in play. (44: p. 148)

Therefore, it is hardly surprising to note the plethora of definitions[2] and theories which have been promulgated in attempts to delineate clearly and explicate carefully this multifaceted, wide-ranging, and highly elusive phenomenon.

In general, two major definitional procedures are extant in the voluminous play literature. The *first* is that of carefully and systematically analyzing the nature and structure of the play occurrence to attempt to outline its essential attributes, components, content, and significance.[3] The *second* major approach consists of attempts to decipher and to clarify the motivational context and structure that precedes, influences, and dictates participation in play. Posited causal explanations derived from this extensive and influential area of play behavior research and investigation include the following hypotheses: surplus energy; instinct practice; life preparation; learning and cognitive devel-

Reprinted from *Journal of the Philosophy of Sport*, VII, (1980), pp. 24–45. Copyright 1981 by the Philosophic Society for the Study of Sport. Reprinted by permission.

opment; recapitulation; relaxation and recreation; generalization and compensation; catharsis; psychoanalytic (the mastery of unpleasant experiences through playful repetitions); competence-effectance (a desire or need to produce effects in the environment); and finally, the triumverate of knowledge-seeking, boredom prevention, and arousal-seeking.

To enumerate, to analyze, and to evaluate comprehensively all aspects of the various fruits of these definitional inquiries, as significant as such a venture undoubtedly would be, is a separate, major research task, far beyond the limits, or for that matter, the concerns of the inquiry at hand. Thus, for the purpose of delineating the focus of the present study, I wish to provide a stipulative definition of the term.

It is here asserted that play may be perceived adequately not as a specific activity or set of activities, but rather as an orientation or way of organizing, experiencing, or relating to the activity. That is, play may be characterized as the context or quality of an activity; it is a stance, a manner of comportment, a fundamental mode of being-in-the-world. Play provides "a syntax, not a vocabulary" (38: p. 94); therefore, although the activity engaged in is not specified, the manner of pursuit is.[4]

There are two major necessary and sufficient components of the play stance. *First,* play is of necessity, a voluntary endeavor which cannot be forced, externally demanded, obligated, or imposed by necessity, coercion, or any form of duty. Indeed, during moments of play, man is fully his own master. *Second,* play is an autotelic activity. That is, play is an intrinsic, noninstrumental, self-contained enterprise which has only "internal finalities which do not transcend it" (14: p. 80) and is participated in for its own sake. Play is not a means to external ends or purposes; it does not further survival, sustenance, pragmatic, or materialistic interests. It is process rather than product oriented. The interest in play is the pursuit of internal values and ends; the reward is in the act. Thus, the prize of play is play itself.

In summary, play is herein characterized as an activity voluntarily undertaken for intrinsic purposes. Participation in any venture, including a game or a sport, in this manner, may therefore be legitimately termed a play occurrence.

II

In contemporary Western culture, the reign of the ideology of work gives us "highly limited permission to be useless" (45: p. 14). Enormous emphasis is placed on man as laborer or producer; everywhere he is fettered or chained to the process of work. Work may be defined as an instrumental or functional activity, exertion, task, operation, or occupation designed to manufacture, to construct, to provide or to accomplish useful results, efforts, goods, or services.

The search for reasons underlying the development and heralding of labor and production as "the ideal, and then the idol, of the age" (20: p. 192) must extend to the realms of both the sacred and the secular. The puritanic tradition of 19th century Protestantism, as an indicator of one source of the former, is succinctly exemplified in the following statement:

> Remember that we are sent into this world, not for sport and amusement, but for labor; not to enjoy and please ourselves, but to serve and glorify God, and be useful to our fellowmen. That is the great object and end of life. In pursuing this end, God has indeed permitted us all needful diversion and recreation. . . . But the great end of life after all is work. (19: pp. 124–125)

It is rather clear that this particular religious orientation[5] places work and play at opposite ends of a continuum, according a positive evaluation to the former and a more negative evaluation to the latter. It should also be noted that "the Protestant ethic linked sacred and secular worlds by regarding success at work as an indication of salvation and avoidance of work as a sign of damnation" (56: p. 8).

The remnants of the religious work ethic; the derivation and construction of a secular version of this code, which facilitated and encouraged the rise and development of the capitalistic structure of the Western world; the significant influences of the Industrial Revolution, when "all Europe donned the boiler-suit" (20: p. 192); the development and aggrandizement of the orderly and hard-working spirit of the American character and republic; and the general ideology of *homo faber* or "man as worker"[6]—all contributed to the increasing acceptance of the assumption that man's expectations and orientation should be framed and nurtured under the category of work and the understanding that he literally manufactures his identity and dignity by his fabrications as a functional entity in the work world.

The permeation, acceptance, and glorification of the spirit of work is readily apparent in contemporary language and discourse:

> It is not an accident that we regularly speak of homework, workbooks, work loads, workouts, workshops, workhorses, schoolwork, task forces, works of art, workrooms, work sheets, work-ups, classwork, work schedules, make-up work, board work, remedial work, course work and committee work. (Harper cited in 16: p. 89)

Man is what he does; his identity is his productivity. The assessment of an individual is conducted, therefore, by a scrutiny of what he has manufactured or attained; academic rank, position in the political or corporate hierarchy, and the length of his vitae or list of credits are all heralded as legitimate indicators of merit. Thus, personal satisfaction, value, and meaning are direct products of man's labor.

These widely acknowledged conceptions cause considerable difficulties. For one, if self-esteem and self-justification are derived predominantly, if not totally, from participation in productive occupations, it is readily apparent that "the most

concentrated points of identity-crisis" in society are to be found when persons are "ostracized from the world of work—the preemployed, the unemployed, and the postemployed." Since work grants identity and status, "those who are excluded from the arena in which values and meanings are produced are exiled from full humanity" (26: p. 123).

This state of affairs is reflected in the widespread belief that moral approval and, for that matter, an adequate income, are to be granted only to persons who are employed.[7] "This morality is captured in the derogatory labels ('welfare bums') applied to people who do not work. Individuals who hold steady jobs are evaluated, and often evaluate themselves, as better than those who do not work" (56: p. 8).

Given the utilitarian, acutely competitive approach of North American and European society—with its dedication to industrious endeavors, efficiency and thrift; "sobriety and rational calculation" (6: p. 10) and rigid discipline; and its unwavering devotion to the proper (i.e., most productive) use of time—it is readily apparent that there is little tolerance or adulation for enterprises perceived to contradict this general orientation.[8,9] While play, at the present time, is deemed permissible and worthwhile for children—because its utilitarian functions of learning, socialization, and general preparation for later life provide rational justification—it is often viewed as "a frivolous throwback to childhood" (58: p. 39) for adults.

A culture or society which praises work, of necessity, considers play to be problematic since "praise of work does not engender praise of play" (45: p. 15). Because play, in effect, produces nothing, neither material goods nor works of service, it is often described as basically empty, sterile, misspent or lost time, rather than as time well applied. Due to its lack of emphasis on practical affairs, it is perceived as being aimless, wasteful, and nonserious;[10] a form of idleness, trifling, or sloth abhorrent to the productive personality; or, perhaps, even as a morally unseemly enterprise characterized by profligate indulgence. Play or, for that matter, other leisure endeavors, often give rise to guilt and embarrassment or elicit shame in persons who seek justification through work (45: p. 13). Consequently, many avoid the opportunity for engagement in such activities by willingly working longer hours, accumulating overtime, taking second jobs, and abbreviating or eliminating vacation periods altogether to return to or remain at work.

Any pragmatic culture so heavily oriented toward productive, utilitarian enterprises will view the adult player as irresponsible, "foolish and incompetent, if not positively demented" (26: p. 128); "will find play to be incomprehensible and dangerous" (45: p. 12); and will tolerate it only with suspicion, guarded restraint, and constraints.

"Since praise of work is the ruling spirit of contemporary man . . . , the world of play is irrelevant and irreverent—irrelevant to the profane world of the worker and irreverent to the magical god of the worker" (45: p. 15). Therefore, play is largely ignored, criticized, disparaged, or even persecuted. For those who inhabit a world of total work, a call to play will sound socially immoral, "as though directed at the very foundations of human society" (52: p. 4). Of course, a call to play is just that, and for that very reason, as I will attempt to demonstrate subsequently, play should be openly, freely, unabashedly, and exuberantly celebrated.

III

Before developing the thesis of this paper further, it should be noted that "there is a current and rather pedestrian view of play, a sort of vulgar interpretation," which perceives play to be an occasional and peripheral phenomenon "on the margin of human life," and grants it, albeit begrudgingly, a restricted, supplementary place in the affairs of man as a recreative pause or temporary "surcease from burdens," through pleasant distraction or diversion, which highlights by contrast the more genuine, important, and serious aspects of life (14: p. 77).

Further, play is frequently posited to serve a prophylactic or therapeutic service as recreation, warding off disasters and ills of the mind and body, and also developing health, fitness, and strength, thereby facilitating increased productivity. It will be helpful here to remember that "recreation," in the root, means literally to "recreate" or "create again." Ecob (9: p. 43), writing more than 60 years ago in a religious journal, urged his readers to understand that "the fundamental and most compelling reason for shorter hours of work, [is] that there may be ample time for the recreating process to restore the waste of vital force, and so make us whole for the next day's labor."[11]

However, if play is utilized as a break in routine for the purpose of returning recuperated to work, it is merely another utilitarian link in the chain, serving as a handmaiden to the productive enterprise, and thereby, demonstrating essentially a work orientation and structure. However, genuine play in its essence is not an instrument for the attainment of external ends, it is not primarily a mental or physical restorative (52: p. 31) and, most assuredly, it is compromised when it is considered as a "sort of Coca-Cola philosophy: 'the pause that refreshes' *in order that* one may do more work" (37: p. 70). Rather, as will be demonstrated subsequently, play is, at heart, use-less.

However, this perception is not widely recognized or acknowledged. A brief amplification of three particularly relevant instances will provide support for this contention. First, there is precious little play to be found in the orientation, content, or activity of many programs or departments of recreation. Frequently, such departments comport themselves as unannounced subdivisions of industrial psychology, charged with the task of making the child or laborer more productive and the school or work environment more tolerable through temporary diversion and relaxation.

Second, faculties of physical education, of course, are also often eligible for this criticism. Here "technocrats of the body," the repair and maintenance men of the human organism, function to tone up, recondition, heal, shape, and train the body (2: p. 90); health, physical fitness, strength, cardiovascular endurance, etc., are highly valued because of the postulated concomitant increases in labor concentration and output, absence of fatigue, and extended work life.

Third, and finally, contemporary, elite, high-achievement sport, although not laying claim to the play spirit, does much to destroy the possibility of its manifestation in other sport forms by its extremely conspicuous example. This form of sport may increasingly be characterized as the experimental science of human productivity. Highly regarded, if not apotheosized in contemporary Western society, the pursuit of excellence—which in its interpersonal forms entails the demonstration of very high degrees of proficiency, surpassing ability, and preeminence in the performance of sporting skills in comparison to the capacities and achievements of others—demands, at the very least, intense effort, concerted dedication, and sacrifice in the preoccupied search for increasingly productive modes and techniques to mobilize totally the athlete to attain maximum output and performance. Enormous ideological and material resources are consumed in the frantic drive for physical excellence, the hunt for new records, and the "manufacturing of champions." Highly specialized and rigid educational programs, laboratories, research institutes, experimental sport centers, and training camps staffed and directed by physiologists, biochemists, doctors, physical educators, psychologists, trainers, and other master technicians and engineers (2: pp. 18-19), work diligently to objectify the athlete's body to produce performance machines subordinated to the goal of ultimate efficiency. Thus, in preparation for athletic endeavors, the body is drilled, trimmed, strengthened, quickened, and otherwise manipulated to improve its fitness and functioning and is often handled as an instrument or utensil to be appropriately directed and mastered.

But where is play?

All three of the previously delineated occurrences or programs produce consequences which are most often negative;[12] such instances and ap-proaches are inappropriate and inadequate to fully comprehend the nature of man's embodied being and the possibilities of celebration inherent in play. In concluding this section, it may be asserted that an obsession with objectivity and productivity in physical efforts and activities renunciates the lived body; represses muscular sensuousness for expressive rather than instrumental ends; focuses exclusively on quantifiable matters to the exclusion of qualitative questions of bodily freedom, sensual gratification, and sexual expressiveness; desensitizes movement as a distinctive source of creative impulses and aesthetic experience; and finally, alienates the individual from his own body.

Several of the forementioned items, of necessity, will be addressed again in subsequent portions of this paper; however, attention must now be focused on a further discussion of some negative results of extrinsic and objective work orientations.

IV

Despite the praise and adulation accorded to work, it is observed, on occasion, that much of modern labor no longer conveys the sense of satisfaction and personal worth that once resulted from the completion of a meaningful task. Although there are variations in the milieu and content of contemporary work structures, there is a remarkable degree of identity. The occupational situation of many contemporary workers is often perceived as an externally controlled and deserted void.

Work on assembly lines and elsewhere is often superficial, repetitive, frustrating, deadening, and meaningless. The fragmentation of labor, demanding only simplistic and automatic responses, and the depersonalization of the laborer often reduce man to a mere assemblage of tasks and functions, and consequently, engender powerful negative and reductive tensions producing perceptions of self-reification, anonymity, estrangement, and personal obliteration. "When the categories of function, efficiency, and output become central for identity, the result is alienation; the individual no longer feels himself to be a sacred nexus of life'' (on Marcel, 26: p. 126).[13]

These negative possibilities and factors all contribute to establishing work and concomitant instrumental orientations as significant contemporary social problems most worthy of careful deliberation, rather than mere unreflective acceptance.[14] Consequently, numerous social philosophers and critics stridently denounce the functional absorption of the individual and the tendency towards denial of self fostered by such environments. Nonetheless, the leveling demands of routine and uniformity frequently transcend the workplace to dictate the nature and modes of activities pursued in other aspects of daily life.

The individual often spends much of his time submerged and cloaked in anonymity, concerned only with assimilating and conforming to the attitudes, opinions, judgments, and role models advocated by the group. Participating solely in average, routine, and mechanical activities, he is engulfed in the communal consciousness of the crowd and its usually undistinguished dictates, and consequently, becomes merely a reflection of social functions and obligations.

In the mass (Kierkegaard's ''the public'' or ''the they'' and Heidegger's *das Man*), for example, everything appears as if it is in the best order. The individual takes his undifferentiated social existence for his whole life; he becomes accustomed to viewing himself in thinglike terms, as merely one unit among many others, as a given substance with predetermined properties and modes of action. Man is ''disburdened'' or ''accommodated'' by the crowd; the choices have already been determined. Participation in this superficial mode of existence and in solely distracting preoccupations and jejune activities, distorts, truncates, or even precludes self-knowledge and often results in self-estrangement.[15]

It should be obvious that the individual completely immersed in objectivity, with little awareness of his unique subjectivity, is unreceptive to avenues and modes of personal existence of a qualitatively different manner. Rather than permitting the individual to obtain insight into his true capabilities and possibilities of free choice or meaningful self-projection, mass dictates tend to foster personal obliteration.

V

With this extended preliminary discussion in hand, I wish to direct my comments beyond the forementioned negative confines to suggest that there is a great deal more available for individuals willing to enter the fields of frolic and to engage in true play activities; that is, more spacious pastures, gently rippling with softer more luxurious grass, saturated with deeper colors, and filled with richer fragrances than was previously described are most assuredly available.

It is herein contended that the realm of play, if participated in openly, offers obvious opportunities to explore alternative modes of awareness, to develop insights into and knowledge of new modes of being, and to explore radically different possibilities perhaps not readily available elsewhere.

During moments of intense, vivid, and individuating engagement made available in play, the individual is provided with numerous occasions to recover himself and to attain a new and more perceptive sense of his own unique, personal existence.

One of the most significant insights to be derived from existential philosophy is the disclosure that man is a ''being-ahead-of himself''; that is, ''being-possible'' and ''being-free for'' are integral ontological components of the human condition. Possibilities[16] are important issues for man and he has a concerned stake in their manifestation.

Sartre, of course, amplified this point by asserting that man is not what he is, but is what he is not. Man's contingency and facticity do not preclude his freedom or ability to ''stretch toward the future.'' ''Possibility is not to be defined by already known limits; the past does not exercise an absolute tyranny over the future'' (26: p. 174).

That is, man is an indeterminate, open question, a "not-yet," with the capacity to transcend present modes of being to structure himself by his choices, actions, and commitments to personal projects.[17]

Although man often avoids recognizing or acting on his possibilities, deliberately or otherwise, if he participates in the world in a state of open awareness, cognizant of the contingencies permeating human existence, possibilities take on a most profound significance. Indeed, "perhaps nothing is so important an object of seriousness than a lost possibility" (11: p. 142).[18] Furthermore, "we experience 'missed opportunities' as missed because we feel that our lives would have been more complete, richer, had we responded when the opening was present" (21: p. 40). Kierkegaard presented an appropriate reflection on this matter: "If I were to wish for anything" Kierkegaard wrote, "I should not wish for wealth and power, but for the passionate sense of the potential, for the eye which, ever young and ardent, sees the possible. Pleasure disappoints, possibility never. And what wine is so foaming, what so fragrant, what so intoxicating, as possibility!" (11: p. 144).

These sentiments, although primarily concerned with the phenomenon and experience of human love, have been echoed and supported recently in several significant philosophical studies[19] which perceive play to be an existentially fundamental occurrence, aptly and succinctly characterized as "an encounter with possibility" (11: p. 141).

Play is heralded as an opportunity and forum for man to experience and to luxuriate in the pursuit of possibilities outside of everyday concerns and contexts and relatively unconstrained by external interventions.

The world of genuine play opens man to new experiences. Hyland (21: p. 38) asserted that the individual's stance in the play situation may be partially distinguished from stances assumed in nonplay encounters by what he termed "responsive openness"—a heightened sense of openness toward the environment and context, as well as the capacity of responding to the possibilities

elicited by his receptivity to the play situation.[20] Here he is not abstracted or distanced in any way from his activity, rather he has the opportunity to perceive freshly, to experience novelty, and to immerse himself wholly. Further, as Keen pointed out, this ability may indeed be one of the defining marks of human dignity:

> In those moments when I am able to rise above compulsion, need, and expectation and allow some novelty to refresh me, I am most certain of my freedom and my potency. I become gracefully free when I become convinced that I have the power to do a new thing. (25: p. 30)[21]

Thus, play may be heralded as a singularly fulfilled, liberating experience, through which man opens doors normally closed, alters his habitual modes of perception, refuses categorically to tolerate premature and limiting closures, views the naked simplicity of the world and entities within it, and inaugurates processes and actions of creative and novel transformation.

To advance to another but very related concept, it must be noted that man is an incarnate subject and that the most decisive trait of human consciousness, coloring all of its manifestations, is that it is an embodied consciousness. Consequently, the actions and motions of the "lived-body," man's insertion and foundation in existence, reveal him as being intimately concerned with his unfolding in the world.

Further, as many phenomenological investigations so capably demonstrated, particularly those of Merleau-Ponty, "nothing is more expressive than the human body" (50: p. 114); it is the locus and vehicle of "an indefinite number of symbolic systems" (35: p. 9). The body provides man with a personally oriented focus for projection and action.

Play, and in particular playful sport, as a vibrant form of human endeavor, reveals the body in its lived concreteness. Configurations and meanings inscribed with shapes and qualities expressive and indicative of the texture of the being of the participant arise by means of the body's power of expression. The player, through exuberant, delightful, joyous and spontaneous movement, gestures, and actions, confronts the world in a fresh manner,[22] engages in dialogue with it, and explores it and himself in a manner pregnant with individual significance.

Thus, it may be stated that the objective and extrinsic approaches previously discussed are inadequate and inappropriate to fully comprehend the unique nature of man's embodied being.[23] The open and aware player experiences and apprehends his body neither as an object nor as a manipulatable, quantifiable instrument; the "lived-subject" not only is sensed but also does the sensing. The body perceived totally as an object is, in a very legitimate sense, drained of its humanity; it is a dead body devoid of its vivifying, expressive, and intentional qualities and abilities.

In addition, it should also be noted that play and sport, through their capabilities of manifesting and transmitting affective states and meanings, may be viewed both as symbolic media and as potentially artistic enterprises capable of stimulating and releasing the creative components of the participant. This thesis will be discussed in more detail in a later section.

In summary, it may be asserted that play is the impulse for, the gate to, and the exercise, instantiation, and essence of freedom.[24] Liberated from mundane, routine confinements; from subordination to the impersonal shackles of constraint and circumstance; and from utilitarian demands, objective orientations, and habitual stances—the true player commits himself totally to the situation at hand and the opportunities to experience possibility[25] by pouring himself wholly and without restraint into the activity to focus on his subjectivity and to luxuriate in the intense, full, lived experience of play.

It will prove to be helpful to the present analysis to discuss play briefly from two additional philosophic perspectives, both relating directly to and based upon the previous investigation of the interconnections between play and possibility: *first,* a systematic theological orientation to the phenomenon and its significance for man; and *second,* an aesthetic perusal of the structure and nature of play. These concerns will be addressed in the subsequent two sections.

VI

In recent times, the question of the nature and significance of human play has emerged as a visible focus of study and discourse in the religious study disciplines under the rubric of "the theology of play." Generally, it may be asserted that the theology of play consists of "an attempt to illuminate the meaning of play through an application of theology, and/or the attempt to clarify theology by applying a play metaphor" (18: p. 48).

The connection between human play and the divine has a long, and perhaps, somewhat surprising history. In *The Laws,* Plato stated that life is most appropriately lived as play: man was "created as a plaything of the gods, and that is the best part of us. All of us, then, men and women alike, must live accordingly, and spend our lives making our play as noble and beautiful as possible" (21: p. 36). The highest goal of human endeavors, thus, is to participate fully in play consecrated to the gods. This insight, coupled with other similar observations variously expressed throughout the history of ideas, including Nietzsche's postulation that "the world *is* the play of Zeus" (13: p. 29), is strongly echoed in selected streams of contemporary Christian theological thought.

Hugo Rahner (54), Jurgen Moltmann (39), Sam Keen (25;26), among several other contemporary theologians,[26] asserted that the creation of the world and man was a meaningful and serious, but also an uncoerced and unnecessary, act. God is free—He is, of course, not constrained by inexorable drives, restraints, compulsions, or laws—

therefore, He creates spontaneously because He wills to do so, not because He must (54: p. 18). The world, thus, cannot be viewed as a "necessary unfolding of God nor an emanation of his being from his divine fullness" (39: p. 17). In other words, the Creation is the result of divine play, that is, of God playing with his own possibilities.

Consequently, it may be contended that man attains the fullest state of awareness and highest form of creative development by demonstrating attributes and qualities and engaging in actions which approximate and imitate those of God through participation in unconstrained, purposeless, and joyful play. Playing corresponds directly to "the ultimate groundlessness of the world" (39: p. 16) as the most appropriate option for man. Similarly to God, man playing in and with the world creates whole new worlds;[27] like the Creation, man's playing is a meaningful outward flowing, an inventive and innovative expression of his freedom, and a festive affirmation of his being. Play, then, is a form of godliness; it is participation in, and consecrated to, the divine. Thus, in play man can echo in a finite manner the infinite joy of the Creator, delight in and celebrate God, become a full "plaything" of the Lord, and exuberantly embrace the nature of his own existence.

A second consideration addressed by the theologians of play concerns itself with an evaluation of the justification and direction of man's worldly endeavors. It is contended that human existence is joyful, at heart, because it is basically and inherently secure in God. Since "grace is a happening rather than an achievement, a gift rather than a reward" (25: p. 145), the individual has already arrived and been accepted as he is. That is, man's existence is "justified and made beautiful" before he is "able to do or fail to do anything." Consequently, man displays and celebrates the meaning of his being not in rendering service, engaging in productive enterprises, or participating in pedantic life styles dedicated toward usefulness or accomplishment, but rather through the far more appropriate nonutilitarian and purpose-free acts of cheerful affirmation, expression, and celebration.

"Play as a world symbol goes beyond the categories of doing, having, and achieving and leads us into the categories of being, of authentic human existence and demonstrative rejoicing in it . . . [through] dancing, singing, and playing" (39: pp. 21, 23–24).

Finally, a third aspect of the theological inquiry into play merits brief mention. Rahner (54: p. 60), for one, repeatedly hailed and extolled play as a manifestation of heartease or an untroubled gladness of the soul; it was perceived as a meaningful prelude to eternity, "a kind of rehearsal, fashioned into gesture, sound or word, of that Godward directed harmony of body and soul which we call heaven" and "the dance of everlasting life" (18: p. 49). Concurrence with Moltmann's (39: p. 35) assertion that "life is not a struggle but preplay, not preparatory labor but prevision of the future life of rejoicing," permits play to be viewed, quite literally, as foreplay and, perhaps, even as "a foretaste of the eschaton" (49: p. 216).

The previously delineated considerations of the positive aspects or attributes of play, among other issues not herein discussed, led Neale (45: p. 176) to assert strenuously that "the goal for the church is to encourage play at all levels. The task of the average person is to continue his playing and allow the spirit of full play to enter into all levels of his adult life." Thus, it may be seen that these theologians emphatically advocate the replacement of the utilitarian or work orientation by the play stance as the most appropriate and definitive perspective on worldly enterprises and modes of being.

Obviously, these brief theological considerations warrant considerably more attention than was possible here.[28] However, hopefully, sufficient indicators have been presented to provide support for the major thrust of this study.

VII

There is currently an almost ecumenical acceptance of play or the element of playfulness as a necessary component of art, and indeed, an extremely long and significant tradition in the history of philosophic thought, from Plato and Aristotle to Kant, Schiller, Santayana, and numerous others, has associated play with aesthetic theory. If in the act of playing man proceeds to formulate new perspectives within which to enjoy, to interpret, and to understand the nature and conditions of his-being-in-the-world, a convincing argument may be forwarded for play as the foundation of art and as an essential ingredient in the artistic process, insofar as it seeks to eschew formalism and rigidity and to keep open its possibilities of comprehension and creativity. Brief mention of three specific aesthetic theories will amplify this contention.

Kant (23: pp. 37–77, 145–181), for example, asserted that the aesthetic experience in man is based upon the interaction of the cognitive faculties of first, imagination, and second, reason and understanding. The imagination formulates images from the perceptual field and the understanding classifies and synthesizes these images. The perception of an aesthetic object or work stimulates these two faculties of apprehension and facilitates their harmonious interaction and unification which is, in turn, the ground for aesthetic pleasure. Thus, for Kant, free play is the unconstrained synthesis and harmonization of the mental powers of imagination and understanding.

Schiller (64), although significantly influenced by Kant,[29] rejected his rather ascetic and one-sided rational orientation to incorporate physical and sensual aspects and concerns absent in much of Kant's work. He perceived play to be a totally absorbing and creative enterprise performing the essential task of reconciliation and harmonization between not simply two mental faculties, but between the two divergent demands or facets of man's nature—reason and the senses.

According to Schiller (64: pp. 64–66, 133–134), to achieve completeness, man is required to develop and to balance both the formal impulse (stemming from his rational nature) and the sensual impulse (stemming from his physical existence or sensuous nature), since both are essential parts of his being. This harmonious middle disposition, or state of organic wholeness, in which man affirms both the physical and the rational, without the constraint or the domination of one by the other, is termed "the play impulse." The play impulse is manifested in or leads to the "living form" of aesthetic activity in which man enthusiastically abandons himself to contemplation and enjoyment "above the fetters of every purposed end . . . in the free movement which is itself end and means."

Play, thus, gives satisfaction to man's creative imagination, nurtures the emotions, excites the soul, and satisfies the senses. This led Schiller (64: p. 80) to assert, in his famous peon of praise to play: "To declare it once and for all, Man plays only when he is in the full sense of the word a man, and he is only wholly Man when he is playing."

To proceed to more contemporary thought, it may be noted that Santayana (61: p. 18), in his discourse on the sense of beauty and aesthetic theory, emphasized that both play and art act as delightful, energizing, and liberating sources of new power which provide opportunities for the modification of human consciousness, the expression of novel and creative acts, and the organization of new modes of joyful sensibility. Indeed, he asserted that "there is an undeniable propriety in calling all the liberal and imaginative activities of man play."

The stance supported by Santayana is highly reminiscent of Schiller's characterization of the activities of the aesthetic man as being free from utility, obligations, practical considerations, and the tyranny of specific, pragmatic ends. Schiller (64: p. 125) stated that the aesthetic impulse builds a "joyous realm of play" which releases man from the shackles of circumstance and constraint. "As long as necessity dictates and want impels, imagination is bound with strong chains to the actual; only when want is satisfied does it develop its unrestrained capacities."

If the three previously delineated sketches are accepted as, at least, indicative and promising,[30] it may be argued that the play and aesthetic experience have much in common: both are unfettered, uncoerced, and distinterested activities releasing the subjectivity of the participant; both provide fresh perspectives and vision, thereby opening up the world and freeing man from the total domination of causality and unreflective, unwavering, and mechanical routines or patterns of action and perception; both provide possibilities for the delight and joy of the participant or viewer completely absorbed and entranced by the activity or object; both are distinct from the everyday, mundane world, if only to gain new perspectives and comprehension; and finally, both possess and demonstrate intrinsic values and ends.

Play is indeed a rich source and protean resource where new paths to understanding and meaning are nurtured in an open field of free expression. Therefore, it may be contended that "human play is a matter of creative imagination and that the creative artist is a player" (37: p. 75).[31]

Thus, it appears to be defensible to assert that play often is the vibrant, living embodiment, to utilize Schiller's terms, of the sensual and the rational, as well as the harmoniously balanced synthesis of form and freedom. It extends beyond pragmatic perspectives, probes beneath superficial surfaces and concerns to address the heart of the matter, thereby permitting a revelational penetration into true being. It is what we believe in and live for.

VIII

It may be asserted that contemporary Western man suffers from the atrophy and debilitation of a "shrunken psyche" (6: p. 12). Socialized and pressed extensively toward instrumental rationality, objective calculation, and sober manipulation, he has repressed and forgotten the jubilation of open and boundless play. However, man is essentially fanciful, graceful, and festive; thus, to become fully human he must regain the ability to

laugh, to dream, to experience wonder, to dance, and to play.

In the orderly, pragmatic, rational, secure, and repressive adult kingdom of Apollo, some sports and games (of course, properly oriented and regulated) are permissible, but enterprises manifesting exuberance, delight, enchantment, revelry, undisciplined enjoyment, and even ecstasy[32]—in other words, instances of full, free, joyous play—are perceived to belong to the domain of Dionysius and are consequently, at the very least, suspect (26: pp. 145, 154).

Nonetheless, it is herein contended that rigid and predominate adherence and homage to Apollonian consciousness involves a "staggering impoverishment of the vital elements" (6: p. 6) essential to open and full human existence: "Poor life, that lacks the elasticity to dart off in prancing enterprises!" (51: p. 22). A reorientation to resurrect the elements of, and to celebrate the capacity for, Dionysian consciousness in vibrant and fulfilled play will alter the barrenness of life, grant transcendence of servitude, dependence, and utility, and radically transform man. Ortega y Gasset emphatically stated that:

Life is an affair of flutes. It is overflow that it needs most. He who rests content with barely meeting necessity as it arises will be washed away. Life has triumphed on this planet because it has, instead of clinging to necessities, deluged it with overwhelming possibilities. (51: p. 21)

Further, if it is agreed that the "abundance of possibilities is a symptom of thriving life," it may be contended that play is a most exceptional mode of being; it is a humus from which man surges creatively forward toward a horizon full of "the lure of infinite distances" (51: pp. 19, 15), beyond stagnation and petrification to cultivate and to explore wondrous fields of possibility.

Entrance into play permits the attainment of the state of balanced and harmonious consciousness manifested by Schiller's aesthetic man and extolled by Nietzsche's Zarathustra, transforms man from producer and accumulator to rejoicer and player, and consequently, provides a readmission to paradise. This state of affairs induced Ortega (51: p. 28) to suggest that the normal hierarchy be inverted to place play and playful sportive activity at the top as "the foremost and creative, the most exalted, serious, and important part of life, while labor ranks second as its derivative and precipitate. Nay more, life, properly speaking, resides in the first alone; the rest is relatively mechanic and a mere functioning."[33]

However, in a world dominated by prudence, diligence, obligation, servitude, necessity, and passivity, play is foreign and the wide recognition of its ontological significance is all but precluded. Play embodies and reflects new, divergent, and radical characteristics and directions; it is a way of "breaking the hammer" (29: p. 72), that is, of removing man from his everyday preoccupations to express doubts concerning the unquestioned relevance and importance of mundane existence; and finally, it announces the "rebirth of patently unproductive festivity and expressive celebration" (6: p. 5).[34] Thus, play and the life of the player are perceived to be irrelevant to the pragmatic world of instrumental concerns and irreverent to those who structure their identity upon, and derive their significance from, successes attained in such efforts.

Consequently, those who refuse to see the joyful colors of the play world and prefer to be deaf to its call will hold the player in disrepute and perceive him to be a fool or a madman. But, as Zorba the Greek (24) so emphatically demonstrated, a touch of madness and the ability to laugh and to dance in the face of contingency[35] and the self-important structure of the social world are essential components of genuine existence, and further, "man must have a little madness or else he will not be free" (60: p. 117). As Keen wrote:

God, but I want madness!
I want to tremble,
to be shaken,

to yield to pulsation,
to surrender to the rhythm of music and sea,
to the seasons of ebb and flow,
to the tidal surge of love.

I am tired of being
hard,
tight,
controlled,
tensed against the invasion of novelty. (25: p. 117)

Surely, to affirm play, and also to concur with Heraclitus, Jesus,[36] Schiller, Huizinga, Fink, and others, that man is only fully man when he plays and that he plays fully only when he plays like a child, in contemporary, achievement-oriented Western society, of necessity, requires more than a touch of madness.

IX

In conclusion, it may be asserted that play is an intrinsically rewarding, purposeless[37] activity which requires no external justification and is located at the center of life, not relegated to its distant perimeter. Indeed, it may be characterized as a rich and vital focal point of diverse lived meanings.[38] It is a *joie de vivre,* an adventurous, festive undertaking which reduces man's provincialism and enlarges his experience by embracing, and penetrating to, the heart of life.

Although it is impossible to delineate fully the diverse components, expressive possibilities, and multitude of infectious delights inherent in the sphere of play, it is readily apparent that it is a most extraordinary and commodious realm—a transubstantiated and wondrous world permeated with serenity, joy, happiness, as well as surprise.

Ultimately, play is an essential, revelatory, liberating, most human enterprise. It is "an affair of flutes" wherein man is provided a grove in which he may listen to the fluid rhythms of inner music, cheerfully express all aspects of his being, including the affirmation of his sensual nature, and luxuriate in the intense, fully-lived release, if not explosion, of his subjectivity. And this is most worthy of praise and celebration, indeed.

Notes

1. Paper presented at the 8th Annual Meeting of the Philosophic Society for the Study of Sport and the International Workshop in Sport Philosophy conducted at Karlsruhe University, Karlsruhe, Federal Republic of Germany, July 6–10, 1980.

   It is necessary to introduce, at the beginning, an important qualifying note. Although nouns and pronouns of the male gender such as "men," "he," and "him" are at times utilized in this paper, the intention is by no means to limit their reference or import specifically to one sex. Rather, the decision not to utilize such neutral terms as "human being" or "human existence" was based solely on the desire not to produce unfortunate and counterproductive confusion with the unique and vibrant denotations and connotations of these specific terms in some of the literature of existential philosophy called upon in certain sections of this essay. Hopefully, the benefits derived from adherence to this policy, in this particular case, will significantly outweigh any quite unintended offense which may be generated.

2. It may be noted that the *Oxford English Dictionary* (42) demonstrates the inevitable difficulties and complications which arise in any definitional investigation of play by utilizing more than 5 full, closely-packed pages to delineate 17 distinctive, major acceptable usages of the term as a noun (with extensive subsets) and 32 additional appropriate applications as a verb. This condition, as indicated by Miller (38: p. 87), has led some critics to assert that the term is frequently utilized as "a wastebasket category of miscellaneous behavior."

3. This methodological approach was utilized by many investigators including Huizinga (20: pp. 13,28), Caillois (3: pp. 9–10; 4: p. 46), Riezler (55), Maheu (31: p. 12), Weiss (68: pp. 138–139), Neale (43: p. 105; 45: p. 65), Fink (14: pp. 80–83), Schmitz (65), Roochnik (58), Hyland (21), Miller (37), Suits (67), and numerous others.

4. For well-considered amplifications, implications, and praise of the "play stance" see Roochnik's (58: pp. 36–41) and Hyland's (21: p. 37) thoughtful philosophic analyses, as well as Miller's (38) interesting anthropological discussion of this topic.

5. The stance discussed here is, to a certain extent, a rather direct reflection of medieval Christian theology which generally condemned all purposeless or unproductive efforts or activities, including play.

6. Sam Keen (26: pp. 121–123) delineated four interpretations and appropriate usages of the term "*homo faber*" and provided an extended description of how the fourth and most popular form is really the most degraded. The four forms are as follows: (1) man is the animal who makes and uses tools; (2) the human mind, no less than the hand, is a toolmaking and tool-using faculty; (3) the chief product of *homo faber* is man himself (i.e., he creates his own identity); and (4) the image of *homo faber* signifies that man is a worker.

7. One notable exception to this general orientation centers upon wealth that is inherited. In such cases, exemption from participation in productive labor enterprises is granted the recipient, at times, without concurrent or consequent negative evaluations; however, any such approval is usually based upon a presumption, often uninvestigated, that the capital and material goods inherited were originally attained and accumulated

through the industrious efforts or shrewd economic investments of the previous members of the family, and thus, legitimately produced in accord with the ethos under discussion. In essence, the seeds of prior labor are permitted to bear fruits in subsequent generations.

8. The opening lines of Dr. Seuss's *The Cat in the Hat Comes Back* illustrated this point:

> This was no time for play.
> This was no time for fun.
> This was no time for games.
> There was work to be done. (37: p. 127)

9. On a somewhat different but related matter, it is interesting to note that, in North American society at least, games of chance and lotteries were generally perceived negatively and were vociferously denied widespread social or legal approval until very recently, largely because they contravened the accepted norms requiring concerted efforts and dedication for the attainment of significant materialistic rewards. However, when the full extent and possibilities of potential "productive" aspects of such ventures were clearly illuminated (for example, the generation of funds for the reduction of taxes, for aid to senior citizens, for church projects, and for cultural and civic enterprises), social acceptance was finally, if somewhat reluctantly, accorded.

10. Miller (37: pp. 103–116) argued that in the history of ideas and theological thought play was not originally perceived to be the opposite of seriousness, but that the intellectually higher principle of rationality forwarded by both Plato and Aristotle subordinated "the virtue of play to the higher virtue of seriousness." For an additional and, at times, contrary discussion of this issue see Hyland (21).

11. Conversely, for the sake of balance and

historical accuracy, it is necessary to state that Collier (5: p. 45), writing in the same journal, discerned that leisure serves a richer, fuller function: "Leisure is not simply a time for recuperation in order to work again, but, on the contrary, it is the time in which we live, grow, and experience our humanhood, if we experience it at all."

12. Brohm (2: pp. 1–36) presented a vociferous and extended denunciation of the objectification and renunciation of the human body in contemporary elite sport programs which culminates with the assertion that such enterprises are forms of "institutionalized celebration of the mortification of the flesh" (2: p. 23). For a further discussion of the limiting, negative, and perhaps even debilitating orientations and consequences of physical education and sport programs dedicated to and obsessed with reification, efficiency, and productivity in the pursuit of excellence, and for suggestions for amelioration of some of the deficiencies, see Meier (34).

13. The literature exploring the concept of alienation is vast. For access to this material, see Schacht's (63) comprehensive analysis, as well as Murchland's (41) and Feuer's (12) studies. For a brief introduction to the analysis of the sources of alienation in labor, in the Marxist sense, see Rinehart (56: pp. 18ff). Finally, the following statement provides insight into the results of two studies on the alienation of labor:

> Robert Dubin's study of the "industrial workers' world" suggests that three out of four industrial workers "did not see their jobs and work places as central life interests for themselves. They found their preferred human associations and preferred areas of behavior outside of employment." Yet another study of industrial workers [David Riesman's "Leisure and Work in Post-

Industrial Socity''] reported that 80 per cent would go on working even if there were no economic need, although the job itself was without meaning or positive satisfaction. These studies point to the problem of alienated leisure. Even when work has ceased to be economically necessary, creatively satisfying, or the focus of meaningful personal relationships, it remains a psychological (or should one say ''theoological'') necessity. (26: p. 143)

14. It is necessary at this point, in an attempt to disarm some potential criticism, to introduce a significant note of qualification. Any utilization of a major differentiation, if not dichotomization, between work and play, as the extent literature concerned with this issue attests, may at times be problematic. Unfortunately, the scope of this paper precludes an exploration of this topic beyond that provided in the text, despite whatever importance such an understanding may possess. However, the purpose and substance of this study, namely, an appreciation of play, are not seriously incapacitated by this state of affairs.

It may be readily acknowledged that not all forms of work possess debilitating consequences or are perceived negatively by the participants, and also that not all forms of play are always free of routinization or superficiality. However, the crucial factor at issue here is the predominant extrinsic or intrinsic orientation of the activity. Any intrinsic rewards generated by the productive work enterprise may be pleasurable and satisfying, but are inessential bonuses, not necessary conditions; conversely, intrinsic motivations and rewards are necessary and essential aspects of the play phenomenon, not fortunate additions. Novak (49: p. 40) addressed this point in the following manner: ''To participate in the rites of play is to

dwell in the Kingdom of Ends. To participate in work . . . is to labor in the Kingdom of Means.'' The forementioned distinction between play and non-play activities, as more fully delineated in earlier sections, is the basis for and informs this study.

15. In a discussion of a thesis to be found in George Konrad's novel *The Case Worker,* Kessler (27: p. 13) stated that ''our urban culture grows more vacant of humane values in proportion to our power to process masses of people through a machinery designed to give them well-being.''

16. Human possibility is here utilized specifically in a manner distinguished from the concepts of empirical or logical possibility; see Stack (66) for a further discussion of this distinction.

17. In a later source, Sartre moved from the unconditional freedom hailed in his earlier writings, particularly in *Being and Nothingness* (62), to a more modified position:

I believe that man can always make something out of what is made of him. This is the limit I would today accord to freedom: the small moment which makes of a totally conditioned social being someone who does not render back completely what his conditioning has given him. (1: p. 22)

18. In one sense, of course, it must be acknowledged that taking action and thereby choosing to actualize one or more possibilities denies, temporarily at least, if not permanently, the manifestation of certain other concurrent possibilities; thus, from this perspective there are always missed possibilities. However, as indicated by the subsequent discussion, the lost possibilities which are at stake and the objects of concern here are those characterized by certain forms, natures, or directions.

19. Cf 11; 14; 21; 40; 43; 58; 62: pp. 580–592.

20. In a *palinode* to his main thesis, Hyland (21: p. 47) acknowledged that, despite its importance, "responsive openness" is a necessary, but not sufficient condition for play since the pickpocket, for one, also demonstrates this quality to a marked degree. Thus, Hyland qualified his statement by introducing the notion of "good" and "bad" forms of "responsive openness," although, regrettably, he did not present an analysis of this distinction.

21. Keen (25: p. 35) amplified this notion by asserting that "a graceful future is one open to psychological, political, and ontological novelty."

22. Novak (49: pp. 137,86) discussed a somewhat similar point in his analysis of the attractiveness and significance of the sport of North American football for the spectator rather than the participant: "To play football wholeheartedly is to live a higher form of life, beyond the ordinary, to drink deep of possibilities of consciousness heretofore neglected." He also stated that "he who has not drunk deep of the virtues of football has missed one of the closest brushes with transcendence that humans are allowed."

23. Further criticism of such approaches, an extended discussion of Merleau-Ponty's phenomenology of the body, plus a consideration of sport in light of these new perspectives are to be found in Meier (33).

24. This sentiment is echoed in numerous philosophical discourses concerned with play: Tillich (37: p. xxx), for example, stated that "play is one of the most characteristic expressions of the freedom of the spirit"; Rahner (54: p. 65) asserted that to play is "to be free, kingly, unfettered and divine"; and Sartre (62: p. 580), of course, specifically viewed play as the release of subjectivity.

25. In fact, Esposito (11: p. 141) asserted that games and sports in general may be perceived as "contrived situations, the purpose of which is to heighten and bring into focus the interplay between possibility and actuality"; the grasp or foothold on a ledge or rock in mountain climbing, for example, contains poignant moments of possibility. Further Morgan (40: pp. 24–30), in an analysis of the notion of possibility largely derived from Esposito, suggested that sport, or better, "sportive activity" may be adequately delineated as the unmediated pursuit of possibilities, predominantly "unconstrained by external impinging factors." In addition, Morgan presented a hierarchical scheme ranking sports according to the degree of mediation of external impinging factors: individual, dual, team, animate nonhuman, inanimate mechanical device— progressively diminishing "the role played by the individual athlete in this evocation of possibility."

26. It is possible to identify at least six theologians who have addressed this particular topic at some length. In addition to the three authors listed, mention must be made of the works of Cox (6;7), Neale (43;44;45), and Miller (36;37). Obviously, limitations preclude a discussion of many of the issues delineated in these works. However, the interested reader is referred to one of the few critical studies of this literature, namely De Caluwe's (8) illuminating study of the positions developed by Rahner, Moltmann, and Neale.

27. Two qualifying notes must be presented concerning the metaphor employed here. First, God's play, in the circumstances under discussion, resulted in the creation of physical entities, a state of affairs very infrequently the case with human play. Second, although man creates new worlds in play, he does not do so totally *ex nihilo* because of the constraints of his facticity; this, of course, is not a factor which limits or binds God.

28. On a somewhat different, but nonetheless

interesting point, it may be noted that, in a recent work, Novak (49: pp. 19,24) argued at considerable length that contemporary sports are forms of natural religion, pregnant with symbolic meaning and other religious qualities; they flow outward "from a deep natural impulse that is radically religious." He asserted that sports create primal symbols and metaphors of cosmic struggle and, thereby, may be perceived legitimately as "rituals concerning human survival on this planet" or as "liturgical enactments of animal perfection and the struggles of the human spirit to prevail."

29. Kant's *Critique of Judgment* (23) was published when Schiller was 30 years of age.

30. The general position previously briefly developed may be supported by numerous herein unspecified ideas and concepts drawn from additional works of aesthetic theory. Of particular merit is the stimulating discussion of the interconnections between play and aesthetics to be found in Nietzsche's *The Birth of Tragedy* (48). Although some of Nietzsche's thoughts on Dionysius and play will be addressed later in this paper, the reader interested in pursuing this topic further is urged to peruse this provocative work. The secondary literature, of course, is extensive. One study of specific relevance to this section, for example, is Roberts's (57) discussion of Santayana's aesthetic theory, in particular, as applied to sport.

31. It should be kept in mind that the intention of this section was not to equate play totally with the aesthetic experience (a plausible position, indeed, but one requiring more extensive discussion and support than was provided herein), but to identify significant similarities in the ontological structures demonstrated or possessed by the two forms of human endeavor.

32. Leonard (30) discussed some of the "hidden dimensions" of play in sport in terms of energy flows, experiences of new clarity, moments of heightened perception and fulfilled presence, peak experiences, and transformed states of consciousness during participation.

33. In fact, Ortega is quite willing to forward a more precise bifurcation:

> We may then divide organic phenomena—animal and human—into two great classes of activity, one original, creative, vital par excellence—that is, spontaneous and disinterested; the other of utilitarian character, in which the first is put to use and mechanized. Utility does not create and invent; it simply employs and stabilizes what has been created without it. (51: p. 17)

34. Cox (6: pp. 10–11,63) asserted that man is *homo festivus:* "man is by his very nature a creature who not only works and thinks but who sings, dances, prays, tells stories, and celebrates." In a later section, he stated that "dance both uses the body to celebrate and also celebrates the body." The interested reader may wish to peruse Cox's (6: pp. 58–67) discussion of the Church and dance. De Caluwe's (8: pp. 110–114) brief analysis of dance as a form of play also provides access to some of the relevant literature.

35. Keen (26: p. 157; 25: p. 160) offered two pertinent reflections on Zorba's dancing and its significance. First, "Zorba dances when the joy or the tragedy of life overflows the capacity of his words." Second, "Religion must return to dance. Perhaps Zorba is the saint for our time."

36. Miller amplified this notion in *Gods and Games:*

> The laughter of the child expresses the joy of freedom, of the sense of adventure, of delight, of pleasure. This must have been what Heraclitus had in mind

when he referred to the end of life as belonging to the little child, and what Jesus meant when he said: "Truly I say to you, unless you receive the kingdom of God as a little child, you cannot enter into it." (37: p. 131)

37. To contend that play is purposeless is to describe it as a self-sufficient enterprise which does not translate to economic or other external concerns. It involves a redistribution of resources and efforts to focus on internal finalities. Indeed, in one sense, it may be postulated that "play posits the non-necessity of the necessary" (46: p. 93). Further, it is a fluid "letting-be of life and meaning," and as Miller (37: p. 151) proposed, it may be the case that "man's noblest and most profound destiny lies in making the central purpose of his life a kind of purposelessness." In sum, then, as far as extrinsic factors are concerned, true play is good for nothing, and therein resides both its essence and merit.

38. Fink (14: pp. 76,83,85) supported this contention. He postulated that play is a "return to the morning freshness of life at its origin"; "a symbolic act of representation, in which human life interprets itself"; and, further, an "action which puts us in the presence of the meaning of the world and of life." For an additional analysis of the rich meanings to be unearthed in the play world, wherein men may "feel the pulse of life's central beat," see Zaner's (69: p. 14) insightful discussion of play as an inherently self-endorsing presentation of what he terms "the moral order."

Bibliography

1. "An Interview with Sartre." *New York Review of Books,* March 26, 1970, pp. 22–31.

2. Brohm, Jean-Marie. *Sport: A Prison of Measured Time.* Translated by Ian Fraser. London: Ink Links, 1978.

3. Caillois, Roger. *Man, Play, and Games.* Translated by M. Barash. New York: The Free Press, 1961.

4. Caillois, Roger. "The Structure and Classification of Games." *Sport, Culture, and Society.* Edited by J. Loy and G. Kenyon. Toronto: Macmillan, 1969.

5. Collier, John. "Recreation." *The Homiletic Review,* 74 (1917), 44–50.

6. Cox, Harvey. *The Feast of Fools: A Theological Essay on Festivity and Fantasy.* New York: Harper and Row, Perennial Library, 1969.

7. Cox, Harvey. *The Seduction of the Spirit.* New York: Simon and Shuster, 1973.

8. De Caluwe, Goederoen. "Theology of Play: A Conceptual Analysis." Unpublished Master of Arts thesis. The University of Western Ontario, London, Canada, 1979.

9. Ecob, James. "Recreation." *The Homiletic Review,* 74 (1917), 43–44.

10. Ehrmann, Jacques. "Homo Ludens Revisited." *Game, Play, Literature.* Edited by Jacques Ehrmann. Boston: Beacon Press, 1968.

11. Esposito, Joseph L. "Play and Possibility." *Philosophy Today,* 18 (1974), 137–146.

12. Feuer, Lewis S. *Marx and the Intellectuals: A Set of Post-Ideological Essays.* Garden City, NY: Doubleday, Anchor Books, 1969.

13. Fink, Eugen. "The Oasis of Happiness: Toward an Ontology of Play." *Game, Play, Literature.* Edited by Jacques Ehrmann. Boston: Beacon Press, 1968.

14. Fink, Eugen. "The Ontology of Play." *Sport and the Body: A Philosophical Symposium.* Edited by Ellen Gerber. Philadelphia: Lea and Febiger, 1972.

15. Fraleigh, Warren P. "The Moving 'I'." *The Philosophy of Sport: A Collection of Original Essays.* Edited by Robert G.

Osterhoudt. Springfield, IL: Charles C Thomas, 1973.

16. Gilbert, Bil. "Imagine Going to School to Learn to Play." *Sports Illustrated,* October 13, 1975, pp. 84–98.

17. Heidegger, Martin. *Being and Time.* Translated by John Macquarrie and Edward Robinson. New York: Harper and Row, 1962.

18. Hoffman, Shirl. "The Athletae Dei: Missing the Meaning of Sport." *Journal of the Philosophy of Sport,* 3 (1976), 42–51.

19. Hogan, William R. "Sin and Sport." *Motivations in Play, Games, and Sports.* Edited by Ralph Slovenko and James Knight. Springfield, IL: Charles C Thomas, 1967.

20. Huizinga, Johan. *Homo Ludens: A Study of the Play-Element in Culture.* Boston: Beacon Press, 1968.

21. Hyland, Drew. "'And That is the Best Part of Us': Human Being and Play." *Journal of the Philosophy of Sport,* 4 (1977), 36–49.

22. Jaspers, Karl. *Existentialism and Humanism: Three Essays.* Edited by Hanns E. Fischer. Translated by E.B. Ashton. New York: Russell F. Moore Co., 1952.

23. Kant, Immanuel. *The Critique of Judgment.* Translated by J.H. Bernard. New York: Hafner, 1966.

24. Kazantzakis, Nikos. *Zorba the Greek.* New York: Simon and Shuster, 1959.

25. Keen, Sam. *To A Dancing God.* New York: Harper and Row, 1970.

26. Keen, Sam. *Apology for Wonder.* New York: Harper and Row, 1969.

27. Kessler, Jascha. "From Eastern Europe: A Book and a Man." *New York Times Book Review,* January 28, 1978, p. 13.

28. Kierkegaard, Soren. *The Present Age.* Translated by Alexander Dru. New York: Harper and Row, 1962.

29. Krell, David F. "Towards an Ontology of Play: Eugen Fink's Notion of Spiel." *Research in Phenomenology,* 2 (1972), 63–93.

30. Leonard, George. *The Ultimate Athlete: Re-visioning Sports, Physical Education and the Body.* New York: Viking, 1975.

31. Maheu, Rene. "Sport and Culture." *International Research in Sport and Physical Education.* Edited by E. Jokl and E. Simon. Springfield, IL: Charles C Thomas, 1964.

32. Meier, Klaus V. "The Kinship of the Rope and the Loving Struggle: A Philosophic Analysis of Communication in Mountain Climbing." *Journal of the Philosophy of Sport,* 3 (1976), 52–64.

33. Meier, Klaus V. "Embodiment, Sport, and Meaning." *Sport and the Body: A Philosophical Symposium: Second Edition.* Edited by Ellen W. Gerber and William J. Morgan. Philadelphia: Lea and Febiger, 1979.

34. Meier, Klaus V. "In Defense of Mediocrity: A Re-visioning of Play in Physical Education." Paper presented to the Philosophy Academy of the National Association for Sport and Physical Education at the annual meeting of the American Alliance for Physical and Health Education, Recreation, and Dance at Detroit, Michigan, April, 1980.

35. Merleau-Ponty, Maurice. *Themes from the Lectures at the College de France 1952–1960.* Evanston, IL: Northwestern University Press, 1970.

36. Miller, David. "Theology and Play Studies: An Overview." *Journal of the American Academy of Religion,* 39 (1971), 349–354.

37. Miller, David L. *Gods and Games: Toward a Theology of Play.* New York: Harper Colophon Books, 1973.

38. Miller, Stephen. "Ends, Means, and Galumphing: Some Leitmotifs of Play." *American Anthropologist,* 75 (1973), 87–98.

39. Moltmann, Jurgen. *Theology of Play.* Translated by Reinhard Ulrich. New York: Harper and Row, 1972.

40. Morgan, William J. "Some Aristotelian Notes on the Attempt to Define Sport." *Journal of the Philosophy of Sport,* 4 (1977), 15–35.

41. Murchland, Bernard. *The Age of Alienation.* New York: Random House, 1971.

42. Murray, James (ed.), *The Compact Edition of the Oxford English Dictionary.* Oxford: Oxford University Press, 1971.

43. Neale, Robert E. "Play and the Sacred: Toward a Theory of Religion as Play." Unpublished Ph.D. dissertation, Union Theological Seminary, New York, 1964.

44. Neale, Robert E. "Play and the Sacred." *Motivations in Play, Games and Sports.* Edited by Ralph Slovenko and James Knight. Springfield, IL: Charles C Thomas, 1967.

45. Neale, Robert E. *In Praise of Play.* New York: Harper and Row, 1969.

46. Netzky, Ralph. "Playful Freedom: Sartre's Ontology Re-Appraised." *Sport and the Body: A Philosophical Symposium: Second Edition.* Edited by Ellen W. Gerber and William J. Morgan. Philadelphia: Lea and Febiger, 1979.

47. Nietzsche, Friedrich. *Thus Spoke Zarathustra.* Translated by R.J. Hollingdale. Harmondsworth, England: Penguin, 1967.

48. Nietzsche, Friedrich. *The Birth of Tragedy and the Case of Wagner.* Translated by Walter Kaufmann. New York: Vintage Books, 1967.

49. Novak, Michael. *The Joy of Sports: End Zones, Bases, Baskets, Balls, and the Consecration of the American Spirit.* New York: Basic Books, 1976.

50. O'Neill, John. "The Spectacle of the Body." *Journal of the Philosophy of Sport,* 1 (1974), 110–122.

51. Ortega y Gasset, Jose. *History as a System and Other Essays Toward a Philosophy of History.* Translated by Helene Weyl. New York: Norton, 1961.

52. Pieper, Josef. *Leisure: The Basis of Culture.* Translated by Alexander Dru. New York: Random House, Pantheon Books, 1964.

53. Proctor, Charles N. and Stephens, R. Rockwell. *Skiing: Fundamentals, Equipment and Advanced Technique.* New York: Harcourt, Brace and Co., 1936.

54. Rahner, Hugo. *Man at Play.* New York: Herder and Herder, 1972.

55. Riezler, Kurt. "Play and Seriousness." *Sport and the Body: A Philosophical Symposium.* Edited by Ellen Gerber. Philadelphia: Lea and Febiger, 1972.

56. Rinehart, James W. *The Tyranny of Work.* Don Mills, Ontario: Longman Canada Ltd., 1975.

57. Roberts, Terence J. "Sport and the Sense of Beauty." *Journal of the Philosophy of Sport,* 2 (1975), 91–101.

58. Roochnik, David L. "Play and Sport." *Journal of the Philosophy of Sport,* 2 (1975), 36–44.

59. Sadler, Jr., William A. "Creative Existence: Play as a Pathway to Personal Freedom and Community." *Humanitas,* 5 (1969), 57–79.

60. Sadler, Jr., William A. "Play: A Basic Human Structure Involving Love and Freedom." *Sport and the Body: A Philosophical Symposium.* Edited by Ellen Gerber. Philadelphia: Lea and Febiger, 1972.

61. Santayana, George. *The Sense of Beauty: Being the Outline of Aesthetic Theory.* New York: Dover, 1955.

62. Sartre, Jean-Paul. *Being and Nothingness: An Essay on Phenomenological Ontology.* Translated and introduced by Hazel Barnes. New York: Philosophical Library, 1956.

63. Schacht, Richard. *Alienation.* Garden City, New York: Doubleday, 1970.

64. Schiller, Friedrich. *On the Aesthetic Education of Man.* Translated with an Introduction by Reginald Snell. New York: Frederick Unger, 1965.

65. Schmitz, Kenneth L. "Sport and Play: Sus-

pension of the Ordinary." *Sport and the Body: A Philosophical Symposium.* Edited by Ellen Gerber. Philadelphia: Lea and Febiger, 1972.

66. Stack, George J. "Human Possibility and Value." *Philosophy Today,* 20 (1976), 95–106.

67. Suits, Bernard. "Words on Play." *Journal of the Philosophy of Sport,* 4 (1977), 117–31.

68. Weiss, Paul. *Sport: A Philosophic Inquiry.* Carbondale, IL: Southern Illinois University Press, 1967.

69. Zaner, Richard M. "Sport and the Moral Order." *Journal of the Philosophy of Sport,* 6 (1979), 7–18.

Bibliography for Sport, Play, and Metaphysics

Ahrabi-Fard, Iradge. "Implications of the Original Teachings of Islam for Physical Education and Sport." Unpublished doctoral dissertation, University of Minnesota, 1974.

Allen, Dorothy J., and Fahey, Brian. (Eds.). *Being Human in Sport*. Philadelphia: Lea & Febiger, 1977.

Alvarez, A. "I Like to Risk My Life." In *Sport and the Body: A Philosophical Symposium*. Edited by Ellen W. Gerber. Philadelphia: Lea & Febiger, 1972.

Amsler, J. "Essai Pour le Sport et le Sacre." *Education Physique et Sport* (1958), 483-488.

Ardley, Gavin. "The Role of Play in the Philosophy of Plato." *Philosophy*, 42 (1967), 226-244.

Arnold, Peter J. *Meaning in Movement, Sport and Physical Education*. London: Heinemann, 1979.

Axelos, Kostas. "Planetary Interlude." In *Game, Play, Literature*. Edited by Jacques Ehrmann. Boston: Beacon Press, 1971.

Banham, Charles. "Man at Play." *Contemporary Review*, 207 (August, 1965), 61-64.

Banks, Gary C. "The Philosophy of Friedrich Nietzsche as a Foundation for Physical Education." Unpublished master's thesis, University of Wisconsin, 1966.

Bannister, Roger. "The Meaning of Athletic Performance." In *International Research in Sport and Physical Education*. Edited by E. Jokl and E. Simon. Springfield, IL: Charles C Thomas, 1964a.

Bannister, Roger. "What Makes the Athlete Run?"

The Australian Journal of Physical Education (March, 1964b), 31-36.

Baum, K. "Der Geist des Sports: Grundfragen einer Psychologie und Philosophie des Sports. Teil: Der Ursport." Unpublished doctoral dissertation, Wurzburg, 1952.

Beisser, Arnold R. "Psychodynamic Observations of a Sport." *Psychoanalytic Review*, 48 (Spring, 1961), 69-76.

Beisser, Arnold R. *The Madness in Sports*. New York: Appleton-Century-Crofts, 1967.

Blumenfield, Walter. "Observations Concerning the Phenomenon and Origin of Play." *Philosophy and Phenomenological Research*, 1 (1941), 470-478.

Bouet, M. "The Function of Sport in Human Relations." *International Review of Sport Sociology*, 1 (1966), 137-140.

Bouet, M. *Signification du Sport*. Paris, 1968.

Bouet, M. "Basic Principles of an Interpretation of High-Performance Sport." In *Sport in the Modern World—Chances and Problems*. Edited by Ommo Grupe, Dietrich Kurz, and Johannes Teipel. New York: Springer-Verlag, 1973.

Burke, Richard. " 'Work' and 'Play'." *Ethics*, 82 (1971), 33-47.

Byrum, Charles S. "Philosophy as Play." *Man and World*, 8 (1975), 315-326.

Byrum, Steven. "The Concept of Child's Play in Nietzsche's 'Of The Three Metamorphoses'." *Kinesis*, 6 (Spring, 1974), 127-135.

Caillois, Roger. *Man, Play, and Games*. Translated by Meyer Barash. New York: Free Press of Glencoe, 1961.

Caputo, John D. "Being, Ground and Play in Heidegger." *Man and World,* 3 (1970), 26-48.

Caspar, Ruth. "A Time for Work: A Time to Play." *Listening,* 16 (Winter, 1981), 18-30.

Caspar, Ruth. "Play Springs Eternal." *New Scholasticum,* 52 (1978), 187–201.

Cherry, Christopher. "Games and the World." *Philosophy,* 51 (1976), 57-61.

Coe, George Albert. "A Philosophy of Play." *Religious Education,* 51 (May/June, 1956), 220-222.

Coomaraswamy, A.K. "Play and Seriousness." *Journal of Philosophy,* 39 (1942), 550-552.

Coutts, Curtis A. "Freedom in Sport." *Quest,* 10 (May, 1968), 68-71.

Cowan, Ed. "Why Sport?" *The Humanist,* 39 (November/December, 1979), 22-28.

Cox, Harvey. "Faith as Play." In *The Feast of Fools: A Theological Essay on Festivity and Fantasy.* Cambridge, MA: Harvard University Press, 1969.

Cox, Harvey. *The Seduction of the Spirit.* New York: Simon and Shuster, 1973.

DeCauluwe, Goederoen. "Theology of Play: A Conceptual Analysis." Unpublished master's thesis, University of Western Ontario, 1979.

DeSensi, Joy. "A Study of Martin Buber's I-Thou and I-It Relationship in Sport." Unpublished doctoral dissertation, University of North Carolina at Greensboro, 1980.

Desmonde, William H. "The Bull-Fight as a Religious Ritual." *American Images,* 9 (June, 1952), 173-195.

Dixon, Peter. *Men Who Ride Mountains.* New York: Bantam, 1969.

Doherty, J. Kenneth. "Why Men Run." *Quest,* 2 (April, 1964), 61-66.

Ehrmann, Jacques. (Ed.). *Game, Play, Literature.* Boston: Beacon Press, 1971a.

Ehrmann, Jacques. "Homo Ludens Revisited." In *Game, Play, Literature.* Boston: Beacon Press, 1971b.

Elena, Lugo. "José Ortega y Gasset's Sportive Sense of Life: His Philosophy of Man." Unpublished doctoral dissertation, Georgetown University, 1969.

Ellis, M.J. *Why People Play.* Englewood Cliffs, NJ: Prentice Hall, 1973.

Ermler, K.L. "Relationship of Existential Freedom to Symbolic Death in Sport." Unpublished doctoral dissertation, State University of New York at Buffalo, 1980.

Fairchild, David. "Man, Mind and Matter: Toward a Philosophy of Sport." *Journal of Thought,* 13 (1978), 225-234.

Fairchild, David L. "What We Are and What We May Be: Reflections on Technology, Play and the Meaning of Contemporary Life." In *Sport and the Humanities: A Collection of Original Essays.* Edited by W.J. Morgan. Knoxville: University of Tennessee, 1979.

Feezell, Randolph. "Play, Freedom and Sport." *Philosophy Today,* 25 (1981), 166-175.

Feezell, Randolph. "Play and the Absurd." *Philosophy Today,* 28 (1984), 319-328.

Fell, Joseph P. "The Ethics of Play and Freedom." In *Heidegger and Sartre: An Essay on Being and Place.* New York: Columbia University Press, 1979.

Felshin, Jan. "Sport and Modes of Meaning." *Journal of Health, Physical Education, and Recreation,* 40 (May, 1969), 43-44.

Fennell, Frank L. "So Runs the World Away: Playtime in Modern America." *Listening,* 16 (1981), 5-17.

Fox, Richard M. "The So-Called Unreality of Sport." *Quest,* 34 (1982), 1-11.

Fraleigh, Sondra H. "Man Creates Dance." *Quest,* 23 (January, 1975), 20-27.

Fraleigh, Warren P. "The Moving 'I'." In *The Philosophy of Sport: A Collection of Original Essays.* Edited by Robert G. Osterhoudt. Springfield, IL: Charles C Thomas, 1973a.

Fraleigh, Warren P. "On Weiss on Records and on the Significance of Athletic Records." In *The Philosophy of Sport: A Collection of Original Essays*. Edited by Robert G. Osterhoudt. Springfield, IL: Charles C Thomas, 1973b.

Fraleigh, Warren P. "Some Meanings of the Human Experience of Freedom and Necessity in Sport." In *The Philosophy of Sport: A Collection of Original Essays*. Edited by Robert G. Osterhoudt. Springfield, IL: Charles C Thomas, 1973c.

Fraleigh, Warren P. "Sport-Purpose." *Journal of the Philosophy of Sport,* II (1975), 74-82.

Franke, E. "Sporting Action and Its Interpretation." In *Sport in the Modern World—Chances and Problems*. Edited by Ommo Grupe, Dietrich Kurz, and Johannes Teipel. New York: Springer-Verlag, 1973.

Furlong, William. "Danger as a Way of Joy." *Sports Illustrated,* 30 (January 27, 1969), 52-53.

Gadamar, Hans-Georg. *Truth and Method*. London: The Seabury Press, 1975.

Garrett, Roland. "The Metaphysics of Baseball." *Philosophy Today,* 20 (1976), 209-226.

Gebauer, G. "The Logic of Action and Construction of the World: Contribution to the Theory of Sport." In *Sport in the Modern World—Chances and Problems*. Edited by Ommo Grupe, Dietrich Kurz, and Johannes Teipel. New York: Springer-Verlag, 1973.

Gerber, Ellen W. "Identity, Relation and Sport." *Quest,* 8 (May, 1967), 90-97.

Graves, H. "A Philosophy of Sport." *The Contemporary Review,* 78 (1900), 877-893.

Gregg, Jerald Rex. "A Philosophical Analysis of the Sports Experience and the Role of Athletics in the Schools." Unpublished doctoral dissertation, University of Southern California, 1971.

Gruneau, Richard. "Freedom and Constraint: The Paradoxes of Play, Games and Sports." *Journal of Sport History,* 7 (1980), 68-86.

Hans, James S. "Hermeneutics, Play, Deconstruction." *Philosophy Today,* 24 (1980), 299-317.

Harper, William A. "Man Alone." *Quest,* 7 (May, 1969), 57-60.

Harper, William A. "Human Revolt: A Phenomenological Description." Unpublished doctoral dissertation, University of Southern California, 1971.

Harper, William A. "On Playing Sport." *Physical Education Review,* 6 (Spring, 1983), 52-57.

Hearn, Francis. "Toward a Critical Theory of Play." *Telos,* 30 (1976-77), 145-160.

Heinegg, Peter. "Philosopher in the Playground: Notes on the Meaning of Sport." *Southern Humanities Review,* 10 (1976), 153-156.

Herman, Daniel J. "Mechanism and the Athlete." *Journal of the Philosophy of Sport,* II (1975), 102-110.

Herrigel, Eugen. *Zen in the Art of Archery*. Translated by R.G.C. Hull. New York: McGraw-Hill, 1964.

Herzog, Maurice. *Annapurna*. New York: Popular Library, 1953.

Hinman, Lawrence M. "Nietzsche's Philosophy of Play." *Philosophy Today,* 18 (Summer, 1974), 106-124.

Hinman, Lawrence M. "On Work and Play: Overcoming a Dichotomy." *Man and World,* 8 (1975), 327-346.

Hoffman, Shirl J. "The Athletae Dei: Missing the Meaning of Sport." *Journal of the Philosophy of Sport,* III (1976), 42-51.

Horkheimer, Max. "New Patterns in Social Relations." In *International Research in Sport and Physical Education*. Edited by E. Jokl and E. Simon. Springfield, IL: Charles C Thomas, 1964.

Houston, Charles S. "The Last Blue Mountain." In *Why Man Takes Chances*. Edited by Samuel Z. Klausner. New York: Anchor Books, 1968.

Houts, Jo Ann. "Feeling and Perception in the Sport Experience." *Journal of Health,*

Physical Education, and Recreation, 41 (October, 1970), 71.

Huizinga, Johan. *Homo Ludens: A Study of the Play Element in Culture.* London: Routledge & Kegan Paul, 1950.

Hyland, Drew A. " 'And That Is the Best Part of Us': Human Being and Play." *Journal of the Philosophy of Sport,* IV (1977), 36-49.

Hyland, Drew A. "Athletics and Angst: Reflections on the Philosophical Relevance of Play." In *Sport and The Body: A Philosophical Symposium* (2nd ed.). Edited by Ellen W. Gerber and William J. Morgan. Philadelphia: Lea & Febiger, 1979.

Hyland, Drew A. "The Stance of Play." *Journal of the Philosophy of Sport,* VII (1980), 87-99.

Hyland, Drew A. "Opponents, Contestants, and Competitors: The Dialectic of Sport." *Journal of the Philosophy of Sport,* XI (1984a), 63-70.

Hyland, Drew A. *The Question of Play.* Washington, DC: University Press of America, 1984b.

Jaspers, Karl. "Sport." In *Man in the Modern Age.* Translated by Eden Paul and Cedar Paul. Garden City, NY: Doubleday, 1957.

Jolivet, Regis. "Work, Play, Contemplation." Translated by Sister M. Delphine. *Philosophy Today,* 5 (Summer, 1961), 114-120.

Kahn, Roger. "Intellectuals and Ballplayers." *American Scholar,* 26 (1957), 342-349.

Keating, James W. "Sartre on Sport and Play." In *Competition and Playful Activities.* Washington, DC: University Press of America, 1978.

Keen, Sam. *To a Dancing God.* New York: Harper & Row, 1970.

Klausner, Samuel Z. (Ed.). *Why Man Takes Chances.* New York: Anchor Books, 1968.

Kleinman, Seymour. "The Nature of a Self and Its Relation to an 'Other' In Sport." *Journal of the Philosophy of Sport,* II (1975), 45-50.

Krell, David Farrell. "Towards an Ontology of Play." *Research in Phenomenology,* 2 (1972), 63-93.

Kretchmar, R. Scott. "A Phenomenological Analysis of the Other in Sport." Unpublished doctoral dissertation, University of Southern California, 1971.

Kretchmar, R. Scott. "Ontological Possibilities: Sport as Play." In *The Philosophy of Sport: A Collection of Original Essays.* Edited by Robert G. Osterhoudt. Springfield, IL: Charles C Thomas, 1973a.

Kretchmar, R. Scott. "Phenomenology of Sport." In *Sport in the Modern World—Chances and Problems.* Edited by Ommo Grupe, Dietrich Kurz, and Johannes Teipel. New York: Springer-Verlag, 1973b.

Kretchmar, R. Scott. "Meeting the Opposition: Buber's 'Will' and 'Grace' in Sport." *Quest,* 24 (Summer, 1975), 19-27.

Kretchmar, R. Scott. "Athletic Courage and Heart: Two Ways of Playing Games." *Journal of the Philosophy of Sport,* IX (1982), 107-116.

Kretchmar, R. Scott, and Harper, William A. "Why Does Man Play?" *Journal of Health, Physical Education, and Recreation,* 40 (March, 1969), 57-58.

Kuezynski, Janusz. "Play as Negation and Creation of the World." *Dialectics and Humanism,* 11 (1984), 137-168.

Kuntz, Paul G. "Paul Weiss: What Is a Philosophy of Sports?" *Philosophy Today,* 20 (Fall, 1976), 170–189.

Lawton, Philip. "Sports and the American Spirit: Michael Novak's Theology of Culture." *Philosophy Today,* 20 (Fall, 1976), 196-208.

Lenk, Hans. "Herculean 'Myth' Aspects of Athletics." *Journal of the Philosophy of Sport,* III (1976), 11-21.

Leonard, George. *The Ultimate Athlete.* New York: Viking Press, 1975.

McLuhan, Marshall. "Games." In *Understand-*

ing Media: The Extensions of Man. New York: Signet, 1964.

Mead, George H. "Play, the Game, and the Generalized Other." In Mind, Self and Society from the Standpoint of a Social Behaviorist. Edited by Charles W. Morris. Chicago: University of Chicago Press, 1959.

Meier, Klaus V. "Authenticity and Sport: A Conceptual Analysis." Unpublished doctoral dissertation, University of Illinois at Urbana-Champaign, 1975.

Meier, Klaus V. "The Kinship of the Rope and the Loving Struggle: A Philosophic Analysis of Communication in Mountain Climbing." Journal of the Philosophy of Sport, III (1976), 52-61.

Meier, Klaus V. "Restless Sport." Journal of the Philosophy of Sport, XII (1985), 64-77.

Meier, Klaus V. "Play and Paradigmatic Integration." In The Many Faces of Play. Edited by Kendall Blanchard. Champaign, IL: Human Kinetics, 1986.

Metheny, Eleanor. Connotations of Movement in Sport and Dance. Dubuque, IA: Wm. C. Brown, 1965.

Metheny, Eleanor. Movement and Meaning. New York: McGraw-Hill, 1968.

Metheny, Eleanor. "The Symbolic Power of Sport." In Sport and the Body: A Philosophical Symposium (2nd ed.). Edited by Ellen W. Gerber and William J. Morgan. Philadelphia: Lea & Febiger, 1979.

Miller, David L. Gods and Games: Toward a Theology of Play. New York: World, 1970.

Mitchell, Robert. "Sport as Experience." Quest, 24 (Summer, 1975), 19-27.

Moltmann, Jurgen. Theology of Play. Translated by Reinhard Ulrich. New York: Herder and Herder, 1972.

Morford, W.R. "Is Sport the Struggle or the Triumph?" Quest, 19 (January, 1973), 83-87.

Morgan, William J. "An Existential Phenomenological Analysis of Sport as a Religious Experience." In The Philosophy of Sport: A Collection of Original Essays. Edited by Robert G. Osterhoudt. Springfield, IL: Charles C Thomas, 1973.

Morgan, William J. "Sport and Temporality: An Ontological Analysis." Unpublished doctoral dissertation, University of Minnesota, 1975.

Morgan, William J. "An Analysis of the Futural Modality of Sport." Man and World, 9 (1976a), 418-434.

Morgan, William J. "On the Path Towards An Ontology of Sport." Journal of the Philosophy of Sport, III (1976b), 25-34.

Morgan, William J. "The Lived Time Dimensions of Sportive Training." Journal of the Philosophy of Sport, V (1978a), 11-26.

Morgan, William J. "A Preliminary Discourse Concerning Sport and Time." Journal of Sport Behavior, 3 (August, 1978b), 139–146.

Moser, S. "Ansatzpunkte Einer Philosophischen Analysedes Sports." In Philosophie un Gegenwart, Meisenham, 1960.

Neale, Robert E. In Praise of Play. New York: Harper & Row, 1969.

Netzky, Ralph. "Playful Freedom: Sartre's Ontology Re-appraised." Philosophy Today, 18 (Summer, 1974), 125-136.

Norbeck, Edward. "Human Play and its Cultural Expression." Humanitas, 5 (Spring, 1969), 43-55.

Novak, Michael. The Joy of Sports: End Zones, Bases, Baskets, Balls and the Consecration of the American Spirit. New York: Basic Books, 1976.

Okrent, Mark. "Work, Play and Technology." Philosophical Forum, 10 (1978-79), 321-340.

Orringer, Nelson Robert. "Sport and Festival: A Study of Ludic Theory in Ortega y Gasset." Unpublished doctoral dissertation, Brown University, 1969.

Ortega y Gasset, José. "Uber des Lebers Sport lochfestlichen Sinn." Jahrbuch des Sports, (1955-56), 9-20.

Ortega y Gasset, José. *Meditations on Hunting.* Translated by H.B. Wescott. New York: Scribners, 1972.

Osterhoudt, Robert G. *An Introduction to the Philosophy of Physical Education and Sport.* Champaign, IL: Stipes, 1978.

Osterhoudt, Robert G. *Sport: A Humanistic Overview.* Tempe: Arizona State University, 1982.

Park, Roberta J. "Raising the Consciousness of Sport." *Quest,* 19 (January, 1973), 78-82.

Pavlich-Roby, Mary. "The Power of Sport." In *Sport and the Body: A Philosophical Symposium.* Edited by Ellen W. Gerber. Philadelphia: Lea & Febiger, 1972.

Perkins, Richard Donald. "Prolegomena to the Study of Play in Nietzsche." Unpublished doctoral dissertation, State University of New York at Buffalo, 1977.

Phillips, Patricia A. "The Sport Experience in Education." *Quest,* 23 (January, 1975), 94-97.

Pieper, Josef. *In Tune With the World: A Theory of Festivity.* Translated by Richard Winston and Clara Winston. New York: Harcourt, Brace & World, 1965.

Progen, Jan. "Man, Nature and Sport." In *Sport and the Body: A Philosophical Symposium* (2nd ed.). Edited by Ellen W. Gerber and William J. Morgan. Philadelphia: Lea & Febiger, 1979.

Rahner, Hugo. *Man at Play.* New York: Herder and Herder, 1967.

Riezler, Kurt. "Play and Seriousness." *Journal of Philosophy,* 38 (1941), 505-517.

Rimmer, Robert. "The Play Ethic." *Free Inquiry,* 3 (Winter, 1982-83), 11-16.

Roochnik, David L. "Play and Sport." *Journal of the Philosophy of Sport,* II (1975), 36-44.

Rossi, Ernest Lawrence. "Game and Growth: Two Dimensions of our Psychotherapeutic Zeitgeist." *Journal of Humanistic Psychology,* 7 (Fall, 1967), 139-154.

Sadler, William A., Jr. "Play: A Basic Human Structure Involving Love and Freedom." *Review of Existential Psychology and Psychiatry,* 6 (1966), 237-245.

Sadler, William A., Jr. "Alienated Youth and Creative Sports' Experience." *Journal of the Philosophy of Sport,* IV (1977), 83-95.

Sadler, William A., Jr. "Creative Existence: Play as a Pathway to Personal Freedom and Community." *Humanitas,* 5 (Spring, 1969), 57-79.

Santayana, George. "Philosophy on the Bleachers." *Harvard Monthly,* 8 (July, 1894), 181-190.

Sarani, Roberts. "The Flash of Spirit." *Quest,* 23 (January, 1975), 78-82.

Schacht, Richard L. "On Weiss On Records, Athletic Activity and the Athlete." In *The Philosophy of Sport: A Collection of Original Essays.* Edited by Robert G. Osterhoudt. Springfield, IL: Charles C Thomas, 1973.

Sheehan, George. *Running and Being: The Total Experience.* New York: Warner Books, 1978.

Shotter, John. "Prolegomena to an Understanding of Play." *Journal of the Theory of Social Behavior,* 3 (1973), 47-89.

Slovenko, Ralph, and Knight, James A. (Eds.). *Motivations in Play, Games and Sports.* Springfield, IL: Charles C Thomas, 1967.

Slusher, Howard S. *Man, Sport and Existence: A Critical Analysis.* Philadelphia: Lea & Febiger, 1967.

Slusher, Howard S. "To Test the Waves Is to Test Life." *Journal of Health, Physical Education, and Recreation,* 40 (May, 1969), 32-33.

Slusher, Howard S. "Existential Humanism and Sport." In *Sport in the Modern World— Chances and Problems.* Edited by Ommo Grupe, Dietrich Kurz, and Johannes Teipel. New York: Springer-Verlag, 1973.

Stevenson, Christopher L. "The Meaning of Movement." *Quest,* 23 (January, 1975), 2-9.

Stokes, Adrian. "The Development of Ball

Games.'' In *Motivations in Play, Games and Sport*. Edited by Ralph Slovenko and James A. Knight. Springfield, IL: Charles C Thomas, 1967.

Stone, Roselyn E. ''Meanings Found in the Acts of Surfing and Skiing.'' Unpublished doctoral dissertation, University of Southern California, 1970.

Stone, Roselyn E. ''Assumptions About the Nature of Human Movement.'' In *The Philosophy of Sport: A Collection of Original Essays*. Edited by Robert G. Osterhoudt. Springfield, IL: Charles C Thomas, 1973.

Stone, Roselyn E. ''Human Movement Forms as Meaning Structures: Prolegomenon.'' *Quest*, 23 (January, 1975), 10-19.

Stone, Roselyn E. ''Of Zen and the Experience of Moving.'' *Quest*, 33 (1981), 96-107.

Studer, Ginny L. ''The Language of Movement Is in the Doing.'' *Quest*, 23 (January, 1975), 98-100.

Thomson, Patricia. ''Ontological Truth in Sport: A Phenomenological Analysis.'' Unpublished doctoral dissertation, University of Southern California, 1967.

Tiger, Lionel. *Men in Groups*. New York: Random House, 1969.

Urbankowski, Bohdan. ''A General Theory of Sport Reality.'' *Dialectics and Humanism*, 11 (1984), 125-136.

Van Den Berg, J.H. ''The Human Body and the Significance of Human Movement.'' In *Psychoanalysis and Existential Philosophy*. Edited by Hendrik M. Ruitenbeck. New York: E.P. Dutton, 1962.

Vernes, Jean Rene. ''The Element of Time in Competitive Games.'' Translated by Victor A. Velen. *Diogenes*, 50 (September, 1965), 25-42.

Wachholz, William H. ''The Nature of Man and the Nature of Competition in Sport and Athletics.'' Unpublished master's thesis, University of Minnesota, 1974.

Walsh, John Henry. ''A Fundamental Ontology of Play and Leisure.'' Unpublished doctoral dissertation, Georgetown University, 1968.

Weiss, Paul. *Sport: A Philosophic Inquiry*. Carbondale, IL: Southern Illinois University Press, 1969.

Weiss, Paul. ''Records and the Man.'' In *The Philosophy of Sport: A Collection of Original Essays*. Edited by Robert G. Osterhoudt. Springfield, IL: Charles C Thomas, 1973.

Weiss, Paul. ''The Nature of a Team.'' *Journal of the Philosophy of Sport*, VIII (1981), 47-54.

Weiss, Paul. ''Some Philosophical Approaches to Sport.'' *Journal of the Philosophy of Sport*, IX (1982), 90-93.

Welter, Katherine A. ''Complete Moments in Sport: A Phenomenological Approach.'' Unpublished master's thesis, Western Illinois University, 1978.

Wenkart, Simon. ''Sports and Contemporary Man.'' In *Motivations in Play, Games and Sports*. Edited by Ralph Slovenko and James A. Knight. Springfield, IL: Charles C Thomas, 1967.

Wenkart, Simon. ''The Meaning of Sports for Contemporary Man.'' *Journal of Existential Psychiatry*, 3 (1963), 397-404.

White, David A. '' 'Great Moments in Sport': The One and Many.'' *Journal of the Philosophy of Sport*, II (1975), 124-132.

Wilkes, James Alexander. ''An Analysis of Jean-Paul Sartre's Use of Play and Sport in *Being and Nothingness*.'' Unpublished master's thesis, University of Western Ontario, 1982.

Wyschogrod, Edith. ''Sport, Death, and the Elemental.'' In *The Phenomenon of Death: Faces of Mortality*. Edited by E. Wyschogrod. New York: Harper and Row, 1973.

Zaner, Richard M. ''Sport and the Moral Order.'' *Journal of the Philosophy of Sport*, VI (1979), 7-18.

Part
IV

Sport and Ethics

Ethical issues deal with questions of value. Value is understood here in the sense of rightness and wrongness. Hence, ethics is a normative or prescriptive discipline as opposed to a descriptive one; that is, it is concerned not with how people actually act (a description of their action), but rather with how they *ought* to act (a prescription of their action).

Accordingly, the theme of the present section is how people ought to act within the context of sport. Three important and timely moral issues will be examined in this regard. The first has to do with the competitive character of sport and how one should treat one's fellow competitors with respect to that character. The second concerns the propriety of using performance-enhancing drugs in sport. And the last addresses the thorny question of how to ensure sexual equality in sport.

Competition, Sportsmanship, Cheating, and Failure

What is the proper competitive thrust of sport, and what mode of moral conduct best fulfills it, are therefore, the foci of the first set of essays of this section. Kretchmar argues that competitive sport involves a communal sharing of a test. Although the element of test in sport is logically distinct from the contest (one can focus on the skillful challenge offered by sport and yet ignore how one's opponent is faring), it is the pivotal basis of competition. For the test mediates the shared interaction that occurs in the contesting, the competing. Hyland argues that although competition in sport more often than not devolves into alienation, it need not do so. Indeed, he contends that competition and friendship are quite compatible, and, more strongly, that competitive encounters steeped in friendship represent the highest (most fulfilling) forms of competitive play.

Keating directs attention to the moral role sportsmanship exercises in competitive sport. Armed with his distinction between sport (a diversion whose aim is the attainment of pleasure) and athletics (an intensely competitive activity whose aim is victory), Keating argues that sportsmanship is not the all embracing moral virtue many take it to be. Its moral applicability is limited, he argues, to the realm of sport where it cultivates the festive, cooperative-competitive spirit of sport. Its applicability to athletics is not a moral one at all, Keating contends, but exclusively a legal one in which it acts as a juridical constraint on the competitive nature of athletics. Feezell's essay questions the radical distinction Keating

219

attempts to draw between sport and athletics. Feezell argues that the attitude of the athlete may be both sportive (festive, playful) and athletic (competitive and serious about winning). Viewed in this more complex, but accurate, way, Feezell ties sportsmanship and competition to the preservation of the play spirit, which he interprets according to Aristotle's conception of the mean: To be a good sport is to be both serious and nonserious in the senses cited above, to avoid the excesses of both caprice and winning.

Pearson introduces the notion of deception in the moral analysis of competitive sport. She distinguishes between *strategic* deception (the attempt to build up in one's opponent the expectation that a certain act will occur when, in fact, another act that disappoints the expectation is intended) and *definitional* deception (contracting to engage in one sort of activity and then engaging in another activity altogether). Pearson concludes that only the latter form of deception is morally suspect because it vitiates the central purpose of sport, namely, to test one's skill. Fraleigh argues in a similar vein. For him, too, the deliberate violation of the rules of sport subverts what sport, as defined by the rules, is all about. This moral prescription against rule-breaking also includes the so-called good foul; that is, fouling one's opponent when it is to one's advantage to do so and without attempting to conceal one's rule-breaking behavior. Such fouls, though widely accepted in sport today, are nonetheless morally unfit, Fraleigh argues, because they disrupt the skill-testing aim of competitive sport. Delattre also regards the violation of the rules as a moral offense on the grounds that it reduces competition to an excessively egoistic order in which one's opponents are treated as means, ignoring their fundamental moral status as ends.

The final two essays of this subsection on competition suggest a significant change in point of departure. Leaman claims that we can clearly specify neither when an instance of cheating has occurred in sport because our dominant notions of cheating are conceptually bankrupt, nor what is morally wrong with cheating. He provocatively suggests that we ought to encourage certain kinds of nondisruptive cheating in sport because it makes it a more intriguing affair. Lehman, in turn, seeks to overturn the view argued by many here that cheating is logically incompatible with winning, that it is logically impossible to win by cheating. Drawing on common cases of rule-breaking in sport (e.g., baseball pitcher Gaylord Perry's penchant for throwing spitballs), Lehman shows that although definite rules were violated no one would argue that the game ceased to be a game because of these violations. By disarming the logical incompatibility thesis he at the same time disarms the use of this thesis to demonstrate that cheating is without qualification an unethical act, that it destroys the fundamental purpose of sport, and so is morally wrong. One who attempts to derive unsportsmanlike behavior, Lehman argues, from the frustration of sport's basic aim is guilty of the same error as one who holds the view that cheating and winning are incompatible: both wrongly assume that one can tell what a game is just by consulting its rule-book. Such logical and moral errors can be avoided, Lehman concludes, only by considering the social contexts in which games are played.

Drugs and Sport

The second cluster of essays of this section takes up the pervasive problem of drug usage in sport. When, if ever, are athletes entitled to take drugs in order to enhance their performance? Simon, after demolishing many of the arguments often cited to support the prohibition of performance-enhancing drugs in sport, concludes that such drugs should be banned because they run counter to the very purpose of athletic competition, which is, in his interpretation, to test the athletic ability of *persons*. Because the improvement in performance owed to drug-taking cannot be attributed to the innate and developed ability of the athlete, but only to the contingent response of the athlete's body to the drug, Simon claims that such drugs have no legitimate place in competitive sport. Although Brown argues that the use of performance-enhancing drugs in sport by children and young people warrants paternalistic intervention, he does not find such intervention defensible in adult sports. He takes this position because he is not convinced that Simon's conception of sport as a mutual quest for excellence is morally privileged over other conceptions of sport that emphasize different kinds of values—for example, the view of sport as a medium for self-exploration and adventure.

Perry's article assesses the fairness of the practice of blood doping in sport. Perry classifies blood doping as a *supplementary* performance enhancer, that is, a tactic that does not *exploit* one's natural abilities, but compensates, and so augments, them. The use of such performance enhancers is fair, on Perry's account, only if it fulfills at least one of the following three conditions: (a) if the supplemented performance diminishes or eliminates other deleterious effects of performance, (b) if the supplemented performance overturns superfluous or otherwise irrelevant hindrances to performance, and (c) if specific ways and devices to supplement or not to supplement performance are agreed on beforehand. Because blood doping has apparently none of the redeeming qualities that other supplementary performance enhancers have, Perry considers its use in sport to be unfair. Hence, he concludes it should be prohibited expect in cases where its use is specified by the rules.

Thompson's article examines a different, but increasingly important, side to the drug question: Under what conditions, if any, is it ethical to require athletes to submit to urinalyses to detect the presence, or lack thereof, of drugs in the body? Thompson argues that the use of such exams is morally justified if they are used to enforce specific rules against banned substances. But under no circumstances, he claims, are such exams justified to detect illegal, recreational drug use by athletes. Hoberman concludes this subsection with an analysis of the basic features of modern, high-performance sport that give rise to, among other things, the use of performance-enhancing drugs. He argues that a certain hidden technological conception of human being underlies contemporary sport, namely, the *body-machine,* which is morally problematic.

Women and Sport

The last group of essays in this section considers the problem of sexual equality in sport. This issue is especially vexing given the apparent physiological advantages men enjoy over women in most sports. It is precisely because the traditional accounts of equal opportunity presume equal potentialities between men and women that English finds them wanting in the case of sport. She offers two proposals to ensure equal opportunity for women in sport. The first is to group individuals by ability alone and provide enough of such ability-groupings to accommodate everyone who wants to participate. English regards this as a good way to distribute the basic benefits of sport (e.g., health, cooperation, character, skill-development, and fun). The second is to group individuals by sex, and so to have separate, protected groups of women's sports. This is a good way, according to English, to distribute the scarce benefits of sport (e.g., fame and fortune). Even though the latter method discriminates against those males whose performance is on par with more able female athletes but less than more able male athletes, English considers it to be a justified practice because the integration of women's sports would have an adverse impact on the self-respect of all women. However, English concludes that because most of our present sports favor the male physique, a society that creates alternative sports that favor the female physique is preferable to one that maintains separate, protected classes of women's sports.

Young's essay spells out the implications of the general exclusion of women from sport. After detailing in what conceptual, practical, and institutional senses women have been barred from sport, she argues that such exclusion limits the full, potential humanity of women as well as the full, potential humanity of sport. Bellioti in turn focuses on English's proposal to distribute the scarce benefits of sport for women. Although sympathetic to much of what English has to say regarding women's right to the basic benefits of sport, Bellioti does not find her argument of self-respect to justify women's access to the distribution of scarce benefits persuasive. Contrarily, Bellioti argues that women, as well as men, ought not respect themselves because of their own or their group's attainments in professional sports, and that as a matter of empirical fact women do not base their self-respect on such professional achievements.

Wenz addresses the problem of human equality in sport, arguing that the answer to this larger problem satisfies the particular problem of sexual equality in sport. Based on the moral perspectives of utilitarianism, egalitarianism, and Rawls' theory of justice, Wenz maintains that the deprofessionalization of sport would better the equality of opportunity of both women and men. He suggests further that action of this sort is, aside from its general salutary effects on human equality, the possible key to overturning inequality in any endeavor where members of groups are biologically disadvantaged. Postow closes this subsection by arguing that sex segregation is not morally required to preserve masculine sports (sports that privilege the male body), to ensure women's equality of opportunity in masculine sports, or to ensure women's self-respect by making possible female stars in masculine sports. With regard to the latter, Postow argues that even if women's self-respect were tied to female athletic stars, such self-respect would be better served by female stars who excelled in sports that favor the female physique.

Additional literature is available on each of the three issues addressed in this section. In the subsection on sportsmanship and cheating general treatments and overviews of sport and ethics can be found in the works of Fraleigh (1984b), Zeigler (1984), Kretchmar (1983), and McIntosh (1979). Osterhoudt (1973) and Sadler (1973) offer direct, critical responses to Keating's essay published here. In addition, Arnold (1983), Coon (1964), and Callisch (1953) independently analyze the notion of sportsmanship. Finally, Wertz (1981) takes a more in-depth look at the cheating problem in sport.

The drug issue in sport has been examined by Grupe (1985), and Beckett (1984). Breivik (in press) considers this issue from the oft-used prisoner's dilemma model. Fraleigh (1984a) responds to the issues raised by Simon and Brown in this volume. Brown (1980) himself more closely examines the use of performance-enhancing drugs by adult athletes. And Moorcraft (1985) looks at the drug question from the athlete's point of view.

Lastly, considerations of equality in competitive sport are addressed by Addelson (1983). Greenberg (1985) and Keenan (1975) focus on the theme of justice. And Ravizza and Daruty (1984) analyze the twin issues of paternalism and sovereignty as they bear on the questions of athlete's rights and the limits of a coach's authority.

COMPETITION, SPORTSMANSHIP, CHEATING, AND FAILURE

From Test to Contest: An Analysis of Two Kinds of Counterpoint in Sport

R. SCOTT KRETCHMAR

Sport thrives on contraries. Where point and counterpoint, thesis and antithesis, and more or less stand out most clearly, sport appears to be its richest. Think of the common sport milieu where East is pitted against West, North against South, the "haves" versus the "have-nots." There is this side and that, home and away, opponents and teammates, winners and losers. Athletes strive to be in contact or apart, here rather than there, now rather than then, and so on. One can barely speak of sport without filling his language with contraries.

Moreover, in sport there appears to have been an invention of new counterpoints. "Shirts," which went for centuries without a clear logical opposite, now have one—"skins." And notions which were thought to have obvious contraries now traffic in the world of sport with new counterpoints. For the opposite of winning is building character; the counterpoint of cheating is stupidity; there is the successful play and its contrary, practice.

But taking language as a primary clue to present hunches about the blood kinship of sport and oppositional relationships is dangerous. Just as the

English language allows one to say, "I love you," at least four times without being redundant, an athlete may be able to say quite sensibly, "I meet opposition in sport, and what is more, I meet opposition in sport." Indeed, in the present paper it is suggested that sport entails two very different kinds of point-counterpoint. It is further maintained that one set of opposites is presupposed by the other.

One basic kind of point-counterpoint,[1] as described by Ogden (2: pp. 53–66), is opposition by scale. This involves one phenomenon ranging in degree from 0 to 100. There is no juxtaposition of logical opposites anywhere between the extremes, but simply more and less of some element as one moves up the scale and down, respectively. Common examples of such opposition are black-white, empty-full and poor-rich. Black, for instance, is the total absence of white and is given a position at the zero end of this hypothetical scale. Black becomes charcoal, gray, light gray, and so on as one moves "up" this scale toward absolute white or the 100 point.

A second kind of point-counterpoint, which is of interest here, is opposition by "cut." (2: pp. 53–66) This places two phenomena on opposite sides of a zero point. When this point is crossed in either direction, a phenomenon immediately changes to its opposite. Opposition by "cut" is

Reprinted from *Journal of the Philosophy of Sport,* II, (1975), pp. 23–30. Copyright 1975 by the Philosophic Society for the Study of Sport. Reprinted by permission.

characteristic of all logical opposites which, by nature, exclude one another. Opposite direction and two of its bases, attraction and repulsion, involve opposition by "cut." Sense-nonsense, possible-impossible, true-false and A-not A exemplify this kind of contrariety. It may be the case that a scale exists on one or both sides of the "cut." For example, different actions are thought to be more or less possible while impossibility would seem to admit of no variation. But the fact remains that the zero point separates two exclusive opposites and does not stand at one extreme of a distinction by degree. While there is some variation on the side of possibility, to continue with the same example, it is *all not* impossibility; the "cut" remains intact.

Sport and the Test

It is commonly recognized that winning and losing are essential to sport. In sport contests one bears witness to his comparative physical prowess. An attempt is made to perform more impressively than another. If successful in this venture, the participant wins; if not, a loss or tie must be recorded.

But there could be no *superior* performance without the possibility for variance in quality among the feats of different performers. One cannot win unless his actions are different *and* noticeably better than another's. While any two human acts would be different (i.e., they occur at separate times and/or places and involve, at least minimally, unique styles), they may not be discernibly superior or inferior to one another. Surely two normally coordinated adults, for instance, who pick up motionless baseballs from the ground do so differently. One person moves more deliberately than the other; one has more rhythm in his movements, and so on. But a person would be hard-pressed to determine who picked up his ball better. Both succeeded quite well.

Thus, while it appears difficult not to do things differently than another, acting in a superior or inferior fashion occurs only in particular situations. It will be argued, in the remainder of this section, that a genuine test provides such minimal (necessary) conditions. The comparisons inherent in the sport contest are unintelligible in the absence of a true test.

A test is an ambiguous phenomenon which is seen as both impregnable and vulnerable. A test "defies" one to solve its riddles. Yet, it "invites" one to try. It offers the challenger both a "yes" and a "no." Its contrariety appears to be an opposition by "cut," not degree.

While tests do vary in their degree of difficulty, each test itself is grounded in an opposition by "cut." Of extreme importance here is the recognition that impregnability and vulnerability are not extremes on a single scale. Impregnability is the facet of a test which indicates that a person might "get it wrong." Vulnerability allows for the possibility that one might "get it right." While an individual could be wrong or right to different degrees, the "cut" remains intact. A mountain climber, for example, who on his first attempt made it halfway to his objective, the summit, and on his second effort traversed three quarters of the distance, failed both times. While his failures differed in degree, they were *both not* successes. The mountain was, in this case, not vulnerable.

Were one to trade this opposition by "cut" for one of degree, a test would become something which is more or less vulnerable or more or less impregnable. But if a "test," to examine the prior possibility, were wholly vulnerable (albeit to different degrees), one's objective would become wholly a foregone conclusion (albeit to different degrees). The climber *will* reach the top of the mountain.

But if a climber tries to reach an easily attainable summit "as fast as possible," a test shows itself once again. To scale this mountain in four hours, for instance, is neither to meet something which is simply more or less vulnerable nor to have a project which is more or less a foregone conclusion. One might fail. The stark opposition by "cut" shows itself clearly.

The testing opposition by "cut" produces an irrevocable sense of uncertainty on the part of the performer. He lives ambiguously toward his test, acting on the one hand as if his project were destined for success but knowing on the other that his gestures may be ineffectual. This uncertainty is an acknowledgement of the twin truths of taking tests —that of the may and may not, making progress and being stymied, solving and trying futilely. The performer's act, then, correlates directly with its object, the test. One lives an expectation of success toward the test's vulnerability and an awareness of possible failure toward the test's impregnability.

Tests simply become unthinkable or unintelligible in the absence of such opposition. As suggested, if something were merely vulnerable, the "test" would become gratuitous facilitation and one's project a foregone conclusion. Nothing would be tested. This is the case with any project which can be done simply, automatically, or without any trouble. On the other hand, if something were merely impregnable, the "test" would become a "state of affairs," and one's project would be wholly futile. Again, nothing would be tested. Immortal feats are not tests for mere mortals.

Thus, neither vulnerability nor impregnability can stand by itself if the test is to exist. To redefine a current cliche, one truly has "no problem" when *either side* of the present oppositional schema is absent, not only when difficulty has fled. Surely an impregnable state of affairs is "no (human) problem."

Yet, the discord created by logical opposites standing, as it were, side by side is bothersome. How can an object reveal itself as both vulnerable and impregnable? And how can the correlating testing act be lived toward both success and failure?

Toward a resolution of this apparent conflict, it can be suggested that a test involves an alternation of vulnerability and impregnability rather than a simultaneity of these factors. This at once avoids the problem of contradiction and retains the contrast offered by the opposites. But this can be no solution. An alternation of vulnerability and impregnability is but an alternation of the foregone conclusion and impossible feat, respectively. Any acceleration of the process only produces a more stroboscopic alternation. The test can never appear. Any revision of this "alternation thesis" which would include overlapping "after effects" is a fatal concession to the present point, for the door to simultaneity and full discord thereby has been reopened.

If an alternation of contraries does not give one a test, there may be some philosophic future in attempting to average the two together. But the mean in this case is a zero point and thus, neither vulnerability nor impregnability. And a test cannot appear at the nil. In other words, a test cannot be described by avoiding references to both "yes" and "no."

In a final argument it could be suggested that the true contraries in this matter are the test and oneself, not elements of the test itself or reflections in the testing act itself. In this schema the actor would constitute the "yes" and the test the "no." Indeed, one often hears talk, for example, about a person confronting a mountain. This would be, supposedly, an individual's courageous affirmation of possibility against the mountain's intransigence. In this case neither the test nor the testing act is internally contradictory, and the sharp opposition by "cut" is preserved.

Yet, this common talk about men and mountains is misleading. If the mountain were simply impregnable, the climber must be (to preserve the opposition) vulnerable. But these attributes both characterize objects, neither one of which, incidentally, is a test. And, of course, the climber wants to take a test, not be one.

The same difficulties obtain on the side of the act. If the climber were to live possibility toward the mountain, the latter must be supposed somehow to exemplify impossibility. But a mountain, of course, cannot live impossibility toward anything, and these two characterizations of acts are individually not those of taking a test. One is the anticipation of a foregone conclusion, the other resignation to the status quo.

Further difficulties are encountered when one tries to match an act's possibility with a mountain's impregnability. In addition to not providing logical opposites, this produces at best a stalemate and at worst a wholly irrational act. In this situation one's capabilities have no arena for their exercise. This supposed testing other cannot be of service, for, as impregnable, it is unable to receive one's skillful thrusts in any way. More to the point, a person who lived simple possibility toward what *he himself* saw to be an unchangeable state of affairs is not obeying the most basic laws of correct thinking. The act and object do not match up. This individual is not just a dreamer, for a dreamer's goals are seen by him as somehow attainable, if only through imaginary acts. This climber, on the other hand, is simply not thinking correctly.

If there is any synthesis to be found "above" the testing thesis (an act's possibility lived toward an object's vulnerability) and antithesis (an act's impossibility lived toward an object's impregnability), it may be described by Fraleigh's terms "sweet tension."[2] Tension on the side of the testing act shows itself as uncertainty. One's testing gesture is forever tentative. It "aims" for success but is never assured of it. The testing act is lived in the mood of "will it happen?"

However, the objective of one's act is not uncertain. Indeed, the very recognition of a test presupposes a *specific, unambiguous act* in virtue of which something is a test. For example, a mountain may show itself as a test, but only against the implicit background of the act of climbing in a certain way to its summit. Without the presence of this specific project, there could be no uncertainty about whether or not *it* can be done.

Tension on the side of the object is encountered as ambiguity. In the manner of an ambiguous figure, the test has two faces. In this case they can be thought of as identical and pointed in opposite directions. The ambiguous profiles at once reveal Ogden's attraction and repulsion. (2: pp. 63–65) As *one* ambiguous object,[3] they are both facing and facing away from one another. They are opposed. But again, the ambiguity is met as a "sweet tension." It is compelling, attractive. The tester is silently called to engage it.

The moment that a mountain climber, for instance, sees an imposing edifice, it can present itself in its full testing ambiguity. There is usually no need on the part of the climber to first measure his own skills and subsequently deduce the testing or non-testing nature of the mountain. One's finite skills *are* one's perspective; they are implicit in meeting the mountain immediately as a test or no test.

As the climb is begun in the face of a true test, one anticipates success in pursuing promising avenues of access. Yet, it is also understood that these very paths may truly be no way to the summit. This "sweet tension" of uncertainty lived toward an ambiguous environment may be resolved momentarily as a particular path is successfully traversed. But uncertainty emerges again as one's gaze falls upon new testing ambiguities in the form of a snow field, steep incline or loose rock. The moment that the discord disappears, the test dissolves. For example, the last half of a mile to the peak may present no problems. One's test disappears in this case precisely one half mile from the summit. The rest of the climb is "exercise."

It may be clearer now why the loss of *testing* uncertainty and ambiguity precludes any possibility for *contesting*. Variance in the quality of two person's performances (thus, permitting victory and defeat) is virtually assured in testing situations. Each "inch" of success is difficult to gain. A person can reveal precisely what he can do, ranging from utter failure to complete success. So long as the testing ambiguity survives, a vast field of potential accomplishment stretches out before the performer. When this ambiguity is lost, the full range of possible success is diminished to just two collecting pools of non-differentiation—the "foregone conclusion" (wherein *everyone* can succeed) and the "state of affairs" (wherein *nobody* can succeed).

While the test provides a basis for contests, it is, in principle, independent from competitive acts.

In other words, a test permits intelligible activity in its own right. When one takes a test he learns "X" about his own skills. This "X" need not stand in relation to another's "X" for it to indicate the state of one's skill. It surely makes sense to talk of someone being successful or unsuccessful without making reference to victories or defeats. One need not lose in a baking contest, for instance, to know that a badly burned pie was unsuccessfully baked.

Billy Jean King, to cite a second example, reported that at times she becomes totally involved with the *test* of tennis and forgets about the relative status of her opponent as an opponent. To paraphrase a portion of her statement, "The ball never comes across the net the same way twice. It is terrifically interesting to deal with the forever new features of the problem." How her opponent is faring is, at least momentarily, irrelevant. Ms. King's "opponent" in such circumstances is providing her with a very rich test, whether or not a contest is being lived between them.

Sport and the Contest

The transition from test to contest is the change from human singularity to community. Simply, it is finding someone with whom one can share a test. In addition, a commitment is made by each side to attempt to better the other's performance. Victory is always victory over someone; defeat is forever suffered "at the hands of," minimally, a second individual.

If a second person and a commitment to excel one another is characteristic of contests, in contrast to tests, it is not difficult to see that a second point-counterpoint is at work here. The contraries in this polarity would appear to be the opponents themselves. One player wants to do this, his adversary that. One team moves east, the other west. There are the winners and the losers. Or as it is sometimes put in contests, "It is either you or me."

This appears to be a second opposition by "cut," a matching of true opposites. But a closer inspection reveals something else. If one wanted to do the opposite of his adversary's efforts to score points, for example, he would *not* be committed to score points, be committed *not* to score points or perhaps, committed to score *non*-points. Of course, this is not the case. Each side wants to score points, more points than the other. Opponents try to do the same thing as one another, only more so. They attempt to pass the same kind of test better, to a greater degree, higher on the scale, than another. Opponents are not essentially opposites but rather very much alike. Their difference is by degree, and it is often slight.

This is not surprising when one considers the derivation of the term "contest" itself. Coming from *com* plus *testari,* meaning to bear witness together, it suggests both human plurality and a common testimony. A minimal two persons must be doing the same kind of thing for valid comparisons of success to be made. It would sound strange for a person to claim victory in a running race to the store even though his adversary used a car or, worse yet, drove to another place. But this contesting "togetherness" is not a community project toward one end, as it would be if two or more persons were trying collectively to pass a test. It is doing the same kind of thing in an attempt to show difference in the direction of superiority.

Thus, contesting opposition would be one of scale. This is a continuous scale running from a hypothetical zero point (utter failure on the test) to 100 (total success on the test). The greatest distinction in the contest is that which exists, for example, between one who "could not get to first base" and another who scored runs as a "matter of habit." Interestingly, the polarity black-white, which is Ogden's archetype for opposition on a continuous scale (2: p. 66), finds its way into such a loser's vocabulary when he complains of being "whitewashed."

Yet it is the subtle distinction between two hues of white, gray, or black which typifies the close contest. So delicate is the distinction that it is often difficult to discern. The exact nature of differences in performance (if any) may be left in doubt until the last moment of the contest. Paradoxically, many behemoths of sport spend hours sending the resounding shock waves of their collisions into the air to symbolize what they see as the great mutually exclusive opposites of the universe—victory and defeat. Yet they may produce but a whisper of difference by degree, only the most subtle of distinctions between themselves. The would be quest for ''A'' rather than ''not-A'' or at least white rather than black turns out to be one for a slightly lighter shade of off-white.

There appear to be two steps taken in moving from test to contest. The first is the development of testing families. It is one tester recognizing another individual as a like tester. It is grounded in the ability to see that someone else can encounter the same test as oneself.

This does not mean that one merely identifies other golfers, swimmers, or mountain climbers as members of a general category. Testing families are much more specific, for golf courses, swimming pools and mountains offer a multitude of different tests. An advanced golfer sees his test, for example, in much different terms than the beginner. A high rough, a heavy cross wind, or a 225 yard distance which must be traversed in a single shot with the ball moving from left to right provides testing ambiguity for the excellent golfer. These same phenomena may be seen by the beginner as impossible situations. The novice cannot exercise his skill in relationship to these situations. In short, the beginner and advanced golfers do not see themselves as members of the same testing family.

This identification of family membership often occurs without knowledge of another's scores or record. There are certain ''signs of the family'' which serve to identify communities of like testers. The quality of another's equipment, the clothes he wears, the stories he tells, and mannerisms in speech, gait, and other body gestures often announce quite loudly the specific testing fraternity

to which he belongs. More telling yet is the manner in which another individual approaches his test. The preparation, deliberation, positioning, and focus of concentration are all family specific. In golf, for example, one can generally watch another merely walk onto the tee and address his ball and thereby recognize the specific community to which he belongs. The eventual swing and result are superfluous for these purposes.

Again, one's own skill is implicit in identifying other members of his testing community. There is usually no need to recall recent scores or otherwise assess one's own skill at taking the test to make this identification. An athlete lives his skill (even if it had changed recently) toward other potential members of his testing family. Their welcome or non-welcome is immediate and is not the end result of a chain of deductions which begin with the measurement of one's own athletic prowess.

The second step in moving from test to contest is making a commitment within a testing family to better one another's performances. This step succeeds the formation of a testing family simply because in the absence of such a community one has at worst no basis for a comparison (two individuals are engaged in taking two different tests) or at best a poor basis for contesting (one side will be ''whitewashed'').

Such a commitment to do better than another is often difficult to observe and, at times, exists only tenuously. One's supposed opponent may become so fascinated with the test itself that the contest is ignored. Or a counterfeit opponent may play for his health, relaxation, or being ''in the great outdoors.'' Victory and defeat, in such situations, are not shared. The contest is not mutually held.

But if two family members are truly contesting, they are interested in each other's progress in taking the test. Their own strategies, rhythms, their very relationship to the test is, in part, dictated by the *other's* performance. Contestants watch one another. The contestants cannot be concerned merely with passing the test, for an opponent may pass it in a superior fashion. The test itself cannot give a contestant sufficient information on what is required of him.

Conclusions

Sport is diverse, even in its basic structure. The two kinds of point-counterpoint examined in this essay undergird two very different kinds of activity. Both are captivating; both have their own "sweet tension." The radical ambiguity of the test, its strident vulnerability and impregnability, as well as the contest's more subtle opposition by degree, the shadings of a little more and a little less, call to those who like to move in an aura of uncertainty.

Notes

1. Point-counterpoint is defined as opposite points, themes, or courses and is used interchangeably with opposition and contrariety in this paper.
2. A phrase used to describe human fascination with sport from Warren P. Fraleigh of the State University College at Brockport, New York.
3. They can be neither back to back nor face to face, for this would eliminate the ambiguity.

Bibliography

1. Kretchmar, R. Scott. "A Phenomenological Analysis of the Other in Sport." Unpublished doctoral dissertation, University of Southern California, 1971.
2. Ogden, C.K. *Opposition: A Linguistic and Psychological Analysis.* Bloomington: Indiana University Press, 1967.
3. Suits, Bernard. "The Elements of Sport," *The Philosophy of Sport.* Robert G. Osterhoudt (ed.). Springfield, Illinois: Charles C Thomas, 1973.

Competition and Friendship

DREW A. HYLAND

I would suppose that nearly everyone who has participated in competitive sports, from sand-lot games through the more organized level of high school and college teams to professional athletics, has had one version or another of the following two experiences. On the one hand, we have experienced that situation in which our competitive play breaks down into alienation. This can of course take on a variety of forms and degrees of intensity. It can be as mild as a slight feeling of irritation when we feel that our opponent has hit us, or perhaps hit a ball *at* us, harder than he or she needed to. Or it can be the stronger and more pervasive feeling which some of us have that we "do better" in competitive sports when we are angry at our opponents, that somehow this spurs us on so that we "really want to win." It can show itself at those times when we hurt someone in competitive play, yet instead of feeling apologetic or at least sympathetic towards our injured opponent, we find ourselves exhilarated. At its extreme form within the context of sports, the game actually degenerates into fisticuffs. In all such cases as these, we have that co-presence of competition and alienation which is so common that it has led some to see a causal relation: competition *causes* alienation. Anyone who has never experienced one form or another of alienation in their competitive play has had an extraordinarily fortunate—not to say sheltered—sporting experience. But there is a second kind of competitive experience which most of

us have also had, one very different from the latter. I refer to that experience of competitive sport in which our relation to our opponent can be that mode of positive encounter which deepens into a form of friendship. Many of our closest friends are people whom we "get to know" in competitive situations. For many of us, playing sports with someone is a way of preserving and deepening an established friendship. Sometimes we can even say that "I never play harder than against my friend," yet even this greater intensity enhances rather than diminishes the positive strength of the relationship. I note with interest that there is less disposition to attribute a causal relation here between competition and friendship; we are rarely informed that competition causes friendship. Still, anyone who has never experienced this sort of friendship in competitive play has had an extraordinarily unfortunate—not to say perverse—sporting experience.

Now the point of these remarks is to enable me to establish what I take to be an apparently obvious but strangely controversial beginning: the empirical news is that both alienation and friendship sometimes accompany competition. This raises a set of questions upon which I should like to reflect in this paper. First, can we speak of a causal relation between either competition and alienation or competition and friendship? If neither, what then is the nature of their respective relations? If both, how can competition be causally tied to such apparently opposite phenomena as alienation and friendship? For that matter, is the direction of the causal relation reversed, that is, do either alienation or friendship *cause* competition?[2] It is impor-

Reprinted from *Journal of the Philosophy of Sport,* V, (1978), pp. 27–37. Copyright 1978 by the Philosophic Society for the Study of Sport. Reprinted by permission.

tant to reiterate that despite the empirical presence of both alienation and friendship in the competition of play, there is and has been a strong tendency to associate competition closely with alienation, and to regard friendship as in tension not just with alienation but with competition itself. Because the relation between competition and friendship is less obvious and perhaps less prevalent, I shall focus on that relation in this paper, though I hope my remarks will be germane to a reflection on the relation of competition and alienation as well.

A second sort of question raised by the co-presence of friendship and alienation in competitive play is this; since both do sometimes occur in play, it would seem to follow that our competitive play ever and again *risks* alienation. (Can we say as well that it risks friendship?) What is the broader significance of this risk-taking element in our competitive play?

I wish to make it clear immediately that these questions are by no means peculiar to the play situation. The relation of competition and alienation, competition and friendship, competition and risk-taking, these are issues of human being itself. At the same time, as I have argued elsewhere, (8: p. 87), the play situation, by its natural intensity and its—sometimes arbitrary—delimitation in space, time, and purpose, can make certain themes more visible than in our ongoing everyday lives. To be sure, play and playful competition can without doubt be engaged in for their own sake; that is compatible with my conviction that the foundational issues of play are not limited to play itself. For this reason, a good part of this paper may seem to wander far from the explicit issue of play. But if I am successful, I will be able to show the intimacy between play and human being by showing how they shed light on *each other*. Let me begin with the following considerations.

The view has been stated by many an armchair philosopher that human beings are "by nature" competitive, by which is usually meant that in one way or another, whether in our business dealings, or our creative projects, our play, or our love affairs, the "competitive instinct" will eventually show itself. Moreover, this thesis, when it is set out with care, seems usually to be coupled with a second thesis about the natural *alienation* of human beings. Thus Hobbes speaks of the "state of nature" as a "war of all against all" (6: pp. 87, 106), and Hegel, in his famous account of the development of self-consciousness in the *Phenomenology of Spirit,* speaks of a primordial "fight to the death" arising out of the desire for recognition (4: pp. 113–114). In perhaps its most popular version, Marx, who does *not* accept the teaching that human being is *by nature* competitive and alienated, still preserves such a close connection between the two that he argues that the removal of competition—through the overcoming of capitalism—will bring about the abolition of alienation (10: pp. 131, 155 et al.).

On the other hand, there is another thesis about human being, usually associated with romanticism, that argues that human beings are by nature friendly, or loving, that only the perversions of society or history bring about the rise of competition or alienation.[3] Significantly, the view that human beings are naturally friendly is usually contrasted to the view that we are by nature competitive.

Perhaps I can now reformulate the guiding themes of this paper at a more fundamental level. Is it the case that there is a necessary connection between human being as competitive and alienation? Or is there a conception of human being which would allow that we be, in a sense, both *by nature* competitive and *by nature* given to friendship? I wish to entertain the thesis that there is indeed such a conception, and moreover, that human play is just the theatre where that complex nature gets most visibly manifested. But the sense of human nature in which competition and friendship are not merely compatible, but closely connected, needs some working out.

Let me begin by delineating two conceptions of the individual which, once again, are usually taken as in tension if not utterly opposed. I shall call them respectively the monadic and the relational.

Briefly, the spokesmen for the monadic conception of the individual argue that human being is—or at least should be—an autonomous, self-reliant monad, whose essence, literally whose being, is intrinsic. To be sure, such individuals will enter into relations with others; this is not a view which argues that becoming a hermit is the *telos* of human existence. But such relationships as people enter will not on this view be literally essential to their nature. Our relations with others may please us, trouble us, amuse or bore us. But they will not make us what we are. As three well-known versions of this view of the individual, I would mention the position presented in Adam Smith's foundational work on capitalism, the *Wealth of Nations* (14: passim, esp. pp. 14, 423, 651), Friedrich Nietzsche's ideal of the *Übermensch*, for whom friendships arise not as a "need" but as a free gift of the "overfulness" of that autonomous individual (11: pp. 168, 173–174, 190, 273), and finally, the individual as presented in the works of Henry David Thoreau, a self-reliant being capable of living as a "world unto himself."[4] Let me emphasize that the spokesmen for this conception present it as desirable, sometimes even as an ideal; and indeed, most of us do experience this sense of autonomy as a positive one. Conversely, we often are troubled when we feel our relations with others to be what we disparagingly call "dependency relationships." Let it suffice to say that this model of the individual has a long, a complex, and we can even say a noble history in our tradition; but no more so than the second conception of which I spoke earlier, that of the relational individual.

According to the spokesmen for the relational individual, we are relational by nature. We are what we are and who we are, positively or negatively, in terms of the name and nature of our relations with others. For example, at the level of social role definition, if I am a father, husband, teacher, and athlete, these definitive roles all refer to modes of relations with others. I want to emphasize that the difference between this view and the former does not depend on whether or not we do relate to others, but on how essential those relations are to our being. As examples of well-known versions of the relational conception of the individual, I would cite the Aristotelian definition of human being as "the political animal" (2: 1253a), its Marxian reformulation as "species being" (10: p. 127 et al), and the standpoint of the existentialist thinker, Martin Buber, who begins his famous book, *I And Thou*, with the teaching that,

"There is no I taken by itself, but only the I of the primary word I-thou and the I of the primary word I-it." (3: p. 4)

As in the case of the monadic individual, so here, the adherents to this view in nearly all cases *affirm it*, see it not only as the natural way for humans to be but as desirable and something to be perpetuated. Indeed, the appeal of participatory involvements, from team sports to nationalism, would hardly be understandable if the conception of the individual as relational did not contain some truth.

The study of the histories of these two viewpoints, the ebb and flow of their dominance, and the efforts to reconcile them would shed considerable light on the development of our tradition. Our purpose here is a more limited one, for which the above sketch will hopefully suffice. We need to ask the relationship, if any, between these conceptions of the individual on the one hand and on the other the themes of competition, alienation, and friendship which are central to the present reflection. I would submit the following thesis, that the conception of the individual as monadic typically and most easily develops an understanding of human being in which competition is present and tends toward alienation, whereas the relational view more easily develops a version of natural friendship, either as original or as a goal. It is not difficult to cite as *prima facie* evidence for these associations some of the previous examples. There is a clear relation between the monadic conception of the individual and the competition of capitalism for Adam Smith, who in order to claim that some *good* will emerge from this situation is forced to the somewhat desperate expedient of the "invisible hand" (14: p. 423). Nietzsche, who clearly argues for the monadic view, accepts and even affirms alienation as part of the life of genuinely creative individuals (11: pp. 168, 190). Again, Marx draws a clear connection between the abolition of alienation under capitalism and the fulfillment of the relational ideal of species being (10: p. 155). Finally, the connection between the relational view and a natural tendency to friendship can be seen in Buber's fundamental thesis that the I-thou relation is the highest possibility for human being (3: passim). If this is plausible, then we must note immediately that the oppositional character of our subject seems to have been deepened. Natural competition and alienation seem grounded in a conception of the individual as monadic, natural friendship in the individual as relational, and these two conceptions seem themselves in fundamental opposition.

But the greatest minds of many a generation have been unsatisfied with this initial opposition. Because both have their appeal, because most of us when we reflect about it want to consider ourselves both monadic, with its connotations of autonomy and authenticity, and relational, with its connotations of community and participation, efforts have been made again and again to argue that the opposition is not irreconcilable, that human being is both monadic *and* relational, a position whose attractiveness is mitigated only by the recognition that it is easier said than justified. Still, numerous efforts at reconciliation of the two positions have been made, and I wish to appeal briefly to one of the most famous, again only with sufficient depth to enable us to relate it to our guiding theme. The position I shall outline might be associated with the Socrates of the Platonic dialogues.

According to the Platonic Socrates in the *Symposium,* the human soul is decisively characterized by eros (love).[5] We are erotic in our very being. Eros, in turn, is characterized by three fundamental aspects. On the one hand, it is incompleteness, partiality. Erotic beings are beings who, in their being, are incomplete, who are not whole. Second,

eros is the experience of, or in its highest instances the explicit recognition of, this incompleteness. Erotic beings experience their incompleteness and the most self-conscious of them recognize it as such. Thirdly, consequent upon the first two aspects, eros is the striving to overcome experienced incompleteness, the striving for the attainment of wholeness out of partiality. Erotic beings, then, are incomplete, experience that incompleteness, and strive to overcome it. This, according to Socrates, is the basic structure of what we call our "love affairs," to be sure, but in fact we use the term "love" to refer to only one of its instances. *All* situations in which we strive to overcome experienced incompleteness, whether of sexuality, of political power, of wealth, or creativity, or of wisdom, all are testimony to our erotic nature. In short, we are erotic through and through.

Now it is not difficult to see how this view attempts to hold that we are both relational and monadic. On the one hand, as incomplete, we are not autonomous; we do not contain the ingredients of completeness within ourselves. We *are* a relation to others—to all other things but especially to other humans—in so far as we see in those others the possibility of fulfillment. I am what I am in terms of the way I experience my eros; my relations with others are the ways in which I seek wholeness. Thus, to use earlier examples, if I am a father, husband, teacher, and athlete, these all testify to ways in which I have experienced incompleteness and strived to overcome it; they are the ways in which I manifest my eros.

On the other hand, my experience of incompleteness, my choice of the ways I shall strive to overcome it, make me what I am as a unique individual. To paraphrase Martin Heidegger's remarks about Dasein, eros is "in each case mine" (5: p. 68). Part of the much discussed striving for "identity" could be construed as the effort to get clear for ourselves about our *own* eros, about our *own* experience of incompleteness and how we will choose to strive after fulfillment. In this sense, to again borrow phraseology from Heidegger, eros is indeed "our ownmost possibility, nonrelational, certain and as such indefinite, not to be out-stripped'' (5: p. 303 et al). In short, our eros makes us each what we are, as individuals, and as such unique. To now put these two points together, we could say that our eros *individualizes* us—makes us each the unique individuals that we are—but it individualizes us *as* relational beings. The beings that get individualized by their eros are relational beings.

To repeat, I have outlined the above sketch of the Socratic understanding of human being only in order to enable us to pursue our theme somewhat further. Hopefully, we are now in a position to ask, if indeed the monadic and relational conceptions of the individual are not irreconcilable, if there is a sense in which human being can be both, what does this suggest about the relationship between competition and alienation on the one hand, which we earlier associated with the monadic individual, and friendship on the other, which we connected most fundamentally with relational individuality? Evidently, it suggests a closer relation than at first appeared. The problem is to work it out adequately.

In order to do so, it will be necessary for me briefly to review two positions I have developed in earlier publications (7: p. 36–49). There I have tried, first, to develop an adequate characterization of what I have called the stance of play, the orientation or mode of comportment we take toward the world and toward other people when we play. I have called that stance ''responsive openness.'' Let me explain as briefly as possible. When we play, whether that play be skiing, tennis, checkers, fishing, or playing house, it seems to me on the one hand that we are more aware of things, more open to possibilities than we are in typically nonplayful situations. To take an obvious example, the person skiing is more aware, more open to, the quality of the snow, the placement of trees, the movements of other people, than is the person, even the same person, slogging through the snow on the way to work. At the same time, the stance of play cannot simply be openness, for as such it could be mere passivity, and play is usually—

though not always—considered an active phenomenon. In addition to openness, the player must also be responsive to what he or she is open to; one must be capable of responding with one's mind and body to that with which our openness presents us. Thus again the skier does not merely ''take in'' the snow, trees, and other people but responds to them with the activity of his or her mind and body. Although these qualities are usually present to some degree in all conscious experience, I find them heightened in situations which we regard as play, and so I have characterized the stance of play as responsive openness.[6] Moreover, this stance can easily be related to the characterization of human being as erotic. Because we are incomplete, because, as I earlier put it, we do not contain the ingredients of completeness within ourselves, we must look to others—to things in the world and to other people—for what fulfillment can be ours. This means, of course, that we must be open to others, aware of their presence, their nature, their possible relation to us. At the same time, again, we cannot merely be open but must respond to that openness, a response which constitutes our erotic effort to seek fulfillment. In this sense, responsive openness is seen to be literally a natural stance, a stance founded in our nature as erotic beings. And so from this standpoint, play as responsive openness can be seen—and recommended—as natural to human being, as one of the most fundamental ways in which we come to be as human.

Second, I have argued (7: p. 44ff) that there is a close kinship between play as responsive openness and the Socratic conception of philosophy as a stance of questioning, or as Socrates regularly puts it, of aporia. Let me again explain briefly. Philosophy, as the love of wisdom, is an explicit, self-conscious manifestation of our erotic nature. As lovers of wisdom, philosophers are distinguished from wise beings (who, suggests Socrates, would have to be gods) (13:203e–204a) by a lack of wisdom, but are distinguished from the nonphilosophers by their having experienced and recognized that lack and the desirability of overcoming it. Now, if, *per impossible,* someone were wise, if, that is, one were capable of giving a comprehensive and consistent account of the whole, the proper mode of discourse for the expression of this wisdom would of course be assertion. The wise person would assert the truth. But according to Socrates, philosophers are not in this position. The proper mode of *philosophic* discourse must be one true to the philosophers' situation as *lacking* wisdom but striving for it. That appropriate mode of speech, indeed the appropriate stance toward the world, is one of questioning, a stance for which Socrates himself becomes famous through the Platonic dialogues. For questioning, the stance of questioning, testifies at once to a lack of wisdom—otherwise we would not need to ask questions—yet at the same time to a striving for it—that is why we question. But one could equally well say, questioning testifies at once to an *openness* to things, yet at the same time to a responsiveness toward what we question openly. The Socratic interrogative stance, or aporia, is thus the philosophic manifestation of responsive openness, which is why several times in the Platonic dialogues philosophy is associated with the highest forms of play (12:276c.d).

To summarize briefly the points needed to develop our theme: It has been suggested, first, that play is characterized by a stance toward our world of responsive openness; second, that this stance is itself founded in the nature of human being as erotic; third, that philosophy is also a manifestation of our erotic nature; fourth, that the appropriate Socratic philosophic stance is one of questioning; and finally, that questioning itself exhibits the stance of responsive openness, and so of play, in the highest degree.

We are now prepared to relate what has been said to the possible reconciliation of competition and friendship. Let us begin with competition. Consider first the original meaning of the word. *Com-petitio* means "to question together, to strive together." Immediately we see that according to the original meaning of the word, competition is in no way necessarily connected to alienation; in-

stead, it is easily tied to the possibility of friendship. It is a questioning of each other *together,* a striving *together,* presumably so that each participant achieves a level of excellence that could not have been achieved alone, without the mutual striving, without the competition. We find the same sense in the related word "con-test," a testing together, where again the notion of togetherness suggests a cooperation which points much more naturally to friendship than to alienation (cf. 9: pp. 23-30). There are, of course, related words which do suggest the elements of alienation. Perhaps the most obvious is "opposition," in which we *posit* ourselves *against* the other, a characterization which clearly makes space for alienation. It is as if the elemental words developed for our play situation indicate the possibility both of alienation and of friendship as naturally tied to play. For our purposes, what we need to emphasize is that competition in its root meaning suggests an affinity more with friendship than with alienation.

Now of course, etymological meanings, though instructive, hardly would be sufficient alone to establish this philosophic point. But there are at least two other considerations which suggest that the connection between competition, questioning, and friendly cooperation is no etymological accident. First, I would remind you of what we could call the existential evidence adduced at the beginning of this paper. From time to time, friendship does arise and is even deepened within the context of competition. To be sure, this establishes no causal relation, but it does testify clearly to the compatibility of the two, and establishes at least the possibility of a closer connection. It is clearly commensurate, for example, with the older conception of friendship as a "demand relationship," wherein friends, far from "not hassling" each other or letting each other "do their own thing," exhibit their friendship through the constant if implicit demand that each be the best that he or she can be. Competition manifestly can be a mode of this form of friendship. Second, the considerations earlier proposed about the relation between eros, responsive openness, play, philosophy, and questioning offer, I believe, a kind of ontological evidence, or perhaps better, an ontological framework within which we can understand that and how competition and friendship, though not necessarily in a causal relation, are nevertheless intimately connected. Competition, as a questioning or striving together, is grounded in our eros, our sense of incompleteness and striving for fulfillment. Here, however, the sense in which that fulfillment is enhanced by and with others is made explicit. In competing with others, our chances for fulfillment are seen as occurring within a framework of positive involvement with, a cooperation with or a friendship with, others. Far from being opposed, competition and friendship are seen to be founded together in our natures as erotic.

At the beginning of this paper, I asked after the relation between competition and friendship, competition and alienation. I specifically wondered whether that relationship was causal. The gist of these reflections is to incline me to answer, no. Competition *causes,* in the sense of efficient causality, neither friendship nor alienation, nor vice-versa. That is not the accurate statement of the relation. Nor is it adequate merely to say they are compatible, that competition is occasionally accompanied by friendship (or alienation). I have argued in my development of the Platonic standpoint that the relationship is more intimate than that, that both are founded together in our nature as erotic. Let me now try to specify that relation. What I am pointing toward, I believe, is a *teleological* relation between competition and friendship. That is, I am saying that competition, as a striving or questioning together towards excellence *in so far as it most adequately fulfills its possibilities,* does so as a mode of friendship. To state it differently, the apotheosis or highest version of competition is as friendship. Moreover, like all good teleologists, I hold the *highest* possibility to be the truly *natural* situation, in the light of which other manifestations of competition, specifically that of alienation, are to be judged defective. According, then, to my teleological account

of competitive play, all competitive play which fails to attain its highest possibility, that of friendship, must be understood as a "deficient mode" of play. This could even be interpreted as implying an ethical injunction: we *ought* to strive at all times to let our competitive play be a mode of friendship.

Now of course, this happy state of affairs can and does break down all too regularly. Our "competition," we could now say, devolves into "opposition," and we experience the common co-presence of alienation and play. Why does such alienation occur? There are no doubt myriad reasons, ranging from the personal psychology of the individual participants, even our moods and what has happened to us before we play, to social convention (it is obviously more acceptable to have fights in hockey games than in basketball games; indeed, one sometimes gets the feeling it is socially expected), to the *Zeitgeist,* the tenor of the times. The point of the preceding remarks is to establish that it is not *natural* that competition lead to alienation; we need not accept it as "part of what competition is," and thus by accepting it implicitly affirm its presence, warrant its perpetuation. Still, to repeat, and by way of assuring you that I am not playing the ostrich with my head in the sand, alienation does occur regularly in competition. It is part of the risk we take when we play competitively, and this leads us to the second of the questions we raised at the outset of this paper, the question of the risk-taking element in competitive play.

Usually, the risk-taking that is taken as thematic in discussions of play is the risk of physical injury and even, as in sports such as car racing, deep sea diving, and rock-climbing, the risk of death (cf. 1: Pages 203–205). To this can be added the psychological risk involved in the possibility of losing, and the effect that might have on our egos. I want now to add to that the risk that is present in nearly all instances of competitive play, the risk that what begins as friendly encounter will end in alienation. Why do we humans, who, we are sometimes told, seek nothing so much as security and self-preservation, for whom insecurity is supposedly one of the most distressing of psychological states, why should we regularly and freely choose to enter into situations—nearly all our play—in which the aforementioned variety of risks are so obviously present? You can no doubt now predict my proposed answer. It is because of our eros.

In competition, wherein we strive together to become more than and better than we are, we question each other together. In so doing, *we call each other and call ourselves into question.* One aspect of our status as erotic is the constant sense of dissatisfaction we have with ourselves in so far as we experience ourselves as incomplete. This dissatisfaction at the sense of lack, this negativity in ourselves, spurs us on to become more than we are. In this way, we constantly hold ourselves open to question. In turn, this calling into question of ourselves, I believe, is at the heart of our willingness, indeed our enthusiasm, to embark upon risk-taking projects, our play foremost among them. We freely choose to take risks because we sense, sometimes consciously, sometimes unreflectively, that risk-taking is a way of engaging in that calling into question of ourselves by which we become what we can become, by which we exhibit our erotic nature. In taking risks, as we sometimes say, we "put ourselves on the line"; risk-full situations *individualize* us, they offer occasions in which we find out who we are in the midst of becoming who we are.[7]

So by way of a brief conclusion we can join together the two sets of questions with which I began this paper. Because of the greater sense of immediacy, of intensity, of immersion that often accompanies play, our playful encounters with others often involve greater, or at least more obvious risks than in other situations. One of the most powerful of such risks is the risk that our play will degenerate into alienation. However, as my latter remarks suggest, this risk is not likely to disappear, for it is part of the very appeal of competitive play, a literally natural consequence of our erotic nature. As erotic beings who play, we will take these risks, and therefore, since a risk without occasional failure soon ceases to be such

a risk, we will occasionally find our play infected with alienation. But the first part of my paper has been intended to support my conviction that we need not and should not find such alienation natural, something to be accepted. Alienation in our competitive play is in every case a failure of the *telos* of competition, and indirectly of our very natures as erotic. Both in its origins and in its goal, its *arche* and its *telos,* competitive play should be one of those occasions where our encounters, intense, immediate, total, are those of friendship, in which we attain to a fulfillment, however momentary, together. A simple conclusion perhaps, a sentiment most of us would like to believe in the face of all too regular evidence to the contrary. The issue this paper has addressed is, can it be grounded in human nature?

Notes

1. An earlier version of this paper was presented at the R. Tait McKenzie Symposium On Sport, University of Tennessee, May 4, 1978.
2. Marx, to take an important example from outside the sporting domain, is profoundly ambiguous on the direction of the causal link between competition and alienation (10: Page 131). My use of "alienation" in this essay is close to Marx's third and fourth senses of alienation developed in the same work: alienation from our "species being" and so from our fellow humans (10: Pages 127, 129).
3. A view perhaps most easily associated with the writings of Rousseau, but pervasive today in both "liberal" and "radical" analyses of society.
4. Perhaps most obviously set out in his famous *Walden* (15: pp. 15–235).
5. (13). See especially the entire speeches of Aristophanes and Socrates, 189b–193d, and 199c–212c.

6. (7). See the "Palinode" for a discussion of difficulties (7: pp. 46–49).

7. See 4: p. 240. We can of course call ourselves into question and take risks alone, as well as with others (cf. 9: pp. 23–31).

Bibliography

1. Alvarez, A. "I Like To Risk My Life," in *Sport And The Body: A Philosophical Symposium,* edited by Ellen Gerber, Philadelphia, Lea and Febiger, 1972.

2. Aristotle, *Politics,* in *Introduction to Aristotle,* edited by R. McKeon, New York, Modern Library, 1947.

3. Buber, Martin, *I And Thou,* translated by R.G. Smith, New York, Charles Scribners Sons, 1958.

4. Hegel, G.W.F., *The Phenomenology of Spirit,* translated by A.V. Miller, Oxford, Clarendon Press, 1977.

5. Heidegger, Martin, *Being And Time,* translated by Macquarrie and Robinson, New York, Harper and Row, 1962.

6. Hobbes, Thomas, *Leviathan,* New York, Bobbs-Merrill, 1958.

7. Hyland, Drew, " 'And That Is The Best Part of Us' Human Being And Play" in *Journal Of The Philosophy Of Sport,* Volume IV, 1977.

8. Hyland, Drew, "Athletics And Angst: Reflections On the Philosophical Relevance of Play," in *Sport And The Body: A Philosophical Symposium,* edited by Ellen Gerber, Philadelphia, Lea & Febiger, 1972.

9. Kretchmar, Scott, "From Test to Contest: An Analysis Of Two Kinds Of Counterpoint In Sport," in *Journal Of The Philosophy Of Sport,* Volume II, 1975.

10. Marx, Karl, *Economic And Philosophic Manuscripts of 1844,* in *Karl Marx: Early Writings,* translated and edited by T.B. Bottomore, New York, McGraw-Hill, 1963.

11. Nietzsche, Friedrich, *Thus Spoke Zarathustra,* in *The Portable Nietzsche,* edited by W. Kaufmann, New York, Viking Press, 1954.

12. Plato, *Phaedrus* in *Platonis Opera,* edited by John Burnet, Oxford, Clarendon Press, 1960, Volume II.

13. Plato, *Symposium,* in *Platonis Opera,* edited by John Burnet, Oxford, Clarendon Press, 1960, Volume II.

14. Smith, Adam, *The Wealth of Nations,* New York, Modern Library, 1937.

15. Thoreau, H.D., *Walden And On The Duty Of Civil Disobedience,* New York, Collier, 1962.

Sportsmanship as a Moral Category

JAMES W. KEATING

Sportsmanship, long and inexplicably ignored by philosophers and theologians, has always pretended to a certain moral relevancy, although its precise place among the moral virtues has been uncertain. In spite of this confusion, distinguished advocates have made some remarkable claims for sportsmanship as a moral category. Albert Camus, Nobel prize winner for literature in 1957, said that it was from sports that he learned all that he knew about ethics.[1] Former President Hoover is quoted as saying: "Next to religion, the single greatest factor for good in the United States in recent years has been sport."[2] Dr. Robert C. Clothier, past president of Rutgers University, paraphrased the words of Andrew Fletcher and commented: "I care not who makes the laws or even writes the songs if the code of sportsmanship is sound, for it is that which controls conduct and governs the relationships between men."[3] Henry Steele Commager, professor of history at Columbia University, has argued that it was on the playing fields that Americans learned the lessons of courage and honor which distinguished them in time of war. Commager sums up: "In one way or another, this code of sportsmanship has deeply influenced our national destiny."[4] For Lyman Bryson, of Columbia University, sportsmanship was of extraordinary value:

The doctrine of love is much too hard a doctrine to live by. But this is not to say that we have not made progress. It could be established, I think, that the next best thing to the rule of love is the rule of sportsmanship. . . . Some perspicacious historian will some day write a study of the age-old correlation between freedom and sportsmanship. We may then see the importance of sportsmanship as a form of enlightenment. This virtue, without which democracy is impossible and freedom uncertain, has not yet been taken seriously enough in education.[5]

Pope Pius XII, speaking of fair play which is widely regarded as an essential ingredient of sportsmanship, if not synonymous with it, has said:

From the birthplace of sport came also the proverbial phrase "fair play"; that knightly and courteous emulation which raises the spirit above meanness and deceit and dark subterfuges of vanity and vindictiveness and preserves it from the excesses of a closed and intransigent nationalism. Sport is the school of loyalty, of courage, of fortitude, of resolution and universal brotherhood.[6]

Charles W. Kennedy was a professor of English at Princeton University and chairman of its Board of Athletic Control. His small volume, *Sport and Sportsmanship*, remains to this day probably the most serious study of sportsmanship conducted in America. Kennedy's commitment to sportsmanship was not merely theoretical and scholarly. As chairman of Princeton's Board of Athletic Control, he severed athletic relations with Harvard when unsportsmanlike conduct marred the relationship.[7] For Kennedy it was not sufficient that sportsmanship characterize man's activities on the athletic field; it must permeate all of life.

> When you pass out from the playing fields to the tasks of life, you will have the same responsibility resting upon you, in greater degree, of fighting in the same spirit for the cause you represent. You will meet bitter and sometimes unfair opposition. . . . You will meet defeat [but] you must not forget that the great victory of which you can never be robbed will be the ability to say, when the race is over and the struggle ended, that the flag you fought under was the shining flag of sportsmanship, never furled or hauled down and that, in victory or defeat, you never lost that contempt for a breach of sportsmanship which will prevent your stooping to it anywhere, anyhow, anytime.[8]

Similar eulogies by other distinguished men with no professional or financial interest in sport or athletics could be multiplied without difficulty, but perhaps the point has already been made. The claims for sportsmanship as a moral category deserve some investigation. It is surprising that the experts in moral theory, the philosopher and the theologian, have seen fit to ignore so substantial an area of human conduct as that occupied by sport and athletics.

Three interrelated problems will be considered in this study: (1) the source of the confusion which invariably accompanies a discussion of sportsmanship and the normal consequences resulting from this confusion; (2) the essence of genuine sportsmanship, or the conduct and attitude proper to sport, with special consideration being given to the dominant or pivotal virtues involved; (3) sportsmanship as applied to athletics—a derivative or analogous use of the term. Once again special

attention will be directed to the basic or core virtues which characterize the conduct and attitude of the well-behaved athlete.

The Source of Confusion and Its Consequences

- fairness courtesy cheerful loser

What is sportsmanship? William R. Reed, commissioner for the Big Ten Intercollegiate Conference, is most encouraging: "It [sportsmanship] is a word of exact and uncorrupted meaning in the English language, carrying with it an understandable and basic ethical norm. Henry C. Link in his book 'Rediscovery of Morals' says, 'Sportsmanship is probably the clearest and most popular expression of morals.' "[9] Would that this were the case. Reed, however, does not define sportsmanship or enumerate the provisions of its code, and the briefest investigation reveals that he is badly mistaken as to the clarity of the concept. The efforts of no less a champion of sportsmanship than Amos Alonzo Stagg presage the obscurities which lie ahead. In addition to a brilliant athletic career at Yale and forty years as head football coach at the University of Chicago, Stagg did a year of graduate work in Yale's Divinity School and would thus seem to have the ideal background of scholarly training in moral theory and vast practical experience to discuss the problem. Yet his treatment leaves much to be desired. He defined sportsmanship as "a delightful fragrance that people will carry with them in their relations with their fellow men."[10] In addition, he drew up separate codes of sportsmanship, or Ten Commandments of sport, for the coach and for the football player and held that both decalogues were applicable to the business world as well. The second, and by far the most unusual, commandment contained proscriptions seldom found in codes of sportsmanship. "Make your conduct a worthy example. Don't drink intoxicants; don't gamble; don't smoke; don't use smutty language; don't tell dirty stories; don't associate with loose or silly women."[11]

Stagg's position is undoubtedly an extreme one, but it calls attention to a tendency all too common among the champions of sportsmanship—the temptation to broaden the concept of sportsmanship until it becomes an all-embracing moral category, a unique road to moral salvation. As always, there is an opposite extreme. Sportsmanship, when not viewed as the pinnacle of moral perfection, can also be viewed as a moral minimum—one step this side of criminal behavior. "A four point program to improve sportsmanship at athletic events has been adopted by the Missouri State High School Activities Association."[12] The first and third provisions of bylaw No. 9 detail penalties for assaults or threats upon officials by players or fans. Such legislative action may be necessary and even admirable, but it is a serious error to confuse the curtailment of criminal activities of this sort with a positive promotion of sportsmanship.

What, then, is sportsmanship? Another approach is by way of the dictionary, everyday experience, and common-sense deductions. Sportsmanship is conduct becoming a sportsman. And who is a sportsman? One who is interested in or takes part in sport. And what is sport? Sport, Webster tells us, is "that which diverts and makes mirth"; it is an "amusement, recreation, pastime." Our problem, then, is to determine the conduct and attitude proper to this type of activity, and this can be done only after a more careful consideration of the nature of sport. Pleasant diversion? Recreation? Amusement? Pastime? Is this how one would describe the World Series, the Masters, the Davis Cup, the Rose Bowl, the Olympic Games, or a high-school basketball tournament? Do the "sport" pages of our newspapers detail the pleasant diversions and amusements of the citizenry, or are they preoccupied with national and international contests which capture the imaginations, the emotions, and the pocketbooks of millions of fans (i.e., fanatics)? It is precisely at this point that we come face to face with the basic problem which has distorted or vitiated most discussions of sportsmanship. Because the term "sport" has been loosely applied to radically different types

of human behavior, because it is naïvely regarded as an apt description of (1) activity which seeks only pleasant diversion and, on the other hand, (2) of the agonistic struggle to demonstrate personal or group excellence, the determination of the conduct proper to a participant in "sport" becomes a sticky business indeed. Before proceeding with an analysis of sportsmanship as such, it is necessary to consider briefly an all-important distinction between sport and athletics.

Our dictionary definition of sport leans upon its root or etymological meaning. "Sport," we are told, is an abbreviation of the Middle English *desport* or *disport,* themselves derivatives of the Old French *desporter,* which literally meant to carry away from work. Following this lead, Webster and other lexicographers indicate that "diversion," "recreation," and "pastime" are essential to sport. It is "that which diverts and makes mirth; a pastime." While the dictionaries reflect some of the confusion and fuzziness with which contemporary thought shrouds the concept of athletics, they invariably stress an element which, while only accidentally associated with sport, is essential to athletics. This element is the prize, the *raison d'être* of athletics. Etymologically, the various English forms of the word "athlete" are derived from the Greek verb *athlein,* "to contend for a prize," or the noun *athlos,* "contest" or *athlon,* a prize awarded for the successful completion of the contest. An oblique insight into the nature of athletics is obtained when we realize that the word "agony" comes from the Greek *agonia*—a contest or a struggle for victory in the games. Thus we see that, historically and etymologically, sport and athletics have characterized radically different types of human activity, different not insofar as the game itself or the mechanics or rules are concerned, but different with regard to the attitude, preparation, and purpose of the participants. Man has probably always desired some release or diversion from the sad and serious side of life. This, of course, is a luxury, and it is only when a hostile environment is brought under close rein and economic factors provide a modicum of leisure that such desires can be gratified. In essence, sport is a kind of diversion which has for its direct and immediate end fun, pleasure, and delight and which is dominated by a spirit of moderation and generosity. Athletics, on the other hand, is essentially a competitive activity, which has for its end victory in the contest and which is characterized by a spirit of dedication, sacrifice, and intensity.

When this essential distinction between sport and athletics is ignored, as it invariably is, the temptation to make sportsmanship an all-embracing moral category becomes irresistible for most of its champions. In 1926 a national Sportsmanship Brotherhood was organized for the purpose of spreading the gospel of sportsmanship throughout all aspects of life, from childhood games to international events.[13] Its code consisted of eight rules:

1. Keep the rule.
2. Keep faith with your comrades.
3. Keep yourself fit.
4. Keep your temper.
5. Keep your play free from brutality.
6. Keep pride under in victory.
7. Keep stout heart in defeat.
8. Keep a sound soul and a clean mind in a healthy body.

The slogan adopted by the Brotherhood to accompany its code was "Not that you won or lost—but how you played the game." In giving vigorous editorial support to the Sportsmanship Brotherhood, the *New York Times* said:

Take the sweet and the bitter as the sweet and bitter come and always "play the game." That is the legend of the true sportsmanship, whether on the ball field, the tennis court, the golf course, or at the desk or machine or throttle. "Play the game." That means truthfulness, courage, spartan endurance, self-control, self-respect, scorn of luxury, consideration one for another's opinions and rights, courtesy, and above all fairness. These

are the fruits of the spirit of sportsmanship and in them . . . lies the best hope of social well-being.[14]

Dictionaries that have suggested the distinction between sport and athletics without explicitly emphasizing it have remained relatively free from this type of romantic incrustation and moral exaggeration in their treatment of sportsmanship. Beginning with nominal definitions of sportsmanship as the conduct becoming a sportsman and of the sportsman as one who participates in sport, they proceed, much more meaningfully, to characterize the sportsman by the kind of conduct expected of him. A sportsman is "a person who can take loss or defeat without complaint or victory without gloating and who treats his opponents with fairness, generosity and courtesy." In spite of the limitations of such a description, it at least avoids the inveterate temptation to make sportsmanship a moral catch-all.

The Essence of Genuine Sportsmanship

Sportsmanship is not merely an aggregate of moral qualities comprising a code of specialized behavior; it is also an attitude, a posture, a manner of interpreting what would otherwise be only a legal code. Yet the moral qualities believed to comprise the code have almost monopolized consideration and have proliferated to the point of depriving sportsmanship of any distinctiveness. Truthfulness, courage, spartan endurance, self-control, self-respect, scorn of luxury, consideration one for another's opinions and rights, courtesy, fairness, magnanimity, a high sense of honor, co-operation, generosity. The list seems interminable. While the conduct and attitude which are properly designated as sportsmanlike may reflect many of the above-mentioned qualities, they are not all equally basic or fundamental. A man may be law-abiding, a team player, well conditioned, courageous, humane, and the possessor of *sang-froid* without qualifying as a sportsman. On the other hand, he may certainly be categorized as a sportsman without possessing spartan endurance or a scorn of luxury. Our concern is not with those virtues which *might* be found in the sportsman. Nor is it with those virtues which *often* accompany the sportsman. Our concern is rather with those moral habits or qualities which are essential, which characterize the participant as a sportsman. Examination reveals that there are some that are pivotal and absolutely essential; others peripheral. On what grounds is such a conclusion reached? Through the employment of the principle that the nature of the activity determines the conduct and attitudes proper to it. Thus, to the extent that the conduct and attitudes of the participants contribute to the attainment of the goal of sport, to that extent they can be properly characterized as sportsmanlike. The primary purpose of sport is not to win the match, to catch the fish or kill the animal, but to derive pleasure from the attempt to do so and to afford pleasure to one's fellow participants in the process. Now it is clear that the combined presence of such laudable moral qualities as courage, self-control, co-operation, and a spirit of honor do not, in themselves, produce a supporting atmosphere. They may be found in both parties to a duel or in a civil war. But generosity and magnanimity are essential ingredients in the conduct and attitude properly described as sportsmanlike. They establish and maintain the unique social bond; they guarantee that the purpose of sport—the immediate pleasure of the participants—will not be sacrificed to other more selfish ends. All the prescriptions which make up the code of sportsmanship are derived from this single, basic, practical maxim: Always conduct yourself in such a manner that you will increase rather than detract from the pleasure to be found in the activity, both your own and that of your fellow participants. If there is disagreement as to what constitutes sportsmanlike behavior, then this disagreement stems from the application of the maxim rather than from the maxim itself. It is to be expected that there will

be differences of opinion as to how the pleasurable nature of the activity can best be maximized.

The code governing pure sport is substantially different from a legalistic code in which lawyers and law courts are seen as a natural and healthy complement of the system. In fact, it is in direct comparison with such a system that the essence of sportsmanship can best be understood. In itself, sportsmanship is a spirit, an attitude, a manner or mode of interpreting an otherwise purely legal code. Its purpose is to protect and cultivate the festive mood proper to an activity whose primary purpose is pleasant diversion, amusement, joy. The sportsman adopts a cavalier attitude toward his personal rights under the code; he prefers to be magnanimous and self-sacrificing if, by such conduct, he contributes to the enjoyment of the game. The sportsman is not in search of legal justice; he prefers to be generous whenever generosity will contribute to the fun of the occasion. Never in search of ways to evade the rules, the sportsman acts only from unquestionable moral right.

Our insistence that sport seeks diversion, recreation, amusement does not imply that the sportsman is by nature a listless competitor. It is common practice for him, once the game is under way, to make a determined effort to win. Spirited competitor that he often is, however, his goal is joy in the activity itself and anything—any word, action, or attitude—which makes the game itself less enjoyable should be eliminated. He "fights" gallantly to win because experience has taught him that a determined effort to overcome the obstacles which his particular sport has constructed adds immeasurably to the enjoyment of the game. He would be cheating himself and robbing the other participants of intense pleasure if his efforts were only halfhearted. Yet there is an important sense in which sporting activity is not competitive but rather co-operative. Competition denotes the struggle of two parties for the same valued object or objective and implies that, to the extent that one of the parties is successful in the struggle, he gains exclusive or predominant possession of that object at the expense of his competitor. But the goal of sporting activity, being the mutual enjoyment of the participants, cannot even be understood in terms of exclusive possession by one of the parties. Its simulated competitive atmosphere camouflages what is at bottom a highly cooperative venture. Sport, then, is a cooperative endeavor to maximize pleasure or joy, the immediate pleasure or joy to be found in the activity itself. To so characterize sport is not to indulge in romantic exaggeration. It is indisputable that the spirit of selfishness is at a very low ebb in genuine sport. Gabriel Marcel's observation concerning the relationship of generosity to joy may even have a limited applicability here. "If generosity enjoys its own self it degenerates into complacent self-satisfaction. This enjoyment of self is not joy, for joy is not a satisfaction but an exaltation. It is only in so far as it is introverted that joy becomes enjoyment."[15] In comparison with sport, athletics emphasize self-satisfaction and enjoyment; sport is better understood in terms of generosity, exaltation, and joy.

Although there is no acknowledgment of the fact, the concern which has been shown for sportsmanship by most of its advocates has been almost exclusively directed to its derivative meaning—a code of conduct for athletes. To the extent that the Sportsmanship Brotherhood was concerned with athletics (and their code of conduct would indicate that was their main concern), their choice of a slogan seems singularly inappropriate. "Not that you won or lost—but how you played the game." Such a slogan can be accommodated in the world of sport, but even there the word "enjoyed" should be substituted for the word "played." Application of this slogan to athletics, on the other hand, would render such activity unintelligible, if not irrational.

"Sportsmanship" in Athletics

Careful analysis has revealed that sport, while speaking the language of competition and con-stantly appearing in its livery, is fundamentally a co-operative venture. The code of the sportsman, sportsmanship, is directed fundamentally to facilitating the co-operative effort and removing all possible barriers to its development. Mutual generosity is a most fertile soil for co-operative activity. When we move from sport to athletics, however, a drastic change takes place. Co-operation is no longer the goal. The objective of the athlete demands exclusive possession. Two cannot share in the same victory unless they are team mates, and, as a result, the problems of competition are immediately in evidence. "Sportsmanship," insofar as it connotes the behavior proper to the athlete, seeks to place certain basic limitations on the rigors of competition, just as continual efforts are being made to soften the impact of the competitive struggle in economics, politics, international relations, etc. But we must not lose sight of an important distinction. Competition in these real-life areas is condoned or encouraged to the extent that it is thought to contribute to the common good. It is not regarded as an end in itself but as the only or most practicable means to socially desirable ends. Friedrich A. Hayek, renowned economist and champion of competition in economics, supports this position:

The liberal argument is in favor of making the best possible use of the forces of competition as a means of co-ordinating human efforts, not an argument for leaving things just as they are. It is based on the conviction that, where effective competition can be created, it is a better way of guiding individual efforts than any other. It does not deny, but even emphasizes, that, in order that competition should work beneficially, a carefully thought-out legal framework is required and that neither the existing nor the past legal rules are free from grave defects. Nor does it deny that, where it is impossible to create the conditions necessary to make competition effective, we must resort to other methods of guiding economic activity.[16]

A code which seeks to mitigate the full force of the competitive conflict can also be desirable in athletics. While an athlete is in essence a prizefighter, he seeks to demonstrate his excellence in a contest governed by rules which acknowledge human worth and dignity. He mistakes his purpose and insults his opponent if he views the contest as an occasion to display generosity and magnanimity. To the extent that sportsmanship in athletics is virtuous, its essence consists in the practice of fairness under most difficult conditions. Since the sportsman's primary objective is the joy of the moment, it is obvious from that very fact that he places no great emphasis on the importance of winning. It is easy for him to be modest in victory or gracious in defeat and to play fair at all times, these virtues being demonstrated under optimum conditions for their easy exercise. The strange paradox of sportsmanship as applied to athletics is that it asks the athlete, locked in a deadly serious and emotionally charged situation, to act outwardly as if he were engaged in some pleasant diversion. After an athlete has trained and sacrificed for weeks, after he has dreamed of victory and its fruits and literally exhausted himself physically and emotionally in its pursuit—after all this—to ask him to act with fairness in the contest, with modesty in victory, and an admirable composure in defeat is to demand a great deal, and, yet, this is the substance of the demand that "sportsmanship" makes upon the athlete.

For the athlete, being a good loser is demonstrating self-control in the face of adversity. A festive attitude is not called for; it is, in fact, often viewed as in bad taste. The purists or rigorists are of the opinion that a brief period of seclusion and mourning may be more appropriate. They know that, for the real competitor, defeat in an important contest seems heartbreaking and nerve-shattering. The athlete who can control himself in such circumstances demonstrates remarkable equanimity. To ask that he enter into the festive mood of the victory celebration is to request a Pagliacci-like performance. There is no need for phony or effusive displays of congratulations. A simple handshake demonstrates that no personal ill-will is involved. No alibis or complaints are offered. No childish excuses about the judgment of officials or the natural conditions. No temper tantrums. To be a good loser under his code, the athlete need not be exactly gracious in defeat, but he must at least "be a man" about it. This burden, metaphorically characterized as sportsmanship, bears heavily upon all athletes—amateur or professional. But there are added complications for the professional. Victories, superior performances, and high ratings are essential to financial success in professional athletics. Too frequent defeat will result in forced unemployment. It is easy, therefore, for a professional athlete to view his competitors with a jaundiced eye; to see them as men who seek to deprive him of his livelihood. Under these circumstances, to work daily and often intimately with one's competitors and to compete in circumstances which are highly charged with excitement and emotion, while still showing fairness and consideration, is evidence of an admirable degree of self-mastery.

Attempts have been made to identify sportsmanship with certain games which, it is contended, were the private preserve of the gentleman and, as a result, reflect his high code of honor.

Bullying, cheating, "crabbing" were all too common in every form of sport. The present movement away from muckerism probably should be attributed in large measure to the growing popularity of golf and tennis. Baseball, boxing, and many of our common sports trace their origin to the common people who possessed no code of honor. On the other hand, golf and tennis, historically gentlemen's games, have come down to us so interwoven with a high code of honor that we have been forced to accept the code along with the game. . . . The effect of the golf code upon the attitude of the millions who play the game is reflected in all our sports.[17]

It is true that in England the terms "gentleman," "sportsman," and "amateur" were regarded as intimately interrelated. The contention that the common people, and consequently the games that were peculiarly theirs, had no comparable code of honor may be correct, but it awaits the careful documentation of some future social historian. One thing is certain, however, and that is that there is nothing in the nature of any game, considered in itself, that necessarily implies adherence to a moral code. Some games like golf and tennis in which the participants do their own officiating provide greater opportunity for the practice of honesty, but if a high code of honor surrounds the "gentleman's games," it is due principally to the general attitude of the gentleman toward life rather than to anything intrinsic to the game itself. The English gentleman was firmly committed to sport in the proper sense of that term and eschewed the specialization, the rigors of precontest preparation, the secret strategy sessions, and professional coaching which have come to be regarded as indispensable for the athlete. "The fact that a man is born into the society of gentlemen imposes upon him the duties and, to some extent, the ideas of his class. He is expected to have a broad education, catholic tastes, and a multiplicity of pursuits. He must not do anything for pecuniary gain; and it will be easily seen that he must not specialize. It is essentially the mark of the bourgeois' mind to specialize."[18] Moreover, "too much preparation is contrary to all English ethics, and secrecy in training is especially abhorrent. Remember that sport is a prerogative of gentlemen. And one of the ear-marks of a gentleman is that he resort to no trickery and that he plays every game with his cards on the table—the game of life as well as the game of football."[19]

It is the contestant's objective and not the game itself which becomes the chief determinant of the conduct and attitudes of the players. If we take tennis as an example and contrast the code of conduct employed by the sportsman with that of the athlete in the matter of officiating, the difference is obvious. The sportsman invariably gives his opponent the benefit of the doubt. Whenever he is not sure, he plays his opponent's shot as good even though he may suspect that it was out. The athlete, however, takes a different approach. Every bit as opposed to cheating as the sportsman, the athlete demands no compelling proof of error. If a shot seems to be out, even though he is not certain, the athlete calls it that way. He is satisfied that his opponent will do the same. He asks no quarter and gives none. As a result of this attitude and by comparison with the sportsman, the athlete will tend toward a legal interpretation of the rules.

The athletic contest is designed to serve a specific purpose—the objective and accurate determination of superior performance and, ultimately, of excellence. If this objective is to be accomplished, then the rules governing the contest must impose the same burdens upon each side. Both contestants must be equal before the law if the test is to have any validity, if the victory is to have any meaning. To the extent that one party to the contest gains a special advantage, unavailable to his opponent, through an unusual interpretation, application, or circumvention of the rules, then that advantage is unfair. The well-known phrase "sense of fair play" suggests much more than an adherence to the letter of the law. It implies that the spirit too must be observed. In the athletic contest there is a mutual recognition that the rules of the game are drawn up for the explicit purpose of aiding in the determination of an honorable victory. Any attempt to disregard or circumvent these rules must be viewed as a deliberate attempt to deprive the contest of its meaning. Fairness, then, is rooted in a type of equality before the law, which is absolutely necessary if victory in the contest is to have validity and meaning. Once, however, the necessary steps have been taken to make the contest a true test of respective abilities, the athlete's sole objective is to demonstrate marked superiority. Any suggestion that fair play obliges him to maintain equality in the contest ignores the very nature of athletics. "If our analysis of fair play has been correct, coaches who strive to produce superior teams violate a fundamental principle of sportsmanship by teaching their pupils, through example, that superiority is more greatly to be desired than is equality in sport. . . . But who today would expect a coach to give up clear superiority—a game won—by putting in enough substitutes to provide fair playing conditions for an opposing team?"[20] Thus understood, sportsmanship would ask the leopard to change its spots. It rules out, as illegitimate, the very objective of the athlete. Nothing shows more clearly the need for recognition of the distinction between sport and athletics.

Conclusion

In conclusion, we would like to summarize our answers to the three problems set down at the outset.

1. The source of the confusion which vitiates most discussion of sportsmanship is the unwarranted assumption that sport and athletics are so similar in nature that a single code of conduct and similar participant attitudes are applicable to both. Failing to take cognizance of the basic differences between sport and athletics, a futile attempt is made to outline a single code of behavior equally applicable to radically diverse activities. Not only is such an attempt, in the nature of things, doomed to failure but a consequence of this abortive effort is the proliferation of various moral virtues under the flag of sportsmanship, which, thus, loses all its distinctiveness. It is variously viewed as a straight road to moral perfection or an antidote to moral corruption.

2. The goal of genuine sport must be the principal determinant of the conduct and attitudes proper to sporting activity. Since its goal is pleasant diversion—the immediate joy to be derived in the activity itself—the pivotal or essential virtue in sportsmanship is generosity. All the other moral qualities that may also be in evidence are colored by this spirit of generosity. As a result of this spirit, a determined effort is made to avoid all unpleasantness and conflict and to cultivate, in

their stead, an unselfish and co-operative effort to maximize the joy of the moment.

3. The essence of sportsmanship as applied to athletics can be determined by the application of the same principle. Honorable victory is the goal of the athlete and, as a result, the code of the athlete demands that nothing be done before, during, or after the contest to cheapen or otherwise detract from such a victory. Fairness or fair play, the pivotal virtue in athletics, emphasizes the need for an impartial and equal application of the rules if the victory is to signify, as it should, athletic excellence. Modesty in victory and a quiet composure in defeat testify to an admirable and extraordinary self-control and, in general, dignify and enhance the goal of the athlete.

Notes

1. *Resistance, Rebellion and Death* (New York: Alfred A. Knopf, Inc., 1961), p. 242.
2. In Frank Leahy, *Defensive Football* (New York: Prentice-Hall, Inc., 1951), p. 198.
3. "Sportsmanship in Its Relation to American Intercollegiate Athletics," *School and Society,* XLV (April 10, 1937), 506.
4. Henry Steele Commager, in *Scholastic,* XLIV (May 8–13, 1944), 7.
5. Lyman Bryson, *Science and Freedom* (New York: Columbia University Press, 1947), p. 130.
6. Pope Pius XII, *The Human Body* (Boston: Daughters of St. Paul, 1960).
7. "Athletic Relations between Harvard and Princeton," *School and Society,* XXIV (November 20, 1926), 631.
8. Charles W. Kennedy, *Sport and Sportsmanship* (Princeton, N.J.: Princeton University Press, 1931), pp. 58–59.
9. William R. Reed, "Big Time Athletics' Commitment to Education," *Journal of Health, Physical Education, and Recreation,* XXXIV (September, 1963), 30.

10. Quoted in J.B. Griswold, "You Don't Have To Be Born with It," *American Magazine,* CXII (November, 1931), 60.

11. *Ibid.,* p. 133.

12. "Sportsmanship," *School Activities,* XXXII (October, 1960), 38.

13. "A Sportsmanship Brotherhood," *Literary Digest,* LXXXVIII (March 27, 1926), 60.

14. *Ibid.,* pp. 60–61.

15. Gabriel Marcel, *The Mystery of Being, Vol. II: Faith and Reality* (Chicago: Henry Regnery Co., 1960), pp. 133–34.

16. Friedrich A. Hayek, *The Road to Serfdom* (Chicago: University of Chicago Press, 1944), p. 36.

17. J.F. Williams and W.W. Nixon, *The Athlete in the Making* (Philadelphia: W.B. Saunders, 1932), p. 153.

18. H.J. Whigham, "American Sport from an English Point of View," *Outlook,* XCIII (November, 1909), 740.

19. *Ibid.*

20. Frederick R. Rogers, *The Amateur Spirit in Scholastic Games and Sports* (Albany, N.Y.: C.F. Williams & Son, 1929), p. 78.

Sportsmanship

RANDOLPH M. FEEZELL

I

There is a movement in contemporary moral philosophy, attempting to return our attention to thinking about the centrality of virtue in the moral life. Until recently the language of virtue had seemingly fallen into disfavor in our 20th-century philosophizing about moral matters. We heard much talk about the naturalistic fallacy, verificationism, the expression of attitudes, prescriptivity, universalizability, the principle of utility, and the like, but little talk about *being* a certain kind of person, having certain dispositions or characteristics that we have always thought to be central to living life in a civilized moral community. In the move toward thinking about lived moral experience, philosophers began talking about issues of pressing social concern, such as abortion, euthanasia, and war. The mistaken impression occasioned in our students and in the community may have been that the return to relevancy, to "real" moral concerns, involved the necessary connection between applied ethics and social ethics. Again, one wonders what happened to the texture of individual moral experience, moral discourse, and moral education, in which we stress the importance of friendliness, compassion, fairness, truthfulness, and reliability. Perhaps an important part of applied ethics involves trying to understand individual virtues. For example, what do we mean or what

are we recommending when we speak of aspects of the virtuous life such as compassion or boldness?

In this context I believe it is relevant to think about the virtue of sportsmanship. Sports have a prevalent place in American cultural life, as well as in numerous foreign countries. Spectator sports set attendance records, yet crowd behavior is often atrocious. More adults participate today in sports with differing degrees of seriousness. There are vast numbers of young people playing sports, coming of age morally, as they devote a large amount of time to their athletic endeavors. Impressive claims are made about the role of sports in the development of character and how important sports are as a preparation for later competitive life. It would be interesting, and indeed important, if one could enlighten us as to what it means to be a good sport. Parents often stress to their children the importance of being a good sport, but it is not apparent what that means.

It should be helpful to start with a few examples before turning to the main arguments of this paper. The paradigm case of a bad sport is the cheater. Consider a high school basketball game. At the end of a close game, a flurry of activity takes place beneath the basket. A foul is called and the coach sees that the referees are confused about who was fouled. He instructs his best foul shooter to go to the free throw line to take the shots although he knows, as does his team and most of the crowd, that another player, a poor foul shooter, was actually fouled. The wrong player makes the free throws and his team wins.[1] In this case the coach has cheated. He has instructed or en-

Reprinted from *Journal of the Philosophy of Sport*, XIII, (1986), pp. 1–13. Copyright 1987 by the Philosophic Society for the Study of Sport. Reprinted by permission.

couraged his players to cheat, and we would say he is a bad sport or, in this instance at least, whether acting out of character or not, he has acted like a bad sport.[2] He has displayed poor sportsmanship.

Why is the cheater a bad sport? What is wrong with cheating? The answer is not difficult to find. Two teams agreed to play the game of basketball, defined by certain rules that constitute what it means to play basketball. By cheating, the coach intentionally broke a rule, thereby violating the original implied agreement. In this sense cheating is a kind of promise-breaking or violation of a contractual relationship. Notice that the moral reason that explains the wrongness of cheating is not unique to playing basketball; an ordinary moral rule has been broken. In the language of virtue, the coach has been found lacking in trustfulness and integrity. He has attempted to gain an unfair advantage by breaking a rule. Perhaps being a good sport is simply an extension of being a good person—in one sense this is an obvious truism—and the meaning of the virtue of sportsmanship is not unique to the activity in question.

Consider some other examples. The intent to injure would usually be a serious moral violation, but acting in such a way that one *might* injure an opponent is often morally ambiguous. Think of a hockey player fighting or a pitcher in baseball throwing one "under the chin." Should one yell at an opponent in hopes of rattling him? Certainly how one responds to defeat or victory is often thought to be an important part of sportsmanship. Should one ever refuse the traditional handshake after the contest? What about running up the score on an opponent or refusing to give credit due to an opponent who has defeated you? In such cases our judgments are more ambiguous and our explanations less obvious. Certainly no rule is violated when one team runs up the score on another, or when a tennis player continually whines, complains, throws his racket, interrupts play, and questions calls. But we want to say this type of behavior is bad form, somehow inappropriate because it violates the nature of what sport is about.

Is there some essential meaning of the virtue of sportsmanship? How can we unify our concept of sportsmanship? Are some aspects of it more central than others? In this paper I will attempt to respond to these questions. First I will critically discuss James Keating's views. Keating (14) first published his analysis of sportsmanship in 1964, and it has become a standard part of the literature in philosophy of sport.[3] As late as 1978, in the introduction to *Competition and Playful Activities* (13), which contains a revised version of his original paper on sportsmanship, he maintained that his view had not been extensively criticized. In speaking of his views of amateurism, winning, and sportsmanship, he said, "To the best of my knowledge there has been no concerted attack upon any of them in the literature" (13: p. iii). I intend to do just that in this paper. Keating has offered an excellent framework within which to initiate an understanding of sportsmanship, but I do not believe he is correct in radically separating sports and athletics. I will conclude the paper with some more positive, less critical suggestions about sportsmanship.

II

Keating's paper is a valuable resource for a number of reasons, not the least of which is his overview of the many and varied claims made about the nature of sportsmanship. Some have made extraordinary assertions about the importance of this notion, as if it is *the* most important virtue in American cultural life. The interpretations of the essence of sportsmanship have included numerous other virtues: self-control, fair play, truthfulness, courage, endurance, and so forth (13: p. 39-42). Keating attempts to unify our understanding by providing a tidy scheme that shows which virtues are essential and which are of only accidental importance. His argument is simple and compelling. Sportsmanship is the conduct that is becoming to a sportsman, or one who engages in sport, so we simply have to understand what sport is. Here we have the crux of the argument, because the term refers to "radically different types of human activity" (13: p. 43). Keating could not be more emphatic in stressing the extreme separation of sport as playful activity and sport as competitive athletic contests. On three different occasions he speaks of them as "radically different types of human activity," and at one point says (13: p. 47) that "a drastic change takes place" when we move from playful activity to athletics.

What, more precisely, is the distinction? Taking hints from dictionary definitions and etymology, Keating argues that sport refers both to the pleasant diversion of play and to spirited competitive athletic contests. To understand the true meaning of sportsmanship, we must carefully distinguish conduct and attitude appropriate to play and conduct and attitude appropriate to athletics.

> In essence, play has for its direct and immediate end joy, pleasure, and delight and which is dominated by a spirit of moderation and generosity. Athletics, on the other hand, is essentially a competitive activity, which has for its end victory in the contest and which is characterized by a spirit of dedication, sacrifice, and intensity. (13:pp. 43-44)

Thus the virtues of the player are radically different from the virtues of the athlete. Insofar as the activity determines the conduct appropriate to it, the player should conduct himself or herself with an attitude of "generosity and magnanimity," keeping in mind his or her obligation to maximize the pleasure of the event and reinforce the ludic character of the activity. Play is essentially cooperative. On the other hand, the athlete is engaged in a competitive struggle whose end is exclusive possession of victory. In the words of G.J. Warnock (23: Ch. 2), this is a situation in which things have the "inherent tendency to go badly"[4] unless moral restraints are put on the rigors of competition. "Fairness or fair play, the pivotal virtue in athletics, emphasizes the need for an impartial and equal application of the rules, if the victory is to signify, as it should, athletic excellence" (13: p. 52). In athletics, generosity and magnanimity are misplaced, as they supposedly are in other areas of life that are essentially competitive. Your opponent expects only that you fairly pursue your self-interest, not that you are to be interested in his or her goal, for you cannot be. Victory is the *telos* of the activity and an exclusive possession. Once the contest ends, the athlete, like the victor or vanquished in war, should face victory or defeat with modesty or a strength of composure.

Since Keating's view of sportsmanship depends so heavily on the sharp distinction between sport as playful activity and sport as athletic competition, we should look more closely at that distinction. How does Keating arrive at it? He begins by citing Webster's definition of sport as "diversion," "amusement," and "recreation." However, since so many sporting events (he mentions, among others, the World Series, the Davis Cup, and even a high school basketball tournament) would be inaccurately described in these terms, there must be another important sense given to this notion. Etymologically, the English forms of the word "athlete" suggest the centrality of contest and the struggle for excellence and victory, so sport, he concludes, must refer to "radically different types of human activity." Although there might already be something misleading about placing such emphasis on etymology and dictionary definitions, the distinction ultimately is a phenomenological one. We should look at lived experience for the basis of the distinction, for play and athletics are radically different "not insofar as the game itself or the mechanics or rules are concerned, but different with regard to the attitude, preparation, and purpose of the participants" (13: p. 43). Now curiosities arise, of a logical, psychological, and moral nature.

Consider one of Keating's own examples, a high school basketball tournament. Suppose Team A is coached by Smith, who views sport as little short of war. The opponent is the enemy, who must be hated and scorned in order to produce maximum intensity and effort. Practices and games are pervaded by a spirit of overarching seriousness. He yells at his players and at referees. He never lets up because he views sport as real life or, if not quite like real life, of great importance as preparation for the harshness of the "real" world. There is a certain ruthlessness in his pursuit of victory and anything goes, short of outright cheating, although even here he is inclined to think that it's alright if you don't get caught. For example, he wouldn't hesitate to run up the score if it might enhance his team's rating and its future tournament seeding. He expects no less from his opponent.

On the other hand, Team B is coached by Jones, whose whole approach to basketball is fundamentally different. He is also a spirited competitor who instills in his player-athletes the value of excellent performance and victory. However, he never forgets that basketball is a game, an arbitrary construction of rule-governed activities invented in order to make possible an intrinsically satisfying activity.[5] For Jones there is always something magical about the world of basketball, with its special order, its special spatial and temporal rhythms. It is set apart from the concerns of ordinary reality. To play and coach basketball is to engage in joyful activities, and the pleasure is increased by improving skills, being challenged to perform well, inventing strategies, and achieving one's goals. He sees the opponent not as an enemy but as a friendly competitor whose challenge is necessary to enhance the pleasurable possibilities of his own play. He realizes it is difficult to sustain the spirit of play within spirited competition, but that is his goal. His seriousness about the pursuit of victory is always mediated by an awareness that basketball is just a game, valuable for the moment, whose value consists primarily in the intrinsic enjoyment of the activity. Fun is an essential element in his understanding of sport.

Are these two coaches engaged in fundamentally different human activities? The example suggests that Keating's distinction is plausible. In one sense, the coaches' attitudes are so dissimilar that we want to say they are engaged in different activi-

ties. But the most important question here is moral, not psychological. I see no reason to take Smith's attitudes as normative. Although the picture of Smith may appear to be overdrawn, it is undoubtedly a correct description of the understanding and attitudes some people have regarding sport. However, it doesn't follow that their attitudes are correct. Keating's argument is logically curious. Recall that play and athletics have been characterized as being radically different with regard to attitudes, but later he states (13: p. 44) that "the nature of the activity determines the conduct and attitudes proper to it." Without further clarification, this appears to be circular and uninformative concerning how our original attitudes toward sport should be formed. I would say that Smith has an impoverished view of sport, an impoverished experience of sport, and it is just such views and attitudes that tend to generate unsportsmanlike behavior in sport.

There are two main problems with Keating's analysis, vitiating his account of sportsmanship, First, because he takes his understanding of play simply from Webster's definition of sport as "diversion," "amusement," and "recreation," he fails to describe adequately the nature of play so as to understand how sport could be seen as an extension of play. Second, and probably because of his limited clarification of play, he incorrectly ascribes a false exclusivity to the psychology of the player and the athlete. The latter point will be discussed first.

The player and the athlete are to be radically distinguished supposedly on the grounds that they differ with regard to attitude, preparation, and purpose. The previous example made such a distinction plausible, but failed to show why one set of attitudes should be normative. In numerous other cases, however, the distinction is difficult if not impossible to make, precisely because the attitudes of the participants are mixed. Consider an ex-college basketball player engaged in a pickup game. Is this person a player or an athlete? What virtues should characterize his conduct? On Keating's model it would be difficult to say. Suppose the basketball player intends to play well, puts out maximum effort, competes hard, and pursues victory. Why? Because he still loves the game and still enjoys the competitive play, the very feel of the activity.

Each game is a unity, the development of a totality with its own finality. Something is at issue, and this is an arena in which the issue at hand will be decisively resolved. He finds the dramatic tensions satisfying, as well as the frolicking nature of running, jumping, and responding to the physical presence of other players. He enjoys the sheer exuberance of the experience. He is serious about his play because such seriousness enhances the activity and heightens the experience. He is serious because the internal logic of the activity demands the pursuit of victory, yet he realizes that in a profound sense his seriousness is misplaced. It doesn't really matter who wins the game, although it does matter that the festivity occurs. Such an attitude toward the pursuit of victory acts as an inner negation of his original seriousness and produces moderation. One might go on here with an extended phenomenological account, but the point is already clear. His attitudes and purposes are extraordinarily complex. He is simultaneously player and athlete. His purpose is to win the contest *and* to experience the playful and aesthetic delights of the experience. His attitudes are at once both playful and competitive, and these color his relationship with his fellow participants. He sees his opponent as both competitor and friend, competing and cooperating at the same time. These are the attitudes that guide his conduct.

Such a fusion of attitudes and purposes may be unsatisfying to some, but I think such a picture of the player-athlete is a truer one than the one offered by Keating. His radical distinction between play and athletics is an excellent example of what Richard Taylor calls polarized thinking. In the context of showing how such thinking leads to metaphysical puzzlement or confusion he says the following:

There is a common way of thinking that we can call *polarization,* and that appears to be the source of much metaphysics. It consists of dividing things into two exclusive categories, and then supposing that if something under consideration does not belong to one of them, then it must belong in the other. "Either/or" is the pattern of such thought, and because it is usually clear, rigorous, and incisive, it is also often regarded by philosophers as exclusively rational. (21: p. 106)

such sharpness and precision are sometimes bought at the expense of truth, for reality is far too loose a mixture of things to admit of such absolute distinctions, and sometimes, both in our practical affairs and in our philosophy, we are led into serious errors, which are fervently embraced just because they seem so clearly to have been proved. (21: p. 107)

Keating offers only one extended example to show what his polarized view of sportsmanship would look like in practice, and his conclusions are odd.

It is the contestant's objective and not the game itself which becomes the chief determinant of the conduct and attitudes of the players. If we take tennis as an example and contrast the code of conduct employed by the player with that of the athlete in the matter of officiating, the difference is obvious. The player invariably gives the opponent the benefit of any possible doubt. Whenever he is not certain, he plays his opponent's shot as good even though he may believe it was out. The athlete, however, takes a different approach. Every bit as opposed to cheating as the sportsman, the athlete demands no compelling proof of error. If a shot seems to be out, the athlete calls it that way. He is satisfied that his opponent will do the same. He asks no quarter and gives none. As a result of this attitude by comparison with the player, the athlete will tend toward a legal interpretation of the rules. (13: p. 50)

I have played tournament tennis and find this example not only unconvincing, it is simply inaccurate in some respects. It bears little comparison to my own experience and that of those with whom I play. First, based on Keating's model, it would be impossible for me to know whether I am a player or an athlete in the context of my tennis playing. I should say I am both, since I compete for victory, but also find great fun in the activity and recognize my opponent as a partner of sorts. Moreover, the conventions of tennis render Keating's example misleading and of little value in helping us to understand sportsmanship. If one is not certain that a ball is out, one plays it. *Only* if one is sure the ball is out is it to be called out. If a call is made but disagreement arises, a let is called and the point is replayed. Giving the benefit of the doubt to the opponent isn't generosity here; it is simply recognizing the relevant conventions. Actually, Keating's description of the so-called athlete sounds suspiciously like an example of bad sportsmanship, since such a person's zeal in the pursuit of victory ignores the unwritten rules of playing without officials and tends to destroy the spirit of play. A more playful spirit would mediate against a zealousness that fuels inappropriate conduct and an ignoring of the rules.

The other main problem with Keating's view of sportsmanship is his account of the nature of play and its relationship to sport. Such a topic demands an extended treatment, and I have attempted to do this elsewhere.[6] Briefly, the most accurate and inclusive phenomenological accounts of experience in sport are those which focus on the nature of play and which show, either explicitly or implicitly, that sport is a formal, competitive variety of human play.[7] I agree with Kenneth Schmitz when he says (18: p. 22) that "sport is primarily an extension of play, and that it rests upon and derives its central values from play." Huizinga's classic account of play stresses that it is an activity freely engaged in when someone metaphorically "steps out" of ordinary life and becomes absorbed in an alternative world of play, with its own order and meaning, constituted by its own rules, experiential rhythms, traditions, tensions, and illusory quality. He also stresses the element of fun as essential. He sums up his account in the following passage:

Summing up the formal characteristics of play we might call it a free activity standing quite consciously outside "ordinary" life as being "not serious," but at the same time absorbing the player intensely and utterly. It is an activity connected with no material interest, and no profit can be gained by it. It proceeds within its own proper boundaries of time and space according to fixed rules and in an orderly manner. (10: p. 13)

Schmitz (18: p. 23) strengthens the analysis of play by distinguishing four types: frolic, make-believe, sporting skills, and games. The movement from frolic to sport is a continuum from less formal, spontaneous, animal-like behavior to more formal activities guided by rules, in which knowledge, preparation, and understanding are called for. In all forms, Schmitz, like Huizinga, stresses the movement from the ordinary to the world of play by a free decision to play. "Such a constitutive decision cannot be compelled and is essentially free. Through it arises the suspension of the ordinary concerns of the everyday world" (18: pp. 24-25). Such a decision constitutes an act of transcendence beyond the natural world, in which a new totality is opened, and experienced with a sense of exhilaration and celebration. Schmitz compares the transcendence of play with religion and art. Also akin to Huizinga's account, Schmitz stresses, especially for the more formal varieties of play, the new order of the world of play with its new forms of space, time, and behavior. It is a "transnatural, fragile, limited perfection. . . . delivering its own values in and for itself, the freedom and joy of play" (18: p. 26). Finally, Schmitz (18: p. 26) argues that it is a "distinctive mode of being. It is a way of taking up the world of being, a manner of being present in the world . . . whose existential presence is a careless joyful freedom."

The problem for the play-theorist of sport is how to connect such a striking description of play with sport. Many think, as Keating seems to, that this account necessarily excludes essential elements of sport, including the striving for excellence and good performance and contesting for victory. But the strength of the play theory of sport is the way in which it can provide both a rich phenomenological account of the experience of play within sports and an explanation of the prominence and appropriate value of good performance and victory. No one would deny that the pursuit of victory is essential in sport; after all, a contest is not mere frolic. But why *do* so many engage in sport? Why do we create our games and begin and continue to play them? The critics of sport give us an important perspective here when they wonder why so many people become obsessed with things like hitting a ball with a wooden stick, or throwing a ball into a hoop, or clubbing a little ball around expansive fairways. They can understand why children, lacking maturity and experience, could enjoy the exuberance of such activities. But grown people? Compared with suffering, friendship, and possible nuclear annihilation because of deep-rooted human conflicts, playing games and treating them with utmost seriousness seems silly. Bernard Suits brings this out well in attempting to define game-playing.

> it is generally acknowledged that games are in some sense essentially non-serious. We must therefore ask in what sense games are, and in what sense they are not, serious. What is believed when it is believed that games are not serious? Not, certainly, that the players of games always take a very light-hearted view of what they are doing. A bridge player who played his cards randomly might justly be accused of failing to play the game at all just because of his failure to take it seriously. It is much more likely that the belief that games are not serious means what the proposal under consideration implies: that there is always something in life more important than playing the game, or that a game is the kind of thing that a player could always have reason to stop playing. (20: p. 14)

The important insight here is that the ''nonseriousness'' at the heart of play is based on the recognition that there are obviously more important values in life than the value of improving sporting skills and winning games. A correct attitude concerning sport would place these values in an appropriate hierarchy. Suits goes on to deny such nonseriousness as the essence of game-playing on the grounds that one could take a game so seriously as to consider it supremely important, taking over one's whole life and forcing one to avoid other duties. But his point is psychological, not moral. Undoubtedly someone *could* have such an attitude but ought not. Suits sees this clearly:

> Supreme dedication to a game . . . may be repugnant to nearly everyone's moral sense. That may be granted; indeed insisted upon, since our loathing is excited by the very fact that it is a game which has usurped the place of ends we regard as so much more worthy of pursuit. (20: p. 15)

Suits concludes his attempt to define game-playing by arguing (20: p. 17) that when we play a game we accept the arbitrary way in which means are used to achieve certain ends—for example in golf our goal is not just to put the ball in the hole but to do it in an extraordinarily limited way—because we simply want to make the activity possible. Evidently such activity, without external practical ends, is intrinsically satisfying.[8]

This analysis leads us to a point where we can see the attitudinal complexity of the player-athlete. We might distinguish between internal and external seriousness. The activity of playful competition calls for pursuit of victory. As Suits suggested, if someone isn't serious in this sense he might be accused of not playing the game at all. On the other hand, there is an external perspective from which the internal seriousness of competition is mediated by an awareness that the activity is a form of play, infused with its own values and qualified by the values of life outside the play-world. The activity engaged in is both competition and play, serious and nonserious. This is the understanding of the activity that gives rise to a more adequate understanding of sportsmanship. The spirit of play may be absent within sport, but it ought not to be if, as has been argued, sport is intimately and in some sense originally related to the playful activity of game-playing. Once again Schmitz offers helpful comments:

> sport can be carried out without the spirit of play. Nevertheless, in the life of individuals and in the history of the race, sport emerges from play as from an original and founding posture. Sport is free, self-conscious, tested play which moves in a transnatural dimension of human life, built upon a certain basis of leisure. . . . There is certainly a return to seriousness in the discipline of formal sport. There is training, performance and competition. But the objectives of sport and its founding decision lie within play and cause sport to share in certain of its features—the sense of immediacy, exhilaration, rule-directed behavior, and the indeterminacy of a specified outcome. (18: p. 27)

Let us turn now to a positive account of the virtue of sportsmanship.

III

In my view, instead of a rigid and precise distinction between play and athletics, we must be content with a fuzzy picture of the fusion of these activities, a picture in which edges are blurred and complexity of attitudes is retained. Keating's view embraces tidiness at the cost of truth. Still we want to ask, What is the essence of sportsmanship? I tend to think that the question is misleading and the phenomenon is dispersed in our experience in innumerable particular instances. We ought to be hesitant about attributing to this notion an abstract unity that is not found in experience. Wittgenstein's admonition that we ought to be suspicious of such talk and appeal to particular cases is well taken here, as always. However, if we view sport as an extension of human play, we can offer an understanding of the virtue of sportsmanship that

will be somewhat more satisfying intellectually, although it will not always generate easily purchased moral recommendations. This shouldn't surprise us.

Keating is right to see that we must understand sportsmanship as conduct flowing from our attitudes, and he is correct in attempting to describe the attitudes appropriate to sport. He is simply incorrect about the attitudes. If sport is understood as an extension of play, then the key to sportsmanship is the spirit of play. Within the arena of competition the play-spirit should be retained. It would be helpful to think of this in Aristotelian terms. Recall Aristotle's description of virtue:

> By virtue I mean virtue of character; for this pursues the mean because it is concerned with feelings and actions, and these admit of excess, deficiency and an intermediate condition. We can be afraid, e.g., or be confident, or have appetites, or get angry, or feel pity, in general have pleasure or pain, both too much and too little, and in both ways not well; but having these feelings at the right times, about the right things, toward the right people, for the right end, and in the right way, is the intermediate and best condition, and this is proper to virtue. Similarly, actions also admit of excess, deficiency and the intermediate condition. (1: 1106b)

In fact, Aristotle's description of the virtuous person reinforces the previous attempt to ascribe a certain psychological complexity to the player-athlete. The courageous or brave person, according to Aristotle (1:1107), is neither excessively fearful, else he would be a coward, or excessively confident, else he would be foolhardy and rash. He feels appropriately fearful, which moderates his confidence, and he feels appropriately confident, which moderates his fear. His virtuous acts are expressions of such moderation and a result of experience and habit. Likewise, the good sport feels the joy and exuberance of free, playful activity set apart from the world, and feels the intensity of striving to perform well and achieve victory. Sportsmanship is a mean between excessive seriousness, which misunderstands the importance of the play-spirit, and an excessive sense of playfulness, which might be called frivolity and which misunderstands the importance of victory and achievement when play is competitive. The good sport is both serious and nonserious, in a sense which by now should be understandable.

Many, if not most, examples of bad sportsmanship arise from an excessive seriousness that negates the play-spirit because of an exaggerated emphasis on the value of victory. Schmitz has a superb comment on such exaggeration:

> The policy of winning at all costs is the surest way of snuffing out the spirit of play in sport. The fallout of such a policy is the dreary succession of firings in college and professional sport. Such an emphasis on victory detaches the last moment from the whole game and fixes the outcome apart from its proper context. It reduces the appreciation of the performance, threatens the proper disposition towards the rules and turns the contest into a naked power struggle. The upshot is the brutalization of the sport. And so, the sport which issued from the play-decision, promising freedom and exhilaration, ends dismally in lessening the humanity of players and spectators. (18: pp. 27-28)

Such exaggeration of victory goes hand in hand with the way we view our relationship to our opponents. The play-spirit will moderate, not negate, the intensity with which we pursue victory, and will introduce a spirit of friendship and cooperation in what would otherwise be a "naked power struggle."[9] Thus, the good sport doesn't cheat, attempt to hurt the opponent, or taunt another. A certain lightness of spirit prohibits uncivil displays of temper, constant complaints to officials, and the like. Throughout the activity, self-control and kinship with others are necessary to maximize the possible values of the play-world.

What does all this mean in more particular instances and over a wider range of examples? Once again Aristotle is helpful. First he insists that it would be misguided to expect an extreme degree of exactness, clarity, or precision in our present moral inquiry. We should expect that degree of precision appropriate to the inquiry, and in ethical theory "it will be satisfactory if we can indicate the truth roughly and in outline" (1: 1094b). In addition, when speaking of moral virtue we seek the mean "relative to us." Virtue is not alike to all people in all situations. Terence Irwin comments:

> Aristotle warns against any misleading suggestion that his appeal to a mean is attended to offer a precise, quantitative test for virtuous action that we can readily apply to particular cases—as though, e.g. we could decide that there is a proper, moderate degree of anger to be displayed in all conditions, or in all conditions of a certain precisely described type. The point of the doctrine, and of Aristotle's insistence of the 'intermediate relative to us,' is that no such precise quantitative test can be found. (1: p. 313)

To see the virtue of sportsmanship as a mean between extremes is not to be given a precise formula for interpreting acts as sportsmanlike or not, but to be given an explanatory and experiential context within which we can learn and teach how we ought to conduct ourselves in sports. From the standpoint of teaching and moral education, an appeal to exemplars of this virtue will always be useful, for they will show us what it means to be playful and cooperative in our sport experience. I cannot see that the moral philosopher is required to do more.[10]

Notes

1. There is, of course, some dispute whether we should say that the cheating coach's

team won. Bernard Suits (20: pp. 12-13) argues that in a strict or logical sense one cannot win by cheating. The game is defined by its rules, so one cannot win the game by breaking the rules since, in that case, one would not be playing the game at all. Craig K. Lehman (15) argues that the conventions of a sport may allow some breaking of the rules (e.g., Gaylord Perry throwing a spitball or an offensive lineman holding) without thinking that the violator has ceased to play the game because of such nonobedience. I am sympathetic to Lehman's arguments, but the so-called "incompatibility thesis" is not crucial to my arguments in this paper. I simply attempt to start with a paradigm example of unsportsmanlike behavior, and the cheating coach is a good place to start since such behavior violates the rules of basketball and the unwritten conventions of proper conduct in the sport.

2. Here I am using the term "bad sport" simply to describe the cheater as someone who displays poor sportsmanship. Bernard Suits (19: Ch. 4) distinguishes the trifler, the cheater, and the spoilsport. What I mean by "bad sport" is not what Suits means by "spoilsport." In the broad sense in which I am using the notion, the trifler, cheater, and spoilsport are all bad sports.

3. Keating's views are extensively discussed in (17). His views are noted by Carolyn Thomas (22) and by Warren Fraleigh (9).

4. Warnock's comments attempt to describe generally "the human predicament" and the way in which morality serves to better the human predicament by countervailing "limited sympathies."

5. See Suits (20).

6. See Feezell (4; 5; 6; 7).

7. See Huizinga (10), Caillois (2), Novak (16), Schmitz (18: p. 22-29), Fink (8: p. 73-83), Esposito (3: p. 102-107), and Hyland (11: p. 94-101), and (12: p. 133-140).

8. The conclusion concerning intrinsic statis-

faction is mine, not necessarily Suits'. I leave open the question whether his account of "lusory attitude" would agree or disagree with this conclusion. See his discussion (19: pp. 38-40, pp. 144-146). His comments on page 40 seem close to the conclusion I offer, but his later comments on professional game playing may lead elsewhere.

9. Drew Hyland (12: pp. 133-139) offers an excellent analysis of how competition always involves the risk of degenerating into an alienating experience, but it need not. Competitive play can be a mode of friendship.

10. I wish to thank members of the editorial board and the editor of the *Journal of the Philosophy of Sport* for their helpful comments.

Bibliography

1. Aristotle, *Nicomachean Ethics.* Translated by Terence Irwin. Indianapolis: Hackett, 1985.

2. Caillois, Roger. *Man, Play, and Games.* Translated by Meyer Barash. The Free Press of Glencoe, 1961.

3. Esposito, Joseph. "Play and Possibility." *Sport and the Body: A Philosophical Symposium. Second Edition.* Edited by Gerber and Morgan. Philadelphia: Lea & Febiger, 1979.

4. Feezell, Randolph M. "Of Mice and Men: Nagel and the Absurd." *The Modern Schoolman,* LXI(4) (May, 1984), 259-265.

5. Feezell, Randolph M. "Play and the Absurd." *Philosophy Today* (Winter, 1984), 319-328.

6. Feezell, Randolph M. "Play, Freedom, and Sport." *Philosophy Today* (Summer, 1981), 166-175.

7. Feezell, Randolph M. "Sport: Pursuit of

Bodily Excellence or Play? An Examination of Paul Weiss's Account of Sport." *The Modern Schoolman,* LVIII(4) (May, 1981), 257-270.

8. Fink, Eugene. "The Ontology of Play." *Sport and the Body: A Philosophical Symposium. Second Edition.* Edited by Gerber and Morgan. Philadelphia: Lea & Febiger, 1979.

9. Fraleigh, Warren. *Right Actions in Sport: Ethics for Contestants.* Champaign, IL: Human Kinetics, 1984.

10. Huizinga, Johan. *Homo-Ludens: A Study of the Play-Element in Culture.* Boston: Beacon Press, 1955.

11. Hyland, Drew. "Athletics and Angst: Reflections on the Philosophical Relevance of Play." *Sport and the Body: A Philosophical Symposium. Second Edition.* Edited by Gerber and Morgan. Philadelphia: Lea & Febiger, 1979.

12. Hyland, Drew. "Competition and Friendship." *Sport and the Body: A Philosophical Symposium. Second Edition.* Edited by Gerber and Morgan, Philadelphia: Lea & Febiger, 1979.

13. Keating, James. *Competition and Playful Activities.* Washington: University Press of America, 1978.

14. Keating, James. "Sportsmanship as a Moral Category." *Ethics,* LXXV (October, 1964), 25-35.

15. Lehman, Craig K. "Can Cheaters Play the Game?" *Journal of the Philosophy of Sport,* VIII (1981), 41-46.

16. Novak, Michael. *The Joy of Sports.* New York: Basic Books, 1976.

17. Osterhoudt, Robert. *The Philosophy of Sport: A Collection of Original Essays.* Springfield, IL: Charles C Thomas, 1973.

18. Schmitz, Kenneth L. "Sport and Play: Suspension of the Ordinary." *Sport and the Body: A Philosophical Symposium. Second Edition.* Edited by Gerber and Morgan. Philadelphia: Lea & Febiger, 1979.

19. Suits, Bernard. *The Grasshopper: Games, Life and Utopia.* Toronto: University of Toronto Press, 1978.

20. Suits, Bernard. "What is a Game?" *Sport and the Body: A Philosophical Symposium. Second edition.* Edited by Gerber and Morgan. Lea & Febiger, 1979.

21. Taylor, Richard. *Metaphysics, Third Edition.* Englewood Cliffs, NJ: Prentice-Hall, 1983.

22. Thomas, Carolyn. *Sport in a Philosophical Context.* Philadelphia: Lea & Febiger, 1983.

23. Warnock, G.J. *The Object of Morality.* London: Methuen, 1971.

Deception, Sportsmanship, and Ethics

KATHLEEN M. PEARSON

At the heart of every athletic activity is the attempt to successfully deceive one's opponent. The thesis presented here is that deception in athletics is not a simple, unitary event. Deception can be analyzed into at least two types: (a) Strategic Deception and (b) Definitional Deception. Finally, a rule of thumb can be established for deciding on the ethics of acts of deception which fall into those two categories.

Strategic Deception

Strategic deception occurs when an athlete deceives his opponent into thinking he will move to the right when he actually intends to move left—that he will bunt the baseball when he intends to hit a line drive—that he will drive the tennis ball when he actually intends to lob it. Examples of this sort of deception are replete in athletic events and need not be elaborated here. The important question is whether these acts of strategic deception are ethical or unethical.

In order to deal with this question, we need a rule of thumb for deciding on the ethics of an act. A standard for deciding if an act of deception is unethical is as follows: If an act is designed by a willing participant in an activity to deliberately

interfere with the purpose of that activity, then that act can properly be labeled unethical.

What is the purpose of athletic activities? Why even have such things as basketball games, football games, tennis games? I suggest that the purpose of these games, in an athletic setting, is to test the skill of one individual, or group of individuals, against the skill of another individual, or group of individuals, in order to determine who is more skillful in a particular, well-defined activity.

How is any particular game defined? A particular game is no more (in terms of its careful definition) than its rules. The rules of one game distinguish it as being different from all other games. Some games may have quite similar rules; however, there must be at least one difference between the rules of one game and those of all other games in order for that game to be distinguished from all other games. If we were to find another game with exactly the same rules between the covers of its rule-book, we would naturally conclude that it was the same game. Thus, problems of identity and diversity of games are decided by the rules for each game. Identical games have identical rules and diverse games have differing rules. A game is identified, or defined, as being just that game by the rules which govern it.

If the purpose of athletics is to determine who is more skillful in a particular game, and if an unethical act is one which is designed to deliberately interfere with that purpose, it is difficult to see how acts of strategic deception could be called unethical. In fact, this sort of deception is at the heart of

Reprinted from *Quest,* XIX, (January, 1973), pp. 115–118. Copyright 1983 National Association of Physical Education in Higher Education. Reprinted by permission.

the skill factor in athletic events. It is the sort of activity which separates the highly skilled athlete from the less skilled athlete, and therefore, is the sort of activity that makes a significant contribution to the purpose of the athletic event. Strategic deception is in no way designed to deliberately interfere with the purpose of athletics.

Definitional Deception

Definitional deception occurs when one has contracted to participate in one sort of activity, and then deliberately engages in another sort of activity. An example of this sort of deception might occur if one were to sign a contract to teach political science, be assigned to a political science class, and then proceed to campaign for a particular political candidate.

How does this parallel an act which might be committed in an athletic setting? The paradigm used here suggests that: (a) Under certain circumstances, the commission of a foul in a game falls into the category of definitional deception; (b) Under certain circumstances, the act of fouling can be labeled as unsportsmanlike; and, (c) Certain kinds of fouls can be linked to acts which can be properly labeled as unethical.

It was established earlier that a game is identified, or defined, as being just that game by the rules which govern it. Furthermore, we are all familiar with the fact that it is in compliance with the rules of a particular game that we commit certain acts, while it is against the rules to commit other acts. When one commits an act that is not in compliance with the rules, he is said to have committed a foul, and a prescribed penalty is meted out in punishment for that act. The ways in which fouls are committed in athletic contests can be separated into two categories. The first category consists of those fouls which are committed accidentally, and the second is composed of those fouls which are committed deliberately.

Let us first consider the case of accidental fouls. According to our rule of thumb, an act must be designed to deliberately interfere with the purpose of the activity in order for that act to be labeled unethical. Since the criterion of intentionality is missing from the accidental foul, that act has no ethical significance. We would ordinarily expect a person to accept the penalty for that foul, but we would not place moral blame on him.

Next, let us turn to the person who deliberately commits a foul while participating in an athletic contest. If the purpose of the contest is to determine who is more skillful in that game we can say that a player has entered into a contract with his opponent for the mutual purpose of making that determination. In other words, he has contracted with his opponent and the audience (if there is one) to play football, for instance, in order to determine who is more skillful in a game of football.

I have argued earlier that a particular game is defined by its rules—that the rules of a game are the definition of that game. If this is the case, a player who deliberately breaks the rules of that game is deliberately no longer playing that game. He may be playing "smutball," for instance, but he is not playing football. This is a case of deliberate definitional deception. These kinds of acts are designed to interfere with the purpose of the game in which they occur. How can it be determined which of two players (or teams) is more skillful in a game if one of the players (or teams) is not even playing that particular game? If the arguments presented here are correct thus far, we can conclude that the intentional commission of a foul in athletics is an unethical act. Ordinarily, when we refer to unethical acts on the part of athletes, we call these acts unsportsmanlike.

Someone might argue, at this point, that the penalties for fouling also are contained within the rulebook for a particular game, and therefore, fouls are not outside the rules for the game. The obvious rebuttal to this position is that penalties for breaking the law are contained within the law books, but no sensible person concludes, therefore, that all acts are within the law. If this were the case, there would be no sense in having laws at all. Similarly, if this were the case with games, there would be no sense in having rules for games. However, since the definition of a game is its rules, if there were no rules for that game there would be no game. Therefore, even though the penalties for fouling are contained within the rule-book for a game, the act of deliberate fouling is, indeed, outside the rules for that game.

A variety of elegant arguments can be produced to indict the deliberate foul. It violates the ludic spirit, it treats the process of playing as mere instrument in the pursuit of the win, and it reflects a view of one's competitor as both enemy and object rather than colleague in noble contest. All of these pleas, however, fall short of the ultimate and most damaging testimony; deliberate betrayal of the rules destroys the vital frame of agreement which makes sport possible. The activity even may go on in the face of such fatal deception, but neither the logic of analysis, nor the intuition of experience permit us to call whatever is left a game—for that is shattered.

Why the Good Foul Is Not Good

WARREN FRALEIGH

Understanding how rules function helps sports participants act appropriately and assists rules-makers state and revise rules. Rules function in relation to a sports contest—an agreed-upon event in which two or more humans oppose one another in attempting to better the other's performance on the same test of moving mass in space and time by means of bodily moves which exhibit developed motor skills, physiological endurance, and socially approved tactics and strategy.[1,2]

How do rules operate to guarantee not only that the contest *exists* but that it may be the *good* contest? In general, rules function in three ways. First, rules contain positive prescriptions for what participants *must do* and what they are *allowed to do*. In basketball, for example, all participants *must* perform actions such as throwing, dribbling and batting the ball and *are allowed to* screen and to choose when they will dribble, pass, or shoot. These prescriptions describe what all other participants must do or can do; thus they define the agreed-upon test which all participants face. Such prescriptive rules may be labeled the *positively prescribed skills and tactics of the contest*.

Second, rules function to identify the within-the-contest goal toward which the performance of the

positively prescribed skills and tactics is aimed. The within-the-contest goal in basketball is to throw the ball through your opponent's basket and to prevent the opponent from throwing it through yours. This is what Suits calls the pre-lusory goal of the game; that is, it is a goal which ". . . can be described before, or independently of, any game of which it may be, or come to be, a part."[3] When such a goal can be described and pursued independently from basketball, and is stated in the rules of basketball, *pre-lusory* takes on another meaning. Specifically, the goal of throwing the ball through your opponent's basket and preventing the opponent from doing it to you means that all participants *know* that all opposing participants will be trying to throw the ball through their basket and prevent them from doing the same *before* the contest begins. Thus rules prescribe both a pre-lusory goal and the lusory means by which that goal may be pursued.[4] These lusory means are described earlier in this article as the positively prescribed skills and tactics of the contest. Together, the pre-lusory goal of basketball and the positively prescribed skills and tactics, as stated in the rules, are agreed upon by all participants when they agree to "play basketball." Further, when people agree to play basketball they *know* that everyone else entering the agreement *knows* what the pre-lusory goal is and what the positively prescribed skills and tactics are. That is why basketball players do not ask "Shall we try to throw the ball through the basket?" or "Shall we dribble, pass, and screen?"

This article is reprinted with permission from the *Journal of Physical Education, Recreation & Dance,* January, 1982, pp. 41–42. The *Journal* is a publication of the American Alliance for Health, Physical Education, Recreation and Dance, 1900 Association Drive, Reston, VA 22091.

Third, rules function to proscribe certain illegal actions. This function is performed by rules statements which identify prohibited actions. Basketball rules, for example, prohibit double dribbles, holding, pushing, tripping, blocking, running with and kicking the ball. Negative proscriptions help to define sport. The inventor of the sport may eliminate certain skills and tactics from the sport, or rulesmakers may add new proscriptions based on the judgment that new skills are inconsistent with the nature of the sport. Basketball rules against goaltending and violations of the free throw lane by an offensive player are proscriptions added by rulesmakers after such actions occurred.

With respect to the contest, rules specify the goal-within-the-contest which all participants must necessarily pursue, the means all participants must use and are allowed to use in purusing that goal, and the means all participants may not legally use to pursue the goal. These three kinds of rules function together, specifying what all participants in principle agree to when they enter a sport contest and what all participants know all other participants in principle agree to. The three functions of rules operate together to ensure that all participants face the same test mutually—that is, that they are *contesting*. Conversely, if *one* opponent fails to pursue the pre-lusory goal of the sport by not performing the required and permitted skills and tactics and/or does perform the prohibited skills and tactics then all participants cannot be facing the same test and, thus, the participants cannot be contesting. Obviously participants who cannot be contesting cannot have a good contest.

If we understand that the sport rules function in three ways to ensure the basis for the good sports contest, then we can comprehend why it is crucial that all participants adhere to the *letter* and the *spirit* of the rules. Because the rules of sport are violated, however, it is necessary to analyze the effects of rules violations on the good sports contest. Essentially three types of rules violations affect the good sports contest. Most commonly, rules may be violated inadvertently and unintentionally. A basketball defensive player, attempt-

ing to attain or maintain a good defensive position against an opponent who feints and then dribbles toward the basket to score, trips the offensive player unintentionally. Inadvertent rules violation temporarily disrupts the good sports contest and does not destroy the agreed-upon mutual test of entering participants. Diligent practice of the positively prescribed skills and tactics of the sport can reduce the incidence of such inadvertent rules violation and enable sports contests to become good or better.

In the second type of rules violation, a participant knowingly and intentionally violates a rule to gain an advantage, but skillfully attempts to do so while avoiding a penalty. For example, a defensive basketball player can skillfully hold without detection an offensive pivot man so that he is unable to move to receive passes thrown to him. Or a golfer can improve his lie secretly, so that his next shot becomes easier to execute well. Such intentional rules violations constitute cheating and result in deliberate disruption of the agreed-upon mutual test. Cheating destroys the good sports contest because

> competing, winning and losing in athletics are intelligible only within the framework of rules which define a specific competitive sport; a person may cheat at a game or compete at it, but it is logically impossible for him to do both. To cheat is to cease to compete.[5]

A person who wins a contest as a consequence of cheating may *say* that he has won but, because cheating is not competing, he speaks incorrectly. In short, one may *correctly* say that a person wins only when he or she has been competing in the contest. The one who has been cheating may not claim victory.

The third type of rules violation occurs when a participant knowingly violates a rule to achieve what would otherwise be difficult to achieve, but violates the rules so as to expect and willingly accept the penalty. A "good" foul in basketball occurs where a defensive player, moving behind an offensive player with the ball who is dribbling for an easy lay up shot, intentionally holds the player, forcing him to shoot two free throws to make the same number of points. Such acts are called *good* because it is in the prudent self-interest of the fouling player to force the opponent to shoot twice from a greater distance to make the same number of points as would have been made by shooting once for a lay up. Violating the rules intelligently occurs if we consider *only* the self-interest of the offending player and team.

How does the "good foul" relate to the rules functions described earlier? The "good" foul is intentionally performing skills proscribed by the rules. Holding is proscribed in basketball rules; also among the proscriptions in basketball rules are intentional fouls which carry a penalty of two shots rather than one shot or one-and-one. But, it is argued, the appearance in the rules of statements about special penalties for intentional fouls makes such acts "part of the game" or "within the rules." It should be clear that the *spirit* of such rules as they were codified by rulesmakers was to eliminate or diminish such actions so that they would *not* be part of the positively prescribed skills and tactics of the game. In short, intentional holding, tripping, and so on are not part of the game or within the rules of basketball although, as stated above, it is at times rational and prudent to do such things when one's own self-interest is all that is considered.

How does the "good" foul relate, then, to the good sports contest? The good foul necessarily detracts from the good sports contest precisely because it changes the nature of the test being faced by all participants without clear agreement, in principle, that the test change is being agreed upon. For it cannot be established unequivocally that agreeing to play basketball means for *all* basketball participants that *everyone* will be performing the "good" foul. The "good" foul is a violation of the agreement which *all* participants know that *all* participants make when they agree to play basketball, namely, that all will pursue the pre-lusory goal of basketball by the necessary and allowable skills and tactics and will avoid use of proscribed skills and tactics.

Even the dominant pattern of socialization of basketball participants cannot avoid the detraction of the "good" foul from the good sports contest. Until such acts are established as agreement in principle by the positively prescribed rules and tactics, it cannot be stated unequivocally that all participants agree to performing the "good" foul by agreeing to play basketball. Agreeing to play basketball does not necessarily mean also agreeing to perform the "good" foul, but it necessarily entails the meaning of performing acts of dribbling, shooting, passing, and so on. In summary, then, intentional violation of the rules done for the purpose of achieving an end otherwise difficult to achieve, but performed in such a way that the violator expects to receive and willingly accepts the penalty, detracts from the good sports contest. Although such intentional violations, of which the "good" foul in basketball is used as *one* illustration, are "good" in terms of the rational self-interest of the violator, they are not good in terms of the good sports contest.

Notes

1. This is a revised definition from Warren P. Fraleigh, "Sport-Purpose," *Journal of the Philosophy of Sport* 2 (1975), p. 78.
2. For a clear exposition on the nature of the sports contest see R. Scott Kretchmar, "From Test to Contest: An Analysis of Two Kinds of Counterpoint in Sport," *Journal of the Philosophy of Sport* 2 (1975), pp. 23–30.
3. Bernard Suits, "The Elements of Sport," in *The Philosophy of Sport,* ed. Robert G. Osterhoudt (Springfield, Ill.: Charles C Thomas Publisher, 1973), p. 50.
4. *Ibid.*, p. 51.
5. Edwin J. Delattre, "Some Reflections on Success and Failure in Competitive Athlet-

ics," *Journal of the Philosophy of Sport* 2 (1975), p. 136.

For a treatment of intentional rules violations see, also, Kathleen M. Pearson, "Deception, Sportsmanship, and Ethics," *Quest,* 19 (January 1973), pp. 115–118; reprinted in this anthology, pp. 459–462.

Major concepts in this paper have been abstracted from Warren P. Fraleigh's book *Right Actions in Sport* (Champaign, Ill.: Human Kinetics Publishers, 1984).

Some Reflections on Success and Failure in Competitive Athletics

EDWIN J. DELATTRE

The initial objects of my reflections are the great and transporting moments of participation in competitive athletics. Reflection on these moments draws our attention to the conditions under which they are possible and to the kinds of people who are capable of achieving them. Reflection on these, in turn, enables us to see at once the touchstone relationship of competitors, and the moral and logical incompatibility of competing and cheating. Most of all we are reminded throughout these reflections that success in competitive athletics is not reducible to winning, nor failure to losing.

Richard Harding Davis was sensitive to the great and transporting moments of participation in competitive athletics. In the late fall of 1895, he wrote a gripping account of the recently contested Yale-Princeton football game. He captured both the involvement of the spectators and the struggle of the participants in revealing ways.

With the score at 16–10 in favor of Yale, but amidst a Princeton comeback, the description proceeds:

It was obviously easy after that to argue that if the Tigers had scored twice in ten minutes

they could score at least once more . . . or even snatch a victory out of defeat. And at the thought of this the yells redoubled, and the air shook, and every play, good, bad, or indifferent, was greeted with shouts of encouragement that fell like blows of a whip on one side and that tasted like wine to the other. People forgot for a few precious minutes to think about themselves, they enjoyed the rare sensation of being carried completely away by something outside of themselves, and the love of a fight, or a struggle, or combat, or whatever else you choose to call it, rose in everyone's breast and choked him until he had either to yell and get rid of it or suffocate. (2: p. 9)

Forgetting "for a few precious moments to think about" oneself, being "carried completely away," can be among the high points of human existence. Yet being so transported in the wrong way, or in the wrong context, becomes fanaticism, irresponsible loss of self-control, even madness. Here we will not concern ourselves with the problematic dimensions of being "carried completely away," since they are not relevant to our reflections.

As the objects of eros are many, we can become passionately involved in diverse pursuits and activities, concerns, persons, even places. Inquiry can be transporting, the quest to discover—was

Reprinted from *Journal of the Philosophy of Sport*, II, (1975), pp. 133–139. Copyright 1975 by the Philosophic Society for the Study of Sport. Reprinted by permission.

anyone ever more obviously carried completely away than the Leakeys at Olduvai George? The love of another, a symphony, dance; the range of our passionate concerns is virtually endless. In this list, of course, is the game: competitive athletics. Because of its special place on this list, which will emerge in our discussion, competitive athletics merit our attention and reflection.

Let us return then to Davis' description for it becomes even more revealing about the transporting moments in competitive athletics:

> The clamor ceased once absolutely, and the silence was even more impressive than the tumult that had preceded it. It came toward the end of the second half, when the light had begun to fail and the mist was rising from the ground. The Yale men had forced the ball to within two yards of Princeton's goal, and they had still one more chance left them to rush it across the line. While they were lining up for that effort the cheering died away, yells, both measured and inarticulate, stopped, and the place was so still that for the first time during the day you could hear the telegraph instruments chirping like crickets from the side line. (2: p. 9)

What is crucial in this passage is not the silence of the crowd, but the occasion for it. The silence is occasioned by the resolution of the game into this moment, this spellbinding moment when the competition is most intense. Think of the moment not as a spectator, but as a competitor. Think of the overwhelming silence of the moments when the game is most of all a test, the moments of significance in the game, the turning points, which all the practice and diligence and preparation point to and anticipate.

Such moments are what make the game worth the candle. Whether amidst the soft lights and the sparkling balls against the baize of a billiard table, on the rolling terrain of a lush fairway or in the violent and crashing pit where linemen struggle, it is the moments when no let-up is possible, when

there is virtually no tolerance for error, which make the game. The best and most satisfying contests maximize these moments and minimize respite from pressure. When competition achieves this intensity it frequently renders the outcome of the contest anti-climactic, and it inevitably reduces victory celebrations to pallor by contrast.

We see here the basic condition of success in competitive athletics. We must be able mutually to discover worthy opponents, opponents who are capable of generating with us the intensity of competition. Exclusive emphasis on winning has particularly tended to obscure the importance of the quality of the opposition and of the thrill of the competition itself. It is of the utmost importance for competitors to discover opponents whose preparation and skill are comparable to their own and who respect the game utterly.

We are recalled to this insight by the applicability to competitive athletics of the phrase "testing one's mettle." The etymological roots of "mettle" are the same as those of metal; indeed these were originally variant spellings of the same word. Just as the quality of a metal ore was determined long ago by the intensity of the color streak produced by rubbing it against a mica-like material called a touchstone, so in competition, one's opponent is his touchstone. In rubbing against a worthy opponent, against his skill, dedication and preparation, the quality of a competitor's mettle is tested.

As all philosophers know, Socrates employed the metaphor of the touchstone in the dialogues. Fellow participants in dialogue are the touchstones by which one tests the epistemic quality of his beliefs. That I have used the same metaphor must not be allowed to obscure the point that inquiry, dialogue, is, without qualification, not competitive. To view inquiry as competition, argument as something won or lost, is to misunderstand both. Dialectical inquiry is the shared and cooperative pursuit of the best approximation of the truth. In successful dialogues, false and confused beliefs are exposed as such, and those who held them benefit by the disclosure of their inadequacy. The testing of one's mettle in competitive athletics is quite another thing. The distinction is vital because when inquiry is treated as competition it is destroyed as inquiry.

Competition, contesting, if you will, thus requires commensurate opponents. The testing of one's mettle in competitive athletics is a form of self-discovery, just as the preparation to compete is a form of self-creation. The claim of competitive athletics to importance rests squarely on their providing for us opportunities for self-discovery which might otherwise have been missed. They are not unique in this by any means—the entire fabric of moral life is woven of such opportunities—but there is no need for them to claim uniqueness. They provide opportunities for self-discovery, for concentration and intensity of involvement, for being carried away by the demands of the contest and thereby in part for being able to meet them, with a frequency seldom matched elsewhere. It is in the face of these demands and with respect to them that an athlete succeeds or fails. This is why it is a far greater success in competitive athletics to have played well under the pressure of a truly worthy opponent and lost than to have defeated a less worthy or unworthy one where no demands were made.

We may appreciate this last point through a final look at Davis' chronicle:

And then, just as the Yale men were growing fearful that the game would end in a tie, and while the Princeton men were shrieking their lungs out that it might, Captain Thorne made his run, and settled the question forever.

It is not possible to describe that run. It would be as easy to explain how a snake disappears through the grass, or an eel slips from your fingers, or to say how a flash of linked lightning wriggles across the sky. (2: p. 9)

We cannot separate the significance of the Yale victory and the Princeton defeat from the fact that there was involved a player capable of such a run. For Princeton to have played well against a team with such a back, to have held a back of such qual-

ity to a single long run, to have required magnificence of Thorne for him to score, is a great success in itself.

How different this is from the occasion for Jack London's concluding lament in his coverage of the Jack Johnson–Jim Jeffries fight:

Johnson is a wonder. No one understands him, this man who smiles. Well, the story of the fight is the story of a smile. If ever man won by nothing more fatiguing than a smile, Johnson won today.

And where now is the champion who will make Johnson extend himself . . . (4: p. 513)

Jeffries was game in that fight, and he took a terrible beating. But the fight was no real competition because the opponents were not commensurate. Worse, Jeffries was ill-prepared, he was not the opponent he might have been. Accordingly, the extent of success possible for Johnson was extremely limited by the time the fight began.

As we noted previously, more is required for successful competition than commensurate opponents. Opponents, to be worthy, must utterly respect the game. Let us return now to explore that claim, for it involves not only important moral considerations but also rather more subtle logical or conceptual ones. An example will help us to expose and deal with both.

It is well known that during his career as a golfer, Bobby Jones several times called penalty strokes on himself. By 1926, he had won the American and British Opens and the American amateur title. In that year he granted an interview on golf style to O. B. Keeler, who asked Jones about those self-imposed penalties:

'One thing more, Bobby. There is a lot of interest in those penalty strokes you have called on yourself. At St. Louis and Brookline and at Worcester—they say that one cost you the championship—and the one at Scioto, in that awful round of 79 when the ball moved on the green—' Bobby held up a warning hand. 'That is absolutely nothing to talk about,' he said, 'and you are not to write about it. There is only one way to play this game.' (3: p. 222)

From the point of view of morality, competitors must consider it unworthy of themselves to break deliberately the rules of the game. When a person violates the rules which govern competition, he treats his opponents as means merely to his end of victory. The symbols of victory have status or meaningfulness only because they stand for triumph in competition; without the opposition, they are worthless. Attainment of these symbols by cheating is therefore the exploitation of those who competed in good faith. Competitors are equally reduced to means merely in cases where the end of the cheater is prize money or gambling profit. Without the competition there can be neither prize nor wager, and the cheater simply uses the bona fide competitors solely for his own gain. Cheating is thus a paradigm case of failure to act with respect for the moral status of persons as ends.

From the point of view of logic, the need for the players' utter respect for the game is equally crucial. Competing, winning and losing in athletics are intelligible only within the framework of rules which define a specific competitive sport. A person may cheat at a game or compete at it, but it is logically impossible for him to do both. To cheat is to cease to compete. It is for this reason that cheaters are the greatest failures of all in competitive athletics, not because of any considerations of winning or failing to do so, but because they fail even to compete.

In the case of golf, as in the Bob Jones example, failure to impose a penalty on oneself where it is required by the rules is to cease to compete at golf. For one can compete with others only in accordance with the rules which govern and define the competition.

Or consider the case of pocket billiards. In all pocket billiard games it is a rule violation to touch any object ball or the cue ball with one's hands or clothing, etc. during play. It is also a violation for the cue to touch any object ball in the execu-

tion of a shot; any player who violates these rules has committed a foul. The penalty for a foul in all cases is termination of one's inning or turn. Now suppose that during a game of straight pool in the execution of a shot where the cue ball must be struck at a steep angle because of an object ball immediately behind it, a player knowingly touches that object ball with his finger, undetected by his opponent or a referee. If he continues to shoot, if he does not terminate his inning voluntarily, he has ceased to compete at straight pool. And because he is no longer competing, he cannot win at straight pool. He may appear to do so, he may pocket the prize money or collect on the wager or carry off the trophy, but since he is not competing any longer, he cannot win. The cheater is logically prohibited from competing and therefore from winning. He can lose by disqualification.[1]

We may wish here to recall Bernard Suits' discussion of rules in "The Elements of Sport." Suits distinguishes the constitutive rules of a game, those which proscribe certain means of achieving the end of the game, from rules of skill which apply to how to play the game well or effectively. He points out that to ". . . break a constitutive rule is to fail to play the game at all." (5: p. 52) He mentions also a third kind of rule, namely the kind of rule which if violated requires the imposition of a specific penalty, the sort of rule we have been discussing. He urges rightly that violating such a rule is neither to fail to play the game nor to fail to play it well, since the penalized action may be nonetheless advantageous to the competitor. But he also notes that such rules are extensions of the constitutive rules. This is the emphasis of my argument. In particular, to commit an act which merits a penalty, to do so knowingly and *not* to incur the penalty is to cease to play the game. To ground a club in golf or to commit a foul in pool is not to cease to play the game. But to ignore the penalty imposed by the rules surely is, and it is in this sense that we understand rules with penalties as extensions of constitutive rules.

Both morally and logically, then, there is indeed only one way to play a game. Grantland Rice makes clear his appreciation of this insight in his autobiography, *The Tumult and the Shouting*. For emphasis, he employs the example of a rookie professional offensive lineman. The athlete responds to Rice's praise for his play during his rookie year by observing that he will be better when he becomes more adept at holding illegally without being caught. Of course, to Rice this confused vision of successful competition is heartbreaking.

We have seen now that success in competitive athletics requires being and discovering worthy opponents, and that worthy opponents must be relative equals with utter respect for the game and their fellow competitors. We have related success to competing well, performing well, under pressure. No one can be a success in competitive athletics if he fails to compete, either by avoiding worthy opposition or by cheating.[2]

Of course, our treatment of competitive athletics is rather narrow; it does not deal with the variety of reasons and purposes people have for engaging in competitive athletics. Our reflections do not really pertain to people who play at competitive games merely for fun or relaxation or exercise, who use, as it were, the format of competitive games for purposes largely indifferent to competing and to winning. We are talking only about people who seek to compete with those whose investment in a game, whose seriousness of purpose and talent, are comparable to their own and who therefore play to win.

Now people vary greatly in talent and available time for preparation, opportunity, training and so on. This means that success in competitive athletics cannot be tied unconditionally to absolute quality of performance. Whether a competitive athlete is a success hinges on numerous relevant factual considerations. We acknowledge this point as part of our sense of fairness through handicapping, establishment of weight divisions in boxing and wrestling, age divisions in junior and senior competition, and division of amateur and professional, to mention only a few.

What then of the athlete as competitor, the ath-lete who competes with equals, who, in the very act of competing, sets victory among his goals? Is winning everything in such competition, the only thing, the sole criterion of success?

We have been told so often enough, and we have seen the young encouraged to believe that winning and success are inseparable, that those who win are "winners" and those who lose, "losers." This view, however, must be tempered by our previous insights; we must not become preoccupied with individual victories to the exclusion of recognition of the importance of patterns of outstanding performance. As Thackeray saw, "The prize be sometimes to the fool. The race not always to the swift." (6: p. 57)

Sometimes performance in victory is mediocre, in defeat awesome. Many super bowls are testimonial to the former. There are countless other examples of mediocrity in victory, from little league games to professional contests. So too of excellence in defeat. To cite only one:

Anyone who saw Wohlhuter's heroic performance in Munich won't soon forget it. In the first qualifying heat, he tripped, and his pipestem body scraped along the track. Scrambling to his feet, he chased after the field—but was shut out by a stride.

'I was startled,' he recalls. 'To this day, I don't even know why or how I went down. When there're 80,000 people watching you, you want to have a good day. I had a choice— walk off the track or give it a try. I chose to be competitive.' (1: p. 48)

To stress victory to the point of overlooking quality of performance is to impoverish our sense of success in competitive athletics.

It matters whether we win or lose. It also matters whether we play the game well or badly, given our own potential and preparation. It matters whom we play against and whether they are worthy of us, whether they can press us to call up our final resources. Satisfaction in victory is warranted only when we have played well against a worthy opponent. Otherwise victory is no achievement, and pride in it is false.

Notes

1. We might ask whether other members of a team are competing if one member is cheating. We would ask immediately whether they knew of it, and deny that they were competing if they knew and did nothing. We would be more perplexed if they did not know. But we would still deny, I think, that the team as a unit was competing. Notice that a team can be disqualified for the violations of one member. The same considerations apply to cheating in the form, say, of recruiting violations.

2. Obviously there is no failure involved in the decision not to participate in athletic or non-athletic competition. Some people are constitutionally unsuited for athletics, some for competition, while others find the demands of games artificial or fabricated and therefore unsatisfying. That there is failure in cheating or in constantly playing unworthy opponents neither suggests nor entails that there is anything wrong with unwillingness to enter at all into competition.

Bibliography

1. Bonventre, Peter. "The Streaker," *Newsweek* (February 17, 1975).
2. Davis, Richard Harding. "Thorne's Famous Run," *The Omnibus of Sport*. Grantland Rice and Harford Powel (eds.). New York: Harper and Brothers, 1932. Reprinted from: "How the Great Game Was Played," *The Journal* (November 24, 1895).
3. Keeler, O.B. "Bobby Jones on Golf Style," *The Omnibus of Sport*. Grantland Rice and Harford Powel (eds.). New York: Harper and Brothers, 1932.
4. London, Jack. "The Story of a Smile," *The Omnibus of Sport*. Grantland Rice and Harford Powel (eds.). New York: Harper and Brothers, 1932.
5. Suits, Bernard. "The Elements of Sport," *The Philosophy of Sport: A Collection of Original Essays*. Robert G. Osterhoudt (ed.). Springfield, Illinois: Charles C Thomas Publisher, 1973.
6. Thackeray, William M. "Sportsmanship," *The Omnibus of Sport*. Grantland Rice and Harford Powel (eds.). New York: Harper and Brothers, 1932.

Cheating and Fair Play in Sport

OLIVER LEAMAN

It is not as easy as it might initially be thought to define cheating in sport, and it is just as difficult to specify precisely what is wrong morally with such behaviour, and why fair play should be prized. In this article I intend to try to throw some light on the notions of both cheating and fair play, and to suggest that stronger arguments than those so far produced in the literature are required to condemn the former and approve the latter.

Let us try to deal first with the definitional problem of what sorts of behaviour constitute cheating, and come to the ethical issue later. Gunther Luschen boldly starts his essay on cheating in sport with this definition:

> Cheating in sport is the act through which the manifestly or latently agreed upon conditions for winning such a contest are changed in favor of one side. As a result, the principle of equality of chance beyond differences of skill and strategy is violated (1976, p. 67).

A problem with this definition is that it omits any consideration of intention. After all, if a player unwittingly breaks the rules and thereby gains an unfair advantage he will not necessarily have cheated. For example, if a boxer has a forbidden substance applied to bodily damage without his

knowledge, then he has not cheated even though the rules have been broken to his advantage. Were he to be penalized or disqualified, it would not be because of his cheating but due to the rules having been broken by those who attend to him in the intervals.

A superior account of cheating is then provided by Peter McIntosh, who claims that:

> Cheating . . . need be no more than breaking the rules with the intention of not being found out . . . Cheating, however, implies an intention to beat the system even although the penalty, if the offender is found out, may still be acceptable (1979, pp. 100–101).

But McIntosh next claims that:

> This definition, however, is too simple. It is not always the written or even the unwritten rule that is broken; tacit assumptions which one contestant knows that the other contestant acts upon may be rejected in order to gain an advantage . . . A more satisfactory definition is that of Luschen (1979, pp. 182–3).

McIntosh's adaptation of Luschen's account makes possible the useful distinction between intending to deceive, which he calls cheating, and breaking the rules without having that intention. He concludes that: "Cheating is an offence against the principles of justice as well as against a particular rule or norm of behaviour" (1979, p. 185). This is presumably because the attempted deception is

Reprinted from *Sport and the Humanities: A Collection of Original Essays* (pp. 25–30), (1981), edited by William J. Morgan, Bureau of Educational Research and Service, University of Tennessee. Reprinted by permission.

an attempt at unfairly putting the cheater in a superior position vis-á-vis the person cheated. This distinction is made clearer if we compare cheating with lying. We may tell someone an untruth without at the same time lying, because we may not intend to present the audience with a proposition which we know not to be true. This comparison suggests that McIntosh's dichotomy is not sufficient since it does not cover those cases where the rules are deliberately broken without any intention to deceive. A player may commit a professional or tactical foul in front of the referee or umpire because he considers that it is better to break the rules and suffer the penalty rather than not to commit the foul at all. Of course, such a player would *prefer* the offense to be unobserved, but cannot reasonably expect it in those circumstances to be overlooked. It is not obvious whether this sort of case is an example of cheating or not. If the intention to deceive is a necessary condition of cheating, then obviously such a case is not one of cheating, for not only did the player not intend to deceive, but he could not even reasonably have expected such an intention to be realized. Yet the rules of the game have been broken, and it might well be argued that it is the intention to break the rules rather than the intention to deceive which will do as a necessary condition of cheating. We can see why this should be so if we return to the analogy with telling an untruth. There is nothing wrong with telling an untruth as such; the fault lies in intending to tell an untruth. If I intend to tell an untruth then my action may or may not deceive you. The falsehood may be so blatant that it is obviously not intended to deceive, but perhaps merely to confuse or gain time. Such a falsehood may nonetheless be called a lie since it seeks to place its author in a position of undeserved superiority vis-á-vis the audience, and this runs against a principle of justice, other things being equal, namely, that the truth ought to be told. If I tell you that p is the case, and I know that p is false, *and* I intend to deceive you with respect to the truth of p, then this is no doubt a more serious lie than if I just intentionally tell an

untruth without attempting to deceive. Other things being equal, we have a right to be told the truth, and if we are lied to then we are not dealt with justly. The injustice is magnified if we are at the same time deceived, or if there is an intention that we be deceived, but the injustice is there whether we are deceived or not, and whether there is any intention to deceive or not.

We may now be a bit clearer about the nature of cheating, but there are nonetheless problems in specifying precisely when a player cheats. Luschen's definition refers to a principle of equality over and above differences in skill and strategy. Using such a definition makes it difficult to give determinate answers to a variety of cases. For example, it might be that player A knows that player B is put off his play by such actions as A's coughing, or doing up his shoe-laces, or altering the pace of the game by doing things which are not directly part of the game, and so on. There are, of course, all sorts of actions which can put players off which are not in themselves illegal. A player may have considerable skill at a game and yet be quite easily beaten by an opponent who understands what sorts of (legal) behaviour the superior player dislikes. If such behaviour is indeed legal, must we say that A is cheating because he is breaking one of the "latently agreed upon conditions for winning such a contest"? It might well be argued that A is cheating since the sorts of skill and strategy which are acceptable in a game involve being better at the motions of the game than one's opponent and successfully exploiting his weaknesses and one's own strengths. Such weaknesses and strengths should be limited to the moves of the game and not to the defects in psychological make-up which are not directly related to the moves of the game. On this view, if B is put off his tennis by A's continual practice of doing up his shoe-laces, and A acts thus because he knows that it puts B off, then A is cheating by acting in this way even though he is not doing anything illegal. (There is naturally a continuum of cases here, where the yelling of hostile imprecations of a sexual nature by A at B would no doubt be adjudged illegal.)

It might be thought that calling A's actions in this sort of case an example of cheating is to go rather too far. After all, perhaps it should be up to a sportsperson to conquer his feelings about slowing a game down by tactics such as A's when such actions are within the rules of the game. B may be a "better" player in terms of skill and strategy than A, yet also more temperamental than A, and A might play on this defect to win more often than B in their contests. This sort of case emphasizes yet again the unsatisfactory nature of the definitions of cheating which Luschen and McIntosh offer. The latter's description involves trying to beat the system and deception, which A's behaviour does not necessarily do. A may take no pains to hide the fact that he is trying to put B off, and he is not trying to beat the system in so far as he is keeping to the explicit rules of the game. So on the McIntosh model A is not cheating at all. On Luschen's account A might be cheating, since he is violating "the principle of chance beyond differences in skill and strategy." However, as we have just suggested, it might be argued that being a good player involves being able to control one's emotional states and overcome annoyances of the time-wasting variety.

What we can conclude is that both accounts fail to tell us how to classify this very common form of behaviour in sport. McIntosh is clear in having to think that A is not cheating, yet this is only because of a simplistic view of the limited possibilities of cheating which is based upon deception and which has already been criticized. Luschen can provide no answer at all. The question of cheating can either be answered in terms of B's obligation as a skillful player to control his temperament (in which case A is not cheating) or in terms of A's behaviour violating a "latently agreed upon" condition for winning a contest (in which case A is cheating). The latter disjunct may seem temptingly acceptable, yet it should be pointed out that there are serious problems with talking about "latent agreements," especially when in practice quite a few players do not act in accordance with such agreements. Non-compliance by some players

makes the problem of identifying precisely what the latent agreement is allegedly about insoluble. In fact, we frequently resort to talking about latent agreements when some people do not want to comply with a behavioural norm and we are trying to prove that they ought to by appealing to some non-explicit rule which they are obliged to follow. Yet this sort of argument is always open to attack by saying that no person is obliged to abide by an agreement, explicit or latent, to which he is not a party.

The tentative conclusion, then, is that there are a good number of difficulties in defining cheating in sport. Now it remains for me to argue that there are similarly many difficulties in specifying precisely what is *wrong* with cheating. It is a commonplace of the literature that cheating in sport is rather like lying in our everyday affairs, and falls under the same moral reproach. That is, if I am not morally entitled to hit someone over the head when competing for a business contract, then I am just as ethically constrained from injuring a competitor in a sporting contest. After all, the practice of sport comes under the same moral rules as the carrying out of any other inter-personal activity (see the work of Aspin, Keenan, Osterhoudt and Zeigler on this topic). Indeed, this rather unexciting comparison has been used to suggest that physical education has a large part to play in moral education. Huizinga has expressed the generally accepted view of what is wrong with cheating in sport by arguing that: "To our way of thinking, cheating as a means of winning a game robs the action of its play-character and spoils it altogether, because for us the essence of play is that the rules be kept—that it be fair play." Aspin makes an interesting observation on this passage. He claims that it ". . . underlines the point about the central virtue of athletic competitions . . . that their whole framework rests upon our desire to see excellence achieved according to rules which attempt to ensure equality, fairness, and impartiality for all" (1975, p. 55). Now, as we have just seen, it is not at all clear what "equality, fairness and impartiality for all" means in a sporting context, nor when they are being denied to a player or players in a contest. It is not a simple matter to determine when the rules of the game are being kept—it depends upon whether a narrower or broader interpretation of the notion of the rules of the game is accepted. So Huizinga's justification of fair play in sport does not as it stands explain why players are morally obliged to reject cheating.

Let us consider a more radical argument concerning fair play. Why should keeping the rules, on whatever interpretation of that expression, be "the essence of play"? In a very basic sense it is obvious that if all or some of the players in a game disobey the rules as a matter of course in their entirety, then they are not playing the game in an ethically dubious manner—they are not playing it at all. Yet this general breakdown of the rules, and consequently of the game, is not what is meant by cheating. The cheater's behaviour is on the whole conforming, since otherwise he would not be allowed to break the rules of the game. Someone who does not in any way conform to the rules of the game will presumably be forbidden, at some stage or other, to continue in it. The cheater seeks to gain an advantage over the opposition in a game and through the game, and so he wants to stay in the game and not destroy it. In addition, those occasions in which he intends to deceive would be robbed of their possible success if it is obvious that he is not adhering to the rules of the game.

If it is acceptable to assert that the presence of cheating in a game does not necessarily invalidate the game, then does it really follow that either the players or the audience should be in favour of fair play in a contest? It might be suggested that many competitions, especially those with some sort of authority present to regulate cheating, would be more interesting if cheating takes place within it, or if several players try to stretch the rules. Such deviant behaviour adds a new dimension to the game which can also add to its interest. Now, I do not want to suggest that cheating cannot disturb the game's rhythm and so make it less interesting to both players and spectators. Perhaps this is what

happens in the majority of cases where cheating is prevalent in sport. Yet it need not be the case in all sporting contests. In so far as the contest is one of wits as well as one of skill and strategy, it can be exciting to compete with and against someone who uses his wits to try to cheat and it can be exciting for an audience to observe such intelligent behaviour.

It might be argued that if both players and spectators have such a laissez-faire attitude to cheating, then they will suffer, or be likely to suffer, harmful influences upon their moral character. We have already referred to the link which is sometimes taken to hold between physical and moral education, to the idea that someone who is taught to break the rules of hockey (or to enjoy watching those rules broken) when it suits his side is more likely to break social rules when it is in his personal interest to do so. Whether any such link exists is an unproved empirical proposition, and there is surely no a priori way of establishing its truth or otherwise. On the other hand, it is surely true that it is possible to inculcate virtues into players and spectators by giving them the opportunity to interact with other people on the sportsfield in a morally acceptable manner and thereby to practice such mutually beneficial roles which they might then apply later in a purely general public context. Yet my argument seems to be that it does not matter how players behave provided that it does not interfere with the interest of the game. Any such claim that sport is amoral in nature would collapse, however, since the actions of players fall under the same very general moral rules as any other sort of behaviour which affects the welfare of others. What I am suggesting is that the fact that people may cheat is part of the structure of sport and is taken into consideration in the rules of the sport, so that cheating in a sport can be built into audience and player perceptions of the game. If it is true that cheating is recognized as an option which both sides may morally take up, then in general the principles of equality and justice are not affected. It may be that player A is a better cheater than player B, yet if cheating is recognized as part of the skill and strategy of the game, then A's advantage is merely an aspect of his being a better player than B. If we dislike the idea of cheating being part of the structure of the game, then perhaps we might consider this passage from Huizinga:

> . . . the game depends upon the temporary acceptance by the players of a set of rules which 'cut off' the activity within the games from events in the 'real' world . . . Play as type of leisure activity . . . entails the temporary creation of a sphere of irreality. . . .

Huizinga's remarks support the idea that cheating in sport need not be compared morally to cheating in our everyday affairs since sport is "just a game" and not simply a reflection of our everyday behaviour. It may be morally acceptable to do certain things in sport which are not acceptable in ordinary life. In his description of violence in hockey, Vaz comments that the:

> . . . implicit objective is to put the opposing star player out of action without doing him serious harm. Illegal tactics and 'tricks' of the game are both encouraged and taught; rough play and physically aggressive performance are strongly encouraged and sometimes players are taught the techniques of fighting. Minimal consideration is given to the formal normative rules of the game, and the conceptions of sportsmanship and fair play are forgotten. . . . Gradually the team is molded into a tough fighting unit prepared for violence whose primary objective is to win hockey games (1972, p. 230).

If this is an accurate description of the general preparation for the playing of professional hockey then both the players and (Vaz suggests) the spectators will expect a skillful player to be good at cheating, where this involves breaking the rules when it is most advantageous to his side. Where such a policy is generally pursued there is no general deception practiced, and players are on equal terms in so far as the conditions for winning the contest are concerned. It is difficult then to see what is morally wrong with such behaviour. After all, it is presumed that the players and spectators are free agents in their participation and attendance. The players know how they are going to behave and the spectators know what they are going to see, namely, cheating carried out when it is considered to be in the best interests of the cheater and his side. If our objection to this practice is to be more than empty romanticism then some stronger arguments in favour of the moral obligatoriness of fair play in sport must be produced.

Perhaps, though, we have unduly stressed what actually happens in some sports at the expense of what ought to happen. That is, if people undertake to play a game, then they may be taken to have understood and agreed to the rules of the game and the principles upon which any fair victory in that game must rest. As Keenan puts it: ". . . if cheating in any form occurs among those parties to the game, they simply fail to adopt the principle of fair play and the morality of justice" (1975, p. 117). As Robert Nozick has expressed this argument: ". . . the principle of fairness . . . holds that when a number of persons engage in a just, mutually advantageous, cooperative venture according to rules and thus restrain their liberty in ways necessary to yield advantages for all, those who have submitted to these restrictions have a right to similar acquiescence on the part of those who have benefited from their submission" (1974, p. 90). Yet what are "the rules of the game" to which players supposedly commit themselves when they enter a game? If we look at the ways in which some sports are played it becomes evident that the rules of the game involve following the formal rules in so far as it is to the advantage of one's own side and breaking them when that is perceived, perhaps wrongly, to be to the side's advantage, where the possibility of suffering a penalty is taken into account. The existence of an authority in games enshrines cheating in the structure of the game; the authority is there to ensure that cheating does not interfere with the principle of fairness in a game. He is there to regulate cheating so that it does not benefit one side more than the other except where one side is more skillful at cheating than the other, and to see that the amount of cheating which takes place is not so great as to change the general form of a particular game. That is, the formal rules of the game must in general be adhered to by all players since otherwise in a clear non-moral sense the game is not being played. But if we are profitably to discuss the notion of the rules of the game, and of cheating and fair play, we must address ourselves to the ways in which players and spectators perceive those rules rather than to an abstract idea of the rules themselves. The next step is to determine what notion of fair play is applicable within the context of the ways in which players actually participate in sporting activities. An injection of realism into philosophical discussions of cheating and fair play in sport is long overdue.

Bibliography

Aspin, D. "Ethical aspects of sport and games and physical education". *Philosophy of Education Society of Great Britain,* 1975, 49–71.

Huizinga, J. *Homo Ludens: A study of the play element in culture.* Boston: Beacon Press, 1950.

Keenan, F. "Justice and sport". *Journal of the Philosophy of Sport,* 1975, 2, 111-123.

Luschen, G. "Cheating in sport". In D. Landers (Ed.) *Social problems in athletics.* Urbana: University of Illinois Press, 1977.

McIntosh, P. *Fair Play: Ethics in sport and education.* Heinemann, London, 1979.

Nozick, R. *Anarchy, state and utopia.* Oxford: Blackwell, 1974.

Osterhoudt, R. "The Kantian ethic as a principle of moral conduct in sport and athletics". In R. Osterhoudt (Ed.) *The philosophy of sport.* Illinois: Charles C Thomas, 1973.

Vaz, E. "The culture of young hockey players: Some initial observations". In A. Taylor (Ed.) *Training: Scientific basis and application.* Quebec: Laval University, 1972.

Zeigler, E. "The pragmatic (experimentalistic) ethic as it relates to sport and physical education". In R. Osterhoudt (Ed.) *The philosophy of sport* (op. cit.).

Can Cheaters Play
the Game?

CRAIG K. LEHMAN

A number of recent philosophers of sport have endorsed the thesis that it is logically impossible to win, or even compete, in a game while at the same time breaking one of its rules (intentionally, at least). For instance, Suits argues:

> The end in poker is not to gain money, nor in golf simply to get a ball into a hole, but to do these things in prescribed (or, perhaps more accurately, not to do them in proscribed) ways: that is, to do them only in accordance with rules. Rules in games thus seem to be in some sense inseparable from ends. . . . If the rules are broken, the original end becomes impossible of attainment, since one cannot (really) win the game unless he plays it, and one cannot (really) play the game unless he obeys the rules of the game. (5: pp. 149–150)

The thesis that cheating in a game is logically incompatible with winning that game may sound initially plausible. I imagine everyone has a vague feeling of having heard it somewhere before—perhaps in high school physical education—but I am going to argue that it is false. Undoubtedly, following some "framework" rules is essential to playing any particular game as we know it, and even violation of rules covering "finer points" may in some cases lead us to say that no game

Reprinted from *Journal of the Philosophy of Sport*, VIII, (1981), pp. 41–46. Copyright 1982 by the Philosophic Society for the Study of Sport. Reprinted by permission.

worthy of the name has taken place, no real winner been determined. But counterexamples to the unqualified incompatibility thesis advocated by Suits and others (1: 4) are not hard to come by.

I

Consider, first, what people ordinarily say about certain sporting events in which deliberate violations of the rules are known (or at least thought) to take place. (I take it for granted that the issue here is the conventional meaning of such phrases as "compete in a game," "win a game," "deliberately violate the rules of a game," etc. Of course someone can stipulate a sense in which it is impossible for cheaters to "really" win, but the nontrivial question is whether this conclusion is implicit in the ordinary meanings of the words.) For instance, many baseball fans believe that Atlanta Braves' pitcher Gaylord Perry throws a spitball. Throwing a spitball is a violation of the rules of baseball. Suppose these fans are right about Perry. Does anyone seriously want to say that no baseball game is ever played when Perry pitches? Should Perry be ineligible for the Hall of Fame on the grounds that he has never won a game, let alone competed, in baseball? Yet this seems to follow if we accept the unqualified thesis that cheating and competing are incompatible. And, of course, cases like Perry's—many of them more elaborate, some of them legendary—can be multiplied indefinitely.

A second point is as follows: Why, if Suits' argument is sound, should only *intentional* violation of rules be relevant to the question of whether genuine participation in a certain game (and hence victory) has taken place? (In the first sentence of this essay, I tried to be charitable by adding intention as a parenthetical condition of the logical-incompatibility thesis, but it will be noted that Suits himself does not say this.) The major premise of Suits' argument, after all, is just that one cannot play a game without following the rules of that game; or in the words of another proponent (4: p. 117) of the incompatibility thesis, "the rules of a game are the definition of that game." But the failure of something to conform to an established definition or set of rules is not abolished by the absence of an intention to nonconformity on the part of its creator. If I draw a four-sided figure with sides of unequal lengths, then I have failed to draw a square, even if I intended to make the sides equal. Thus, it seems that even unintentional violations of the rules of a game should lead us to say that no game (and hence no victory) has occurred, if the usual argument for the logical-incompatibility thesis is correct.

This points the way to more counterexamples. Amateurs almost certainly commit unwitting violations of some rule or other in any game they play, especially while learning. Even in major professional sports, sharp-eyed commentators (and instant replays) often expose accidental violations of the rules, but no one is tempted to say that no game has therefore occurred. Indeed, in team sports, the presence of just one secret cheater on a squad whose members otherwise intend to follow the rules religiously would render the whole team logically incapable of winning.

Let me approach the matter from a different direction. In "Some Reflections on Success and Failure in Competitive Athletics," Delattre, another defender of the logical-incompatibility thesis, remarks:

Both morally and logically, then, there is only one way to play a game. [That is, by the rules.] Grantland Rice makes clear his appreciation of this point in his autobiography, *The Tumult and the Shouting*. For emphasis, he employs the example of a rookie professional lineman. The athlete responds to Rice's praise for his play during his rookie year by observing that he will be better when he becomes more adept at holding illegally without being caught. Of course, to Rice this confused vision of successful competition is heartbreaking. (1: p. 137)

Now, admittedly, I cannot quite work up a broken heart over this incident, but that is not the main point. My question is rather, what kind of confusion did Rice think his lineman had fallen prey to—conceptual confusion, of the sort which fails to notice the impossibility of round squares and married bachelors, or (alleged) moral confusion of the sort which places winning (or, more precisely, "winning") ahead of playing strictly by the rules? The thesis that cheating and competing are logically incompatible would require the former interpretation (and then, perhaps, we should think of the lineman as heartbreakingly stupid), but I strongly suspect that Rice was disappointed in his lineman's alleged moral confusion. I also suspect that the logical-incompatibility thesis draws part of its appeal from being conflated with the moral thesis; Delattre, for instance, speaks of Rice as appreciating "this point," when there are really two points involved.

II

When one cannot see a pattern to them, counterexamples often seem like trivial nit-picking. In this case, however, I think there is a clear pattern, though perhaps not a particularly profound one. The counterexamples all seem to stem from social custom or convenience (i.e., utility). Games are played within a framework of social practices and priorities, and violations of rules must be assessed within this framework to determine whether competition and victory, in the normal sense of the words, have occurred.

Hence, the spitball and offensive holding are a part of the game of baseball and football, respectively, and are techniques sometimes practiced by winners in those sports. Custom seems the primary reason why a game in which the spitball rule is violated is still baseball: The folklore of the game abounds with gleefully told stories of doctored pitches, bats, playing fields, etc., and booing the umpire (i.e., the embodiment of the rules) is a hallowed tradition. On the other hand, the fact that offensive holding can occur in a game of football seems to be mainly a concession to utility: There is simply no practical way for the officials to see everything that occurs in the interior of the line, and the game would probably be much less enjoyable to watch if all the infractions were punished (i.e., the offense would be continually frustrated by penalties, if not by the defensive line).

Of course, as I conceded at the outset, a game cannot be played if too many of its rules are violated. There would be no point in calling an activity a game of baseball if none of the rules of baseball were followed, and it is certainly hard to imagine the point when only a few of the rules are followed. Admittedly, too, one can imagine a society of sanctimonious sports purists who allow that a certain game is played only if every rule of that game is strictly followed. But perfect adherence to every rule is not usually essential to the occurrence of a given game, with a genuine winner.

Between the two extremes of angelic obedience to rules and destruction of a game by wholesale violation of its rules is an interesting set of borderline cases, as in professional wrestling: Here, rules against punching, kicking, strangling, etc., are routinely violated, so that even if the outcome were not fixed, there would be considerable question about whether the resulting show was wrestling.

In the social context of certain ultra-violent science-fiction movies, the objective of sport usually seems to be the provision of spectacles of mayhem; perhaps in those societies, ''illegal'' biting and choking would seem as innocuous as the spitball does in American baseball. But in the actual context of our society, I am not sure what to say about professional wrestling.

So, although I concede that at some (probably hard-to-define) point, excessive rule violations become incompatible with playing a given game, and that there also may be certain ideal cases in which exacting conformity to rules is essential, I maintain that (due to social custom and convenience) it is not in general necessary to the playing or winning of games that every rule of those games be obeyed. Pearson (4: p. 116), however, yet another defender of the logical-incompatibility thesis, remarks that ''a particular game is no more (in terms of its careful definition) than its rules.'' She then goes on, in best Lockean fashion,[1] to state the corollary that ''problems of identity and diversity of games are decided by the rules for each game. Identical games have identical rules and diverse games have differing rules.'' But if I am correct, it should be possible to imagine different games with identical rules (because they are played in the context of different social customs and utilities), and identical games with differing rules (because social customs and utilities negate the difference of rules ''in practice''). For example, it seems conceivable (although I do not know this to be the case) that Japanese baseball players are much more earnest about following the rules of the game than American players are. If the spitball were more widely used than it is in American baseball, and if its effect were greater than I think it is, I can easily imagine a Japanese player saying that, because of the spitball, Americans play a different game. In my view, this would be the literal truth rather than just a manner of speech. Also, of course, it is simple to imagine the cases of differential enforcement of rules canceling out differences in rules.

III

So far I have been concentrating on the thesis that cheating and competing are logically incompatible. But the logical-incompatibility thesis often serves as a premise (or at least a background assumption) in moral arguments designed to show that cheating is, without qualification, unethical and/or unsportsmanlike. I therefore want to conclude this essay with a brief examination of one such argument.

The most explicitly worked-out version of this argument that I know of is advanced by Pearson:[2]

I have argued earlier that a particular game is defined by its rules—that the rules of a game are the definition of that game. If this is the case, a player who deliberately breaks the rules of that game is deliberately no longer playing that game. . . . These acts [i.e., deliberate violations of rules] are designed to interfere with the purpose of the game. If the arguments presented here are correct thus far [and it has been asserted earlier that (1) "the purpose of these games is to test the skill of one individual, or group of individuals, against another . . ." and (2) "If an act is designed by a willing participant in an activity to interfere with the purpose of that activity, then that act can properly be labelled unethical"] we can conclude that the intentional commission of a foul ["an act that is not in compliance with the rules"] in athletics is an unethical act. Ordinarily, when we refer to unethical acts on the part of athletes, we call these acts unsportsmanlike. (5: pp. 116–117)

The major premise of this argument [i.e., item (2) in the brackets] is reminiscent of Kant's second illustration of the first form of the categorical imperative; Pearson also speaks elsewhere of players entering into a contract with their opposition. Obviously, however, discussion of such fundamental principles is beyond the scope of this essay. I grant them for the sake of argument. But consider the other premises.

Understood narrowly enough, I would have no quibble with the assertion that the rules of a game "define" that game; my point has only been that in certain contexts, breaking the rules that "define" a game will not entail that one is not playing that game. Suppose, however, that I am wrong, and the logical-incompatibility thesis is correct. It will still not follow that a player who deliberately breaks the rules of a game is deliberately no longer playing that game. For "deliberately" introduces an intentional context, and validity is not preserved in intentional contexts. (The man behind the arras was Polonius, but it does not follow that in deliberately killing the man behind the arras, Hamlet was deliberately killing Polonius). Similarly, if someone is too "confused" to appreciate the logical-incompatibility thesis, he or she may deliberately violate a rule without deliberately opting out of the game.

Still, someone might reply, this is irrelevant to Pearson's main point. If her ethical major premise is correct, and if the purpose of games is to test the skill of the participants, then if we just add the premise that someone who deliberately violates the rules of a game is deliberately interfering with a test of the skill of the participants, without trying to deduce it from the logical-incompatibility thesis, the conclusion can still be secured. To be sure, some qualifications might be needed to take care of cases in which rules are deliberately broken for some unusual reason, but the idea would be that in deliberately throwing a spitball (or so we suppose), Perry is deliberately interfering with a test of the batter's skill at hitting a (legal) pitch. In general, cheaters know very well that they are trying to minimize an opponent's chances in a test of skill.

Nevertheless, even if these emendations are allowed, I think the argument is still infected with the same disease I was trying to cure in the last section. For how does one establish that *the* purpose of a game is a test of its participant's skill? So far as I can see, only by supposing a certain romanticized social context in which custom and convenience dictate that games are played solely to test the player's skill within a certain framework of rules. But that, I would argue, is not the social context of most sports as *we* know them. Indeed, to the extent that it is intelligible to talk of sports having purposes at all (an assumption which apparently goes undefended), sports seem to be multipurpose. Baseball, for example, serves the purposes of providing an income for owners and players, an afternoon's diversion for the casual fan, another installment in a unique kind of larger-than-life drama for a passionate devotee of "the national pastime." Of course, competing in or observing an event in which there are tests of skill basically within the framework of a set of (very complicated) rules is a main purpose of almost everyone concerned with baseball, but a pure test of skill featuring saintly observance of every rule is *the* purpose of baseball only to a few purists.

Thus, I think that Pearson's attempt to derive unsportsmanlike conduct from some kind of frustration of the purpose or goal of a game implicitly falls victim to the same oversight as the thesis that cheating and competing are logically incompatible: It assumes that one can read off what a game (or the purpose of a game) is just by examining the rule book. Admittedly, rule books for games do not contain statements of purposes for those games. But they do set down conditions for winning, and they do proceed on the assumption that the rules are rigorously followed; this makes the hypothesis that the purpose of a game is to determine a winner according to its rules by far the most obvious hypothesis.

I suspect, then, that no argument that makes deliberate violation of rules a sufficient condition for unsportsmanlike conduct is likely to apply to many of the sports we know. And this seems to me as it should be: I have no reason to believe that Perry, if he throws a spitball, or offensive linemen, if they hold, are generally regarded as poor sports by their peers or the fans. On the contrary, it seems likely that many of them are regarded as displaying all the essentials of good sportsmanship. Sportsmanship seems to transcend the rulebook, not only in the sense of sometimes requiring more than adherence to the rules, but also in the sense of sometimes permitting less.

Notes

1. See (3), esp. Bk. II, Ch. 27, sec. 8, "Idea of identity suited to the Idea it is applied to."
2. For similar views, see (1: 2). Keating does not defend the logical-incompatibility thesis, but he does tie unsportsmanlike conduct to frustration of the goal of sport.

Bibliography

1. Delattre, Edwin J. "Some Reflections on Success and Failure in Competitive Athletics." *Journal of the Philosophy of Sport,* II (1976), pp. 133–139.
2. Keating, James W. "Sportsmanship as a Moral Category." *Ethics,* LXXV (October 1964), pp. 25–35.
3. Locke, John. *Essay Concerning Human Understanding.* Many editions.
4. Pearson, Kathleen. "Deception, Sportsmanship, and Ethics." *Quest,* XIX (January 1973), pp. 115–118.
5. Suits, Bernard. "What is a Game?" *Philosophy of Science,* XXXIV (June 1967), pp. 148–156.

Good Competition and Drug-Enhanced Performance

ROBERT L. SIMON

Competition in sport frequently has been defended in terms of the search for excellence in performance.[1] Top athletes, whether their motivation arises from adherence to the internal values of competition or desire for external reward, are willing to pay a heavy price in time and effort in order to achieve competitive success. When this price consists of time spent in hard practice, we are prepared to praise the athlete as a worker and true competitor. But when athletes attempt to achieve excellence through the use of performance-enhancing drugs, there is widespread condemnation. Is such condemnation justified? What is wrong with the use of drugs to achieve excellence in sport? Is prohibiting the use of performance-enhancing drugs in athletic competition justified?

The relatively widespread use of such drugs as anabolic steroids to enhance performance dates back at least to the Olympics of the 1960s, although broad public awareness of such drug use seems relatively recent. Anabolic steroids are drugs, synthetic derivatives of the male hormone testosterone, which are claimed to stimulate muscle growth and tissue repair. While claims about possible bad consequences of steroid use are controversial, the American College of Sports Medicine warns against serious side effects. These are believed to include liver damage, atherosclerosis, hypertension, personality changes, a lowered sperm count in males, and masculinization in females. Particularly frightening is that world-class athletes are reportedly taking steroids at many times the recommended medical dosage—at levels so high that, as Thomas Murray (4: p. 26) has pointed out, under "current federal regulations governing human subjects . . . no institutional review board would approve a research design that entailed giving subjects anywhere near the levels . . . used by the athletes."

The use of such high levels of a drug raises complex empirical as well as ethical issues. For example, even if steroid use at a low level does not actually enhance athletic performance, as some authorities claim, it is far from clear whether heavy use produces any positive effects on performance. At the very least, athletes who believe in the positive effects of heavy doses of steroids are not likely to be convinced by data based on more moderate intake.

As interesting as these issues are, it will be assumed in what follows that the use of certain drugs does enhance athletic performance and does carry with it some significant risk to the athlete. Although each of these assumptions may be controversial, by granting them, the discussion can concentrate on the ethical issues raised by use of performance-enhancing drugs.

Reprinted from *Journal of the Philosophy of Sport*, XI, (1984), pp. 6–13. Copyright 1985 by the Philosophic Society for the Study of Sport. Reprinted by permission.

I. What Is a Performance-Enhancing Drug?

If we are to discuss the ethics of using drugs to enhance athletic performance, we should begin with a clear account of what counts as such a drug. Unfortunately, a formal definition is exceedingly hard to come by, precisely because it is unclear to what substances such a definition ought to apply.

If it is held to be impermissible to take steroids or amphetamines to enhance performance, what about special diets, the use of coffee to promote alertness, or the bizarre practice of "blood doping," by which runners store their own blood in a frozen state and then return it to their body before a major meet in order to increase the oxygen sent to the muscles?

It is clear that the concept of an "unnatural" or "artificial" substance will not take us very far here, since testosterone hardly is unnatural. Similarly, it is difficult to see how one's own blood can be considered artificial. In addition, we should not include on any list of forbidden substances the use of medication for legitimate reasons of health.

Moreover, what counts as a performance-enhancing drug will vary from sport to sport. For example, drinking alcohol normally will hurt performance. However, in some sports, such as riflery, it can help. This is because as a depressant, alcohol will slow down one's heart rate and allow for a steadier stance and aim.

Rather than spend considerable time and effort in what is likely to be a fruitless search for necessary conditions, we would do better to ignore borderline cases and focus on such clear drugs of concern as amphetamines and steroids. If we can understand the ethical issues that apply to use of such drugs, we might then be in a better position to handle borderline cases as well. However, it does seem that paradigm cases of the drugs that are of concern satisfy at least some of the following criteria.

1. If the user did not believe that use of the substance in the amount ingested would increase the chances of enhanced athletic performance, that substance would not be taken.

2. The substance, in the amount ingested, is believed to carry significant risk to the user.

3. The substance, in the amount ingested, is not prescribed medication taken to relieve an illness or injury.

These criteria raise no concern about the normal ingestion of such drugs as caffeine in coffee or tea, or about medication since drugs used for medicinal purposes would not fall under them (1). The use of amphetamines and steroids, on the other hand, do fall under the criteria. Blood doping seems to be a borderline case and perhaps this is as it should be. It is employed only to enhance performance, is not medication, is not part of any normal training routine, yet seems to pose no significant risk to the user.[2]

However, the important issue for our purposes is not the adequacy of the three criteria as a definition for, as I have suggested, any search for a definition in the absence of the correct normative perspective will likely turn out to be a fruitless hunt for the nonexistent snark. Rather, the major concern is not with defining performance-enhancing drugs but with evaluating their use. In particular, it is one thing to claim that the three criteria (or any other proposed set) are satisfied to a particular degree. It is quite another to make the normative claim that use of the substance in question is morally questionable or impermissible.

Why should the use of possibly harmful drugs solely for the purpose of enhancing athletic performance be regarded as impermissible? In particular, why shouldn't individual athletes be left at liberty to pursue excellence by any means they freely choose?

II. Performance-Enhancing Drugs, Coercion, and the Harm Principle

One argument frequently advanced against the use of such performance-enhancing drugs as steroids is based on our second criterion of harm to the user. Since use of such drugs is harmful to the user, it ought to be prohibited.

However, if we accept the ''harm principle,'' which is defended by such writers as J.S. Mill, paternalistic interference with the freedom of others is ruled out. According to the harm principle, we are entitled to interfere with the behavior of competent, consenting adults only to prevent harm to others. After all, if athletes prefer the gains that the use of drugs provide along with possible side effects to the alternative of less risk but worse performance, external interference with their freedom of choice seems unwarranted.

However, at least two possible justifications of paternalistic interference are compatible with the harm principle. First, we can argue that athletes do not give informed consent to the use of performance-enhancing drugs. Second, we can argue that the use of drugs by some athletes does harm other competitors. Let us consider each response in turn.

Informed Consent

Do athletes freely choose to use such performance-enhancing drugs as anabolic steroids? Consider, for example, professional athletes whose livelihood may depend on the quality of their performance. Athletes whose performance does not remain at peak levels may not be employed for very long. As Carolyn Thomas (6: p. 198) maintains, ''the onus is on the athlete to . . . consent to things that he or she would not otherwise consent to. . . . Coercion, however, makes the athlete vulnerable. It also takes away the athlete's ability to act and choose freely with regard to informed consent.'' Since pressures on top amateur athletes in national and world-class competition may be at least as great as pressures on professionals, a comparable argument can be extended to cover them as well.

However, while this point is not without some force, we need to be careful about applying the notion of coercion too loosely. After all, no one is forced to try to become a top athlete. The reason for saying top athletes are ''coerced'' is that if they don't use performance-enhancing drugs, they may not get what they want. But they still have the choice of settling for less. Indeed, to take another position is to virtually deny the competence of top athletes to give consent in a variety of sports related areas including adoption of training regimens and scheduling. Are we to say, for example, that coaches coerce athletes into training and professors coerce students into doing work for their courses? Just as students can choose not to take a college degree, so too can athletes revise their goals. It is also to suggest that *any* individual who strives for great reward is not competent to give consent, since the fear of losing such a reward amounts to a coercive pressure.

While the issue of coercion and the distinction between threats and offers is highly complex, I would suggest that talk of coercion is problematic as long as the athlete has an acceptable alternative to continued participation in highly competitive sport. While coercion may indeed be a real problem in special cases, the burden of proof would seem to be on those who deny that top athletes *generally* are in a position to consent to practices affecting performance.

Harm to Others

This rejoinder might be satisfactory, critics will object, if athletes made their choices in total isolation. The competitive realities are different, however. If some athletes use drugs, others—who on their own might refrain from becoming users—are "forced" to indulge just to remain competitive. As Manhattan track coach Fred Dwyer (3: p. 25) points out, "The result is that athletes—none of whom understandingly, are willing to settle for second place—feel that 'if my opponent is going to get for himself that little extra, then I'm a fool not to.'" Athletes may feel trapped into using drugs in order to stay competitive. According to this argument, then, the user of performance-enhancing drugs is harming others by coercing them into becoming users as well.

While the competitive pressures to use performance-enhancing drugs undoubtedly are real, it is far from clear that they are unfair or improperly imposed. Suppose, for example, that some athletes embark on an especially heavy program of weight training. Are they coercing other athletes into training just as hard in order to compete? If not, why are those athletes who use steroids "coercing" others into going along?[3] Thus, if performance-enhancing drugs were available to all, no one would cheat by using them; for all would have the same opportunity and, so it would be argued, no one would be forced into drug use any more than top athletes are forced to embark on rigorous training programs.

Perhaps what bothers us about the use of drugs is that the user may be endangering his or her health. But why isn't the choice about whether the risk is worth the gain left to the individual athlete to make? After all, we don't always prohibit new training techniques just because they carry along with them some risk to health. Perhaps the stress generated by a particularly arduous training routine is more dangerous to some athletes than the possible side effects of drugs are to others?

Arguably, the charge that drug users create unfair pressures on other competitors begs the very question at issue. That is, it presupposes that such pressures are morally suspect in ways that other competitive pressures are not, when the very point at issue is whether that is the case. What is needed is some principled basis for asserting that certain competitive pressures—those generated by the use of performance enhancing drugs—are illegitimately imposed while other competitive pressures—such as those generated by hard training—are legitimate and proper. It will not do to point out that the former pressures are generated by drug use. What is needed is an explanation of why the use of performance-enhancing drugs should be prohibited in the first place.

While such arguments, which describe a position we might call a libertarianism of sports, raise important issues, they may seem to be open to clear counter-example when applied in nonathletic contexts. Suppose for example that your co-workers choose to put in many extra hours on the job. That may put pressure on you to work overtime as well, if only to show your employer that you are just as dedicated as your colleagues. But now, suppose your fellow workers start taking dangerous stimulants to enable them to put even more hours into their jobs. Your employer then asks why you are working less than they are. You reply that you can keep up the pace only by taking dangerous drugs. Is the employer's reply, "Well, no one is forcing you to stay on the job, but if you do you had better put in as many hours as the others" really acceptable?

However, even here, intuitions are not a particularly reliable guide to principle. Suppose you have other less stressful alternatives for employment and that the extra hours the others originally work without aid of drugs generate far more harmful stress than the risk generated by the use of the stimulant? Perhaps in that case your employer is not speaking impermissibly in telling you to work harder. If not, just why does the situation change when the harmful effects are generated by drugs rather than stress? Alternatively, if we think there should be limits both on the stress generated by pressures from overtime *and* the risks created by drug use, why not treat similar risks alike, regardless of source? Similarly, in the context of sport, if our goal is to lower risk, it is far from clear that the risks imposed by performance-enhancing drugs are so great as to warrant total prohibition, while the sometimes equal risks imposed by severe training regimens are left untouched.

Harm and the Protection of the Young

Even if athletes at top levels of competition can give informed consent to the use of performance-enhancing drugs, and even if users do not place unfair or coercive competitive pressures on others, the harm principle may still support prohibition.

Consider, for example, the influence of the behavior of star athletes on youngsters. Might not impressionable boys and girls below the age of consent be driven to use performance-enhancing drugs in an effort to emulate top stars? Might not high school athletes turn to performance-enhancing drugs to please coaches, parents, and fans?

Unfortunately, consideration of such remote effects of drug use is far from conclusive. After all, other training techniques such as strict weight programs also may be dangerous if adopted by young athletes who are too physically immature to take the stress such programs generate. Again, what is needed is not simply a statement that a practice imposes some risk on others. Also needed is a justification for saying the risk is improperly imposed. Why restrict the freedom of top athletes rather than increase the responsibility for supervision of youngsters assigned to coaches, teachers, and parents? After all, we don't restrict the freedom of adults in numerous other areas where they may set bad examples for the young.

III. Drugs and the Ideal of Competitive Sport

Our discussion so far suggests that although the charges that use of performance-enhancing drugs by some athletes harms others do warrant further examination, they amount to less than a determinative case against such drug use. However, they

may have additional force when supported by an account of competitive sport which implies a distinction between appropriate and inappropriate competitive pressures. What we need, then, is an account of when risk is improperly imposed on others in sport. While I am unable to provide a full theory here, I do want to suggest a principled basis, grounded on an ethic of athletic competition, for prohibition of paradigm performance-enhancing drugs.

My suggestion, which I can only outline here, is that competition in athletics is best thought of as a mutual quest for excellence through challenge (2: pp. 133–139). Competitors are obliged to do their best so as to bring out the best in their opponents. Competitors are to present challenges to one another within the constitutive rules of the sport being played. Such an account may avoid the charges, often directed against competitive sports, that they are zero-sum games which encourage the selfish and egotistical desire to promote oneself by imposing losses on others.

In addition, the ideal of sport as a *mutual* quest for excellence brings out the crucial point that a sports contest is a competition between *persons*. Within the competitive framework, each participant must respond to the choices, acts, and abilities of others—which in turn manifest past decisions about what one's priorities should be and how one's skills are to be developed. The good competitor, then, does not see opponents as things to be overcome and beaten down but rather sees them as persons whose acts call for appropriate, mutually acceptable responses. On this view, athletic competition, rather than being incompatible with respect for our opponents as persons, actually presupposes it.

However, when use of drugs leads to improved play, it is natural to say that it is not athletic ability that determines outcome but rather the efficiency with which the athlete's body reacts to the performance enhancer. But the whole point of athletic competition is to test the athletic ability of persons, not the way bodies react to drugs. In the latter case, it is not the athlete who is responsible for the gain. Enhanced performance does not result from the qualities of the athlete *qua* person, such as dedication, motivation, or courage. It does not result from innate or developed ability, of which it is the point of competition to test. Rather, it results from an external factor, the ability of one's body to efficiently utilize a drug, a factor which has only a contingent and fortuitous relationship to athletic ability.[4]

Critics may react to this approach in at least two different ways. First, they may deny that drug use radically changes the point of athletic competition, which presumably is to test the physical and mental qualities of athletes in their sport. Second, they may assert that by allowing the use of performance-enhancing drugs, we expand the point of athletic competition in desirable ways. That is, they may question whether the paradigm of athletic competition to which I have appealed has any privileged moral standing. It may well be an accepted paradigm, but what makes it acceptable?

Drugs and Tests of Ability

Clearly, drugs such as steroids are not magic pills that guarantee success regardless of the qualities of the users. Athletes using steroids must practice just as hard as others to attain what may be only marginal benefits from use. If performance enhancers were available to all competitors, it would still be the qualities of athletes that determined the results.

While this point is not without force, neither is it decisive. Even if all athletes used drugs, they might not react to them equally. The difference in reaction might determine the difference between competitive success and failure. Hence, outcomes would be determined not by the relevant qualities of the athletes themselves but rather by the natural capacity of their bodies to react to the drug of choice.

Is this any different, the critic may reply, from other innate differences in athletes which might

enable them to benefit more than others from weight training or to run faster or swing harder than others? Isn't it inconsistent to allow some kinds of innate differences to affect outcomes but not the others?

Such an objective, however, seems to ignore the point of athletic competition. The point of such competition is to select those who do run the fastest, swing the hardest, or jump the farthest. The idea is not for all to come out equally, but for differences in outcome to correlate with differences in ability and motivation. Likewise, while some athletes may be predisposed to benefit more from a given amount of weight training than others, this trait seems relevant to selection of the best athlete. Capacity to benefit from training techniques seems part of what makes one a superior athlete in a way that capacity to benefit from a drug does not.

Competition and Respect for Persons

At this point, a proponent of the use of performance-enhancing drugs might acknowledge that use of such drugs falls outside the prevailing paradigm of athletic competition. However, such a proponent might ask, "What is the *moral* force of such a conclusion?" Unless we assume that the accepted paradigm not only is acceptable, but in addition that deviance from it should be prohibited, nothing follows about the ethics of the use of performance-enhancing drugs.

Indeed, some writers seem to suggest that we consider new paradigms compatible with greater freedom for athletes, including freedom to experiment with performance-enhancing drugs. W.M. Brown seems to advocate such a view when he writes,

Won't it [drug use] change the nature of our sports and ourselves? Yes. . . . But then people can choose, as they always have, to compete with those similar to themselves or those different. . . . I can still make my actions an 'adventure in freedom' and 'explore the limits of my strength' however I choose to develop it. (1: p. 22)

I believe Brown has raised a point of fundamental significance here. I wish I had a fully satisfactory response to it. Since I don't, perhaps the best I can do is indicate the lines of a reply I think are worth considering, in the hope that it will stimulate further discussion and evaluation.

Where athletic competition is concerned, if all we are interested in is better and better performance, we could design robots to "run" the hundred yards in 3 seconds or hit a golf ball 500 yards when necessary. But it isn't just enhanced performance that we are after. In addition, we want athletic competition to be a test of *persons*. It is not only raw ability we are testing for; it is what people do with their ability that counts at least as much. In competition itself, each competitor is reacting to the choices, strategies, and valued abilities of the other, which in turn are affected by past decisions and commitments. Arguably, athletic competition is a paradigm example of an area in which each individual competitor respects the other competitors as persons. That is, each reacts to the intelligent choices and valued characteristics of the other. These characteristics include motivation, courage, intelligence, and what might be called the metachoice of which talents and capacities are to assume priority over others for a given stage of the individual's life.

However, if outcomes are significantly affected not by such features but instead by the capacity of the body to benefit physiologically from drugs, athletes are no longer reacting to each other as persons but rather become more like competing bodies. It becomes more and more appropriate to see the opposition as things to be overcome—as mere means to be overcome in the name of victory —rather than as persons posing valuable challenges. So, insofar as the requirement that we respect each other as persons is ethically fundamental, the prevailing paradigm does enjoy a privileged perspective from the moral point of view.

It is of course true that the choice to develop one's capacity through drugs is a choice a person might make. Doesn't respect for persons require that we respect the choice to use performance enhancers as much as any other? The difficulty, I suggest, is the effect that such a choice has on the process of athletic competition itself. The use of performance-enhancing drugs in sports restricts the area in which we can be respected as persons. Although individual athletes certainly can make such a choice, there is a justification inherent in the nature of good competition for prohibiting participation by those who make such a decision. Accordingly, the use of performance-enhancing drugs should be prohibited in the name of the value of respect for persons itself.

Notes

1. This paper was presented at the Olympic Scientific Congress in Eugene, Oregon (July, 1984) as part of a symposium, sponsored by the Philosophic Society for the Study of Sport, on the use of performance-enhancing drugs in sport. Some of the material in this paper is included in Robert L. Simon, *Sports and Social Values* (Englewood Cliffs, NJ: Prentice-Hall, 1985), and published by permission of Prentice-Hall.
2. The ethical issues raised by blood doping are discussed by Perry (5).
3. The charge of coercion does seem more plausible if the athlete has no acceptable alternative but to participate. Thus, professional athletes with no other career prospects may fit the model of coercion better than, say, a young amateur weight lifter who has been accepted at law school.
4. Does this approach have the unintuitive consequence that the dietary practice of car-

bohydrate loading, utilized by runners, also is ethically dubious? Perhaps so, but perhaps a distinction can be made between steroid use, which changes an athlete's capabilities for athletically irrelevant reasons, and dietary practices, which enable athletes to get the most out of the ability they have.

Bibliography

1. Brown, W.M. (1980). ''Ethics, Drugs and Sport.'' *Journal of the Philosophy of Sport,* VII, 15–23.

2. Delattre, Edward. (1975). ''Some Reflections on Success and Failure in Competitive Athletics.'' *Journal of the Philosophy of Sport,* I, 133–139.

3. Dwyer, Fred. (1982). ''The Real Problem: Using Drugs to Win.'' *The New York Times,* July 4, 2S.

4. Murray, Thomas H. (1983). ''The Coercive Power of Drugs in Sports.'' *The Hastings Center Report,* 13, 24–30.

5. Perry, Clifton. (1983). ''Blood Doping and Athletic Competition.'' *International Journal of Applied Philosophy,* 1, 39–45.

6. Thomas, Carolyn E. (1983). *Sport in a Philosophic Context.* Philadelphia: Lea & Febiger.

Paternalism, Drugs, and the Nature of Sports

W.M. BROWN

During the marathon run at the 1972 Munich Olympics, Frank Shorter is said to have sipped decarbonated Coca-Cola provided along the route by his assistants as he headed for a gold medal. Clearly, for Shorter, caffeine was the drug of choice for that most demanding of running events. Since that time, caffeine has become one of an increasingly long list of banned drugs no longer permitted by the International Olympic Committee for competing athletes.[1] The list includes both a variety of chemically synthesized drugs as well as naturally occurring substances that are artificially prepared for human use.[2] The central issue of the use of such substances is not their so-called recreational use, the most prominent example of which is probably the widely publicized use of cocaine by some professional athletes. (Alcohol is apparently not currently a prohibited drug for Olympic athletes.) Rather, the issue is the use of drugs to enhance the benefits of training and to improve peak performance in competition.

Controversy on this issue centers on several factors which have both an empirical aspect and a moral one. The empirical questions concern both the effectiveness of drug use for training and competition and the possible harm such use can have for users.[3] The moral questions concern the appropriateness of the use of drugs in sports, especially when their use is seen as a kind of cheating, a breach of principles of fair play. It is sometimes claimed, too, that the use of drugs in sports is somehow unnatural or incompatible with the very nature of sports. I intend to discuss these matters, but from the perspective of the moral principle of paternalism that I believe motivates many people who are concerned with this issue. First I want to look closely at the issue of drug use in sports by children and young people—cases which may appear to justify paternalistic choices—and then turn to the harder case of the paternalistic control of drug use by adults in sports.

Even John Stuart Mill (7), in his sustained attack on paternalistic restrictions on individual liberty, limited the application of his principles to mature individuals, adults in the full possession of their cognitive and emotional capacities. In the case of children, and perhaps others whose mature development of these capacities and a wider experience of life's possibilities has yet to be achieved, restrictions on individual liberty may be justified as preventing significant harm that might not otherwise be recognized and avoided. In such cases it seems clear that paternalistic interference is not only permissible but may indeed be obligatory to prevent harm and allow for a full flourishing of the child's potential development. Of course, judgment must be balanced: An important part of growing up is making mistakes and learning from them. All parents know the anguish of allowing failure to help guide the maturation of their children. Following Joel Feinberg and Gerald Dworkin, we can distinguish between ''soft'' and ''hard'' paternalism (2;3;4).[4]

Soft paternalism is defined by Dworkin (3: p. 107) as ''the view that (1) paternalism is sometimes justified, and (2) it is a necessary condition for such justification that the person for whom we are acting paternalistically is in some way not competent.'' The key element here is clearly the determination that the person for whom we are acting is in fact not acting voluntarily, perhaps due to various circumstances including immaturity, ignorance, incapacity, or coercion. It may be that the nonvoluntary character of the behavior is evident or justifiably assumed on other grounds. This is typically the case with young children; but it is sometimes also true of adults whose situation makes clear that their actions are not fully voluntary. The more problematic cases are those of adult behavior that is not obviously nonvoluntary, but whose consequences are potentially dangerous or serious enough to call for careful deliberation. In these cases, as Feinberg (4: p. 8) suggests, we may be justified in intervening at least temporarily to determine whether the conduct is voluntary or not.

If soft paternalism is most clearly relevant to intervention in the lives of children and incompetent persons, hard paternalism must deal with cases of fully voluntary action and show nevertheless that paternalism is justified. Here we may have every reason to suppose that the action in question is voluntarily undertaken by someone who has carefully appraised the consequences, weighed all available information, is emotionally responsive to the circumstances, but still opts to act in ways that involve the probability of serious harm, degradation, or impairment of opportunity or liberty. The most frequently cited cases are of those who seek to sell themselves into slavery, or persist in ignoring basic safety precautions such as wearing helmets while riding motorcycles. I shall return to the hard paternalistic thesis and its application to the case of adult sports after considering first the view of the soft paternalist and its application to the case of children and young people and their

participation in sports. I shall not be directly concerned with the soft paternalist attitude toward adult sports except as an extension of its application to the case of children.

The soft paternalist argues that limitation of one's liberty is justified when one's behavior or actions are not fully voluntary because they are not fully informed, or because one is not fully competent or is in some relevant way coerced. All of these factors may plausibly be seen as present in the case of children's sports. By virtue of their youth, limited education, and inexperience, young people may frequently act in imprudent and potentially harmful ways, ways that may have unforeseen but long-term or irreversible consequences. Before considering the case of drugs, let me review several other cases in which the soft paternalist has what seems to be a strong argument for intervention or control of the young athlete's participation in sports.

The first kind of situation can best be called ''safety cases.''[5] These involve efforts by coaches, trainers, parents, and others to ensure that young players are provided with proper safety equipment and that they use it while engaged in playing the sport. Especially in contact sports such as football or hockey, such equipment as helmets and padded uniforms may be essential to protect the players against serious injury. Other sports may require other kinds of precautions. For example, swimmers may be prohibited from training alone in a pool, runners may be required to wear proper shoes, contact lenses may be forbidden, and so on. Some of these precautions may simply be prescribed by thoughtful parents or coaches, but others may be written into the rules of the sports by athletic associations, schools, or boards of education, thereby restricting participation to those who are properly equipped, or prohibiting certain kinds of play as too dangerous.

Indeed, most of the rules governing contact between players are formulated with the intention of ensuring the safety of enthusiastic and energetic players. The reasons for these requirements and rules are evident. Young athletes are frequently marvelously competent and talented in performing the intricate or arduous or swift feats called for in their sports. But they are typically equally unaware of their own limitations, their susceptibility to injury, and the long-term consequences of injuries to their development or effective participation. What justifies intervention in these cases, of restrictions on what young athletes may do, is precisely the belief that they are thus being prevented from harming themselves and that on mature reflection they themselves will come to see the reasonableness of the restrictions now placed on them. As their own experience broadens, and as their knowledge of themselves and their actions deepens and their values mature, they are, we anticipate, likely to join in accepting the restrictions they may have seen before as irksome and unnecessary.

A second set of cases I propose to refer to as "health cases." Insofar as injuries are closely connected with our views of health, there is clearly a considerable overlap between these two types of cases. Nevertheless, I believe there are some significant differences that warrant a separate category. Even in the absence of injuries and of circumstances likely to promote them, other matters of health rightly should concern the parent or coach of young athletes. I have in mind here matters that concern training, medical examinations and corresponding medical treatment or therapy, and nutrition and rest. They may involve the need for periodic medical examinations, the proper treatment of injuries, insistence on adequate nutrition and rest, and thoughtful organizing of training schedules that carefully consider the age, preparation, and health of the athlete.

In these cases, the young person typically lacks information to make adequate judgments—information that may be the purview of specially trained persons with long experience working with athletes and others. Furthermore, the young person is not generally expected even to be aware of his or her own ignorance or of the importance of acquiring medical or other information at an age when health may be taken for granted. Moreover,

even when information is available, its significance may not be readily appreciated, habits of restraint and caution may be ill-formed, and self-discipline in maintaining therapeutic or training regimens may be minimal. The opposite may also occur. Youthful determination may manifest itself in excessive restraint, debilitating training, or stubborn persistence. Here ancient wisdom of balance, moderation, measure or variation may be the needed antidote, provided by more experienced people who insist on more wholesome approaches to sports preparation.

Of course, other factors than ignorance and inexperience may need to be overcome in paternalistic control of youthful sports. Peer and perhaps especially adult pressures are often a critical factor that adult advisors must deal with firmly and sensitively. One other important distinction should be mentioned here. So far, I have ignored the difference between health as the absence of disease or injury and health as a positive feature of growth and development. If it is clear that adults are justified in controlling the sports activities of young people in the interest of preventing injuries or speeding recuperation, and in maintaining the health of their children and students in the sense of keeping them injury-free and minimally healthy, it is also plausible that they are justified in seeking a greater degree of health or fitness for them. This seems to involve more centrally an educational function, though this feature is clearly present in the other two kinds of cases I have discussed, and I now turn to consider what might be called "educational cases."

Sports in our schools and universities, even when they involve intercollegiate competition, are almost invariably associated with departments of physical education. I mention this because it seems that a neglected but focal role for parents and coaches is educational, and the educational function goes far beyond the training of skills to include the inculcation of attitudes and values, the dissemination of information, and the formation of habits of mind as well as of body. It is difficult to illustrate cases in which paternalistic issues arise here, because the guidance of parents and coaches is often so subtle and pervasive as to be unnoticed by those it influences. Its character as interfering with or controlling the behavior of unwilling charges is more difficult to discern. Nevertheless, I think there are some fairly clear cases.

One type of case brings us back to efforts to prevent injury and to foster wholesome development by prescribing training schedules and nutritional standards designed to maximize training effectiveness. The effort here should never be merely to prescribe, but also to educate by explaining the rationale for the requirements, presenting the evidence available to substantiate the judgments, and requiring that the student understand as much as possible how the decisions were made. What can be expected here will vary with the age and educational level of the student; but resistance can often be expected, not only to following the requirements but to making efforts to understand them. I offer no formula for success in these efforts. As in all educational contexts many options are available to gifted teachers: cajolery, punishment, rewards, example, the inducements of affection, friendship, and respect, and lessons of failure and success. But I do wish to stress that these efforts are made because we believe the lessons should be learned, willingly or not, in the gym and playing field as well as the classroom. In doing so we counter the thoughtless or irrational or emotionally immature behavior of our students with paternalistic measures we believe are acceptable to fully rational and emotionally mature individuals.

A second type of educational case involves values. I have in mind instances of cheating or foul play in which adults may intervene to correct unfair, dishonest, or unsportsmanlike actions. Here again the goal is not merely to remedy or referee but is fundamentally educational. We should seek to instill values of fairness and honesty, countering whatever tendencies to the contrary we observe on the grounds that such action is not in the best interest of the players, whatever they may think about it. The development of values like the acquisition of knowledge in general is but one aspect of the central aim of education, which is the discovery of self-knowledge. Since, especially in young people, this is inextricably bound up with what they will become as well as with what they now are, the paternalistic guidance by adults must both inform and shape in light of what the adults believe to be the characteristics of persons in the fullness of their cognitive and emotional powers.

We are now ready to discuss control of the use of drugs by children and young people as an aspect of their participation in sports. Although I think a good general case can be made for proscribing drug use by young people, and even that a recreational use of drugs has some negative relevance to participation in sports, I plan to limit my remarks to a consideration of the use of drugs to influence athletic training and performance. I have not hesitated to offer here what I consider to be defensible moral judgments on the topics and issues I have raised. My point is not to insist that these judgments are unavoidable, but to suggest that they correspond with widely held intuitions relating to the acceptability of paternalism in regard to children and their sports activities.

Two aspects of drug use can be distinguished in advance, one being the use of drugs as medication. When medical treatment does not prevent sports participation entirely, it may significantly curtail that involvement. And when injury or illness requires medication which nevertheless will allow some sports activity, the decisive criterion will be improvement of the participant's health, not athletic achievement. There may also be times when use of medication is unrelated to sports and seems in no way to affect participation, except perhaps to allow it where otherwise it might not be possible. (An example might be drugs used to control mild epilepsy.) Here, too, the primary concern is the health and safety of the child. Such use may enhance participation in the limiting sense of making it possible, but where the purpose and effect of such usage is limited to medically justifiable ones, we may reasonably disregard this trivial enhancement. In the event that a medication did significantly improve performance over what would otherwise be expected, we could consider it in the next category.

This category involves cases in which drugs are used by otherwise healthy people for the express purpose of enhancing training or competition. There are a number of reasons why such usage should be prohibited. Foremost, of course, are the clear threats to the health and safety of the persons taking them. Among the many drugs available to athletes are some that have a powerful effect on the balance of the hormonal system, such as testosterone and other steroids, or human growth hormone, or L-dopa and β-blockers which can stimulate such hormones. Psychomotor or central nervous system stimulants can have a variety of powerful effects on the human body. Young people are especially vulnerable not only to the primary effects of such drugs but also to many deleterious side effects and to possible long-range effects that in many cases are only now beginning to be determined.[6] Damaging effects on growth patterns, and on psychosocial development, are probable high risks of such drugs for children and young people—risks far outweighing any possible benefits of temporary superior athletic prowess.

I should mention that in this respect, drugs are not different in kind, though perhaps in degree, from other features of sports which conflict with our values of health for young people. Arduous and extreme training methods, excessively rough contact between players, and insufficient recuperation or recovery from illness or injury, for example, may all violate our reasonable standards of wholesome athletics. Indeed a paramount concern for any tendency to overemphasize achievements in young people's sports is that it encourages a disregard for the health and balanced development of the young players.

I suspect that these judgments are relatively uncontroversial. But I now want to renew our discussion of the relation of such possible drug use and the development of attitudes and values by young players which I have already defended as among the legitimate paternalistic concerns of guardians and athletic supervisors. Drug use of the kind we are discussing (and of course many other features of training and competition) is clearly associated with winning, indeed with winning at virtually all costs. The chief consideration will always be how use of drugs will enable a young athlete to develop more quickly and effectively the strength, speed, or endurance needed to win, and how subsequent use will provide an improved competitive performance. This attitude is one that we can fairly consider to be nearly a defining characteristic of professionalism as it has come to be understood.

This use of drugs therefore carries with it, or encourages the development of, attitudes and values that conflict with those we hope to instill in children and young people through their very early participation in athletics. Among these latter values are sportsmanship, honesty, fairness, self-reliance as well as cooperation, grace under pressure, and health. Others could also be mentioned. But a central value is that of experiencing achievement through personal effort, of responding willfully to challenge, and thereby of coming to realize, that is, both to create and to understand, one's self, the complex bundle of skills, dispositions, beliefs, values, and capacities which constitute a personality.

Merit in a young athlete should reflect factors that are fully within his or her control. Ability and achievement should be a reflection of the amount of effort and self-motivation that are consonant with a normal life not characterized by fanaticism (an unreasonable purposiveness). We seek to stress a history of training and competitive effort that may to some extent cancel the uncontrollable differences among people so that superior skill is the result of a growing strength or personal resolve. In our paternalistic limiting of the freedom of young athletes, we are not emphasizing freedom to do anything or to have anything done to one, but rather the freedom of self-determination which accords with ideals of a reasoned, autonomous, well-balanced life, led in relation to a sensible ranking of values. It is because success due to some special technique or technology is only marginally reflective of athletic skill or training or motivation that we discount it or forbid it in the repertoire of young athletes.[7]

I want to emphasize that sports are not the only context in which these values are developed; indeed, they may not even be the best one. But they are a place, and for many people a very important one, where this learning process does occur. The conflict raised by drug usage of the kind we are discussing is that, by emphasizing one value over all others, it skews the context of learning and growth so as to deny sufficient credibility to other values. Moreover, it may conflict directly with efforts to encourage the young athlete to grasp the relation between personal effort and achievement so closely tied to both the experience of joy, excitement, and satisfaction of the athletes themselves, and to a similar appreciation by spectators.

It should be clear that we can extend the claims of soft paternalism, which I have so far discussed in regard to children, to various cases of adult behavior which presume incapacity of some sort, for example, ignorance, lack of opportunity or resources, or immaturity. But these are the easy cases for the soft paternalist and I shall not dispute them here. The difficult cases are surely those that give us every reason to believe that the actors are rational, informed, emotionally mature adults. The soft paternalist in turn must dispute such presumptions. We could of course hold that adult athletes who take drugs to enhance training or performance are in some way irrational, that they do not fully appreciate the dangers of such actions or the seriousness of side effects, or cannot adequately weigh the evidence that drug usage is not beneficial to performance. Moreover, we could claim that such athletes, in addition to ignoring relevant information, are unable to resist the pressures of others to succeed at all costs, that their weakness of will warrants paternalistic interference.

But such a reply is unconvincing, at least in many readily imaginable cases. It cannot be the very use of drugs which is the sole evidence for irrationality or self-destructiveness or weakness of will, on pain of begging the central question. And

the evidence, once in, is very unlikely to support the claim that all cases of drug use are nonvoluntary in the requisite way. Rather, the truth seems to be that in these cases other values come into play. Adult values and motivations are not always the same as those we may encourage for young people. Adult life *is* more complicated, and though we intend the training in values and skills of childhood and youth to carry over to maturity, we are well aware that they will inevitably compete with other values that are often at odds with those we can reasonably insist on earlier. Often for adults winning *is* more important, and the circumstances of life may encourage a new range of motives: fame, wealth, power, social mobility, patriotism, pride of class, or race or ideology.

We may not accept such values or wish to encourage such motivations but, in a free society they are permissible; we may not deny them, to those who choose them, on grounds of paternalism. Where such values predominate, the risks of drugs may be outweighed by the benefits they may bring. Perhaps we come here to one of the sources of the distinction between ''amateur'' and ''professional.'' If so, the distinction does not match the one I am suggesting between the values of youth and adulthood. Some professional skills and the knowledge of professional experience are clearly applicable to youth sports, and, conversely, professional values need not conflict with other values. It is always a matter of emphasis, role, age, commitments, and goals that determine which values dominate.

Indeed, even in our approach to sports for children, and especially of youths, we will at some point begin to anticipate some of the competing values that will increasingly vie for their attention and commitment as they grow older. As always, there are important questions of timing, emphasis, role, and age. But teachers and parents must at some point help facilitate the transition to full autonomy at which earlier limits to freedom can no longer be tolerated.

The soft paternalist could of course insist that where drug use or sports activities carry with them high risk, even risk of death or permanent injury, we are justified in intervening to prevent serious costs to the rest of us even when the athletes are willing to take the risks.[8] But society does not typically support the costs of such injury, and we could in any case require proper insurance for the athletes. Moreover, the psychic cost to others is surely minimal and, even in cases such as boxing, it is normally outweighed by the psychic gains of the spectator; the vicarious thrill and excitement, the shared pride, the satisfactions of knowledgeable viewing. In any case the balance of risks and benefits concerning drug usage is not likely to be clear. Efforts are no doubt being made to control for undesirable side effects, and the benefits may often need to be measured only in fractions of seconds. And why should we single out one class of risks when others, perhaps equally great, are already tolerated for the sake of excellence? Finally though it involves interference in the lives of others, such a response does not seem paternalistically motivated.

At this point, we may resort to something like a principle of ''hard'' paternalism if we are to persist in our efforts to control the choices and options of athletes. We are in effect seeking to impose on those who resist it an alternative set of values. But what would justify such an imposition? There seems no reason to suppose that taking risk in sports, even great risk, is inevitably irrational, self-destructive, or immature, as we have seen. Nor is it plausible to suggest that we forbid all of the sports which involve such risk, such as mountain climbing, sky-diving, or even boxing. As Mill argued, such intervention in people's lives would itself be a greater wrong than the possible injury of activities voluntarily chosen.

It may nevertheless be argued that the use of drugs is somehow inconsistent with the nature of sports, and that sports in turn are linked with a broader set of values—a conception of the good life—which is betrayed by the use of drugs, so that interference in the choices of athletes in this respect is done to preserve a greater good, one they may have lost sight of in their preoccupation with the more narrow concerns of training and competition. Such an argument a priori, as I have argued elsewhere, is not cogent (1). There is, I believe, no single conception of sports on which we need agree. In competitive sports we stress fairness and balanced competition; but in more solitary pursuits these values seem irrelevant. In the case of drugs, fairness may dictate equal access and widely available information. But even this is not clear: athletes and coaches seem justified in keeping secret their training regimens, and even, when permitted by the rules, equipment modifications.

Often, too, we stress human factors such as determination, fortitude, and cooperativeness over risk taking and technology. But in other cases—luge, skiing, mountain climbing, hang-gliding—risk and technology dominate. We believe in the capacity of sports to promote health and fitness, but many originated in the practice of war and routinely involve stress and injury, sometimes death. We fashion rules and continually modify them to reduce hazards and minimize serious injury, but few would seek to do so entirely. Perhaps we are tempted to require in athletes only what is natural. But our sports have evolved with our technology and our best athletes are often unnaturally, statistically, endowed with abilities and other characteristics far beyond the norm. It seems artificial indeed to draw the line at drugs when so much of today's training techniques, equipment, food, medical care, even the origin of the sports themselves, are the product of our technological culture.

Nevertheless, something more may be said for the claim that sports reflect a broader set of values. In discussing the justification of paternalism in coaching the young, I have stressed the formation of the values of honesty, fairness, and autonomy, values central to my conception of personhood. But they are not the only ones that might be stressed. Obedience, regimentation, service to others, or sacrifice might have been proposed. These, too, in the proper context, might also be developed together with the skills of athletics. The values, perhaps even a conception of what is good for human life, are associated with sports, not because of their nature, but due to the way we choose to play them. We can indeed forbid the use of drugs in athletics in general, just as we do in the case of children. But ironically, in adopting such a paternalistic stance of insisting that we know better than the athletes themselves how to achieve some more general good which they myopically ignore, we must deny in them the very attributes we claim to value: self-reliance, personal achievement, and autonomy.

Notes

1. The current ban on caffeine is defined in terms of a maximum level in urine of 15 μg/mL. For athletes this certainly means no direct ingestion of caffeine tablets, but also a need to avoid combinations of coffee, soft drinks, and over-the-counter medications like Anacin or Empirin which could lead to excessive accumulations of the drug.
2. A good example of such substances is the hormone testosterone. Since it occurs naturally in the body, it has been difficult to detect exogenous testosterone. A new test, however, now measures the ratio of testosterone to a metabolite, epitestosterone, which normally occur in a one-to-one ratio. Since exogenous testosterone isn't converted as readily to epitestosterone, it changes the ratio. The IOC requires the ratio of testosterone to its epimer in urine to be less than six to one. See Zurer (10).
3. Much of the evidence available to athletes in this regard is anecdotal, based on the personal experience of coaches, trainers, a few sports physicians, and the athletes themselves. The research literature is skimpy and the results conflicting. See Zurer (10) for a brief discussion of the conflicting views on the evidence. See also Williams (9).

4. These articles are conveniently reprinted in (8). Dworkin makes the distinction between ''soft'' and ''hard'' paternalism in (3). A slightly broader definition of paternalism is defended by Gert and Culver (5). (A version of this article appears in 6: Ch. 7.)
5. Dworkin (3: p. 108) uses this rubric, but for a different type of case.
6. Among the side effects of anabolic steroids are acne and liver tumors. For children and adolescents who are still growing, premature bone fusing and precocious puberty are likely results. See Zurer (10: pp. 73–75).
7. I'm grateful to Bill Puka for discussing this point with me, though in a somewhat different context.
8. Dworkin (3: p. 109) briefly discusses this argument for a different kind of case.

Bibliography

1. Brown, W.M. (1980). ''Drugs, Ethics, and Sport.'' *The Journal of the Philosophy of Sport,* VII, 15–23.
2. Dworkin, Gerald. (1972). ''Paternalism.'' *The Monist,* 56, 64–84.
3. Dworkin, Gerald. (1983). ''Paternalism: Some Second Thoughts.'' *Paternalism.* Edited by Rolf Sartorius. Minneapolis: University of Minnesota Press.
4. Feinberg, Joel. (1971). ''Legal Paternalism.'' *Canadian Journal of Philosophy,* 1, 106–124.
5. Gert, Bernard, and Culver, Charles. (1976). ''Paternalistic Behavior.'' *Philosophy and Public Affairs,* 6, 45–57.
6. Gert, Bernard, and Culver, Charles. (1982). *Philosophy in Medicine: Conceptual and Ethical Issues in Medicine and Psychiatry.* New York: Oxford University Press.
7. Mill, J.S. (1978). *On Liberty.* Indianapolis: Hackett Publ.

8. Sartorius, Rolf. (1983). *Paternalism.* Minneapolis: University of Minnesota Press.

9. Williams, Melvin H. (1974). *Drugs and Athletic Performance.* Springfield, IL: Thomas.

10. Zurer, Pamela S. (1984). ''Drugs in Sports.'' *Chemical and Engineering News,* April 30, pp. 69–79.

Blood Doping and Athletic Competition

CLIFTON PERRY

During the 1976 Olympic Games it was suggested that certain athletes, notably long distance runners, had secured their gold, silver and bronze metals through natural ability, arduous training and blood doping. Blood doping is a process by which an athlete increases his blood volume and his supply of erythrocytes. This is usually accomplished through a four step process. First, the athlete engages in high altitude training for a period of approximately six weeks. This increases the athlete's red blood cell count and consequently the oxygen transporting capacity of the blood. Second, the athlete removes up to a pint of blood and freezes it. The freezing preserves the blood for later use. Third, the athlete resumes training for a period sufficient to replace the lost blood and red blood cells to a level achieved in the first step. Finally, the athlete reintroduces the blood extracted in the second step. This gives the athlete a blood volume and erythrocyte count not possible naturally. Although there may be a problem with blood viscosity, it is suspected that increasing the oxygen transporting capacity of the blood helps physical performance. If the benefits of an increased hemoglobin count outweigh the detriment of increased blood viscosity, then blood doping is sure to greatly enhance an athlete's performance in competition.

Reprinted from Clifton Perry, "Blood Doping and Athletic Competition," *The International Journal of Applied Philosophy,* Vol. 1, No. 3 (Spring 1983), 39–45. Reprinted with permission of the Editor.

Nevertheless, some concern has been expressed regarding the ethical status of blood doping. It has been charged that blood doping brings an unfair advantage to the athlete who so trains. After all, the athlete who so trains secures a level of performance not secured naturally. If such performance enhancers as steroids and amphetamines are proscribed, why then should anyone think that blood doping is permissible? In the course of this paper the reasons for and against blood doping shall be investigated with the hope of presenting a tentative answer to the above question.

Usually one has done something unacceptable in sports competition when one has violated the rules of the game. The rules proscribe certain acts which constitute transgressions of the intended purpose of the activity. Such transgressions constitute unfair advantages for the competitor. For instance, in running a marathon, the runner must cover, on foot and only on foot, twenty-six and two tenths miles. If a runner covers any portion of the distance by means other than by foot, e.g., by auto, the runner has taken an unfair advantage. Of course, not all advantages are unfair. A runner who takes advantage of his unusually long stride has not taken an unfair advantage in the race. The difference would seem to be that while taking advantage of a long stride does not inhibit the qualitative appraisal of the runner in terms of speed per distance, taking the auto does. Given that the intended purpose of the marathon is to qualitatively distinguish between competitors in terms of speed over a course of twenty-six and two tenths miles, the runner who takes the auto, while still crossing the finish line, fails to do so in a way which would enable us to appraise his performance for the distance and thereby rank him against the other runners.

There are other sorts of advantages which are exploited by athletes but are not considered unfair, e.g., some of the techniques of training. Some of the training equipment and training techniques are highly sophisticated and extremely artificial, e.g., artificial track surfaces, air shoes, etc. Nevertheless, the scarce access to the advantages, be they artificial or not, is not sufficient reason for disallowing them. For example, not every long distance runner has access to the better coaches and the best equipment. Not every runner has the economic funds necessary to cover the expense of a sufficient period of high altitude training. Finally, not every athlete has knowledge concerning the physical benefits of carbohydrate loading (A regimen whereby carbohydrates are not eaten for the first three days of a six day period prior to a race, depleating the glycogen supply in the muscles. The athlete then eats nothing but carbohydrates for the next three days during which time the body overcompensates and stores three to four times as much glycogen as it would normally). It is not, however, considered unfair to fully exploit the advantages which accrue from the use of these training devices and techniques.

What then is the difference between fair and unfair advantages in sports competition? It is doubtful that the artificial—natural distinction is very helpful since artificial track surfaces, air shoes, and sophisticated training techniques are usually considered fair but are, nevertheless, artificial. Accessibility should similarly prove unhelpful. For instance, if all competitors had access to an auto for a portion of the race, although we might rate each athlete in relation to one another, we could not rate them against the required conditions of the race. Thus, rather than having merely one athlete transgressing the race requirements, we would have all of them doing it. Rather, it would seem

that the difference is more properly described in terms of enhancing one's performance through supplementation as opposed to the exploitation of one's natural abilities. In the latter case, the body's capacity to perform is not enhanced but utilized or exploited to achieve some level of performance. In the former case, the capacity is supplemented such that the performance is, at least in part, the result of the supplementation. High altitude training, carbohydrate loading, interval training, etc. would appear to all to be appropriate examples of securing a particular performance level through exploitation. In such cases, enhanced performances are secured not by compensating or supplementing the body but by having the body adjust to changes in environmental factors. Taking an auto in a boat race, placing heavy metal weights in one's boxing glove etc., all appear to be examples of achieving a specific performance level through supplementation. Although there are other ways of taking unfair advantage of other competitors, e.g., tripping opponents during a boat race or otherwise ensuring that one's opponents perform poorly through means independent of individual capacity, one way which does not seem unfair is the simple exploitation of one's natural abilities.

To effectively test the thesis differentiating fair from unfair methods in sports competition the presented distinction should at least be able to account for the easy intuitive cases of fair and unfair advantages. Unfortunately, this, at least initially, seems to be where the presented distinction fails. For example, certain running shoes, certain track surfaces (e.g., the track surface at Harvard University), certain poles used in pole-vaulting, do not exploit the athlete's capacity but supplements his or her performance. Athletes are not better vaulters when particular poles are used but vaulting limits are consistently higher with the use of these poles. Runners have not become faster runners when running on certain track surfaces but their times are consistently lower on the particular surfaces. Finally, if there is any truth to the belief that the curve lasted air shoes actually improve running times (as is commonly believed with regard to the use of spikes on most track surfaces) it is not because the runner actually has secured an ability to run at faster speeds, but rather because the shoes have merely supplemented his or her performance. It thus appears that the above distinction would classify as unfair, things which most believe to be fair or at least not clearly unfair.

The problem appears compounded in the other direction as well. Although the distinction would eliminate the use of drugs designed to merely enhance performance through supplementary stimulation, e.g., amphetamines, it does not appear capable of classifying the use of anabolic steroids as unfair. Insofar as anabolic steroids do not simply supplement one's performance but rather enhance one's capacity to perform, such steroids would appear to escape the stigma of unfairness. But this surely violates the very standards and intuitions employed in appraising the use of anabolic steroids in athletic training.

Perhaps the previously proposed distinction may be amended so as to eliminate the noted problems. It might be suggested that where performance is enhanced through supplementation but is nevertheless accepted, then it must fulfill at least one of three functions. First, the augmented performance must come about as a result of the endeavor to eliminate the deleterious effects which are associated with the practice of the sport. For instance, good running shoes have the second or double effect of augmenting running speeds. Their primary end is to assuage the shock of heel impact, prevent mid-foot pronation, reduce medial stress and various other problems connected with running. It just so happens that when some of the above noted problems are eliminated, so are the incumbrances upon maximal speed. Officials with the Harvard track likewise reported that, while times were better, injuries were reduced by fifty percent.

Second, the enhanced performance may be seen as the reaction to an undesired inhibitor to better performances. Unlike the first condition, the second allows for aggressive measures to be implemented primarily in order to augment the athlete's

performance. The reason is that the athlete's performance prior to the innovation to enhance such, was inhibited through conditions which should not have obtained in the first place. For example, through supplementation, ultra-lightweight racing flats enhance racing times. But the improved speeds were favorably received because the prior restrictions to such improved speeds, i.e., the weight of the running shoe, were seen primarily as irrelevant to qualitative appraisal of the athlete's running ability.

Finally, the enhanced performances may simply be the result of an agreed upon elimination or addition of an empirical factor. It may simply be agreed upon to permit spikes or the extremely flexible poles during a particular track or field meet. During the athletic event, enhanced performances may be reported but insofar as the purpose of the meet is to qualitatively appraise each athlete's performance given the conditions, employing such conditions need not be considered unfair. Problems arise only when the records obtained under such favorable conditions are used to usurp previous records where such advantages were not permitted or known.

We might also amend the proffered distinction by arguing that enhanced capacities are either quite different from merely exploited capacities (and therefore proscribed for exactly the same reason supplemented enhanced performances are proscribed) or are allowed but only insofar as they are not deleterious. Although we might be able to eliminate the use of anabolic steroids by appeal to the requirement of not being deleterious (anabolic steroids elevate enzyme levels in the liver) it is quite important which of the above disjunctions is accepted. It would seem that if enhanced capacities are permitted, then blood doping in not being deleterious would be permitted irrespective of the fate of other capacity enhancers, e.g., anabolic steroids. If, on the other hand, enhanced capacities are disallowed, so also would be the fate of blood doping.

It is, however, unclear whether blood doping is, in fact, a capacity enhancer or a supplementary performance enhancer. It might first be suggested that blood doping has much more in common with mere performance enhancers than it has with capacity enhancers. The effects of blood doping are not dispositionally connected with the long range effects of athletic training. Indeed, the extra quantity of blood will, within a short period of time, be eliminated from the body without *any* remaining changes to the individual's capacity. This is what mere performance enhancers do and what capacity enhancers do not do. Of course, the effects of training can also be lost. Cardio-respiratory training effects and muscle tone may, for instance, be significantly attenuated through prolonged bed rest. Nevertheless, there is a difference between the loss of performance output through the loss of a mere performance enhancer and the loss of a capacity through inactivity. In the former case, the loss in the performance level is due to the body's return to homeostasis. There is nothing the athlete can do by way of performance to retain the former level of performance. In the latter case, the loss in the performance level is not due to the body's return to homeostatis since a well trained athletic body usually is homeostatic. Indeed, this is precisely why, in the latter case, performance will usually be sufficient to retain the performance level. Consequently, unless blood doping is either used to assuage pain, eliminate unnatural performance inhibitors or is granted for a given particular athletic endeavor, then the fate which befalls other performance enhancers should also befall blood doping. Since under normal conditions it seems that none of the above conditions obtain with regard to blood doping, i.e., blood doping does not assuage pain, eliminate what is generally considered to be unnatural performance inhibitors or has been generally permitted within a particular race for purposes of qualitatively appraising a group of blood doping athletes against a given distance, blood doping seems to be undesirable.[1]

To make matters worse, if blood doping were permitted, then the unfavorable consequence of allowing 'artificial blood' would seemingly follow. That is, if it is permissible to augment one's per-

formance by increasing the oxygen transporting ability of the blood, then perhaps the use of Fluosol-DA would also prove acceptable. However, the use of a blood substitute seems unacceptable. Blood doping like the supplementary performance enhancer Fluosol-DA should surely be rejected since the blood substitute would debar the qualitative appraisal of the athlete's actual ability. But if a blood substitute would be rejected, and the use of such follows from the accepted use of blood doping, then it would appear that blood doping should be similarly rejected.

The attempted *reductio ad absurdum* argument might nevertheless be questioned on two accounts. It might first be argued that the *reductio* argument fails because Fluosol-DA is a more efficacious transporter of oxygen than hemoglobin.[2] As such, Fluosol-DA would enhance performance even if a given quantity were used to replace, as opposed to supplement, the same quantity of blood. This cannot, of course, be said about blood doping. Therefore to castigate the use of Fluosol-DA is not, *ipso facto,* to deprecate the use of blood doping.

The counterargument seems entirely correct with regard to replacement. However, it is not clear that the argument is germane with respect to supplementation. We might, that is, experience some difficulty in allowing the replacement of blood with Fluosol-DA in athletic competition because such a replacement would constitute a mere performance enhancer. But if replacement of blood with Fluosol-DA would be a mere performance enhancer so also would be the supplementation of blood with Fluosol-DA. Yet in the case of supplementation, the use of Fluosol-DA would simply do more efficaciously what blood doping is designed to do, namely, transport more oxygen than an exploited capacity is capable of transporting. If it is permissible to so supplement the body's performance by means of blood doping, why would it be wrong to do exactly the same thing in a more effective manner?

Second, it might be contended that the *reductio* fails because whereas blood doping facilitates physical performance through the introduction of a natural material which is actually indigenous to the body, the introduction of Fluosol-DA is neither indigenous nor natural. It seems that two remarks can be made concerning this last defense of blood doping. First, it is somewhat unclear whether or not it is being maintained that blood doping is permissible because it is natural (rendering the condition of being natural both necessary and sufficient for acceptability). The latter disjunct appears false. Many artificial things are found quite acceptable in sports competition, e.g., racing shoes, synthetic tracks, etc. Consequently, if the use of Fluosol-DA is in fact looked upon unfavorably in sports competition, it must be for reasons other than its being an artificial rather than a natural addition. It would seem that the reason Fluosol-DA may be found unacceptable is that it constitutes a clear example of a supplementary performance enhancer without also possessing any of the redeeming qualities noted above. But now we have returned full circle to the argument which was initially used to impugn the virtues of blood doping, namely, that Fluosol-DA is merely a more effective supplementary performance enhancer than blood doping and if blood doping were allowed, why not Fluosol-DA? Consequently, it would seem that being natural is not only not necessary for acceptability in sports competition but neither is it sufficient. Indeed, to simply maintain that being natural is sufficient for acceptability in the midst of the blood doping issue might well constitute an example of begging the question.

Whatever the fate of the *reductio* it might be further argued that although blood is natural to the body, the quantity of blood secured through blood doping is not. One need only consider such conditions as thrombocytopenia (a decrease in the platelets in circulating blood) in order to appreciate that it is not the item alone which figures into what is and what is not natural to the individual.[3]

If the above is not a caricature, then blood doping appears to be a mere supplementary performance enhancer. Without the other necessary redeeming qualities blood doping seems to suffer the same fate as other performance enhancers which lack acceptability. Given the tenability of the remarks, it would seem that blood doping should be rejected as unfair in sports competition (at least in all competition which does not include such under the rule specifications) or at least that the burden of proof rests with those who wish to maintain that blood doping is appropriate in athletic competition.

Notes

*I wish to recognize the assistance and financial support of the Program on Human Values and Ethics and the National Endowment for the Humanities, grant number ED-32072-78-652.

1. It is conceivable that blood doping might be allowed under the third condition and perhaps where oxygen was in short supply, i.e., at very high altitudes, smog laden cities, etc., the second condition might also be satisfied.

2. Kevin Tremper, Alan Friedman, Edward Levine, Ron Lapin and Debra Camarillo. ''The Preoperative Treatment of Severely Anemic Patients with a Perfluorochemical Oyxgen-Transport Fluid, Fluosol-DA,'' *The New England Journal of Medicine.* Vol. 307, No. 5. July 29, 1982, pp. 277–283.

3. Thrombocytopenia may result in any or all of the following: bleeding into the skin, mucosal bleeding, bleeding into the central nervous system and of course anemia with all of its associated problems.

Privacy and the Urinalysis Testing of Athletes

PAUL B. THOMPSON

Under what conditions, if any, is it ethical to require athletes to submit to urinalysis examinations? An answer to this question involves careful consideration as to the purpose of the examination, as well as an understanding of the athlete's right to privacy. The issue of urinalysis provokes serious questions regarding the separation of athletic activity from the athlete's personal life. Does a coach or team official have a right or responsibility to insure that an athlete's private conduct does not compromise his or her ability to perform in sport? If so, are there limits to this authority which would indicate the permissibility of requiring urinalysis examinations?

Urinalysis is a laboratory procedure which identifies the chemical composition of a urine sample. The procedure has become controversial in athletics because urinalysis can reveal the presence of drugs in an athlete's urine. This controversial use of urinalysis should not be confused with the non-controversial procedure of analyzing a urine sample as a part of a regular physical examination. Controversial use of urine sampling also break down into two discrete categories. Urinalysis has been required of competitors in track and field events in order to identify the presence of stimulants, pain killers, steroids, and other drugs which are assumed to alter the competitive equilibrium of the sport. Rampant drug use among professional athletes has prompted the suggestion that urinalysis might be used to detect the use of illegal and dangerous substances among athletes. The ethical analysis of these two different uses of urine testing requires differentiation on several key points.

I shall assume without argument that privacy is not a form of property, and hence that privacy rights must not be confused with property rights. An argument for this position is made by Larry May (2). This assumption is important for the discussion of urinalysis testing since, if privacy were merely a form of property, one might argue that privacy rights are surrendered to an employer or official under the contract which a professional athlete signs, or under the implicit contract of amateurism. The point of the assumption is to demand that privacy rights be renounced specifically, and not as part and parcel of a standard employer/employee relationship. There must be some reason specific to the activity of sport which supports the abnegations of privacy. We would not tolerate urinalysis as a matter of course as a condition of employment in a bank, a factory, or a hamburger stand. The fact that it is contemplated as a requirement for participation in sport, needs, therefore, to be justified by some condition or phenomenon

Reprinted from *Journal of the Philosophy of Sport*, IX, (1982), pp. 60–65. Copyright 1983 by the Philosophic Society for the Study of Sport. Reprinted by permission.

313

which distinguishes sport from other forms of human activity.

The use of urine sampling in the enforcement of a drug ban is largely an issue for the philosophy of competition. Although there may be controversy over *whether* a drug should be banned in a given sport, once the ban has been imposed as a condition of competition there is little question about the ethicality of using urinalysis as a means of enforcement. When entering a competition, an athlete makes an implicit commitment to abide by the rules of the competition, and also to respect the measures required to secure fairness in the enforcement of rules. Clearly, the collection of urine samples provides an objective and impartial means for the enforcement of rules prohibiting the use of certain specific drugs.

It must, of course, be admitted that the decision as to whether a drug ought or ought not to be banned can be tortuous and riddled with philosophical difficulties. It will depend upon our knowledge about the effects of the drug in question, but also upon our conception of sport itself. When does an advance in sports medicine alter the conditions of competition so drastically that, effectively, a *new* sport is defined? How do we define the conditions of competition for a given sport? Do these conditions imply a "natural" or nonenhanced concept of physical fitness? These are questions which will probably be answered on a sport-by-sport and drug-by-drug basis (1). Such questions do not, however, play a role in determining the ethicality of urine sampling once it has been established that the use of a particular substance is inconsistent with the conditions of competition for a sport.

The use of urinalysis to detect banned substances falls within the scope of rule enforcement; hence one might object that urinalysis is inconsistent with philosophies of sport which stress amateurism and voluntary compliance with rules. This is tantamount to suggesting that enforcement of rules is secondary to certain esthetic considerations in the ideal of sportsmanship. It is difficult to imagine a sport so conceived (on an ideal of pure sportsmanship) in which the question of urinalysis could arise at all. Urine testing for banned substances, by its very nature, is a practice applicable only to sports where competition has been formulated in terms of rather precise rules and enforcement procedures.

The more difficult and topical issue involves the use of urinalysis to determine whether an athlete is using illegal or dangerous drugs recreationally. Revelations of drug use made by well-known athletes have brought this issue to prominence in the sports press (cf. 3: pp. 66–82). Urinalysis has been proposed as a means of identifying athletes who use drugs. This proposal has been met with protests citing an athlete's right to privacy as a protection against involuntary testing for drug use (4; 5).

In order to understand the ethical questions involved in such an application of urine testing, several points must be clarified. First, urinalysis for detecting illegal drug use differs from urinalysis for detecting banned drugs in important respects. When a drug is banned, the prohibition of that drug becomes a part of the definition of the sport in question. Banned drugs are drugs used to affect the competitive outcome of a sport. The illegal drugs in question are not ingested in order to affect the outcome of the sport; hence they have no place in defining the conditions of competition for a sport. Since the drugs are not banned on competitive grounds, officials have no referential authority over their use; hence officials have no justification for initiating a procedure designed to detect their use. Athletes are presumed to use these drugs "on their own time," so to speak, and an athlete violates no rules of traditional sports by doing so.

Second, the use of urinalysis specifically to detect illegal substances can be distinguished from urine tests conducted in the course of regular physical examinations. Since the doctors who conduct such examinations will have knowledge of an athlete's drug use, a confidentiality issue arises in regard to the conditions under which this knowledge can and should be disclosed. This is a difficult issue for medical ethics, but it can and should be differentiated from the ethical question of ordering an athlete to undergo urinalysis specifically for the purpose of identifying illicit drug use.

Third, there may be occasions in which coaches or other athletic officials have clear *in loco parentis* responsibility for their athletes. Under such a situation, coaches may be responsible for the moral as well as physical development of their charges. This conception of the coach-athlete relationship is doubtlessly grounded in the philosophical view that a primary goal of athletics is "character development." It is a philosophical view which is probably on the wane in many phases of contemporary sport, and it is clearly inoperative in the professional sports where urinalysis has been proposed. Professional coaches have no responsibility for the moral development of their players. This point is worth mentioning since a coach or team official who did have clear *in loco parentis* authority could quite plausibly construe this to include authority to see that an athlete was not violating any laws. Even in such a case it is difficult to imagine a situation in which the mutual respect between coach and athlete implied by the *in loco parentis* responsibility could have deteriorated badly enough to make urinalysis justifiable.

Given a situation in which coaches and team officials have no special mandate to watch over an athlete's moral development, are there any sport-related special circumstances which could justify forced urinalysis? There are two relevant possibilities. First, since team officials assume some responsibility for the physical development of athletes, testing for drug use might be interpreted as helping athletes stay in optimal physical condition. Second, a team official might cite a negative impact on team morale or cohesiveness as a justification for the investigation of drug abuse.

The first possibility suggests that, in the long run, urinalysis is in the interest of the athlete himself. It will be argued that a drug user can be given counseling and treatment which will help him or her avoid further abuse. The ethical force of this suggestion is to argue that what at first glance appears to be a clear breach of an athlete's privacy rights can be justified in light of the overriding goodness of its consequences—namely that it helps him or her overcome a drug problem. Cast in this light, the argument is an example of the classic utilitarian problem of forcing someone to do something for their own good; it is a practice which utilitarians have concluded does more harm than good. The weakness of the "helping" argument is shown by examining its probable consequences.

It is clear that a policy of conducting urine tests and referring drug abusers to treatment centers will be helpful indeed for athletes desirous of treatment, but there is no need for urinalysis to identify this group. The problem arises with regard to athletes identified as drug abusers who do not wish treatment. Presumably these athletes will be presented with the alternative of accepting forced treatment or of losing some privilege (probably all opportunities to compete). If there is no penalty for "failing" one's urine test, there is no reason to conduct a test. We may speculate with some degree of assurance that some athletes forced into treatment will later be very grateful and agree that the identification and treatment of their drug use have been helpful. These people are helped at the expense of those who either refuse treatment and suffer for it, or accept the condition of treatment but continue to resent the intrusion into their privacy and claim that the treatment is of little value. Even those who are helped are robbed of their autonomy as moral agents. It is hard to imagine why a coach's responsibility to train and condition players justifies such an abrogation of basic moral respect. The idea of helping athletes by forcing them to undergo urinalysis is also founded on the dubious assumption that all instances of drug use are health problems. Illicit drugs have become an insidious social problem precisely because *some* people have the capacity to resist the debilitating effects of drug use, even over relatively long periods of use.

In the matter of professional team sports, the claim that urinalysis is in the health interests of the player can be taken rather differently. Since the professional team athlete is in the employ of the team owner, and since the team owner derives profits (indirectly) from the athletic performance of such employees, the owner may claim that the health of the athlete is a matter of his (the owner's) financial interest. Such a claim breaks down to two components. One is a general claim regarding employer/employee relations; but this is merely the illegitimate preference of the employer's financial interest over the employee's privacy rights (discussed previously). The more difficult question here is whether the nature of sport itself, the requirement of a physical performance from an employee, alters the basic employer/employee relationship in such a way that an owner can be said to have a legitimate claim.

The strongest argument in favor of such a view is by analogy to other well established sports practices. Current and former training measures have been accepted as more or less legitimate infringement upon the athlete's privacy. At one time, restrictions against sexual intercourse before a game (in extreme cases, throughout an entire season) were widespread. Even more commonly, athletes are subjected to periodic weight checks. Athletes who fail to meet a specified weight can be subject to fines and even firings.

The analogy to restrictions on sexual intercourse is particularly á propos, since this training rule has largely fallen into disuse for reasons directly relevant to the issue at hand. While it is reasonable to suppose that some athletes suffer reduced performance after relatively recent sexual activity it is doubtful that all or even most do. Since the issue is athletic performance, and *not* the underlying moral attitudes toward sex and/or drug use, the athlete should be judged on the basis of performance. Athletes who perform well regardless of sexual activity or occasional drug use would be unjustly restricted by training practices which infringe upon their private life to no apparent purpose. Those who are negatively affected can and should be disciplined or criticized for their reduced performance, and *not* for the private indiscretions which contribute to reduced performance.

The analogy to weighings breaks down for simi-

lar reasons. The history of sport is littered with stories of paunchy quarterbacks and outfielders who nevertheless deliver stellar performances. No team owner would have fired Babe Ruth for failing to make a weight limit. The issue, again, is performance. It seems more plausible that an athlete and a trainer might agree on an ideal weight, and that the weight check will be made as a means of monitoring compliance with this explicit contract. By analogy, it seems reasonable to condone an explicit agreement between a trainer and an athlete with a history of drug problems which involves periodic urinalysis as a means of monitoring compliance. The ethics of such agreements are entirely different from those of general and mandatory testing for drug use, since by assenting to the contract, the athlete submits to the test voluntarily, and hence, it is no invasion of privacy. This exception naturally assumes that the athlete has not been coerced into accepting the contract.

The final argument for forced urinalysis appeals to a philosophical concept of team spirit or morale. This justification can itself be broken into two principles. One might claim that individual athletes represent the whole; that is, a team, an organization or institution, or the sport itself. As such, officials of the sport have a "right" to insure that its representatives are of appropriate moral fiber. This form of argument is so patently paternalistic that it deserves little serious analysis. Although it might justify sanctions against known offenders, it can hardly be used to justify the extreme measure of taking urine samples in order to identify individuals who might be potential embarrassments to the whole.

A more serious argument involves the idea that individuals using drugs have a negative effect on the camaraderie and spirit so often noted with respect to team sports. The critical question, which is unresolved, is whether there is any demonstrable link between drug use and team spirit. At the very least, it seems that this argument cannot justify urinalysis as a matter of course. Some confessed drug abusers have played on championship teams. One may also speculate that the ignomy of being subjected to urinalysis might have a worse effect on morale than minor cases of drug abuse, but philosophically, such considerations are beside the point.

The appeal to team spirit assumes a dubious premise with regard to an individual athlete's personal autonomy. It requires an athlete to regard at least some aspects of his or her personal life as subservient to the team concept; furthermore, it gives team officials license to regulate personal affairs in advance of a clear indication that impacts upon the team are involved. While some philosophical visions of the team concept would certainly give credence to the first part of this assumption, the second part is tantamount to a surrender of all privacy rights whatsoever. This totalitarian vision of sport is surely inconsistent with the traditional spirit of athletic competition.

In conclusion, urinalysis can be defended ethically when it has been clearly established as a procedure for enforcing the rule of a given sport. This can be so only when the use of a drug or substance has been determined to be inconsistent with the normal conditions of competition for that sport. There are no special sports-related circumstances which justify the use of urinalysis to identify users of illegal drugs. The normal privacy rights enjoyed by everyone protect athletes from this intrusion into their private lives.

The intentions of the authority conducting a urinalysis are, thus, the critical factor in determining the ethicality of the test. When the purpose of the test is to insure compliance with the regulations of a sport, it poses no threat to privacy. Privacy, in other words, cannot be cited in order to prevent referees from detecting cheating. An individual's decision to participate implies consent to referential authority. Privacy rights, however, can and are cited in restricting the access of officials into the lives of individuals for the purpose of identifying and proving criminal activity. This restriction should apply most strongly when the investigating parties are not duly appointed public authorities, but persons who derive authority through the regulatory offices of sport or as employers of athletes. As such, when the intention of an official conducting a urine test is to identify criminal activity, as opposed to rule violations, the official has usurped the athlete's right to a life beyond sport. The criterion of intention also shows why a medical utilization of urinalysis is acceptable, since the examining physician's intent is to certify the physical well-being of the athlete, and not to ascertain facts about his or her private activities.

The privacy rights of athletes and the possible abridgement of these rights through urinalysis raise philosophical questions about sport and competition which go beyond the scope of the present paper. Given the analysis in terms of intention, the governing bodies of a given sport could technically redefine a sport so as to make the criminal activity of an athlete off the field a violation of the rules of the sport. The purpose for this would not be to justify the expulsion of known criminals; there is strong precedent in sport to establish an official's right to do this already. Rather, the rule change would be to give officials a clear authority to pry into the private activities of athletes by making these activities part and parcel of the sport. Needless to say, such a tactic runs counter to the intuitive concept of sport which, presumably, guides our understanding of rules in sport.

The issue of urinalysis is thus a crucial one in that it could alter the very concept of sport which informs the organization of competitive activity in our society. It is at the cutting edge of issues which ask us to evaluate the distinction between sport and life. Given the current delineation of that distinction, the intention of the official conducting the test determines its moral validity. The ill-considered demand for urinalysis as a way to identify criminal activity is, at best, morally unjustifiable. At worst it may undermine the philosophical foundations of competitive sports.

Bibliography

1. Brown, W.M. "Ethics, Drugs and Sport." *Journal of the Philosophy of Sport,* 7 (1980), 15–23.

2. May, Larry. "Privacy and Property." *Philosophy in Context,* 10 (1980), 40–53.

3. Reese, Don, and John Underwood. "I'm Not Worth a Damn." *Sports Illustrated,* June 14, 1982, pp. 66–82.

4. "Schram Favors Exams for Drugs." *The Dallas Morning News,* July 20, 1982, p. B1, B3.

5. "Schram Backs Checks for Drugs." *Houston Chronicle,* July 21, 1983, Section 2, p. 4.

Sport and the Technological Image of Man

JOHN M. HOBERMAN

On November 16, 1985, the President of the Federal Republic of Germany, Richard von Weizsäcker, addressed a meeting of the West German National Olympic Committee on the subject of modern sport. Mr. von Weizsäcker's long and carefully reasoned presentation offers an ideal framework for my own remarks on the anthropological consequences of scientific sport, and for that reason I would like to cite some of its key passages.

Mr. von Weizsäcker begins by noting, first, the fantastic success of modern sport as a form of culture and, second, the inner logic that constitutes its driving force, which he equates with the Olympic motto "citius, fortius, altius." "This inner law of sport," he states, "this constant comparative process, constitutes the dynamic and the fascination of sport. It is an expression of the dynamic character of Western civilization which, through science and technology, has given shape to world civilization as we know it." The fundamental law of this civilization is the performance principle, which is linked in turn to the idea of virtually endless progress. The charisma of sport grows directly out of its promise of limitless performances, and here is where the trouble begins.

The problem, says Mr. von Weizsäcker, is that

Presented at a symposium on "Ethical Issues in the Treatment of Children and Athletes with Human Growth Hormone," sponsored by the University of Texas Ethics Lectures Series, University of Texas at Austin, April 26, 1986. Printed by permission.

whereas science and technology can be progressively transformed, the human body cannot be. The temptation to treat the human body as if it were a machine comes into conflict with our most basic ideas of what a human being should be, and the result of this conflict is a reckoning with the idea of human limits. "That the specific limits which have been set by nature itself should not be exceeded is beyond all doubt," he states. "What remains in question is precisely how these limits are to be defined." We do know, however, that in some circles the temptation to exceed these limits has become overwhelming. "The danger that specific body-types will be developed for specific sport disciplines is no longer a matter of science fiction; for this reason we can already see on the horizon the danger that specific athletic types will be bred by means of more or less concealed chemical or even genetic manipulations."

Mr. von Weizsäcker's prescription for this difficult situation is what he calls "a clear and binding ethics of sport" resulting from a kind of self-interrogation. Sport, he says, "will be able to preserve its humanizing influence and contribute to human dignity only if, as it develops, it resists this pressure, if it recognizes its own inner laws, if it sees and accepts these limits. For sport itself stands on a threshold. In the long run it will master this situation only if it recognizes it as an existential issue rooted in moral premises. Its worldwide success does not release sport from the obligation to examine its own deepest premises. On the contrary, it is precisely this almost limitless success which forces sport to reflect both on its premises and its limits'' (1).

My own point of departure is the idea that modern high-performance sport is a global monoculture whose values derive in large measure from the sphere of technology. My central theme is the relationship between sport and what I have called the technological image of man. It is my view that the comprehensive technologizing of high-performance sport contains, and in some ways conceals, an agenda for human development for which high-performance athletes serve as ideal models. It is also my opinion that this anthropological agenda is a sinister one that transcends, even as it includes, the cultivation of certain body-types for sportive purposes. High-performance sport has become an exercise in human engineering that aims at producing not simply an athletic type, but a human type as well.

Sport as we know it has existed for about a century, and during that time it has been increasingly shaped by a technological order for which it is also a potent symbol in two oddly contrasting ways. On the one hand, athletic charisma originates in a dynamic body whose machinelike dimension is its aura of force or speed. This body, energized by an unquantifiable will, is the symbolic catapult or projectile that performs in stadiums around the world.

On the other hand, the body of the athlete has become, quite literally, a laboratory specimen whose structure and potential can often be measured in precise quantitative terms. This is the materialistic interpretation of the sportive body, whose machinelike dimension is its accessibility to rational analysis. For example, the *body composition analyzer* describes the body in terms of water, fat, and other tissues, and measures basal metabolism. The *force platform* measures biomechanical force by placing the athlete on a surface containing sensors that feed data on tiny pressure changes to a computer. Using these data, a scientist can advise an athlete on how to change his or her movements to obtain better results. A

digitizer is a computerized device that can express human movement in computer language; a scientist translates the cinematographic record of an athlete's movements into a body of data that can be reproduced on a computer screen in the form of a moving stick figure. The separate movements that make up the performance can be quantified and related to each other mathematically so that a strategy for maximum performance can be designed. It is then up to athletes to develop into the hypothetical ideal self the machine has told them they can be.

These and other technological procedures are the concealed dimension of modern high-performance sport. But even if the public knew more about them, it is unlikely that they would be resented, because they measure the human organism rather than change it directly. The notorious procedures, alluded to by Mr. von Weizsäcker, are those that change, or threaten to change, the human body or human behavior to promote athletic performance.

Anabolic steroids are used to accelerate muscle growth, accelerate healing after surgery or injuries, and increase the emotional intensity with which an athlete can train. Human growth hormone is being used increasingly in the hope that it will produce larger bodies. So-called beta-blockers, which are normally used to tranquilize pigs before slaughter, are taken by competitive marksmen to depress the pulse rate and produce an even state of consciousness to insure a steady hand (2). Amphetamines are used by professional ice-hockey players in the United States and in Europe to produce feelings of aggression, which will presumably enhance their performances during games. Experienced observers, including physicians, have pointed to symptoms such as dilated pupils and "blankly staring faces like those of wax figures" (3). In Europe professional bicycle racers have used substances as dangerous as heroin, strychnine, and cortisone to improve performances (4). Some overstimulated athletes have actually gone berserk, attacking competitors and, in the case of a Belgian bicycling champion, his own children. It has been long rumored that certain substances have been used to arrest the physiological development of prepubescent female gymnasts in order to preserve their flexibility (5). And finally, blood doping, also known as blood boosting or blood packing, involves the transfusion, or reinfusion, of whole blood or packed red blood cells into an athlete for the purpose of increasing endurance (6).

Because of the premium it places on sheer performance, the high-performance sport community is attracted to these technologies even as it recognizes the traditional objections to their use. "Our ethical and moral rules," a Swedish strength coach said in 1984, "have maintained that one must not administer anything to the body. But I view the hormonal substances as a progressive development comparable to the use of fiberglass poles by pole-vaulters" (7). It is important to recognize the charismatic appeal of this claim. In 1983 Frederick C. Hatfield, the scientific editor of *Muscle & Fitness,* offered the following manifesto: "Drugs are not inherently evil—misuse and abuse by people give them that connotation. I believe that drugs have been, are and will continue to be an important source of man's salvation. I also believe that there can be no nobler use for drugs than improving man's performance capabilities. Society demands bigger, faster and stronger athletes. The sacrosanctity of the sports arena, however, has been a hindrance to meeting this demand" (8). Here, too, we encounter an awareness of a cultural obstacle, the "sacrosanctity of the sports arena," which must be removed if human potential is to be realized. By now it is too late to remind these visionaries—or the International Olympic Committee—that the founder of the modern Games, Pierre de Coubertin, viewed the prospect of the superdeveloped athlete with horror (9). Untroubled by such concerns, the performance-oriented visionary like Dr. Hatfield substitutes for the sacrosanctity of tradition the sacrosanctity of the performance principle, and we should be honest enough to recognize that at this point in its history our civilization provides us with very little

in the cultural mainstream that can match the performance principle in mass appeal. For this reason it is not particularly difficult to predict the course of this debate for the foreseeable future. It is likely that a kind of athletic Nietzscheanism like that of Dr. Hatfield will strain against certain prohibitions, primarily of religious origin, which prescribe that the human image should remain inviolate. It is also possible to predict that for many athletic coaches this is going to be a very difficult period, simply because they will be faced with a contradictory set of demands. On the one hand, they will be expected to represent traditional values at a time, at least in the United States, when such values are associated by many people with religious orthodoxy. On the other hand, the inexorable logic of the performance principle will demand improved performances, which will require in turn the application of new technologies.

What we can confirm as of today is, first, that the manipulative sport technologies are poisoning relationships throughout the world of high-performance sport, and second, that they are here to stay. "The non-doped athlete," the West German sport physician Wolfgang Pförringer stated in 1983, "will soon be a thing of the past. And the sport physician who refuses to prescribe drugs will be excluded from high-performance sport" (10). Professor Willdor Hollmann, head of the Cologne Institute for Sport Medicine and Circulatory Research and recent president of the German Association of Sport Physicians, said in 1985: "Never again, not even in the remote future, will we see a type of high-performance sport without doping problems" (11).

The technologies I have briefly discussed up to this point are inflicting intolerable strains on several kinds of relationships within the world of high-performance sport. The best known relationship that is exacerbated by these technologies is that between athletes and the bureaucracies that administer both their competitions and the drug-testing procedures that are becoming a standard feature of high-level athletic competition. Increasingly, however, we are seeing public accusations being directed by athletes, trainers, and officials against athletes, trainers, and officials of different nationalities. And in some cases athletes will accuse athletes of their own nationality. As Professor Hollman put it in 1984: ''No one trusts anyone any more. Every athlete asks himself what the other one crouching next to him in the starting blocks is doing, what kinds of things he has been taking in the course of his training in order to win. And if the athlete who asks himself this stands there completely clean and loses, then he may later call himself a fool for having behaved in this way'' (12).

At the European championship competition in marksmanship held in Yugoslavia in September 1985, the possible use of beta-blockers was the main topic of conversation. Despite the lack of clear-cut evidence of cheating, the status of two world-record marks was left in doubt (13).

In October 1984 the captain of the Swedish Ice-hockey Association, Leif Boork, accused Soviet hockey players of using anabolic steroids. ''I cannot prove that the Russians are doping themselves with specific reports from real sources,'' he said. ''My claim is based on general observations and impressions. For example, Russian ice-hockey players constantly show inexplicable weight-changes from one season to another'' (14).

In February 1985 the Swedish discus-thrower Ricky Bruch presented evidence before the doping commission of the Swedish National Sport Association indicating that doping of one kind or another was being practiced within something like twenty different sports in Sweden. Reactions to these allegations were mixed. The commission's legal expert professed shock when told that young athletes were taking potentially lethal doses of insulin. The commission's chairman, on the other hand, dismissed the evidence as ''nothing special,'' and stated that he could not understand ''why Ricky is being so dramatic about this'' (15). Whether this remark reflected a healthy scepticism or a terminal cynicism is hard to say.

Most public accusations, however, build upon already existing feelings of national rivalry; and it is only too clear how sport research has come to be seen as being analogous to military research. As if to illustrate this point, a prophetic parable of scientific sport and its demoralizing effects comes to us from the Swedish Ski Games held in March 1985. For the first time in skiing history, an Italian team had won a major relay race in international competition. Then, as snow and darkness descended on the town of Falun, the whispering began.

The Italian victory, a Swedish journalist wrote, could be ascribed to any or all of three factors: the financial health of the Italian ski association; its technological ingenuity (a new paraffin wax); or its medical staff—''a much discussed and sensitive area.'' In particular, one Professor Conconi had experimented with blood doping and had ''helped,'' among others, Alberto Cova, the 1984 gold medalist in the 10,000 meter run. In short, the Swedish skiers found themselves wondering about who—and what—they had been skiing against.

An older, and still nebulous, blood doping controversy has clouded the spectacular career of the Finnish runner Lasse Viren, double gold medalist at 5,000 and 10,000 meters at both the 1972 and 1976 Olympic Games. Confessions by other Finnish runners over the past several years suggest that Viren's repeated denials that he was blood doped cannot be taken at face value. In 1981 the steeplechaser Mikko Ala-Leppilampi stated that blood doping carried him into the 1972 Olympic final round of his event. And in 1983, prompted by a religious awakening, Kaarlo Manninka confessed that he owed his two silver medals at the 1980 Moscow Games, for the 5,000 and 10,000 meter runs, to blood doping (16). Even before these public statements, Viren's relationship with some of his fellow competitors had been spoiled by rumors about his participation in blood doping procedures.

From a technological standpoint, the key relationship within the world of high-performance sport binds athletes to their physicians, and here too the performance-enhancing technologies are having a profound effect. If the high-performance athlete is technology's version of the ideal citizen, then the high-performance sports physician is technology's version of the ideal healer; and his or her life, too, has become a complicated one.

First, the division between technology-oriented and technology-resisting athletes reflects a similar division within the camp of the sport physicians, and disagreements among the physicians produce confusion among athletes. When two West German former athletes published an "Anti-Doping Pamphlet" last November, one of them commented: "It is alarming that we had to produce this manifesto ourselves, and that it was not officials or doctors who did it. But they are clearly incapable of doing so, because they are divided" (17). Public disagreements, and even feuding, among high-performance sport physicians are particularly evident in West Germany, where these affairs are closely followed in the press. Following the 1984 Olympic Games, during which West German athletes experienced an injury rate of as much as 75%, there was public feuding between the official team physician, Dr. Joseph Keul, and a controversial colleague, Dr. Armin Klümper, who was himself blamed for the withdrawal from Olympic competition of a promising bicycle racer whom he had injected with anabolic steroids on account of an injury (18). West German Olympic officials withdrew him rather than risk his disqualification through testing for banned substances.

At this point we should recall Dr. Pförringer's prediction that "the sport physician who refuses to prescribe drugs will be excluded from high-performance sport." Such exclusion may well be emotionally intolerable for physicians whose association with high-performance athletes is a matter of personal importance. Others are undoubtedly motivated by the intoxicating conviction that the pursuit of limitless performance is akin to transforming men into gods. The devoted sports physician who abstains on principle from prescribing banned substances can hardly hope to compete with a physician like Armin Klümper, who has become a cult figure for many West German athletes. Equally important is the fact that, although he is correctly viewed by the West German sport establishment, and its physicians, as a renegade, he is a charismatic one, "the father figure of German sport," as one famous decathlete once put it (19).

A less dramatic dissenter from the official anti-substance position is the sports physician Heinz Liesen, who, like Dr. Willdor Hollmann, holds a position at the Institute for Sports Medicine and Circulatory Research at the German Sport College in Cologne. Dr. Liesen, who may be termed a conforming dissenter, is restrained from prescribing anabolic steroids by the rules that are imposed on him rather than by any principled doubts about their use, because he regards hormones as natural substances analogous to vitamins. It is with sarcasm that he notes, "We are indeed moral theologians in the area of sport" (20).

But the most interesting figure of all is Dr. Willdor Hollmann, and what makes him interesting is his profound ambivalence about high-performance sports medicine in general. On the one hand, it is clear that he regards high-performance sport as a kind of disaster zone that is also an integral part of modern civilization; and he has specifically criticized the International Olympic Committee (21) for promoting what he has called "a totally commercialized professional sport circus" (22). "We have reached the maximum," Dr. Hollmann has stated, "the athletes have entered the biological border zone" (23). On the other hand, it is also clear that Dr. Hollman is being forced by developments within sport science to flirt with the possibility of becoming a conscientious objector to high-performance sports medicine as a whole (24). Nevertheless, he has refused the boycott option, stating that it remains his duty to serve his patients (25).

The central ambiguity of high-performance sports medicine may be posed as a question: Is this medical practice humane or is it functional? Is the physician there to serve the patient as a human being who is considered to be somehow different from his or her athletic self, or is the physician there to maximize performance on the assumption that the person is indeed identical to the athlete?

This ambiguity also appears in the area of sport psychology, which I regard as the ultimate sport technology. After her defection from East Germany and its sports establishment, the sprinter Renate Neufeld made the following observation: "We never went to the club psychologists on our own. True, they could influence our precompetition emotional states and calm us down. But we knew that they were there primarily to get the last reserves out of you" (26).

The fact that sport psychology is a manipulative psychology points to the question of what psychology is and what it ought, and ought not, to be. In West Germany sport psychology is sometimes referred to, I think appropriately, as "psychodoping." What follows is a description of one of its techniques by the sport psychologist Henner Ertel: "Through a receiver in one ear we send a continuous barrage of nonsense questions to the part of the brain which handles conscious perception, until it has virtually ceased functioning. Simultaneously, through a second receiver in the other ear, we send simple messages to the unconscious which penetrate directly because the conscious mind is blocked off" (27). Such attempts at psycho-engineering raise the most fundamental questions about what human beings are and what should and should not be done to them, particularly by physicians. It is becoming increasingly evident that sport science means the shaping of mind and behavior in conformity with technological norms. For this reason an examination of the human model toward which these developments point is of the utmost significance. Our first step will be to look briefly at the meaning of the term technology. We will then conclude with a short discussion of sport psychology and its latent implications.

The pursuit of the record performance, or the supreme performance, is a celebration of the logic of technological civilization. For this reason, any investigation of modern sport must include a reckoning with what the German philosopher Martin Heidegger called "the question concerning technology" (1955) and subsidiary questions concerning the technologizing of human movement, which Heidegger never chose to address.

In "The Question Concerning Technology" and *What Is Called Thinking* (1954), Heidegger offers two fundamental arguments about technology. First, he states that we have scarcely begun to recognize the effects of technology on human beings, and he goes to great lengths to emphasize our helplessness in this regard. We remain particularly "unfree and chained to technology," he says, when we regard it as something "neutral," because this attitude "makes us utterly blind to the essence of technology" (28).

Heidegger's second major point is that "the essence of technology is by no means anything technological. Thus we shall never experience our relationship to the essence of technology so long as we merely conceive and push forward the technological, put up with it, or evade it" (29). The meaning of technology is not equivalent to the mechanical apparatus that somehow contains it. "Our age is not a technological age because it is the age of the machine; it is an age of the machine because it is the technological age. But so long as the essence of technology does not concern us, in our thought, we shall never be able to know what the machine is" (30). Our disposition toward technology, of which we are unaware, precedes the artifacts that we take technology to be.

The most important characteristic of modern high-performance sport is that it is a global monoculture whose values derive in large measure from the sphere of technology. Because sport confronts us with the question concerning technology, and because its complexity as a cultural phenomenon exceeds even what the link to technology entails, sport must be regarded as one of the great and intractable problems for humanistic scholarship.

The technologized body of the high-performance athlete belongs to a larger category of technologized bodies including the bodybuilder, the cosmonaut, and the physically ordinary person who appears in many advertisements in the United States, standing next to or seated upon a training machine whose purpose is to suggest the technological glamour of high-performance sport. To subject one's body to the machine is to participate in the spirit of the age. But this can be done in a number of ways. Bodybuilders use machines to make their bodies take on the condition of metal or stone. Cosmonauts use machines to make their bodies adapt to other machines they will pilot and inhabit. Athletes use machines to make their bodies function with the efficiency of a machine. And physically ordinary purchasers of training machines enter into a relationship with the machines so as not to be excluded from the dimly intuited dynamic of their own civilization. This is what makes their machines articles of fashion. The dynamic they represent transcends mere fashion, because they are the essence of technology in Heidegger's sense.

Sport science does not physically hybridize humans and machines; as of today there is no sportive equivalent to Dr. Frankenstein's monster. Instead, sport science treats the human organism as though it were a machine, or as though it ought to be a machine. This technologized human organism comprises both mind and body, for which there are distinct sets of strategies. The implicit demand of these strategies, in my view, is a streamlined and decomplexified image of the human being.

Scientific sport in this sense can be understood in terms of Jacques Ellul's concept of technique as it is elaborated in *The Technological Society (La Technique ou L'enieu du Siécle,* 1954). Like Heidegger, Ellul senses within technology a logic that is engulfing us. And, like Heidegger, he distinguishes sharply between the machine and the logic it conceals (technique). What separates Ellul from Heidegger is the former's willingness to present us with an exhaustive description of that hidden logic, which both inhabits and surpasses the machine.

Technique, says Ellul, is "the *totality of methods rationally arrived at and having absolute efficiency* (for a given stage of development) in *every* field of human activity." Technique is efficient procedure per se, an irresistible and homogenizing force that "has taken over all of man's activities." It "is efficient and brings efficiency to everything,"

striving for "the mechanization of everything it encounters." "Technique has become autonomous; it has fashioned an omnivorous world which obeys its own laws and which has renounced all tradition." Its "refusal to tolerate moral judgments" is due to the fact that it "has only one ordering principle: efficient ordering" (31). Technique, in short, is a ubiquitous *modus operandi* that has seduced modern civilization without a struggle.

"In every conceivable way," says Ellul, "sport is an extension of the technical spirit. Its mechanisms reach into the individual's innermost life, working a transformation of his body and its motions as a function of technique and not as a function of some traditional end foreign to technique, as, for example, harmony, joy, or the realization of spiritual good. In sport, as elsewhere, nothing gratuitous is allowed to exist; everything must be useful and must come up to technical expectations" (32). Although somewhat too categorical, Ellul's diagnosis of modern sport is essentially correct. Why has the world chosen as its predominant physical culture competitive sport rather than expressional dance? What makes the modern body an efficiently performing body rather than a different sort of body?

The tyranny of technique is evident in a recent development within cross-country skiing, which has been revolutionized at its highest competitive level by the skating technique invented by the Finnish skier Pauli Siitonen. The advent of the Siitonen technique has already had two effects. First, it has quickly erased a traditional style at the higher competitive levels of the sport. And second, it has presented every high-performance athlete in the sport with a dilemma: whether to continue with a familiar and less efficient style, or risk injury and considerable discomfort while adjusting to the new and more efficient style. Jochen Behle, for years West Germany's best long-distance skier, has scandalized his trainers by refusing to adopt Siitonen's technique. "Does Behle not have the right," *Der Spiegel* asked a West German sport physician, "to decide for himself what is or is not appropriate for his own body?'' Of course he does, said the doctor. ''But an athlete who receives state support is also expected to increase his efficiency by learning new techniques. If that seems too risky to him, then he must withdraw to the second rank'' (33). Long associated with the state-supported sport cultures of the Socialist bloc, this sort of thinking has become a global norm. On either side of the East/West divide, the body is treated as though it were a machine.

Finally, let us return to the psychological dimension of sport science. Doping techniques in particular illustrate the profoundly psychosomatic character of much sport science. Psychogenic effects are highly ambiguous, because neither the athletes nor their trainers can be sure whether a perceived improvement in performance may not derive from the power of suggestion. For this reason it is necessary to speak of the technologizing of the human organism as a whole rather than of the body alone.

Sport science is very much interested in the modelling of mental processes. Hypnotherapy and other techniques are used to promote positive thinking, to flatten consciousness into one dimension—that of automatic performance. ''Psychology,'' an American athlete stated in 1980, ''is for people who don't believe in themselves.'' Thinking is antithetical to athletic efficiency. ''I need to get mindless in races,'' a world-class American sprinter said in 1979. ''I tend to get caught up in the visuals, in the race's esthetics.'' But this sort of reflective involvement is counter-productive. There is much evidence to suggest that, as a subculture, the world of high-performance sport is profoundly hostile to any sort of mental complication. The most important fact about modern sport, viewed as an anthropological phenomenon, is the hostility to introspection its goals and techniques require, and this is its truly disturbing dimension.

How can we make sense of the athlete whose identity emerges from the spirit of technology? What can we say when the speed skier, whose goal is to hurtle down a mountainside at 200 kilometers per hour, employs introspective techniques such as

Zen, tai chi, and transcendental meditation to produce a functional state of mind he describes as ''a blank wall and a positive attitude''? In fact, the speed skier is but one variation of a human type that dates from the beginning of the twentieth century and whose purpose is to incarnate the cultural dynamic inherent to technology.

Every important sport doctrinaire of the early decades of this century interprets sport as only one expression of a new sensory reality associated with the frenetic character of modern life. This is the real meaning of modern sport, and this is what accounts for its infiltration by technological norms, by what Ellul calls technique. It is seldom noted that the sportive-dynamic body played a significant role in avant-garde movements like Italian Futurism and German Expressionism. Both ideologies, and especially Futurism, were infatuated with athleticism, the idea of the record performance, and the theme of *speed*.

Sport incorporates the man-machine synthesis because it is a *modernism*. F.T. Marinetti, the most important theorist of Futurism, worshipped both athletes and machines. ''We believe,'' he wrote in 1911, ''in the possibility of an incalculable number of human transformations, and without a smile we declare that wings are asleep in the flesh of man.'' In the fantasies of Marinetti, the technologized athlete of the future appears in a nascent state. What is more, he intuits the anthropological consequences of such transformations. ''This nonhuman and mechanical being, constructed for an omnipresent velocity, will be naturally cruel, omniscient, and combative'' (34). Like the athlete, the jet pilot, and the cosmonaut, Marinetti knows that psychology is an impediment to the dynamic life, and that the dignity of man is to exist as a machine.

Notes

1. ''Der Sport befindet sich in einer Grenzsituation,'' *Süddeutsche Zeitung,* November 18, 1985.

2. "Notizen aus L.A.," *Süddeutsche Zeitung,* August 6, 1984.

3. "Wie die Stiere," *Der Spiegel,* January 14, 1985.

4. "Mediziner: Da wird Wahnsinn zur Methode," *Die Welt,* July 14, 1983.

5. "Unheimliche Angst," *Der Spiegel,* February 22, 1982.

6. See especially Harvey G. Klein, M.D., "Blood Transfusion and Athletics: Games People Play," *The New England Journal of Medicine,* March 28, 1985.

7. "Styrkeexpert vill legalisera anabola steroider," *Svenska Dagbladet,* September 12, 1984.

8. Letter from Frederick C. Hatfield, Ph.D., *Sports Illustrated,* September 26, 1983.

9. Pierre de Coubertin, *Essais de psychologie sportive* (Lausanne and Paris: Librairie Payot, 1913), p. 133.

10. "Mediziner: Da wird Wahnsinn zur Methode," *Die Welt,* July 14, 1983.

11. "Unheilsamer Drang," *Der Spiegel,* April 8, 1985.

12. "'Doping ist wie ein Buschfeuer'," *Süddeutsche Zeitung,* February 1, 1984.

13. "Weltrekord-Schützen unter Dopingverdacht," *Süddeutsche Zeitung,* September 9, 1985.

14. "Boork anklagar Sovjet för doping," *Svenska Dagbladet,* October 12, 1984.

15. "Ricky Bruch anklagar svenska stjärnor," *Svenska Dagbladet,* February 3, 1984.

16. "Schweiger kommen ins Gerede," *Süddeutsche Zeitung,* November 29, 1984; see also "Medelmåttor världsbäst," *Dagens Nyheter* (Stockholm), May 30, 1985.

17. "Ein neues Signal im Kampf gegen das Doping," *Süddeutsche Zeitung,* November 22, 1985.

18. "'Siegen um jeden Preis'," *Der Spiegel,* November 26, 1984.

19. *Ibid.*

20. "Zuviel Theater um Anabolika," *Süddeutsche Zeitung,* January 23, 1985.

21. "Sportärzte kritisieren Samaranch," *Süddeutsche Zeitung,* October 29, 1985; "'Gefahren durch Flickschusterei'," *Der Spiegel,* November 4, 1985.

22. "Der Sport ist wie ein ungepflügtes Land," *Süddeutsche Zeitung,* January 30, 1985.

23. "'Typen wie aus dem Panoptikum'," *Der Spiegel,* July 23, 1984.

24. "'Gefahren durch Flickschusterei'," *Der Spiegel,* November 4, 1985.

25. *Ibid.*

26. Quoted in John M. Hoberman, *Sport and Political Ideology* (Austin: University of Texas Press, 1984), p. 212.

27. "Die Psycho-Spiele," *Stern,* August 2, 1984.

28. Martin Heidegger, "The Question Concerning Technology," in *The Question Concerning Technology and Other Essays* (New York: Harper Colophon Books, 1981), p. 4.

29. *Ibid.*

30. Martin Heidegger, *What Is Called Thinking?* (New York: Harper Torchbooks, 1972), p. 24.

31. Jacques Ellul, *The Technological Society* (New York: Vintage Books, n.d.), pp. xxv, 4, 5, 12, 14, 97, 110.

32. *Ibid.,* p. 384.

33. "Urlaube nach zwei, drei Tagen zu Ende," *Der Spiegel,* January 28, 1985.

34. R.W. Flint, ed. Marinetti: *Selected Writings* (New York: Farrar, Straus and Giroux, 1972), p. 91.

Sex Equality in Sports

JANE ENGLISH

What constitutes equal opportunity for women in sports? Philosophers have developed three major positions concerning equal opportunity, but they have focused on fields in which the sexes are either known or assumed to have equal potentialities. In sports, some relevant differences between the sexes, though statistical, do appear to be permanent. All three of the most widely held views on equal opportunity are deficient when applied to this area. Since there may be other permanent differences between the sexes, in such areas as spatial perception or verbal ability, it is useful to examine the problems of equal opportunity in sports.

I

One account of equal opportunity identifies it with nondiscrimination. On this view, if we do not pay any attention to the race of applicants to law school, for example, then our admissions are "color blind" and give blacks equal opportunity. Admission should be based on characteristics relevant to law school, such as intelligence and grades, while irrelevant characteristics such as sex and race should be ignored entirely. Most philosophers have rejected this account as too weak. If women lack motivation because they never see female lawyers on television, "sex blindness" alone will not

provide equal opportunity. Although "formal" equality is necessary for justice, it is not sufficient. These philosophers would permit temporary violations of this ideal, but only in the transition to a just society.

When applied to sports, however, their view proves inadequate. If our sports were made sex-blind, women would have even less opportunity to participate than at present. Given equal incentives and more role models, women would have more interest in athletics, but few would qualify for high school, college, professional and Olympic teams. Statistically speaking, there are physiological differences between the sexes that are relevant to sports performance. Remedial programs and just institutions cannot obliterate all differences in size and strength. So far from being necessary for equal opportunity, sex-blindness can actually decrease it.

A second account of equal opportunity identifies it with equal chances. Oscar and Elmer are said to have equal opportunity to become brain surgeons if it is equally probable that they will become brain surgeons. Most philosophers have rejected this conception of equal opportunity as too strong. If Oscar is a genius with great manual dexterity and Elmer is uncoordinated and slightly retarded, then they should not have an equal chance to become brain surgeons. Our society is not unjust if it encourages Oscar and discourages Elmer from this profession, because these skills are relevant to the job.

When we turn to women in sports, however, the model of equal probabilities seems to have some merit. Sports offer what I will call *basic benefits* to which it seems everyone has an equal right:

Reprinted from Jane English, "Sex Equality in Sports," *Philosophy & Public Affairs* 7 no. 3 (Spring 1978). Copyright © 1978 by Princeton University Press. Reprinted by permission of Princeton University Press.

health, the self-respect to be gained by doing one's best, the cooperation to be learned from working with teammates and the incentive gained from having opponents, the ''character'' of learning to be a good loser and a good winner, the chance to improve one's skills and learn to accept criticism—and just plain fun. If Matilda is less adept at, say, wrestling than Walter is, this is no reason to deny Matilda an equal chance to wrestle for health, self-respect, and fun. Thus, contrary to the conclusion on the example of the brain surgeon, a society that discourages Matilda from wrestling is unjust because it lacks equal opportunity to attain these basic benefits.

The third account of equal opportunity calls for equal chances in the sense of equal achievements for the ''major social groups.'' Blacks have an equal opportunity to be lawyers, on this view, when the percentage of lawyers who are black roughly equals the percentage of blacks in the population. Like the ''equal probabilities'' view, this one calls for equal chances, but it interprets this by averaging attainments across the major social groups.

When this third account is applied to sports, it seems to have the undesirable consequence that a society is unjust if less than half its professional football players are women. If we had to provide sufficient incentives or reverse discrimination to achieve this result, it would create a situation unfair to 170-pound males. (They may even clamor to be recognized as a ''major social group.'') More important, it seems wrong to argue that a low level of health and recreation for, say, short women, is compensated for by additional health and recreation for tall women; one might as well argue that women are compensated by the greater benefits enjoyed by men. Rawls and Nozick have argued against utilitarianism by pointing out that society is not a ''macro-individual'' such that the benefits of some persons cancel out the sufferings of others. But the major social groups are not macro-individuals either. Proponents of the third account have not, to my knowledge, replied to this objection.

Beyond the basic benefits of sport, some ath-

letes reap the further benefits of fame and fortune. I shall call these the *scarce benefits* of sport. The term is not meant to imply that they are kept artificially scarce, but that it is simply not possible for prizes and publicity to be attained equally by everyone at once. Although everyone has an equal right to the basic benefits, not everyone can claim an equal right to receive fan mail or appear on television. For this, having the skill involved in the sport is one relevant factor. In short, I shall maintain that the second account, equal probabilities, should be applied to the basic benefits; whereas the third model, proportional attainments for the major social groups, should be applied to the scarce benefits. And I shall construct an argument from self-respect for taking the ''average'' across the major social groups in the case of scarce benefits.

II

The traditional accounts of equal opportunity are inadequate because men and women are physiologically different in ways relevant to performance in sports. What is a fair way to treat physiologically disadvantaged groups? Two methods are in common use, and I shall suggest a third option.

One common method is to form competition classes based on a clear-cut physiological characteristic, such as weight or age, well known to be a hindrance in the sport in question. For example, middleweight boxers receive preferential treatment in the sense that they are permitted to move up and compete against the heavyweights if they desire, while the heavyweights are not permitted to move down into the middleweight class.

Sex is frequently used to form separate competition groups. If we apply the boxing model, several conclusions about this practice follow. Women should be allowed to ''move up'' and compete against the men if they wish. Since sex is not relevant to performance in all sports, the sport should be integrated when it is not. For example, it is probably irrelevant in dressage, riflery and car racing. In other sports, the differences between the sexes may be too small to justify separate classes—as in diving and freestyle skiing. In still others, the sexes have compensating differences. In channel swimming, for instance, men are advantaged in strength, but women profit from an insulating layer of fat. Additional sports could be integrated if the abilities characteristic of the two sexes were valued equally. In many areas, such as swimming, it is simply unknown whether the existing differences are due to permanent physiological characteristics or to cultural and social inequalities. Additional empirical research is needed before it will be known where integration is appropriate.

An objection to the use of groupings by sex is that it discriminates against those males whose level of performance is equal to that of the abler females. For example, if we have a girls' football team in our high school, is it unfair to prohibit a 120-pound boy who cannot make the boys' team from trying out for the girls' team? If we provide an additional team for boys under 140 pounds, does that discriminate against girls under 100 pounds? Against short boys over 140 pounds? It is impossible to provide a team for every characteristic that might be relevant to football performance. The objection has force because the differences between the sexes are only statistical. Our 120-pound boy is being penalized for the average characteristics of a major social group to which he belongs, rather than being treated on the basis of his individual characteristics.

The justification for maintaining separate teams for the sexes is the impact on women that integration would have. When there are virtually no female athletic stars, or when women receive much less prize money than men do, this is damaging to the self-respect of all women. Members of disadvantaged groups identify strongly with each other's successes and failures. If women do not attain roughly equal fame and fortune in sports, it leads both men and women to think of women as naturally inferior. Thus, it is not a right of women tennis stars to the scarce benefits, but rather a right of all women to self-respect that justifies their demand for equal press coverage and prize money.

This provides a justification for applying the third account of equal opportunity to the distribution of scarce benefits. It also explains why the "major social groups" have this feature, while arbitrary sets of individuals do not. A group singled out for distinctive treatment and recognized as a class tends to develop feelings of mutual identification which have an impact on the members' self-respect. It also affects the respect and treatment they get from others. In an androgynous society, we might be as unaware of a person's sex as we now are of left-handedness. Then roughly equal attainments would no longer be required, on my reasoning, for unequal attainments would not injure self-respect. Conversely, although there is some evidence of late that blacks have physiological traits such as a longer calf that give them an advantage in jumping and sprinting, I do not conclude that we should form separate track or basketball leagues for whites, since the self-respect of whites is not endangered by this modest advantage possessed by blacks.

III

A different method often used to give the disadvantaged equal access to the basic benefits of sport is to group individuals by ability alone. This occurs when we find second and third string games, B-leagues, intramural meets or special matches for novices or amateurs. Groupings by age, sex, or weight are often just attempts to approximate ability groupings in a convenient and quick way. When convenience is the intent, then, it must not be rigidly imposed to keep talented girls off the first string.

Groupings by ability are much easier to justify than groupings by the specific characteristics just discussed. There is no discrimination against less able members of the dominant group. Ability groupings take into account all the traits that may affect performance. Competition with those close to one's own ability usually provides the most incentive and satisfaction, except where style of play is very different. It is imperative to make recreational leagues on all levels of skill available to people of all ages, sexes, income levels, and abilities, because everyone has an equal right to sport's basic benefits.

Groupings by ability must not lead to disrespect for those playing in the lower ability groups, however. Sports is an area in which we have tended to confuse respect with what has been called "esteem." I may have a low (and accurate) estimate of myself as a tennis player without losing respect for myself as a person. Although competition does entail winners and losers, it does not entail disrespect for the losers. Much has been said recently about this among other evils of competition. But competition per se is not bad. It offers fun, excitement, entertainment, and the incentive to perform at one's best. The problems arise when losers are scorned or discouraged from playing, and when winning becomes the end rather than the means to basic benefits. It is ironic that sports, long recommended for building character and teaching how to be a good loser and winner, have often taught aggression and elitism. Experts have become idols and millionaires, while the rest of us watch rather than participate. With effort, the entry of women into sports could foster a reawakening to these values, which are widely shared but have been lost lately in the shuffle of big business sports. Some such reawakening is necessary if ability groupings are to be effective.

IV

So far I have assumed that women are a physiologically disadvantaged group in need of protection or special handicaps. In recent years, women have been making impressive progress in narrowing the gap between male and female performance. But there are apparently some permanent biological differences that affirmative action and consciousness raising will never change: women are smaller than men, they have a higher percentage of fat, they lack the hormones necessary for massive muscle development, they have a different hip structure and a slower oxygenation rate.

Before we conclude that women are permanently relegated to inferiority, however, let us note that what is a physiological disadvantage in one activity may be an advantage in others: weight is an asset to a Sumo wrestler and a drawback for marathon running; height is an aid in basketball but not on the balance beam. In some sports, women have natural advantages over men. The hip structure that slows running gives a lower center of gravity. Fat provides insulation and an energy source for running fifty-mile races. The hormones that hinder development of heavy muscles promote flexibility. Even small size can be an asset, as jockeys and spelunkers know.

An example of an athletic activity which emphasizes the female advantages is ballet. Some ballerinas can stand on one toe while extending the other leg up into a vertical position where it touches the ear! While admittedly few women can do this, even fewer men can. Men are simply physiologically disadvantaged in the body flexibility that ballet emphasizes. Perhaps the most extreme example of a sport favoring women's natural skills is the balance beam. Here, small size, flexibility and low center of gravity combine to give women the kind of natural hegemony that men enjoy in football.

This suggests a third approach to aiding physiologically different groups. We should develop a variety of sports, in which a variety of physical types can expect to excel. We tend to think of the possible sports as a somewhat fixed group of those currently available. Yet even basketball and football are of very recent invention. Since women have been virtually excluded from all sports until the last century, it is appropriate that some sports using women's specific traits are now developing, such as synchronized swimming.

This method is different from forming handicapped groups or second-string leagues, and it is superior in its impact on the self-respect of the affected groups. It contributes to a woman's self-respect to see or read about the best women golfers. But this pride is tempered by the knowledge that they are "only" the best *women*. The very need for a protected competition class suggests inferiority. The pride and self-respect gained from witnessing a woman athlete who is not only the best woman but the very best athlete is much greater. Perhaps most white male readers have not experienced this sort of identification characteristic of "minority" groups. But it is clearly displayed in the extraordinary interest in gymnastics among adolescent girls inspired by Olga Korbut, and the pride blacks derived from Jackie Robinson.

V

In calling for the development of new sports, I am suggesting that our concept of "sports" contains a male bias. Historically, this is understandable, because sports were an exclusively male domain, probably based on war and hunting, and actually used to assert male dominance. The few athletic activities permitted to women—mostly forms of dance—were not thought to fall under the *concept* of sport, and are still classified as arts or entertainment instead. Speed, size, and strength seem to be the essence of sports. Women *are* naturally inferior at "sports" so conceived.

But if women had been the historically dominant sex, our concept of sport would no doubt have evolved differently. Competitions emphasizing flexibility, balance, strength, timing, and small size might dominate Sunday afternoon television and offer salaries in six figures. Men could be clamoring for equal press coverage of their champions.

Here it might be argued that our concept of sport cannot be altered to make women equal, because speed, strength, and size are inevitable elements

of *spectator* appeal. But it is participating rather than watching that is central to sport. Although speed is exciting, so is precision. Nor do audiences always choose to watch the experts. More important, spectator interest is a cultural product, tending to follow rather than lead media attention.

VI

The just society, in my view, would contain a greater variety of sports than we now have, providing advantages for a wider range of physical types. The primary emphasis would be on participation, with a wealth of local teams and activities available to all, based on groupings by ability. Only where style of play is very different would groupings by weight, age, or sex be recommended. The goal would be to make the basic benefits of health, teamwork, and fun equally available to everyone. Just distribution of the scarce benefits is somewhat more complex. Level of skill, audience appeal, and the self-respect of major social groups all have to be considered.

Current problems of the real world are far removed from such a utopia. Rights to the basic benefits dictate immediate changes in the distribution of our sports resources. Most obvious is the need for equal facilities—everything from socks to stadiums. If this means we must disturb a "Pareto optimal" situation—selling the football team's videotape machine if we are to provide a jogging path for the middle-aged—so be it. More subtle is the need for equal incentives. As well as equal scholarships and prizes, women need peer approval and changed sex-role stereotypes.

In short, I have suggested a division of the benefits of sport into the "basic" and the "scarce" ones. From the assumption that everyone has an equal right to the basic benefits of health and recreation, I have argued that the access to participator sports should not be based upon having the ability to play the sport well. And this ability is only one factor in the attainment of the scarce benefits. Since I believe that the right of women to roughly half of the scarce benefits, overall, stems from the right to self-respect, I have argued that a society which invents alternative sports using women's distinctive abilities and which rewards these equally is preferable to a society which only maintains protected classes for women in sports at which men are advantaged.

The Exclusion of Women From Sport: Conceptual and Existential Dimensions

IRIS MARION YOUNG

Conceptual and normative issues about women's relation to sport have not been given nearly enough attention by either philosophers or feminists. Jane English began to take up these issues in her paper "Sex Equality in Sport."[1] This paper, which is dedicated to Jane's memory,[2] develops those issues further.

In Section I, I argue that insofar as our culture defines woman's body as object, the culture necessarily excludes women from its concept of sport. In Section II, I discuss the institutional and practical exclusion of women from sport in our society. Section III argues that insofar as our culture excludes women from both the idea and reality of sport, it excludes us from full participation in humanity itself. Hence inclusion of women in both the idea and institutions of sport is a fundamental condition of women's liberation. Finally, in Section IV I argue that the cultural exclusion of women from the idea and reality of sport has given sport a masculinist bias which prevents sport itself from exhibiting its potential humanity. Hence the inclusion of women in the idea and institutions of sport is a fundamental condition for the humanization of sport.

Reprinted from *Philosophy in Context*, Vol. 9, (1979), pp. 44–53. Copyright 1979 by *Philosophy in Context*, Cleveland State University, Cleveland, Ohio 44115. Reprinted by permission.

I

The most basic aspect of woman's existence in a male dominated society, according to de Beauvoir, is that the symbols and institutions of the society define woman as the Other. Masculinist culture defines woman as immanence as opposed to transcendence, determinate nature as opposed to the self-chosen subject.[3] This symbolic elaboration of woman as the Other identifies the female body as mere body-object, as opposed to the body-subject which is the man.

The ideal of feminine beauty is variable, but certain demands remain constant; for one thing, since woman is destined to be possessed, her body must present the inert and passive qualities of an object. Virile beauty lies in the fitness of the body for action, in strength, agility, flexibility; it is the manifestation of transcendence animating a flesh that must never sink back upon itself . . .

. . . Her body is not perceived as the radiation of a subjective personality, but as a thing, sunk deeply in its own immanence; it is not for such a body to have reference to the rest of the world, it must not be the promise of things other than itself; it must end the desires it arouses.[4]

335

There is little question that the status of women has undergone alteration in the present century, and to a large degree it has been progressive change. There has been little weakening, however, of the masculinist identification of the feminine body as object. Indeed, I believe it can be argued that the objectification of the female body in contemporary American culture is greater than that of many cultures, but I will not make that argument here. In any case, the symbolic media of contemporary society convey an image of the female body as mere flesh. Those aspects of a woman's body most gazed at and discussed, and in terms of which she herself all too often measures her own worth, are those which least suggest action—neck, breasts, buttocks, etc. Contemporary film, advertising, popular literature and periodicals, and countless other media objectify the female body as sexy, passive flesh. They use this objectification of the female body, moreover, as means of sensualizing other objects, thus making them desirable. Finally, while norms of dress retain much of the liberality that emerged in the sixties, in recent years there has been a revival of "feminine" styles which tend to make the female body inactive, both in appearance and reality.

Now sport is a notoriously slippery concept, and I do not wish here to enter the discussion about how it should be defined.[5] Whatever else it is or is not, however, sport is the achievement of a non-utilitarian objective through engagement of bodily capacities and/or skills. In sport, at least ideally, the body is spontaneous subject and the subject is wholly embodied. The identity of body and active subjectivity reaches its paradigm in sport; the very stance, muscles, movement and directionality of the athlete exhibit directly her or his intentions and projects. To be sure, the body-subject underlies all human activity, and many activities, such as physical labor, require skill, strength and dexterity in the use of the body's capacities. Athletic activity, however, abstracts the body's movement and accomplishment from its normal involvement in the complex web of natural and social goals; sport calls upon the body's capacities and skills merely for the sake of determining what they can achieve.

By its nature, then, sport exhibits the essential body-subject. Masculinist culture defines women, on the other hand, as the essential body-object. Thus in a culture which defines woman as Other, sport and woman are mutually exclusive concepts. This suggests that the sense of incompatibility between women and sport which still dominates in our society is not a social accident, but a conceptual and symbolic necessity. To the degree that in our society the female body is objectified, women must be excluded from the concept of sport. It follows that if there is a particular female person participating in sport, then, either she is not "really" a woman, or the sport she engages in is not "really" a sport. These two interpretations of the phenomenon frequently occur in our society, often together.[6]

II

Not only have women been excluded from the idea of sport, the institutions and practices of sport to a large degree still exclude women as well. The causal relationship between the cultural symbols of sport and the institutions of sport are indeed complex, and I do not wish to develop those here. I shall merely describe aspects of the exclusion of women from sport and practice.

The degree to which young girls are discouraged from engaging in physical activity, often in very subtle ways, has been noted in much recent literature.[7] To a large degree the sanction on girls' physical activity does have the effect of reducing the level of physical activity of girls, especially relative to boys. There is however, a certain girlhood culture of resistance. Many preadolescent girls engage in some physically challenging play such as jumping rope, roller skating, bike racing, various bouncing ball games, hop scotch, and countless other games. Our society does not take these girls' games seriously as sport, however, and by the time we reach ten or eleven we have put them away as childish things. The sort of physical play in which girls typically engage has institutional form only in the world of the girls themselves; the girls engage in their play "spontaneously" largely without the help, notice, guidance and institutionalized resources of the larger society.

Specifically what our society largely denies girls is access to the organized and institutionalized sport which it takes for granted as an essential part of the boy's childhood and adolescent environment. Boys generally play at games institutionalized in the larger society. From an early age parents, older children, teachers and coaches provide them the opportunity to develop their athletic skill in a self-conscious way. The society encourages, recognizes, develops and rewards the physical activity and achievement of boys, at the same time it discourages and often ignores that of girls.

The absence of institutionalized sport for girls and women, coupled with the active sanction against their physical activity that girls often experience, does much to develop in us a sense of ourselves as weak, frail, sedentary. Exclusion from sport as the paradigm of physical engagement with the world is not merely something that *happens* to girls, however. We also actively choose ourselves as inactive bodies.

The female person who grows up in a society which defines the female body as object rarely escapes developing a bodily self-image in conformity with that definition. As she passes through the years of adolescence she increasingly experiences the sexually objectifying gaze of men and the measuring gaze of other women which assess her in terms of her "feminine beauty." When others look upon us in this way it is difficult not to regard ourselves from the same objectifying point of view. More often than not we actively take up our identity as body-objects. We regard our bodies as mannequins to be pruned, shaped, dressed and painted.[8] A number of psychological studies report that women have significantly higher bodily awareness than men.[9]

This body image has a definite impact on our potential for sport. In his book on sport, Paul Weiss considers the question of why women take an interest in sport less frequently than men. He answers that each sex naturally stands in a different relation to its body. Men are more abstract and intellectual than women. While women are capable of intellectual endeavors, in general, "a woman is less abstract than a man because her mind is persistently ordered toward bodily problems."[10] The very process of maturing, Weiss claims, brings women into natural unity with their bodies, whereas the intellectual tendency of men sets them in tension with and separated from their bodies. Men seek to engage in sport in order to resolve this tension and achieve a unity with their bodies. Women tend to be less interested in sport, because we already have this unity.

Despite the obviously sexist and mystifying character of this metaphysical appeal to male and female natures, there is a grain of truth in Weiss' explanation of why women tend to be interested in sport less than men. The reason does lie in part in the relation in which women stand to our bodies. To the degree that we choose ourselves as body-objects, we find it difficult to become enthusiastic body-subjects and frequently do not desire to challenge our bodies in sport. The mutual exclusivity of women and sport which exists at the ideal level thus enters the experience and self-definition of women themselves.

III

The major symbols and institutions of sport in our society continue by and large to exclude women. This exclusion of women from sport implies our exclusion from full participation in humanity, at both the symbolic and practical levels. Mary E. Duquin has suggested that sport symbolizes human transcendence of nature in the establishment of culture. Following Ortner, she claims that virtually all cultures associate woman with nature and man with culture.[11] The exclusion of women from sport, then, symbolizes the exclusion of women from humanity itself as the cultural transformation of nature.[12]

Along similar lines, Eleanor Metheny argues that sport symbolizes human freedom. She argues that sport abstracts from the constraints and requirements of the natural and social world in which we seek to enact particular material goals. In such everyday action one must submit to the constraints of external ends, worldly resistances and unintended consequences. In sport, on the other hand, the conditions, rules and restraints, as well as the goals, are self-chosen, and one engages one's body capacities purely for the sake of showing them at their best. In this way sport serves as a symbol of freedom.[13] If sport stands in this way as a symbol of freedom, then the exclusion of women from the idea of sport implies our exclusion from the idea of human freedom.

The dominant ideology of formal equality denies the feminist claim that our society excludes women from full participation in humanity. Our exclusion from most aspects of humanity is subtle and slippery. The explicit conceptual and symbolic exclusion of women from sport, coupled with sport's symbolization of transcendence and freedom, provide us with one of those few instances in our culture where the equation of humanity with masculinity appears explicitly.

Exclusion of women from the institutions and practices of sport, moreover, has a real effect on our opportunity to develop our human capacities. The female person who defines herself and is defined by others as fragile, weak, awkward and passive, and who receives little encouragement to engage her body in physical activity, will more often than not become weak, awkward, and physically timid. As I have developed elsewhere, feminine bodily existence under these conditions is characterized by contradictory structures of bodily comportment and spatiality. Sexist society excludes us by definition and in practice from developing ourselves as free body subjects.[14]

If, as Merleau-Ponty argues, the basic structures of human existence—consciousness, intentionality,

purposiveness, etc.—have their foundation in the body as acting and expressing subject,[15] then the inhibition of women's development of our body subjectivity implies a profound inhibition of our humanity.[16] In our society athletic activity is one of the few institutionalized opportunities a person has for developing a sense of himself or herself as a vigorous, powerful, skillful, coordinated and graceful body. In contemporary advanced industrial society laboring activity, and even to a large extent military activity, rely little on physical virtues of strength, agility and coordination. Thus in our society sport has a more crucial role in the founding of body subjectivity than perhaps it has had in the past. The exclusion, including the self-exclusion, of women from participation in sport thus prevents us from realizing fundamental aspects of our humanity.

From the above considerations it follows that a fundamental condition of the liberation of women is our full inclusion in both the idea and reality of sport. For the exclusion of women from sport not only deprives us of important human opportunities, it gives a fundamental advantage to men. The same society which discourages the physical development of women actively encourages man's exercise of physical strength and skill. There can be little doubt that such differential access to physical power is a significant element in the social power men have over women, as well as the social justification of this power distribution.

From several points of view, then, the call for full inclusion of women in the symbols and institutions of sport may represent a demand more fundamental and far reaching than demands for simple justice, like equal pay for equal work or shared housework, despite the importance of these other demands.[17] If the exclusion of women from the concept of sport symbolizes our exclusion from humanity itself, and if our exclusion from the institutions of sport contributes in a basic way to a sense of weakness, body-objectification and physical timidity among women, then the inclusion of women in the symbols and institutions of sport is a basic aspect of our full participation in humanity.

IV

The exclusion of women from the symbols and institutions of sport has consequences not only for the condition of women, but for the nature of sport itself. Because sport excludes women at the same time that it serves as a foundation of masculinist privilege and ideology, the masculinist bias which permeates the symbols and institutions of sport in our culture blunts and deforms its potential human significance.

English has pointed out how the very kinds of sport which exist in our society reflect this masculinist bias. The most celebrated and most practiced sports put a premium on height, mass, strength and speed—attributes in which on the average men will tend to excel over women. The sport imagination has not even begun to tap the possibilities latent in the physical capacities in which women will tend to excel over men.[18] Most of the sports played today have their origins in male experiences in sex segregated activities, such as hunting or warfare. None have arisen from the specific activities of women or from women's specific experience.

Perhaps more importantly, in contemporary society sport appears to carry nearly the full weight of the meanings of masculinity. Most masculinist societies contain a number of institutions in which a man can show himself a "real" man, and from which women are excluded. In contemporary society, however, sport remains one of the few institutions which explicitly serves this function, and hence it is overburdened with a masculine image. Contemporary society, moreover, provides few contexts in which physical fighting among men is socially sanctioned, yet it continues to associate masculinity with being the strongest and best fighter. In this way as well sport must bear the brunt of the associations of masculinity.

Numerous writers lament the contemporary equation of sport and masculinity as distorting both sport and men. They declaim the overly aggressive character of contemporary sport, its excessively competitive character, the typical emphasis on winning at all costs, the high pressure under which (usually male) athletes work.[19] To the degree that sport and sportsmen are under high pressure in our society to "prove" themselves, be aggressive, and pursue winning in a highly rationalized and technologized fashion, it would seem that sport presently lacks some of the freedom which Metheny claims for it.

These undesirable features of contemporary sport practices, which many writers explicitly associate with the masculinist bias of sport, stand in marked contrast to the virtues which philosophers have attributed to sport in recent years. Philosophers analyze sport as part of the aesthetic realm; sport, they argue, embodies virtues of form, rhythm, drama, beauty and grace. Just as often they claim for sport fundamental moral qualities: justice, fairness, cooperation, sense of community and so on.[20] To the degree that these accounts fail to pose the alleged virtues of sport as what sport *should* be, rather than what it is and has been, they function as ideological justifications for the institutions of sport as they presently exist.[21]

As long as sport must carry nearly the full weight of masculinist images, it cannot also realize its potentially aesthetic and moral qualities. Inclusion of women in the symbols and institutions of sport, then, is a necessary condition for the humanization of sport. Mere inclusion of women in the existing concept and institutions of sport, however, is not sufficient. Sports programs for women today frequently model themselves on and measure themselves by the standards of sports programs which have traditionally been reserved for men. There is more justice in this situation than in the exclusion of women entirely, but the masculinist bias of sport is not thereby removed.

Duquin suggests that only when sport becomes androgynous in its symbolic meaning and real content will sport have achieved its human possibilities. Androgyny in sport means for her the encorporation of virtues typically associated with women into the symbols and practices of sport—such as expressiveness and grace—along with a corresponding decline in the present overly aggressive and instrumentalist aspects of sport which are typically associated with masculinity.[22]

The mere entrance of women in sport in greater numbers—even in masculinist sport—will, in my opinion, begin to break down the masculinist meaning of sport; perhaps this process has already begun, though it is too early to tell. Both the liberation of women and the liberation of sport, however, require in addition the invention of new sports and the inclusion in our concept of sport of physical activities presently outside or on the boundaries of sport.

Notes

1. *Philosophy and Public Affairs,* Vol. 7 (1978) no. 3, pp. 269–277.
2. Jane English died in 1978 while climbing the Matterhorn. In her much too short career, Jane English contributed a great deal to the development of feminist studies in philosophy. She edited two anthologies in the area, as well as published several papers. Her death came as a great shock and loss to the community of women philosophers.
3. *The Second Sex* (New York: Vintage Books, 1974), especially Chapter IX.
4. *Ibid.,* p. 178.
5. For some examples of different approaches to this problem, see Ellen Gerber, ed., *Sport and the Body: A Philosophical Symposium* (Philadelphia: Lea and Febiger, 1972), especially the articles in Part I, "The Nature of Sport."
6. See Jan Felshin, "The Dialectics of Woman and Sport," in Gerber, Felshin, Berlin and Wyrick, *The American Woman In Sport,* Reading, MA: Addison-Wesley Publishing Co., 1974), pp. 179–210.
7. See, for example, Lenore J. Weitzman, "Sex Role Socialization," in Freeman, ed., *Woman: A Feminist Perspective* (Palo Alto, CA: Mayfield Publishing Co., 1975), pp. 105–144.
8. For an account of the connection of this body self-image and sexual objectification, and of the effect of both on the oppression of women, see Sandra Lee Bartky, "Psychological Oppression," in Sharon Bishop and Marjorie Weinsweig, ed., *Philosophy and Women* (Belmont, CA: Wadsworth Publishing Co., 1979), pp. 33–41.
9. Seymour Fisher cites a number of studies coming to this conclusion, and reports some of his own, in *Body Experience in Fantasy and Behavior* (New York: Appleton-Century-Crofts, 1970), especially pp. 525–540.
10. Paul Weiss, *Sport: A Philosophical Inquiry* (Carbondale: Southern Illinois University Press, 1969), p. 217.
11. Sherry B. Ortner, "Is Female to Male as Nature is to Culture?" In Rosaldo and Lamphere, ed., *Woman, Culture, and Society* (Stanford University Press, 1974), pp. 67–88.
12. Mary E. Duquin, "Effects of Culture on Women's Experience in Sport," *Sport Sociology Bulletin,* Vol. 6, no. 1, Spring 1977.
13. Eleanor Metheny, "The Symbolic Power of Sport," in op. cit. Gerber, *Sport and the Body,* pp. 221–227.
14. Iris Marion Young, "Throwing Like a Girl: A Phenomenology of Feminine Body Comportment, Motility and Spatiality," *Human Studies,* Vol. 3, 1980.
15. Maurice Merleau-Ponty, *The Phenomenology of Perception* (New York: The Humanities Press, 1962), especially Part I, Chapters 3 and 4.
16. Perhaps it should be pointed out here that insofar as the development of bodily expressiveness is inhibited in men, their humanity is also inhibited.

17. Francis Keenan, in "Justice and Sport," *Journal of the Philosophy of Sport,* Vol. II, 1975, pp. 111–123, calls for equality for women in sport, and appears to see this call as comparable to these other demands.

18. See English, op. cit., and Weiss, chapter 13.

19. See Marc Feigen Fasteau, *The Male Machine* (New York: McGraw-Hill, 1974), chapter 9; Harry Edwards, *Sociology of Sport* (Homewood, IL: The Dorsey Press, 1973); Arnold R. Reisser, *The Madness in Sports: Psychosocial Observations on Sports* (New York: Appleton-Century-Crofts, 1967), especially chapters 14 and 16.

20. See the relevant sections in op. cit. Gerber, *Sport and the Body;* there are numerous papers in the *Journal of the Philosophy of Sport* which develop these themes as well.

21. Cf. Felshin, op. cit.

22. Mary E. Duquin, "The Androgynous Advantage," in Carole A. Olgesby, ed., *Women and Sport: From Myth to Reality.*

Women, Sex, and Sports

RAYMOND A. BELLIOTTI

Jane English (2) has presented several arguments related to sexual equality in athletics. Crucial to these arguments is the distinction between basic and scarce athletic benefits. Basic benefits are those to which everyone has an equal right; scarce benefits are those to which everyone does not have an equal right. Examples of basic benefits are health, the self-respect to be gained by doing one's best, learning cooperation and competition by working with teammates and battling against opponents, and the opportunity to improve one's skills. Examples of scarce benefits are fame and fortune. It is clear that basic benefits, at least in theory, can be available to all and are achievable by all; scarce benefits by their very nature cannot be attained by all (2: pp. 270–71).

I

English (2: p. 273) advances the following argument in defense of the claim that women have a justifiable demand for equal coverage and prize money:

The Argument From Self-respect
1. Members of disadvantaged groups identify strongly with each other's successes and failures.
2. If women do not attain roughly equal fame and fortune in sports, it leads both men and women to think of women as naturally inferior.
3. When there is a wide disparity in these attainments between men and women, this is damaging to the self-respect of all women.
4. All women have a right to self-respect. This right to self-respect justifies the demand for equal press coverage and prize money for women.

Premises (1) and (4) can be quickly accepted. Self-respect is an indispensable factor for both enjoying our lives and living fruitfully with others. And, surely, it is true that individuals are often classified into groups, and that this group affiliation often leads them to be treated in particular ways and also leads them toward certain expectations and goals—hence the call for "role models" by many advocates for affirmative action.

Premises (2) and (3) are much less convincing. Even if the performances of the most capable women in sports in which objective performance measurement is possible (e.g., golf and bowling) are below the performances of the most capable men, we should not conclude that women are naturally inferior. Past cultural and social inequalities may well account for at least some of the disparity. And if women do not attain equal fame and fortune because of this performance disparity and because of market conditions, this need and should not lead anyone to conclude that women are *naturally* inferior as athletes; and it should certainly not lead anyone to conclude that women are inferior *people*.

Reprinted from *Journal of the Philosophy of Sport,* VI, (1979), pp. 67–72. Copyright 1979 by the Philosophic Society for the Study of Sport. Reprinted by permission.

Why should *all* women lose self-respect because of a dearth of female athletic stars or because professional women athletes receive less prize money than men receive? It is only when society teaches us that our self-respect is connected integrally with athletic attainments that this might occur. It is one thing to say that members of disadvantaged groups identify strongly with each other's successes and failures, and quite another to say that unequal financial attainments in athletics will result in a loss of self-respect for all members of the group.

The fact is that we should not respect ourselves because of our own or our group's attainments of fame and fortune in professional sports; we should respect ourselves and those we identify with on the basis of the kind of people we are, the kind of moral lives we lead, and the characters we possess. And the strange part of all this is that English (2: p. 274) seems to recognize this later in her article, for she states, ''I may have a low (and accurate) estimate of myself as a tennis player without losing respect for myself as a person.'' Here she is certainly correct.

All women may have low estimates of themselves as athletes and athletic attainers without losing respect for themselves or their sisters as people. There simply is no necessary connection between a person's athletic attainments and that person's degree of self-respect; and there should not be any empirical connection. Again, there is an empirical connection only if society as a whole or the major social group itself teaches and values athletic performance measured by fame/fortune as an important aspect of the group's or individual's self-respect. But society and the major social groups need not and should not teach this and, hence, there need be and should be no empirical connection between athletic attainments and self-respect.

However, it should be rejoined that even if there is no *necessary* connection between athletic attainments and group self-respect, and even if there *should* be no empirical connection, there still *is* an empirical connection, at least in our society.

But I think that this is false, at least in the case of women. Do all women, or even a majority of women, really lose self-respect because Chris Evert Lloyd does not make as much money as Bjorn Borg; or because Nancy Lopez is in a lower tax bracket than Jack Nicklaus; or, if we look to the past, because Mickey Wright received far less press coverage and prize money than did Arnold Palmer? I would conjecture that the vast majority of women could care less about Chris Evert Lloyd and Nancy Lopez, and that very few even know who Mickey Wright was. I believe that the majority of women do not even take an active interest in female professional sports, much less lose self-respect because of disparities in female and male sports attainments. So, I do not think there is any empirical connection between female athletic attainments and female self-respect.

II

English (2: p. 270) identifies properly the role of self-respect in athletics when she states that ''self-respect (is) to be gained by doing one's best.'' The notion of individual self-respect being connected with effort expended in fulfilling athletic potential is much sounder than the attainment principle (3). Much athletic ability is natural, personally undeserved, and such that we cannot take credit generally for our possession of it. It seems inappropriate and mistaken to allow our self-respect to hinge upon so arbitrary a factor. However, much of what we personally deserve is directly determined by the effort and energy we expend in certain pursuits. That is why we often praise a less gifted competitor who is making the most of her ability and denigrate a more talented performer who seems to be an underachiever.

Athletics, if it is to be a factor in determining our self-respect, should be valued for its basic, and not for its scarce, benefits.

The argument from the right to self-respect does not concentrate on equality of performance between men and women professional sports stars, but rather upon equality in press coverage and financial rewards. To those who believe that fame/fortune in professional sports should be proportionate to performance, it would not seem unjustified to compensate women less, or to allow them less media coverage, if the reason for doing so is not simply that they are women, but rather that they do not perform as well. At least in some sports objective performance is clearly measurable and comparable (e.g., golf, bowling, and skeet shooting); in other sports (e.g., basketball, tennis, and baseball) the top men professionals are held uncontroversially to be significantly superior to the top women. One could argue that the whole point of awarding prize money and lavishing fame is to single out the most proficient athletic performers. To reward equally the best men and women in a sport, when the former are objectively better performers than the latter, is to stray from the correlation of reward and performance.

I am assuming that in any occupation, professional athletics or otherwise, if females demonstrated that they could perform comparably to the top males, then unequal recognition and pay would clearly be justified, unless some special market conditions could be cited. Suppose that women could demonstrate this parity of performance, but were still denied equal recognition and pay. How would they respond? Rather than losing self-respect, I suspect, they would be outraged, angered, and indignant. Women under these circumstances would have no reason to lose self-respect, since they would have proven they were just as capable as comparable males. No one would conclude that women were naturally inferior in any respect. So I think that (2) is false. The connection between thinking women naturally inferior is connected, if it is connected at all, with inferior athletic *performance* and not inferior athletic *fame* and *fortune*. Further, as I have previously tried to indicate, even inferior performance in athletics need not lead everyone to conclude that women are *naturally* inferior athletes; and it should lead no one to conclude that they are inferior human beings.

Let us suppose that women could be shown to be inferior performers to comparable males in *all* occupations in which both groups labored. What would be the response of women in this case if they were recognized and rewarded less? The response might well be a loss of self-respect, since they might be led to conclude (rightly or wrongly) that women were naturally inferior to men in certain important skills. But note two things: (1) This loss of respect would be connected with inferior performance much more than with inferior fame/reward; (2) This loss of self-respect would not occur if women were judged inferior in only one, or a few, occupation(s), since they could point to other occupations in which they equalled or surpassed comparable male performers. So, again, I conclude that premises (2) and (3) are, at best, overstatements, and, at worst, simply false.

III

Recognition and monetary reward for athletics and all occupations are determined to a large extent by market conditions. Public demand for, and attendance at, sports contests determine in large part the money available to be awarded as prizes and the amount of media coverage for the event. But, of course, public interest can be altered by the media; increased media coverage of an event can have an important effect on increasing public demand for these types of events.

Do females have a justified demand for increased media coverage as a means of thwarting their loss of self-respect? Let us consider the case of high fashion models. There are several women who have recently become famous as models: Jean Shrimpton, Twiggy, Margeaux Hemingway, and Farrah Fawcett-Majors, among others. There are no relatively famous male fashion models. Female models at this level receive substantially more pay than male models. Yet this situation has not led all men to lose self-respect for several reasons: (1) Men are not taught that the rewards and recognition of this occupation are an integral part of their group's self-respect; (2) Even if it could be shown that male models perform less capably than their female counterparts—although I do not know how, if at all, the performances of models are measured—men can still point to other, more important, occupations in which they excel. Hence, they need not think themselves naturally inferior people; and (3) Men have been conditioned to regard all aspects of fashion less important to them than to women.

But suppose it were possible via an intensive program of public relations gimmickry to make fashion very important among men. Suppose by focusing a great deal of media coverage upon male fashion that the market could be manipulated and male demand for fashion increased greatly. Men would suddenly demand equal fame and recognition for male fashion models, since the self-respect of all men will be diminished if parity is not attained. However, the performance of male fashion models still lags behind the performance of comparable female models. So additional media and market manipulation is required in order to protect the self-respect of all men, and parity is achieved.

Would we really want all this to occur? I judge that if market and media manipulation in fashion is justified at all it should be concerned with deemphasizing the importance of fashion consciousness among both men and women. An individual's make-up, clothes, and sartorial style should play a very small role in determining one's self-respect. And so too with professional athletics. Instead of manipulating media and market influences to achieve a parity of fame and fortune for female stars whose objectively measured performances are inferior to comparable male stars, we might consider manipulating these influences (if at all) to achieve a deemphasis on professional sports themselves. Again, an individual's and a group's self-respect need not and should not be connected with the monetary attainments of professional athletic stars.

IV

Much of what English says is very perspicacious. The emphasis on athletics should be participation and not spectating; expenditures for big time male high school and college sports ought to be cut in deference to increasing the opportunities for participation for females, non-varsity males, and the community as a whole; equal opportunity for the *basic* benefits of athletics must be available to all; and sports other than those of traditional male domain should be considered valuable (2: p. 275).

However, she is wrong in arguing that the scarce benefits of athletics must be equalized for women in order to maintain the self-respect of all women. She is wrong because: (1) The attainments of top professional athletes need not and should not be a significant factor in determining the self-respect of all women; (2) As an empirical matter of fact, these attainments *are not* an important factor in the way the vast majority of women determine their respect for themselves; (3) Unequal objective performances, *ceteris paribus,* should not be rewarded and recognized equally; (4) Society should be more concerned with teaching us to identify our self-respect with our moral traits and characters, rather than vicarious identification with professional sports stars; and (5) Even if I am incorrect about the truth of (1)–(4), to say that X (women) have a right to Y (self-respect) and that Z (parity in attainments for female sports stars) is necessary for Y, it does not follow that X have a right to Z or a justified claim to Z.

To say that someone has a right to life and right to privacy, and to establish that certain things are necessary for that someone to continue living or continue to have privacy, does not establish that the person has a right or justified claim to these certain things.[1] Among other considerations, some of these necessary things may require that others perform supererogatory acts, and no one has a *right* that others perform supererogatory acts for her. Parity for female sports stars in terms of financial attainments may well require supererogatory acts on the part of society, especially in view of the fact that these stars have not demonstrated parity in terms of objectively measured performance.

There may be other arguments that can be advanced in support of equalizing the scarce benefits of professional sports (e.g., as *compensation* for past cultural and social deprivations); I suspect that these would not be successful. Finally, it seems clear that English's argument from the right to self-respect fails, or so I am claiming.

Notes

1. For clarification of this point and related notions see my "Negative Duties, Positive Duties, and Rights" (1).

Bibliography

1. Belliotti, Raymond A. "Negative Duties, Positive Duties, and Rights." *The Southern Journal of Philosophy,* XVI (1978), 581–588.
2. English, Jane. "Sex Equality in Sports." *Philosophy and Public Affairs,* VII (1978), 269–277.

Human Equality in Sports

PETER S. WENZ

Issues of social justice are among the most intellectually challenging to both the ethicist and philosopher of law, especially when there appear to be permanent, biologically determined differences of ability and potential among the people and between the groups for whom justice is sought. Such is the case between men and women in the realm of sports. The problem of providing justice in this area has been the topic of popular magazine articles,[1] federal[2] and state[3] legislation, adjudication[4] and philosophical contemplation.[5] But the heart of the matter has yet to be discussed. I will attempt to do this by first reviewing some of the current issues in this area, then exploring the relationship between the use and exchange values of athletic participation, and finally proposing a radical solution which is defended on utilitarian, egalitarian and Rawlsian ethical grounds. The result will be an approach to promoting social justice and equality amongst biologically diverse groups which may be applicable beyond the area of sports.

Contemporary Issues

One of the first issues concerning sex equality in sports was, and still is, monetary. Traditionally, schools have spent much more money on men's than on women's athletic programs. Schools tended to fund a greater number of men's sports in

the first place. They also went to the expense of entering more men's than women's teams in interscholastic competition, and gave members of these teams such extra benefits as free laundry service and enlarged coaching staffs. Finally, "men's" sports—those traditionally reserved for male competition, especially football—are the most capital intensive in terms of both the equipment needed to play the game and the facilities needed to accommodate spectator interest. The unsurprising result of these disparities is that women and men were not, and for the most part still are not, afforded equal athletic opportunities at school.

One response to this situation is to attack the monetary issue directly, insist that women's athletic programs be funded at levels equal to men's. But it is unclear what this might mean. If it means that all of the same sports are to be funded for both men and women, and at the same level, there is a problem. One result of sex discrimination in the past is that women have been convinced to take less seriously the desirability and even the possibility of developing their own athletic abilities. One of the worst aspects of social inequality is the internalization of their inferior status on the part of disadvantaged people. The problem this poses for the equal funding of athletics is that there are at present likely to be fewer women than men interested in spending many after-school hours engaged in athletics. So, equal funding of women and men would likely result in greater per capita expenditures for women than men. This may be viewed as unjust.

Also, women and men have been tracked into many different sports, women into field hockey

First published in *The Philosophical Forum*, Volume XII, Number 3, Spring 1981, pp. 238–250. Reprinted by permission.

and softball and men into football and baseball, for example. This, too, is most likely reflected in current patterns of participation preferences among men and women so that even if men's and women's programs were funded equally, whether on a per-team or per-capita basis (it's not obvious which it should be), the sports funded would still not be identical. This would cause three difficulties for effecting sex equality in sports. First, the traditionally male sports are more capital intensive, especially when you include the facilities needed to accommodate spectator interest. One might try to circumvent this problem by claiming that because the school stadium is used by women for field hockey as well as by men for football, it is not a football stadium. The capital investment it represents should not, therefore, be attributed to men's as opposed to women's athletics. But this is a sham. The stands could be much smaller and cheaper if designed to accommodate only the number of spectators wanting to see women's field hockey.

The second problem is also a result of disproportionate spectator interest in men's rather than women's athletic competition. If funding is the issue, and that was the issue with which we began, spectator interest in men's athletics can be translated into gate receipts which, it might be argued, could justifiably be spent disproportionately on those sports generating the funds. Rawls' theory of justice might be invoked, improperly I hope later to show, in support of such a position. The disadvantaged—women's field hockey—are treated justly when the advantaged make additional gains, so long as the disadvantaged also gain in the process. So, increased funding of the football program in response to its gate receipts would seem justified, if this was a device used to generate more money for athletics generally, including women's field hockey.

However, further emphasis on traditionally popular men's athletic programs exacerbates the problem of disproportionate spectator interest in men's athletics generally. This is troublesome not only because it allows the gate receipt argument

to be used to justify even greater funding for football (a second round of the same reasoning), but also because it reinforces the pressure in our culture for women to discount their athletic abilities. If the rest of society is interested primarily in men's athletics, perhaps women athletes, and potential athletes should be also. Thus, the rich get richer and the poor get pom poms. For this reason, Rawls, who values self-respect preeminently, would probably abjure the view that increased funding of men's sports is justified when some of the increased gate receipts are given to women's athletics.

In sum, fostering sex equality in sports through changed funding patterns is problematic at best. In some cases it is not clear which changes would be just and which unjust. Finally, funding alone cannot address the problems of motivation, self-concept and self-respect among women that are the legacy of past injustices. This is apparent from the fact that equal funding of men's and women's athletic programs is a ''separate but equal'' position. It is now normally considered unjustified when applied to different races because separate is considered inherently unequal when applied to groups between whom there is a history in the dominant culture of invidious contrast. Because there is just such a history in the dominant culture concerning men and women's athletics, separate athletic programs for men and women might be inherently unequal. This is illustrated concretely and poignantly by cases of women wanting to compete on men's athletic teams for the increased prestige and competition this would allow.[6]

It might appear, then, that altered funding patterns could be supplemented or replaced altogether by the integration of athletics. The difficulty is that for many sports, including most of those popular in the United States, the biological differences between men and women give men a statistical advantage. These sports include strength and speed and often height and weight among the traits helpful for successful competition. Although some women are stronger, faster, taller and heavier than some men, on the average men are stronger, faster, taller and heavier than women. So some proponents of women's athletics fear that sex-integrated athletic programs will result in even fewer women participants and less funding for and concentration upon the development of women athletes.[7]

In short, given all the variables present in the current situation, the optimal course of action is neither obvious nor agreed upon.

Use Value and Exchange Value in Sports

One philosophic strategy for approaching such situations is the elaboration of an ideal state of affairs which, were it to be realized, would constitute a solution to the problem. The solution is often ideal in the sense that no one knows how its realization might be effectively promoted; aspects of the society which create the problem in the first place might render impractical even *attempts* to directly effect the ideal's realization. Nevertheless, the ideal has an important function. As various policies which are amenable to practical implementation are reviewed and considered, those which would move the society toward the ideal might be preferred to those with an opposite or neutral tendency.

The ideal in this case can be explained by applying to sports Adam Smith's distinction between value in use and value in exchange.[8] The exchange value of a sport to an individual is the fame and fortune he or she derives from participating in that sport. Such rewards result from, but are extrinsic to the athletic activity in question. The activity itself, the rules in accordance with which it is carried out, the physical qualities and interpersonal cooperation it calls for and so forth, could all be exactly the same whether or not the rewards of fame and fortune are offered for participation. This is because fame and fortune result not from the activity itself, but from the interest others show in one's participation. This interest results in ad-

miration for the participant and a willingness to monetarily compensate him or her for participating. Someone deriving fame and fortune by participating in a sport under these conditions exchanges his or her participation for these other goods. Thus, they constitute the exchange value for that individual of participating in that sport.

The use value of a sport to an individual, by contrast, is the value to that individual which is intrinsic to his or her participation in that sport. It is dependent on the formal rules of the game, the mores in accordance with which it is played, the qualities of physical coordination and interpersonal cooperation it calls for, and its competitive nature. The values resulting from participation normally include development of motor skills and improvement of bodily health, as well as the enhancement of self-esteem which results from overcoming difficulties. In addition, participation can be character building, teaching the individual to accept criticism, be a good winner and a good loser and, in team sports, a cooperative person. Finally, participation can be fun. Because these goods, which constitute the use value of a sport to a given individual, do not depend on rewards offered by others, they are intrinsic rather than extrinsic to the athletic endeavor.

Though there are exceptions, it will be assumed here that the use value of most sports for most people who voluntarily participate in them is positive. Possible exceptions might include an extremely dangerous sport, like hang-gliding, or moto-cross competition for an epileptic. Generally, however, the use value of voluntary participation is positive.

The aggregate use value of a sport is the total use value of that sport to individuals in a society over a given period of time, such as a year. It is the sum of the sport's use values to all individuals in that society who participated in that sport during that time period. Since the use value of athletics is assumed to be generally positive, the aggregate use value is positively related to the number of people and the time spent by those people participating in that sport during that time period.

The aggregate exchange value of a sport is the total fame and fortune accruing to participating individuals due to this participation. It is positively related to the spectator interest in that sport, because fame and fortune accrue to participants only when others care enough to witness the sport being played that they offer these rewards to participants.

The relationship between the aggregate use and aggregate exchange values of a sport, that is, between the population's interest in playing and watching it, is the topic of the remainder of this section. Generally, people who enjoy participating in a sport come to enjoy watching others play. Having played the sport themselves they can empathize, kinesthetically in some cases, with the players they are watching. Spectators can appreciate, admire and enjoy the players' skills when they have, by playing the sport themselves, attempted to develop and exercise those same skills. They can also better understand and therefore appreciate player strategy and team cooperation if they have played the sport themselves. For all these reasons, it is more likely that someone who has played basketball but not hockey will prefer watching basketball to hockey on television when both are available. Thus, it seems that participation in a sport, its (aggregate) use value in a given population, increases spectator interest and therewith the (aggregate) exchange value of the services of excellent players.

It is doubtful, however, that watching and playing a sport are mutually supporting. I shall argue in the remainder of the section that whereas playing increases watching, watching tends to depress rather than increase the level of participation. I call this the inverse relationship thesis (IRT). Stated fully the thesis is that, all other things being equal, an increase in the use value of a sport causes an increase in its exchange value. But its increased exchange value tends to depress its use value. In this causal direction the use and exchange values are inversely relational. This means that any conditions which cause an increase in the use value of a sport will cause a greater such increase if other conditions operate to prevent the exchange value from increasing, as well. More important, it also

means that any conditions which cause a decrease in a sport exchange value will, other things being equal, cause an increase in its use value.

This inverse relationship thesis (IRT) is central to the argument of this paper. Nevertheless, I will not claim to have demonstrated its truth in the arguments which follow. Considerable investigation by social scientists is required for its refutation or confirmation. I do claim, however, that the arguments which follow in this section make the IRT exceedingly plausible, and that subsequent arguments from it to further conclusions demonstrate its importance to any consideration of equality in sports.

The first argument for the IRT is that watching can serve as a vicarious outlet for urges to participate, thereby dissipating those urges before they can reach the level at which they would be acted upon. Thus, someone who sometimes plays basketball may find it easier to forego playing if he or she can watch others play. This is analogous to the claim, made by those who argue against legal restrictions on the availability of pornography for adults. They claim that watching pornography, rather than inciting people to sex crimes, dissipates the urge to commit such crimes, because it affords people vicarious sexual involvement which serves to replace actual involvement. The evidence gathered to support this claim indirectly favors the view that watching a sport decreases the level of participation.

The same view is supported by a very different consideration. The exchange value of an individual's athletic endeavors is generally directly related to his or her level of proficiency. The function is not linear, of course, but it is generally true that the exchange value increases with proficiency. A society in which the exchange value of participation for those who are proficient is very high is a society in which there is greater spectator interest in that sport. It is also one in which the level of proficiency that becomes normative is very high. As people increasingly watch something done with great proficiency, they tend to think it normal that the activity in question be carried on at that level of proficiency. But as the normative level of proficiency increases beyond what most people are capable of attaining, people are discouraged from participating. Lacking respect for the level of their own attainment, participation is ego-damaging. Conversely, as the norms of proficiency are increasingly established by an individual for himself or herself, or by that individual's peers, participation is encouraged and can be expected to increase. Thus, the exchange value of participating in a given sport in a given society probably varies inversely with its use value.

Another consideration is that as the exchange value, and so the level of spectator interest in a sport, increases, the organization of participation in that sport tends to become increasingly institutionalized. The reason for this is not hard to find. Spectator interest can be translated into a market demand. In a profit-minded society, people tend to organize themselves and others so as to meet the market demand and gain monetary rewards. What is more, the institutional organization of the sport does not stay at the professional level. It is replicated at lower levels. Professional baseball results ultimately in Little League. Football and basketball are played interscholastically in organized leagues at the grade school level.

It might seem that such organization and institutionalization of a sport might increase its aggregate use value in society as schools and other organizations prompt children to join athletic institutions (organized teams and leagues). The predominant tendency, however, is probably just the opposite. Institutionalized sports notoriously discriminate in favor of the most athletically talented individuals. Development of skills of the less talented is often ignored. The norms of performance of the more talented become normative for the group as a whole, with the consequence that the less talented are not only ignored but dispirited. The net effect of the institutionalization of sports that results from emphasis on its exchange value is therefore predominantly to discourage rather than encourage widespread participation, to decrease rather than increase its aggregate use value in society.

In sum, three reasons have been advanced to support the inverse relationship thesis, the conten-tion that the aggregate use value of a sport ordinarily decreases with an increase in its aggregate exchange value: (1) Watching a sport can serve as a vicarious outlet which dissipates urges to participate. (2) The norms of excellence increase with a sport's exchange value, discouraging the participation of the less talented. And, (3) as the exchange value increases the sport is increasingly institutionalized, which also puts a premium on talent and discourages the participation of others.

Some examples may be helpful at this point. It is commonly thought, and I have no reason to doubt, that a larger percentage of the American population played baseball in the earlier part of the century than at present. Its professionalization and institutionalization have increased its aggregate exchange value while decreasing its aggregate use value. Jogging, by contrast, is not very institutionalized and has very little exchange value at present. It is not much of a spectator sport. People set norms of proficiency for themselves and engage in the activity informally. Its exchange value is low and its use value high. It is what might be called a folk-sport.

Sports that might seem to constitute counterexamples are golf and tennis. Their use and exchange values have increased simultaneously in recent years, in direct rather than inverse relation to one another. These are sports in which participation is found particularly enjoyable by a large percentage of the people in our culture who are introduced to them. But until recently participation in them was reserved for the relatively wealthy primarily because of the expense, much as is still the case with equestrian events. A major proximate cause of their increased use value, I submit, has been the decreased expense of participating in them.

Since World War II, the percentage of the average family's income spent on food and housing has declined somewhat, leaving more disposable income for recreation of all sorts. More important, the expansion of the public sector beginning with the New Deal has manifested itself in public works projects which include public recreation facilities, among them, tennis courts and golf courses. People are paying for these facilities with their taxes, diminishing considerably the differential cost of participation versus non-participation. In addition, tennis was first played on grass, which is very difficult to maintain at the required quality level, then on clay, which also requires considerable maintenance. Now, most people play on asphalt, which is much cheaper to maintain. The developing technology of lawn care has made golf course maintenance less expensive also, though the change is less dramatic here. Those developments, I believe, are primarily responsible for the increased use value of golf and tennis. The availability of tennis and golf as spectator sports, especially on television, is a consequence, not a cause of their increased use value. This is consistent with the IRT.

To see this, let us conduct a thought experiment. Imagine a dramatic increase of television time devoted to equestrian events. If the cost of participating remained about the same, so, I believe, would participation. Now imagine instead a dramatic decrease in that cost. Participation would increase dramatically even in the absence of increased television coverage. Then, of course, responding to increased participation, television coverage would follow suit. This kind of media response is currently occurring in the case of racquet ball. In sum, just as media coverage would not be necessary for people to increase their participation in equestrian events were their expense dramatically reduced, so media coverage was not necessary for the increased use values of tennis and golf.

Finally, consider the case of soccer. It is not a folk-sport in this country, so its use value is so low that its professionalization and institutionalization can increase that value. (Goodness knows why this is happening. Perhaps it is spurred on by the same folks who want us to think metric, namely, multinational corporations. I suppose they want us to play soccer so that everyone will be able to get along at international-employee picnics. These are only conjectures, of course.) The point is that the use value of sports is great only in folk-sports anyway. Institutionalization holds the level of participation in any sport below that of a folk-sport. So high use value cannot be attained through institutionalization. High use value in a sport occurs only when the culture is allowed to take up its own folk-sports, spurred on by the usual forces involved in cultural evolution. In our country this does involve commercialism, and producers of jogging shoes and racquetball racquets have been doing an excellent job of late.

I hope at this point to have made the IRT very plausible. The important part of the thesis is that, other things being equal, a decrease in exchange value will *ordinarily* cause an increase in use value. The qualification "ordinarily" is included because absolute universality is not essential. Only the strong predominance of the tendency for decreased exchange values to increase use values is necessary. The usefulness of the IRT for subsequent arguments will not be diminished if an exceptional sport is found not to conform to it. Having made the qualification, I will neglect its reiteration.

Ethical Arguments

Because the exchange value of athletic participation includes esteem from others, it can probably never be reduced to zero. Nor would it be desirable to do so. I will argue, however, that eliminating the *major* source of exchange value, financial rewards for athletic participation, is desirable. What is more, the desirability can be deduced from egalitarianism, John Rawls' theory of justice and the most popular forms of utilitarianism when they are combined with the IRT.

Consider first the ethical view that average utility ought to be maximized. Imagine a society in which, like our own at this time, the monetary aspect of the exchange value of athletic participation is very great for the exceptionally gifted athlete. Because those who reap these scarce benefits are very few, a matter of thousands in a society of millions, these benefits do not constitute much of the utility in the society as a whole. This is especially the case because those exchanging their participation in athletics for really large monetary rewards constitute only a small fraction of those thousands receiving any monetary rewards at all. Consequently, the loss of this aspect of the exchange value of sports in society would, taken by itself, have a minute effect upon the average level of utility in the society as a whole. More important from the perspective of average utility would be the effect on spectators. People are spectators, presumably, because they enjoy watching sports. If people are prevented from reaping monetary rewards from athletic participation, it would seem that there would be less athletic competition for would-be spectators to watch, hence a considerable drop in average utility.

If the exchange and use values of athletic participation are inversely related, however, such a drop in average utility would almost surely not occur. The general level of proficiency among athletes whose play is being watched would, on the whole, be drastically reduced. But it is not at all clear that one's enjoyment as a spectator is primarily or even very largely a function of the level of proficiency of the athletes being watched. A close contest, personal acquaintance with the contestants and personal presence at the site of competition are each as significant a determinant of spectator enjoyment as is the level of the contestants' proficiency. And two of these would be increased, for those who chose to be spectators, if athletes were not paid for their participation. By drastically reducing the exchange value of sports, the use value would be greatly increased. This means that many more people would be playing more of the time in more locations. Those who chose to be spectators would more often be able to witness athletic events in person because such events would more often be taking place nearby and the cost of admission would be little (to cover maintenance of the grounds, for example) if anything. And since more people would be participating in athletics, it would more often be possible to view contests among people with whom the spectator is personally acquainted.

So there is no reason to suppose that the enjoyment of those who chose to be spectators would be diminished if athletes were not paid.

It is the aggregate of spectator enjoyment which would be reduced, not the average. It would be reduced because fewer people would be spectators as more, if use value is inversely related to exchange value, voluntarily askew watching in favor of participating. But if, as I have argued, sporting events would be as available and enjoyable for spectators as at present, the predominance of participation would signal that people gain even more enjoyment from participation. This would represent a broad based net gain in utility that would, because it affects so many people, have a greater effect on average utility than all of the preceding considerations.

In sum, the loss of utility to professional athletes would be more than compensated for by the gain in utility on the part of the large proportion of the population who would voluntarily exchange watching for participating.[9] Those who continued to watch would at worst be affected neutrally. So, if the inverse proportionality thesis is correct, the proponent of maximizing average utility should adopt the ideal of a society in which athletes are debarred from being paid for their athletic participation.

Those who, like Richard Brandt and Nicholas Rescher, believe that utilitarian considerations should be combined with egalitarian considerations have a stronger reason for reaching the same conclusion. For this is a case in which utility and equality go hand-in-hand. The gain in utility is broad-based. It accrues to the large number of people who voluntarily exchange watching for participating. The loss in utility, besides being smaller than the gain, includes the loss to those making substantial sums from their athletic participation. There is thus a leveling effect. The relative have-nots gain and the haves lose.

Rawls has an even stronger reason for adopting the ideal of a society in which athletics is de-professionalized. An example will make this clear. Rawls is interested in maximizing the level of welfare of the representative individual from society's least advantaged group. Welfare is gauged in terms of what he calls primary goods, wealth, power, liberty and, importantly self-respect. Suppose, then, that we group people by sex. (We could get the same results grouping people by age, size or weight.) Suppose, further, that the aggregate of use value and of exchange value accruing to women from sports is less than the corresponding values accruing to men. Finally, suppose that the exchange value of athletic participation for exceptionally gifted individuals in the society is great. These suggestions probably accord well with the actual situation in our society at this time. But this is not essential since the same conclusion can be drawn from plausible alternate assumptions.

On these suppositions women are the worse off group. De-professionalizing sports would result in a greater loss of wealth to men than to women because men have more to lose. But if the inverse relationship thesis, and the accompanying utilitarian calculations presented above are correct, utility would be increased by de-professionalization, even for men. The loss to male professional athletes would be more than compensated for by the gain to many more other men in terms of the use value of sports. Rawls' particular emphasis on the primary good of self-respect and his employment of what he calls the Aristotelian Principle both serve to strengthen this conclusion. For the loss among men would be primarily financial, whereas the gain would be, through greater athletic participation, in the realms of self-confidence and self-respect, as these come, in accordance with the Aristotelian Principle, from progressive mastery of skills and development of talents.

A fortiori, the position of women would be improved by the de-professionalization of athletics. They have less to lose financially and more to gain in terms of self-confidence and self-respect. So if Rawls advocates maximizing primary values among the most deprived group, and women are the most deprived group (when we group by sex), then he should advocate the de-professionalization of athletics.

The same conclusion would follow were the ag-

gregate exchange value of women's athletic participation equal to that of men. In such a case women would have as much to lose financially as men from de-professionalization. But they would still have more to gain than men in terms of the self-respect that comes from the use value of sports. And even men gain more than they lose by de-professionalization. So women would still be the most deprived group whose accumulation of primary goods would be maximized by banning financial rewards for athletic participation. Like men, they would gain more in self-respect than they lost financially. Such a ban would, therefore, still follow from Rawl's theory when combined with the inverse relationship thesis.

Conclusion

In sum, if the inverse relationship thesis is correct, the de-professionalization of sports is ethically mandatory from the utilitarian, egalitarian and Rawlsian ethical perspectives. Two conclusions follow from this. First, empirical, social scientific research designed to test the IRT is in order. Second, if the IRT is correct, sex equality in sports is a by-product of and impossible without the more general human equality in sports that results from an emphasis on use over exchange values. This prompts, without in any way confirming, the following conjectural generalization concerning social equality between members of groups which are, as groups, biologically unequal. The equality of the groups can be approached only as a general egalitarianism among individuals, taken as individuals, is approached through a concentration on use rather than exchange values.

Sangamon State University

Notes

1. Rose De Wolf, ''The Battle for Good Teams,'' *Women Sports,* I (July 1974), pp. 61-63; in *Sex Equality* ed. Jane English

(Prentice-Hall, 1977), pp. 231–238.

Ellen Weber, "Boys and Girls Together: The Coed Team Controversy," *Women Sports,* I (September, 1974), pp. 53–55.

Brenda Fasteau, "Giving Women a Sporting Chance," *Ms. Magazine,* July, 1973.

Ann Crittenden Scott, "Closing the Muscle Gap," *Ms. Magazine,* September, 1974, pp. 49–55, 89.

Mariann Pogge, "From Cheerleader to Competitor," *Update,* Fall, 1978, pp. 15–18.

2. Title IX of the *1964 Civil Rights Act* as amended 42 U.S.

3. Michigan, Connecticut, New Jersey, Indiana, Minnesota and Nebraska have statutes providing for the integration of non-contact sports at the high school level.

4. *Hollander v. Connecticut Interstate Athletic Conference,* Superior Court of New Haven Co., Conn., March 29, 1971.

Haas v. South Bend Community School Corp., 289 N.E. 2d 495 (Ind. 1972).

Bucha v. Illinois High School Association, 351 F. Supp. 69 (N.D. Ill. 1972).

N.O.W. Essex County Chapter v. Little League Baseball, 127 N.J. Superior, 22, 318A. 2d, 33 (1974).

5. Jane English, "Sex Equality in Sports," *Philosophy and Public Affairs,* VII (Spring, 1978).

6. De Wolf, pp. 232 ff.

7. De Wolf, p. 235.

8. This is similar but not identical to Jane English's distinction between the basic and scarce benefits of sports.

9. More remote effects can be ignored because they are so problematic and might, for that reason, as likely favor one side as another. Also, those which can be counted on, like the losses to promoters of professional athletics, lawyers for professional athletes and others dependent on professional athletics for a living, will largely be matched by gains for those who produce the athletic equipment used by increasing numbers of participants.

Women and Masculine Sports

B.C. POSTOW

Supporters of the antiandrogynist, or "vive la difference," ideal of gender identification may understandably find encouragement and reassurance in the contemplation of sports. Sports have traditionally been regarded as an unequivocally masculine endeavor—a training ground for manly skills and attitudes. Nature itself seems to support the antiandrogynist position, for in sports anatomical differences between men and women are undeniably relevant, giving men a very considerable statistical superiority over women. I shall investigate the various senses in which sports may plausibly be called masculine, and I shall argue that the fact that sports do qualify as masculine in these senses yields no support to the antiandrogynist ideal. The antiandrogynist position holds that people ought to maintain a distinction between the masculine and the feminine either to conform to some good natural order or to foster and preserve distinct gender identities for reasons of mental health or social welfare. My investigation will reveal no natural order which is *prima facie* worthy of efforts for its preservation. I shall also argue against the view that the desirability of preserving distinct gender identities justifies maintaining any sort of distinction between men's and women's sports (e.g., by subtly discouraging women's participation, or even by maintaining sex segregation in teams). I shall also argue, on the other hand, that the natural male advantage in most sports must be acknowledged and dealt with in a way not pro-

vided for within well-known androgynist ideals of individual excellence.

Joyce Trebilcot (9: pp. 71–72) distinguishes between two androgynist ideals: monoandrogynism, or *M* for short, and polyandrogynism, or *P* for short. According to *M,* each individual should develop both traditionally masculine and traditionally feminine personality traits and should engage in both traditionally masculine and traditionally feminine activities. According to *P,* it is desirable for any individual who is inclined to do so to conform to the ideal approved by *M,* but it is equally desirable for an individual who is inclined to do so to develop only "masculine" or only "feminine" personality traits and to engage only in "masculine" or only in "feminine" activities. With respect to women and sports, *M* would naturally lead us to believe that it is desirable for women to participate in "masculine" sports; *P* would naturally lead us to believe that it is equally desirable for women to participate in "masculine" sports as not to participate in them. Both *M* and *P* seem to lead us astray here because they are limited to ideals of individual excellence and do not deal with the larger social reality. I shall argue that unlike most activities, some sports are masculine[1] in a sense that I shall call masculine$_d$, which does give women a moral reason *not* to support or participate in them.

First, I will define the senses in which sports may be called masculine and then inquire whether the fact that a sport is masculine in any of these senses provides a reason for women not to engage in it or to engage in it differently or separately from men. At least four different features or clus-

Reprinted from *Journal of the Philosophy of Sport,* VII, (1980), pp. 51–58. Copyright 1981 by the Philosophic Society for the Study of Sport. Reprinted by permission.

ters of features of a sport might reasonably be referred to in calling a sport masculine. One such cluster of features was isolated by Eleanor Metheny, who analyzed those sports (e.g., wrestling, weight-lifting, long-distance running, and most team sports) from which Olympic rules have excluded women. She lists these features as follows:

An attempt to physically subdue the opponent by bodily contact

Direct application of bodily force to some heavy object

Attempt to project the body into or through space over long distances

Cooperative face-to-face opposition in situations in which some body contact may occur. (7: p. 49)

Perhaps these features are believed to be especially appropriate physical expressions of aggression, power, and effectiveness, which are seen as especially masculine. Whatever the explanation, however, it does seem that a native speaker would be likely to call sports which possess these features masculine or even supermasculine, although sports may also be characterized as masculine on other grounds. Metheny has shown that some features which identify a sport as masculine are characterizable solely in terms of the behavior required of participants by the rules of the game. To determine whether a sport has these features, one should refer to the rules of the game rather than to the characteristic attitudes of participants or to the societal function served by the sport. Any sport requiring the behavior depicted by Metheny's list or some similar list[2], then, will be called masculine$_a$.

A second cluster of features which may prompt people to call a sport masculine concerns the attitude with which the sport is characteristically played and which is thought to be necessary for playing the sport well. This attitude includes "aggressiveness, competitive spirit, stamina, and discipline" all focused on winning or setting rec-

ords.[3] Devotion to a team is also a contributing factor. These elements of attitude constitute a "mode which is understood to conform to an image of masculinity no less strong in contemporary America than in ancient Greece" (6: pp. 184; 187). Sports which are characteristically played in this mode and which it is commonly thought must be played this way to be played well, will be called masculine$_b$ sports. All sports may be masculine$_b$ to a greater or lesser degree, but sports such as football, in which approved aggressiveness includes a readiness to injure an opponent, seem to qualify as masculine$_b$ to an especially high degree.

Another feature which may be thought to qualify a sport as masculine is its use as a vehicle of masculine gender identification. A sport will be termed masculine$_c$ if participation in it in our society functions to engender or reinforce a feeling of identity and solidarity with men as distinct from women. Baseball and football are two sports which have traditionally served this function in our society, largely by being designated as activities especially appropriate for boys and men and inappropriate or questionably appropriate for girls and women. Swimming and volleyball would not qualify as masculine$_c$ sports.

Of course, masculine$_b$ sports and masculine$_c$ sports are somewhat related in that masculine$_b$ sports are by definition well suited to socialize males in accordance with the particular ideal of masculine gender identity embodied in the masculine$_b$ attitudinal mode. Nevertheless, an activity which is masculine$_b$ to the highest degree would fail to be masculine$_c$ if it were approved for women and men equally and without role differentiation.[4] Such a sport would socialize both women and men in accordance with the masculine$_b$ attitudinal mode, but it would not socialize men as a group distinct from women. Little League baseball has traditionally been masculine$_c$, but sex-integrated Little League baseball should cease to be masculine$_c$ even if it remains masculine$_b$.

Another reason for which sports may be thought masculine is their definition of athletic excellence in terms of developed capacities, such as strength and speed, in which men naturally have a considerable statistical advantage over women. A sport will be called masculine$_d$, then, if it is such that due to biological factors, most men are significantly better at it than most women, and the best athletes in it are men. Examples of masculine$_d$ sports are football, baseball, basketball, and tennis, which strongly emphasize upper-body strength (10: p. 96). Not all sports are masculine$_d$. On the balance beam, "small size, flexibility and low center of gravity combine to give women the kind of natural hegemony that men enjoy in football" (5: p. 275), and in long-distance swimming women have the natural advantages of long-term endurance, buoyancy, insulation, and narrow shoulders (10: p. 98). Still, the vast majority of our sports, including the most prestigious ones, are masculine$_d$.

Does the fact that a sport is masculine in any of the senses explained above provide a moral reason for women not to engage in it or to engage in it differently or separately from men? The features which make a sport masculine$_a$ seem generally to be morally neutral,[5] and insofar as they are neutral, I take it to be uncontroversial that these features per se provide no moral grounds for women to observe any limitations on participation, or to participate separately from men. Of course, masculine$_a$ sports are generally also masculine$_d$[6]; this fact is arguably grounds for sex segregation and will be subsequently dealt with.

In my opinion, there is nothing intrinsically immoral in participating in masculine$_b$ sports in a masculine$_b$ way, but if there is a superior ideal, there is a moral reason to pursue that ideal rather than the masculine$_b$ ideal. Mary Duquin (4: pp. 101–102) depicts a superior ideal of sport which combines instrumental and expressive attitudes and behavior. In ideal sport, "the participant feels a sense of fulfillment when participating, as well as when winning. She feels joy, strength, thrill, competence and control when sporting whether in practice or competition. She performs ethically, drawing her ethics from her own self-conscience. . . . She performs with confidence and comradeship." Now, all masculine$_b$ sports seem capable

of being played in a nonmasculine$_b$ way.[7] Therefore, those with moral objections to the masculine$_b$ attitudinal mode have no reason to refrain from masculine$_b$ sports, but only (at most) to refrain from participation with those who subscribe to that ideal. This might well preclude participation in professional or even subsidized athletics,[8] but it need not preclude mixed teams of men and women, for not all men subscribe to the masculine$_b$ ideal. Nothing that has been said supports the antiandrogynist position, for women have not been shown to have any less right than men to play masculine$_b$ sports in a masculine$_b$ way against men. Insofar as Duquin's ideal is accepted as superior to the masculine$_b$ ideal, however, M must be preferred to P, for P would approve of the masculine$_b$ ideal equally with Duquin's ideal.

I shall assume for the sake of argument the positive value of masculine orientation and solidarity for males. It may be thought that women should refrain from participating in masculine$_c$ sports, or at least be relegated to second-class status in them, for we have seen that a sport ceases to be masculine$_c$ if women are fully integrated in it. But sport is not the only way to forge masculine orientation and solidarity,[9] and exclusion from the dominant sport culture is directly and indirectly detrimental to women in many ways.[10] Thus, even if masculine orientation and solidarity for males are of undoubted net value, women would betray their own dignity as agents with rights as important as those of men by accepting limitations on participation or second-class status for the purpose of preserving popular sports as masculine$_c$ male preserves. Those who disagree with me may object that sport is not, as I have alleged, merely one of many possible vehicles of masculine orientation in our society. Arnold R. Beisser (2: pp. 194–195) argues that sport's emphasis on strength, together with its separation of male from female roles, makes it uniquely suited to relieve the tensions created by the facts that men have lost much of their fatherly authority and their status of sole breadwinner and that male strength is almost obsolete, even though "the cultural expectations of masculinity have remained fixed as they were in pioneer days." Notice, however, that the function of sport to which Beisser is here drawing our attention is not merely the formation or reinforcement of masculine gender identity, but rather the relief of a tension generated by the dissonance between reality and the ideology of "pioneer days" that men deserve respect and authority because of their physical strength. Insofar as sports serve as a safety valve to relieve the pressure caused by the dissonance between this ideology and reality, they help to preserve the ideology. Because this ideology is patently unworthy of preservation, Beisser's observation cannot be used to show that the fact that sports are masculine$_c$ is a good reason for women to refrain from participation in them or to accept second-class status in them.

As I indicated at the beginning of the paper, the fact that a sport is masculine$_d$ does, I think, provide some reason for women not to support or engage in it. The number and prestige of sports in which men have a natural statistical superiority to women, together with the virtual absence of sports in which women are naturally superior, help perpetuate an image of general female inferiority which we have a moral reason to undermine. An obvious way to undermine it is to increase the number and prestige of sports in which women have a natural statistical superiority to men or at least are not naturally inferior. Thus, there is reason, at least where this can be done without undue personal sacrifice, for women to withdraw energy and support from masculine$_d$ sports and to turn instead toward other sports—preferably ones in which women naturally excel. It seems clear, however, that women who enjoy or are well-suited to masculine$_d$ sports are not obligated to abstain from them in order to popularize sports in which women excel, for that end can be achieved without such sacrifices.

My moral intuitions become less definite when we turn to a problem of current interest raised in school athletics by the male advantage in masculine sports. It seems unfair to bar from men's teams those women who can make the grade, for this would deny those women equality of opportunity to compete, defined as freedom from legal or other socially imposed restrictions. But if women should be free to compete against men, then it seems that men should also be free to compete against women. In masculine$_d$ sports, allowing men to compete against women would expose women to a drastically reduced probability of receiving the moderately scarce athletic resources, such as access to facilities and coaching, that go with making a team. This too seems unfair. Equality of opportunity qua freedom from socially imposed restrictions on one's ability to compete seems to work against equality of opportunity qua probability, given the same level of effort, of actually receiving the benefits of the sport. The first kind of equality of opportunity seems required by the ideal of fair competition; the second kind of equality of opportunity seems required by the students' prima facie equal rights to what Jane English (5: p. 270) calls the basic benefits of sports, such as health and fun. A scheme supported by Richard Alan Rubin that each sport should have three independent teams offers a possible compromise. The varsity team "would consist of the best male and female athletes. . . . The remaining two teams would consist of athletes of lesser ability and would be separated by sex" (8: p. 566). In Rubin's scheme, women interested in participating on a team in a masculine$_d$ sport would still have roughly half as much probability of making some team (i.e., either varsity or second string) as men have, because men would make up all or almost all of the varsity and all of the men's team, whereas women would be almost exclusively confined to the women's team. This might be acceptable, however, if Rubin is right that "virtually everyone interested would be able to compete." Preserving one team for women and one for men would, at any rate, avoid the drastic reduction in women's chances of participating that would result from having only mixed teams. Rubin's scheme also avoids the drastic denial of formal equality of competitive opportunity for men that would result if a team were reserved for women but not for men. Of course, one might wish to strike the compromise differently, sacrificing men's rights to formal equality of opportunity in favor of women's rights to equal probability of receiving the benefits of sports. This could be done by having only one second string team which either barred men completely or put a quota on them.

A possible problem with both these compromise schemes is that they are probably illegal under the ERA (8: pp. 573–574).[11] Another objectionable feature is that they tie probability of receiving the basic benefits of a sport to natural aptitude. Men and women with unsuitable physiques do not have an equal probability of receiving the basic benefits of sports, compared with more athletically gifted men and women. A way to grant fully everyone's *prima facie* claim (even those with unsuitable physiques) to an equal right to the basic benefits of participating in the school sports which she or he most enjoys, and still to grant fully everyone's *prima facie* claim to equal formal freedom to compete, would be to sever the connection between winning a place on a team and being granted access to moderately scarce athletic resources. In team sports, either enough teams could be available at every ability level to accommodate everyone who wanted to play and who was willing to turn out for practice (with scarce athletic resources simply spread as thinly as necessary to go around), or there could be at least one team for each ability level, with membership in the teams determined by some form of lottery that equalized the probability of being on a team for everyone who wanted to play and was willing to turn out for practice. There would, in these schemes, be no apparent need for sex separation, because women would not be deprived of an equal chance for athletic benefits by being made to compete with men. Of course, the best athletes would stand to lose a great deal compared with the usual arrangement which makes access to scarce athletic resources a reward of winning competitions. Perhaps a sound argument could be made that the social desirability of helping the best athletes develop to their fullest

potential overrides the *prima facie* claim of athletically ill-endowed people to an equal right to the benefits of the sports they enjoy. In this case, a scheme like Rubin's would be preferable.

In professional athletics, there may appear to be a special reason for maintaining single-sex teams in masculine$_d$ sports. Jane English (5: p. 273) argues that "when there are virtually no female athletic stars, or when women receive much less prize money than men do, this is damaging to the self-respect of all women." But this argument is open to several objections. Raymond A. Belliotti (3: pp. 68, 71) seems correct in stating that "we should not respect ourselves because of our own or our group's attainments of fame and fortune in professional sports," and that "as an empirical matter of fact, these attainments *are not* an important factor in the way the vast majority of women determine their respect for themselves." Furthermore, if women's self-respect were dependent on the existence of female athletic stars, it would seem more helpful to have stars in female-biased sports, where the very best athletes are women, than in masculine sports, where the very best athletes are men.

In closing, let me recapitulate the major positions I have taken in this paper: (1) The anti-androgynist position is incorrect: women have as much right as men to engage in any masculine sport in any sense of that term and do not have any duty to accept second-class status; (2) sex segregation is not morally required in sports on grounds of its usefulness in preserving masculine$_c$ sports, nor is it morally required on grounds of its usefulness in maintaining women's equality of opportunity in masculine$_d$ sports, or on grounds of serving women's self-respect by making possible female stars in masculine$_d$ sports; (3) because they are ideals of purely individual excellence, both forms of androgynism discussed by Trebilcot lead us astray concerning the desirability of women participating in masculine sports. Neither form of androgynism takes account of the fact that men do naturally have a very considerable statistical advantage over women in performing prestigious activities such as masculine$_d$ sports, and that women have reason to counter the general image of male superiority fostered by those activities by withdrawing support from the activities and promoting activities in which women have a natural advantage over men.[12]

Notes

1. I intend the word "masculine" itself to be neutral between the androgynist and antiandrogynist ideals. I shall at this point cease to put the word in quotes. This may seem to favor the antiandrogynist position, but it would have favored the androgynist position to use quotes at every occurrence. I have decided that it is fairest to err, if err I must, by allowing my choice of punctuation to favor the position with which I have least sympathy.

2. One suggestion for tinkering with the list is to delete Metheny's third item and to add "the use of deadly force against animals" to capture bull-fighting and hunting.

3. Duquin (4: pp. 97–98) is here speaking of the instrumental orientation (i.e. focus on winning) which she says has characterized sports up to the present. She argues that sports have been regarded this way because they have been regarded as masculine, and "society has traditionally expected males to be instrumental, not expressive."

4. The fact that females must be excluded for a sport to be "masculine$_c$" is obvious also to the promoters of sports as a vehicle of masculine socialization. Duquin (4: p. 90) cites the following examples: A. Fisher, "Sports as an Agent of Masculine Orientation," *The Physical Educator,* 29 (1972), p. 120, and P. Werner, "The Role of Physical Education in Gender Identification," Ibid., p. 27.

5. The use of deadly force against animals (see

note 2 above) seems morally objectionable to me—equally objectionable for men as for women, of course.

6. Possible exceptions are sports in which there is an "attempt to project the body into or through space over long distances," for if the distances are long enough male strength may be countered by female endurance, light weight, and tolerance for heat (10: p. 98).

7. It seems that if soccer can be played noninstrumentally, then any sport can. I know that soccer can from my participation in a series of soccer games played by a mixed-sex faculty group at my own institution. Although we played our best and cheered enthusiastically when our team scored a goal, most of us did not keep track of the number of goals scored, and did not know which team had won the game when it was close.

8. Duquin (4: p. 102) cites a psychological study which supports the view that extrinsic incentives in athletics may impede a noninstrumental approach: M. R. Lepper, D. Greene, and R. Nisbett, "Undermining Children's Intrinsic Interest with Extrinsic Reward: A Test of the Overjustification Hypothesis," *Journal of Personality and Social Psychology,* 8 (1973), p. 129.

9. Some other ways are the wearing of clothing socially defined as male attire, behavior which is demanded of and reserved for males by etiquette, the different roles assigned to men and women in dancing and other mixed-sex activities, participation in groups and ceremonies from which women are excluded, and participation in activities in which males and females engage separately (e.g., sex-segregated clubs). I do not wish to defend all of these as morally unobjectionable.

10. This is argued in detail by Iris Young in an unpublished manuscript, "Social Implications of the Exclusion of Women from

Sport.'' Drawing on Beauvoir, Merleau-Ponty, and Eleanor Metheny, she argues (to put her argument very roughly) that because sport is activity *par excellence,* to be regarded as an inappropriate participant in sport is to be regarded as less than a human subject or conscious agent. Furthermore, she argues, exclusion from the dominant sport culture carries serious cultural disabilities in business, politics, and everyday life.

11. Other possible drawbacks of the plan favored by Rubin are expense, dilution of talent, and difficulty of finding schools to compete with at the lower levels. See (1).

12. For very helpful bibliographical suggestions and other comments, I am much indebted to Mary Vetterling-Braggin, Madge Phillips, William Morgan, and Joan Hundley. This paper will appear in *'Femininity', 'Masculinity' and 'Androgyny': A Modern Philosophical Discussion,* edited by Mary Vetterling-Braggin. It is printed here with the permission of Littlefield, Adams & Co., copyright 1981.

Bibliography

1. Association of American Colleges, Washington, D.C. Project on the Status and Education of Women. ''What Constitutes Equality for Women in Sport? Federal Law Puts Women in the Running.'' April 1974.

2. Beisser, Arnold R. ''The American Seasonal Masculinity Rites.'' *Sport Sociology: Contemporary Themes.* Edited by Andrew Yiannakis et al. Dubuque, IA: Kendall/Hunt Publishing Co., 1976.

3. Belliotti, Raymond A. ''Women, Sex, and Sports.'' *Journal of the Philosophy of Sport,* 6 (1979), 67–72.

4. Duquin, Mary E. ''The Androgynous Advantage.'' *Women and Sport: From Myth to Reality.* Edited by Carole A. Oglesby. Philadelphia: Lea & Febiger, 1968.

5. English, Jane. ''Sex Equality in Sports.'' *Philosophy & Public Affairs,* 7 (1978), 269–277.

6. Felshin, Jan. ''The Dialectic of Woman and Sport.'' *The American Woman in Sport.* By Ellen W. Gerber et al. Reading, MA: Addison-Wesley Publishing Co., 1974.

7. Metheny, Eleanor. ''Symbolic Forms of Movement: The Feminine Image in Sports.'' *Connotations of Movement in Sport and Dance.* Dubuque, IA: Wm. C. Brown Publishing Co., 1965.

8. Rubin, Richard Alan. ''Sex Discrimination in Interscholastic High School Athletics.'' *Syracuse Law Review,* 25 (1974), 535–574.

9. Trebilcot, Joyce. ''Two Forms of Androgynism.'' *Journal of Social Philosophy,* 8 (1977), 4–8. Reprinted in *Feminism and Philosophy.* Edited by Mary Vetterling-Braggin et al. Totowa, NJ: Littlefield, Adams and Co., 1977.

10. Wood, P.S. ''Sex Differences in Sports.'' *The New York Times Magazine,* May 18, 1980.

Bibliography for Sport and Ethics

Addelson, K.P. "Equality and Competition: Can Sports Make a Woman of a Girl?" In *Women, Philosophy, and Sport: A Collection of New Essays.* Edited by B.C. Postow. Metuchen, NJ: Scarecrow Press, 1983.

Alapack, R. "Distortion of a Human Value: Competition in Sport." *Journal of Physical Education,* 72 (March, 1975), 118-119.

Arnold, Peter J. "Sport, Moral Education, and the Development of Character." *Journal of Philosophy of Education,* 18 (1983a), 275-281.

Arnold, Peter J. "Three Approaches Toward an Understanding of Sportsmanship." *Journal of the Philosophy of Sport,* X (1983b), 61-70.

Asinof, Eliot. "1919: The Fix Is In." In *The Realm of Sport.* Edited by Herbert Warren Wind. New York: Simon and Schuster, 1966.

Aspin, David. "Ethical Aspects of Sports and Games in Physical Education." *Proceedings of the Philosophy of Education Society of Great Britain,* 9 (1975), 49-71.

"Athletics and Morals." *Atlantic Monthly,* 113 (February, 1914), 145-148.

Bailey, C. "Games, Winning and Education." *Cambridge Journal of Education,* 5 (1975), 40-50.

Banham, Charles. "Man at Play." *Contemporary Review,* 207 (August, 1965), 61-64.

Beckett, A. "Philosophy, Chemistry and the Athlete." *New Scientist,* 103 (1984), 18.

Beisser, Arnold R. *The Madness in Sports.* New York: Appleton-Century-Crofts, 1967.

Bend, Emil. "Some Functions of Competitive Team Sports in American Society." Unpublished doctoral dissertation, University of Pittsburgh, 1970.

Borotra, J. "A Plea for Sporting Ethics." *Bulletin of the Federation International d'Education Physique,* 48 (1978), 7-10.

Boutilier, Mary, and SanGiovanni, Lucinda. *The Sporting Woman.* Champaign, IL: Human Kinetics, 1983.

Bowen, Wilbur P. "The Evolution of Athletic Evils." *American Physical Education Review,* 14 (March, 1909), 151-156.

Breivik, Gunnar. "The Doping Dilemma: Some Game Theoretical and Philosophical Considerations." *Sportswissenschaft* (in press).

Broekhoff, Jan. "Sport and Ethics in the Context of Culture." In *The Philosophy of Sport: A Collection of Original Essays.* Edited by Robert G. Osterhoudt. Springfield, IL: Charles C Thomas, 1973.

Brown, W.M. "Ethics, Drugs, and Sport." *Journal of the Philosophy of Sport,* VII (1980), 15-23.

Brown, W.M. "Comments on Simon and Fraleigh." *Journal of the Philosophy of Sport,* XI (1984), 33-35.

Calisch, Richard. "The Sportsmanship Myth." *Physical Educator,* 10 (March, 1953), 9-11.

Code, Lorraine B. "Is the Sex of the Knower

Epistemologically Significant?'' *Metaphilosophy,* 12 (1981), 267-276.

Code, Lorraine B. ''Responsibility and the Epistemic Community: Women's Place.'' *Social Research,* 50 (1983), 537-555.

Coon, Roger. ''Sportsmanship: A Worthy Objective.'' *Physical Educator,* 21 (March, 1964), 16.

Cooper, W.E. ''Association: An Answer to Egoism.'' *Journal of the Philosophy of Sport,* IX (1982), 66-68.

Deatherage, Dorothy. ''Factors Related to Concepts of Sportsmanship.'' Unpublished doctoral dissertation, University of Southern California, 1964.

Diggs, B.J. ''Rules and Utilitarianism.'' *American Philosophical Quarterly,* I (January, 1964), 32-44.

Edwards, Harry. *Sociology of Sport.* Homewood, IL: Dorsey Press, 1973.

Eggerman, Richard W. ''Games and the Action-Guiding Force of Morality.'' *Philosophical Topics,* 13 (1985), 31-36.

Fairchild, David L. ''Creative Sports: Antidote to Alienation.'' *Journal of the Philosophy of Sport,* V (1978), 57-62.

Földesi, Tamas, and Földesi, G.S. ''Dilemmas of Justness in Top Sport.'' *Dialectics and Humanism,* 11 (1984), 21-32.

Fraleigh, Warren P. ''An Examination of Relationships of Inherent, Intrinsic, Instrumental, and Contributive Values of the Good Sports Contest.'' *Journal of the Philosophy of Sport,* X (1983), 52-60.

Fraleigh, Warren P. ''Performance-Enhancing Drugs in Sport: The Ethical Issue.'' *Journal of the Philosophy of Sport,* XI (1984a), 23-29.

Fraleigh, Warren P. *Right Actions in Sport: Ethics for Contestants.* Champaign, IL: Human Kinetics, 1984b.

French, Marilyn. *Beyond Power: On Women, Men, and Morals.* New York, NY: Summit, 1985.

Gehlen, A. ''Sport and Gesellschaft.'' In *Das Grosse Spiel.* Edited by U. Schuttz. Frankfurt: 1965.

Gerber, Ellen W., Felshin, Jan, Berlin, Pearl, and Wyrick, Waneen. *The American Women in Sport.* Reading, MA: Addison-Wesley, 1974.

Gould, Carol C. *Beyond Domination: New Perspectives on Woman and Philosophy.* Totowa, NJ: Rowman & Allenheld, 1984.

Graves, H. ''A Philosophy of Sport.'' *Contemporary Review,* 78 (1900), 877-893.

Greenberg, J., Mark, Melvin, and Lehman, Darrin. ''Justice in Sports and Games.'' *Journal of Sports Behavior,* 8:1 (1985), 18-33.

Grim, P. ''Sports and Two Androgynisms.'' *Journal of the Philosophy of Sport,* VIII (1981), 64-68.

Grupe, O. ''The Problem of Doping or the Influence of Pharmaceutics on Performance in Sports from the Standpoint of Sport Ethics.'' *SNIPES Journal,* 8 (January, 1985), 51-56.

Harding, Sandra, and Hintikka, Merrill B. *Discovering Reality: Feminist Perspectives on Epistemology, Metaphysics, Methodology, and Philosophy of Science.* Reidel, 1983.

Hartman, Betty Grant. ''An Exploratory Method for Determining Ethical Standards in Sport.'' Unpublished doctoral dissertation, Ohio State University, 1958.

Hearn, Francis. ''Toward a Critical Theory of Play.'' *Telos,* 30, (Winter, 1976-77), 145-160.

Held, Virginia. ''Feminism and Epistemology: Recent Work on the Connection Between Gender and Knowledge.'' *Philosophy & Public Affairs,* 14 (1985), 296-307.

Herman, Daniel J. ''Mechanism and the Athlete.'' *Journal of the Philosophy of Sport,* II (1975), 102-110.

Hoben, Allan. ''The Ethical Value of Organized Play.'' *Biblical World,* 39 (March, 1912), 175-187.

Hogan, William R. "Sin and Sports." In *Motivations in Play, Games and Sports*. Edited by Ralph Slovenko and James A. Knight. Springfield, IL: Charles C Thomas, 1967.

Holmstrom, Nancy. "Do Women Have a Distinct Nature?" *Philosophical Forum*, 14 (Fall, 1982), 77-94.

Hosmer, Millicent. "The Development of Morality Through Physical Education." *Mind and Body*, 21 (June, 1914), 156-163.

Hult, Joan S. "The Philosophical Conflicts in Men's and Women's Collegiate Athletics." *Quest*, 32 (1980), 77-94.

Hundley, Joan. "The Overemphasis on Winning: A Philosophical Look." In *Women, Philosophy and Sport*. Edited by B.C. Postow. Metuchen, NJ: Scarecrow Press, 1983.

Hyland, Drew. "Playing to Win: How Much Should It Hurt?" *The Hastings Center Report*, 9:2 (1979), 5-8.

Johnson, George E. "Play and Character." *American Physical Education Review*, 31 (1926), 981-988.

Kaplan, Janice. *Women and Sports*. New York: Viking Press, 1979.

Keating, James W. "Sportsmanship as a Moral Category." *Ethics*, 75 (1964), 25-35.

Keating, James W. "Athletics and the Pursuit of Excellence." *Education*, 85 (March, 1965a), 428-431.

Keating, James W. "The Heart of the Problem of Amateur Athletics." *Journal of General Education*, 16 (1965b), 261-272.

Keating, James W. "The Ethics of Competition and its Relation to Some Moral Problems in Athletics." In *The Philosophy of Sport: A Collection of Original Essays*. Edited by Robert G. Osterhoudt. Springfield, IL: Charles C Thomas, 1973.

Keating, James W. *Competition and Playful Activities*. Washington, DC: University Press of America, 1978.

Keenan, Francis. "Justice and Sport." *Journal of the Philosophy of Sport*, II (1975), 111-123.

Kellor, Frances A. "Ethical Value of Sports for Women." *American Physical Education Review*, 11 (September, 1906), 160-171.

Kennedy, Charles W. "The Effect of Athletic Competition on Character Building." *American Physical Education Review*, 31 (1926), 988-991.

Kennedy, Charles W. *Sport and Sportsmanship*. Princeton, NJ: Princeton University Press, 1931.

Kew, F.C. "Values in Competitive Games." *Quest*, 29 (Winter, 1978), 103-112.

Kohn, Alfie. "Why Competition?" *The Humanist*, 40 (January/February, 1980), 14-15, 49.

Kretchmar, R. Scott. "Ethics and Sport: An Overview." *Journal of the Philosophy of Sport*, X (1983), 21-32.

Laughter, Robert James. "Socio-Psychological Aspects of the Development of Athletic Practices and Sports Ethics." Unpublished doctoral dissertation, Ohio State University, 1963.

Lemaire, Lyn. "Women and Athletics: Toward a Physicality Perspective." *Harvard Women's Law Journal*, 5 (1982), 121-142.

Lenk, Hans. "Alienation, Manipulation and the Self of the Athlete. In *Sport in the Modern World—Chances and Problems*. Edited by Ommo Grupe, Dietrich Kurz, and Johannes Teipel. New York: Springer-Verlag, 1973.

Lucas, J.R. "Moralists and Gamesman." *Philosophy*, 34 (January, 1958), 1-11.

MacGuigan, Maryellen. "Is Woman a Question?" *International Philosophical Quarterly*, 13 (1973), 485-505.

Massengale, John Denny. "The Effect of Sportsmanship Instruction on Junior High School Boys." Unpublished doctoral dissertation, University of New Mexico, 1969.

McBride, P. *The Philosophy of Sport*. London: Health Cranton, 1932.

McCormick, Richard A. "Is Professional Boxing Immoral?" *Sports Illustrated*, 17 (November 5, 1962), 70-82.

McIntosh, Peter. *Fair Play: Ethics in Sport and Education.* London: Heinemann, 1979.

McMurty, John. "Philosophy of a Corner Linebacker." *The Nation,* 212 (January 18, 1971), 83-84.

McMurty, John. "The Illusions of a Football Fan: A Reply to Michalos." *Journal of the Philosophy of Sport,* IV (1977), 11-14.

Michalos, Alex C. "The Unreality and Moral Superiority of Football." *Journal of the Philosophy of Sport,* III (1976), 22-24.

Mihalich, Joseph C. *Sport and Athletics: Philosophy in Action.* Totowa, NJ: Rowman & Littlefield, 1982.

Miller, Donna Mae. "Ethics in Sport: Paradoxes, Perplexities, and a Proposal." *Quest,* **32** (1980), 3-7.

Montague, Ashley. *The Humanization of Man.* New York: World Publishing, 1962.

Moorcraft, D. "Doping: The Athlete's View—Dilemmas and Choices." *Olympic Review* (October, 1985), 634-635.

Morgan, William J. "An Analysis of the Sartrean Ethic of Ambiguity as the Moral Ground for the Conduct of Sport." *Journal of the Philosophy of Sport,* III (1976), 82-96.

Muhammad, Elijah. *Message to the Blackman in America.* Illinois: Muhammad Mosque of Islam No. 2, 1965.

Nash, Jay B. "The Aristocracy of Virtue." *Journal of Health, Physical Education, and Recreation,* 20 (1949), 157, 216-217.

Nelson, William N. "The Principle of Fair Play." Unpublished doctoral dissertation, Cornell University, 1972.

Oberteuffer, Delbert. "On Learning Values Through Sport." *Quest,* 1 (December, 1963), 23-29.

Oberteuffer, Delbert, Michielli, Donald, and Carlson, Joseph. "Sportsmanship—Whose Responsibility?" In *Anthology of Contemporary Readings.* Edited by Howard S. Slusher and Aileene S. Lockhart. Dubuque, IA: Wm. C. Brown, 1966.

Oelschlagel, G. "Karl Marx und die Korperkultur." *Theorie und Proxis der Korperkultur,* 17 (1968), 394-401, 587-594.

Ortega y Gasset, José. "The Ethics of Hunting." In *Meditations on Hunting.* Translated by H.B. Wescott. New York: Scribner's, 1972.

Osterhoudt, Robert G. "The Kantian Ethic as a Principle of Moral Conduct in Sport." *Quest,* 19 (January, 1973a), 118-123.

Osterhoudt, Robert G. "On Keating on the Competitive Motif in Athletics and Playful Activity." In *The Philosophy of Sport: A Collection of Original Essays.* Edited by Robert G. Osterhoudt. Springfield, IL: Charles C Thomas, 1973b.

Osterhoudt, Robert G. "In Praise of Harmony: The Kantian Imperative and Hegelian *Sittlichkeit* as the Principle and Substance of Moral Conduct in Sport." *Journal of the Philosophy of Sport,* III (1976), 65-81.

Plessner, H. *Die Funktion des Sports in der industriellen Gesellschaft.* Wissenschaft und Weltbild 262 sgg., 1956.

Postow, B.C. "Masculine Sports Revisited." *Journal of the Philosophy of Sport,* VIII (1981), 60-63.

Postow, B.C. (Ed.). *Women, Philosophy and Sport: A Collection of New Essays.* Metuchen, NJ: Scarecrow Press, 1983.

Postow, B.C. "Sport, Art and Gender." *Journal of the Philosophy of Sport,* XI (1984), 52-55.

Potter, Stephen. *The Theory and Practice of Gamesmanship.* New York: Bantam Books, 1965.

Proost, Jan. "The Concept of Fair Play in Homer's Greece." Unpublished master's thesis, University of Toledo, 1972.

Ralls, Anthony. "The Game of Life." *Philosophical Quarterly,* 16 (January, 1966), 23-24.

Ravizza, Kenneth, and Kathy Daruty. "Paternalism and Sovereignty in Athletics: Limits and Justifications of the Coach's Exercise of Authority Over the Adult Athlete.'' *Journal of the Philosophy of Sport,* XI (1984), 71–82.

Rawls, John. ''Two Concepts of Rules.'' *Philosophical Review,* 64 (January, 1955), 3–32.

Reader, Mark, and Wolf, Donald. ''On Being Human.'' *Political Theory,* 1 (1973), 186–202.

Reddiford, G. ''Morality and the Games Player.'' *Physical Education Review,* 4 (1981), 8–16.

Richardson, Deane E. ''Ethical Conduct in Sport Situations.'' *Proceedings of the Sixty-Fifth Annual Meeting of the National College Physical Education Association.* San Francisco, CA: 1962.

Rivello, J. Roberto. ''Rules and Ethical Actions.'' *Actia,* 3 (1975), 9–12.

Roberts, Terence J. ''An Examination of the Moralities of Athletics and Play.'' Unpublished master's thesis, University of Windsor, Canada, 1973.

Roberts, Terry, and Galasso, P.J. ''The Fiction of Morally Indifferent Acts in Sport.'' In *The Philosophy of Sport: A Collection of Original Essays.* Edited by Robert G. Osterhoudt. Springfield, IL: Charles C Thomas, 1973.

Rodnon, Stewart. ''Sport, Sporting Codes, and Sportsmanship in the Work of Ring Lardner, James T. Farrell, Ernest Hemingway and William Faulkner.'' Unpublished doctoral dissertation, New York University, 1961.

Roemer, Eleanor. ''And Some Are More Equal than Others: The Exemption of Revenue Producing Sports From Title IX.'' *Philosophical Studies in Education,* (1979), 73–83.

Rogers, Frederick Rand. *The Amateur Spirit in Scholastic Games and Sports.* Albany, NY: C.F. Williams & Sons, 1929.

Royce, Josiah. *Some Relations of Physical Training to the Present Problems of Moral Education in America.* Boston: The Boston Normal School of Gymnastics, ca. 1908.

Sadler, William A. ''A Contextual Approach to an Understanding of Competition: A Response to Keating's Philosophy of Athletics.'' In *The Philosophy of Sport: A Collection of Original Essays.* Edited by Robert G. Osterhoudt. Springfield, IL: Charles C Thomas, 1973.

Schaef, Anne Wilson. *Women's Reality.* San Francisco, CA: Winston Press, 1981.

Scott, Jack. *The Athletic Revolution.* New York: Free Press, 1971.

Scott, Jack. ''Sport and the Radical Ethic.'' *Quest,* 19 (January, 1973), 71–77.

Shaw, John H. ''The Operation of a Value System in the Selection of Activities and Methods of Instruction in Physical Education.'' *Proceedings of the Fifty-Ninth Annual Meeting of the College Physical Education Association,* Daytona Beach, Florida, 1956.

Shea, Edward. *Ethical Decisions in Physical Education and Sport.* Springfield, IL: Charles C Thomas, 1978.

Simmons, A. John. ''The Principle of Fair Play.'' *Philosophy & Public Affairs,* 8 (1979), 307–337.

Simon, Irving. ''A Humanistic Approach to Sports.'' *The Humanist,* 43 (July/August, 1983), 25–26, 32.

Simon, Robert L. *Sports and Social Values.* Englewood Cliffs, NJ: Prentice-Hall, 1985.

Smith, Ronald A. ''Winning and a Theory of Competitive Athletics.'' In *Sport and the Humanities: A Collection of Original Essays.* Edited by William J. Morgan. Knoxville, TN: University of Tennessee, 1979.

Soble, Alan. ''Feminist Epistemology and Women Scientists.'' *Metaphilosophy,* 14 (1983), 291–307.

Spencer, Herbert. *The Principles of Ethics,* Vol. 1. New York: D. Appleton and Company, 1910.

Spelman, Elizabeth V. "Woman as Body: Ancient and Contemporary Views." *Feminist Studies,* 8 (1982), 109–132.

Stearns, Alfred E. "Athletics and the School." *Atlantic Monthly,* 113 (February, 1914), 148–152.

Stewart, C.A. "Athletics and the College." *Atlantic Monthly,* 113 (February, 1914), 153–160.

Suenens, L. "The Alienation and Identity of Man." In *Sport in the Modern World—Chances and Problems.* Edited by Ommo Grupe, Dietrich Kurz, and Johannes Teipel. New York: Springer-Verlag, 1973.

Suits, Bernard. "The Grasshopper: A Thesis Concerning the Moral Idea of Man." In *The Philosophy of Sport: A Collection of Original Essays.* Edited by Robert G. Osterhoudt. Springfield, IL: Charles C Thomas, 1973.

Suits, Bernard. "Sticky Wickedness: Games and Morality." *Dialogue,* 21 (1982), 755–760.

Thomas, Carolyn E. "Do You 'Wanna' Bet: An Examination of Player Betting and the Integrity of the Sporting Event." In *The Philosophy of Sport: A Collection of Original Essays.* Edited by Robert G. Osterhoudt. Springfield, IL: Charles C Thomas, 1973.

Thomas, Carolyn E. "Sports Equality: A Case of Mistaken Identity." In *Sport and the Humanities: A Collection of Original Essays.* Edited by William J. Morgan, Knoxville, TN: University of Tennessee Press, 1979.

Thomas, Carolyn E. *Sport in a Philosophic Context.* Philadelphia: Lea & Febiger, 1983a.

Thomas, Carolyn E. "Thoughts on the Moral Relationship of Intent and Training in Sport." *Journal of the Philosophy of Sport,* X (1983b), 84–91.

Thomas, Duane L. "A Definitional Context for Some Socio-Moral Characteristics of Sport." *Journal of the Philosophy of Sport,* III (1976), 22–24.

Turbeville, Gus. "On Being Good Sports in Sports." *Vital Speeches,* 31 (1965), 542–544.

Turin, Stephanie L. *Out of the Bleachers: Writings on Women and Sport.* New York: The Feminist Press, 1979.

Tutko, T., and Burns, W. *Winning is Everything and Other American Myths.* New York: Macmillan, 1976.

Underwood, John. "The True Crisis (Is Sport Crooked?)." *Sports Illustrated,* 18 (May 20, 1963), 16–19, 83.

Underwood, John. *The Death of an American Game: The Crises in Football.* Boston: Little, Brown, 1979.

UNESCO. *Sport, Work, Culture. Report of the International Conference of The Contribution of Sports to the Improvement of Professional Abilities and to Cultural Development.* Helsinki, Finland, August 10–15, 1959.

Valentine, Eugene. "Lombardi on Winning." In *Sport and the Humanities: A Collection of Original Essays.* Edited by William J. Morgan. Knoxville, TN: University of Tennessee, 1979.

Vetterling-Braggin, Mary. "One Form of Anti-Androgynism." *Journal of the Philosophy of Sport,* VIII (1981), 55–59.

Vetterling-Braggin, Mary. (Ed). *"Feminity," "Masculinity," and "Androgyny": A Modern Philosophical Discussion.* Totowa, NJ: Littlefield, Adams & Co., 1982.

Weiss, Paul. *Sport: A Philosophic Inquiry.* Carbondale, IL: Southern Illinois University Press, 1969.

Wertz, S.K. "The Varieties of Cheating." *Journal of the Philosophy of Sport,* VIII (1981), 19–40.

Wertz, S.K. "The Preservation of Sport." In *Topical Problems of Sport Philosophy.* Edited by Hans Lenk. Köln: Institut fur Sportswissenschaft, 1983.

Wilton, W.M. "An Early Consensus on Sportsmanship." *Physical Educator,* 20 (October, 1963), 113–114.

Young, Iris Marion. "Throwing Like a Girl: A

Phenomenology of Feminine Body Compartment, Mobility and Spatiality.'' *Human Studies,* 3 (1980), 137–156.

Zaner, Richard M. ''Sport and the Moral Order.'' *Journal of the Philosophy of Sport,* VI (1979), 7–18.

Zeegers, Machiel. ''The Swindler as Player.'' In *Motivations in Play, Games and Sports.* Edited by Ralph Slovenko and James A. Knight. Springfield, IL: Charles C Thomas, 1967.

Zeigler, Earle F. ''The Pragmatic (Experimentalistic) Ethic as it Relates to Sport and Physical Education.'' In *The Philosophy of Sport: A Collection of Original Essays.* Edited by Robert G. Osterhoudt. Springfield, IL: Charles C Thomas, 1973.

Zeigler, Earle F. ''Coach and Athlete—In Each Other's Power.'' *National Association for Physical Education in Higher Education Proceedings,* 1 (1980), 56–65.

Zeigler, Earle F. *Ethics and Morality in Sport and Physical Education.* Champaign, IL: Stipes, 1984.

Part
V

Sport and Social-Political Philosophy

Social and political philosophy encompasses a wide range of normative and critical questions. In Anglo-American circles, it is concentrated largely on issues of "rights," "obligations," the limits of state authority, and justice. In continental circles, it is based more on general prescriptions about the structures of social and political institutions and their fundamental legitimacy. Whereas the former more or less presupposes the basic institutions of liberal, democratic society, the latter calls into question the very foundations of these social, political institutions. The focus of the present selection of essays on sport follows an essentially continental bent. That is, it is centrally concerned with the role sport plays in either sustaining or challenging the social and political structures of bourgeois society.

The first essay of this section begins on a rather grand note. Ortega divides human activity into two categories. The first, and most primary category is the spontaneous and exuberant activity of play; the second, derivative category is the utilitarian, practical activity of labor. In Ortega's view, the creative sources and energies of human life, including labor, are all drawn and modified from play. Moreover, it is from the creative fund of play, he contends, that the first, prehistorical social organizations and the state emerged. Ortega's play theory of the state stands in direct opposition to the labor based theories of radical and Marxist thinkers.

Horkheimer's piece on sport ignores its seamy side and concentrates on its liberating social features. Horkheimer regards sport to be a renunciation of instrumental reason, and he argues that sport is a fundamental expression of freedom, which belongs with the likes of art, philosophy, and all the "productive springs" of the imagination. It is in these expressive forms of cultural life, according to Horkheimer, that our best hopes for an alternative, truly humane life, lie. Horkheimer's view of leisure and popular culture is quite at odds with the views commonly ascribed to him by even his more sympathetic commentators.

Lenk challenges the claim advanced by certain Neo-Marxists that sport replicates the performance principle of capitalist society. Such a view, Lenk maintains, overlooks the potential for individual development and self-confirmation possible in sport. This potential for self-development exhibits none of the repressive features claimed by the neo-Marxists, and their failure to differentiate among the widely divergent forms of achievement displayed, for example, in sport seriously damages, according to Lenk, the credibility of their attack.

Lasch also takes to task the so-called radical, Marxist, and neo-Marxist critics of sport, but not, as for Lenk, because of their radical perspective, but because they fail to realize their radical intentions. The critics go wrong, according to Lasch, because they misconstrue the source of the modern degradation of sport and concentrate their attack on sport's alleged promotion of bourgeois virtues (e.g., militarism, chauvinism, sexism), which are now quite obsolete. The real root of the degradation of sport, argues Lasch, has to do with the destruction of its illusion of reality and its investment of a futile activity with utter seriousness. This destruction is, Lasch argues, part and parcel of a society that degrades work, and in so doing creates in people the need for distraction and crude sensationalism. Such is the source of the transformation of contemporary sport into a mass spectacle.

Morgan's essay attacks the primacy accorded labor in capitalist social orders. He argues that such primacy, anchored as it is in the profit motive of capitalism, accounts for the inability of such societies to deliver on their promise of the good life, the abundant life envisaged in capitalism's notion of utopia. This is because the profit motif of capitalism presupposes scarcity, as opposed to abundance, as its *modus operandi.* He concludes that the dystopian consequences entailed by present society's utopian aspirations can only be avoided by a new conception of the flourishing life, a conception of utopia premised on play as opposed to labor.

Parry's essay, the final selection of this section, looks at recent developments in the sociology of sport, particularly its relatively recent adoption of Marxist paradigms of analysis. Within the Marxist camp, he pays special attention to the new hegemonic theory of sport as chiefly represented by the work of the British theorist John Hargreaves. Although finding much of Hargreaves' work to his liking, Parry laments the virtual absence of strategic concerns and thinking in such work. Rather than writing books for petty-bourgeois intellectuals, he points out, hegemonists should be developing strategies for forging class consciousness and counterinstitutions. Parry also reproaches hegemony theory for simply assuming the truth of Gramsci's work (the theoretical father of hegemony theory) and the falsity of alternative Marxist positions.

The social-political study of sport is obviously still in the developing stage. Not unexpectedly what literature there is in this area is largely sociological in nature, and so lacks philosophical precision and sophistication. Nonetheless, a critical corpus of work is gradually emerging. Rojek (1985) and Hoberman (1984) provide a comprehensive, in-depth overview of the various social-political theories of sport. The hard-line, orthodox Marxist approach to sport is represented in the works of Brohm (1978), Rigauer (1981), and Beamish (1981, 1982, 1985). The views of Alt (1982), Gruneau (1983), and Hargreaves (1986) comprise the best of the hegemonic literature on sport. Critical theoretical perspectives are especially prominent in the analyses of Hearn (1976), and Morgan (1985, 1983). Liberal, democratic-tending views of sport can be found in Guttmann (1978), and Simon (1985). And finally, Eichberg's writings, whose maverick style makes them difficult to classify, deserve mention, particularly his analysis (1984) of the Western colonization of Third World sports.

The Sportive Origin
of the State

J. ORTEGA y GASSET

I

Scientific truth is characterized by its exactness and the certainty of its predictions. But these admirable qualities are contrived by science at the cost of remaining on a plane of secondary problems, leaving intact the ultimate and decisive questions. Of this renunciation it makes its essential virtue, and for it, if for nought else, it deserves praise. Yet science is but a small part of the human mind and organism. Where it stops, man does not stop. If the physicist detains, at the point where his method ends, the hand with which he delineates the facts, the human being behind each physicist prolongs the line thus begun and carries it on to its termination, as an eye beholding an arch in ruins will of itself complete the missing airy curve.

It is the task of physics to ascertain for each fact occurring here and now its principle, that is to say the preceding fact that causes it. But this principle in its turn has a principle, and so down to a first original principle. The physicist refrains from searching for first principles, and he does well. But, as I said, the man lodged in each physicist does not resign himself. Whether he likes it or not, his mind is drawn towards the last enigmatic cause of the universe. And it is natural that it should be thus. For living means dealing with the world, turning to it, acting in it, being occupied with it. That is why man is practically unable, for psychological reasons, to do without all-round knowledge of the world, without an integral idea of the universe. Crude or refined, with our consent or without it, such a trans-scientific picture of the world will settle in the mind of each of us, ruling our lives more effectively than scientific truth.

The past century, resorting to all but force, tried to restrict the human mind within the limits set to exactness. Its violent effort to turn its back on last problems is called agnosticism. But such endeavor seems neither fair nor sensible. That science is incapable of solving in its own way those fundamental questions is no sufficient reason for slighting them, as did the fox with the high-hung grapes, or for calling them myths and urging us to drop them altogether. How can we live turning a deaf ear to the last dramatic questions? Where does the world come from, and whither is it going? Which is the supreme power of the cosmos, what the essential meaning of life? We cannot breathe confined to a realm of secondary and intermediate themes. We need a comprehensive perspective, foreground and background, not a maimed scenery, a horizon stripped of the lure of infinite distances. Without the aid of the cardinal points we are liable to lose our bearings. The assurance that we have found no means of answering last questions is no valid excuse for callousness towards them. The more deeply should we feel,

Reprinted from *History as a System and Other Essays Toward a Philosophy of History* (pp. 13–32), 1961, New York: W.W. Morton Company. Copyright 1961 by the W.W. Morton Company. Reprinted by permission.

down to the roots of our being, their pressure and their sting. Whose hunger has ever been stilled with the knowledge that he could not eat? Insoluble though they be, these problems will never cease to loom on the vault of night, stirring us with their starry twinkle—the stars, according to Heine, are night's restless golden thoughts. North and South help to orient us despite their being not precisely cities to which one can buy a railroad ticket.

We are given no escape from last questions. In one fashion or another they are in us, whether we like it or not. Scientific truth is exact, but it is incomplete and penultimate and of necessity embedded in another ultimate, though inexact, truth which I see no objection in calling a myth. Scientific truth floats in a medium of mythology; but science taken as a whole, is it not also a myth, the admirable myth of modern Europe?

II

One of these last questions, and probably that of strongest influence on our daily destinies, is the idea we hold of life. The nineteenth century, utilitarian throughout, set up a utilitarian interpretation of the phenomenon of life which has come down to us and may still be considered as the commonplace of everyday thinking. According to it, the fundamental activity of life consists of a response to and satisfaction of imperative needs; and all manifestations of life are instances of this activity—the forms of animals as well as their movements, man's mind as well as his historical works and actions. An innate blindness seems to have closed the eyes of this epoch to all but those facts which show life as a phenomenon of utility, an adaptation. Modern biology and recent historical investigations, however, have exploded the current myth and given rise to a different idea, in which life appears with a more graceful gesture.

According to this idea, all utilitarian actions aiming at adaptation, all mere reaction to pressing needs, must be considered as secondary vital functions, while the first and original activity of life is always spontaneous, effusive, overflowing, a liberal expansion of pre-existing energies. Far from being a movement enforced by an exigency—a tropism—life is the free occurrence, the unforeseeable appetite itself. Darwin believed that species equipped with eyes have been forthcoming in a millennial evolutionary process because sight is necessary or convenient in the struggle for existence against the environment. The theory of mutation and its ally, the Mendelian theory, show with a certainty hitherto unknown in biology that precisely the opposite is true. The species with eyes appears suddenly, capriciously as it were, and it is this species which changes the environment by creating its visible aspect. The eye does not come into being because it is needed. Just the contrary; because the eye appears it can henceforth be applied as a serviceable instrument. Each species builds up its stock of useful habits by selecting among, and taking advantage of, the innumerable useless actions which a living being performs out of sheer exuberance.

We may then divide organic phenomena—animal and human—into two great classes of activity, one original, creative, vital par excellence—that is, spontaneous and disinterested; the other of utilitarian character, in which the first is put to use and mechanized. Utility does not create and invent; it simply employs and stabilizes what has been created without it.

If we leave aside organic forms and consider only the actions of living beings, life always presents itself as an effort, but an effort of two different kinds, one made for the sheer delight of it, as Goethe says:

Das Lied, das aus der Kehle dringt,
Ist Lohn, der reichlich lohnet;

the other compulsory, an exertion in which we are urged on and worn out by a necessity imposed on us and not of our invention or desire. If the classic instance of the obligatory effort which strictly satisfies a need is to be found in what man calls work, the other, the effort *ex abundantia cordis,* becomes most manifest in sport.

We thus feel induced to invert the inveterate

hierarchy. Sportive activity seems to us the foremost and creative, the most exalted, serious, and important part of life, while labor ranks second as its derivative and precipitate. Nay more, life, properly speaking, resides in the first alone; the rest is relatively mechanic and a mere functioning. To give a concrete example: the true vital phenomenon is the development of an arm and its possible movements. Once the arm with its possibilities exists, its motion in a given case is simply a mechanical matter. In the same way the eye, having come into being, sees in accordance with the laws of optics; but one cannot make an eye with optical laws. Queen Christina of Sweden remarked to Descartes, who upheld the mechanical nature of living beings, that she had never seen her watch give birth to baby watches.

This must by no means be understood as though utilitarian reaction did not in its turn inspire the sportive power, providing it with stimuli for new creations. What I want to say is that in every vital process the first impulse is given by an energy of supremely free and exuberant character, in individual life as well as in history. In the history of every living entity we shall always find that life at first is prodigal invention and that it then selects among the possibilities thus created, some of which consolidate in the form of useful habits. Merely passing in review the film of our own lives reveals our individual destinies to be the result of the selection made by actual circumstances among our personal possibilities. The individual we grow to be in the course of our lives is only one of the many we might have been but had to leave behind —lamentable casualties of our inner army. It is important to enter existence with ample possibilities in order that we may oblige destiny, the fatal pruning knife, always to leave us with some sturdy shoots intact. Abundance of possibilities is a symptom of thriving life, as utilitarianism, the attitude of confining oneself to the strictly necessary, like the sick man who begrudges every expenditure of energy, discloses weakness and waning life.

Success in life depends on amplitude of possibilities. Every blow we receive must serve as another impulse towards new attempts.

My reader will forgive me. I never conceive of this idea without its bringing back to memory the triumphant scene which the circus clowns of my childhood used to perform. A clown would stroll in with his livid, floured face, seat himself on the railing, and produce from his bulky pocket a flute which he began to play. At once the ringmaster appeared and intimated to him that here one could not play. The clown, unperturbed, stalked over to another place and started again. But now the ringmaster walked up angrily and snatched his melodious toy from him. The clown remained unshaken in face of such misfortune. He waited till the ringmaster was gone, and plunging his hand into his fathomless pocket produced another flute and from it another melody. But alas, inexorably, here came the ringmaster again, and again despoiled him of his flute. Now the clown's pocket turned into an inexhaustible magic box from which proceeded, one after another, new musical instruments of all kinds, clear and gay or sweet and melancholy. The music overruled the veto of destiny and filled the entire space, imparting to all of us with its impetuous, invincible bounty a feeling of exultation, as though a torrent of strange energies had sprung from the dauntless melody the clown blew on his flute as he sat on the railing of the circus. Later I thought of this clown of the flute as a grotesque modern form of the great god Pan of the forest whom the Greeks worshiped as the symbol of cosmic vitality—serene, goat-footed Pan who plays the sacred syrinx in the sinking dusk and with its magic sound evokes an echo in all things: leaves and foundations shiver, the stars begin to tremble, and the shaggy goats dance at the edge of the grove.

Let us say without further ado, then, that life is an affair of flutes. It is overflow that it needs most. He who rests content with barely meeting necessity as it arises will be washed away. Life has triumphed on this planet because it has, instead of clinging to necessities, deluged it with overwhelming possibilities, so that the failure of one may serve as a bridge for the victory of another.

The expression most fragrant with the scent of

life, and one of the prettiest in the dictionary, is to my mind the word "incitement." It has no meaning except in the disciplines of life. Physics does not know of it. In physics one thing does not incite another; it causes it and the cause produces an effect in proportion to itself. A billiard ball colliding with another imparts to it an impulse in principle equal to its own; cause and effect are equal. But when the spur's point ever so lightly touches its flank, the thoroughbred breaks into a gallop, generously out of proportion to the impulse of the spur. The reaction of the horse, rather than a response to an outer impulse, is a release of exuberant inner energies. Indeed, a skittish horse, with its nervous head and fiery eye, is a splendid image of stirring life. Thus we imagine the magnificent stallion whom Caligula called *Incitatus* and made a member of the Roman Senate.

Poor life, that lacks the elasticity to dart off in prancing enterprises! Sad life, that lets the hours pass in lassitude, the hours which should flash like quivering foils. A melancholy fate for a Spaniard to live in an epoch of Spanish indolence and to remember the charger's rearing and the tiger-leaps of which in better times Spain's history consisted. Where has her vigor gone? Does it await resurrection in her hoary soil? I want to believe it; and resigned to feed on images, since nothing else is left to me, I draw comfort from this:

Córdoba is one of those cities whose soil is saturated with historical memories. Under the present quiet and humble town sleeps what remains of six civilizations: Roman, Gothic, Arabic, Hebrew, Spanish of the classic and of the romantic periods. Each of them may be epitomized in one august name: Seneca, Alvaro, Averroes, Maimonides, Góngora, Duque de Rivas. And all these treasures of creative power lie buried under the drowsy surface. Córdoba is a rosebush with its roots in the air and its roses underground.

Now it happened a few years ago that as workmen were digging in the patio of a palace belonging to a lady of ancient descent, on Claudio Marcelo Street, their spades struck against a hard object. They looked closer and saw something like the ear of a bronze horse. They dug on, and there emerged before their wondering eyes the splendid head of a horse and then the beginning of an equestrian statue of Roman style—perhaps the statue of Claudius Marcellus himself. They apprised the lady, she informed herself of the possible cost of the excavation and, finding it prohibitive, ordered the statue to be covered with earth again. And there he remained in his tomb, incredible though it seems, the Spanish *Incitatus* with his fine strong neck and his sensitive, foam-flecked mouth. But as the Breton fishermen, when leaning over the sides of their boats on calm afternoons, believe that they hear bells ringing from the bottom of the sea, thus one might fancy that if one held one's ear to the ground one would hear the desperate subterranean neighing of that great bronze horse.

But we have to continue our way.

III

Youth!—In some not too distant future I hope to quarry the rich vein of secrets we come upon in psychology of youth. In general, the time is ripe for a resolute attack on the great biological themes of childhood, youth, maturity, senility.

I beg leave to prophesy for the near future a converging of scientific attention on the problem of ages common to all organisms, not only plants, animals, and human beings. Before long, one of the great themes of thought will be the tragic fact of the aging of races. Then will biology become aware of the necessity of starting the analysis of the secret of life from the obvious, though unheeded, fact of the inevitability of death.

Here we are concerned only with a feature peculiar to the psychology of youth.

In attempting to distinguish different phases in the mental development of a child, one would have to look for an inner activity free from influences of the will and the environment and would have to study the changes this activity has undergone year by year. Dreams, for example. Analysis of dreams suggests a division into three periods. First the child dreams that he plays alone. At the second stage a new personage enters the scene, another child, but this child plays only the role of a spectator; it is present to watch the dreamer play. Then comes a third and last period, close to puberty, when the child's dreams are invaded by a whole group of boys who play with him, and into whose turbulent band his individual person merges.

Indeed, one of the forces decisive in the adolescent soul, and one which still gains strength in that of the full-grown youth, is the desire to live together with other boys of the same age. The isolation of infancy breaks down, and the boy's personality flows out into the coeval group. He no longer lives by himself and for himself; he no longer feels and wishes as an individual; he is absorbed by the anonymous personality of the group which feels and wishes for him. That is why youth is the season of friendship. Boys and young men, still unformed as individuals, live submerged in the group of the young which drifts undivided and inseparable over the fields of life wherever the wind may carry it. I call this urge to sociability the instinct of coevality.

One day a boy of twelve, sensitive and limpid of soul, who is near to my heart, came to his mother and said: "Mamma, tomorrow we are all going on an excursion with the school, boys and girls. I want my suit to be pressed. You must give me a silk handkerchief and five pesetas for candies." Knowing her son as a rough-and-ready young man, the mother, surprised at so much urbanity, asked what it was all about. And the boy candidly replied: "You know, Mamma, we have begun to like the girls." Now, he himself did not yet like the girls. What had happened was that the group of schoolboys as such had felt the first stir of the curiosity of sex, a vague presentiment of the charm of femininity and the dynamic grace of the struggle between the man's gallant wooing and the coyness of the woman. The first impulse of puberty had appeared in the group before it had appeared in the individual, and the lively band,

glowing with solidarity like a football team, had decided to join battle against the eternal feminine. Needless to say, when on that famous day their valiant troop came up against the pertness of the maidens, they were dumbfounded, and could not even muster enough courage to brandish the sweet bribe of candies.

Human history seems to proceed with a double rhythm: the rhythm of age and the rhythm of sex. In some epochs the youthful influence prevails; others are ruled by mature men. At any rate, directly after the formless form of human society which sociologists call the horde, we find a society endowed with a beginning of organization, the principle of which is that of age. The social body has grown in numbers, and from a horde it has developed into a tribe. Primitive tribes are divided into three social classes which are not economic, as socialistic dogma would have it, but are the groups of youth, maturity, and old age. No other distinctions have yet developed. The family, in particular, is still unknown; so much so, in fact, that all members of the class of the young call themselves brothers, naming all those of the older class father. The first social organization divides the tribe not into families, but into so-called age-classes.

Among these three ages, however, the one that predominates through power and authority is not the class of the mature men, but that of the youths. In fact, this is frequently the only class, and a number of facts, which it is unnecessary to detail here, show beyond doubt that it is the first to be organized. What has happened in the transition from the shapeless horde to the organized tribe?

The hordes had been roaming for years without coming upon each other. The number of individuals of the human species on the whole planet was still exceedingly small. But there must have befallen an unusually prolific epoch which densified the population enough to bring the hordes closer together. This increase in population is a symptom of higher vitality in the species, and of growing perfection of its faculties.

Now it comes to pass that the boys of two or

three neighboring hordes, driven by the desire for coeval comradeship, decide to unite and to live together—obviously not for the purpose of remaining idle. Youth is sociable, and at the same time eager for hazardous enterprises. Infallibly, one of a temperament more imaginative or bold or deft than the rest will rise among them and propose the great venture. They all feel, without knowing why, a strange and mysterious disgust for the familiar women of their own blood with whom they live in the horde and an appetite sharpened by imagination for the others, those alien women, unknown, unseen, or only fleetingly espied.

And now one of the most prodigious events of human history takes place, an event from which gigantic consequences have sprung. They decide to rape girls of distant hordes. But that is no gentle enterprise. A horde does not meekly tolerate the abduction of its women. To rob them one has to fight; and war is born for the service of love. War calls for a leader and necessitates discipline, thus bringing into being authority, law, and social structure. But unity of leadership and discipline entails and fosters unity of spirit, a common concern in the great problems of life. And we find, as a matter of fact, that the ceremonies and rituals of the cult of magic powers originate in these associations of youths.

Life in common begets the idea of building a permanent and spacious dwelling, an abode different from the occasional den and the simple shelter against the wind. The first house built by man is not a home for the family, still nonexistent, but a casino for young men. Here they prepare for their expeditions and perform their rituals; here they indulge in chanting, drinking, and wild banquets. Whether we approve of it or not, the club is older than the family, the casino older than the domestic hearth.

Mature men, women, and children are prohibited on pain of death from entering the casino of the young, which ethnologists, because of its later forms, call the bachelor house. It is all mystery, secret, taboo. For, surprisingly enough, these primitive associations of youths took on the character of secret societies with iron discipline, in which the members through severe training developed proficiency in war and hunting. That is to say, the primeval political association is the secret society; and while it serves the pleasures of feasting and drinking, it is at the same time the place where the first religious and athletic asceticism is practiced. We must not forget that the literal translation of the word "asceticism" is "training exercise." The monks took it over from the sport vocabulary of the Greek athletes. *Ascesis* was the regime of the life of an athlete, and it was crammed with exercises and privations. Thus we may well say that the club of the young is not only the first house and the first casino, but also the first barrack and the first monastery.

The deities, as I have said, are the gods of the hunter, the animals; and their cult is of orgiastic and magic character. Man wins the good will of the sacred animal powers by imitating animal forms and movements. On the solemn days of the god's great festivals the youthful band cover their faces with horrid masks and animal heads and dance through the fields in wild ecstasy. They hurl a piece of wood into the air which, swinging at the end of a cord, produces a weird noise at the sound of which women and children scatter, for they are forbidden to see the fantastic troop of dancers as it departs in drunken rapture for a raid on alien women. The mask that is worn at festivals is also the costume of war. Festivals, hunts, and wars long remained indistinguishable. That is why almost all primitive dances are stylized hunting or warlike gestures.

All these remarks which space here compels me to set down in a somewhat breathless manner are no mere hypotheses of my own. Every act we have described may, in its essentials, be occurring somewhere on the earth in this moment.

We have seen, then, that the first human society is precisely the opposite of a reaction to imposed necessities. It is an association of the young for the purpose of raping the women of alien tribes and performing all sorts of barbarous exploits. Rather than a parliament or a cabinet of bigwigs, it resembles an athletic club.

What in refined epochs of decadence and romanticism was to become the dream of the *princesse lointaine* in rough and primitive times gave rise, as we have seen, to the first organization of society. It brought about exogamy, that is to say, the primary nuptial law which commands the seeking of a wife outside the circle of blood relations. The biological importance this has had for the human species need hardly be stressed. The first matrimony was robbery, rape—of which symbolical traces remain in many later wedding ceremonies and even in the vocabulary of love itself, since the impetuous desire of love is called rapture.

IV

We have found that the clubs of the young introduced into history the following phenomena: exogamy, war, authoritative organization, training or asceticism, the law, cultic associations, the festival of masked dances or carnival, and the secret society. And all this indistinguishably merged into one phenomenon provides the irrational historical origin of the state. Again we see that in the beginning there is vigor and not utility.

There can be small doubt, however, that this epoch of unrestricted and uncontrolled predominance of tempestuous youth was a hard and cruel time. The rest of the social mass must find some defense against the martial and political associations of the young. They find it in the association of the old—the senate. The mature men live with the women and children of whom they are not, or do not know they are, the husbands and the fathers. The woman seeks the protection of her brothers and her mother's brothers. She becomes the center of a social group contrasting with the club of the young males. Here we come upon the first family, the matriarchal family, which, as a matter of fact, is of defensive and reactive origin and opposed to the state. Henceforth, the principles of equal age and equal blood will strive against each other in history. When one rises the other sinks, and vice versa.

In this brief outline I have sought to use the origin of the state as an instance of the creative power inherent in the activity of sport. It was not the worker, the intellectual, the priest, properly speaking, or the businessman who started the great political process, but youth, preoccupied with women and resolved to fight—the lover, the warrior, the athlete.

New Patterns in Social Relations

MAX HORKHEIMER

At the start I should like to mention a few of the reasons, given by modern thinkers, for the significance of sport. First, I would say, one reason lies in the change in the nature of daily work: industrialization, motorization, automatization demand of the average man more preciseness, more trustworthiness, more ability to change from one assignment to another, more patience, but less spontaneity, less personal interest, less physical effort. The second reason is that individuals have a feeling that their functions, despite their importance, as well as they themselves, have become interchangeable; that is why they are longing to be respected for achievements which are due to their personal efforts as individuals. Another reason is the need of the man in the lonely crowd to have real, that is, meaningful contact with others, possibly comradeship, to assert himself, to share things with others, to have common ideals. Furthermore, there is less cultural distance between the social groups now than one hundred years ago. Achievement has become the yardstick for everybody: individuals, communities, nations, social systems, even ideologies. Sport, says the sociologist, is a society all of its own; it is maintained by work like society at large, but work in sport is a game in the other society, a kind of game that stirs up and keeps busy the energies of both active and passive participants. This society of its own—and here is a questionable side of the importance of sport in the modern world—or rather the ethics of this new society, are used as a kind of substitute for any moral yardstick. Anything seems to be justified if it is done in a sportsmanlike manner, if there is some sporting spirit and fair play in it. Even a bloody war, or the gruesome fights between gang and gang or clique and clique.

Among the criticisms of sport today, one of the most frequent ones concerns the interest of powerful agencies and of nations in what is going on in sports. This is indeed criticized very much, and I should like to read to you a little passage which I found when I became interested in sports; it is taken from the *Encyclopaedia of Social Science*. "The importance of sport in modern society," this encyclopaedia says, "lies not so much in its value as a means of recreation, an educational or even a military discipline, but in its economic implications. The problem confronting students of leisure and recreation is chiefly one of regulation, whether through private voluntary effort, or through legislation of a large-scale business, an enterprise which is based on specialization and professionalism, ruthless competition, exploitation of performers and exaggerated publicity." You see that there is indeed much criticism regarding the interest shown by the big agencies. But we must be clear: without their help to stimulate and organize sport, there would not be sport like we have in our days. This kind of interest is good and bad at the same time.

Reprinted from E. Jokl and E. Simon, editors, *International Research in Physical Education* (pp. 173–185), 1964. Courtesy of Charles C Thomas, Publisher, Springfield, Illinois.

385

Now let me look into this whole problem the way I see it, and again, I ask for your indulgence because I have thought about it only as a social scientist and I shall be raising a number of questions. In particular I shall say that, from the point of view of the social sciences we know very little about sports in many respects, and that we should have many more studies and much more research made on this phenomenon called sport.

Whoever studies the changes which have taken place during the last century in the way of life of the industrialized countries is immediately struck by the change in the functions of the family. The family forms a cell, the structure of which bears witness to the impact of the transformations which society as a whole has undergone. Inversely, the changes in the structure of the family have made their impact on the structure of society. At the beginning of the century there could still be found, not only in the countryside, but often in towns too, what sociology terms "the extended family." At least in the so-called middle-classes, the businessman, the industrialist, the owner of a small factory too, looked upon his family as being not only his wife and children, but also his parents and his brothers and sisters; he felt himself to a certain extent responsible for those of the family who were incapable of maintaining themselves. Quite often all lived in one household together with the servants, who might stay for many years with the same family. The bank manager who gave the head of the family credit for his business and advice as to his finances, the lawyer, and, last but not least, the doctor, had all for a long time been closely connected with the family. This cell gave the child the impression of a social reality more durable than the individual himself. It gave him a sense of security favourable for the development of his aptitudes. He was an integral part of it, as it was an integral part of him. Looking after it, enriching it, continuing it, was the task which took up his whole life, giving it a positive meaning, which was not artificial but real. It was simply taken for granted. This "family feeling" permeated all the activities of the individual, professional

and non-professional even outside the narrow sphere of the family. Thus the idea of sport, too, was grounded on and at the same time limited by the ties which bound the individual to his family. The society of that time did not make the same demands on sport which it does today.

The social mechanisms which have brought about this change in the family are too well known for me to expound them here. I will therefore confine myself to mentioning the following ones: the amazing development of technology, motorization and automation; the progressive falling-off in the importance of the small independent industry and of the human qualities which it called for; the linking of many functions in the work-process; equality of men and women on a legal footing; the tendency towards full employment. The relationship between men and women, or to use a term which is in itself a significant one, "marriage partners," as well as the relationship between parents and children—who are now the sole elements forming the family—has become more rational, more conscious, more limited. Without the partners themselves having anything to do with it, the family, which had been an end in itself, has become an instrument. All the feelings which derived from the basic "family feeling" have been affected by the disintegration of the former family cell; although the family may still be regarded as an obligation by those who are conscious of their responsibilities, it no longer gives a meaning to life. However, the need to find a meaning to life has grown all the greater, as there are no other sources which can satisfy it.

The results of this change are to be seen particularly clearly in the sphere of religion. How is the conception of Our Father in Heaven and the identification of the believer with the Son, of love and respect for one's neighbour, to determine the behaviour of the individual if the circumstances, which formerly contributed during the period of childhood to bestow meaning on the notions of Father and Son, have become so prosaic and so impoverished. For the majority the sole aim which necessity dictates is the individual career, and since this is primarily the concern of the individual alone, the latter senses a void in his life, is ill at ease, experiences often that inward despair which is one of the characteristics of the mood of modern man. The increase in juvenile delinquency, the tendency toward nationalist outbidding by the Left or the Right, the surface optimism which corresponds, however, to a deep-felt cynicism, originate in the crisis which our civilization is undergoing, in which the transformation of the family plays a vital role.

Clearly sport figures among those activities which help young people to overcome the difficulties of present-day society. Teaching, in particular of traditional subjects, because of the lack of solid relations between school and family, is considered, even in the lower classes, exclusively as a preparation for future professional life; the higher up the scale of education one goes, the more this is accepted as an inevitable evil. The school-teachers, and more so the professors, impart to their pupils knowledge both useful and useless; much of it is useless—one has only to think of how the philologists and historians of our colleges and universities needlessly overburden the future teachers. Outside the school but in connection with it, sport groups have begun to form. Even if the creation and the development of these groups may sometimes reveal grave deficiencies, even if they are liable to cause psychological harm to students who are handicapped or physically weak, this belonging to a team is a factor of great importance in the lives of school children and young people. The understandable demands of the health insurances that the sports group of school children should be supervised by a teacher, may hinder, however, the formation of free groups, which are often to be preferred.

I should like to say a word on the function of small groups in general. It is among his fellows, in sport and play, that the individual finds what for a long time neither home nor school, much less the crowded lecture-halls and seminars of the university, have satisfactorily given him, namely the opportunity to assert himself by continual con-frontation with others; to assert himself not only physically, but, equally, through his character, his mind and his emotions. In the common effort which unites them, he is encouraged to reveal his different instincts, his preferences and his antipathies and, at the same time, to master them. He learns to put himself forward in an open and honest manner, to recognize and admit his own weaknesses and to accept those of others. Sociologists and psychologists have repeatedly told us that the mass of spectators at contests and matches are practicing a catharsis, that is to say, they are letting off in a harmless manner their aggressive instincts. Now this is all the more true and fulfills a more productive purpose for the small group practicing sport. To externalize their instincts in a form which is acceptable to others also means, for the adolescents in the small group, to develop these instincts, to give them a certain form, in a sense to *"civilize"* them. It is hardly necessary for me to stress that the psychological process involved brings with it certain dangers. Education in the team and by the team is in no way comparable to the multilateral development of the child in the cultivated bourgeois family of the 19th century; to the continual confrontation of father and son from childhood through puberty to maturity. It is true that there is some resemblance between the sense of community, and the comradeship which excludes rivalry on the one hand, and, on the other, the respect and veneration for the father, which finally triumph over envy and jealousy. However, the emotional development of the adolescent within the group is accomplished more simply and energetically. The individual is compelled by force of circumstances to adapt at all costs. He learns far less of the content and of the reactions which stem from the cultural tradition; he is less hampered by problems of feelings; but he learns more quickly what is essential, the mechanisms with which he will henceforth always react to his surroundings. It is perhaps here that we see the superior educative value of the group. Subtleties of attitude towards the rest of the world; nuances in motivation, which were formally the aim of education, would be today—and all the more in the society of the future—a ridiculous burden, shackles, the equivalent of provincial peculiarities in former times. I must confess, however, that this is a problematic advantage.

The ever-increasing educative value of the sport group in schools and universities is only one of the many reasons for the unusual role which sport plays in modern society. It is, so to speak, a natural product of society; it was spontaneously generated to counteract certain dangers and deficiencies which appeared in the course of the mutation of society. It is pointless in this context to speak of financial interests, those of commerce and of industry, of hotels and of travel agencies, of agencies of international propaganda, of the mass media and of national lotteries. I think that eventually these influences are justified, at this juncture in our civilization which I have been describing. Furthermore they help to extend the radius of the action of sport into those milieux which have become, as it were, "vacua," blank areas, under the impact of technological progress and of the changes in social structures which it has produced. This influence can be particularly beneficial in the loneliness of old age, when human relations tend to become colourless and superficial, or in the organization of leisure-time—Freizeit, loisirs—which clearly shows us that the conception of the individual subject is antiquated and vague. I do not hesitate to express my conviction that in all the fields we have been considering here, sport can do at least as much as an art and a literature which have almost become museum pieces. The more light is thrown on the functions and possibilities of life in a sporting community, the more necessary it will become to make sport the subject of very serious theoretical and empirical studies, a subject for scientific research. Anyone who is a little acquainted with the literature, is well aware that, apart from a few treatises and some excellent articles, science reveals an astonishing gap when it comes to the question of sport. Today, confessing as I do my ignorance on the subject, I can do little

more than raise a number of questions which, in my opinion, deserve a serious scientific answer.

The first question which occupies me concerns the relationship between the athletes themselves, between the athletes and the trainer, the coach, and finally the relationship between the athletes and either the opposing team or their individual opponents. As far as I can judge, the relations between the athletes in the same group are certainly positive ones. They seem to be better in the younger teams than in those which are already at the stage of competing in public; better in the smaller groups than in the large ones; better at secondary-school age than at college or university age. It goes without saying that conditions will be different in different countries. The sport situation in the United States has been the best studied. The problematic aspects have been constantly brought forward and discussed. It has been ascertained that football in particular has assumed a very important role in colleges and universities. "In higher education," to quote the Director of a college on the West coast of the United States, "there is a need for an integrating force, for a common ground, by reference to how the various studies can be coordinated. Neither science nor religion can fill this role. The curriculum has become more complex; there are numerous branches which can be chosen. Few students have the same time-table. . . . In our times of intellectual and social disintegration it is . . . football which unites all the studies. . . . Football is more than a spectacle, it has become a symbol. . . . From a loftier standpoint you could say that football has become the spiritual centre of the modern campus." At the university, however, sport is already tottering on the verge between an amateur hobby and a professional activity. The group is still, it is true, fairly free, open, devoting itself to the game without ulterior motive. "College football" you may read in a recent report "has neither the studied grace nor the untamed violence of the professional game; the quarterback stars are not yet the routine professionals who read the Wall Street Journal, belong to the P.T.A. and get telegrams of good wishes from their insurance agents on their birthdays. Their game is still a game. They make mistakes and if they ever do become professional, most of them have to start their training all over again.''

There are two problems which anyone who takes college football seriously should consider. The first is that football already exerts a strong influence on the pupils in their final classes at high school. A former head coach at a large university, the University of Southern California asserts that ''In spite of all the solemn promises of purity, college football has already all the blemishes which professional football acquired when it became a big commercial business.'' This means to say that the successful team draw the students and makes good publicity; it is even a source of donations and endowments. Even state institutions, says the coach, always need more money. The danger lies most of all in the increasingly marked preference which is shown for scholarship candidates who are promising players, in the transformation of open playing groups into teams wearing the colours of their institution, which even on the college sports ground take over the same functions as town, industry, or state teams. The more institutional, commercial, political and national interests infiltrate into the sport group, and the more they condition the relations of the players among themselves, of these with the players of rival teams and between players and spectators, the less free and profitable these human relations will become. It would be wrong not to recognize that the interest of private and official bodies in sport is a desirable, and even necessary condition for the realization of the subjective and objective potentialities of sport, which attract children and particularly adolescents, and incite them to take an active part in sports. Nevertheless we should be aware of these powers.

The second danger is that the power of integration which sport exercises today favours only a limited number of the members of the institution, particularly as they advance from grade to grade at school or from semester to semester at the university. ''The proportion of students who actively participate in the diverse disciplines of sports is so small,'' says Mr. Robert Hutchins, former president of the University of Chicago, ''that it is hard to say, even if this sporting activity were a game instead of a business, whether or not it improves the health or the morality of university life.''

The relations with the opponent, which I shall come back to, affect above all teams of youths and adults. They are of fundamental importance for the evaluation of the social and psychological functions of sports. With regard to relations between opponents, I should like to quote an observation which I owe, among many other things to my friend, William Jones. The more intense the contact between the opposing parties in a sporting exercise, the less psychological aggression there is, even if the contest is relentless. The boxer, in throwing a punch, does not feel himself to be attacking an enemy. His opponent is at the same time his partner. And even if the struggle is very earnest, if everything is at stake, there is no hatred. It has also been observed that the real sportsman is more interested in his performance, more interested in what he succeeds objectively in doing, than in his opponent; that is to say, the difference, the antagonism between the other and the self, tends to disappear from sport, taken in the best sense of the word. Of course, one cannot lay this down as a general rule; and above all it applies only to the immediate protagonists in the sport drama.

The relations between the members of a team and their trainer, as also those between the trainers of different teams, have hitherto been little explored. The trainers, or coaches, are generally professionals, very rarely are amateurs to be found among them. The coaches are grouped in professional associations. But when they find themselves with their team face to face with a rival team and a rival coach on the playing field, they are not only opponents, in many cases they are enemies. The much debated problem of amateurs and professionals, which I will not try to analyse here, might be studied particularly with regard to coaches. I do not think personally that the professional is necessarily any more a business-man than the so-called amateur. It is true that for the professional it is not just the match itself which is at stake, it is also his position, his job, his name, his prestige. Prestige always has its material value; which is why it has been said, and rightly so, that the limits between amateurism and professionalism are fluid, or more precisely, illusory. Whoever gives some thought to the subject will come to the conclusion in our present-day rationalist and pragmatic age, the dream of a prestige stripped of all material advantages will never constitute a sufficient social attraction. The number of people who would be prepared, for the sake of a prestige of this kind, to devote to sport the time which they might have spent in earning money in some other way, will never form a group significant enough to engage the attention of a statistician.

The coach not only fills the role of the teacher at school, but the relations between him and his team are even more closely knit than those between the teacher and his pupils, in fact it could be said that he fulfills for his team some of the functions of the priest and of the officer. The way in which in a basketball match—one of the most differentiated games in modern sport—he selects and replaces his players, and gives them their instructions, is sufficient indication of the extent to which he must know the game, the capabilities of his men, and what fine perceptions he must have in order to be a good coach.

The referee or umpire on the other hand is never a professional; most of them have never been regular team-members. They are usually keen sports club members, whose ambition it is to become referees and perhaps even international referees. In spite of vociferous protests on the part of a dissatisfied public, in spite of all the criticisms to which he is subjected, even at the risk of having empty bottles hurled on to the playing field and of the match developing into a free-for-all fight, the referee is always to the forefront of the game; he must travel widely, and he looks upon his office

as a great honour. I think it would be a very interesting study to question local and international referees on their lives, to inquire into the motives which guide them and into their ideas in general.

I have deliberately mentioned the referee before the captain and the champion of the team. For the star-athlete is an even more important element. Sometimes the star-athlete—by means of his public —can have more influence over the referee than the referee has over him. Star-athletes—if my information is accurate—are very often sensitive, irritable, temperamental, just like the "stars" in other spheres. And like the latter they are not even always the best performers. For while the other members of the team are generally linked by friendship, the relations of the champion with the ordinary athlete are often—as also in other fields— problematic. The "stars," as I have said before, exercise considerable influence on the spectators. In a match which took place, I am told, in Alexandria, between a team from Egypt and one from Spain, a fist-fight broke out among the spectators; but the two most popular players from the two opposing teams declared on the public address system that they were friends and straight-away peace was restored among the audience. One could say much about this psychological phenomenon, namely the impulse to follow the man with the greatest reputation. We have a number of complex studies on audience reactions at the cinema and in other mass gatherings. I myself have made studies on this question or helped in editing such studies. Often the results have brought to light new facts, quite different from those we had foreseen in our hypotheses. Allow me to give you an example, even if it is not connected with sport. I remember a film against capital punishment, which showed a particularly cruel example of legal murder. My colleagues and myself knew that this film had been a considerable box-office success in several of the provincial towns, although we knew too that the majority of the inhabitants were in favour of capital punishment. Delighted at the influence of this truly humanitarian film we sent students to interview local cinema managers. The chief question was: "Why has this film against execution had a longer run than any of the other films?" The reply was always the same: "Oh, was it a film *against* capital punishment? In any case, the subject of the film was an execution, wasn't it?"

If I am not mistaken, inquiries into the reactions of the audience at sports meetings should produce more humane results. We should not let ourselves be led astray by the fevered shouting, frenzied applauding and furious whistling which goes on in the sports grounds throughout the world: the spectators always prefer to see victory rather than defeat, though of course one is not possible without the other. The joy exhibited at the victory of the athlete or athletes with whom a particular section of the audience identifies itself does not betoken—though there are a few exceptions—hatred for the opponent. In fact, it often happens that joy for a victory is mixed with respect and sympathy for the beaten side. Stronger than the desire to see one's own side win is, perhaps, the hope of having a glimpse of perfection, or at least something approaching it. I am under no delusions; this idea, I know, is paradoxical. When one considers the resemblance between on the one hand the plebs and dignitaries who peopled the circuses of Ancient Rome and on the other the crowds which nowadays pack the sports stadia, it seems ridiculous to talk of anything other than aggressive instincts. However, the escape from loneliness, from the atmosphere of the home, from daily routine and drab duties; the hankering to be together with fellow townsmen or countrymen, may be complementary motives. Nationalism in particular, universal religion of the modern age, is considered by many authors to be the chief motivation of the crowds which come to the sports grounds throughout the world. Nevertheless I believe that there are many more objective elements, psychological and sociological, contained in sport and in the sporting public than historians and many writers would have us believe. The inquiries almost always ask the same questions: how many matches does the average man go to, what percentage is there of participants of the same age, of the

same social group, of men and women—of course there are always more men. What should be studied above all are motives, characters and behaviour. Practical inferences for the development of sport and of other spheres of culture could result from studies of this kind. The wish so justifiably expressed by M. René Maheu in his speech in Rome three years ago, that sport might one day reach those heights which it might only attain through culture, cannot be realized without the aid of methodical thinking. The same can be said of the words of Jean Prévost a year before that in Finland: "Sport too has its humanist aspects." And Maheu on the same occasion went on to say: "These humanist aspects should be taught like the other humanities, like the other cultural disciplines." But in order to teach them—let me add—we have first to find them and formulate them.

May I say in a word how difficult it is to explain theoretically the role of nationalism in sport. If, by nationalism we mean not an attachment to cultural traditions, legitimate pride in the great works and achievements of the civilization to which we belong—in which case nationalism may well be linked with horror for the misdeeds of the same civilization—but if we mean the blind affirmation of the will for national domination which goes hand in hand with the hatred of all those who think differently, the individual ego being inflamed by the collective ego, then nationalism and sport are definitely in opposition. "The morality of sport" writes a young sociologist, "is shown in its attempt to neutralize certain values. There must be a winner and a loser, but victory or defeat should not be assessed *in moral terms.*" And this same morality, "which is expressed in conceptions such as *fairness, team-spirit, etc.,*" in positive or negative values, tends towards pluralism, towards the open society in which that which is different, too, is prized. "The sporting spirit," says this author, "should offer and guarantee each group equality of chances to show its worth and to participate in the exercise of power."

In sports competitions one can observe how the spectator at first identifies himself with his own side, but afterwards often transfers his sympathies to the weaker team, especially if it is making every effort to catch up on the advantage which the other team has over it. So it is encouraged in every possible way. "The uneasiness which takes hold on us when we see political events which are contrary to the rules of democratic practice" so the same author continues, "certainly originates from this feeling: this is not sporting." Similar examples soon lead us to the conclusion that the rules of sportsmanship and mentality of the sportsman, which it is true are violated only too often, constitute the modern expression of the former great cultural traditions, of Christianity, as also of the Age of Enlightenment in France and of the philosophy of Immanuel Kant. Without this sporting spirit one cannot imagine the existence of fair and peaceful competition between nations.

It has often been said that sport should not become an aim, but should remain an instrument. To me the first idea seems right and the second one wrong. As long as it is only an instrument, and consciously recognized as such, it may be used in the service of profit, politics, egotism or just as a pastime. Whether it serves health is, in my view, problematic. But all these ends, whether good or problematic, will destroy sport if they are allowed to dominate it totally, will prevent its being an expression of freedom. In this respect sport is like art, literature and philosophy, and all the springs of the productive imagination. To preserve its freedom, to allow it to make its own decisions and dictate its own regulations, in spite of all the powerful influences from outside, seems to me to be the historic task of all those who are seriously concerned with sport. I admit that I do not feel at all optimistic. Nevertheless, seeing that in our modern civilization, threatened on all sides, and suffering from the decadence of the family and of other sources of culture, sport has become, for the reasons which I have mentioned, a kind of world in itself, a society within society, we should stake our hopes on it. We all know that sport, too, has been considerably affected by the cultural crisis. I have omitted to illustrate this in detail but I think that we must devote ourselves above all to discovering and strengthening its non-pragmatic and consequently productive elements, and I know that many of you think as I do, and are in a better position to take steps towards this end than I.

Toward a Social Philosophy of Achievement and Athletics

HANS LENK

To date, no comprehensive philosophy of achievement behavior has been developed. Nevertheless, the new critical generation and the so-called establishment agree about one thing: both believe that we live in an "achieving society" guided by the "performance principle" (or "the principle of achievement"). Social ranks and opportunities, advancement, remuneration, and influence have been assessed and allotted solely on the basis of personal professional performance. A society that assigns roles and ranks to its members on this principle is called an "achieving society" (McClelland).

On the above points both sides are in agreement. However, on other issues there is a parting of minds: While the new protest generation considers all workers to be yoked under the inhuman and also unnecessary pressure or even "terror" of performance and the compulsion of productivity which ought to be eliminated as quickly as possible, the members of the Establishment resolutely plead for the preservation of the "performance principle" which, as they claim, has brought us

prosperity and economic security. Anyone who preaches defeatism regarding production, performance, and achievement, is, they say, plainly asocial and irresponsible in view of the need to raise productivity for the future welfare of mankind.

There is something "human, all too human" about these all-or-nothing dichotomies which are highly convenient for dividing people into supporters and opponents, into members of ingroups and outgroups: hedonists and hippies versus ascetic puritans. Performance or pleasure? The hedonists plead: "Then we prefer to choose pleasure"; the puritans reply: "We don't want any socioeconomic catastrophe—therefore we are for performance."

Apparently, however, performance, as it is claimed by the critics, always also involves the pressure of productiveness and "pressure for achievement." Pleasure or the compulsion of achievement, this alternative seems to be the only one: puristic thinking in terms of alternatives on both sides—whether from the Left or the Right. Yet thinking in terms of totality is, in fact, always wrong. Reality is not that simple. This line of thought leads too easily to totalitarianism.

This kind of thinking in clichés is typical of that argument which is used ideologically for the apparently theoretical justification of one's own values as well as for the rejection of those of others.

393

"Performance" is strongly imbued with emotions depending upon interests and social values of the person pronouncing upon it; to some people it is a concept of quality, a price tag, which even advertising uses suggestively: in the year of the last Olympic Games some service stations used the slogan "Performance decides" for advertising purposes. By advocating competition and by talking about performance the advertisement created, or attempted to create, the illusion of achievement. The other connotations of this word of many meanings, "Leistung," i.e. performance (achievement), were also—implicitly at least—suggested in one way or another. On the other hand, the social critics, who saw through this trick, rejected all ideas of competition, all merits in training to improve performance, as ideological perfidy on the part of holders of power or the ruling class to maintain their established privileges and positions. They even regarded the reference to successful achievement as conservative ideology.

The criticism of the performance principle and the model of the "achieving society" is transferred ready-made to athletics. Particularly in the so-called late capitalist system athletics are regarded by the critics as a "national and international demonstration of the performance potential and the ideology of achievement of the political and economic system." Athletics would, they say, serve "to restore and preserve physical fitness . . . which, in turn, is exploited in the process of work." This criticism claims that the popular sports find their function in "canalizing aggressions (which mainly arise in the process of work) into harmless channels"; that is to say they have a "bread-and-circus function." Even school sports ("as the acknowledged reservoir for the training of new sports champions," who would also be used by other people as tools of the capitalist system) are alleged to contribute "decisively to the stabilization and consolidation of this capitalist system." These assertions come from a resolution put forward by the Young Socialists of West Germany at their party conference some years ago. This socialist criticism can be summarized as follows: "A society which has made a point of converting the concept of achievement through the performance principle into an ideology cannot avoid applying it in sports, too. This ideologically irrational performance principle is reflected in sport in just the same way as it is in the processes of industrial work and production. The top sportsmen, as muscle-machines and symbolic reflections of the political and economic system that they represent, become mechanical medal-producers." Two years earlier a document of the Socialist German Students' Association (SDS) had already regarded "the performance in sports as an indirect encroachment of social repression" itself. All that the Young Socialists did was to repeat this sweeping judgment in more intelligible language.

Yet even such an otherwise deliberate author as Günter Grass recently expressed the opinion that the "dictatorship of the performance principle" was becoming increasingly reflected in competitive sports. A substitute 'arms race' was taking place in all the nations that go in for sports and especially for the Olympics. The sportsmen were not motivated solely by "personal ambition": "It is the collective performance principle that drives them." "Athletics do not provide a release from pressures. They are the result of the pressures to which competitive societies submit themselves. They have trained crack sportsmen by means of blind compliance in order to be represented by them." Yet, "where achievement does not help to solve social problems it creates additional social problems. Achievement on principle makes excessive demands on those from whom it is extorted, devours and dissipates their strength, their health and their time, senselessly produces a surplus, mixes poison in the air and the water and creates slag piles which not even weeds can make turn green." "Misapplied social ambition" would call for excessive output also in sport. It was not only the professionally employed who were subjected to "professional coercion" and "the terror of performance," but also the crack sportsmen who "make their bodies available for the interests of others."

Are athletics to be regarded as the most conducive instantiating model of the performance principle, as the clear reflection of the "achieving society," as the open embodiment of systematic coercion to compete, with all the manifestations of socio-pathological and psycho-neurotic compulsion? What the performance principle" means, in this alleged interpretation, is compulsion to perform. The total cliché permits no differentiation. Competitive sports are competitive terrorism. Pleasure in performance—that is unknown. One author, Rigauer, had already described the methods of training for sports as "repressive . . . systems of operational instructions": "To practise competitive sports means that one must perform in order to fulfill society's expectations of (one's) performance" (p. 18).

But does performance in sports actually and totally come under the "performance principle" in the sense used by the social critics? Can criticism be transferred from the business sphere to competitive sports so simply without further distinction? As always, analysis is more difficult than general pro-and-contra clichés.

In the first place the talk about "*the* performance principle" is by no means unambiguous. Marcuse uses it in his book *Eros and Civilization* (p. 115) in at least three different meanings. In one place he says: "The definition of the standard of living in terms of automobiles, television sets, airplanes and tractors is that of the performance principle itself." In this first meaning he equates "performance principle" with the principle of economic competition and with the contention that the society is stratified in accordance with the economic criteria of profit and success. In the second meaning Marcuse denotes only the "extra," or surplus, repression exerted above and beyond that required for ensuring an appropriate standard of living, i.e., the enforced, "alienated" labour, as coming under the "performance principle." Finally, in the third case Marcuse also interprets the "performance principle" for our society and for our culture as a principle of the identity of the personality, as a principle of self-presentation and

self-confirmation, even self-constitution. He does not subordinate artistic achievements to the performance principle but to the "criticism of the performance principle."

What, then, is the Marcusean position which makes sense regarding achievement in sports? The relationship of sports to the "performance principle" naturally differs according to each of the three interpretations. According to the first interpretation the amateur's achievement in sports does not, in fact, belong to the performance principle, apart from few highly earning athletes or professionals who determine and enhance their status on the "performance market" partly through the sale of their mercenary "goods" called "performance." And in the second version, too, achievement in sports does not come under the performance principle if one disregards coercive measures by the directors of associations or sanctions in the form of threats that a sports scholarship would be withdrawn if an athlete does not turn up at a training course or a meet, etc. According to this interpretation normal achievement in sports is even a part of a "libidinally" hued, or tinged, activity in Marcuse's sense: the athlete does, in fact, personally aspire to this particularly strongly and attaches intense emotional value and feelings of delight to it, even if it is to some extent a question of an abstract "delight" at success in the future and a "delight" at the performance achieved. In this interpretation, achievement in sports would have to be classed, according to Marcuse's definition, precisely with what he calls "criticism of the performance principle"—an obvious absurdity as compared with the normal usage of the language. In competitive sports one would actually have a "libidinally" hued and constituted activity in a culture subordinated to the play impulse, which is what Marcuse calls for in place of the listless monotony of the assembly-line work of factories of today.

It is completely wrong to suppose that every achievement in sport is the result of pressure to perform, that every performance in sport is extorted from the athlete. Hardly anyone makes more demands upon himself than the sportsman himself. This assessment and this experience of the athlete should not be ignored—not even if it is contended that this attitude towards performance was manipulated in his early childhood. The differences between the fact that the athlete aspires to high achievements in sports and strives for success on the one hand and the attitude toward compulsory labour or toward the maintenance of production norms at the assembly-line on the other simply cannot be ignored. Purely sociological criticism all too often fails to take into account this crucial difference. Evaluated attitudes are, however, constitutive for these differences. Mark Twain was puzzled long ago as to why to gum up paper-bags was work, yet the climbing of Montblanc was sport.

In the third interpretation of the performance principle given by Marcuse, in which it is explained as a criterion of self-assertion, achievement in sports is most certainly included in the "performance principle." Everything said about "libidinally" hued and constituted activity would also be applicable here.

Before this explanation can be gone into more fully, however, it is necessary first to discuss, in view of the general criticism of social critics of the "performance principle" in the professional field, how far this criticism applies to performance in sports. This criticism might be briefly summarized: The social-philosophical criticism of the professional "performance principle" is directed, firstly, against the compulsory character of the routine work which is extorted unilaterally from the worker contrary to his interests and abilities; secondly, against the non-attributability of the result of complex production processes, of a "performance," of an accomplished work to the person producing it; thirdly, against the lacking, but falsely claimed equality, of opportunities in education and employment; and, fourthly, against the inhumanity of a hypostasized perfect implementation of the "performance principle."

On the transferability of point 1 of this criticism what may be said is this: Achievement in sports is not as a rule (apart from extreme exceptions) extorted from the individuals under pressure; it corresponds to the maximum extent to the interests and abilities of the athlete.

On point 2: As a result, success or performance as well as achievement in sports is still to be attributed exclusively to the individual as his own work—in contrast to the "performance on the assembly-line." Only the individual athlete can accomplish the achievement, the performance is unmistakably effected by a personal feat—it cannot be accomplished by surreption and trickery. National help in fostering and funding can facilitate it, but cannot be a substitute for it. Even if the rate of success of the performance decreases in comparison with that of better assisted competitors—the individual accountability for the performance is thereby not diminished nor is its emotional content. Every attraction for the athlete himself, the effort to succeed, the pleasure in performance, and the pride in achievement and the importance of all these for proving and confirming oneself cannot be simply argued away. They are psychic realities.

On point 3: The equality of opportunities in competitive sports is, indeed, also impeded by national and social promotional measures, but it is still more nearly achieved than in the professional "start in life." This certainly applies primarily to the participants from countries somewhat on an equal footing of fostering athletic improvement. However, this also applies to the already motivated and experienced sportsmen themselves, and not to all who could potentially take part in a competition. The points of criticism that were directed against the applicability of the performance principle in the professional sphere can, therefore, hardly be transferred to sports and achievement in sports—and, by the way, also not to professional work in general but only to some specific forms, admittedly still deplorable ones—e.g., assembly-line work. (But there are initiatives under way to improve human conditions of factory work—and they should be supported intensively.) Not only emotional preoccupation but also personal accountability and attributability are completely guaranteed in athletic achievement. Equality of opportunity is, within limits, relatively easier to achieve here than in any other social sphere.

The fourth point of the criticism, which was directed against the all-too-perfect implementation of the performance principle and against a total "achieving society," can likewise not be utilized as an argument against competitive sports as a social phenomenon. For the latter by no means requires a total "achieving society," even if, as a social segment, it is organized in restricted aspects in accordance with the criteria of achievement. Sport by no means requires that all other social spheres should be regulated and evaluated according to the criteria of performance nor that every single person has to be regarded only as an object of productiveness of achievements, even if an evaluation of the individual in his performance role prevails within the very disciplines relating to competitive sports.

Perhaps one could advance some more detailed arguments against the gross conception of athletics as the ideal model of the "achieving society" in general such as was advocated by Adam and v. Krockow.

Adam describes "the attitude towards achievement in sports as a model . . . for . . . the attitude to proficiency in general": Advancement on the social scale as a result of an objective and impartial comparison of performance reconciles the initially seemingly antagonistic principles of equality and of differentiated assignment of ranks. In an ideal "achieving society," according to Adam, "all orders of precedence would be based on comparative performance." Absolute objectivity of comparison (especially of different kinds of performance) is impossible. But this objectivity can most nearly be achieved in a model manner in competitive sports (through measurement, contriving a decisive situation or counting successful attempts—less or hardly at all objectively through assessment of points and scores on the basis of subjective decisions). "The mechanism of self-affirmation" through one's own performance stabilizes, according to Adam, the "feeling of one's own value"—particularly in the overcoming of intentionally induced feelings of listlessness and obstacles in training for sports. In athletics, moreover, the attitude toward achievement is trained in an exemplary manner and, in Adam's opinion, that is essential for the preservation of the species and for the balance of fortune of mankind in view of the problems of the growing population.

Whilst Adam analyses the model of competitive sports more from a sociopedagogic perspective, v. Krockow (1962, p. 58 ff., 52 ff.) goes in more for a sociological and sociophilosophical interpretation: "Athletics—a product of the industrial society"; v. Krockow expands this almost trivial sociological proposition to the philosophical one "that competitive sports . . . are the symbolically concentrated representation of the society's basic principles." It is in sport that "exactitude," "ideality," "objectivity," equality of opportunities, measurability and comparability, spectacularness and general intelligibility represent symbolically more clearly than anywhere else the principles of differentiation in performance (i.e., attribution of a social rank on the grounds of individual achievements); the same is true, according to v. Krockow, of the principle of competition and yet also of the equality of opportunities for success. "Performance, competition and equality. What makes modern sport so pregnant with symbolism and so fascinating is not at least the exactness, not to mention the ideality, with which it realizes these basic principles of the industrial society" (1972, p. 94). V. Krockow (*ibid.* p. 96) even asserts: "Sport gives expression to the principles of the industrial society far better than the latter itself does": the objectivity and also the transparency of the comparison of performances, which are nearly perfectly realized in sport, are not exhibited by anything like so completely and visibly in any of the other fields of the complex, almost unsurveyable industrial society. The achievements of the research-worker can only be assessed by experts, the celebrities of our publicity-conscious society create the illusion of achievements, often through acts of self-advertisement. Yet here—in sport—"the record jump is transmitted optically into every house, intelligible to everyone and measured three times over" (*ibid.* p. 95).

Thus, we apparently have sport as the ideal-typical (purely idealized, trenchantly demonstrated) model of the so-called "achieving society." This model thesis seems attractive: it not only explains the fascination of sport and its stormy development parallel with the industrial society itself. It also enables one to understand the protest of the new social criticism, which criticizes the so-called performance principle and competitive sports jointly in a like manner. Moreover, this model thesis is compatible with the relative separation or "extra-worldly demarcation" (v. Krockow) of the sphere of sport from the so-called vicissitudes of life, from the sphere of work. Model character and relative own-worldliness can very well go together.

On the other hand, this model thesis also encounters certain difficulties: What is too easily overlooked is the fact that the so-called "achieving society" is intrinsically a "success society," sometimes of sham achievements sold by means of publicity and of careers, all the more so because professional and social achievement can scarcely be attributed any longer to the individual alone: team, boom and system constitute the determinants of general social achievements. Somewhat exaggeratedly one might say: We no longer live in the idealized, publicly proclaimed "achieving society" but in a "success society": the really personally accomplished achievement counts less in the acquiring of status than do the social effects of achievements, the success or even the semblance of achievement or of talent, or in certain cases the publicity given to alleged achievements (e.g. election successes). Publicity as a substitute for achievement? Is social success already proof of achievement? Certainly, this overall equating of publicity, success and achievement applies, if at all, primarily to representatives of the upper middle classes, to employees laden with responsibilities and to promotion-seeking "performance men." For the lower classes the requirements of production are increasingly converted into standardized and routinized functions of super-

vision of standards which do not allow the individual to stand out from the rest and to distinguish himself through his own efforts, for their main requirement seems to be, rather, the avoidance of acts of disruption and the adherence to average norms as far as possible without any loss due to friction. Whereas social climbers are more inclined to regard the attitude to performance from the point of view of ability to achieve social success, for members of the lower classes the required "performance orientation" seems to consist exclusively in the postulate of allocation and subordination to complex organizational processes with as little disruption as possible.

Ichheiser as early as 1930, in his book *Kritik des Erfolges (Criticism of Success),* made a clear distinction between ability to perform and ability to succeed. He also drew attention to the mechanism of deception whereby the Machiavellian exploitation of the ability to succeed and the concomitant, but mostly concealed, violations of norms imperceptibly favour those who are already able to succeed or who are privileged, and he pointed out that this is not regarded as, let us say, a sign of plain good fortune but is considered by others (and by those concerned themselves) to be a personal achievement.

The sociological requirements of the socio-psychological factors of all these variations of the "performance principle" have not yet been sufficiently examined. It is only in the most recent period that the psychological theory of attribution (Weiner and others) has been going more closely into these questions, in that it is examining the cognitive conditions under which particular types of personality attribute success to themselves as personal achievements or are more inclined to believe that they owe it to fortunate circumstances.

Are the above-mentioned deviations from the idealized "performance principle" the reason for the special fascination of athletics? Does achievement in sports still represent relatively purely, as it were, something which is no longer to be found in the assessment of professional and public achievement: the individual accountability and attributability, the "joyful" experience and "pleasure" in success, the fact that the possibility of deception and corruption does not exist as a rule or else is subjected to strict controls, and the absence of real dependence in the sense of submission to power?

The new criticism of sport mostly relates the outlined character of sport (as a model for the ideal principles of an achieving society) exclusively or predominantly to the so-called capitalist or late capitalist societies. This is undoubtedly a biased restriction as socialist industrial societies or, to put it better, state capitalist systems of society are even more dedicated to the raising of production norms and are inclined to make even more severe demands on the individual for the fulfilment of such norms. Naturally, that also applies to athletics in the socialist countries.

The social criticism of sport is not directed against every demand for achievement but only against the ideology of the achieving society which subordinates all other requirements to the raising of production and achievement and which is oriented to the assurance and creation of privileges of a class-conditioned kind: In particular, a striving for achievement that is motivated by the class struggle is expressly approved by the critics.

Admittedly, a total achieving society would be terrible: the competition of all against all in all activities—man\preying upon man (homo homini lupus)—would make Hobbes' primordial vision come true. The "achieving society" is only a Utopian model which cannot be truly brought into existence, although in some areas, as in sport, it is one ideal orientational symbol among others and is additional to other models for guidance. It can certainly only be applied to limited social spheres and also only in a restricted degree that would be ideally typical (in the sociological meaning of the word after Max Weber); in fact it applies exclusively to social spheres that are distinguished by their comparative competitiveness. It is certainly not desirable to judge a person as a whole solely by his performances in limited social spheres, whether the latter relate to his profession or, say,

to sport. Nor should all the members of a society be subjected to the necessity of achievement even in limited spheres. The "achieving society," which serves as a model in a good many respects, must not become the "compulsorily productive and achieving society" in every respect. A model like this one can only give limited guidelines for limited applicability conditions. Yet, it is true that even our society still cannot dispense with certain constrictions on achievement for quite a long time. That, however, is another matter.

But science, art, and sport could be spheres of performance for individually differentiated possibilities of distinction, and they could be opportunities for enjoyable, libidinally motivated and hued (Marcuse) activities, which could be conducive to self-confirmation, social self-assertion and, in this way, to the stabilizing development of the personality. The pedagogical applications obviously are at hand. The younger Marx's anthropology of the creative, freely evolving human being, as displayed in the ideal image of the scientist and the engineer, is in every way also comparable with the ideal image of the role of the competitive athlete, whose free "self-chosen activity" and whose opportunity to fashion his performance freely and in a certain sense to reflect and unfold his personality therein, ought not to be replaced by a thesis of compulsion for a perfect and excessive performance in competitive sport. That is by no means to deny that in a good many kinds of sports and disciplines, which are especially subjected to public interest and public pressure, one may discern tendencies of a quasi-moral public pressure on performance or the authoritarianism of a corporate dirigistic power and corresponding influences on athletes.

There is no doubt that the new criticism of sport is right in one respect: the concept of the "achieving society" as well as that of the so-called "performance principle" have hitherto been simply taken for granted and have not been more closely examined from the sociophilosophical point of view. This also leads to the partly grotesquely unworldly and excessively incisive black-and-white analysis of athletics. A hitherto nonexistent philosophy of achievement would still have a lot of work to do here in respect to more precise distinctions, necessary differentiations and balanced judgments.

What becomes clear after this analysis is this: one cannot simplify the matter as the German writer Günter Grass does and just assert that the "collective performance principle" impels or compels the athletes as forcefully as it does people in the professional field and that "performance terror" and "compulsion by the object in question" ("Sachzwang") would prevent them from making their own decisions and determining their own actions. Apart from extreme cases which are not to be denied, the athlete identifies himself to a very great extent with his athletic achievements—especially those in training, which scarcely attract public attention. He finds pleasure in the fulfilment of tasks which demand of him all his energy subject to a calculated risk. He identifies himself completely with this subjectively and freely chosen attitude of his.

The thesis of compulsion can, therefore, only fall back on a thesis of manipulation: to the effect that the competitive sportsmen were, in fact, drilled through educational influences in early childhood into adopting the competitive attitude, which our culture positively prizes, and into internalizing the "achieving principle." Certainly, athletes are not more manipulated here than anyone else who has grown up in the Western industrial society. Surely almost all education, then, had to be regarded as manipulation—and nobody could then be called free, for everybody would be "manipulated" in every respect. Viewed empirically, manipulation could hardly be separated from education. In fact, merely relative freedom is identifiable by the fact that the person who is already competent to judge responsibly subscribes to a decision, adopts it as his own, and even defends it. From the point of view of moral philosophy this must be accepted as his opinion, even if the decision to be defended should in some cases prove to be a pleasant illusion.

Obviously, acute problems arise in the case of young adolescents who are not yet able to perceive and assess the problems of an excessive training for performance. Nowadays there are a good many disciplines, ranging from swimming to gymnastics, in which such an intensive regimen of training is required, even at the youthful age of 10 to 12 years, that manifestations of narrow-mindedness, regimentation and dependence on the authoritarian decisions of the parents or coach cannot be precluded in all cases. Nevertheless, the guiding aim in every case should be to avoid forcing even the child to act against his own will, but as often as possible to discuss critically with him (albeit in a preparatory manner) the intelligible problems of the training and gradually to develop his powers of discernment so that the child will later on be able to form his own, relatively independent opinions and to make his own decisions. A coach, too, must be prepared to point out the problems to an athlete and, in some cases, to advise him rather to choose another way of self-development if sports seem to be too onerous to that boy or girl.

Quite apart from that, the achievement of the highest performance is scarcely possible if one does not completely identify oneself with the training and with the significance of this activity.

Self-determined motivation of performance (so far as it is relatively possible) is always preferable in every respect to extraneously determined pressure to perform. Thus, the "democratic" style of coaching founded on the ideal of participatory decisions is by no means a Utopian fiction: It was already introduced and further developed in a good many kinds of team sports quite a long time ago, especially with respect to the Olympic Gold Medal crews of the successful rowing coach, Karl Adam, although it ought to have been more difficult to guide a team towards this objective than, say, an athlete concerned with a single discipline. The possibility of practicing exemplarily "democratic" behavior in a small group of sportsmen shall not be gone into further here.

At any rate, it is clear that the mere system-stabilizing compensatory function of sport and its alleged function to serve only as a vehicle for the regeneration of the labour force, as well as the diverting, manipulating and "depoliticizing" effect of athletics, cannot properly represent *all* the aspects of this complex social and psycho-social phenomenon, as the critics claim.

It is true that the star athletes are also regarded as representatives of the nation, but this function is primarily projected onto them by public opinion. This does not, however, mean that they become just "mechanical medal-producers," "efficient muscle-machines," pampered beasts of top level performance and "reproduced symbols of the political and economic system" and nothing else. Not only are their psychic experiences and the significance of sport for the development and stabilization of their personalities to be looked at in another light, but sport also acquires another meaning in its cultural-philosophical aspect: as a modern Herculean-Promethean myth of daring, energetic action, it embodies the dynamic character of the archetypal roles of the contest and of competitiveness in a symbolical manner resembling the way in which life was reflected for the ancient Greeks in some of their great classical dramas of fate. Yet this interpretation of competitive sport has still only been mentioned. It cannot be presented in detail here; an attempt has been made elsewhere (by the author in 1972) to indicate its main outlines.

The socio-philosophical discussion of sport and of the attitude towards achievement has only just begun. To extricate it from the mere polarization of thinking in black and white, of "pro and contra," is the task of a detailed analysis and criticism in the future. What is particularly noteworthy is the fact that society, which regards itself as an "achieving society," does not possess any kind of elaborated, let alone well-founded, philosophy of the types of attitudes towards achievement. A wide field of activity remains open here for bold philosophical theses and critical considerations.

Bibliography

Adam, K.: Nichtakademische Betrachtungen zur einer Philosophie der Leistung. In *Leistungssport* II (1972) No. 1, pp. 62–68.

Bohme, J.-O., Gadow, J., Güldenpfennig, S., Jensen, J., Pfister, R.: *Sport im Spätkapitalismus.* Frankfurt, 1971.

Gebauer, G.: "Leistung" als Aktion und Prasentation. In *Sportwissenschaft* 1972, pp. 182–203.

Grass, G.: Sport ohne Stoppuhr. In DSB (ed.): *Deutscher Sport* 2, München 1971, p. 18 ff.

Hack, L.: Was heisst schon Leistungsgesellschaft? In *Neue Kritik* 7, No. 3 (1966), pp. 23–32.

Ichheiser, G.: *Kritik des Erfolges.* Leipzig, 1930.

Jungsozialisten: Stellungnahme zum Sport in der Resolution zum Parteitag Bremen 1971. In Jungsozialisten: *Bremer Parteibeschlüsse.* Bonn, 1971, pp. 20–24.

Krockow, C. von: Der Wetteifer in der industriellen Gesellschaft und im Sport. In Ausschuss deutscher Leibesetzieher (ed.): *Der Wetteifer,* Frankfurt/Wien 1962, pp. 48–63 (Limpert).

Krockow, C. von: *Sport und Industriegesellschaft.* München, 1972 (Piper).

Lenk, H.: *Leistungsmotivation und Mannschaftsdynamik.* Schorndorf/Stuttgart, 1970 (Hofmann).

Lenk, H.: *Philosophie im technologischen Zeitalter.* Stuttgart, Berlin, Köln, Mainz, 1971 (2nd ed.) (Kohlhammer).

Lenk, H.: *Werte, Ziele, Wirklichkeit der modernen Olympischen Spiele.* Schorndorf/Stuttgart, 1964, 1972 (2nd ed.) (Hofmann).

Lenk, H.: *Leistungssport: Ideologie oder Mythos?* Stuttgart, Berlin, Köln, Mainz, 1972 (Kohlhammer).

Lenk, H.: Achievement Motivation and Performance Sport. *Journal of World History* XIV (1972a), pp. 239–249.

Lenk, H.: Sport, Achievement, and the New Left Criticism. In *Man and World* (1972 b), pp. 179–192.

Lenk, H.: Trees, Tournaments, and Sociometric Graphs. *International Review of Sport Sociology* VI (1971), pp. 175–204.

Lenk, H.: Alienation, Manipulation, and the Athlete's Self. In Grupe, O. (ed.): *Sport in our World—Chances and Problems.* (Scientific Conference in the Connection with the Olympic Games in Munich 1972) Berlin, Heidelberg, New York (Springer 1973), pp. 8–18.

Lenk, H. (ed): *Technokratie als Ideologie.* Stuttgart, Berlin, Köln, Mainz, 1973 (Kohlhammer).

Lenk, H., Gebauer, G., Franke, E.: Perspectives of the Philosophy of Sport. In Grupe, O., Kurz, D., Teipel, J.M.: *The Scientific View of Sport.* Berlin, Heidelberg, New York (Springer 1972), p. 29–58.

Lenk, H., Moser, S., Beyer, E. (eds.): *Philosophie des Sport.* Schorndorf/Stuttgart, 1973 (Hofmann).

Lenk, H.: *Social Philosophy of Athletics.* Champaign, Illinois, 1979 (Stipes Publishing Co.).

Marcuse, H.: *Eros and Civilization.* Boston 1955; reprinted: London (Sphere Books).

McClelland, D.C.: *The Achieving Society.* Princeton, 1961 (van Nostrand).

Offe, C.: *Leistungsprinzip und industrielle Arbeit.* Frankfurt, 1970 (Europäische Verlagsanstalt).

Rigauer, B.: *Sport und Arbeit.* Frankfurt, 1969 (Suhrkamp).

Slusher, H.S.: *Man, Sport, and Existence.* Philadelphia, 1967 (Lea & Febiger).

Vanderzwaag, H.J.: *Toward a Philosophy of Sport.* Reading/Mass., 1972 (Addison & Wesley).

Weiss, P.: *Sport—a Philosophic Inquiry.* Carbondale-Edwardsville, London-Amsterdam, 1969 (Southern Illinois University Press).

The Degradation of Sport

CHRISTOPHER LASCH

The Spirit of Play Versus the Rage for National Uplift

Among the activities through which men seek release from everyday life, games offer in many ways the purest form of escape. Like sex, drugs, and drink, they obliterate awareness of everyday reality, but they do this not by dimming awareness but by raising it to a new intensity of concentration. Moreover, they have no side effects, hangovers, or emotional complications. Games simultaneously satisfy the need for free fantasy and the search for gratuitous difficulty; they combine childlike exuberance with deliberately created complications. By establishing conditions of equality among the players, according to Roger Caillois, games attempt to substitute ideal conditions for "the normal confusion of everyday life."[1] They re-create the freedom, the remembered perfection of childhood, and mark it off from ordinary life with artificial boundaries, within which the only constraints are the rules to which the players freely submit. Games enlist skill and intelligence, the utmost concentration of purpose, on behalf of activities utterly useless, which make no contribution to the struggle of man against nature, to the wealth or comfort of the community, or to its physical survival.

The uselessness of games makes them offensive to social reformers, improvers of public morals, or functionalist critics of society like Veblen, who

saw in the futility of upper-class sports anachronistic survivals of militarism and prowess. Yet the "futility" of play, and nothing else, explains its appeal—its artificiality, the arbitrary obstacles it sets up for no other purpose than to challenge the players to surmount them, the absence of any utilitarian or uplifting object. Games quickly lose their charm when forced into the service of education, character development, or social improvement.

Today the official view of the beneficial, wholesome effects of sport, which has replaced the various utilitarian ideologies of the past, stresses their contribution to health, fitness, and hence to the national well-being, considered as the sum of the nation's "human resources." The "socialist" version of this ideology hardly differs from the capitalist version promulgated, for example, by John F. Kennedy in his tiresome pronouncements on physical fitness. Attempting to justify the creation of his President's Council on Youth Fitness (headed by the Oklahoma football coach, Bud Wilkinson), Kennedy cited the consistent decline of strength and fitness as measured by standard tests. "Our growing softness, our increasing lack of physical fitness, is a menace to our security." This attack on "softness" goes hand in hand with a condemnation of spectatorship.

Socialist pronouncements sound depressingly similar. The Cuban government announced in 1967 that sport should be considered part of the "inseparable element of education, culture, health, defense, happiness and the development of people and a new society." In 1925, the central committee of the Soviet Communist party declared that sport should be consciously used "as a means of rallying the broad masses of workers and peasants around the various Party Soviet and Trade Union organizations through which the masses of workers and peasants are to be drawn into social and political activity.'' Fortunately, people of all nations intuitively tend to resist such exhortations. They know that games remain gloriously pointless and that watching an exciting athletic contest, moreover, can be emotionally almost as exhausting as participation itself—hardly the ''passive'' experience it is made out to be by the guardians of public health and virtue.

Huizinga on Homo Ludens

Modern industry having reduced most jobs to a routine, games take on added meaning in our society. Men seek in play the difficulties and demands—both intellectual and physical—they no longer find in work. It is not perhaps monotony and routine in themselves that take the enjoyment out of work, for any job worth doing entails a certain amount of drudgery, but the peculiar conditions that prevail in large bureaucratic organizations and increasingly in the modern factory as well. When work loses its tangible, palpable quality, loses the character of the transformation of matter by human ingenuity, it becomes wholly abstract and interpersonal. The intense subjectivity of modern work, exemplified even more clearly in the office than in the factory, causes men and women to doubt the reality of the external world and to imprison themselves in a shell of protective irony. Work now retains so few traces of play, and the daily routine affords so few opportunities to escape from the ironic self-consciousness that has itself assumed the qualities of a routine, that people seek abandon in play with more than the usual intensity. ''At a time when *image* is one of the most frequently used words in American speech and writing,'' Joseph Epstein notes in a recent essay on sports, ''one does not too often come upon the real thing.''

The history of culture, as Huizinga showed in his classic study of play, *Homo Ludens,* appears from one perspective to consist of the gradual eradication of the play element from all cultural forms—from religion, from the law, from warfare, above all from productive labor.[3] The rationalization of these activities leaves little room for the spirit of arbitrary invention or the disposition to leave things to chance. Risk, daring, and uncertainty—important components of play—have no place in industry or in activities infiltrated by industrial standards, which seek precisely to predict and control the future and to eliminate risk. Games accordingly have assumed an importance unprecedented even in ancient Greece, where so much of social life revolved around contests. Sports, which satisfy also the starved need for physical exertion—for a renewal of the sense of the physical basis of life—have become an enthusiasm not just of the masses but of those who set themselves up as a cultural elite.

The rise of spectator sports to their present importance coincides historically with the rise of mass production, which intensifies the needs sport satisfies while creating the technical and promotional capacity to market athletic contests to a vast audience. But according to a common criticism of modern sport, these same developments have destroyed the value of athletics. Commercialization has turned play into work, subordinated the athlete's pleasure to the spectator's, and reduced the spectator himself to a state of vegetative passivity—the very antithesis of the health and vigor sport ideally promotes. The mania for winning has encouraged an exaggerated emphasis on the competitive side of sport, to the exclusion of the more modest but more satisfying experiences of cooperation and competence. The cult of victory, proclaimed by such football coaches as Vince Lombardi and George Allen, has made savages of the players and rabid chauvinists of their followers. The violence and partisanship of modern sports lead some critics to insist that athletics impart militaristic values to the young, irrationally inculcate local and national pride in the spectator, and serve as one of the strongest bastions of male chauvinism.

Huizinga himself, who anticipated some of these

arguments but stated them far more persuasively, argued that modern games and sports had been ruined by a "fatal shift toward over-seriousness." At the same time, he maintained that play had lost its element of ritual, had become "profane," and consequently had ceased to have any "organic connection whatever with the structure of society." The masses now crave "trivial recreation and crude sensationalism" and throw themselves into these pursuits with an intensity far beyond their intrinsic merit. Instead of playing with the freedom and intensity of children, they play with the "blend of adolescence and barbarity" that Huizinga calls puerilism, investing games with patriotic and martial fervor while treating serious pursuits like games. "A far-reaching contamination of play and serious activity has taken place," according to Huizinga. "The two spheres are getting mixed. In the activities of an outwardly serious nature hides an element of play. Recognized play, on the other hand, is no longer able to maintain its true play-character as a result of being taken too seriously and being technically over-organised. The indispensable qualities of detachment, alertness, and gladness are thus lost."

The Critique of Sport

An analysis of the critique of modern sport, in its vulgar form as well as in Huizinga's more refined version, brings to light a number of common misconceptions about modern society and clarifies some of the central issues of this study, especially the nature of spectacle and the difference between spectacle and other kinds of performance, ritual, and contest. A large amount of writing on sports has accumulated in recent years, and the sociology of sport has even entrenched itself as a minor branch of social science. Much of this commentary has no higher purpose than to promote athletics or to exploit the journalistic market they have created, but some of it aspires to social criticism. Those who have formulated the now familiar indictment of organized sport include the sociologist Harry Edwards; psychologist and

former tennis player Dorcas Susan Butt, who thinks sport should promote competence instead of competition; disillusioned professional athletes like Dave Meggyesy and Chip Oliver; and radical critics of culture and society, notably Paul Hoch and Jack Scott.[4]

A discussion of their work helps to isolate what is historically specific to the present cultural malaise. The critics of sport, in their eagerness to uncover evidence of corruption and decline, attack intrinsic elements of athletics, elements essential to their appeal in all periods and places, on the erroneous assumption that spectatorship, violence, and competition reflect conditions peculiar to modern times. On the other hand, they overlook the distinctive contribution of contemporary society to the degradation of sport and therefore misconceive the nature of that degradation. They concentrate on issues, such as "over-seriousness," which are fundamental to an understanding of sport, indeed to the very definition of play, but peripheral or irrelevant to their historical development and contemporary transformation.

Take the common complaint that modern sports are "spectator-oriented rather than participant-oriented." Spectators, in this view, are irrelevant to the success of the game. What a naive theory of human motivation this implies! The attainment of certain skills unavoidably gives rise to an urge to show them off. At a higher level of mastery, the performer no longer wishes merely to display his virtuosity—for the true connoisseur can easily distinguish between the performer who plays to the crowd and the superior artist who matches himself against the full rigor of his art itself—but to ratify a supremely difficult accomplishment; to give pleasure; to forge a bond between himself and his audience, which consists in their shared appreciation of a ritual executed flawlessly, with deep feeling and a sense of style and proportion.[5]

In all games, particularly in athletic contests, display and representation constitute a central element—a reminder of the former connections between play, ritual, and drama. The players not only compete; they enact a familiar ceremony that reaffirms common values. Ceremony requires witnesses: enthusiastic spectators conversant with the rules of the performance and its underlying meaning. Far from destroying the value of sports, the attendance of spectators makes them complete. Indeed one of the virtues of contemporary sports lies in their resistance to the erosion of standards and their capacity to appeal to a knowledgeable audience. Norman Podhoretz has argued that the sports public remains more discriminating than the public for the arts and that "excellence is relatively uncontroversial as a judgment of performance."[6] More important, everyone agrees on the standards against which excellence should be measured. The public for sports still consists largely of men who took part in sports during boyhood and thus acquired a sense of the game and a capacity to distinguish among many levels of excellence.

The same can hardly be said for the audience for artistic performance, even though amateur musicians, dancers, actors, and painters may still comprise a small nucleus of the audience. Constant experimentation in the arts has created so much confusion about standards that the only surviving measure of excellence is novelty and shock value, which in a jaded time often resides in a work's sheer ugliness and banality. In sport, on the other hand, novelty and rapid shifts of fashion play a small part in games' appeal to a discriminating audience.

Yet even here, the contamination of standards has already begun. Faced with rising costs, owners seek to increase attendance at sporting events by installing exploding scoreboards, broadcasting recorded cavalry charges, giving away helmets and bats, and surrounding the spectator with cheerleaders, usherettes, and ball girls. Television has enlarged the audience for sports while lowering the level of its understanding; at least this is the operating assumption of sports commentators, who direct at the audience an interminable stream of tutelage in the basics of the game, and of the promoters who reshape one game after another to conform to the tastes of an audience supposedly incapable of grasping their finer points. The

American League's adoption of the designated-hitter rule, which relieves pitchers of the need to bat and diminishes the importance of managerial strategy, provides an especially blatant example of the dilution of sports by the requirements of mass promotion. Another is the "Devil-Take-the-Hindmost Mile," a track event invented by the San Francisco *Examiner,* in which the last runner in the early stages of the race has to drop out—a rule that encourages an early scramble to avoid disqualification but lowers the general quality of the event. When the television networks discovered surfing, they insisted that events be held according to a prearranged schedule, without regard to weather conditions. One surfer complained, "Television is destroying our sport. The TV producers are turning a sport and an art form into a circus."[7] The same practices produce the same effects on other sports, forcing baseball players, for example, to play World Series games on freezing October evenings. The substitution of artificial surfaces for grass in tennis, which has slowed the pace of the game, placed a premium on reliability and patience, and reduced the element of tactical brilliance and overpowering speed, commends itself to television producers because it makes tennis an all-weather game and even permits it to be played indoors, in sanctuaries of sport like Caesar's Palace in Las Vegas. Television has rearranged the athletic calendar and thus deprived sports of their familiar connection with the seasons, diminishing their power of allusiveness and recall.

As spectators become less knowledgeable about the games they watch, they become sensation-minded and bloodthirsty. The rise of violence in ice hockey, far beyond the point where it plays any functional part in the game, coincided with the expansion of professional hockey into cities without any traditional attachment to the sport—cities in which weather conditions, indeed, had always precluded any such tradition of local play. But the significance of such changes is not that sports ought to be organized, as a number of recent critics imagine, solely for the edification of the players and that corruption sets in when sports begin to be played to spectators for a profit. No one denies the desirability of participation in sports—not because it builds strong bodies but because it brings joy and delight. It is by watching those who have mastered a sport, however, that we derive standards against which to measure ourselves. By entering imaginatively into their world, we experience in heightened form the pain of defeat and the triumph of persistence in the face of adversity. An athletic performance, like other performances, calls up a rich train of associations and fantasies, shaping unconscious perceptions of life. Spectatorship is no more ''passive'' than daydreaming, provided the performance is of such quality that it elicits an emotional response.

It is a mistake to suppose that organized athletics ever serve the interests of the players alone or that professionalization inevitably corrupts all who take part in it. In glorifying amateurism, equating spectatorship with passivity, and deploring competition, recent criticism of sport echoes the fake radicalism of the counterculture, from which so much of it derives. It shows its contempt for excellence by proposing to break down the ''elitist'' distinction between players and spectators. It proposes to replace competitive professional sports, which notwithstanding their shortcomings uphold standards of competence and bravery that might otherwise become extinct, with a bland regimen of cooperative diversions in which everyone can join regardless of age or ability— ''new sports for the noncompetitive,'' having ''no object, really,'' according to a typical effusion, except to bring ''people together to enjoy each other.'' In its eagerness to remove from athletics the element that has always underlain their imaginative appeal, the staged rivalry of superior ability, this ''radicalism'' proposes merely to complete the degradation already begun by the very society the cultural radicals profess to criticize and subvert. Vaguely uneasy about the emotional response evoked by competitive sports, the critics of ''passive'' spectatorship wish to enlist sport in the service of healthy physical exercise, subduing or

eliminating the element of fantasy, make-believe, and play-acting that has always been associated with games. The demand for greater participation, like the distrust of competition, seems to originate in a fear that unconscious impulses and fantasies will overwhelm us if we allow them expression.[8]

The Trivialization of Athletics

What corrupts an athletic performance, as it does any other performance, is not professionalism or competition but a breakdown of the conventions surrounding the game. It is at this point that ritual, drama, and sports all degenerate into spectacle. Huizinga's analysis of the secularization of sport helps to clarify this point. In the degree to which athletic events lose the element of ritual and public festivity, according to Huizinga, they deteriorate into ''trivial recreation and crude sensationalism.''[9] Even Huizinga misunderstands the cause of this development, however. It hardly lies in the ''fatal shift towards over-seriousness.'' Huizinga himself, when he is writing about the theory of play rather than the collapse of ''genuine play'' in our own time, understands very well that play at its best is always serious; indeed that the essence of play lies in taking seriously activities that have no purpose, serve no utilitarian ends. He reminds us that ''the majority of Greek contests were fought out in deadly earnest'' and discusses under the category of play duels in which contestants fight to the death, water sports in which the object is to drown your opponent, and tournaments the training and preparation for which consume the athletes' entire existence.

The degradation of sport, then, consists not in its being taken too seriously but in its trivialization. Games derive their power from the investment of seemingly trivial activity with serious intent. By submitting without reservation to the rules and conventions of the game, the players (and the spectators too) cooperate in creating an illusion of reality. In this way the game becomes a representation of life, and play takes on the character of play-acting as well. In our time, games—sports in particular—are rapidly losing the quality of illusion. Uneasy in the presence of fantasy and illusion, our age seems to have resolved on the destruction of the harmless substitute gratifications that formerly provided charm and consolation. In the case of sports, the attack on illusion comes from players, promoters, and spectators alike. The players, eager to present themselves as entertainers (partly in order to justify their inflated salaries), deny the seriousness of sport. Promoters urge fans to become rabid partisans, even in sports formerly ruled by decorum, such as tennis. Television creates a new audience at home and makes "live" spectators into participants who mug for the camera and try to attract its attention by waving banners commenting on the action not on the field but in the press box. Sometimes fans interject themselves into the game more aggressively, by dashing onto the field or tearing up the stadium after an important victory.

The rising violence of crowds, routinely blamed on the violence of modern sports and the habit of taking them too seriously, arises, on the contrary, out of a failure to take them seriously enough—to abide by the conventions that should bind spectators as well as players. After the exciting match between Vilas and Connors, in the 1977 finals of the U.S. Open at Forest Hills, an unruly crowd spilled onto the court immediately after the last point and thus broke the hours of tension that should have been broken by the traditional handshake between the players themselves—incidentally allowing Connors to escape from the stadium without acknowledging his rival's victory or taking part in the closing ceremonies.[10] Repeated transgressions of this kind undermine the illusion games create. To break the rules is to break the spell. The merging of players and spectators, here as in the theater, prevents the suspension of disbelief and thus destroys the representational value of organized athletics.

Imperialism and the Cult of the Strenuous Life

The recent history of sports is the history of their steady submission to the demands of everyday reality. The nineteenth-century bourgeoisie suppressed popular sports and festivals as part of their campaign to establish the reign of sobriety. Fairs and football, bullbaiting, cockfighting and boxing offended middle-class reformers because of their cruelty and because they blocked up public thoroughfares, disrupted the daily routine of business, distracted the people from their work, encouraged habits of idleness, extravagance, and insubordination, and gave rise to licentiousness and debauchery. In the name of rational enjoyment and the spirit of improvement, these reformers exhorted the laboring man to forsake his riotous public sports and wakes and to stay at his hearth, in the respectable comfort of the domestic circle. When exhortation failed, they resorted to political action. In early nineteenth-century England, they were opposed by a conservative coalition that crossed class lines, the commoners having been joined in the defense of their "immemorial" enjoyments by traditionalists among the gentry, especially the provincial gentry not yet infected with evangelical piety, sentimental humanitarianism, and the dogma of enterprise. "What would be the Consequence," they asked, "if all such Diversions were entirely banished? The common People seeing themselves cut off from all Hope of this enjoyment, would become dull and spiritless . . . : And not only so, but thro' the absolute Necessity of diverting themselves at Times, they would addict themselves rather to less warrantable Pleasures."[11]

In the United States, the campaign against popular amusements, closely associated with the crusade against liquor and the movement for more strict observance of the Sabbath, took on the character of an ethnic as well as a class conflict. The working class, largely immigrant and Catholic, struggled, often in uneasy alliance with the "sporting element" and with "fashionable society," to defend its drink and its gambling against the assault of middle-class respectability. In mid-nineteenth-century New York, for example, the Whig party identified itself with enterprise, improvement, sobriety, piety, thrift, "steady habits," "book-learning," and strict observance of the Sabbath; while the Democrats, at once the party of rural reaction and the party of the immigrant masses, appealed among other constituencies to the sporting set—in Lee Benson's characterization, to lovers of "hard liquor, fast women and horses, and strong, racy language."[12] The passage of blue laws, which rendered many popular amusements illegal and drove them underground, testifies to the political failure of the alliance between sport and fashion. Middle-class reformers enjoyed the advantage not merely of superior access to political power but of a burning sense of moral purpose. The spirit of early bourgeois society was deeply antithetical to play. Not only did games contribute nothing to capital accumulation, not only did they encourage gambling and reckless expenditure, but they contained an important element of pretense, illusion, mimicry, and make-believe. The bourgeois distrust of games reflected a deeper distrust of fancy, of histrionics, of elaborate dress and costume. Veblen, whose satire against middle-class society incorporated many of its own values, including its hatred of useless and unproductive play, condemned upper-class sports on the grounds of their "futility"; nor did he miss the connection between sport and histrionic display: "It is noticeable, for instance, that even very mild-mannered and matter-of-fact men who go out shooting are apt to carry an excess of arms and accoutrements in order to impress upon their own imagination the seriousness of their undertaking. These huntsmen are also prone to a histrionic, prancing gate and to an elaborate exaggeration of the motions, whether of stealth or of onslaught, involved in their deeds of exploit."[13]

Veblen's satire against the "leisure class" miscarried; in America, where leisure found its only justification in the capacity to renew mind and body for work, the upper class refused to become a leisure class at all. Fearful of being displaced by the rising robber barons, it mastered the art of mass politics, asserted its control over the emerging industrial corporations, and embraced the ideal of the "strenuous life."[14] Sports played an important part in this moral rehabilitation of the ruling class. Having suppressed or driven to the margins of society many of the recreations of the people, the *baute bourgeoisie* proceeded to adapt the games of its class enemies to its own purposes. In the private schools that prepared its sons for the responsibilities of business and empire, sports were placed at the service of character building. The new ideology of imperialism, both in England and in the United States, glorified the playing field as the source of qualities essential to national greatness and martial success. Far from cultivating sport as a form of display and splendid futility, the new national bourgeoisie—which at the end of the century replaced the local elites of an earlier day—celebrated precisely their capacity to instill the "will to win."[15]

At a time when popular preachers of success were redefining the work ethic to stress the element of competition, athletic competition took on new importance as a preparation for the battle of life. In a never-ending stream of books turned out to satisfy the rising demand for sports fiction, popular authors upheld Frank Merriwell and other athletes as models for American youth. The young man on the make, formerly advised to go into business at an early age and to master it from top to bottom, now learned the secret of success on the playing field, in fierce but friendly competition with his peers. Proponents of the new strenuousness insisted that athletics trained the courage and manliness that would promote not only individual success but upper-class ascendancy. "In most countries," according to Theodore Roosevelt, "the 'Bourgeoisie'—the moral, respectable, commercial, middle class—is looked upon with a certain contempt which is justified by their timidity and unwarlikeness.[16] But the minute a middle class produces men like Hawkins and Frobisher on the seas, or men such as the average Union soldier in the civil war, it acquires the hearty respect of others which it merits." Roosevelt believed that sports would help to produce such leaders; at the same time he warned his sons not to regard football, boxing, riding, shooting, walking, and rowing as "the end to which *all* your energies must be devoted, or even the major portion of your energies."

Athletic competition also laid the foundations of national greatness, according to ideologues of the new imperialism. Walter Camp, whose tactical innovations at Yale brought into being the modern game of football, argued during World War I that the "grand do-or-die spirit that holds the attack on the one yard line was what made Chateau-Thierry."[17] General Douglas MacArthur echoed these platitudes in World War II: "Upon the fields of friendly strife are sown the seeds which, on other days, on other fields, will bear the seeds of victory."[18] By this time, however, the cult of the strenuous life was as obsolete as the explicit racism that once informed imperialist ideology. MacArthur himself was an anachronism in his flamboyance and his reactionary faith in clean living and high thinking. As American imperialism allied itself with more liberal values, the cult of "manly arts" survived as an important theme only in the ideology of the far right. In the sixties, reactionary ideologues extolled athletics as "a fortress that has held the wall against radical elements," in the words of the head football coach at Washington State University; or as Spiro Agnew put it, "one of the few bits of glue that holds society together." Max Rafferty, California superintendent of schools, defended the view that "a coach's job was to make men out of wet-behind-the-ears boys" and tried to reassure himself that "the love of clean, competitive sports is too deeply imbedded in the American matrix, too much a part of the warp and woof of our free people, ever to surrender to the burning-eyed, bearded draft-card-burners who hate and envy the athlete because he is something they can never be—*a man*."[19]

Corporate Loyalty and Competition

Left-wing critics of sport have made such statements the focus of their attack—another sample of the way in which cultural radicalism, posing as a revolutionary threat to the status quo, in reality confines its criticism to values already obsolescent and to patterns of American capitalism that have long ago been superseded. Left-wing criticism of sport provides one of the most vivid examples of the essentially conformist character of the "cultural revolution" with which it identifies itself. According to Paul Hoch, Jack Scott, Dave Meggyesy, and other cultural radicals, sport is a "mirror reflection" of society that indoctrinates the young with the dominant values. In America, organized athletics teach militarism, authoritarianism, racism, and sexism, thereby perpetuating the "false consciousness" of the masses. Sports serve as an "opiate" of the people, diverting the masses from their real problems with a "dream world" of glamour and excitement. They promote sexual rivalry among males—with "vestal virgins" leading the cheers from the sidelines—and thus prevent the proletariat from achieving revolutionary solidarity in the face of its oppressors. Competitive athletics force the "pleasure oriented id" to submit to "the hegemony of the repressed ego" in order to shore up the nuclear family—the basic form of authoritarianism—and to divert sexual energy into the service of the work ethic. For all these reasons, organized competition should give way to "intramural sports aimed at making everyone a player." If everyone "had fulfilling, creative jobs, they wouldn't need to look for the pseudo satisfactions of being fans."[20]

This indictment, offensive in the first place in its assumption that cultural radicals understand the needs and interests of the masses better than the masses themselves, also offends every principle of social analysis. It confuses socialization with indoctrination and takes the most reactionary pronouncements at face value, as if athletes automatically imbibed the right-wing opinions of some of their mentors and spokesmen. Sport does play a role in socialization, but the lessons it teaches are not necessarily the ones that coaches and teachers of physical education seek to impart. The mirror theory of sport, like all reductionist interpretations of culture, makes no allowance for the autonomy of cultural traditions. In sport, these traditions come down from one generation of players to another, and although athletics do reflect social values, they can never be completely assimilated to those values. Indeed they resist assimilation more effectively than many other activities, since games learned in youth exert their own demands and inspire loyalty to the game itself, rather than to the programs ideologues seek to impose on them.

In any case, the reactionary values allegedly perpetuated by sport no longer reflect the dominant needs of American capitalism at all. If a society of consumers has no need of the Protestant work ethic, neither does it need the support of an ideology of racism, manliness, and martial valor. Racism once provided ideological support for colonialism and for backward labor systems based on slavery or peonage. These forms of exploitation rested on the direct, unconcealed appropriation of surplus value by the master class, which justified its domination on the grounds that the lower orders, disqualified for self-government by virtue of racial inferiority or lowly birth, needed and benefited from their masters' protection. Racism and paternalism were two sides of the same coin, the "white man's burden."

Capitalism has gradually substituted the free market for direct forms of domination. Within advanced countries, it has converted the serf or slave into a free worker. It has also revolutionized colonial relations. Instead of imposing military rule on their colonies, industrial nations now govern through client states, ostensibly sovereign, which keep order in their stead. Such changes have made both racism and the ideology of martial conquest, appropriate to an earlier age of empire building, increasingly anachronistic.

In the United States, the transition from Theodore Roosevelt's jingoism to Woodrow Wilson's liberal neocolonialism already spelled the obsolescence of the older ideology of Anglo-Saxon supremacy. The collapse of "scientific" racism in the twenties and thirties, the integration of the armed forces in the Korean War, and the attack on racial segregation in the fifties and sixties marked a deep-seated ideological shift, rooted in changing modes of exploitation. Of course the relation between material life and ideology is never simple, least of all in the case of an ideology as irrational as racism. In any case, de facto racism continues to flourish without a racial ideology. Indeed it is precisely the collapse of de jure racism in the South and the discovery of de facto racism in the North, sheltering under the ideology of tolerance, that distinguishes the most recent phase of the race problem in the United States. The ideology of white supremacy, however, no longer appears to serve any important social function.

"Martial machismo," as Paul Hoch calls it, is equally irrelevant to an age of technological warfare. The military ethic, moreover, required the athlete or soldier to submit to a common discipline, to sacrifice himself for the good of a higher cause; and it thus suffers the general erosion of organizational allegiance in a society where men and women perceive the organization as an enemy, even the organizations in which they work. In sport as in business, group loyalties no longer temper competition. Individuals seek to exploit the organization to their own advantage and to advance their interests not merely against rival organizations but against their own teammates. The team player, like the organization man, has become an anachronism. The contention that sport fosters an unhealthy spirit of competition needs to be refined. Insofar as sport measures individual achievement against abstract standards of excellence, encourages cooperation among teammates, and enforces rules of fair play, it gives expression to the competitive urge but also helps to discipline it. The crisis of athletic competition today derives not from the persistence of a martial ethic, the cult of victory, or the obsession with achievement (which some critics still see as the "dominant sports creed"), but from the collapse of conventions that formerly restrained rivalry even as they glorified it.

George Allen's dictum—"winning isn't the most important thing, it's the only thing"—represents a last-ditch defense of team spirit in the face of its deterioration.[21] Such pronouncements, usually cited as evidence of an exaggerated stress on competition, may help to keep it within bounds. The intrusion of the market into every corner of the sporting scene, however, re-creates all the antagonisms characteristic of late capitalist society. With the free-agent draft, the escalation of athletic salaries, and the instantaneous stardom conferred by the media on athletic success, competition among rival organizations has degenerated into a free-for-all. It is no wonder that criticism of competition has emerged as the principal theme in the rising criticism of sport. People today associate rivalry with boundless aggression and find it difficult to conceive of competition that does not lead directly to thoughts of murder. Kohut writes of one of his patients: "Even as a child he had become afraid of emotionally cathected competitiveness for fear of the underlying (near delusional) fantasies of exerting absolute, sadistic power." Herbert Hendin says of the students he analyzed and interviewed at Columbia that "they could conceive of no competition that did not result in someone's annihilation."[22]

The prevalence of such fears helps to explain why Americans have become uneasy about rivalry unless it is accompanied by the disclaimer that winning and losing don't matter or that games are unimportant anyway. The identification of competition with the wish to annihilate opponents inspires Dorcas Butt's accusation that competitive sports have made us a nation of militarists, fascists, and predatory egoists; have encouraged "poor sportsmanship" in all social relations; and have extinguished cooperation and compassion. It inspires Paul Hoch's plaintive cry: "Why bother scoring or winning the game at all? Wouldn't it be enough just to enjoy it?" In all likelihood, the same misgivings lie behind Jack Scott's desire to find a proper "balance" between competition and cooperation. "Competitive sport is in trouble," Scott says, "when the balance is tipped toward competition." An athlete should strive for accomplishment, according to Scott, but not "at the expense of himself or others." These words express a belief that excellence usually *is* achieved at the expense of others, that competition tends to become murderous unless balanced by cooperation,

and that athletic rivalry, if it gets out of hand, gives expression to the inner rage contemporary man desperately seeks to stifle.

Bureaucracy and "Teamwork"

The prevalent mode of social interaction today is antagonistic cooperation (as David Riesman called it in *The Lonely Crowd*), in which a cult of teamwork conceals the struggle for survival within bureaucratic organizations. In sport, the rivalry among teams, now drained of its capacity to call up local or regional loyalties, reduces itself (like the rivalry among business corporations) to a struggle for shares of the market. The professional athlete does not care whether his team wins or loses (since losers share in the pot), as long as it stays in business.

The professionalization of sport and the extension of professional athletics into the universities, which now serve as a farm system for the major leagues, have undercut the old "school spirit" and have given rise among athletes to a thoroughly businesslike approach to their craft. Athletes now regard the inspirational appeals of old-fashioned coaches with amused cynicism; nor do they readily submit to authoritarian discipline. The proliferation of franchises and the frequency with which they move from one locality to another undermines local loyalties, both among participants and spectators, and discourages attempts to model "team spirit" on patriotism. In a bureaucratic society, all forms of corporate loyalty lose their force, and although athletes still make a point of subordinating their own achievements to those of the team, they do so in order to promote easy relations with their colleagues, not because the team as a corporate entity transcends individual interests. On the contrary, the athlete as a professional entertainer seeks above all to further his own interests and willingly sells his services to the highest bidder. The better athletes become media celebrities and supplement their salaries with endorsements that often exceed the salaries themselves.[23]

All these developments make it difficult to think

of the athlete as a local or national hero, as the representative of his class or race, or in any way as the embodiment of some larger corporate unit. Only the recognition that sports have come to serve as a form of entertainment justifies the salaries paid to star athletes and their prominence in the media. As Howard Cosell has candidly acknowledged, sports can no longer be sold to the public as "just sports or as religion. . . . Sports aren't life and death. They're entertainment."[24] Even as the television audience demands the presentation of sports as a form of spectacle, however, the widespread resentment of star athletes among followers of sport—a resentment directed against the inflated salaries negotiated by their agents and against their willingness to become hucksters, promoters, and celebrities—indicates the persistence of a need to believe that sport represents something more than entertainment, something that, though neither life nor death in itself, retains some lingering capacity to dramatize and clarify those experiences.

Sports and the Entertainment Industry

The secularization of sport, which began as soon as athletics were pressed into the cause of patriotism and character building, became complete only when sport became an object of mass consumption. The first stage in this process was the establishment of big-time athletics in the university and their spread from the Ivy League to the large public and private schools, thence downward into the high schools. The bureaucratization of the business career, which placed unprecedented emphasis on competition and the will to win, stimulated the growth of sports in another way. It made the acquisition of educational credentials essential to a business or professional career and thus created in large numbers a new kind of student, utterly indifferent to higher learning but forced to undergo it for purely economic reasons. Large-scale athletic programs helped colleges to attract such students, in competitive bidding for enrollments, and to entertain them once they enrolled. In the closing years of the nineteenth century, according to

Donald Meyer, the development of an "alumni culture" centering on clubs, fraternities, alumni offices, money drives, homecoming ceremonies, and football grew out of the colleges' need not only to raise money in large amounts but to attract "a clientele for whom the classroom had no real meaning but who were by no means ready to send their sons out into the world at age eighteen."[25] At Notre Dame, as Frederick Rudolph has pointed out, "intercollegiate athletics . . . were consciously developed in the 1890s as an agency of student recruitment." As early as 1878, President McCosh of Princeton wrote to an alumnus in Kentucky: "You will confer a great favor on us if you will get . . . the college noticed in the Louisville papers. . . . We must persevere in our efforts to get students from your region. . . . Mr. Brand Ballard has won us great reputation as captain of the football team which has beaten both Harvard and Yale."

In order to accommodate the growing hordes of spectators, the colleges and universities, sometimes aided by local business interests, built lavish athletic facilities—enormous field houses, football stadiums in the pretentious imperial style of the early twentieth century. Growing investment in sports led in turn to a growing need to maintain a winning record: a new concern with system, efficiency, and the elimination of risk. Camp's innovations at Yale emphasized drill, discipline, teamwork.[26] As in industry, the attempt to coordinate the movements of many men created a demand for "scientific management" and for the expansion of managerial personnel. In many sports, trainers, coaches, doctors, and public relations experts soon outnumbered the players. The accumulation of elaborate statistical records arose from management's attempt to reduce winning to a routine, to measure efficient performance. The athletic contest itself, surrounded by a vast apparatus of information and promotion, now appeared almost incidental to the expensive preparation required to stage it.

The rise of a new kind of journalism—the yellow journalism pioneered by Hearst and Pulitzer, which sold sensations instead of reporting news—helped to professionalize amateur athletics, to assimilate sport to promotion, and to make professional athletics into a major industry. Until the twenties, professional sports, where they existed at all, attracted little of the public attention lavished on college football. Even baseball, the oldest and most highly organized of professional sports, suffered from faintly unsavory associations—its appeal to the working class and the sporting crowd, its rural origins. When a Yale alumnus complained to Walter Camp about the overemphasis on football, he could think of no better way of dramatizing the danger than to cite the example of baseball: "The language and scenes which are too often witnessed [in football games] are such as to degrade the college student and bring him down to a par with or even lower than the average professional baseball player."

The World Series scandal of 1919 confirmed baseball's bad reputation, but it also set in motion the reforms of Kenesaw Mountain Landis, the new commissioner brought in by the owners to clean up the game and give it a better public image. Landis's régime, the success of the eminently respectable and efficient New York Yankees, and the idolization of Babe Ruth soon made professional baseball "America's number-one pastime." Ruth became the first modern athlete to be sold to the public as much for his color, personality, and crowd appeal as for his remarkable abilities. His press agent, Christy Walsh, developer of a syndicate of ghost writers who sold books and articles under the names of sports heroes, arranged barnstorming tours, endorsements, and movie roles and thus helped to make the "Sultan of Swat" a national celebrity.

In the quarter-century following World War II, entrepreneurs extended the techniques of mass promotion first perfected in the marketing of college football and professional baseball to other professional sports, notably hockey, basketball, and football. Television did for these games what mass journalism and radio had done for baseball, elevating them to new heights of popularity and at the same time reducing them to entertainment.

In his recent study of sport, Michael Novak notes that television has lowered the quality of sports reporting, freeing announcers from the need to describe the course of play and encouraging them instead to adopt the style of professional entertainers. The invasion of sport by the "entertainment ethic," according to Novak, breaks down the boundaries between the ritual world of play and the sordid reality from which it is designed to provide escape. Broadcasters like Howard Cosell, who embody the "virulent passion for debunking in the land," mistakenly import critical standards more appropriate to political reporting into the coverage of sports. Newspapers report the "business side" of sports on the sports page, instead of confining it to the business section where it belongs. "It is important," Novak argues, ". . . to keep sports as insulated as we can from business, entertainment, politics, and even gossip. . . . The preservation of parts of life not drawn up into politics and work is essential for the human spirit." Especially when politics has become "a brutal, ugly business" and work (not sport) the opiate of the people, athletics alone, in Novak's view, offer a glimpse of the "real thing." They take place in a "world outside of time," which must be sealed off from the surrounding corruption.[27]

Leisure as Escape

The anguished outcry of the true fan, who brings to sports a proper sense of awe only to find them corrupted from within by the spread of the "entertainment ethic," sheds more light on the degradation of sports than the strictures of left-wing critics, who wish to abolish competition, emphasize the value of sports as health-giving exercise, and promote a more "cooperative" conception of athletics—in other words, to make sports an instrument of personal and social therapy. Novak's analysis, however, minimizes the extent of the problem and misconstrues its cause. In a society dominated by the production and consumption of images, no part of life can long remain immune from the invasion of spectacle. Nor can this invasion be blamed on the spirit of debunking. It arises, in a paradoxical fashion, precisely out of the attempt to set up a separate sphere of leisure uncontaminated by the world of work and politics. Play has always, by its very nature, set itself off from workaday life; yet it retains an organic connection with the life of the community, by virtue of its capacity to dramatize reality and to offer a convincing representation of the community's values. The ancient connections between games, ritual, and public festivity suggest that although games take place within arbitrary boundaries, they are nevertheless rooted in shared traditions to which they give objective expression. Games and athletic contests offer a dramatic commentary on reality rather than an escape from it—a heightened reenactment of communal traditions, not a repudiation of them. It is only when games and sports come to be valued purely as a form of escape that they lose the capacity to provide this escape.

The appearance in history of an escapist conception of "leisure" coincides with the organization of leisure as an extension of commodity production. The same forces that have organized the factory and the office have organized leisure as well, reducing it to an appendage of industry. Accordingly sport has come to be dominated not so much by an undue emphasis on winning as by the desperate urge to avoid defeat. Coaches, not quarterbacks, call the plays, and the managerial apparatus makes every effort to eliminate the risk and uncertainty that contribute so centrally to the ritual and dramatic success of any contest. When sports can no longer be played with appropriate abandon, they lose the capacity to raise the spirits of players and spectators, to transport them into a higher realm of existence. Prudence, caution, and calculation, so prominent in everyday life but so inimical to the spirit of games, come to shape sports as they shape everything else.

While he deplores the subordination of sport to entertainment, Novak takes for granted the separation of work and leisure that gives rise in the first place to this invasion of play by the standards of the workaday world. He does not see that the degradation of play originates in the degradation of work, which creates both the need and the op-

portunity for commercialized "recreation." As Huizinga has shown, it is precisely when the play element disappears from law, statecraft, and other cultural forms that men turn to play not to witness a dramatic reenactment of their common life but to find diversion and sensation. At that point, games and sport, far from taking themselves too seriously, as Huizinga mistakenly concluded, become, on the contrary, a "thing of no consequence." As Edgar Wind shows in his analysis of modern art, the trivialization of art was already implicit in the modernist exaltation of art, which assumed that "the experience of art will be more intense if it pulls the spectator away from his ordinary habits and preoccupations."[28] The modernist esthetic guarantees the socially marginal status of art at the same time that it opens art to the invasion of commercialized esthetic fashion—a process that culminates, by a curious but inexorable logic, in the postmodernist demand for the abolition of art and its assimilation to reality.

The development of sport follows the same pattern. The attempt to create a separate realm of pure play, totally isolated from work, gives rise to its opposite—the insistence, in Cosell's words, that "sports are not separate and apart from life, a special 'Wonderland' where everything is pure and sacred and above criticism," but a business subject to the same standards and open to the same scrutiny as any other.[29] The positions represented by Novak and Cosell are symbiotically related and arise out of the same historical development: the emergence of the spectacle as the dominant form of cultural expression. What began as an attempt to invest sport with religious significance, indeed to make it into a surrogate religion in its own right, ends with the demystification of sport, the assimilation of sport to show business.

Notes

1. Roger Caillois, "The Structure and Classification of Games," in John W. Loy, Jr., and Gerald S. Kenyon, *Sport, Culture, and*

Society (New York: Macmillan, 1969), p. 49.

2. capitalist and socialist versions of the ideology of national fitness
John F. Kennedy, "The Soft American" (1960), reprinted in John T. Talamini and Charles H. Page, *Sport and Society: An Anthology* (Boston: Little, Brown, 1973), p. 369; Philip Goodhart and Christopher Chataway, *War without Weapons* (London: W. H. Allen, 1968), pp. 80, 84.

3. Johan Huizinga, *Homo Ludens: A Study of the Play Element in Culture* (Boston: Beacon Press, 1955 [1944]), pp. 197–98, 205; Huizinga, *In the Shadow of Tomorrow* (New York: Norton, 1936), p. 177.

4. recent criticism of sports
Harry Edwards, *The Sociology of Sport* (Homewood, Ill.: Dorsey Press, 1973) and *The Revolt of the Black Athlete* (New York, Free Press, 1969); Dorcas Susan Butt, *Psychology of Sport* (New York: Van Nostrand Reinhold, 1976); Dave Meggyesy, *Out of Their League* (Berkeley: Ramparts Press, 1970); Chip Oliver, *High for the Game* (New York: Morrow, 1971); Paul Hoch, *Rip Off the Big Game: The Exploitation of Sports by the Power Elite* (New York: Doubleday, 1972); Jack Scott, *The Athlete Revolution* (New York: Free Press, 1971).

5. This does not mean that virtuosity is the principal component of sport. In implying a comparison, here and elsewhere, between athletic and musical performances, I wish to make just the opposite point. A performer who seeks merely to dazzle the audience with feats of technical brilliance plays to the lowest level of understanding, forgoing the risks that come from intense emotional engagement with the material itself. In the most satisfying kind of performance, the performer becomes unconscious of the audience and loses himself in his part. In sport, the moment that matters is what a former basketball player describes as the moment "when all those folks in the stands don't count." The player in question, now a scholar, left big-time sport when he discovered he was expected to have no life outside it, but he retains more insight into the nature of games than Dave Meggyesy, Chip Oliver, and other ex-athletes. Rejecting the simple-minded radicalism according to which "commercialization" has corrupted sports, he says: "Money [in professional sports] has nothing to do with capitalism, owners, or professionalism. It's the moment in some games where it doesn't matter who's watching, all that counts is that instant where how you play determines which team wins and which team loses."

If virtuosity were the essence of sport, we could dispense with basketball and content ourselves with displays of dunking and dribbling. But to say that real artistry consists not of dazzling technique but of teamwork, timing, a sense of the moment, an understanding of the medium, and the capacity to lose oneself in play does not of course mean that games would have the same significance if no one watched them. It means simply that the superior performance has the quality of being unobserved.

6. Podhoretz on excellence
quoted in Michael Novak, *The Joy of Sports* (New York: Basic Books, 1976), p. 176.

7. track and surfing/Scott, *Athletic Revolution*, pp. 97–98.

8. In any case, the fashionable chatter about the need for greater participation in sports is entirely irrelevant to a discussion of their cultural significance. We might just as well assess the future of American music by counting the number of amateur musicians. In both cases, participation can be an eminently satisfying experience; but in neither case does the level of participation tell us much about the status of the art.
"new sports for the noncompetitive"; "Games Big People Play," *Mother Jones,* September-October 1976, p. 43; see also Terry Orlick, *The Cooperative Sports and*

Games Book: Challenge without Competition (New York: Pantheon, 1978).

9. Huizinga, *Homo Ludens,* p. 48.

10. Vilas–Connors match
I am indebted for these suggestions to Herbert Benham.

11. nineteenth-century campaign against popular amusements
Robert W. Malcolmson, *Popular Recreations in English Society, 1750–1850* (Cambridge: Cambridge University Press, 1973), p. 70.

12. Lee Benson, *The Concept of Jacksonian Democracy* (New York: Antheneum, 1964), p. 201.

13. Thorstein Veblen, *The Theory of the Leisure Class* (New York: Modern Library, 1934 [1899]), p. 256.

14. Goodhart and Chataway, *War without Weapons,* pp. 4–5, 28–29.

15. The founder of the modern Olympics, Pierre de Coubertin, admired the English and attributed their imperial success to the character-building influence of athletics. "Is Arnoldism applicable in France?" he wondered. Philip Goodhart and Christopher Chataway, in their account of the rise of this new cult of sports, character development, and empire, make it clear that the new view of sports was a middle-class view that unfolded in opposition to both aristocratic and popular traditions. Whereas cricket, boxing, and horse racing had been identified with gambling, the middle class attempted to use sports to promote respectability, patriotism, and manly vigor.

16. "In most countries, the 'Bourgeoisie' . . . major portion of your energies." Elting E. Morison, ed., *The Letters of Theodore Roosevelt* (Cambridge, Mass.: Harvard University Press, 1951), 2: 1444; 3: 615.

17. "grand do-or-die spirit . . . Chateau-Thierry." Donald Meyer, "Early Football," unpublished paper.

18. "Upon the fields of friendly strife . . . seeds of victory."
quoted in Scott, *Athletic Revolution,* p. 21.

19. reactionary rhetoric
ibid., pp. 17–21; Hoch, *Rip Off the Big Game,* pp. 2–4.

20. Although the clichés alluded to here can be found throughout the radical critique of sports, Hoch's book provides them in richest profusion and expresses them in the purest revolutionary jargon. See *Rip Off the Big Game,* pp. 7, 18, 20, 122, 154, 158, 162–6, 117.

21. "dominant sports creed"
Edwards, *Sociology of Sport,* p. 334. Cf. Jerry Rubin, *Growing (Up) at Thirty-seven* (New York: M. Evans, 1976), p. 180: "The ethic of competition, achievement, and domination is the core of the American system."

22. Heinz Kohut, *The Analysis of the Self* (New York: International Universities Press, 1971), p. 196; Herbert Hendin, *The Age of Sensation* (New York: Norton, 1975), p. 167.

23. Butt, *Psychology of Sport,* pp. 18, 32, 41, 55–58, and *passim;* Hoch, *Rip Off the Big Game,* p. 158; Jack Scott, "Sport" (1972), quoted in Edwards, *Sociology of Sport,* p. 338.

24. Cosell/quoted in Novak, *Joy of Sports,* p. 273.

25. alumni culture/Meyer, "Early Football"; Frederick Rudolph, *The American College and University* (New York: Vintage, 1962), p. 385.

26. Walter Camp
Meyer, "Early Football."

27. Novak, *Joy of Sports,* ch. 14.

28. Edgar Wind, *Art and Anarchy* (New York: Knopf, 1963), p. 18.

29. "sports are not separate . . . above criticism" quoted in Novak, *Joy of Sports,* p. 276.

Play, Utopia, and Dystopia: Prologue to a Ludic Theory of the State

WILLIAM J. MORGAN

There is a certain schizophrenia apparent in our contemporary regard for work and play. On the one hand, we celebrate the advance of technology insofar as it progressively releases us from the burden of labor and opens up the free and potentially joyous life of play; on the other, we rail against technological progress as it takes away our jobs and enforces us to live, at best, an uneventful life of indolence thinly disguised as leisure, at worst, a traumatic life of feared penury. On the one hand, we pride ourselves on the number of hours that have been sliced off the work week from its noted excesses in the incipient period of industrialization; on the other, we spend the hours off the job, hours won not only by technological advances but by hard negotiating and bitter sacrifices by labor unions, working at yet another job to make ends meet, or engaged in extracurricular activities whose demeanor and style are virtually indistinguishable from our everyday work pursuits. Given the choice of free time or maximizing personal gain, we invariably choose the latter while we exalt the former.

The positive side of this schizophrenia founds our dream of a better future life, our vision of

utopia, while the negative side feeds our darker, seamier view of the future, our vision of dystopia. The former, grander view grew out of an age happier than our own when the view was widely held that a life of material abundance was within the ready reach of all humankind. All that was required to secure this "good life," so it was thought, was to unleash the productive forces of labor whose technological sophistication provided the key to the satisfaction of the general needs of the populace. The only remaining obstacles to salvation, it was thus argued, were technical ones. The prospect of such a quantitatively rich life emboldened us to think of the coming post-industrial age as the age of human deliverance, of the ideal life freed from the yoke of scarcity.

Out of the womb of this sanguine view, however, has sprung an increasingly pessimistic vision of the human condition, of a life less than prodigal. This vision of paradise lost has been nourished principally by the insight that most of our technical-productive gains have been inextricably coupled with significant losses. This insight is itself a product of numerous realizations now apparent in the contemporary age: the technological encroachment of certain natural limits to growth (e.g., finite mineral resources, tolerances in our ecological systems, physical constraints such as the laws of thermodynamics) which poten-

Reprinted from *Journal of the Philosophy of Sport,* IX, (1982), pp. 30–42. Copyright 1983 by the Philosophic Society for the Study of Sport. Reprinted by permission.

tially imperil the long-term survival prospects of the human species, the institutionalization of scarcity in the form of inequitable modes of social distribution which render the relation between material production and the general satisfaction of human needs problematic, the increasingly clear tendency of present forms of material growth and expansion to disrupt world stability thereby creating enmity among the various peoples of the world and an ever greater disparity between the "haves" and the "have nots," and the fact that despite great technological advances people are working as hard as before (with the mental tyranny of work replacing its previous physical tyranny) and as long as, and in some cases longer than before (save the noted anomalous period spanning the Industrial Revolution). Consequently, most of our outstanding technical and productive achievements, such as the fact that more people are living a materially prosperous life than ever before, must be framed in terms of their nullifying opposites, that more people are dying of starvation and general plunder than ever before. It is these wedded antinomies of advance and decline, production and destruction, liberation and repression, which undermine our optimism in the future, and stir our complacency that the only significant problems remaining are technical ones. Dystopia, rather than utopia, is their imminent product.

The emergence of the theme of dystopia out of the theme of utopia poses a dilemma which is the basis of the present paper: namely, that the ideological forces and institutions which built modern human civilization cannot sustain it. That is, the material growth suppositions of our modern sociopolitical systems, shared by liberal and state capitalism (pseudo-socialism) alike, and their respective basis in labor as the animus and regulator of social life, are the source of the antinomies previously cited. What I will argue in the present paper, then, is that the dystopian consequences of the utopian aspirations of modern society, as well as the schizophrenia that fuels them, are not accidents but necessary products of its economic infrastructure. I will argue further, in accord with the

mandate implicit in the latter, that what is required here is nothing short of a paradigm change, a new conception of the flourishing life congenial both to the material possibilities of the present age and the genuine possibilities of human life. I will then suggest play as just such a "radical," new conception of the good life, and argue for its social implementation as the grounds for breaking the pernicious union of production and destruction. I will finally argue, as a corollary of the above, that any advanced industrial society which subscribes to the preeminence of labor (material production) over play, and regards such preeminence as perfectly rational, is to be viewed as suffering from a social pathology which must be extirpated if the qualitative course of human civilization is to be assured. First, however, the central terms of the investigation, work and play, require some clarification.

I

Work and play may be understood and fashioned, for present purposes, in terms of two general strata of human life. These strata, which do not exhaust the content of human becoming but comprise its major divisions, include, respectively, the realms of necessity and possibility. Work finds its niche in the former, play in the latter.

The realm of necessity is so-termed given the subordinate status of possibility within its domain. That is, all possibilities entertained herein are understood to be tied to certain basic necessities which determine their efficacy, and delimit their scope. Such necessities comprise the primal imperatives of life itself: its daily sustenance and material continuance. As such, this realm encompasses the round of human activities that commonly fall under the province of ordinary life. Principal among them, and serving as their constitutive source, however, is work. For work itself springs from the mandate of life to reproduce itself. Its central features, therefore, can be gleaned from this fact. Thus, work's material style and orientation, its attempt to inscribe a human form on a natural object to accentuate its utility, its logic of domination by which it regulates its interchange with nature in the effort to master it, and its instrumental valuation of the ensemble of natural and human objects—all follow from its grounding in necessity.

Similarly, the realm of possibility is defined not by the absence, but by the subordinate status of one of the elements of its dialectic—in this instance necessity. Whatever efficacy necessity has here is a product of possibility. This realm is quite obviously not inclusive of our daily round of activities, but of a special, narrower, class whose main triumvirate consists of art, religion and philosophy. Play, however, is their constitutive source, and serves as their paradigmatic activity. For play is steeped in possibility; indeed its being is contingent on its severance of all ties to the world born of practical exigency. It is by breaking such ties and by placing in their stead its own exigency and necessity (in the form of rules), that play constitutes itself as a rather special encounter with possibility (in the form of gratuitous obstacles to be overcome). The very status of such limits (rules) as imperatives, however, follows only from the fact that they allow for the pursuit of a possibility not otherwise available. Here again the main features of play can be read off its dominant element. Thus, play's nonmaterial orientation, its disinterest in impregnating an object with a human form for any utilitarian purpose, its noninstrumental order of reason which countenances its interest in objects only as tests to wrest a moment of possibility from them, and its intrinsic valuation of such activity, all follow from its grounding in possibility.

With the above distinction in hand, the argument for the ensuing analysis can now be better framed. The core of that argument will rest on the claim that capitalism, whatever its form, has a vested interest in the dominion of the realm of necessity (work) over the realm of possibility (play). Such dominion manifests itself in the guise of scarcity—here defined as the disparity between human needs and wants, and the resources (natural and technical) requisite to their satisfaction. I will argue that capitalism is based on the principle of scarcity, and that this fact accounts for its contribution to the dilemma outlined above, and its inability to rescue us from it.

II

It is hardly a secret that the driving force of capitalism is profit.[1] Hence, the capitalist invests in production not out of any noble gesture to improve the lot of humankind but to secure a profit. Marx termed this acquisitive drive the "law of capitalist accumulation." And the point to be made here is that the law of accumulation is capital's law of scarcity. That is, it is the "mechanism" by which a dissonance between human needs and productive output is ensured. For the need to expand capital, which harbors within itself no limiting features save certain benign self-correcting measures, gives rise to new and ever greater productive efforts whose results it is prepared from the outset to dismiss as insufficient. This apparently insatiable goad to produce is rooted in a specific form of labor, wage-labor.

The laborer in a capitalistic society, owing to its private property relations, must sell its labor in order to live. This selling of labor, however, as Marx realized, not only inaugurates the process of capitalistic production but determines its general complexion as well. That is, Marx discovered in the exchange of labor for a wage the key to the bourgeois law of accumulation. For unlike all other exchanges in capitalism, the exchange of labor for a wage is not, and cannot be an equivalent one. Rather, the wage the laborer receives for transferring its productive activity to the capitalist is always less than the value that labor produces. By thus turning over its productive capacity to the capitalist, relinquishing thereby all claims to the products that ensue from its activity, the laborer yields to the capitalist a value in excess of the wage received—what Marx calls surplus-value. And it is the appropriation of this surplus-value (un-requited labor) which makes possible the goal of capitalist accumulation, and so, the very existence of capitalism itself.

The law of capitalist accumulation can now be more precisely characterized as the effort to extract as much surplus-value as possible. Considered in terms of labor, this means expanding that part of the normal working day in which the worker directly serves the capitalist's acquisitive interests and works, in effect, gratis (surplus-labor), and holding constant or contracting that part in which the worker produces the equivalent value of its wage (necessary-labor). The capitalist can exact a greater portion of surplus-labor, and so surplus-value, in any one of three ways: by paying less than full value for labor (less than a subsistence wage); by lengthening the working day, that is, adding on to its surplus-labor part; by altering not the length but the parts of the working day, that is, shrinking its necessary in favor of its surplus part. The history of capitalism shows that it has not been adverse to resorting to any one of these measures. With the development of advanced capitalism, however, the two former measures have largely been discarded owing principally to the increasing rationalization of production, which exposed the counter-productive effects of immiserating the worker physically, socially and economically, and the growing power of labor itself (labor unions, etc.). Hence, the chief means used to extract surplus-value in modern capitalism is to revolutionize the productive forces, to increase their productivity. By raising the productivity of labor, and holding constant the length of the working day, the capitalist is assured of its requisite surplus-value. Moreover, the technological sophistication of labor not only serves the capitalist's profit interests by allowing a greater part of the working day to be given over to surplus-labor, it also serves those interests by depressing wages; that is, by displacing ever greater numbers of the work force, by rendering their services obsolete, the demand for labor falls and, therefore, its price.

It hardly needs to be reiterated here that the modern capitalist strategy of augmenting capital by enhancing productive prowess depends, as all such strategies do, on the operation of the principle of scarcity. With respect to the capitalists themselves, scarcity is, as noted, incarnate in their law of accumulation which supersedes the productive forces they set in motion. But the functioning of this law requires that the workers act in consonance with the principle of scarcity as well. Indeed, the acquisitive goals of capitalism can only be realized if the workers feel some compulsion to produce at ever greater levels. In the early phases of capitalism, the immiserated status of the worker virtually guaranteed its cooperation in the private productive ventures of the capitalists. But with the coming of advanced industrial society, and the concomitant increase in the standard of living of the workers—which always occurs disproportionately with the concentration of wealth, the task of providing a goad to produce becomes more subtle, though no less urgent.

Here, as always, supplying such a goad requires the transformation of a potential condition of abundance into one of scarcity. For the threat posed to capitalism by the economic growth of the workers is a lessened propensity to work. Such a propensity is premised on abundance, on a parity between productive output and needs and wants. Parity of this sort is obviously incongruous with the surplus-labor demanded by capitalism. It must, therefore, give way to disparity. This is accomplished by removing all constraints producers are likely to place on their income, by, in other words, expanding their needs. Thus, the need to contrive in its producers ever greater needs, to drive them to fresh new sacrifices and new forms of gratification, is vital to the operation of capitalism. Such inducements to scarcity are most effective, as Galbraith noted, when they lead workers into indebtedness, a state which makes them especially reliable and earnest producers (2: p. 350). All of this presupposes the production of an ever greater stock of unnecessary artifacts and services and, correlatively, a growing emphasis on the scientific management of needs.

The tactic of augmenting capital by enhancing

production is not, however, as Marx detected, unproblematic. Indeed, at bottom it harbors a contradiction which manifests itself by throwing production into periodic crises of expanding proportion. The contradiction has to do with the fact that capitalism tends, on the one hand, toward an unlimited development of the productive forces which, on the other, comes into conflict with its more limited aim—the expansion of capital. The latter is more limited insofar as it must convert its productive results into capital, that is, its products must be sold to capitalize further productive ventures. Given, then, the stimulus to unlimited production, and the disproportionate social organization of wealth, it follows that the productive output of capitalism will at certain recurring points outstrip its capacity to absorb such production. When this happens production is brought to a standstill, and thereby the appropriation of surplus-value. This confirms our earlier claim that scarcity is crucial to the functioning of capital; for the crisis in question here is a crisis of abundance, indeed superabundance, in which the supply of goods exceeds the demand for them. The fact that such abundance does not redound to the worker, whose scarce resources are accentuated in such cases since the cessation of production is synonymous with the cessation of its sustenance, does not overturn this point but merely shows the extent to which capitalism is based on profit rather than the general satisfaction of human needs.

The crisis of overproduction is thus immanent to capitalism itself. It can be remedied only by inducing scarcity. But the ability of capitalism to manage such crises grows, in exact proportion to the recalcitrance of surplus-production (abundance) to yield to scarcity, more problematic. Its point of diminishing return is reached with the fruition of the development of production, namely automation. The automation of production sharpens the contradiction embodied in overproduction as one between capital's positing of human labor as the measure and source of wealth and its diminution of human labor as an integral element of production. Expressed from the worker's vantage point, the contradiction pivots on the worker's dependence on work for its sustenance, and the tendency of capital to eliminate the source of that sustenance. Marx was not unaware of the potential revolutionary effects of automation as the following passage from the *Grundrisse* attests:

> to the degree that large industry develops, the creation of real wealth comes to depend less on labor time . . . than on the power of the agencies set in motion during labor time, whose 'powerful effectiveness' . . . depends . . . on the general state of science and on the progress of technology. . . . As soon as [human labor] . . . has ceased to be the great well-spring of wealth, labor time ceases and must cease to be its measure, and hence exchange-value [must cease to be the measure] of use-value. (7: pp. 704-5)

Thus, with the onset of automation, and the corresponding deflection of human labor from a direct producer role to a subordinate supervisorial and maintenance role, it becomes impossible to measure the productive output of an individual and so to assess a wage for it. Further, since the accumulation of capital is derived from surplus human labor which is ultimately derived from the unequal exchange of labor for a wage, the displacement of human for machine labor, which unlike its human counterpart exchanges for its equivalent value, dissolves the generative source of wealth in capitalism. At this point, the strategy of extracting surplus-value by increasing productive capacity turns into its opposite. It is not clear capitalism of any form has a remedy for this.

III

Play assumes quite diverse forms in liberal and bureaucratic state capitalism. All of its various manifestations, however, conform to a basic instrumental pattern imposed on it by capital.[2] This undergirding pattern is composed of two interrelated elements: the first underlies the marginal social status play enjoys in capitalism, the second its metamorphosis into a productive force. Unpacking each of these elements provides the key to understanding the role and significance of play in modern society.

The modern role forged by capital for play was just that, a recent product of the advance of industrial society and its indigenous social relations. It should be noted, therefore, that the initial response of capitalism to play was one of bald suppression. That is, prior to its revision of the instinctual apparatus of the pre-bourgeois human agent, building the new industrial order of capitalism required the overt repression of play. In an age in which a life not conspicuously devoted to utility was considered suspect, and in which intellectuals and others peripherally related to the productive affairs of mainstream life now sought an identity (intellectual workers) and justification rooted in these very affairs, play could only be regarded as an antipode of the emerging new society. It was, accordingly, anathematized as the enemy of "modernity," and as something to be despised and ridiculed rather than esteemed. Shoring up the erratic work habits of the workers, honing their productive capacity and discipline, curbing their imprudent expenditure of time, energy, and money, all required, it was argued, the eradication of play.[3] The advent of advanced industrial society, however, made this posture obsolete.

The modern sanction of play as instrumental activity was hastened by the new integrative wave of mature capitalism. That sanction, however, was a conditional one contingent on maintaining some separation and apartness between play and the central productive apparatus of society. Such separation issues from the acquisitive drive of capitalism itself which employs the productive forces not to ameliorate the struggle for existence but to intensify it. It creates this struggle anew by converting disposable time into the scarce time of surplus-labor. The dependence on surplus-labor, therefore, mandates that play be driven into the interstices of human life, into its periphery. Here it lies in the shadow of work. And here capital-

ism fashions for it a certain diversionary and escape status, and at the same time exercises control over its intrusion into the productive affairs of human life. For as Marcuse (5: p. 47), for one has observed, the control of play is a function of the length of the working day. The exploitation of surplus-labor accomplishes this control particularly well.

It is clear from the above that in capitalism one does not work in order to play, but that one works in order to work again. But this requirement of surplus-labor, which consigns play to the borders of human life, does not entail that play simply languish there. On the contrary, the ingenuity of capitalism consists in its uncanny ability, quite transparent in its notion of surplus-labor, to make the superfluous a condition of the necessary. This strange power of inversion intrinsic to capital, which according to Marx (8: p. 156) accounts for the mystifying fact that within its ken "everything is itself something different from itself," endows the amorphous diversionary status of play with a concrete instrumental form. That is, it turns play into a productive force. Here its quality of "apartness" simply designates its rank as a subsidiary productive activity. Play thus stands in this inverted scheme of things in a parasitic relation to work, which means that it has no purpose or sense of seriousness of its own save that which it derives from work.[4]

The specific productive functions assumed by play in advanced bourgeois society number principally three: restorative, compensatory, and prophylactic function. These are to be taken neither as mutually exclusive nor as exhaustive of the possible instrumental uses of play in capital. It should be further observed that each of these subordinate functions are derived from the immanent requirements of capitalism itself and are not, therefore, intrinsic to play. This is quite consistent with its parasitic status in capital.

As implied in our previous remarks, all three functions of play are a response to capital's mode of development of the productive forces. They presuppose, as such, the continuous degradation of work in which it becomes progressively more fragmented, routinized and abstract. The ingression of machine labor, which caps this development, merely exacerbates the stultifying effects of such labor. Labor is thus gradually stripped of its palpable challenge to transform nature in imaginative, nurturant ways. This is further aggravated by the planned obsolescence and deliberate shoddiness of the artifacts it produces, a fact which accounts for its inordinate dependence on the scientific and intuitive guile of advertising to find or create a market for its products. The cumulative effect of all of this is to create, even in the most content and naive of laborers, the need for an escape, a diversion from work. Play provides just such an escape. And it is in this capacity that it respectively restores, compensates and releases the laborer from his bondage to alienated work.

The most obvious requirement engendered by the reduction of work to a monotonous stretch of abstract labor is the need for a recuperative period. Play, as the spare or empty time left over from work, readily satisfies this need. The decision to play in this instance does not entail a conscious abstention from work, as it did for the pre-bourgeois human being,[5] but a simple capitulation to the rigors of production. Such rigors mandate an expanding level of production and, correlatively, provision for the worker to recreate, to refresh itself. Play here is clearly not the aim of work, its telos, but merely its prop. It serves, therefore, as an appendage to production, taking on its same instrumental laws and characteristics.

The cretinization of work also issues in the need for compensation. The principal form of recompense for labor in capitalism is the wage. The demand for a better wage is, therefore, the typical response to the further degradation of work. But the structural constraints on wages levied by the production of surplus-value, and the growing debilitating mental and physical effects of alienated labor, render mere financial remuneration inadequate. Hence, the reliance on play and kindred leisure activities as supportive compensatory devices. Play is construed in this manner as an

entitlement for arduous work, as a reward for the mental and physical tyranny of labor. Such reward can obviously be channeled in a recuperative direction. Nonetheless, it is still possible to tease out a pure compensatory sense to play here. This consists, more precisely, in its capacity to serve as a "substitutive satisfaction" for work. The gratuitous obstacles and challenges of play thus take the place of the exogenous challenges formerly posed by work. Since the tendency of capital is to dissolve the sense of struggle, daring and risk associated with work, the ability of play to endow life with another sense of struggle and overcoming looms large in the advance of bourgeois society.

The alienation of work gives rise further to the use of play as a kind of safety valve. This prophylactic use of play is engendered by the build-up of tensions and frustrations indigenous to alienated labor. Such potentially disruptive forces must be contained in a society predicated on the extraction of surplus-value. And it is play which furnishes such containment as an escape by which these repressed tensions can be vented. Play here is a form of therapy which purges these tensions of their perturbative effects. In doing so, it makes the established social order, and its norms of repression, more palatable to the human psyche. But its task of mollifying repression grows more difficult as our sensibilities are further jaded by ruinous work. In response, play devolves into mere spectacle, a base display bordering on crude sensationalism and the vicarious thrills provided by violence, gambling, media blitzes, circus-like side-shows and paid entertainers. The reduction of play to a spectacle marks its assimilation into the amusement industry and its entertainment ethic whose main purpose seems to be the deflection of human thought and action from its substantive core, the trivialization of all of human life. The packaging of play as yet another commodity to be sold for its spectacle potential, with all its attendant paraphernalia (clothing, equipment, etc.), coincides with the consumer orientation of mature capitalism, to be contrasted with its early thrift orientation, which requires the creation of ever new markets to absorb its productive capabilities.

Capital's transformation of play into a handmaiden of work means ultimately, however, that its fate lies in the twists and turns of production and the fortuitous ebb and flow of the market. Since the odyssey of production in capital is replete, as noted, with crises of overproduction wrought by the technological enhancement of labor, play too is prey to such crises. Yet it is in such crises that play sheds its productive roles, and in so doing becomes an important economic, political and social problem for capitalism. This is so in two senses. First, the phenomenon of overproduction reveals that the development of capitalism tends toward the production of an abundance which is inimical to its preservation. It is the creation of this abundance which, in turn, makes possible the ascendance of play over work by removing the temporal constraints imposed on the former as a spare time activity. Second, this ascendance of play is to be distinguished from the operation of its instrumental predecessor in capitalism. That is, the form of play set loose by the production of abundance stands outside the web of instrumental laws peculiar to capitalistic production. This pure form of play, rooted as it is in a different rational and axiological order, is impervious to the assimilative, integrative tendencies of advanced capitalism. It constitutes, as such, a constant threat to capitalism and its notion of the flourishing life. The mobilization of forces against the rise of (pure) play is, therefore, a task not lightly regarded by bourgeois ideologists.[6]

Capital's corrective response is, of course, to manipulate behavior to conform to the canons of scarcity. In the case of overproduction, it does this crudely by severing the laborer's source of sustenance, its job. This blunt economic transformation of abundance into acute scarcity more than compensates for its accidental relinquishment of temporal control over play, now further augmented by this move. Play is thereby effectively reduced to a dreaded residue of overproduction.

Its emergence, therefore, is not an occasion of joy or celebration, but of dread and impoverishment. As Bertrand Russell notes:

> Suppose that at a given moment, a certain number of people are engaged in the manufacture of pins. They make as many pins as the world needs, working (say) eight hours a day. Someone makes an invention by which the same number of men can make twice as many pins as before. But the world does not need twice as many pins. Pins are already so cheap that hardly any more will be bought at a lower price. In a sensible world, everybody concerned in the manufacture of pins would take to working four hours instead of eight, and everything else would go on as before. But in the actual world this would be thought demoralizing. The men still work eight hours, there are too many pins, some employers go bankrupt, and half the men previously concerned in making pins are thrown out of work. There is, in the end, just as much leisure as on the other plan, but half the men are totally idle while half are still overworked. In this way it is insured that the unavoidable leisure shall cause misery all around instead of being a universal source of happiness. (11: pp. 16-17)

As effective and swift as the above economic manipulation of scarcity is, its ultimate capacity to contain play stems from capital's coordination of individual consciousness with its social consciousness. That is, by reconciling the private interests of individuals with the public interests and requirements of capitalism, it is able to cast a negative spell over play which is more pervasive and deep-seated than any simple economic measure. For it is through such coordination of consciousness that the threat posed to capitalism by abundance becomes a threat to the individual as well. Automation, therefore, not only calls into question the meaning and efficacy of the system, but the meaning and efficacy of the individual's life. In a society which prides itself on the "equal liability of all to work,"[7] and in which one's self-worth and anchor in society—not to mention the very structure of one's day—is rooted in work, its decrease can only be viewed with suspicion. The source of that suspicion, and what is at stake here, is not merely the pride of the workers, nor a concern over what they might do with their newly found free time, but their very humanity. For that humanity has been subtly molded and managed by capitalism, such that the limits of being human have been rendered co-extensive with those of work. Hence, technology's usurpation of those limits, and the exogenous struggles that found them, is construed as a usurpation of our humanness, of its immanent sense of purposiveness. Play is once again made a dreaded residue of overproduction. But this dread, unlike its economic counterpart, admits of no redemption and knows no legitimation since it is founded on the loss of our (productive) humanity. Play in this instance cannot rescue our humanity, but only confirm its loss.

The worker's internalization of the social requirements of capitalism thus explains its well known opposition to advanced technology. Capitalism, in short, makes it in the rational self-interests of the workers, both economically and spiritually, to oppose such technology either through the calculated underuse of existing technology, or the blockage of new technology. That such opposition reflects the interests of the system as well is evident from its dependence on human labor to realize its acquisitive goals. If that is not evidence enough, the role of the state in these matters makes this patently clear. For the state constructs as its litmus test for the implementation of new technology whether such technology will at least create as many jobs as it eliminates. Technical progress becomes, therefore, a human calamity, and the free time of play is transmuted into the coerced time of waiting for work, or the empty time of mourning our loss of human purpose.

IV

Implicit in our preceding criticism of the inverted ratiocination of capital is a view of the proper, truly rational relation of work to play. The gist of this rational relation is, as its opposite in capital, teleological. But the direction of the relation is here reversed, that is, play is the telos of work. Play, in other words, is the end or aim of work. In claiming such, much more is being claimed than the simple fact that work sometimes just happens to eventuate in play, as it periodically does in capitalism, but that the very reason for working is to "free up" time for playing, that, more precisely, work naturally inclines, free of social impediments, toward play. This view does not entail any conflation of work and play, but is premised on the absence of such conflation. The dissolution of all substantive differences between work and play is rather part of the ideological, assimilative repertoire of advanced capitalism. Work and play remain, then, opposites on this rendering but concordant rather than discordant ones. Their complementary status is a function of the teleological relation that we have alleged holds between them in which work, and its development of the material substratum, is made subordinate to the accession of play and its realm of possibility.

The bare outlines of a new, rational successor to capitalist society can be read off the above relation. Such a society would, of course, be based on play rather than work, and abundance rather than scarcity. From a production standpoint, it would assume the same goals of the so-termed "steady state" which is characterized by its equilibrium between wants and resources, and production and consumption. Certain constraints on material growth, and on the quantum of goods produced at any given time would, accordingly, have to be levied in consideration of human and ecological needs. Technology would not immediately cease, but its scope would be altogether different.[8] Instead of serving a vital role in the perpetuation of the struggle for life, it would be employed as a liberating force to progressively diminish the obligations and burdens of labor. This is in keeping with the new qualitative notion of wealth operative in this society which equates wealth not with "exchange-value," with the capacity to purchase the necessaries and conveniences of life, but with free, disposable time. The standard of wealth here subscribed to that "less is more" makes it clear that the procurement of the necessities of life is the prerequisite, but not the content of a free society. Such content belongs rather to play whose proliferation is the guiding aim of this social system. Hence, a steady state society presupposes constancy only in terms of material growth. Beyond this, and indeed because of this, it presupposes a great profusion of the human spirit and its wellspring, play.

That in fact work and play operate more often than not at loggerheads with one another does not undermine the cogency of the above view, and the new society it presages, but illustrates rather graphically its pathological repression. Such repression is endemic to capitalism and its law of accumulation. The operation of this law guarantees the primacy of the economic struggle for life, and so, the opposition of work and play. This can be termed pathological precisely because it deflects the order of human endeavor from its proper rational course only in order to serve its own social, vested interests. What we collectively produce, therefore, acts as a material force against our liberation. Labor, in turn, functions not by redressing the claims of necessity but by reproducing its claims in perpetuity. It is in this manner that not only play but labor itself is stripped of its rational meaning, and authentic significance. For by negating the self-canceling dynamic of labor, by imposing arbitrary strictures on its self-effacing task of satisfying human needs, labor is reduced to a servile enterprise much akin to the celebrated task of Sisyphus. The extent to which capitalism

bases itself on such a use of labor, and commits itself to such an inverted rational order, is the extent to which the pathology rages within it.

Having said all this, I do not wish to suggest that the transition envisaged here from a work- to a play-based society will be an easy one to make. It must initially overcome the ideological resistance of the prevailing social order. Such resistance is not to be taken lightly; for capitalism has been so successful in promulgating its acquisitive pathology as a universal, rational standard of human life that Freud's concern over the sustenance of human civilization owing to humankind's "natural" aversion to work is no longer a real concern. It is thus clear that no simple, reformist measure, such as the popular efforts to humanize work, will do. As long as the structural laws of capitalism remain unscathed, the problems sketched here will not disappear. It is also clear that not just any radical measure will suffice either. Thus, Marx's pure socialist order, which in the contemporary political arena constitutes the only developed radical alternative to capitalism, does not fit the bill. This is so since, as Marx (9: p. 81; 6: p. 119) himself proclaims, the organization of this society is "essentially economic," and labor is regarded, accordingly, not only as a "means of life" but as "life's prime want." What is required here, therefore, is a dose of critical, imaginative thinking, a thinking freed of the aberrations of modern society, of its inversion of means and ends, of its contrivance of a "natural" aversion to play. There are, fortunately, historical precedents to build on, but not, of course, to replicate. Most notable among these is, perhaps, Aristotle's linkage of the "well-ordered" state to leisure, and Hegel's notion of the modern state which sought to break the reduction of the social and the political to the economic. The difficulty of the task notwithstanding, I think it is not claiming too much to say that the very destiny of humankind *may* very well depend on the construction of a social order conducive to the rational realignment of work to play.

Notes

1. The gist of this analysis of capitalism, as will become quite apparent in the ensuing discussion, is of a decidedly Marxist flavor.

2. This instrumental notion of play qualifies, given our earlier characterization, only as a quasi-play form.

3. On this point, see Frank Hearn (3: pp. 207, 213).

4. The accomplishment of this metamorphosis of play should not go unnoticed. For, on the one hand, what was formerly regarded as a paradigm of an unproductive endeavor, as its highest instantiation, has now been transformed into a hybrid productive force. And, on the other, this influx of play was achieved without tarnishing the legitimation of the prevailing social order. That is, not only was capital able to make provision for play without relinquishing control over its disposition, it was also able to subtly consummate this control by turning play into its opposite.

5. The pre-bourgeois human agent's abstinence from work was based on a different, noncapitalistic notion of affluence. There are, in this regard, two basic paths to affluence (the ready satisfaction of human needs): want less or produce more. Primitive humans, as Marshall Sahlins has shown in his brilliant book *Stone Age Economics* (12: p. 2), by and large chose the former route, not as a matter of prudential restraint, or as a way of augmenting personal wealth, but as a concerted, conscious decision to live a life as free of work as possible. The choice to abstain from work was also common among the ancient Greeks who, e.g., if they lacked the requisite wealth, avoided work by winnowing their basic life requirements. The decision to limit one's needs did not, however, guarantee affluence—that would be claiming too much. But even when genuine scarcity reared its ugly head, its claims were considered to be a private affair to be disposed of, accordingly, by one's self and family. Prior to the burgeoning of capitalism, therefore, scarcity was either resolved by wanting less, or simply consigned to the realm of private life.

6. Unless specified otherwise, all further references to play will be to its pure, noninstrumental, sense.

7. The "equal liability of all to work" is a precept most characteristic of advanced capitalism. Thus, in the early stages of capitalism the liability to work was shouldered principally by the lower working class, leaving the upper class managers and entrepreneurs to devote their time to leisure pursuits. It was this disparity which precipitated Veblen's stinging critique of the slovenly manner of the leisured upper class. But in mature capitalism this critique is obsolete; for as Galbraith (2: p. 350), among many others, has noted, today's corporate managers often work harder than their employees and show a capacity to work which outstrips "even the most imaginative possibilities for the acquisition and use of goods and services." In a very real sense, then, there is no longer any leisure class. This point notwithstanding, the vast majority of such corporate managers, while they do not find their work completely onerous, do not find it intrinsically satisfying either. As Maccoby (4: p. 177) found, "none expressed the deep commitment [in their work] of a scientist passionately searching for the truth."

8. For a more complete account of the role of technology in a steady-state society see Meadows (10: p. 182).

Bibliography

1. Arendt, Hannah. *The Human Condition.* Chicago: University of Chicago Press, 1969.
2. Galbraith, John Kenneth. *The New Industrial State.* New York: New American Library, 1972.
3. Hearn, Frank. "Remembrance and Critique: The Uses of the Past for Discrediting the Present and Anticipating the Future." *Politics and Society,* 5 (1975), 201-27.
4. Maccoby, Michael. *The Games-Man: The New Corporate Leader.* New York: Simon and Schuster, 1976.
5. Marcuse, Herbert. *Eros and Civilization.* Boston: Beacon Press, 1966.
6. Marx, Karl. *Critique of the Gotha Program, in Marx and Engels: Basic Writings on Politics and Philosophy.* Edited by Lewis S. Feuer. Garden City, New York: Doubleday Co., 1959.
7. Marx, Karl. *Grundrisse.* Translated by Martin Nicolaus. New York: Vintage Books, 1973.
8. Marx, Karl. *The Economic and Philosophic Manuscripts of 1844.* Translated by Martin Milligan. New York: International Publishers, 1972.
9. Marx, Karl. *The German Ideology.* Translated by Clemens Dutt. In *Marx and Engels: Collected Works Volume* V. New York: International Publishers, 1976.
10. Meadows, Donella H., et al. *The Limits to Growth.* New York: New American Library, 1975.
11. Russell, Bertrand. *In Praise of Idleness and Other Essays.* London: Allen and Unwin, 1935.
12. Sahlins, Marshall. *Stone Age Economics.* Chicago: Aldine-Atherton, 1972.

Hegemony and Sport

S.J. PARRY

This paper[1] starts with recent developments in the sociological study of sport, which have paralleled developments in the parent discipline and other subdisciplines. "Positivist" or "functionalist" or "bourgeois" sociology (as well as economics and politics) have given ground to Marxist or Neo-Marxist approaches to the extent that the latter have achieved authoritative preeminence in certain areas. Let me illustrate this by presenting an analytical model and providing an example from studies of world economical development before suggesting a certain parallel in sport sociology.

Paradigm Construction in Sociology and the Sociology of Sport

In *The Two Marxisms* Alvin Gouldner (10: p. 289ff) constructs a Marxist critique of Marxism, attempting to explain its historical development and to provide an analytical framework for its reconstruction and future development. His principal metatheoretical tool is a theory of the development of social theory, and specifically a theory of the evolution of Marxism through three stages. The first stage is one of "paradigm coalescence," during which the theory seeks to differen-

tiate itself by attacking opponents and by defining itself in dramatic and forceful terms. The second stage is an application of the paradigm to empirical study, during which the paradigm encounters "anomalies" which either challenge it, or for which it can offer no explanation. The third stage is "paradigm normalisation" during which definitive textbooks are written to transmit the theory in its "classic" form to future generations.[2]

This model is neatly applied to the development of the "Neo-Marxist" underdevelopment theory. At the stage of paradigm coalescence, the theory establishes its identity through comparison and contrast with classical Marxism and with bourgeois "modernization theory." During the second stage, the theory serves as a novel instrument for inquiry into actual states of affairs in the real world, when its utility and explanatory power will be tested, and its real or apparent limitations exposed. In fact, this particular paradigm stimulated a massive amount of empirical work which, in turn, stimulated a variety of challenges to the paradigm. "Paradigm normalisation" seems to have occurred already—the classic texts are written—but this, of course, does not mean that the argument is over. This stage is but a moment in the dialectical process, and so long as some variant of the paradigm serves explanatory purposes, the theoretical argument will proceed in parallel.

Foster-Carter (9: pp. 81-93) has painted a detailed picture of the process of paradigm coalescence as against both bourgeois modernization theory and traditional Marxism. To take just the former for our present purposes, the originally

Reprinted from *Journal of the Philosophy of Sport*, X, (1983), pp. 71–83. Copyright 1984 by the Philosophic Society for the Study of Sport. Reprinted by permission.

dominant bourgeois "modernization" theories, for example, the stage theory of W.W. Rostow (31) were characterized as:

1. ahistorical—this category of "traditional society" was seen as unhelpful, indeed obfuscatory.
2. astructural—it presupposed "national society" as a unit, as if everyone could "take off" if we all helped a little.
3. conflict-free—an evolutionary and peaceful transition between "stages" was assumed.
4. ideological—while claiming to be value-free and scientific, it actually served Western interests.

The underdevelopment theory, however:

1. related historical evidence to the developmental career of specific societies to demonstrate the causes of under-development.
2. took the world as the unit of analysis, in order to demonstrate the mechanism of "structural surplus-sucking."
3. emphasized the historical role of social revolution, and reintroduced it (in part) as a prescription, while developing an account of the contribution of class struggle.
4. insisted on a "scientific" approach to problem-solving, which exposed the ideological nature of such concepts as "development" (e.g., Amin's (1: p. 18) observation that "At the centre growth *is* development, but at the periphery, growth may lead to disarticulation").

A parallel set of characterizations and critiques can be discerned in John Hargreaves's discussion of bourgeois approaches to the sociology of sport, both "the dominant one" (functionalism) and "the second approach within mainstream sociology" (interactionism). The principal criticism of interactionism is that it is *astructural*—no consideration is given to the character of the social order within

which patterns of individual action-seeking are located. Functionalism sees sport as adapting to society's requirements and integrating individuals into institutions and role expectations, as well as utilizing a concept of "social needs" which confuses the needs of specific groups with the needs of all. To this extent the analysis is *conflict-free*—there is no class analysis of social power. It is also *ideological*: "the approach tends to be conceptually related to a social engineering perspective, sometimes very explicitly in policy-inspired research, but mostly implicitly in work which claims to be scientifically neutral" (19: p. 37). Additionally, Hargreaves's main illustration of the weakness of the approach (19: pp. 37-38) is a superb example of an historical analysis of the relationship between the developmental career of certain sport forms and the changing patterns of the political, social, and economical order in which they are embedded. That is to say, it points to the *ahistorical* character of functionalistic analysis.

Thus it can be seen that Hargreaves's discussion follows a recognizable strategy as a contribution to the coalescence of the paradigm he wishes to promote. In a fairly usual pattern he has sought to differentiate his approach from that of the bourgeois tradition which has dominated the sociological study of sport. The next strategic move, however, is to repeat the process against other foes: alternative Marxist approaches. This is particularly important in view of the perception of what constitutes Marxism which is held by its critics. For example, Roberts (30: Chapter 6) sees it as a theory which seeks to explain social reality by a simplistic reference to the interests of a single dominant class. And Guttman's (13: Chapters 2 and 3) Weberian approach is outlined in contrast with Classical Marxism and Critical Theory (which he calls "Neo-Marxism"). Now, Hargreaves shares in many of the criticisms brought forward by such anti-Marxists. In his discussion of Critical Theory (19: pp. 41-44), which he elsewhere refers to as Correspondence Theory (18: p. 104), he deprecates its pathological view of human behavior, its *deterministic* and *ahistorical* perspective, and its inability to account for the difference between sport in state socialist and capitalist societies (its *acontextuality*). In his discussion of structuralist Marxism (19: pp. 44-46) which he elsewhere refers to as Reproduction Theory (18: p. 104) he criticizes it as *conflict-free* (for it gives no account of how control may be problematic for dominant groups), *elitist* (since we have to distinguish between the ideologically duped masses and the intellectual elite who alone, with the aid of their "science," can see through the ideological veil which all culture presents) and as seeing individuals as *passive* recipients and bearers of "structures" rather than as active centres of consciousness.

We have now arrived at a list of objectionable features which are to serve as contrasting elements with the new paradigm, which Hargreaves considers will avoid the failings of other Marxisms, thus accommodating some of the more usual bourgeois criticisms, and will confront bourgeois theories with a model of the sociological study of sport whose explanatory power will demonstrate a compelling range, depth, and complexity. This new paradigm he calls Hegemony Theory which as applied to sport, owes much to its development within the sociology of culture, as well as of course, to its original creator, Antonio Gramsci.

Gramsci's Contribution to Marxist Theory

The Marxist tradition has had to address the question: How is the remarkable survival power of the capitalist system to be explained? Marx had "predicted" the inevitable collapse of capitalism as a result of successively more serious crises arising from internal contradictions in the system. Crisis-ridden it may be, close to collapse it has seemed to be, but it still limps along.

Marx sometimes wrote as if he expected revolutionary change to occur the day after tomorrow. For example, in 1848 he spoke of Germany as

being "on the eve of a bourgeois revolution" which was to be "but the prelude to an immediately following proletarian revolution" (cited in 26: p. 160). Lenin and other Bolshevik leaders, prior to the Russian revolution, assumed that "without aid from the international world revolution, a victory of the proletarian revolution (in Russia) is possible." The Bolsheviks had seen themselves as but one actor on the world stage, and had expected (and had thought themselves to *require*) parallel developments elsewhere. "Otherwise we would perish," said Lenin (cited in 22: p. 22). Yet, despite such expectations and hopes, capitalism has persisted in just those parts of the world seen by Marx as ripening earliest, and this condition has required explanation by subsequent theorists. As Sassoon remarked:

Authoritarian, mechanical Marxists are now few and far between. The old assumptions of what for many years was widely considered Marxism have been thrown aside: the economy as the direct source of historical change, with ideas and culture the mere reflection of economics; the state as an instrument of a class; the "great bang" or crisis theory of the downfall of capitalism; ideology as something which is used to blind the population to its "true" interest; the vanguard party, the dictatorship of the proletariat, etc. etc. (32: p. 9)

Against this background of a reappraisal of Classical Marxism, both in view of problems relating to the coherence of its internal logic, and in view of its apparent lack of success in interpreting and changing the real Western world, the work of Gramsci looms large. The main body of his published work, *The Prison Notebooks*, was written in fragmentary fashion during the eleven years immediately preceding his death. "We must prevent this brain from functioning for twenty years," Mussolini is reported as saying, but during his incarceration, and despite the necessity to deceive the censor by adopting code-like devices, he succeeded in filling 33 notebooks, or some 2,350 printed pages (24: p. 73). However, the nature of these notes and the conditions under which they were written, demand of any reading of Gramsci that it be a reconstruction, an interpretation. This we shall now attempt.

There had been a tendency to examine the possibility that capitalism had somehow succeded in resolving its internal contradictions. My own view is that Marx himself can be held partially responsible for this trend: for rational intervention is only possible given understanding, and Marx had provided the intellectual tools and analyses which alerted the bourgeoisie to the possibility of its own demise. However, Gramsci

concentrated on how the advanced capitalist order was increasingly able to contain the threats generated by these inherent self-destructive tendencies through the manipulation of mass consciousness. Owing to its subtle control over "civil society" . . . The bourgeois class . . . has established an ideological "hegemony." Condemned to perceive reality through the conceptual framework of the bourgeoisie, the masses wear their chains willingly. (8: pp. 472-73)

There are terms used here which require explanations. First, *civil society* is distinguished from political society in that the former encompasses all those social institutions and relationships that are based on consent, as opposed to coercion. Anderson (2: p. 21) presents an "explicit set of oppositions":

Political society	Civil society
Force	Consent
Domination	Hegemony
Violence	Civilization

Civil society, the site of the exercise of hegemony, "comprises all the 'so-called private organisations' like political parties, trade unions, schools, church, voluntary and cultural associations and the family, as opposed to the public character of the state" (33: p. 83). Political power

may now be construed as residing not simply in the coercive and repressive apparatus of the state, but as being exercised at all levels of society. It is coercion plus hegemony; "there is not one aspect of human experience which escapes politics, and this extends as far as 'common-sense' " (27: p. 201).

For Gramsci, politics is "the central human activity, the means by which the single consciousness is brought into contact with the social and natural world . . ." For "every man, in as much as he is active, i.e., living, contributes to modifying the social environment in which he develops . . . in other words, he tends to establish 'norms', rules of living and of behaviour" (21: pp. 22-23). We are *all* political beings—even to do "nothing" is to collude in the perpetuation of a state of affairs, and hence to do *something*. For Gramsci then, sociological analysis must include not just the understanding and interpretation of public institutions, but also the political analysis of the organization of consent.

Thus, secondly, *hegemony* is "political leadership based on the consent of the led, a consent which is secured by the diffusion and popularisation of the world view of the ruling class" (3: p. 352). It is "an order in which a certain way of life and thought is dominant, in which one concept of reality is diffused throughout society in all its institutional and private manifestations, informing with its spirit all taste, morality, customs, religious and political principles and all social relations" (35: p. 587). Third, it is:

primarily a *strategy* for the gaining of the active consent of the masses through their self-organisation, starting from civil society, and in all the hegemonic apparatuses: from the factory to the school and the family. And this has the aim of creating a collective political will, at once national and popular: a historic bloc of socialism. (4: p. 119)

Now, these differing definitions give at least a hint of the difficulty involved in interpreting

Gramsci's remarks, and the contested nature of discussions surrounding his work. In the present context, however, I don't really think that much at all hangs on whether we see hegemony as a *relation*, a sociopolitical *situation*, or as a political *strategy*, for each is a facet of the others. Hegemony is a political strategy which employs a relation of intellectual and moral leadership in order to bring about a state of affairs in which a certain group holds dominance.

This account of state power as "hegemony protected by the armour of coercion" (11: p. 263) has important implications for revolutionary strategy. First, it will not do simply to advocate the seizure of political power, for the capitalist class exercises power through both the state and civil society. It is necessary to achieve both political power and hegemony. This is what distinguishes potential revolutionary situations in the West (e.g., the recent election in Italy) from Lenin's Russia: "In Russia, the state was everything, civil society was primordial and gelatinous; in the West, there was a proper relation between state and civil society and when the state trembled a sturdy structure of civil society was revealed" (11: p. 238). That is to say, in contradistinction to classical Marxism, Gramsci holds that a serious economic crisis in an advanced capitalist country will not necessarily result in a serious political crisis, since hegemonic structures may remain intact. Second, this suggests that a revolutionary strategy will employ a 'war of position' rather than a 'war of manoevre' (11: pp. 238-39). "The working class will only be able to advance in an economic crisis if it has made substantial progress in breaking the hegemony of the ruling class and in building up its own hegemony" (33: p. 86). The task will be to employ a long-term strategy of counter-hegemonic incursions. The work of the "organic intellectual" will be one of "developing counter-institutions and a counter-culture such that people no longer would breathe bourgeois ideology every time they came into contact with the cultural atmosphere" (29: p. 39). Third, a part of this strategy will be to transcend the immediate eco-nomical interests of the working class in the more long-term interest of forging alliances among a broad range of social strata, so as to create a "national-popular" front under the hegemonic leadership of the working class. "In short, it is necessary to win the 'hearts and minds' of the majority *before* the conquest of state power" (3: p. 473). The "war of manoevre" (the actual transfer of state power) would simply be one moment in the "war of position" (the gradual struggle to break the hegemonic power of the ruling class).

Finally, the overall purpose of the strategy looks towards ". . . creating the terrain for a subsequent development . . . towards the realisation of a superior, total form of modern civilisation" (11: p. 133). This new, socialist, society would not simply rely on the socialization of economic life automatically to transform political and social relationships, but would continue to develop its hegemonic ideals of active, participatory democracy, a socialized economy, and the relocation of the life of the mass of human beings from the Realm of Necessity to the Realm of Freedom.

Before closing this section, I should say a word about Gramsci's approach to ideology, although I am reluctant to enter into an extensive discussion here.[3] G. Williams's (35: p. 7) definition of hegemony makes it clear that the dominant conception of reality which is diffused throughout society operates not simply through a set of beliefs, ideals, or values, but also through those inscribed in actual social practices. What people *do* is an expression of ideology. In this way what strikes people as "common sensical" or "natural" in their experience and interpretation of, and engagement in, the social world may well be the most secure repository of ideology. As R. Williams says:

> "hegemony" goes beyond "ideology." What is decisive is not only the conscious system of ideas and beliefs, but the whole lived social process . . . It is a lived system of meanings and values . . . which as they are experienced as practices are reciprocally confirming. It

thus constitutes a sense of reality for most people in the society. (36: pp. 109-110)

Gramsci introduced into the study of "culture" an awareness of the necessity of relating particular cultural practices to patterns of power, influence, and domination, and an awareness that such practices could be interrogated for their ideological content.

The Hegemony Theory of Sport

We are now in a position to return to the Hegemony Theory and to attempt to construct it by drawing out the implications of some of Hargreaves's "contrasting elements" and of some of Gramsci's ideas, and relating them to some of the work which has applied such insights to the analysis of sport. To begin with, we can expect Hegemony Theory to look at both political society and civil society at various levels. As well as investigating state control, state funding, and state organizations it will investigate voluntary associations, folk idioms, and the actual practices of sporting participants and spectators. In so doing, it will have special regard for the active meaning-makings of agents, as well as investigating the specific ways in which dominant ideology is inscribed in practice. That is to say, it will operate with an extended concept of power and domination, involving both coercion and the organization of consent, together with a sensitivity to the occurence of active resistance or negotiation in a class war of position. It will not assume a "superior" perspective in view of its intellectually privileged position, but will expect to discover within forms of resistance an incipient strategy. Above all, it will see sport in its widest possible historical and structural context, in an attempt to explain how and why the domination of a particular class comes to be expressed through sporting practice in such a way that its values become part of our notions of what is "natural" or "common sense." Here are some examples:

1. It is a commonplace of Marxist theorizing that the maintenance of divisions between subordinate groups contributes to the maximal efficiency of the capitalist system. Clarke & Clarke's (6: pp. 63, 71) thesis is that sport enshrines the doctrine of competitive individualism as the "natural human condition," and supports nationalism, racialism, and sexism. It reproduces and transmits dominant ideological themes and values, which are then 'concentrated' when given media coverage, since its representation is informed by values such as spectacle, drama, personalization, and immediacy.

2. To take up one of those themes, Paul Willis (37: pp. 117, 130) argues that beliefs about sport and gender "combine into one of the few privileged areas where we seem to be dealing with unmediated 'reality'." Of course women are biologically different; of course women cannot perform as well as men, at least in certain sporting activities— but the taking up and emphasizing of these differences means that "an ideological view comes to be deposited in our culture as a common-sense assumption—'of course women are different and inferior'."

3. Bringing out other features of the explanatory goals of Hegemony Theory, John Clarke (7) seeks to explain the rise of "skinhead" culture and football hooliganism with reference to historical changes in the social structure of Britain. In particular he discusses the "embourgeoisement" of the working-class, the "bourgeoisification" of formerly working-class activities, and the breakdown in patterns of (inner-city) working-class life. The response of this section of working-class youth is active, creative and confrontive: "The skinheads' creation of a style involved a reassertion of the old traditions, a defence of that culture which seemed threatened with contamination by middle class styles and values" (7: p. 16). The "traditional Saturday meeting

place of the class" must be seen as a "site of struggle," a venue for the enactment of what have been called "resistance rituals" (15). Football hooliganism must be seen as a counter-hegemonic practice: "a microcosmic reflection of the attempt to defend the culture against the encroachment of the bourgeoisie" (6: p. 17).

4. In his discussion of sport as a ritual and dramatic expression of hegemony, Hargreaves (18: pp. 126-27) emphasizes that the symbolic meaning of West Indian cricket is different for the "white-oriented elite" and the "black lower classes": "For the former . . . cricket is a symbol of the perfectly ordered society, with its complex rules and the ideology of obedience and authority . . . For the latter, however, it is one of the few sources of solidarity and pride uniting 'us'." Again, with reference to British sport as understood by dominant and subordinate classes: "As far as the former is concerned sport is a striking metaphor for an idealised capitalism, which asserts that it works . . . for the latter, sport is more a metaphor for how life should be—an implicit condemnation of a society that does not work so well for them" (18: pp. 133-34).

The point here seems to me to be that there is no simple, straightforward way in which sport is "ideological." Its intrinsic character carries with it no particular ideological force. What matters is whether or not, and the way in which, a given ideology can *appropriate* a particular form, *colonize* it, and present it as expressive of itself as opposed to some other ideology. This sense in which, for example, sport can become "different" within different contexts and hegemonies is well expressed by Chantal Mouffe:

It is therefore, by their articulation to a hegemonic principle that the ideological elements acquire their class character which is not intrinsic to them. This explains the fact

that they can be 'transformed' by their articulation to another hegemonic principle. (28: p. 193)

Examples could be multiplied here in order to attempt to show in what ways our identified characteristics of Hegemony Theory are worked out in specific studies, but I hope there are enough here to give a flavor of the theory in action.

Some Observations and Criticisms

To begin with, we should welcome this fresh departure in the study of sport. It is hard to see how the introduction of a perspective which has been thought to be so powerful in investigating other areas of culture could fail to illuminate the area of sport. It promises to clarify, in this underresearched, but important constituent of mass culture, the relationships between ideology, power, domination, social class, the marshaling of mass opinion through "naturalizing" practices, and the symbiosis between sport and the media. However, there are some observations and criticisms that I would like to make under a number of headings.

Alternative Perspectives, Explanation, and Evidence

The problem of paradigm coalescence is that it adopts the method of the elimination of alternatives. Each alternative is presented schematically in such a way as to reveal its faults, and then it is assumed that if the new paradigm apparently avoids those errors it must advance our understanding. There is little attempt to argue out the case, or to justify the adequacy of the new paradigm: characteristically it is simply asserted. For example, Hargreaves (19: p. 47) asserts that "what in fact I am proposing is an approach which leaves open the possibility of relating sport as an element in culture to the structure of hegemony." He does this without discussing Gramsci's work at all. The concept of "hegemony" which will provide the lynch-pin of the new paradigm is presented by both Jennifer and John Hargreaves (19: pp. 14, 47) through the justifiably famous passage in Williams's work *Marxism and Literature* (36: p. 110).

So, there is some attempt to engage alternative perspectives, but unfortunately this seems to occur mainly in the early stages of the argument, and with the dismissive purpose of pejorative contrast. Simultaneously, a version of Gramsci is accepted uncritically as a starting point for analysis, so that it seems as though you must be wearing the correct kit before you can play. Surely there must at some stage be an attempt to confront the question "Does his theory of hegemony function as an adequate explanation of social order in the West?" (8: p. 476). Although Hegemony Theory asserts this, it is still open to us to ask "Is it true that the dominant class in Britain exerts 'hegemony'?" In attempting to answer the question, presumably we would conduct some sort of empirical inquiry as to whether the working class had been "co-opted" or whether it were "resisting." Of course, *both* sets of evidence would indicate the presence of hegemony, since co-option is its explicit aim, and resistance can be contrastively assumed to be an embryonic realization of hegemonic oppression, born of working-class experience. But now, if the working class is "passive" or "obedient" or "colludes," why should this be assumed to be a manifestation of hegemony? The class may well be fairly satisfied with its lot in present circumstances; or it may be cowed by fear of the consequences for it of unemployment. And if it resists, why should that be assumed, *a priori*, to be anything more than petty crime or hooliganism. Interpretations of Gramsci are contradictory here: Femia (8: p. 481) sees in the masses "latent instincts of rebellion, which are often expressed in deviant behaviour and which comprise, in embryonic form, an alternative *Weltanschauung*." But Bates (3: p. 365) asserts that "Gramsci severely criticised those left-wing intellectuals who justify the petty crimes and immorality often associated

with an oppressed class." And he goes on to quote Gramsci's clear warning against a sentimental ennobling of "inferior" conduct: "Revolutionaries must learn to distinguish between behaviour which is revolutionary and behaviour which is simply criminal."

The point is that we cannot just read into deviant behavior the variety of political significance we would wish to observe, and it is perhaps here that we would expect Hegemony Theory to confront conflicting evidence from non-Marxist paradigms. In fact, we should *require* it to do so, or to stand accused of selectivity of evidence. Analogously to the "football hooliganism" issue, A. Hargreaves and Hammersley (16: p. 143) conclude their discussion of C.C.C.S. statements on antischool working class youth thus: "At best, they are a spurious attribution of inchoate 'radical' insight to rebellious pupils. At worst, they exist as entirely unsubstantiated assertions about dormant revolutionary potential." For it to advance our understanding, the Hegemony Theory must do more than simply paint plausible pictures of possible political positions. It must also explain *why* its own explanation should be preferred to alternatives, with reference to evidence other than that which is conveniently self-referenced.

Isomorphism

The analysis often takes the form of repeating an account which has been (or might have been) given in another context, or with reference to a subject other than sport. Since the object of study is "historical and class significance in different sets of social relations" (34: p. 153) the research task is to discern general features of social reality inscribed in various cultural forms. There are two problems here: first, it will not do simply to describe only certain similarities, homologies, or other relationships between sport and wider society. We shall also need some account of the *significance* of these similarities. It is true that some theorists in the past have asserted the radical disjunction between sport and the rest of society, but even if we concede the falsity of that position, and agree that sport in a capitalist society reflects more general social arrangements and values, we still need to ask to what extent such a relationship supports the Hegemony Theory. Does football really become a different activity in different societies, or does it remain by and large the same activity, but wrapped and presented differently in different cultural contexts—and if the latter, who would expect anything else? Of course, sociologists have an occupational stake in expanding the significance of sociological characterization and explanation, but we shouldn't let them get away with it too easily. Second, the drawing of such parallels or the demonstration of such similarities is an analytically irresponsible device, since it relies upon the selection of only those features of activities, or only that evidence, which supports the thesis of similarity. And this is necessarily the case, since the specification of initial conditions (central features of the hegemonic ideology) has to be structured in some way, such that it *demands* selectivity of attention and evidence.

Understanding, Strategy, and the Task of the Intellectual

My use of the word "understanding" in the last paragraph of the subsection Alternative Perspectives, Explanation and Evidence was deliberately in a "passive liberal" sense of the term, suggesting a personal cognitive grasp of a phenomenon. A Gramscian concept of understanding, however, would emphasize the *dialectical* quality of such cognitive activity, and would have a class strategy written into it. "Understanding," here would mean "cognitive mastery the purpose of which is criticism of the phenomenon and its rearticulation to the needs of the revolutionary working class." In view of this, Hargreaves's (19: p. 54) final sentences sound strangely muted: "It is now time for the analysis of sport to shift . . . to a more critical and advanced level of understanding. It *may* be that on the way something concrete can also be accomplished with respect to the way that sport

itself is practised." It seems to me that Hargreaves has coerced himself into such a weak conclusion because there is scarcely any consideration in his work of revolutionary strategy. Precisely *what* is to be accomplished? How is sport to be rearticulated to working-class hegemony? Through what agency? To what end? What new form will it take? Given that the task is the subversion of existing bourgeois hegemonic structures, probably by forming class alliances and waging a war of position, how is this to be *specified*? What should I do *tomorrow*?

Of all this there is nothing in the (admittedly infant) Hegemony Theory literature. Possibly I am being unfair in expecting Hargreaves to do everything in a short essay,[4] but I think there is more to it than that. Gramsci's theory placed a particular emphasis on the role of "organic intellectuals," whose precise task it was to develop counter-hegemonic struggles in virtue of their critical understanding. How are we then to situate the work of Hegemony Theorists themselves? Why are they writing books and articles primarily for the consumption of petty-bourgeois academicians such as ourselves, rather than developing counter-institutions rooted in popular consciousness? There is a possibility that their strategy is to forge class alliances by co-opting some of us, but I suspect that there is genuinely little in the way of strategic thinking going on, for good reason.

Marxism, Economics, and Culture

To begin with, it seems to me that in recent years cultural studies have taken on board a range of Marxist concepts, methodologies, and problems but, as it were, piecemeal and half-heartedly.[5] To borrow an analogy from elsewhere, the Marxification of cultural studies has been built up through successive revisions of bourgeois theories and, like a Russian doll, the final outer layer has essentially the same shape as the innermost one. If this allegation has any truth in it, we may expect to see 'hegemony' used as a neat, handy device of some explanatory assistance, but essentially uprooted from the "philosophy of praxis" within which Gramsci developed it. To begin with Gramsci (11: p. 161): "for though hegemony is ethical-political, it must also be economic, must necessarily be based on the decisive function exercised by the leading group in the decisive nucleus of economic activity." I don't really see how there could be a more explicit statement of the importance of the economic in Gramsci's analysis, but this does not square with Hargreaves's (18: p. 117) perception: "Gramsci's in practice paid relatively little attention to the mode of production in his theory." Having, in so many words, put that problem out of the way, he is now free to go on to develop his own view of sport as ritual and drama, but we must ask now to what extent his account can be called "Marxist" at all. I would advance two conditions (at least) of a view's being Marxist: (a) That it has a central concern with praxis; with changing things as well as interpreting them; with revolutionary strategy. (b) That it has a central concern with the economic logic of capitalism. As Ingham remarks:

> The logic, surely, is ever present and cannot be relegated to some last instance in determination, and experience . . . is not purely independent of the logic. Is not a concern for the relationships between capital's logic and lived experience . . . the crux of Gramsci's contribution? (23: pp. 205-6)

Neither of these conditions, to my mind, has yet been adequately addressed by the Hegemony Theory.

One thing remains to be said: as well as presupposing the truth of Gramscian Marxism, Hegemony Theory implicitly assumes the falsity of other positions. However, since we are not presented with a full frontal assault on liberal-democratic values, we have no clear idea as to *why* we should engage in counter-hegemonic activity.

Does the working class as a whole (and not just small samples of skinheads) *prefer* "modern" sport and its media presentation? If so, why? How would Hegemony Theory seek to dissuade members of that class from their preference? If not, what can or should they do about changing the nature of sport? These are some of the questions which need to be addressed if Hegemony Theory is to speak to those not already converted. That is to say, Hegemony Theory will not attain hegemony among sociological theories of sport unless it seeks to extend itself beyond the corporate stage so as to build a popular alliance around its central theses. Whether it can do this *and* retain its 'Marxist' credentials remains to be seen.

Notes

1. A paper read at the Annual Conference of the Philosophic Society for the Study of Sport held at King's College, London, England, July 7-9th, 1983.
2. The origin of this account is quite clear: its central concepts appear in Kuhn's (25) chapter titles.
3. See (5), passim, but especially Hall et al. (14).
4. See his forthcoming book (20).
5. An example of this is Clarke's (7: pp. 17-18) elementary confusion of the bourgeoisie with the middle class.

Bibliography

1. Amin, S. Accumulation on a World Scale. New York & London: *Monthly Review Press*, 1974.
2. Anderson, P. "The Antinomies of Antonio Gramsci." *New Left Review,* 100 (1976), 5-78.
3. Bates, T.R. "Gramsci and the Theory of Hegemony." *Journal of the History of Ideas,* 36 (1975), 351-366.

4. Buci-Glucksmann, C. "Hegemony & Consent: A Political Strategy." *Approaches to Gramsci*. Edited by A.S. Sassoon. London: Writers and Readers Publishing Cooperative, 1982.

5. Centre for Contemporary Cultural Studies. *On Ideology*. London: Hutchinson, 1978.

6. Clarke, A., and Clarke, J. "Highlights and Action Replays: Ideology, Sport and the Media." *Sport, Culture & Ideology*. Edited by J. Hargreaves. London: Routledge and Kegan Paul, 1982.

7. Clarke, J. "Football Hooliganism and The Skinheads." C.C.C.S. *Stencilled Paper* No. 42, University of Birmingham, 1973.

8. Femia, J.V. "The Gramsci Phenomenon: Some Reflections." *Political Studies*, 27 (1979), 472-483.

9. Foster-Carter, A. "Neo-Marxist Approaches to Development and Underdevelopment." *Sociology and Development*. Edited by de Kadt and Williams. London: Tavistock Publications, 1974.

10. Gouldner, A. *The Two Marxisms*. London: Macmillan, 1980.

11. Gramsci, A. *Selections from Prison Notebooks*. Edited by Q. Hoare and G. Nowell Smith. London: Lawrence & Wishart, 1971.

12. Gruneau, R.S., and Cantelon, H. (eds.). *Sport, Culture and the Modern State*. Toronto: University of Toronto Press, 1982.

13. Guttman, A. *From Ritual to Record*. New York: Columbia University Press, 1978.

14. Hall, S., et al. "Politics and Ideology: Gramsci." *On Ideology*, London: C.C.C.S., Hutchinson, 1978.

15. Hall, S., and Jefferson, T. (eds.). *Resistance Through Rituals*. London: C.C.C.S. Hutchinson, 1976.

16. Hargreaves, A., and Hammersley, M. "C.C.C.S. Gas! Politics and Science in the Work of the C.C.C.S." *Oxford Review of Education*, 8 (1982), 139-144.

17. Hargreaves, Jennifer (ed.). *Sport, Culture & Ideology*. London: Routledge and Kegan Paul, 1982.

18. Hargreaves, J. "Sport and Hegemony." *Sport, Culture and the Modern State*. Edited by R. Gruneau and H. Cantelon. Toronto: University of Toronto Press, 1982.

19. Hargreaves, J. "Sport, Culture and Ideology." *Sport, Culture and Ideology*. Edited by J. Hargreaves. London: Routledge and Kegan Paul, 1982.

20. Hargreaves, J. *Sport and Hegemony in Britain*. London: Macmillan, 1983, forthcoming.

21. Hobsbawm, E.J. "Gramsci and Marxist Political Theory." *Approaches to Gramsci*. Edited by A.S. Sassoon. London: Writers and Readers Publishing Cooperative, 1982.

22. Howe, I. (ed.). *The Basic Writings of Trotsky*. Mercury Books, 1964.

23. Ingham, A. "Sport, Hegemony and the Logic of Capitalism: Response to Hargreaves and Beamish." *Sport, Culture and the Modern State*. Edited by R. Gruneau and H. Cantelon. Toronto: University of Toronto Press, 1982.

24. Joll, J. *Gramsci*. London: Fontana, 1977.

25. Kuhn, T.S. *The Structure of Scientific Revolutions*. Chicago: University of Chicago Press, 1962.

26. Laski, H.J. (ed.). *Communist Manifesto*. London: Allen and Unwin, 1948.

27. Mouffe, C. (ed.). *Gramsci and Marxist Theory*. London: Routledge and Kegan Paul, 1980.

28. Mouffe, C. "Hegemony and Ideology in Gramsci." *Gramsci and Marxist Theory*. Edited by C. Mouffe. London: Routledge and Kegan Paul, 1980.

29. Piccone, P. "Gramsci's Hegelian Marxism." *Political Theory*, 2 (1974), 32-45.

30. Roberts, C. *Contemporary Society and the Growth of Leisure*. London: Longman, 1978.

31. Rostow, W.W. *The Stages of Economic Growth*. Cambridge: Cambridge University Press, 1960.

32. Sassoon, A.S. (ed.). *Approaches to Gramsci*. London: Writers and Readers Publishing Cooperative, 1982.

33. Simon, R. "Gramsci's Concept of Hegemony." *Marxism Today,* 22 (March 1977), pp. 78-86.

34. Taylor, I. "On the Sports Violence Question: Soccer Hooliganism Revisited." *Sport, Culture and Ideology*. Edited by J. Hargreaves. London: Routledge and Kegan Paul, 1982.

35. Williams, G.A. "The Concept of Hegemonia in the Thought of Antonio Gramsci: Some Notes on an Interpretation." *Journal of the History of Ideas,* 21 (1960), 586-599.

36. Williams, R. *Marxism and Literature*. Oxford: Oxford University Press, 1977.

37. Willis, P. "Women in Sport in Ideology." *Sport, Culture and Ideology*. Edited by J. Hargreaves. London: Routledge and Kegan Paul, 1982.

Bibliography for Sport and Social-Political Philosophy

Alt, John. "Beyond Class: The Decline of Industrial Labor and Leisure." *Telos,* 28 (1976), 55–80.

Alt, John. "Sport and Cultural Reification: From Ritual to Mass Consumption." *Theory, Culture, and Society,* 1 (1982), 93–107.

Balbus, Ike. "Politics as Sports: The Political Metaphor in America." *Monthly Review,* 26 (1975), 26–39.

Beamish, Rob. "Central Issues in the Materialist Study of Sport as a Cultural Practice." In *Sociology of Sport: Diverse Perspectives.* Edited by Susan L. Greendorfer and Andrew Yiannackis. Champaign, IL: Leisure Press, 1981a.

Beamish, Rob. "The Materialist Approach to Sport Study." *Quest,* 33 (1981b), 55–71.

Beamish, Rob. "Sport and the Logic of Capitalism." In *Sport, Culture and the Modern State.* Edited by Hart Cantelon and Richard Gruneau. Toronto, Canada: University of Toronto Press, 1982.

Beamish, Rob. "Understanding Labor as a Concept for the Study of Sport." *Sociology of Sport Journal,* 2 (December, 1985), 357–364.

Bourdieu, Pierre. "Sport and Social Class." *Social Science Information,* 17 (1978), 819–840.

Bray, Cathy. "Sport, Capitalism, and Patriarchy." *Canadian Woman Studies,* 4 (1983), 11–13.

Brohm. J.M. *Sport: A Prison of Measured Time.* London: Ink Links, 1978.

Cantelon, H. "The Reproductive and Transformative Potential of Sport: Comparative Analyses Utilizing the Weberian Concept of Domination and Rationalization." In *Proceedings of the Second International Seminar on Comparative Physical Education and Sport.* Edited by John Pooley, Halifax: Delhousie Printing Center, 1980.

Cantelon, Hart, and Gruneau, Richard (Eds.). *Sport, Culture and the Modern State.* Toronto, Canada: University of Toronto Press, 1982.

Critcher, Charles. "Radical Theorists of Sport: The State of Play." *Sociology of Sport Journal,* 3 (1986), 333–343.

De Wachter, Frans. "Are Sports a Factor for Peace?" In *Topical Problems of Sport Philosophy.* Edited by Hans Lenk. Scharndorf: Huffman, 1983.

Eichberg, Henning. "Olympic Sport: Neocolonization and Alternatives." *International Review for the Sociology of Sport,* 19 (1984), 97–106.

Gruneau, Richard. "Freedom and Constraint: The Paradoxes of Play, Games, and Sports." *Journal of Sport History,* 7 (1980), 68–86.

Gruneau, Richard. "Sport and the Debate on the State." In *Sport, Culture, and the Modern State.* Edited by Hart Cantelon and Richard Gruneau. Toronto, Canada: University of Toronto Press, 1982.

Gruneau, Richard. *Sports, Class and Social Development.* Amherst: University of Massachusetts Press, 1983.

Gruneau, Richard. "Commercialism and the Modern Olympics." In *Five Ring Circus:*

Money, Power and Politics at the Olympic Games. Edited by Alan Tomlinson and Gary Whansel. London: Pluto Press, 1984.

Guttmann, Allen. *From Ritual to Record: The Nature of Modern Sports.* New York: Columbia University Press, 1978.

Hall, M.A. "How Should We Theorize Sport in a Capitalist Patriarchy?" *International Review for the Sociology of Sport,* 20 (1985), 109–116.

Hargreaves, Jennifer. (Ed.). *Sport, Culture and Ideology.* London: Routledge and Kegan Paul, 1982.

Hargreaves, John. *Sport, Power and Culture.* New York: St. Martin's Press, 1986.

Hart-Nibbrig, Nand, and Cottingham, Clement. *The Political Economy of College Sports.* Lexington, ME: Lexington Books, 1986.

Hearn, Francis. "Toward a Critical Theory of Play." *Telos,* 40 (1976–77), 145–160.

Heinila, K. "Sports and International Understanding—A Contradiction in Terms." *Sociology of Sport Journal,* 2 September, 1985), 240–248.

Hoberman, John. *Sport and Political Ideology.* Austin, TX: University of Texas Press, 1984.

Hoberman, John. *The Olympic Crisis: Sports, Politics and the Moral Order.* New Rochelle, NY: Aristide D. Caratzas, 1986.

Hughes, Robert, and Coakley, Jay. "Mass Society and the Commercialization of Sport." *Sociology of Sport Journal,* 1 (1984), 57–63.

Ingham, Allan. "Sport, Hegemony, and the Logic of Capitalism." In *Sport, Culture and the Modern State.* Edited by Hart Cantelon and Richard Gruneau. Toronto, Canada: University of Toronto Press, 1982.

Ingham, Alan, and Hardy, Stephen. "Sport, Structuration, Subjugation and Hegemony." *Theory, Culture and Society,* 2 (1984), 85–103.

Johnson, Arthur T., and Frey, James H. (Eds.). *Government and Sport: The Public Policy Issues.* Totawa, NJ: Rowman and Allanheld, 1986.

Jones, S.G. "Sport, Politics and the Labour Movement: The British Workers' Sport Federation, 1923–1935." *British Journal of Sports History,* 2 (September, 1985), 154–178.

Lipsky, Richard. *How We Play the Game: Why Sports Dominate American Life.* Boston: Beacon Press, 1981.

Lipsky, Richard. "The Political and Social Dimensions of Sports." In *American Sport Culture.* Edited by Wiley L. Umphlett. Cranbury, NJ: Bucknell University Press, 1985.

McKay, Jim. "Hegemony, the State and Australian Sport." In *Power Play: Essays in the Sociology of Australian Sport.* Sydney, Australia: Hole and Ironmonger, 1986a.

McKay, Jim. "Marxism as a Way of Seeing: Beyond the Limits of Current 'Critical' Approaches to Sport." *Sociology of Sport Journal,* 3 (1986b), 261–272.

Morgan, William J. "Toward a Critical Theory of Sport." *Journal of Sport and Social Issues,* 7 (1983), 24–35.

Morgan, William J. "Labor, Sport, and Critical Theory: A Response to Beamish." *Sociology of Sport Journal,* 1 (1985a), 68–81.

Morgan, William J. " 'Radical' Social Theory of Sport: A Critique and a Conceptual Emendation." *Sociology of Sport Journal,* 2 (March, 1985b), 56–71.

Morgan, William J. "Social Philosophy of Sport: A Critical Interpretation." *Journal of the Philosophy of Sport,* 10 (1985c), 33-51.

Postow, Betsy C. (Ed.). *Women, Philosophy, and Sport: A Collection of New Essays.* Metuchen, NJ: Scarecrow Press, 1983.

Rigauer, Bero. *Sport and Work.* Translated by Allen Guttmann. New York: Columbia University Press, 1981.

Riordan, James. "Sport and Communism—On the Examples of the USSR." In *Sport, Culture and Ideology.* Edited by Jennifer Hargreaves. London: Routledge and Kegan Paul, 1982.

Rojek, Chris. *Capitalism and Leisure Theory.* New York: Tavistock, 1985.

Salamun, Kurt. "Kritische Gesellschaftstheorie und Sportkritik der Neuen Linken." In *Topical Problems of Sport Philosophy.* Edited by Hans Lenk. Schorndorf: Verlag Karl Hufmann, 1983.

Simon, Robert. *Sports and Social Values.* Englewood Cliffs, NJ: Prentice Hall, 1985.

Theberge, Nancy. "A Critique of Critiques: Radical and Feminist Writings on Sport." *Social Forces,* 60 (1981), 341–353.

Theberge, Nancy. "Joining Social Theory to Social Action: Some Marxist Principles." *Arena Review,* 8 (1984), 11–19.

Wheeler, Robert. "Organized Sport and Organized Labor." *Journal of Contemporary History,* 13 (1978), 191–210.

Whitson, David. "Sport and Hegemony: On the Construction of the Dominant Culture." *Sociology of Sport Journal,* 1 (1984), 64–78.

Whitson, David. "Structure, Agency and the Sociology of Sport Debates." *Theory, Culture, and Society,* 3 (1986), 99–106.

Part VI

Sport and Aesthetics

Within the general category of axiology, or the theory of value, aesthetics coexists with ethics and socio-political philosophy. Whereas ethics concerns itself with questions of what is good and how people ought to act, and socio-political philosophy with the question of what is the common good, aesthetics is that discrete branch of philosophical inquiry that concerns itself with beauty or the beautiful, especially in works of art, and with questions of taste and standards of value in judging art.

Modern aesthetic theory has predominantly limited itself to the rigorous investigation of three particular areas of inquiry: the nature and significance of works of art; the processes of producing and experiencing art; and the certain aspects of nature and human production usually considered to be outside of the realm of art, which nonetheless often evoke an aesthetic experience during contemplation of their forms or sensory qualities (e.g., sunsets, flowers, mountain peaks, machinery, and the human form).

This section of the book is concerned largely with the question of the legitimacy, or the lack thereof, of considering and including the aesthetic and artistic aspects of various forms of sport production, experiences, or contemplation within one or more of the three previously delineated areas of aesthetic inquiry.

Sport has long been considered to be a worthy subject for artists; that is, its potential as an object of beauty to be represented in some created art form, for the purposes of evoking an aesthetic experience in the viewer, has frequently been recognized. Indeed, some of the finest examples of this state of affairs may be found among the remnants of the ancient Greeks who gave particularly avid representation to sport and athletes in various art forms. In addition, Edgell (1944), Metzl (1962), and Masterson (1974) all document and analyze a number of contemporary works of art that employ sport as their subject matter for just such purposes.

However, more important than the itemization of the representation of sport in art is the significant question of whether or not sport is in and of itself an art form; that is, as a form of cultural, and even aesthetic, expression, does sport fulfill the criteria applied to art forms such as sculpture, painting, and dance? To respond adequately to this query concerning the nature of sport, it is helpful, as a prelude, to discuss first the concept of play.

There is a long and significant tradition in the history of philosophic thought, from Plato and Aristotle, to Kant, Schiller, Santayana and numerous others, which has associated play with aesthetic theory. If in the act of playing man proceeds to formulate new perspectives within which to enjoy, to interpret, and to understand the nature and conditions of his being in the world, a convincing argument may be forwarded for play as the foundation of art and as an essential ingredient in the artistic process, insofar as it eschews formalism and rigidity to keep open its possibilities of comprehension and creativity.

This section, thus, begins with an excerpt from Schiller's important and still influential *Letters on the Aesthetic Education of Man*. Although almost two centuries have elapsed since its original publication, this work is noteworthy for Schiller's astute perception, which is just currently receiving the recognition due it, that play is a totally absorbing and creative enterprise that performs the essential task of reconciling and harmonizing the two divergent facets of man's nature, namely, the rational and the sensual. According to Schiller, to achieve completeness, man is required to develop and balance both the formal impulse (stemming from his rational nature) and the sensual impulse (emanating from his physical nature), because both are essential aspects of his being. This harmonious middle disposition, or state of organic wholeness, in which man affirms both the physical and the rational, without the constraint or domination of one by the other, is termed the *play impulse* or *play instinct* by Schiller. In turn, the play impulse is manifested within or leads to the *living form* of aesthetic activity, in which man is provided the opportunity to satisfy his creative imagination, nurture the emotions, excite the soul, and satisfy the senses. This state of affairs led Schiller to assert the following, in his famous paean of praise to play: "To speak out once for all, man only plays when in the full meaning of the word he is a man, and *he is only completely a man when he plays.*"

This theme is echoed frequently in more contemporary writings that contend that many, if not all, the liberal and imaginative activities of man may properly be termed play. Indeed, there is currently an almost ecumenical acceptance of the element of playfulness, if not entrance into the realm of play, as a necessary prerequisite component of artistic endeavors. To leave the domain of play and to turn more directly to the consideration of contemporary philosophic inquiries into sport, it is necessary to note that relevant literature of the past two decades has concerned itself predominantly with the delineation of the aesthetic experience of and within sport, as well as with the identification of similarities and differences between sport and art.

The philosopher who has addressed the topic of the connections between sport and aesthetic theory most frequently and in greatest detail is undoubtedly Best, thus, two of his works are herein included. In the initial entry, Best lays the groundwork for considering the aesthetic potential of sport forms by forwarding two crucial distinctions: first, between *purposive* and *aesthetic* sports; and second, between *artistic* and *aesthetic* endeavors. He contends that much of the literature concerned with regarding sport as a form of art is confused by a failure to recognize, in particular, the significance of the second differentiation. According to Best, the aesthetic is primarily an evaluative concept applied to spectators' perceptions, whereas the artistic is principally a participant concept much narrower in scope in that it presupposes that an artifact was produced with a definitive expressive intent in mind. Further, although any sports activity can be viewed from an aesthetic perspective, only select sport forms lay claim to the aesthetic as a central element (e.g., springboard diving and gymnastics).

In most competitive sports, such as football or tennis, Best contends that the aesthetic element is incidental to the ongoing activity and resolution of the contest. Further, with respect to the concept of the artistic, he flatly precludes the inclusion of sport on the grounds that, even in activities that emphasize aesthetic components, the major requisite feature for inclusion in this category is absent. According to Best, any art form whatsoever must allow for the possibility of the expression of a conception of a life issue, such as moral, social, or political problems; such a possibility is simply not intrinsic to any sport. In the last portion of his chapter, in which he rebukes writers who enact an illicit "slide" from such terms as *beautiful* and *graceful* to art, he concludes by contending that whereas sport can indeed be the subject of art, art cannot be the subject of sport.

Kupfer takes issue with some important aspects of Best's position. He argues that not only the qualitative or judged sports, but also the competitive or purposive sports contain essential aesthetic components. The dramatic possibilities and qualities inherent to purposive sports, due to necessary social interaction and opposition, uncertainty of outcome, tension development, and final resolution, and at times culminating in a 'great moment' long remembered in the collective consciousness of sports fans, makes these activities eligible for aesthetic attention and serious axiological inquiry. Roberts also disagrees with Best's assertion that purposive sport has no inherent aesthetic dimension, as well as his contention that the complete identification of means and end is the important feature that distinguishes the concept of art from that of sport. Roberts contends that Best's supposed differences between means and ends are simply the result of an equivocal application of radically different modes of description applied to sport and art; namely, that Best describes art in exclusively particular terms, whereas he describes sport in exclusively general terms. Further, Roberts claims that once this equivocation is righted, the ''differences'' evaporate.

Boxill continues the debate by arguing against the import of four specific reasons or features put forward by Best in support of his previously delineated position. First, that the concern for the demonstration of skill in the sense of technical efficiency in sport overshadows the essential artistic ingredients of style, grace, and form. Second, that the strong desire for victory in competitive sport overshadows the aim of representing beauty. Third, that even if one of the aims of sport is beauty, it is not the sole aim. And fourth, that even when athletes aim at beauty, they are not consciously making any statement about the human condition. In addition, Boxill discusses how issues of gender discrimination influence or determine the outcome of each of the previously enumerated items.

The formal responses of Kupfer and Best to Boxill's efforts are included in this section. Kupfer, although concurring with much of Boxill's analysis, asserts that it is not necessary to argue as strenuously that sport is an art form in order to establish it as a rich source of aesthetic value; in other words, her fundamental purpose can be achieved without necessarily establishing sports' artistic credentials. Kupfer contends that rather than identifying effect with aim, based upon the suggested distinction between the aesthetic and the artistic, Boxill should be satisfied with a rigorous description of the aesthetic parameters of sport.

Wertz's brief piece also contests an assertion to be found throughout much of Best's work, namely, that the context of an action determines its description. Wertz claims that Best's contextualist demands are too restrictive, unreasonable if not extreme, and simply unsympathetic to modern times. Instead, he asserts that, to ascribe meaning to actions in sports, it is necessary to study the identifying marks presented within the nature of the action itself, including the intention of the participants and the context.

It is only appropriate that Best be afforded the opportunity to respond. In the final entry of this section, Best chastises Wertz for misrepresenting his contention that the essential character of an action is inextricably related to the normal context of its occurrence. He also addresses other criticisms to be found in Wertz's articles and concludes, once again, that sport, even of the aesthetic kind, is not art. In addition, he also rebukes Boxill for completely ignoring the central aspect of his argument, namely, the crucial distinction between the aesthetic and the artistic. Following a very brief comment on Kupfer's piece, Best reiterates his firm conviction that, although sport can indeed be superb aesthetically, it is simply not a form of art.

Obviously, there is more to be said about this particular debate; consequently, the interested reader is directed to the additional entries authored by Best and Wertz listed in the bibliography at the end of this section. At this point, however, mention should be made of additional significant works concerned with the entire topic of aesthetic theory and its application to sport, which may profitably be consulted.

The early literature on sport and art was concerned principally with attempting to demonstrate the existence of an affinity or relationship between the two. Thus a number of writers have modified or expanded upon Schiller's original theory to apply it directly to sport. Santayana (1955) emphasized that both play and art act as delightful, energizing, and liberating sources of new power that provide opportunities for the modification of human consciousness, the expression of novel and creative acts, and the organization of joyful sensibility. Further, the articles by Seward (1944) and Hein (1968, 1970) are noteworthy examples of this type of philosophical analysis. In addition, two meritorious selections that discuss sport as a form of artistic cultural expression are those by Maheu (1963) and Jokl (1974).

More recent philosophical efforts have addressed the larger questions concerning the aesthetic or artistic merits of sport itself. Reid's (1970, 1980) work provides a critical foundation for such efforts. Whiting and Masterson's (1974) anthology includes many pieces that studiously examine the aesthetic possibility of sport. Osterhoudt's (1973) collection also includes a section on aesthetics that considers the topic from theoretical perspectives ranging from Aristotelian to Hegelian reflections on the nature of art. Keenan's (1973) informative paper, contained in this collection, explores the dramatic possibilities and attributes of sport by applying Aristotle's six formal elements of tragedy to the spectacle of the sports contest. In addition, Thomas (1979b) also explores the tragic dimension of sport, whereas Kaelin (1968) discusses the aesthetic qualities inherent to the ''well-played'' game from the point of view of the interested spectator.

Roberts' (1979b) essay explores the study of the aesthetic properties of sport through the medium of established symbol systems such as language and art; in particular, he restricts his attention to one form of symbolism in sport, that of representation. Numerous other essays attempt to establish sport fully within the legitimate boundaries of a performing art (Kuntz, 1977; Masterson, 1983). Souriau's (1983) recently translated work presents an interesting extended analysis of the aesthetics of movement that has obvious implications for sport. Also worthy of perusal are Arnold's (1979) book on movement as a source of personally significant experience, as well as his article (1985) contrasting the performer's perspective on the aesthetic aspects of sport with that of the spectator's. Admittedly, not all relevant matters have been addressed herein; indeed, with the sparse and inconclusive treatment of the subject to be found in the existent literature, there is much room for further research aimed at delineating more fully the aesthetic qualities and artistic parameters possible or contained within various sport forms.

Play and Beauty

FRIEDRICH VON SCHILLER

I approach continually nearer to the end to which I lead you, by a path offering few attractions. Be pleased to follow me a few steps further, and a large horizon will open up to you, and a delightful prospect will reward you for the labor of the way.

The object of the sensuous instinct, expressed in a universal conception, is named Life in the widest acceptation; a conception that expresses all material existence and all that is immediately present in the senses. The object of the formal instinct, expressed in a universal conception, is called shape or form, as well in an exact as in an inexact acceptation; a conception that embraces all formal qualities of things and all relations of the same to the thinking powers. The object of the play instinct, represented in a general statement, may therefore bear the name of *living form*; a term that serves to describe all aesthetic qualities of phenomena, and what people style, in the widest sense, *beauty*.

Beauty is neither extended to the whole field of all living things nor merely enclosed in this field. A marble block, though it is and remains lifeless, can nevertheless become a living form by the architect and sculptor; a man, though he lives and has a form, is far from being a living form on that account. For this to be the case, it is necessary that his form should be life, and that his life should be a form. As long as we only think of his form, it is lifeless, a mere abstraction; as long as we only feel his life, it is without form, a mere impression. It is only when his form lives in our feeling, and his life in our understanding, he is the living form, and this will everywhere be the case where we judge him to be beautiful.

But the genesis of beauty is by no means declared because we know how to point out the component parts, which in their combination produce beauty. For to this end it would be necessary to comprehend that *combination itself*, which continues to defy our exploration, as well as all mutual operation between the finite and the infinite. The reason, on transcendental grounds, makes the following demand: There shall be a communion between the formal impulse and the material impulse—that is, there shall be a play instinct—because it is only the unity of reality with the form, of the accidental with the necessary, of the passive state with freedom, that the conception of humanity is completed. Reason is obliged to make this demand because her nature impels her to completeness and to the removal of all bounds; while every exclusive activity of one or the other impulse leaves human nature incomplete and places a limit in it. Accordingly, as soon as reason issues the mandate, "a humanity shall exist," it proclaims at the same time the law, "there shall be a beauty." Experience can answer us if there is a beauty, and we shall know it as

Reprinted from "Letter XV" in *Essays and Letters*, Vol. VIII. Translated by A. Lodge, E.B. Eastwick and A.J.W. Morrison. London: Anthropological Society, 1882.

soon as she has taught us if a humanity can exist. But neither reason nor experience can tell us how beauty can be and how a humanity is possible.

We know that man is neither exclusively matter nor exclusively spirit. Accordingly, beauty as the consummation of humanity can neither be exclusively mere life, as has been asserted by sharp-sighted observers, who kept too close to the testimony of experience, and to which the taste of the time would gladly degrade it; nor can beauty be merely form, as has been judged by speculative sophists, who departed too far from experience, and by philosophic artists, who were led too much by the necessity of art in explaining beauty; it is rather the common object of both impulses, that is of the play instinct. The use of language completely justifies this name, as it is wont to qualify with the word play what is neither subjectively nor objectively accidental, and yet does not impose necessity either externally or internally. As the mind in the intuition of the beautiful finds itself in a happy medium between law and necessity, it is, because it divides itself between both, emancipated from the pressure of both. The formal impulse and the material impulse are equally earnest in their demands, because one relates in its cognition to things in their reality and the other to their necessity; because in action the first is directed to the preservation of life, the second to the preservation of dignity, and therefore both to truth and perfection. But life becomes more indifferent when dignity is mixed up with it, and duty no longer coerces when inclination attracts. In like manner the mind takes in the reality of things, material truth, more freely and tranquilly as soon as it encounters formal truth, the law of necessity; nor does the mind find itself strung by abstraction as soon as immediate intuition can accompany it. In one word, when the mind comes into communion with ideas, all reality loses its serious value because it becomes *small*; and as it comes in contact with feeling, necessity parts also with its serious value because it is *easy*.

But perhaps the objection has for some time occurred to you. Is not the beautiful degraded by this, that it is made a mere play? and is it not reduced to the level of frivolous objects which have for ages passed under that name? Does it not contradict the conception of the reason and the dignity of beauty, which is nevertheless regarded as an instrument of culture, to confine it to the work of being a mere play? and does it not contradict the empirical conception of play, which can coexist with the exclusion of all taste, to confine it merely to beauty?

But what is meant by a *mere play*, when we know that in all conditions of humanity that very thing is play, and *only* that is play which makes man complete and develops simultaneously his twofold nature? What you style *limitation*, according to your representation of the matter, according to my views, which I have justified by proofs, I name *enlargement*. Consequently I should have said exactly the reverse: man is serious *only* with the agreeable, with the good, and with the perfect, but he *plays* with beauty. In saying this we must not indeed think of the plays that are in vogue in real life, and which commonly refer only to his material state. But in real life we should also seek in vain for the beauty of which we are here speaking. The actually present beauty is worthy of the really, of the actually present play-impulse; but by the ideal of beauty, which is set up by the reason, an ideal of the play-instinct is also presented, which man ought to have before his eyes in all his plays.

Therefore, no error will ever be incurred if we seek the ideal of beauty on the same road on which we satisfy our play-impulse. We can immediately understand why the ideal form of a Venus, of a Juno, and of an Apollo is to be sought not at Rome, but in Greece, if we contrast the Greek population, delighting in the bloodless athletic contests of boxing, racing, and intellectual rivalry at Olympia, with the Roman people gloating over the agony of a gladiator. Now the reason pronounces that the beautiful must not only be life and form, but a living form, that is, beauty, inasmuch as it dictates to man the twofold law of absolute formality and absolute reality. Reason also utters the decision that man shall only *play* with beauty, and he *shall only play* with *beauty*.

For, to speak out once for all, man only plays when in the full meaning of the word he is a man, and *he is only completely a man when he plays*. This proposition, which at this moment perhaps appears paradoxical, will receive a great and deep meaning if we have advanced far enough to apply it to the twofold seriousness of duty and of destiny. I promise you that the whole edifice of aesthetic art and the still more difficult art of life will be supported by this principle. But this proposition is only unexpected in science; long ago it lived and worked in art and in the feeling of the Greeks, her most accomplished masters; only they removed to Olympus what ought to have been preserved on earth. Influenced by the truth of this principle, they effaced from the brow of their gods the earnestness and labor which furrow the cheeks of mortals, and also the hollow lust that smoothes the empty face. They set free the ever serene from the chains of every purpose, of every duty, of every care, and they made *indolence* and *indifference* the envied condition of the godlike race; merely human appellations for the freest and highest mind. As well the material pressure of natural laws as the spiritual pressure of moral laws lost itself in its higher idea of necessity, which embraced at the same time both worlds, and out of the union of these two necessities issued true freedom. Inspired by this spirit the Greeks also effaced from the features of their ideal, together with *desire* or *inclination*, all traces of *volition*, or, better still, they made both unrecognizable, because they knew how to wed them both in the closest alliance. It is neither charm, nor is it dignity, which speaks from the glorious face of Juno Ludovici; it is neither of these, for it is both at once. While the female god challenges our veneration, the godlike women at the same time kindles our love. But while in ecstasy we give ourselves up to the heavenly beauty, the heavenly self-repose awes us back. The whole form rests and dwells in itself—a fully complete creation in itself—and as if she were out of space, without advance or resistance; it shows no force contending with force, no opening through which time could break in. Irresistibly carried away and attracted by her womanly charm, kept off at a distance by her godly dignity, we also find ourselves at length in the state of the greatest repose, and the result is a wonderful impression for which the understanding has no idea and language no name.

Sport—The Body Electric

JOSEPH H. KUPFER

Willie Stargell is "Pops," elder statesman of Pittsburgh's baseball team, the Pirates. His powerful body and mind as much as his age qualify him to be the team's leader. "Stargell Stars" for outstanding play grace his teammates' caps and even opposing players seek him out for his company and advice. Yet despite his weighty presence at first base, he is lighthearted, perhaps to a fault. At least, the umpires during the 1979 Championship Series (prelude to the World Series) found fault with him for "horsing around" with the opposing team's base runners; he was reprimanded for chatting, teasing, and playing good natured tricks on them. When asked about this by a reporter, Stargell first noted that the base runners never complained but seemed to enjoy fraternizing with him at first base. He concluded the interview archly, observing that it was awfully funny how people forget that just before every ball game, the umpires shout "Play ball!"; they never yell "Work ball!" It is a game, even if played for pay.

The problem with contemporary sports, especially in America, is that they have become too serious, or we have become too serious about them. Our attitude toward sports has been infected by their "professionalization": league expansion, salary and prize money escalation, media and consumer gluttony. Sports is a major industry, big

Reprinted from *Experience as Art: Aesthetics in Everyday Life* (pp. 111–140, 203–206) by Joseph H. Kupfer, 1983 by permission of the State University of New York Press. Copyright 1983 State University of New York Press, Albany, New York.

business. In fact, *analyzing* the professionalizing of sports, especially in its "non-professional" incarnations in our schools and Little Leagues, has itself become a business. By now we are too familiar with the "Little League Father Syndrome" and the machinations of athletic recruiting on all levels. Easy pickings for sports debunkers.

1. Professionalization and Play

What calls for greater scrutiny lies hidden in this sports boom. The professionalization of sports reaches deep into what we appreciate in it—regardless of level of play. The "professionalized" fan has become obsessed not only with the details of sport as a business (salary arbitration, lawsuits, cable TV "packages") but with the business*like* side of sports: such bottom-line items as scores, wins, rankings. These consequences, abstracted from the actual events of the game, loom larger than the play which produces them. Our eyes are so fixed on end results that we lose sight of the means by which they come about—the "play" is no longer the thing. This seems a natural concomitant of the professionalization of sports. Former athletic director of De Paul University, Father Gielow makes the following comment:

> If college athletics is just big business, that's no good, even though I realize it needs a lot

455

of very shrewd moves to pull it off. But never, because of my background, my priesthood, would I agree with something at the expense of good solid values.

A serious question has to be raised: Does a student deserve a better ticket than a trustee? I think the students come first, I think that got me in a little trouble. I hate to say that I'm a victim. I don't want to agree so fast, because that saddens me. But it may be true.[1]

Something has gone wrong in our colleges. Not only is it virtually impossible for a (nonscholarship) workaday student to go out for the team, but he may not even get to see play those who are paid to play.

In this process we are losing something profound on the side of aesthetic appreciation: direct aesthetic appreciation of sport and consequently what sport has to offer for the aesthetic enhancement of daily life. Too often, we look to sport to satisfy our most obvious, private needs, with the result that we attend more to ourselves than to the sporting event before us. Our egos obscure much of the game from our own perception.

The traditions and rituals of the different sports are a wonderful thing, but without appreciation of the aesthetic of the sporting event the traditions and rituals are easily corrupting. They breed shallow enjoyments and self-enclosure when we look to sports merely as outlets for our aggression or as symbols of our strength. Rather than entrench the provincialism of narrow identifications, sport's rituals can enlarge us by embodying universal aspects of human movement and drama. For many of us, the traditions and ceremonies of sport have supplanted those of religion, creating new forms of congregation as we gather in stadia, arenas, and parks to witness the familiar forms reenacted.

The idea was that the ballpark—any ballpark— was a sanctuary. Once inside it, people were safe. Time stood still. The rules didn't change, like they did on the outside. There were no surprises. There was no death. Fanning liked to think that if somebody who had lived and died, say, in the 1920s or 1930s or 1940s could return to earth and walk inside a major league baseball park, they would feel immediately at home, and have the comforting assurance that a continuity had been upheld since their passing.[2]

The rites and sacraments of sport provide a stable structure for our enjoyments and anguish. Change occurs within the confines of the rules and traditions and so is always brought within an orbit of manageability often missing from the disruptions in our everyday patterns of life. What sport *can* be, then, is an aesthetic ritual of the body. This occurs when we attend to the incredible range and grace of human movement that sports are capable of exhibiting. As aesthetic ritual of the body, sport can inform our everyday movement and awareness of movement. Whether or not we actually participate in sports ourselves, our daily rhythms can be informed by appreciating the aesthetic sport has to offer. Simply watching sports is not enough for this to happen, it all depends on how we watch and what we watch for.

. . . . I had gone each lonely Sunday to the Polo Grounds where Gifford, when I heard the city cheer him, came after a time to represent to me the *possible*, had sustained for me the illusion that I could escape the bleak anonymity of life.[3]

There is nothing wrong with sport as a vehicle for dreaming, but it easily nourishes unrealistic projections of our personal desires or needs. Self-indulgent, we live on the unreal succor of fantasy. It is important to realize that, although unreal, such projections do not signify a playful apprehension of sport. They are too practical in the sense of self-serving. Absorption in fantasy clouds how sport can portray the possible in nonillusory, creative ways when appreciated as play: when its rhythms and proportions inform us of an aesthetic movement latent in our daily lives. Rather than dwelling on idiosyncratic illusions of success or fame, we can accept sports' invitation to celebrate our bodies' exuberance in movement—for the sheer fun of it.

• • •

What I want to suggest is that in the loss of the playful we deprive ourselves of entrance into the aesthetic dimension of sport. Sport especially lends itself to aesthetic appreciation because it is so naturally playful. The imperatives of the decidedly practical make aesthetic appreciation difficult in our everyday experience. Forced by need or moral constraint, we rarely are free simply to act for the sake of enjoyment of the activity: its inherent qualities, tensions, and resolutions. But something as nonpractical as sport should unambiguously invite our aesthetic attention. The sport situation is in a very obvious sense outside the "real" world. It is set up for the purpose of enjoying bodily activity toward no further extrinsic end.

In sports, we set up procedures, sometimes as games, and "pretend" that the activity and outcome are important. As Haywood Hale Broun phrases it, we enter into a "shared delusion." Because we set the rules of the activity and its consequences emerge according to these rules, we most completely define our freedom in play. Perhaps this is why such activities "disport" us, carrying us away from the everyday. We are quite literally free in *structuring* the play as well as in deciding *whether* to play (since not compelled by necessity). Broun nicely sees what is wrong with cheating in this respect: It puts us back in the real world[4]—the game becomes *really* important, pretense is lost. The goals and purposes of sport are not real; they serve no practical need outside the sporting arena. What real use is served in putting golf balls into holes or swatting tennis balls back and forth across a net? In this respect, sport takes the pretense of theatre one step further. Where theatre presents real ends and activities in a pretend setting, the significance of even the ends and activities are pretended in sport.

2. Individual Sports

A. Quantitative/Linear

Some sports obviously bear the practical stamp of their useful origins. Where once man ran or threw or jumped or swam in order to secure food, fight enemies, or explore surroundings, sport isolates these bodily movements for their own sake. Man now plays at activities that were once part of a practical enterprise, but in order to be transformed into sport, their practical value must be severed and the body appreciated simply as moving against the natural limits of space and time. Space and time form the matrix of all bodily activity, but in sports such as those which involve running, throwing, jumping, and the like, they stand out as the means by which man's measure is to be taken. Such sports in a way replace useful ends by *measurement:* how far the shot is put, the javelin thrown; how quickly the course run or swum (perhaps this is appropriate since counting or numbering is itself a practical activity). This kind of sport, then, is linear or quantitative in nature; its performance naturally includes quantification of time and/or space.

The nonaesthetic significance of the quantitative nature of these sports is clear. For one thing, the measurability of feats enables fairly accurate comparisons of different performances—performances separated spatially or temporally. We can compare a mile run in America to a mile run in Australia, or a mile run today with one run forty years ago, because people or machines *record* rather than *judge* accomplishment. Consequently, records are compiled and sometimes take on a life of their own. We can enjoy reading the records of performers whom we have never seen; indeed, one of the delights of linear sports lies in noting the progress human beings have made during the history of the sport. Progress in the mile run since Roger Bannister first broke the four minute "*barrier,*" moreover, is human progress, since the obstacles—space and time—are common to the species. To run a mile in less than four minutes or to put a sixteen pound shot sixty-five feet is the same anywhere,[5] making the same demands on the performer. And while hitting .400 in baseball or throwing forty touchdown passes in a football season can be compared with past performances, the issue is always clouded. These measures cannot be as pure since they are determined by an effort made against, and often with, other people rather than the abstractable dimensions of space and time. But this delight in records and progress in speed or strength is not itself an aesthetic delight. As interesting and enjoyable as record-keeping can be, it can distract us from the performance itself and encourage in us the anti-aesthetic penchant for counting and numbering.[6] The fascination with magnitudes, great and small, threatens to obscure the beauty of sports.

In aesthetic appreciation of the linear sports we grasp the relation between the human movement and the numerical result. The movement itself tends to be repetitious: either continuously—as in the swimmer's stroke or runner's gait—or serially—as in throwing, jumping, or vaulting sports. What we look for is the smooth, fluid motion that suggests effortlessness. No wasted energy, no superfluous movement—just as the compression of words makes a poem trim and lean. "Rhetorical flourishes . . . fussily blur the ideal of a straight, direct line to conclusion."[7] On one level, we appreciate the smooth fluid style because it simply *appears* to require less effort for the same result that a jerky one gains. Thus, a truly fast runner, for example, *could* still be aesthetically deficient if he ran with extraneous rolls, jerks, or flailing. But this is sports, after all, and not dance, so we have an eye for results. Because appearance is connected with measurement, we implicitly judge that the herky-jerky performer *would* have done even better were he more fluid. Grace really is efficient; the aesthetic value of continuous, rhythmic movement has a measurable payoff. Measurement palpably confirms what our eyes intuitively register. Bob Beamon *seemed* to *fly* in his 1968 Olympic execution of the long-jump and *in fact* broke the existing record by over two feet!

But perhaps there is a larger perspective also at work in our aesthetic appreciation of linear, quantitative sports.

Perhaps part of our aesthetic delight lies in the unwinnable struggle with nature. Progress in these sports is ultimately infinite. We can forever shave microseconds off our times, add millimeters to our distances. On the fringes of our awareness is the Sisyphean spectacle of human beings exhausting their resources against the natural limits of physical movement. If we turn away from the particular records involved and look at the overall effort, then space and time are seen as the boundaries of all of our *own* daily movements. And in our own graceful, efficient moments, their limits seem to shrink. When we sprint for the bus or leap over a puddle, we feel ourselves, however transiently, masters of our physical world.

B. Qualitative/Formal

In sports such as diving and figure skating, we are further removed from real world concerns of usefulness and measurement. The athlete performs *in* rather than *against* nature. Not worried about amounts of space covered or time elapsed, we attend exclusively to the *look* of the body in motion. Everyone dives the same distance in roughly the same time. These are qualitative or "formal" sports whose excellence is equivalent to beauty of movement. Measurement does not provide an added aesthetic relation or means of assessment (although degree of difficulty does). In these formal sports, we admire the fluid execution of varied, difficult movement: the spring and flip of the gymnast in her floor exercise, the skater's transition from a leaping double axel to the helix-like spin. Because difficult, we can appreciate the skill needed to perform these sequences. They are *aesthetically* noteworthy, however, because they display the suppleness and graceful strength of the human body. It is not the difficulty in itself that is aesthetically valued; rather, it is a performance with "the grace that makes strength the agent of art."[8] The linear sports are more limited in what they can exhibit, more focused on the struggle against our natural limitations. They seem workmanlike, whereas the formal sports provide contexts for liberation of movement—flight and gliding, air and ice. Here the human seems almost transformed into a creation of liquid motion.

The requirements of staging formal, qualitative sports as competitions reveal their fundamentally aesthetic nature. These competitions require judges, not recording officials who function as auxiliaries or substitutes for machines. Human beings must *evaluate* the performance of the athlete; *aesthetic judgment* is required. It must then undergo strained translation into numerical grading. The counting must be derived from the aesthetic judgment, indicating that the aesthetic, not the scoring or number, is fundamental in such sports. In the linear sports, on the other hand, keeping track of numbers is part of watching the performance itself and not a separate effort to be added on.

This is simply to say that counting is not integral to our appreciation of these formal sports the way it is to our enjoyment of the linear sort. Their central thrust is formal; their contribution to our everyday life is to be found in the grace with which human beings can accomplish varied, difficult movements. Aesthetic appreciation of these sports (and there is hardly any other kind of appreciation insofar as we are actually watching the performance) inevitably enlivens us to the body in motion—whether our own or another's. Thus does a skater's spin accentuate and complete our pivot to close the garage door or pirouette in slipping into an overcoat. Perhaps we even recapitulate the slalom skier's subtle weight shift when we veer out of someone's way in a grocery aisle. Appreciating the quality of movement of the most magnificent members of our species imprints, ever so delicately, images that are patterns for our own motion. Scale and degree are the only differences. If appreciating painting can enhance our everyday perception of light and color, why should we not expect appreciation of a gymnast like Olga Korbut to enhance our appreciation of physical movement, including our own?

The corollary of this is an aesthetic sensitivity to our environment as opportunity for movement and perception. Is it in fact conducive to aesthetic perception, movement, and perception-in-movement? Do our buildings, for instance, invite rhythmic movement of body or eye? Instigating aesthetic awareness of ourselves as moving in space and time, formal sports make us critics of environments that thwart fluidity and grace in movement. Aesthetic appreciation of sport, then, can combat the increasing *disembodiment* of modern life. Working at desks, encased in buildings and autos, pushing the buttons of appliances—*we lose touch.*[9] Perhaps more than any other single activity, qualitative sports reveal our bodies as more than useful machines, as an aesthetic medium with which we ought to be in intimate touch.

3. Competitive Sports

Competitive sports are the most popular, and for good reason. Only they require human opposition, offense and defense, for their play. Only they are *essentially social.* As we shall see in the next section, this added element of human confrontation (and cooperation) multiplies the aesthetic possibilities of competitive sports. While linear and formal sports *can* be engaged in competitively (and competition can enhance their performance), human opposition is not essential for their performance. We can run, pole vault, or dive quite well all by ourselves. But hitting a tennis ball against a wall or shooting a basketball is practice—it is not playing the game of tennis or basketball. To do that, opponents are needed.

Competitive sports transform the central features of both linear and formal sports by incorporating them within the structure of a game. As in linear sports, counting is a natural part of the play of competitive sports. Because brought about by overcoming human opposition, it is "scoring." And of course there are aspects of the game which can be isolated and measured, such as how fast a player can run or throw a ball. But such feats are subordinated to and transformed in the play of the game. We run to get to the football, jump to snare a basketball rebound, throw to get a base runner out. Achieving great magnitude without playing well ironically underlines the primacy of playing the game: With his 100-miles-per-hour fastball, Nolan Ryan is nevertheless much less effective than slower, more crafty pitchers (his lifetime won-loss record hovers about the mediocre .500 level). We appreciate "linear" accomplishments in competitive sports as *constitutive of the* play. Competitive sports, in fact, make the linear more playful, less feat-like by embedding it in a game.

Form as well as number is integrated into a larger fabric. Just as competitive sports transform the stark exertion of linear performances, so do they subordinate the "pure" grace of movement characteristic of the formal sports. We appreciate the athlete's balletic movements not in isolation, simply for their own sake, but within the framework of competitive play. A graceful jump and throw is marred by going off-target; it is supposed to serve a purpose internal to the game. The game thereby discloses the function inherent in grace. The best plays are graceful and while many who play well lack in grace, their good performance is not achieved *because* of their awkwardness. It is rather because they have compensated for the lack of grace and manage to "get the job done."

It is just because competitive sports have internal purposes whose final result is scoring or the thwarting of a score that we come to think of them as purposeful—aimed at winning by outscoring the opponent(s). The late football coach, Vince Lombardi, is reported to have said: "Winning isn't the most important thing; it's the only thing." Winning at games seems somehow more important than winning in a linear or formal performance. Perhaps the term "performance" is a clue as to why. In linear and formal sports the athlete really *performs*, alone.[10] She may perform better than another but does not really "win" at something. Competitive sports, however, are *contests* between or among people, more like a human drama. Perhaps this is why Lombardi could sound plaus-

ible when he warned his football players that their "manhood was on the line" when they took the field. We seem to forget that winning the game is a goal *imaginatively* set up and accepted expressly for the purpose of playing the game, "as if" it were important.[11]

The reply, of course, is that for the professional athlete it *is* important. Granted. But why must professionalization infect all levels and appreciations of the game? Why have we spectators and amateur players forgotten that it is "as if" winning were important?

The irony is that while scoring/winning has been overemphasized, it has also been unwittingly underplayed. Overemphasized *apart* from the play of the game, it has been underexposed as an aesthetic constituent of the game. In examining the stress on winning apart from the play of the game, we need to see how it results from a mistaken understanding of scoring/winning as the *purpose* of playing. Because of this misunderstanding, playing the game is viewed as merely the means to the distinct, dominant end of winning. But we are mistaken if we think that winning is "an identifiable aim or purpose which is of far greater importance than the way it is accomplished."[12] The mistake will become apparent as we take a brief detour and recall the place of purposes in everyday activities.

The first thing to note is that the purpose of an everyday activity is the reason or basis for engaging in it. The activity *exists* for the sake of its purpose. We shingle our roofs in order to keep the inside of our homes dry; we take medicine in order to restore health. Were it not for the purposes of keeping our homes dry or restoring health we would not engage in these respective activities. But scoring is not the *raison d'etre* of competitive sport. It was not that in virtue of which the sport came to exist or is engaged in. "The play's the thing" and it *includes* scoring and winning. Since neither scoring nor winning is the reason or basis for competitive sport, it cannot be its purpose.

Scoring/winning is not, therefore, an end which could be accomplished by some other means; consequently, it is not distinguishable from or "external" to the game itself. Practical purposes in the everyday, however, are independent of their means and are rightly said to be the purposes *of* their activities since they are attainable by some other means. The practical activity is itself subordinated to the goal as its instrument. There are other ways besides shingling of keeping homes dry, other ways of restoring health besides taking medicine. These just seem the best, given our circumstances, resources, and know-how. But it would be ridiculous to suggest that we might try to score or win by some other means than playing the game of basketball or baseball. Another way of putting this idea is to say that we do not independently value scoring or winning and only subsequently alight upon the playing of this game simply as a means to the score or the win. Scoring is not an end which could be accomplished by some other avenue because what it *means* "to score" depends upon the particular kind of game being played. Obviously, scoring in tennis is defined by the structure of the game of tennis, and so on for the other sports.

Why then have so many people thought that scoring/winning is the purpose of sports? I believe that this sort of thinking rests on a confusion. People confuse two ways in which purposes relate to activities: as the goal *of* and as a goal *within* an activity. An activity may serve some purpose or function external to it—as in the cases of shingling and taking medicine. A purpose or end may, on the other hand, be included within an activity, regardless of whether the activity as a whole serves any further (external) purpose. This is the case with "taking tricks" in bridge; singing a harmonic in a barbershop quartet; or achieving validity in an argument. These are purposes *within* their respective activities. Scoring is not a purpose *of* sport but is an end *within* the play of the game, in fact, created as part of the game. By confounding these two sorts (and loci) of purpose, people falsely conclude that the play in competitive sport is purposeful in the sense of serving an end external to it.[13]

When a purpose is the purpose *of* an activity, it defines the activity. But when a purpose is a purpose *within* an activity, as part of it, the activity defines it! The subordination or dependency relation is reversed. The purpose *of* an activity helps distinguish it from others. The purpose of keeping one's home dry gives meaning to shingling; the purpose of restoring health distinguishes taking medicine from taking hallucinogenic drugs. But the mere fact that a goal is scored or a game won cannot define or differentiate one sport from another. On the contrary, the differentiation proceeds the other way 'round. The scoring (internal purpose) is distinguished by the manner of play of this or that particular kind of game. Sports are differentiated internally, by what is *required* to score, by the manner of play whose issue is scoring. The form or structure of the particular sport is the basis for our choosing to watch or play *it* rather than another. And it is this particular structure, then, which defines its internal purpose of scoring or winning.

What is crucial, especially from the aesthetic point of view, is *how* the score/win is made, not *that* it is made. To score or win as the result of accident or shabby play can by no stretch of the imagination be thought as achieving the "purpose" of competitive sport. Yet this would be of no matter if winning or scoring were in fact its purpose.[14] Even a professional athlete can transcend the practical concern for victory because of aesthetic interest. Speaking of those rare, magical moments when playing basketball was more like dancing than working, Bill Russell notes that those "spells" were fragile:

> An injury would break them, and so would a couple of bad plays or a bad call by a referee. Once a referee broke a run by making a bad call in my favor, which so irritated me that I protested it as I stood at the foul line to take my free throws. . . . He looked at me as if I was crazy, and then got so angry that I never again protested a call unless it went against me. . . . Sometimes the feeling would

last all the way to the end of the game, and when that happened I never cared who won. . . . I don't mean that I was a good sport about it—that I'd played my best and had nothing to be ashamed of. . . . When the game ended at that special level, I *literally* did not care who had won.[15]

Ideally, scoring or winning is valued as a sign of excellence in play because it is characteristic of excellence. Scoring or winning is part of our understanding of good play; the team that plays well *deserves* to win, the way a virtuous person deserves happiness. If by some strange change in nature good play went consistently unrewarded with scoring/winning, then we would modify the game so that it was—or just stop playing. Our very concept of playing the game would change.

Overemphasis on scoring and outcome in general focuses attention on ends at the expense of their connection with means—*how* the outcomes are achieved. This invites an attitude of expedience and inattention to the very conditions which produce the consequences we value so inordinately. It also disconnects the particular outcome—such as a thwarted scoring attempt—from subsequent events. The outcome, then, is sundered from its prior context and future effects. Too often ". . . so-called means remain external and servile and so-called ends are enjoyed objects whose further causative status is unperceived."[16] Sport ought not reinforce such discontinuities in experience. Rather, it should occasion the transformation of cause-effect relationships into those of means-consequence. This is epitomized in play, in which the connections between means and ends is the chief source of delight, as it constitutes the situation's *meaning*. When we concentrate on ends, such as scoring or winning, at the expense of their means, therefore, the activity loses meaning for us. We then miss the fact that ". . . fulfillment is as relative to means as means are to realization."[17]

Rather than feed our growing obsession with results irrespective of how obtained, sports should give us an opportunity to see how events grow out of one another, how means enter into ends and ends further shape the future. When viewed playfully and as play, sports crystallize the way the purposes of scoring/winning are defined by the activities which produce them (and in turn determine subsequent events). It matters for all the world whether the 5-4 score was the result of a seesawing contest or the termination of a last-minute, furious rally (by *either* team). Perhaps we are too worried, in life as in sport, about the "score" and not enough about the quality of play.

The score itself is but an abstraction from the play. It tells us important information at a glance, like a newspaper headline, but is misleading even as a summary of play. This is because the score alone cannot tell us how and when the scoring did and *did not* occur; it is necessarily mute about non-scoring play, play which is sometimes the best in the game. "The score," therefore, indifferently represents widely different means and manner of play, abstracting from the way in which opposition is surmounted or frustrated. Put this way, it is odd to think that scoring/winning is more important than what it took to score the goal, defend the goal, or win the game. When this happens, games become uninteresting producers of statistics (not even justified in linear sports, where it is more natural). We revel in total football yardage, yearly and lifetime home runs, average rebounds per game of basketball—not noticing whether the yardage was piled up against weak opponents or the home runs hit when the game was out of reach. We make a fetish of quantity, number, accumulation. Infatuation with sheer magnitude is far more crippling and insidious than any fetish of sexual accoutrement. It keeps our attention on an ever-receding horizon, never on the moment. In sport it not only distracts us from the game's beauty but it even muddies the aesthetic role of scoring/winning. But what exactly is that role?

Scoring serves to define and articulate *overcoming opposition*. It helps determine the completeness of play and thereby the overall form of the game. It gives a closure to our experience of sport often lacking in everyday life. Unlike everyday life, sport gives us conclusive conclusion: to a game, a series, a season, a career. To appreciate the conclusion, though, we must see it as the fulfillment of what has preceded: whether it be a surprise 15th-round knockout by the apparent "loser" (as when Mike Weaver floored John Tate for a share of the heavyweight boxing championship in 1980) or the seemingly inevitable culmination of a football team's consistently superior play.

It is only when the play of the game is subordinated to external ends such as money or ego that scoring or winning is valued irrespective of the quality of play. In origin and ideal, games have no purpose other than the delight taken in their play. To play a game for monetary or personal gain, while not necessarily disastrous to its aesthetic appreciation, is always to introduce a purpose or basis foreign to the game itself. Scoring or winning, then, become independent purposes of the game only when extrinsic purposes become motivations to perform or watch. Our aesthetic expectations are satisfied when scoring and victory complete excellent play. Sport, then, provides clear-cut occasions for the joining of the useful (purpose-achieving) and the aesthetic (aesthetic execution of the play). When this happens our aesthetic appreciation seems to be of a second order, a "meta-appreciation" of the harmonizing of the practical with the aesthetic. Perhaps this harmony instantiates, as Kant would put it, the union of necessity (*needed for* a practical purpose) and freedom (the *free play* of the imagination which characterizes aesthetic experience). At any rate, we delight in victory which results from luck or shabby play only when we have some ulterior stake in the outcome. The more important these ulterior purposes are to us, the more we respond as if the umpire were indeed shouting "Work ball!", whether or not we are aware of it.

4. Social Drama

The complications introduced by human opposition multiply the aesthetic possibilities in competitive sports—dramatic possibilities due to social interaction. Nature provides a fairly constant standard or domain for linear and formal sports, but people must react and adjust to one another in competition. It is always a game of mutual re-adaptation and combination. A boxer must adjust to the weaving reaction of his opponent to his own initial, feinted jab; a defensive lineman must slip an attempted block in order to set up the tackle his linebacker will try to make. And this gives rise to a stunning variety of movements, rhythms, and situations. The social nature of games adds dramatic complexity just as the society of others complicates our daily lives.

In the individual sports, we focus on the human body: its motion and rhythms. In social sports the individual's movement is necessarily related to another's as well as to the movement of what ties them together—puck, shuttlecock, ball. Embedded in a contest, the athlete's movements and rhythms are taken up into the larger movements and rhythms of the game, creating a correlative mood or atmosphere.

Some games[18] are tense, stingy encounters in which defense dominates and scores are hard earned, as if squeezed from a resistant world. Our attention is tight in such contests, screwed to each moment since any play can be decisive. Ideally, their conclusion is a clean, incisive play, snapping the taut mood with its clarity. At the other extreme are sprawling, brawly affairs, scoring barrages threatening to last forever. There is a sense of luxury, opulence—always in danger of lapsing into the slackness that inflated wealth brings. These encounters "feel" lighter; we become almost giddy with the quantity of results and length of play. These two extremes mirror the poles of our everyday experience: now a seeming superabundance of riches, then a meager portion of sustenance.

At the beginning of a game, of course, we cannot know what is in store. What begins as a wide open slugfest can abruptly turn tense with firm defense. We look back on squandered chances and at our own false sense of luxury in scoring as we gather the two phases into an aesthetic whole. The shift of mood is itself an aesthetic transition gently felt as it happens, fully savored in retrospect.

On rare occasions, contests provide us with several shifts: in tempo, rhythm, or "dominance." The latter yields a sense of tug-of-war as one reversal succeeds another. Writing of the prize-fight in which Rocky Marciano relieved Jersey Joe Walcott of the heavyweight championship, A.J. Liebling notes that in the first nine rounds the lead changed hands three times: "Walcott to Marciano in the third round, Marciano to Walcott in the seventh, Walcott to Marciano in the ninth."[19] Walcott then came back briskly to capture the eleventh and twelfth rounds, "the fourth switch in plot." This seesawing ended with Marciano's short, lethal left hook in the thirteenth round.

As with many *potentially* aesthetic experiences, games often fail to fill out into discernible wholes possessed of strong aesthetic qualities. Some never find a rhythm and in others tension is all but dissipated in early lopsidedness or lackadaisical play. The latter mars the drama of a game by destroying that particular dimension of rhythm which depends upon crispness of execution. An aesthetically complete game, moreover, requires balance between the opponents, otherwise the emotional tone will flatten. "Torpid" and "loose" do not so much characterize an emotional mood as indicate a lack of one. Without approximate equality, at least in a given encounter, the game as a whole goes slack; there is little anticipatory quickening as events do not seem to harbor interesting future possibilities. Aesthetic attention is then rewarded only episodically in the close or spectacular play. Such games gradually degenerate into their linear and formal components; we thrill to a long pass in football or an acrobatic shot in tennis, but that is all.

Balance, however, does not mean "sameness." Contrasting styles within balanced, even performances provide aesthetic richness. In *Levels of the Game*, John McFee reflects upon the difference between Arthur Ashe's flamboyant, "all-out" play and Clark Graebner's conservative, steady game of tennis. The contrast between Ashe's "shot-making" and Graebner's "play-making" was accentuated by the further contrast *within* each of the opponents. Ashe's flamboyant play was accompanied by a cool, calm demeanor, while Graebner's steady game was played demonstratively, heatedly. The dramatic tension between style and temperament *in* each of the players magnified the pair of differences *between* them. The sharp differences between each man's technical style and character lead the spectator to such dramatic speculations as: Can Ashe afford to play with abandon *because* he is so controlled, so cool? Aesthetic expectations were fulfilled in this particular match when Ashe triumphed with a series of low-percentage, high-voltage shots. Perhaps Ashe would not have had the opportunity or been moved to such dazzling display against a less steady opponent. And this is something we should be alive to, for it enlivens the drama of the contest.

Just *this* opponent makes the sort of demand on the individual (or team) which presses him to his utmost effort. There is a cooperative basis to all competition, at the very least on the level of fair play and agreeing to compete. But more, it is a "contest" in which each *tests* the other and *testifies* to his effort and ability. Each depends upon the other to bring the best out of him, as in a friendship or educational exchange. In this way the opponents are united, forming a whole whose opposition is also a cooperation.

> Every so often a Celtic game would heat up so that it became more than a physical or even mental game, and would be magical. . . . *Both* teams had to be playing at their peaks, and they had to be competitive. . . . It never started with a hot streak by a single player, or with a breakdown of one team's defense. It usually began when three or four of the ten guys on the floor would heat up. . . . The feeling would spread to the other guys, and we'd all levitate.[20]

The dynamics of such interaction are as important an aesthetic dimension of sport as the graceful flick of the tennis backhand or the daring streak of the base stealer. In such situations are we likely to see "peak performances," tensions reaching toward crescendo after crescendo. Continuing his description of those games when everyone "heated up," Russell notes his need for both teams to keep the rhythm moving:

> Then the game would just take off, and there'd be a natural ebb and flow that reminded you of how rhythmic and musical basketball is supposed to be . . . and I'd actually be rooting for the other team. When their players made spectacular moves, I wanted their shots to go into the bucket. . . .[21]

In such tensions, give and take, and finally resolutions, competitive sports exhibit something of real-life struggle and resolve. Now obviously the drama of sport is considerably less than that of either real life or the theatre, but in its way it offers what they cannot. The dramatic development in sport is a distilled, circumscribed version of reality's. The unravelling of events is confined by the form of the game, its rules "shrinking" conflict to manageable proportions. The confrontations of the game are simple and starker because physically enacted. Because more obvious, almost a caricature of everyday life, the drama of sport indirectly suggests the greater subtleties found in the everyday. Sport can give clear and definite conclusion to dramatic confrontation in a way not possible within the ambiguities of either real or theatrically portrayed life, as if the rules and physical movement of the game supplant the complexities of plot and character. Yet precisely because of this, it can point to the bases for ambiguity and indefinite resolution in our daily dramas.

When aesthetically rich in dramatic qualities, the game builds to a consummation. The delicate balance between offenses and defenses establishes a rhythm which is fulfilled in its conclusion. The strengths and weaknesses of the opponents exhibited throughout reach their final reckoning in the outcome which is in doubt until the last possible moment[22] and the closing of the uncertain story can then be experienced as a climax, not simply a terminus of motion. Such a conclusion seems to put all the scoring and smaller duels and tensions in their "proper" dramatic place. Thus do we retrospectively hold the entire game before us, looking for omens, portents of what seems at the climax to have been inevitable.

Of course not all games fill out so nicely; they can fail to develop aesthetically for many reasons: ". . . But if the play of the Minneapolis Miniatures depresses us by its sloppiness, so, curiously, the precise rigidities of the Soviet Army Six depress us by their mechanical evenness."[23] Broun nicely points out the two extremes that the genuinely aesthetic avoids—loose aimlessness and mechanical rigidity. These are the extremes our daily activities tend toward: the meandering, pointless browse through the shopping mall; the overly circumscribed routine of a student's classroom schedule. The aesthetic mean combines the structure which is exaggerated in the mechanical with the freedom which is dissipated in the directionless. At its best, sport demonstrates the place of improvisation in the competition; jazz-like, the competitors respond in the moment to the opponent's own modification in play.

We must improvise in the face of human opposition in a way less called for in the linear or formal sports. The greater constancy and predictability of nature demand less alteration in strategy or immediate performance. But when Julius Erving finds his path to the basket blocked by a surprise move by the opposition, he suddenly veers at a tangent, shifts the ball to his left hand and with a swoop flicks the ball off the backboard as he has never done before. Invention by the other begets answering, unrehearsed creativity. Sometimes the result is a spontaneous variation in bodily motion that can alter the flow and rhythm of the whole game. The beauty of improvisation is magnified, moreover, when the social dimension is elevated, when *teams* play the game.

• • •

In team sports, each individual must adapt to the play of his mates as well as to his opponents'. This increased range of human interaction enlarges the game's aesthetic. As in art proper, we have the chance to see the parts integrated into an organic whole when players' movement and ability are complementary. In memorable teams, noted for their teamwork, the whole really is more than the sum of its parts. The Bill Russell-led Boston Celtics come quickly to mind; each player realized his excellence because of his relationships with the rest of the team's members. Each developed fully through his fellows' play: on the fast break, switching defense, or simply moving without the ball.

The play of the Celtics contrasted sharply with that of the contemporaneous Los Angeles Lakers who were led by three exceptional individuals (Jerry West, Elgin Baylor, and Wilt Chamberlain). They excelled *as* individuals; when one had the ball he put on a show—a solo performance. While their individual virtuosity was aesthetically breath-taking, they did not conspire to create an aesthetically integrated team.

Balance is needed within a team (as well as between teams) in order to achieve the cohesiveness of aesthetic unity. When the team members seem to be functioning as parts of one organism, the individuals' movements are felt to be determined by and attuned to the rhythm of the whole team. The action of each member of the Celtics' "fast break," for instance, seemed essentially suited to those of the others: Heinsohn's defense freed Nelson to help Russell rebound and then pass to Jones, who assisted Havlicek on his lay-up. It is practically impossible to give "credit" to one without including the contributions of the rest; they so jell that we can hardly tell where one's play begins and another's leaves off.

The excellent play of team members is a direct function of their interaction, as they flourish under one another's influence. The relationship among the players resembles that found among parts of a work of art: words in a poem enhancing one another's meaning; harmony complementing a musical composition's melody. On the experiential level, we perceive the cohesiveness of team play as the gracefulness of a "larger" organism; we experience something that may be thought of as inter-active grace. This is what I was getting at above in describing a Celtic "fast break," when individual grace of movement is absorbed into the fluidity of the team's flow. We see it in the continuity of a smooth relay in baseball when the infielder takes the outfielder's throw and, pirouetting, relays the ball to home plate. The path of the ball is a straight line from the outfielder to home plate, the infielder a seemingly magical conduit.

Where the linear sports call our attention to time or distance, competitive sports emphasize *timing* and *place*. The timing and location of a pass in football or hockey is usually more important than its speed or distance: *Where* a ball is hit and *when* a pass is made is crucial. By incorporating them into its structure, games transform sheer speed and distance into timing and location. The old base-ball exhortation to "hit 'em where they ain't" signifies placing the ball deftly, not merely whacking it hard or far.

"Timing" refers not only to the play among the teammates, but also to the occasion within the course of the game itself. Does the spectacular catch stave off a rally? Does the brilliant lob win the tennis match? The building and sustaining of dramatic tension obviously depend upon *when* the play is (or is not) made. We appreciate what does *not* happen as much as what does, just as a pause or inaction in the theatre punctuates speech or behavior. We savor chances missed, imaginatively rearranging events. Our mouths fill with "if only's": if only he had hit the home run in the eighth inning when two men were on base instead of in the fifth when no one was; if only he had not fumbled on fourth down with one yard to go for a touchdown. Without a sense of timing there is no appreciation of a game's decisive play: ". . . Every game's got its own special moment . . . that defines all that's happened before it and all that's gonna happen after it."[24] To feel, to perceive such decisive moments immediately, without cognitive analysis, is what aesthetic sensibility is all about. Surely there can and should be a carry-over to a sense of timing in our everyday lives, an immediate perception of opportunities lost, friendships ignited, deceptions uncovered. The turning points in games publicly dramatize the defining moments in our lives that we are so apt to miss for what they really are, so blind are we to the drama of our own living.

• • •

The batter swings and lofts a long fly down the foul line. At the last second the ball veers foul by a foot. What luck! Good luck for one team, bad for the other. Perhaps. It depends on why the ball sliced foul. The pitcher may have succeeded in fooling the batter ever so slightly and that slight advantage is spatially translated into one foot foul (or one foul foot, for the team at bat). As in daily life, what seems to be luck often is the result of talent or effort well-timed. This is the sense of Branch Rickey's aphorism, "Luck is the residue of design." Careful attention discovers the little displays of intelligence that make up the design. But if the ball is blown foul by a sudden gust of wind? Surely that is not the residue of design. And surely when a player gets a favorable outcome from what is plainly a blunder, he is "lucky" in the ordinary sense of the word. The drama of competitive sports includes the hand of chance, just as does the drama of everyday life. Another's illness becomes our opportunity; a wind-blown hat occasions intimacy; or a power failure dims our business plans. Sport does not distort the aesthetic role of luck, it merely unclutters our perception of it.

• • •

The Green Bay Packers are one yard from a touchdown and victory with seconds to play on the frozen tundra of Wisconsin. The ball is snapped for the last play of the championship game; Jerry Kramer, lineman, gets a tentative toe-hold, pushes the defensive tackle slightly off balance, and Bart Starr, the quarterback, squirms into the end zone. The audience erupts. They have

not only witnessed but have taken part in a "Great Moment in Sports!"

The dramatic qualities of sport are pinpointed in "great moments," those performances which stand out in the collective memory of its fans. Like classics in the art world, these moments become almost but not quite hackneyed, trotted out in film clips and reminiscing banter. For all their repetition, however, Beethoven's Fifth Symphony, Orson Welles' "Citizen Kane," and Hamlet's Soliloquy are nonetheless great moments in art. We may rely on them too much, asking them to provide more enrichment than they are capable of, but that is our failure, not theirs.

As with a work of art, a great moment in sport may well take more than a moment. Don Larsen's "perfect" pitching performance in the 1956 World Series took a couple of hours, as did Wilt Chamberlain's 100-point basketball outing. But the paradigm of the great moment is probably just that—a split-second catch, shot, or pass—a moment frozen in time. Only the moment freezes time and takes our breath away. The moment of excellent performance consummates all that has come before, rounding out our expectations, resolving the game's conflicts.

As its name indicates, great moments are a matter of timing; they come at crucial moments, usually in important games. Not only is the play dramatically timed, but it is a dramatic response to demanding play by the opposition. Unless Vic Wertz blasts a baseball nearly 400 feet, Willie Mays cannot make his spectacular back-to-homeplate catch during the 1954 World Series; unless Joe Frazier is boxing like a juggernaut, Muhammad Ali is not forced to display all his ring virtuosity (perhaps lack of worthy opposition deprived Marciano of his greatest moments). After a wonderful hockey play-off game between the North Stars and the Islanders, columnist Dave Anderson wrote:

> Hockey, or any game, is seldom played at that [Great Moment] level because the exquisite elements which create that level seldom fall

together. Such a game requires two quality teams at peak performance competing for high stakes in a cauldron of emotion. And at that level, the outcome is almost incidental.[25]

The Great Moment is epitomized in a moment because in a moment our attention is riveted. Time seems frozen for our breathless appreciation as we attend fully and are filled. The possibility of a great or even a *good* moment should quicken our attention, keeping us more alert than usual and perhaps altering our usual level of discrimination. The technical innovations of television (such as "instant replays," slow-motions, and stop-actions), even television itself, lessen the premium of careful observation. We need not be "on our toes" when we know that videotape replays will show us the outstanding play from several angles, at varying speeds, over and over. Whereas, "being there" means being on the lookout. And, of course, when we are on the lookout for the great play, we see so much more: the shifting of the boxer's feet; the football player's subtle change of speed; the deceptive dip of the tennis racquet. Being ready for the great moment quickens us to the movement in each moment upon which the great performance ultimately rests. And this is really what aesthetic attention is all about: noticing the features and qualities of whatever is present to us.

Dramatic tension screws our senses to the present, and this is good, but aesthetic attention in the first place discovers the minute dramas within each moment—whatever the significance of the situation. Aesthetic attention in sports can and does affect our everyday perceptions of physical movement. Watchful for a great moment, we are awakened to the flows and interruptions within each, however mundane. At a jazz concert recently, a stagehand climbed down a ladder after adjusting some lights. On the last rung something went wrong, he stumbled backwards, and smashed into the bass violin—irreparably damaging it. Most of us saw only the thunderous climax of his movement and gasped our concern. But a friend just

quietly nodded, seeing this "awful moment" prefigured in each of the stagehand's earlier, little, awkward steps. While careful attention may mean fewer surprises, it will be because we see how movements unfold out of one another.

5. Micro-Rhythms, Meta-Rhythms

The "great moment" shines at one end of the temporal continuum for aesthetic appreciation of sport. But, we can appreciate such long-range projects as the mazy turns of a team's history or an athlete's blossoming career as well as the quick and bright. This continuum also has a spatial counterpart, ranging from the flashing glint of a skater's blade to the panoramic surges of soccer teams. As in everyday life, we manage to appreciate a fair share of the micro-rhythms, accents on the "small" end of the continua: the left-right, jab-hook tattoo of a boxer's "combination"; the promise of the poised racquet, stick, or bat. Sometimes we perceive a pause and anticipate the accented beat that is to follow. When the baseball pitcher chooses ". . . not to throw on a man [to trap the base runner off base]. Whole thing about *base* stealing. It's like a dance."[26]

The turns and twists, leaps and lunges comprise episode events within the larger contexts of games, competitions, seasons. Appreciating each moment need not preclude seeing how the moments build upon one another until, finally, a season or career has come to a close. Does the star performer go out blazing like a meteor, the way Ted Williams and Rocky Marciano did? Or does he "hang on," a sorry reminder of what he once was? Even serious injury can add a dramatic dimension when seen in the context of a player's whole career and place in the game. Thus, Chuck Bednarik's crippling tackle of Frank Gifford ". . . was the rather brutal homage the league was paying him for catching one too many passes, for winning one too many times. . . ."[27] Yet the drama of Gifford's football career was not over; defiantly, it reversed field, as he was wont to do, for he returned to play, sometimes spectacularly, yet another day. It takes an effort of memory and imagination to grasp with aesthetic firmness the events which make up team or individual biographies, but it can be done. Such breadth of apprehension is needed lest the meta-rhythms of the sport escape.

Within the meta-rhythms of sport, time and place are redefined. Their meaning is modified by the seasons and locales of the different sports. Each has its time and its place—in the sun, on the urban concrete, or under the creaking rafters.

> Perhaps if sports have their inner rhythms, . . . there is a larger rhythm, like Ecclesiastes' list of the times for this and the times for that. Perhaps if baseball is the game that runs its leisured way through the whole of hopeful spring and lazy summer, football should be the game of brief intensity, a search for a great day.[28]

But with the professionalization of sports their seasons have become blurry. They no longer unambiguously claim their own time, so that the relationships among them have lost their clarity, their meta-rhythm gone slack. Basketball and hockey stretch deep into May when the balmy weather makes rink and court the wrong place to play or watch. Conversely, baseball's slow flow threatens to freeze in October winds. Why lay this loss at the doorstep of professionalization? Because longer schedules are largely responsible for loss of seasonal hegemony, and longer schedules are the result of league expansions and television commitments. Of course, league expansion and television contracts add up to more revenue—professionalization includes commercialization. Abetting the cause of "more" is the gradual loss of the outdoors as setting for such sports as soccer, football, and baseball. "Indoor" (American) soccer and domed stadia have brought these sports "in from the cold," out of their natural seasonal niches. When any sport can be played any place we are in danger of forgetting their distinctive aesthetic personalities and the way their differences harmonize in the yearly round of play.

6. Aesthetic Attitude

The notion of the "aesthetic attitude" helps distinguish aesthetic orientation and valuation from a variety of other possibilities. The aesthetic attitude is different, for example, from the economic, social, or historical. Each kind of attitude is characterized by its respective value and therefore determines the sort of appreciation likely to be had. For example, we can view a piece of land as an investment, a site for low-rent housing, or the scene of a Civil War battle. But when we attend to the piece of land simply for its appearance, its contours and colors, texture and rhythms, then we take the aesthetic attitude toward it. We turn away from a host of everyday interests and look for aesthetic relations and qualities.

> We may say of all these nonaesthetic interests, and of "practical" perception generally, that the object is apprehended with an eye to its origins and consequences, its interrelations with other things. By contrast, the aesthetic attitude "isolates" the object and focuses upon it—the "look" of the rocks, the sound of the ocean, the colors in the painting. . . . Its whole nature and character are dwelt upon.[29]

The same applies in sports. The aesthetic aspects and values are distinct from whatever practical interests we may bring to the performance or contest. To appreciate a sport aesthetically is likely, moreover, to conflict with viewing it from a practical standpoint; the interests of the "professional" athlete or spectator incline him least toward aesthetic appreciation. It is difficult, for example, to appreciate the grace of a boxer who is demolishing the home town boy. And when we are playing another team for a prize or money it is practically impossible to value their teamwork. The aesthetic attitude requires that we "distance" ourselves a bit from such realistic, everyday concerns.

So far so good, but we must further distinguish different expectations and orientations *within* the aesthetic attitude itself. It is not appropriate to expect the same aesthetic riches from different art forms or styles. We should not expect to find the same sort of aesthetic values in a sonata as we anticipate finding in a symphony.

So Spenser's great *Faerie Queene* is ignored because fools try to read it as though it were a sonnet of Donne, for the *Queene* is a medieval tapestry, and one wanders about in it. An epic is not an epigram.[30]

Even within the same medium, then, our general aesthetic attitude should be specifically determined by the form and style of the particular object or performance at hand.

And so it goes for appreciating the aesthetic qualities of sports. There are inherent structural differences among sports: A sprint is over in a flash while a marathon takes hours, and hockey is virtually continuous movement while baseball and football have pauses after each play. It should be no surprise, therefore, that aesthetic potentials vary from sport to sport, some variations greater than others. This is why it is foolish to expect or demand similar aesthetic rewards from structurally different sports.

And yet this is exactly at the heart of much popular (misplaced) criticism of particular sports or particular performances of them. We hear people faulting baseball, for example, for slowness of pace or deliberateness of action. Spectators more than likely are looking to baseball to supply the aesthetic qualities more easily found in such sports as football or basketball; only the season changes for such spectators. But this is like faulting a war movie for showing violence or a surrealistic painting by Dali for being "weird." Part of the general description of the aesthetic attitude is that it includes a "sympathetic" openness to the object or event before us. For sport, this means giving the structure of the particular game or activity a chance to show what it has to offer.

Because it has come in for much harsh criticism by today's fast-paced generation, baseball is a good candidate for close examination (and if I dwell too long on its "innings and outs," forgive an enthusiast). To appreciate baseball, we must first cultivate a sense of its setting—a park, a field, or "grounds." Its context is that of a leisurely outing during which we bask in the sun, enjoying friends and food.[31] There is no rush. We are to savor the moments of player and manager decision, the slow building of tension as the batter repeatedly steps out of the box, trying to guess the pitcher's mind while at the same time upset his rhythm.[32] Contributing to its patient pace is baseball's atemporal nature. Structured by outs and innings, baseball does not move to a game-clock, so there is no rush, no frantic play against time. Relaxing in the abundance of time, we are suddenly brought up sharp by the explosive home run or the flashing double play. The quick steal or rapid pick-off stands out within the game's overall easy pace.

The regular tempo and even, staid pace of baseball are determined by its structure. Former baseball player, Ken Harrelson, once pointed out that baseball is the only sport in which the defense controls the ball by putting it in play. Conversely, once the defense commences the action, only the offense can score. There is no immediate, sudden transition from offense to defense or defense to offense. Each team waits to "take its turn" and we must wait for this regular alternation to occur. In football, basketball, hockey, or tennis, however, a sudden shift in advantage can occur; either side can mount an attack at any time regardless of who happens to "possess" or put in play the object of "interest" (literally, that which connects and engages the two sides). But in baseball, scoring opportunity (and number of outs) is fixed. And because the defense controls the ball, the sense of order and fixity is increased; the offense must wait, it cannot take matters into its own hands by initiating play.

It may be stretching a point, but I think that the fixity and orderliness of baseball are reinforced by its circularity. Scores occur when players go *around* the bases, returning home, and the game progresses by going "through" each team's *recurring* batting order. Goal-sports (football, lacrosse, basketball, hockey, soccer, and the like) are linear: Play moves back and forth, surging and ebbing. In most, space is consumed and finally invaded by the ball or puck at the goal. The players on each team do not "wait" around, but are in the thick of the linear flow all the time. It is not just that the action is continuous, but each player is in or near the action continually.

The aesthetic appreciation, and therefore the criticism, of a particular sport must, then, be appropriate to the possibilities of that sport's particular aesthetic. Bill Russell notes, for example, that basketball is played essentially in the air, and football is a game of territory. We can, of course, still find aesthetic fault with a baseball game, but not because it lacks those aesthetic qualities displayed by other sports. We should fault a game for lacking such aesthetic qualities it is capable of.[33] While baseball's aesthetic may not appeal to everyone, just as a waltz tempo may not suit polka lovers, its pace and rhythms should be felt in relation to its general structure. Its aesthetic possibilities are determined by its style and structure. The aesthetic moral of this extends all the way into our daily activities: We should not expect a lecture to offer the same rewards as party chitchat, or a walk in the woods to provide what a plunge in the surf can. Our minds and bodies move within determining contexts which, like those in sport, structure time and space.

7. Participation

"What attracted me was the sound of the swish, the sound of the dribble, the feel of going up in the air."[34]

What is *distinctive* about each sport, and what should shape our aesthetic expectations as spectators, should also contribute to the aesthetic enjoyment of participating. So Bradley might have included the sound of a shot being blocked, the feel of the ball flicking off the fingertips, or the look of a spinning, weaving lay-up. Basketball: Its textures and rhythms are so different from those of tennis or football, running or swimming; we simply "feel" different playing in each one.

More Americans are participating in more sports but we do not seem playful about it. We compete to win tournament and trophy, or work on shape and health. Eyes fixed on glory, waistline, and heartbeat, we do not pay much attention to the aesthetic qualities inherent in participating in the sport itself. We do not play. When we play our senses are alive. Not only is the body the receiver of sensory news from the environment, but it is itself an *object* of sensory awareness. This is especially true in individual sports in which no response to others is called for.

Isolated with and within his body in its environment, the performer is free to appreciate the rhythms he makes with it. The runner, for instance, can appreciate from the "inside" the pattern his arm, leg, and breath movement creates. For him, shifting, breathing, and muscular exertion are viscerally felt and heard, whereas spectators can only infer this experience from what they see. Even the weariness of muscles and, finally, pain can be appreciated by the performer as the accompaniment of motion.

The grace that the spectator only sees the performer feels. Moreover, he feels it as instigated by himself since he is "in charge." He controls the angle of the dive, the thrust of the pole before the vault, the rhythms of the run. The kinesthetic experience that results, therefore, is *felt as the result* of the athlete's own will or choice. Slicing into the water, soaring up to the bar, or loping across a meadow are experienced as the completion of mental as well as physical concentration. When the body does the mind's bidding, the aesthetic of performance includes mental-physical continuity. We experience ourselves as one. Attending to our body's movement is also attending to our control. This requires harmony between our active and passive capacities: responding to our present performance, readied by current feedback for subsequent movement. This "self-communication" is experienced immediately as "listening" to our body, which shapes the messages we then send it. Continuity in movement results from moving in *response* to antecedent motion; we are, in effect, responding to ourselves.

In individual sports we can attend to the coordination of the whole body's movement. The hand-eye coordination so crucial in social sports and everyday tasks is virtually nonexistent. Especially rhythmic are such "repetitive" sports as swimming and running, in which the same motion is repeated; arms and legs, trunk and head, are synchronized in a pattern of beats and rests, thrusts and recoveries. Consider the coordination involved in the rhythms of swimming the crawl: head turns, inhaling; right arm pulls down, left arm reaching; kick-kick; face down, exhaling; left arm pulls, right arm lifting from side; kick-kick. No wonder we can be so attuned to our bodies' rhythms that we experience a meditative refreshment.

We also tune in to our interaction with the environment. Consider swimming again, where environment plays such a significant aesthetic role, so palpably does it depart from our ordinary surroundings. Not only are we moving through a "foreign" medium when we swim, but we are horizontal rather than upright, buoyed up. Supported from below, feeling lighter than normal, the water envelopes and caresses us. Its softening effect includes opacity of sight and diffuseness of light: a striking sensuous context for the rhythms established by breathing and by head, trunk, and limb movement. We beat out these rhythms as we slide through a medium that resists and then fluidly yields to the pull of our arms and the push of our legs.

Our participation in social sports, on the other hand, is informed more by other people than environment; rather, other people comprise our environment. Here we must react and adjust to what others, opposition or teammates, are doing, as well as anticipate what they *will* do. As we run to the ball in tennis, we must anticipate where our opponent will be on the other side of the net. The

response to ourselves paramount in individual sports is now situated within the larger context of social response. The "aesthetic" field of perception and initiation of movement is widened. It is further deepened when teammates are added and we must adapt cooperatively to their response to us— all of which aims at overcoming the opposition!

Spectators, as we have noted, appreciate continuously recoordinated and readjusted play, but their perceptions do not issue in any immediate physical response on their part (unless standing, shouting in appreciation). It is the continuity between perception and physical response that adds an aesthetic dimension to participation. Similarly, the participant not only feels the dramatic tension, as does the audience, but must play *in* it. "Grace under pressure" is an exquisite aesthetic experience with which the audience can perhaps sympathize. But when we ourselves are playing, our running, throwing, leaping, or shooting are crystallized by the pressure of competition.

As much as our enthusiasm for victory has warped our appreciation of sports, keeping score does dramatically structure our participation. The score informs our perception of the situation and our anticipation of action. It adds directionality, a sense of "building" to the play. Whether we play in a seesaw contest, a game in which one team doggedly claws back from repeated setbacks, or one in which a comfortable margin suddenly, inexplicably melts away, keeping score with winning and losing in mind certainly provides a felt horizon to our play.[35]

This directionality, however, is typical of a conventional Western aesthetic. If and when we forego keeping score in our play, we tend to tune in to the rhythms and other nonlinear components of the game. When we appreciate playing a game in this way, our orientation is more akin to an African or Eastern aesthetic perspective. Such a nonlinear, nonincremental aesthetic has clearly influenced twentieth-century Western art: threads of meaning, swatches of color, patches of sound laid side by side or end to end but with no "escalating" or "progressing." Describing John Coltrane's play on the tenor saxophone in the early '60s, Leroi Jones writes:

The seeming masses of sixteenth notes, the *new* and finally articulated concept of using whole groups or clusters of rapidly fired notes as chordal insistence rather than a strict melodic progression . . . to try to play almost every note of the chord separately, as well as the related or vibrating tones that chord produced. The result, of course, is what someone termed 'Sheets of Sound.'[36]

Can we sometimes, forgetting the score, not worrying about winning, give ourselves up to the rhythms, grace, and body-tempo of the game so that we experience "sheets of movement"? In such moments we would feel how the rhythms change and modify one another. We might sense our energies and actions as part of a flowing repetition rather than building toward a climax or progressing along a linear route.

But perhaps the ideal of aesthetic playing should involve both the progressive aspect of competition *and* appreciation for directionless "players" of play. Maybe neither has to sacrificed and we can savor their roles in the dramatic build-up without forfeiting a "non-Western," nonincremental enjoyment in the horizontal dimensions of play. Every now and then Bill Russell seemed to have both; his peak moments were realized through intense competition but the competition sent him "over" its edge, into the horizontal textures of play.

At that special level all sorts of odd things happened. The game would be in a white heat of competition, and yet somehow I wouldn't feel competitive—which is a miracle in itself. . . . The game would move so quickly that every fake, cut and pass would be surprising, and yet nothing could surprise me. It was almost as if we were playing in slow motion. During those spells I could almost sense how

the next play would develop and where the next shot would be taken.[37]

Notes

1. *New York Times*, March 8, 1981.
2. Ron Powers, *Toot-Toot-Tootsie, Good-Bye* (New York: Delacorte Press, 1981), p. 112.
3. Frederick Exley, *A Fan's Notes* (New York: Simon and Shuster, 1977), p. 231.
4. Heywood Hale Broun, *Tumultuous Merriment* (New York: Richard Manek, 1979), p. 20.
5. This is, of course, subject to a mild qualification. Variations in conditions such as a "following wind" in track do make a difference to performance and are taken into account.
6. A boyhood friend of mine actually gave up watching sports in favor of poring over their epiphenomena—statistics. The numerical results became more fascinating than the events which produced them.
7. David Best, *Philosophy and Human Movement* (London: Allen and Unwin, 1978), p. 110).
8. Broun, p. 80.
9. John McDermott, *The Culture of Experience* (New York: New York University Press, 1976), pp. 166-167.
10. Although games, golf and bowling are really individual sports, since no opponent is necessary for their play; where present, the opponent plays *beside* rather than against or with another. They also seem to be more emphatically numerical than competitive game sports, counting the number of strokes or pins being more essential to the play of the game.
11. My thanks for this go to Professor Melvin

Rader, who was kind enough to comment on an earlier draft of this chapter.

12. David Best, "The Aesthetic in Sport," *British Journal of Aesthetics,* Vol. 14, No. 3 (Summer 1976), p. 199.

13. The question of purposefulness is clarified by the Kantian distinction between purpose and purposivity. Art is purposive but not purposeful. This means that it displays those properties such as we find in objects which exist in order to serve an external purpose, but it does not in fact serve any such purpose. The unity of art works does not derive from something external to themselves, i.e., a function, as does, say, a telehone or car. Although a work of art does not exist in order to serve some external end, it may contain within itself aims or purposes, as for example literary works in which the narrator or characters act or speak in order to attain some end. The purely purposive then may include purposes within it without as a whole being subservient to an extrinsic purpose or end. Sport is like art in being purposive but without external purpose. We engage in the activity or its viewing for its own sake.

14. Paul Ziff, "A Fine Forehand," *Journal of the Philosophy of Sport,* Vol. I (September 1974). Ziff seems to view performance in some sports, including the competitive, as "counting," i.e., important only with regard to scoring. He maintains that form matters (as a "grading factor") *only* in the qualitative, formal sports. He writes that ". . . if one manages somehow to sink the ball expeditiously enough one may end up a champion" (p. 101). He is obviously viewing sporting events only with a concern for their outcome, with a "professional" attitude, for he continues: "It is not looks but points that win a tennis match" (p. 104). My question for Ziff is: But is it points that make a tennis match good or worth watching?

15. Bill Russell (with Taylor Branch), *Second Wind: The Memories of an Opinionated Man* (New York: Random House, 1979), p. 157.

16. John Dewey, *Experience and Nature* (New York: Dover, 1958), p. 370.

17. Dewey, p. 397.

18. What counts as a particular stingy or luxurious game is, of course, relative to the nature of the sport; thus, an 8-6 score in professional hockey is heavy with scoring, while a 75-70 score in professional basketball is a very tight contest.

19. A.J. Liebling, *The Sweet Science* (New York: Viking Press, 1956), p. 97.

20. Russell, pp. 155-156.

21. Russell, p. 156. Note here how scoring contributes yet is subordinated to the game's *aesthetic* qualities.

22. For a more detailed account of cooperation inherent in competition and the role of suspense in sports, see Warren Fraleigh's "On Weiss on Records and on the Significance of Athletic Records," *Philosophic Exchange,* Vol. I, No. 3 (Summer, 1972), pp. 105-111, and E.F. Kaelin's "The Well-Played Game: Notes Toward an Aesthetics of Sport," *Quest,* No. 10 (May 1968), pp. 16-28.

23. Broun, p. 155.

24. Powers, p. 224.

25. *New York Times News Service,* May 21, 1981.

26. Powers, p. 224.

27. Exley, pp. 348-349.

28. Broun, pp. 118-119.

29. Jerome Stolnitz, "The Aesthetic Attitude," *Introductory Readings in Aesthetics* (New York: Free Press, 1969), John Hospers, ed., p. 20.

30. Paul Ziff, "Reasons in Art Criticism," *Philosophy Looks at the Arts* (New York: Scribner's, 1962), Joseph Margolis, ed., p. 176.

31. See Roger Angell's *The Summer Game*

(New York: Popular Library, 1978). Powers suggests, in *Toot-Toot-Tootsie, Good-Bye*, that there are also aesthetic aspects of a ballpark's relation to its urban context:

> He'd come up in the days of the great old upright neighborhood ballparks—Ebbets Field, the Polo Grounds, old Sportsman's Park, Crosley Field—the old square-bottom parks that were . . . fitted like tiles into the existing mosaic of the city . . . and settling, over the decades, into the stew of summer urban life. . . . (p. 7)

32. Defending baseball's pace, Broun remarks:

> That very slowness of which some fans complain is twisting the nerves of players (and fans) as they seem endlessly to contemplate the possibilities of triumph, defeat, or disgrace that are possible with every pitch. . . . The beautiful balances of the game produce a sawtooth of success and failure. (p. 77)

33. This must, of course, be qualified, since a sport *could* be rejected totally as too meager in aesthetic dividends. But we must be especially wary of implying in such wholesale dismissal that it is the structure of the sporting activity that is responsible for our aesthetic dissatisfaction. As with the rejection of a kind of music or style of painting, the fault may lie more with the audience than the object of apprehension.

34. John McPhee quoting Bill Bradley (former star player for Princeton and the New York Knickerbockers) in *A Sense of Where You Are* (New York: Farrar, Strauss, and Giroux, 1965), p. 75.

35. The closing of his career intensified the competitive horizon Bill Russell felt in playing against Wilt Chamberlain.

> I was acutely aware that my career was ending, and I wanted to leave on a high. . . . I was offended the instant Wilt left the game. I didn't think he'd been hurt that badly, and even if he was, I wanted him in there. We were close—so close—to finishing with a great game . . . I thought to myself, ''This is my last game. Make me earn it. Come on out here.''

36. *Black Music* (New York: Morrow, 1968), pp. 58-59.

37. Russell, p. 156.

The Aesthetic in Sport

DAVID BEST

Introduction

There appears to be a considerable and increasing interest in looking at various sporting activities from the aesthetic point of view. In this chapter I shall examine a central characteristic of paradigm cases of objects of the aesthetic attitude, namely works of art, in order to see to what extent it is applicable to sport. Finally, I shall consider the question of whether sports in general, or at least those sports in which the aesthetic is ineliminable, can legitimately be regarded as forms of art. It will be shown that discussion of this topic is confused by a failure to recognise the significance of the distinction between the aesthetic and the artistic.

The Aesthetic Point of View

It might be asked whether all sports can be considered from the aesthetic point of view, when one takes account of the great and increasingly varied range of such activities. That question at least can be answered clearly in the affirmative, for any object or activity can be considered aesthetically—cars, mountains, even mathematical proofs and philosophical arguments.

This raises a point discussed in Chapter 5, that it is less conducive to error to regard the aesthetic

Reprinted from *Philosophy and Human Movement* (pp. 99–122) by David Best, 1978, London: Allen & Unwin. Copyright 1978 by Allen & Unwin Ltd. Reprinted by permission.

as a way of perceiving an object or activity than as a constituent feature of it. I mention this because the term 'aesthetic content' is often used, and it carries the misleading implication that the aesthetic is some sort of element which can be added or subtracted. In order to clarify the point it may be worth considering a way in which the notion of aesthetic content was once defended. It was argued that the aesthetic cannot be merely a point of view since this fails to account for the fact that some objects and activities are more interesting aesthetically than others. Thus, it was said, there must be aesthetic content since, for instance, the appearance of a car could be affected by altering physical features of it, and in a similar way gracefulness could be added to or subtracted from a movement.

A factor which may well contribute to confusion on this issue is a failure to distinguish two ways in which 'aesthetic' is used. These can be broadly characterised as (1) evaluative, and (2) conceptual. An example of the former is: 'Borzov is an aesthetic athlete.' This is to use the term in a positive evaluative way, and is roughly equivalent to 'graceful', or 'aesthetically pleasing'. But it is clearly the latter usage which is our concern, and this includes both the beautiful and the ugly; the graceful and the clumsy; the aesthetically interesting and the aesthetically uninteresting. Thus whatever one's opinion of the appearance of the car, it has to be considered from the aesthetic point of view in order for any relevant judgement to be offered.

Now certainly it does not necessarily indicate

a misapprehension to use the term 'aesthetic content'. It depends what is meant by it, and there are two possibilities:

(1) To assert that A is part of the content of B would normally imply that A is a constituent feature or component of B, and that therefore a close examination of B will reveal it. This naturally leads to the kind of error discussed in Chapters 5 and 6. For, since statements about aesthetic content cannot be supported by empirical investigation, there will be a strong temptation to assume either that the aesthetic content is non-physical and somehow lying behind the physical object or activity, or that the aesthetic is a purely subjective content, not in the object itself but solely in the mind of the perceiver. And since in neither case can any sense be given to the notion of justification of aesthetic judgements, this is to reduce them to vacuity.

(2) However, if the term 'aesthetic content' is used to make the point that it is only by reference to objective features that aesthetic judgements can be justified, then the notion is unexceptionable. There is a complex issue here, which involves the distinction between physical movements and actions . . . To make the point briefly, precisely the same physical movements may be aesthetically pleasing in one context yet displeasing in another. For example, one may regard a series of movements in a dance as poor aesthetically until it is pointed out that one has misinterpreted the performance. Under the different interpretation they can now be seen as superb. Although there is no physical difference in the movements, the revised judgement is based upon the way in which the new interpretation has determined a different context. Nevertheless, the new interpretation and aesthetic judgement depend solely upon *objective* aspects of the movements. (I consider the nature of the objective reasons given in support of aesthetic judgements in another book, 1974.)

Thus aesthetic judgements are certainly answerable in this way to observable physical features, and if the point of using the term 'aesthetic content' is to emphasise the fact no confusion need arise. However, since it is so frequently used in, or with the misleading implications of, the former sense, it is, in my view, wiser to eschew the term.

The Aesthetic Concept

Although anything can be considered from the aesthetic aspect, some activities and objects are more centrally of aesthetic interest than others. Works of art, to take a paradigm case, are primarily of aesthetic interest, although even they can be considered from other points of view. For instance, paintings are commonly considered as an investment. Hence we need to ask what distinguishes the aesthetic from other ways of looking at objects. One important characteristic is that the aesthetic is a non-functional or non-purposive concept. To take a central example again, when we are considering a work of art from the aesthetic point of view we are not considering it in relation to some external function or purpose it serves. It cannot be evaluated aesthetically according to its degree of success in achieving some such extrinsic end. By contrast, when a painting is considered as an investment, then it is assessed in relation to an extrinsic end, namely that of maximum appreciation in financial value.

This characteristic of the aesthetic immediately raises an insuperable objection to theories which propose an oversimple relation between sport and the aesthetic by identifying them too closely. For example, it is sometimes claimed that sport just *is* an art form (for examples, see Anthony, 1968), and it has been suggested that the aesthetic is the concept which unifies all the activities subsumed under the heading of physical education (see Carlisle, 1969). But there are many sports, indeed the great majority, which are like the painting considered as an investment in that there is an aim or purpose which can be identified independently of the way it is accomplished. That is, the *manner* of achievement of the primary purpose is of little or no significance as long as it comes within the rules. For example, it is normally far more important for a football or hockey team *that* a goal is scored than *how* it is scored. In very many sports of this kind the over-riding factor is the achievement of some such independently specifiable end, since that is the mark of success.

This non-purposive character of the aesthetic is often misunderstood. Such a misunderstanding is manifested in the commonly supposed consequence that therefore there can be no point in art. The presupposition underlying this misunderstanding is that an activity can intelligibly be said to be of point or value only in relation to some external purpose towards which it is directed. Now in cases where such an extrinsic end is the primary consideration, evaluation does depend on it. As we have seen, a painting considered solely as an investment would be evaluated entirely according to its degree of success in achieving maximum capital appreciation. Where the attainment of the end is the over-riding consideration, the means of attaining it obviously becomes relatively unimportant. It would not matter, for instance, what sort of painting it was as long as the end was realised. Similarly, if someone should wish to improve the petrol consumption of his car by changing the carburetter, the design of the new one and the materials from which it is made would be unimportant as long as it succeeded in giving maximum mileage per gallon.

However, the purpose of art cannot be specified in this way, although the misapprehension we are now considering stems from the mistaken assumption that the point of an activity *must* somehow be identifiable as an end or purpose distinct from the activity itself. Yet where art, or more generally the aesthetic, is concerned, the distinction between means and end is inapplicable. For instance, the question 'What is the purpose of that novel?', can be answered comprehensively only in terms of the novel itself. It might be objected that this is not entirely true, since the purpose of some novels could be given as, for example, exposing certain deleterious social conditions. But this objection misses the point I am trying to make,

for if the purpose is the external one of exposing those social conditions then in principle it could equally well, or perhaps better, be realised in other ways, such as the publication of a social survey or a political speech. The report of the social survey is evaluated solely by reference to its purpose of effectively conveying the information, whereas this would be quite inappropriate as a standard for the aesthetic evaluation of a novel. To put the same point another way, from the point of view of efficient conveying of information, the precise form and style of writing of the report is unimportant except in so far as it affects the achievement of that purpose. One report could be as good as another, although the style of writing or compilation was different from or even inferior to the other. There could not be a parallel situation in art in which, for example, one poem might be said to be as good as another although not so well written. This is an aspect of the complex problem of form and content in the arts. To put it briefly, there is a peculiarly intimate connection between the form of an object of aesthetic appreciation, i.e. the particular medium of expression, and its content, i.e. what is expressed in it. So that in art there cannot be a change of form of expression without a corresponding change in what is expressed. It is important to recognise that this is a logical point. For even if one way of writing the report were the clearest and most efficient, this is a mere contingent matter since it is always possible that a better method may be devised. But it is not a contingent matter that the best way of expressing the content of Solzhenitsyn's *One Day in the Life of Ivan Denisovich* is in the particular form of that novel, i.e. it would make no sense to suggest that its content could be more effectively conveyed in another way. So that the question becomes: 'What is the purpose of this particular way of exposing the social conditions?' The end cannot be specified as 'exposing such and such social conditions', but only as 'exposing such and such social conditions in this particular way and no other'. And to give a comprehensive account of what is meant by 'in this particular way and no other' one would have to produce nothing less than the whole novel. The end cannot be identified apart from the manner of achieving it, and that is another way of saying that the presupposition encapsulated in the question, of explanation in terms of purposive action directed onto an external end, is unintelligible in the sphere of aesthetics. In short, in an important sense the answer to 'What is the purpose of that novel?' will amount to a rejection of the question.

A further objection, which has important implications for the aesthetic in sport, might be that in that case how can we criticise a work of art if it can be justified only in terms of itself and there is nothing else with which it can be compared? There is a great deal to be said about the common misapprehension that to engage in critical reasoning is necessarily to generalise (see Bambrough, 1973). It is sufficient for my argument to recognise that critical appreciation of art consists largely in giving reasons why particular features contribute so effectively to or detract from *this particular* work of art. The important point for our purposes is to see again that the end is inseparable from the means of achieving it, for any suggested improvement is given in terms of the particular work of art in question. Another way of putting this point is to say that every feature of a work of art is relevant to the aesthetic assessment of it, whereas when we are judging something as a means to an end, there are irrelevant features of the means, or equally effective alternative means, of achieving the required end. To say that X is an irrelevant feature is always a criticism of a work of art, whereas this is not true of a functional object.

It is true that the aim in a sport cannot be considered in isolation from the rules or norms of that particular sport. Scoring a goal in hockey is not just a matter of getting the ball between the opponents' posts, but requires conformity to the laws of the game. Such requirements are implicit in the meaning of the term 'scoring a goal'. Nevertheless, in contrast to a work of art, within those limits there are many ways of achieving the end, i.e., of scoring a goal, in hockey.

The Gap: Purposive and Aesthetic Sports

At this point we need to direct our attention to the difference between types of sporting activities with respect to the relative importance of the aesthetic. On the one hand, there are those sports, which I shall call 'purposive' and which form the great majority, where the aesthetic is normally relatively unimportant. This category would include football, climbing, track and field events, orienteering and squash. In each of these sports the purpose can be specified independently of the manner of achieving it as long as it conforms to the limits set by the rules or norms—for example, scoring a goal and climbing the Eiger. Even in such sports as these, of course, certain moves or movements, indeed whole games or performances, can be considered from the aesthetic point of view, but it is not central to the activity. It should be recognised that this is a logical point. For example, an activity could obviously still count as football even if there were never a concern for the aesthetic. By contrast, it could not count as football if no one ever tried to score a goal. That is, in these sports it is the independently specifiable purpose which at least largely defines the character of the activity, and the aesthetic is incidental.

On the other hand, there is a category of sports in which the aim cannot be specified in isolation from the aesthetic, for example, synchronised swimming, trampolining, gymnastics, figure-skating and diving. I shall call these 'aesthetic' sports since they are similar to the arts in that their purpose cannot be considered apart from the manner of achieving it. There is an intrinsic end which cannot be identified apart from the means. Consider, for example, the notion of a vault in formal gymnastics. The end is not simply to get over the box somehow or other, even if one were to do so in a clumsy way and collapse afterwards in an uncontrolled manner. The way in which the appropriate movements are performed is not incidental but central to such a sport. That is, the aim cannot be specified simply as 'getting over the box', but only in terms of the manner of achievement required. Indeed, aesthetic norms are implicit in the meaning of terms like 'vault' and 'dive', in that to vault over a box is not the same as to jump over it, or to get over it somehow or other. Although such terms as 'vault' are not employed in Modern Educational Gymnastics, the same issue of principle applies. There may be greater flexibility in the possibilities of answering a particular task in Educational as compared with more formal gymnastics, yet it is still important to consider how, aesthetically, the task is answered. Clumsy, uncontrolled movements would not be regarded as contributing to an adequate way of answering the task, whichever of the indefinite number of ways may be chosen. Similarly, not any way of dropping into the water would count as a dive. One would have to satisfy at least to a minimal extent the aesthetic requirement built into the meaning of the term for a performance to count as even a bad dive.

The distinction, then, is clear. A purposive sport is one in which within the rules or conventions, there is an indefinite variety of ways of achieving the end which at least largely defines the game. By contrast, an aesthetic sport is one in which the purpose cannot be specified independently of the manner of achieving it. For instance, it would make no sense to suggest to a figure-skater that it did not matter *how* he performed his movements, as long as he achieved the purpose of the sport, since that purpose inevitably *concerns* the manner of performance. It would make perfectly good sense to urge a football team to score goals without caring how they scored them. Perhaps the point can be made most clearly by reference to the example given above, of the aesthetic norms built into terms such as 'vault' and 'dive', for whereas not *any* way of dropping into the water could count as even a bad dive, *any* way of getting the ball between the opponents' posts, as long as it is within the rules, would count as a goal, albeit a very clumsy or lucky one.

There is a common tendency to distinguish between these two types of sports in terms of competition. For example, in an interesting article on this topic, Reid (1970) distinguishes between what I have called purposive and aesthetic sports in the following way:

> Games come at the end of a kind of spectrum. In most games, competition against an opponent (individual or team) is assumed . . . At the other end of the spectrum there are gymnastics, diving, skating . . . in which grace, the manner in which the activity is carried out, seems to be of central importance.

Against this, I would point out that competition in Olympic gymnastics, skating and diving can be every bit as keen as it can be in Rugby football. Reid is adopting the prevalent but mistaken practice of contrasting the competitive with the aesthetic. Yet, for instance, it is quite apparent that, on occasion, competition between dance companies, and between rival dancers within the same company, can be as intense and as nasty as it can in ice-hockey. Moreover, to take a paradigm case, there are competitive music festivals, in which a similar spirit may be engendered. The great Korean violinist, Kyung-Wha Chung, after winning first prize in one competition, remarked: 'It was one of the worst experiences of my life, because competitions bring out the worst in people.'

Closing the Gap

We can now return to the original question concerning the characterisation of the aesthetic way of looking at sport. By examining the paradigm cases of sports in which the aesthetic is logically inseparable from what the performer is trying to achieve, we might hope to discover aspects of this way of considering them which can be found to apply even to purposive sports, when they are looked at aesthetically.

In figure-skating, diving, synchronised swimming, trampolining and Olympic gymnastics it is of the first importance that there should be no wasted energy and no superfluous movements. Champion gymnasts, like Nadia Comaneçi and

Ludmilla Tourischeva, not only perform striking physical feats, but do so with such remarkable economy and efficiency of effort that it often looks effortless. There is an intensive concentration of the gymnast's effort so that it is all directed precisely and concisely onto that specific task. Any irrelevant movement or excessive expenditure of energy would detract from the quality of the performance as a whole, just as superfluous or exaggerated words, words which fail to contribute with maximum compression of meaning to the total effect, detract from the quality of a poem as a whole.

However, even in the case of the aesthetic sports there is still, although no doubt to a very limited extent, an externally identifiable aim; for example the requirements set by each particular movement, and by the particular group of movements, in gymnastics. Now it might be thought that it would be justifiable to regard such stringencies as analogous to, say, the form of a sonnet. That is, it may be thought more appropriate to regard them as setting a framework within which the performer has the opportunity to reveal his expertise in moving gracefully than as an externally identifiable aim. There is certainly something in this notion, but it is significant that there is no analogy in aesthetic sports with poetic licence. The poet may take liberties with the sonnet form without necessarily detracting from the quality of the sonnet, but if the gymnast deviates from the requirements of, for instance, a vault, however gracefully, then that inevitably does detract from the standard of the performance. Nevertheless, the main point for our purposes is that even if, in the aesthetic sports, the means never quite reaches the ultimate of complete identification with the end which is such an important distinguishing feature of the concept of art, it at least closely approximates to such an identification. The gap between means and end is almost, if not quite, completely closed.

Now I want to suggest that the same consideration applies to our aesthetic appreciation of sports of the purposive kind. However successful a sportsman may be in achieving the principal aim of his particular activity, our *aesthetic* acclaim is reserved for him who achieves it with maximum economy and efficiency of effort. We may admire the remarkable stamina and consistent success of an athlete such as Zatopek, but he was not an aesthetically attractive runner because so much of his movement seemed irrelevant to the ideal of most direct accomplishment of the task. The ungainliness of his style was constituted by the extraneous rolls or jerks which seemed wasteful in that they were not concisely aimed at achieving the most efficient use of his energy.

So to consider the purposive sports from the aesthetic point of view is to reduce the gap between means and end. It is, as nearly as possible, to telescope them into the ideal of unity. From a purely purposive point of view any way of winning, within the rules, will do, whereas not *any* way of winning will do as far as aesthetic considerations are concerned. There is a narrower range of possibilities available for the achievement of an end in an aesthetically pleasing way, since the end is no longer simply to win, but to win with the greatest economy and efficiency of effort. Nevertheless, the highest aesthetic satisfaction is experienced and given by the sportsman who not only performs with graceful economy, but who also *achieves* his purpose. The tennis player who serves a clean ace with impeccable style has, and gives to the spectator, far more aesthetic satisfaction than when he fractionally faults with an equally impeccable style. In the case of the purposive sports there is an independently specifiable framework, i.e., one which does not require the sort of judgement to assess achievement which is necessary in the aesthetic sports. Maximum aesthetic success still requires the attainment of the end, and the aesthetic in any degree requires direction onto that end, but the number of ways of achieving such success is reduced in comparison with the purely purposive interest of simply accomplishing the end in an independently specifiable sense.

This characteristic of the aesthetic in activities which are primarily functional also applies to the examples cited earlier of mathematical proofs and philosophical arguments. The proof of a theorem in Euclidean geometry or a philosophical argument is aesthetically pleasing to the extent that there is a clean and concisely directed focus of effort. Any over-elaborate, irrelevant, or repetitious section, in either case, would detract from the maximum economy in achieving the conclusion which gives greatest aesthetic satisfaction. Rhetorical flourishes, however aesthetically effective in other contexts, such as a political speech, detract aesthetically from a philosophical argument by fussily blurring the ideal of a straight, direct line to the conclusion. The aesthetic satisfaction given by rhetoric in a political speech is related to the latter's different purpose of producing a convincing or winning argument rather than a valid one.

The aesthetic pleasure which we derive from sporting events of the purposive kind, such as hurdling and putting the shot, is, then, derived from looking at, or performing, actions which we take to be approaching the ideal of totally concise direction towards the required end of the particular activity. Skiing provides a good example. The stylish skier seems superbly economical, his body automatically accommodating itself, apparently without conscious effort on his part, to the most appropriate and efficient positions for the various types and conditions of terrain. By contrast, the skiing in a slalom race often appears ungainly because it looks forced and less concisely directed. The skier in such an event may achieve greater speed, but only by the expenditure of a disproportionate amount of additional effort. Similarly, athletes at the end of a distance race often abandon the smooth, graceful style with which they have run the greater part of the race. They achieve greater speed but at disproportionate cost, since ungainly, irrelevant movements appear— the head rolls, the body lurches, and so on. In rowing, too, some oarsmen can produce a faster speed with poor style but more, if less effectively produced, power. Even though it is wasteful, the net effective power may still be greater than that of the oarsman who directs his more limited gross power with far more efficiency and therefore with

more pleasing aesthetic effect. It is often said that a good big 'un will beat a good little 'un. It is also true in many sports, unfortunately, that a poor big 'un may well beat a far better little 'un.

Perhaps these considerations do something to explain the heightened aesthetic awareness which is achieved by watching slow-motion films and television replays, since (1) we have more time to appreciate the manner of the performance, and (2) the object of the action, the purpose, in an extrinsic sense, becomes less important. That is, our attention is directed more to the character of the action than to its result. We can see whether and how every detail of every movement in the action as a whole contributes to making it the most efficient and economical way of accomplishing that particular purpose. A smooth, flowing style is more highly regarded aesthetically because it appears to require less effort for the same result than a jerky one. Nevertheless, as was mentioned above, achievement of the purpose is still important. However graceful and superbly directed the movements of a pole-vaulter, our aesthetic pleasure in his performance is marred if he knocks the bar off.

One additional and related factor is that some people naturally move gracefully whatever they may be doing, and this may contribute to the aesthetic effect of their actions in sport. If I may be pardoned for the outrageous pun, Muhammad Ali provides a striking example.

Several questions remain. For example, why are some sporting events regarded as less aesthetically pleasing than others, i.e., where we are not comparing actions within the same context of direction onto a common end, but comparing actions in different contexts? For instance, in my view the butterfly stroke in swimming, however well performed, seems less aesthetically pleasing than the crawl. Perhaps this is because it looks less efficient as a way of moving through the water, since there appears to be a disproportionate expenditure of effort in relation to the achievement. A similar example is race walking which, even at its best, never seems to me to be an aesthetically pleasing event. Perhaps, again, this is because one feels that the same effort would be more efficiently employed if the walker broke into a run. In each of these cases one is implicitly setting a wider context, seeing the action in terms of a wider purpose, of movement through water and movement over the ground respectively. But what of a sport such as weight-lifting, which many regard as providing little or no aesthetic pleasure, although it is hard to discover a wider context, a more economical direction on to a wider or similar end in another activity, with which we are implicitly comparing it? Perhaps the explanation lies simply in a general tendency to prefer, from an aesthetic point of view, sports which allow for smooth, flowing movements in the achievement of the primary purpose. Nevertheless, for the devotee, there are, no doubt, 'beautiful' lifts, so called because they accomplish maximum direction of effort.

Now the objection has been made against my account that it fails to differentiate the aesthetic from the skilful. I think two points are sufficient to overcome this objection. First, as a careful reading of the chapter will reveal, my argument, if valid, shows that in sport the two concepts are certainly intimately related, but it also shows that they are not entirely co-extensive. I have marked some ways in which they diverge.

The second and more important point is this. Even if it were true that my argument had not revealed a distinction between the two concepts, that would not constitute an objection to it. For why should not those features of an action in virtue of which it is called skilful also be those in virtue of which it is called aesthetically pleasing? Wittgenstein once wrote: 'Ethics and aesthetics are one.' Whether or not one would want to accept that statement will depend on Wittgenstein's argument for it. One cannot simply dismiss it on the grounds that it *must* be self-defeating to offer a characterisation of the aesthetic which also characterises the ethical.

The supposed objection seems to incorporate the preconception that to have characterised the aesthetic is to have specified those essential features which can be shared by no other concept. This would be like denying that ginger can be an essential ingredient in ginger cakes on the ground that it is *also* an ingredient in ginger ale. The objector produced no argument, but simply assumed that an account which also fitted the skilful could not be adequate as an account of the aesthetic. So, in response to this supposed objection, I could simply reply: 'You are right, I concede that my argument does not entirely distinguish the aesthetic from the skilful. But so far from constituting an objection to my argument, what you have provided amounts to a rough summary of it.'

Context and Aesthetic Feeling

The foregoing argument raises two related considerations which have an important bearing upon the notion of aesthetic *experience* in sport. First, a movement cannot be considered aesthetically in isolation, but only in the context of a particular action in a particular sport. A graceful sweep of the left arm may be very effective in a dance, but the same movement may look ugly and absurd as part of a service action in tennis, or of a pitcher's action in baseball, since it detracts from the ideal of total concentration of effort to achieve the specific task. A specific movement is aesthetically satisfying only if, in the context of the action as a whole, it is seen as forming a unified structure which is regarded as the most economical and efficient method of achieving the required end.

Secondly, there is a danger of serious misconception arising from a mistaken dependence upon feelings as criteria of aesthetic quality, whether in sport or in any other activity, including dance and the other arts. This is part of the misconception to which we alluded in Chapter 6, and consists of taking the feeling of the performer or spectator as the ultimate arbiter. Yet, as we have seen, any feeling is intelligible only if it can be identified by its typical manifestation in behaviour. This is what Wittgenstein (1953) meant by saying that an inner process stands in need of outward criteria. Thus, in the present case, it is the observable physical movement which identifies the feeling and not, as is often believed, the inner feeling which suffuses the physical movement with aesthetic quality or meaning. The feeling could not even be identified if it were not normally experienced in certain objectively recognisable circumstances. One should resist the temptation, commonly encountered in discussion of dance and other forms of movement, to believe that it is how a movement feels which determines its character or effectiveness, whether aesthetic or purposive. That it feels right is no guarantee that it is right. Inexperienced oarsmen in an 'eight' are often tempted to heave their bodies round violently in an attempt to propel the boat more quickly, because such an action gives a feeling of much greater power. Yet in fact it will upset the balance of the boat and thus reduce the effectiveness of the rowing of the crew as a whole. The most effective stroke action can best be judged by the coach who is watching the whole performance from the bank, not by the feeling of the individual oarsmen or even of all the crew. Similarly, in tennis and skiing, to take just two examples, the feeling of an action is often misleading as to its maximum efficiency. A common error in skiing is to lean into the slope and at a certain stage in his progress a learner starts to make turns for the first time which feel very good. Yet, however exhilarating the feeling, if he is leaning the wrong way he will be considerably hampered from making further progress, because in fact he is not directing his efforts in the most effective manner. There are innumerable other such examples one could cite, and this, of course, has important implications for education. If the arbiter of success in physical activities is what the students feel, rather than what they can be observed to do, it is hard to see how such activities can be learned and taught.

However, to refer to an objection which we considered in Chapter 6, it is important not to misunderstand this point by going to the opposite extreme, for I am not saying that we cannot be guided by such feelings, or that they are of no value. My point is that they are useful and reliable only to the extent that they are answerable to patterns of behaviour which can be *observed* to be most efficiently directed onto the particular task. This reveals the connection between this and the preceding point, for it is clear that the character and efficiency of a particular movement cannot be considered in isolation from the whole set of related movements of which it forms a part, and from the purpose towards which they are, as a whole, directed. Thus the context in which the movement occurs is a factor of an importance which it is impossible to exaggerate, since the feeling could not even be identified, let alone evaluated, if it were not normally experienced as part of an objectively recognisable action.

In this respect I should like to question what is often said about the aesthetic attitude, namely that it is essentially or predominantly contemplative. Reid (1970), for instance, says: 'In an aesthetic situation we attend to what we perceive in what is sometimes called a "contemplative" way.' Now it may be that a concern with the arts and the aesthetic is largely contemplative, but I see no reason to deny, indeed I see good reason to insist, that one can have what are most appropriately called aesthetic *feelings* while actually performing an activity. There are numerous examples, such as a well-executed dive, a finely timed stroke in squash, a smoothly accomplished series of movements in gymnastics, an outing in an 'eight' when the whole crew is pulling in unison, with unwavering balance, and a training run when one's body seems to be completely under one's control. For many, the feelings derived from such performances are part of the enjoyment of participation, and 'aesthetic' seems the most appropriate way to characterise them. Reid says that 'a dancer or actor in the full activity of dancing or acting is often, perhaps always, in some degree contemplating the product of his activity'. Later, he says of games players: 'There is no time while the operation is going on to dwell upon aesthetic qualities . . .

Afterwards, the participant may look back upon his experience contemplatively with perhaps some aesthetic satisfaction.' Again, of the aesthetic in cricket, he remarks: 'The batsman may enjoy it too, although at the moment of play he has no time to dwell upon it. But to produce exquisite strokes for contemplation is not part of his dominating motive as he is actually engaged in the game . . .' Yet the batsman's aesthetic experience is not necessarily dependent upon his having time at the moment of playing the stroke to 'dwell upon it', nor is it limited to a retrospective contemplation of his performance. If he plays a perfectly timed cover drive with the ball flashing smoothly and apparently effortlessly from the face of his bat to the boundary, the aesthetic satisfaction of the batsman is intrinsic to what he is doing. The aesthetic is not a distinct but perhaps concurrent activity, and it need not depend upon detached or retrospective contemplation. His experience is logically inseparable from the stroke he is playing, in that it is identifiable only by his particular action in that context. And it is quite natural, unexceptionable, and perhaps unavoidable to call such an experience 'aesthetic'. 'Kinaesthetic' or 'tactile' would not tell the whole story by any means, since producing the same physical movement in a quite different context, for instance in a laboratory, could not count as producing the same feeling. Indeed, it is significant that we tend naturally to employ aesthetic terms to describe the feelings involved in such actions. We say that a stroke felt 'beautiful', and it was so to the extent that it was efficiently executed in relation to the specific purpose of the action in the sport concerned. Many participants in physical activities have experienced the exquisite feeling, for instance, of performing a dance or gymnastic sequence, of sailing over the bar in a pole vault, or of accomplishing a fluent series of Christis with skis immaculately parallel. It is difficult to know how to describe these feelings other than as 'aesthetic'. It is certainly the way in which those of us who have taken part in such activities tend spontaneously to refer to them. So, although I do not wish to deny that contem-

plation is an important part of the aesthetic, I would contend that it is not exhaustive. It is by no means unusual to experience aesthetic feelings, properly so called, while actually engaged and fully involved in physical activities. Moreover, many of us who have derived considerable pleasure from a wide variety of sporting activities would want to insist that such aesthetic experience constitutes a large part of the enjoyment of participation.

The Aesthetic and the Artistic

In the case of the purposive sports, then, as the actions become more and more directly aimed, with maximum economy and efficiency, at the required end, they become more and more specific, and the gap between means and end is to that extent reduced. That is, increasingly it is less possible to specify the means apart from the end. In these sports the gap will, nevertheless, never be entirely closed in that there cannot be the complete identification of means and end, or more accurately perhaps, the inappropriateness of the distinction between means and end, which obtains in the case of art. For even if in fact there is a single most efficient and economical way of achieving a particular end, this is a contingent matter. The evolution of improved high-jumping methods is a good example. The scissor jump was once regarded as the most efficient method, but it has been overtaken by the straddle, the Western roll and the Fosbury flop.

There remains an interesting question. The aesthetic sports have been shown to be similar to the arts with respect to the impossibility of distinguishing means and ends. Does this mean that such sports can legitimately be regarded as art forms? I should want to insist that they cannot, for two reasons. First, as we have seen, there is good reason to doubt whether the means/end distinction ever quite becomes inappropriate, although it almost reaches that point, even in the aesthetic sports. That is, unlike dance, in these sports there is still an externally specifiable aim even though, for instance, it is impossible entirely to specify what the gymnast is trying to achieve apart from the way in which he is trying to achieve it. Perhaps this is what some physical educationists are getting at when they say, rather vaguely, that a distinction between gymnastics and dance is that the former is objective while the latter is subjective.

However, it is the second reason which is the more important one, and this concerns the distinction which is almost universally overlooked or oversimplified, and therefore misconceived, between the aesthetic and the artistic. The aesthetic applies, for instance, to sunsets, birdsong and mountain ranges, whereas the artistic tends to be limited, at least in its central uses, to artifacts or performances intentionally created by man—*objets trouvés*, if regarded as art, would be so in an extended sense. Throughout this chapter I have so far followed the common practice of taking 'aesthetic' to refer to the genus of which the artistic is a species. My reason for doing so is that any other difference between the two concepts is of no consequence to my main argument, since their logical character with respect to the possibility of distinguishing between means and end is the same. However, in order to consider the question of whether any sport can justifiably be regarded as an art form a more adequate distinction between the aesthetic and the artistic is required, and on examination it becomes clear that there is a much more important issue here than is commonly supposed. I can begin to bring out the issue to which I refer by considering Reid's answer to the question. He is prepared to allow that what I call the aesthetic sports may justifiably be called art, but in my view his conclusion is invalidated because his own formulation of the distinction overlooks a crucial characteristic of art. He writes (1970):

When we are talking about the category of art, as distinct from the category of the aesthetic, we must be firm, I think, in insisting that in art there is someone who has made (or is mak-

ing) purposefully an artifact, and that in his purpose there is contained as an essential part the idea of producing an object (not necessarily a 'thing': it could be a movement or a piece of music) in some medium for aesthetic contemplation . . . the movement (of a gymnast, skater, diver), carried out in accordance with the general formula, has aesthetic quality fused into it, transforming it into an art quality . . . The question is whether the production of aesthetic value is intrinsically part of the purpose of these sports. (If so, on my assumptions, they will be in part, at least, art.)

This certainly has the merit of excluding natural phenomena such as sunsets and roses, but some people might regard his exclusion of *objets trouvés* as somewhat difficult to justify. What, in my view, is worse, this conception would include much which we should be strongly disinclined to call 'art'. For example, a wallpaper pattern is normally designed to give aesthetic pleasure, but it would not on that account, at least in the great majority of cases, be regarded as art. Many such counter-examples spring to mind; for instance the paint on the walls of my office, the shape of radiators and spectacles, and coloured toilet paper. In each case the intention is to give aesthetic pleasure, but none is art (which is not necessarily to deny that, in certain unusual circumstances, any of them could be considered as art, or as part of a work of art).

Reid has done sufficient in my view to show clearly that the great majority of sports cannot legitimately be regarded as art. For the *principal* aim in most sports is certainly not to produce performances for aesthetic pleasure. The aesthetic is incidental. And if it should be argued against me that nevertheless such purposive sports *could* be considered from the aesthetic point of view, my reply would be that so could everything else. Hence, if that were to be regarded as the distinguishing feature of art then *everything* would be art, and thus the term 'art' would no longer have any application.

Nevertheless, Reid's formulation fails, I think, because he overlooks the central aspect of the concept of art which underlies the fact that there are cases where one may appreciate a work of art aesthetically but not artistically. To understand the significance of this point, consider the following example. Some years ago I went to watch a performance by Ram Gopal, the great Indian classical dancer, and I was enthralled by the exhilarating quality of his movements. Yet I did not appreciate, because I could not have understood, his dance artistically, for there is an enormous number of precise meanings given to hand gestures in Indian classical dance, of which I knew none. So it seems clear that my appreciation was of the aesthetic not the artistic.

This example brings out the important characteristic of the concept of art which I particularly want to emphasise, since it is generally overlooked by those who conflate 'aesthetic' and 'artistic'. Moreover, the failure to recognise it is probably the main source of misconceived distinctions between the two terms. I shall first outline the point roughly, and go on to elucidate it more fully in relation to other claims made for sport as art.

It is distinctive of any art form that its conventions allow for the possibility of the expression of a conception of life situations. Thus the arts are characteristically concerned with contemporary moral, social, political and emotional issues. Yet this is not true of the aesthetic. I think it is because he does not recognise the significance of this point that Reid is prepared to allow that the aesthetic sports may legitimately be regarded as art forms. But it is this characteristic of art which is my reason for insisting that even those sports in which the aesthetic is intrinsic, and which are therefore performed to give aesthetic satisfaction, cannot justifiably be considered as art. For in synchronised swimming, figure-skating, diving, trampolining and gymnastics, the performer does not, as part of the convention of the activity, have the possibility of expressing through his particular medium his view of life situations. It is difficult to imagine a gymnast who included in his

sequence movements which expressed his view of war, or of love in a competitive society, or of any other such issue. Certainly if he did so it would, unlike art, *detract* to that extent from his performance.

Of course there are cases, even in the accredited arts, such as abstract paintings and dances, where we are urged not to look for a meaning but simply to enjoy the line, colour, movement etc., without trying to read anything into them. But it is intrinsic to the notion of an art form that it can at least *allow for* the possibility of considering issues of social concern, and this is not possible in the aesthetic sports. Incidentally, if I am right that the activities of art and sport are quite distinct, this poses problems for those who suggest that the aesthetic sports may provide one method of, perhaps an introduction to, education in the arts, although of course this is not in the least to cast doubt on their aesthetic value. At their best these sports are undoubtedly superb aesthetically, but they are not, in my view, art.

Sport and Art

Partly in order to bring out more fully the important characteristic of the concept of art which I have just outlined, and partly because of the widespread misconception on the issue, I should like further to elucidate my reasons for denying the common supposition that sport can legitimately be considered as art.

As we have seen, it is clear that there is a distinction between the aesthetic and the artistic, even though it may be difficult precisely to delineate it. Yet, in the literature on sport, one still very frequently encounters an illicit slide from such terms as 'beautiful' and 'graceful' to 'art'. An author will refer to a general interest in the beauty of the movement in various sporting activities, and will assume implicitly or explicitly that this entitles such activities to be considered as art. Anthony (1968) and Reid (1970) give several examples, and the same confusion runs through Carlisle (1969) who writes, for instance, that 'various forms of dance are accepted as art forms and aesthetic criteria are also applied in other activities, e.g., ice-skating, diving, Olympic gymnastics and synchronised swimming'. A more recent example is Lowe (1976) who writes: 'By analysing dance, as one of the performing arts, with the object of deducing the aesthetic components . . . a step will be taken closer to the clarification of the beauty of sport as a performing art.' So far as I can understand this, Lowe seems to be guilty of the confusion to which I refer, since clearly 'beauty' and its cognates do not necessarily imply 'art'. To say that a young lady is beautiful is not to say that she is a work of art.

For the reasons already given, I submit that, despite the amount of literature on the topic, we should finally abandon this persistent but misguided attempt to characterise sport *in general* as art. Quite apart from what seems to me the obvious misconception involved, I just do not see why it should be thought that sport would somehow be endowed with greater respectability if it could be shown to be art.

There is, of course, a much more convincing case to be made for the credentials of the aesthetic sports as art, although even here I do not think it succeeds. My rejection of the case hinges on the way I have characterised the distinction between the aesthetic and the artistic. It would seem that any attempt to draw this distinction in terms of definition, or by reference to particular kinds of objects or performances, is almost certainly doomed to failure. Hence I distinguish the two concepts by drawing attention to a characteristic which is central to any legitimate art *form*, rather than to a work of art within that medium. Thus, to repeat the point, my own formulation is that any art form, properly so-called, must at least *allow for* the possibility of the expression of a conception of life issues, such as contemporary moral, social and political problems. Such a possibility is an *intrinsic* part of the concept of art, by which I mean that without it an activity could not count

as a legitimate art form. It is certainly a crucial factor in the ways in which the arts have influenced society. Examples abound. For instance, it is reported that during the occupation of France in the war a German officer, indicating the painting *Guernica*, asked Picasso, 'Did you do that?' To which Picasso replied, 'No, you did.'

By contrast, such a possibility is not intrinsic to any sport. However, this point has been misunderstood, as a result of which it has been argued against me that in sport, too, there can be comment on life issues. The commonest example cited was that of black American athletes on the rostrum at the Olympic Games, who gave the clenched-fist salute for Black Power during the playing of the national anthem. But this does not constitute a counter-example, since such a gesture is clearly *extrinsic* to, not made from within, the conventions of sport as such. The conventions of art are in this respect significantly different from those in sport, since it is certainly intrinsic to art that a view could be expressed, for instance on colour discrimination, as in Athol Fugard's plays about the issue in South Africa.

We have seen that since aesthetic terms such as 'beauty' are often applied to sport, it is sometimes erroneously supposed that therefore sport is art. A similar misconception occurs with respect to the terms 'dramatic', 'tragic', and their cognates. These terms are used in a notoriously slippery way, hence it certainly cannot be assumed that they are used in other contexts as they are in art. For instance, if I were to leap up during a meeting, shout abusive terms, and hurl a cup through a window, that would certainly be dramatic, but I am modest enough to assume that no one would regard it as artistic.

It is an understood part of the convention that tragedy in a play happens to the *fictional characters* being portrayed, and not to the actors, i.e., the living people taking part. By contrast, and ignoring for a moment the issue of whether it would be legitimately employed in such a context, 'tragedy' in sport *does* happen to the participants, i.e. to the living people taking part. For example, let us imagine that I am playing the part of Gloucester, in the play *King Lear*. In the scene where his eyes are put out it is agonising for the character in the play, Gloucester; not for me, the actor. There is no comparable convention in sport such that it would make sense to say of a serious injury in Rugby that it occurred to the full-back, and not to the man who was playing full-back. While in Canada recently I was given an interesting illustration of the point. A party of Eskimos, attending a performance of *Othello*, were appalled to see what they took to be the killing of people on the stage. They had to be reassured by being taken backstage after the performance to see the actors still alive. The Eskimos had assumed that different actors would be required for each performance.

To put the point roughly, it is a central convention of art, in contrast to sport, that the object of one's attention is an *imagined* object. Thus a term such as 'tragic', used of art, has to be understood as deriving its meaning from that convention. Yet, although this is a central convention of art, it is overlooked or misconstrued by most of those who argue that sport is art, or drama. This omission vitiates a good deal of the literature on the topic. Reid (1970) gives several examples, including that of Maheu, who claims that 'spectator sports are the true theatre of our day'; Carlisle (1969) who supports the contention that cricket is 'an art form both dramatic and visual'; Kitchin, who in an article on 'Sport as drama' writes of international soccer: 'This is the authentic theatre in the round, from which Hungary's Manager made a thirty-yard running exit with both hands clenched over his eyes . . . Soccer is drama without a script.' Similarly, Keenan (1973) in an article entitled 'The athletic contest as a "tragic" form of art', writes: 'There is no doubt that athletic contests, like other human endeavours, provide drama. No one would question whether Bannister's effort which produced the first sub-four-minute mile was dramatic.' But I would seriously question whether, indeed I would deny that, 'dramatic' is being used here in the same sense as when it occurs in the context of discussion of a play, since the relevant convention is lacking. That there is no comparable convention in sport can be brought out most clearly by the lack of any analogue with a fictional character. What happens to Gloucester does not happen to the person playing the part of Gloucester. The analogue in sport would have to be something like: 'What happened to Hungary's Manager did not happen to the man who held the position as manager', and 'What happened to the athlete who completed the first sub-four-minute mile did not happen to Bannister, who took part in the race', both of which are palpably absurd.

There are two common uses of the term 'tragic' which are outside, and which therefore should not be confused with its use within, the conventions of drama:

(1) Where the term is used, for instance, of serious injury to a sportsman, the analogue in a play would be serious injury to an actor, for example in an accident during a duelling scene. 'Tragic' in this sense does not depend on conventions at all, whether sporting or artistic, but is used to refer to a poignantly sad and distressing event in real life, such as a seriously crippling or fatal accident or illness.

(2) On the other hand, in the irritatingly prevalent but barbarously debased sense of the term where 'tragic' is used, for instance, of the failure of a sportsman to achieve a success on which he had set his heart, the analogue in drama would be not some tragic event in a play but, for instance, the failure of an actor in a crucial role, or his failure to obtain a role which he earnestly wanted. It is still quite different from the use of the term within the conventions of drama. Strangely enough, Keenan (1973) recognises this point to some extent, yet fails to realise that it undermines his whole case. He writes: 'We can truly sympathise with classic efforts of athletic excellence that end in tragedy. They parallel the difficult episodes in life.' As one example, he cites an Olympic marathon race:

The amazing Pietri entered the stadium with an enormous lead on the field, needing only to negotiate the last 385 yards to win. His effort had left him in an obvious state of extreme physical fatigue . . . The crowd cheered lustily for him to continue, to fight off the fatigue, to win. His final collapse came near the finish line as the eventual winner . . . was just entering the stadium.

This example, so far from supporting Keenan's case reveals the fatal flaw in it, for 'tragedy' here is used in the latter sense adumbrated above, and is totally different from the way the term is used within and as part of the conventions of drama. The point can be brought sharply into focus by recognising that a poignantly tragic moment in drama is a *triumph*, a mark of *success*, for an actor, whereas, by contrast a 'tragic' moment in sport is a *failure*, even if a noble and courageous failure, for the competitor.

The importance of the conventions of art can be brought out in another way, by reference to the use of the term 'illusion'. In the context of the arts 'illusion' is not employed as it would be of, for instance, a mirage. One actually, if mistakenly, believes that an oasis is there, whereas one does not actually believe that someone is being murdered on a stage. Or at least, if one should actually believe that someone is being murdered this significantly reveals a failure to grasp one of the most important conventions of drama. The term 'illusion' is used in a different, if related, sense in the context of art. I say that the sense is related because, for instance, the actors, theatre management and producer, by means of lighting, stage effects and a high standard of acting, try to induce the audience to suspend their disbelief, as it were. Nevertheless, as Scruton (1974) puts it, our experience of representation and expression in art 'derives from imagination, not belief'.

Of course this is not in the least to deny that it is possible to be imaginative in sport, although I have been rather surprisingly misunderstood in this respect. What it does deny is that there are analogous conventions in sport such that the participants have to be imagined, as one has to imagine the characters in a play or novel.

In short, the misconception of those writers who persist in what I firmly believe are misguided attempts to argue that sport is an art form, stems from their ignoring or misconstruing the crucial importance of the *art* aspect of a work of art. For instance, one commonly experiences emotional responses to both artistic and sporting performances, and as both spectator and performer. Now, emotional feelings can be identified only by criteria, of which the most important is what is called the 'intensional object', i.e. the kind of object towards which the emotion is directed. In the case of art, the intensional object cannot be characterised in isolation from the relevant conventions. The point becomes particularly clear, perhaps, when we think how we can be moved by completely non-naturalistic works of art, such as surrealism, abstract expressionism, and an allegory such as *Le Petit Prince* by St-Exupéry.

Now of course with respect to sport, too, the intensional object cannot be characterised independently of the conventions of that particular kind of activity. The point was brought home vividly to me when for the first time I watched an American Football match, which was a keenly contested local derby between two rival high schools. There was considerable partisan excitement, but I was unable to share in it because I did not understand the game. As an even clearer example, a friend in Jasper told me of his experience, while working in the North West Territories, of trying to teach the local Eskimos how to play soccer. He was frustrated, apparently, by their inability to understand, or at least refusal to accept, that the purpose of the game was to defeat the opposing team. The Eskimos were much too genial to adopt such an uncivilised, competitive ethos, hence if a team were winning, members of it would promptly score in their own goal in order to be generous to their opponents.

So one certainly needs to understand the conventions of sport, too, in order to become emotionally involved in the appropriate way. But the conventions of sport are in important respects very different from those of art, even in the case of aesthetic sports such as figure-skating. The champion skater John Curry has strongly expressed his conviction that figure-skating *should* be regarded as an art form, and the superb Canadian skater, Toller Cranston, is frequently quoted as a counter-example by Canadians. He, too, apparently, has often insisted that figure-skating is an art. However, this contention is based on a confusion, and in my opinion it would be clearer to conceive of them as two quite distinct kinds of activity. Then we should have on one hand the *sport* of figure-skating, and on the other hand the *art* of modern dance on ice, which these skaters want to create as a new art form. It is interesting that Toller Cranston is said to have expressed annoyance at the limitations imposed by the conventions and rules of the *sport*, and has made his point forcefully by *deliberately* performing his figure-skating in several competitions *as* an art form. For instance, in response to the music he had flouted the canons of the sport by performing movements which *did* express his view of life situations. But it is significant that, much to his further chagrin, he *lost* marks for doing so. In my view the judges were quite right. The context of sport, even an aesthetic sport, is not appropriate for art. It is significant, perhaps, and tacitly concedes my point, that John Curry has put his convictions into practice by creating 'The John Curry Theatre of Skating'.

Now it might be objected that in denying in this way that sport can legitimately be regarded as art I am simply being stipulative. That is, it might be said that this is arbitrarily to lay down how the term 'art' should be used. This objection is of the same kind as that which was discussed in Chapter 4 with respect to the use of 'intellectual', and it can be met in a similar way. Certainly philosophers cannot legislate how words should be used, and what is to count as correct usage. 'Artistic' could be used as synonymous with 'aesthetic', and there could be no *philosophical* objection to what I regard as barbarously degenerate uses such as 'the art of cooking'. The philosophical point is that, however the term may be used, this will not *remove*, even although it may blur, the relevant distinction. That is, if 'art' were to be used as

broadly as this, there would still be a distinction between those forms of activity which have, and those which do not have, intrinsic to their conventions, the possibility of comment on life issues in the way described. And in such a case, it would be necessary to employ some other term to mark those which have this kind of convention. Hence it seems to me much less conducive to confusion to restrict 'art' to such activities.

To repeat the point, then, in my opinion it is high time we buried once for all the prolix attempts to show that sport is art. It may be of interest to point up illuminating similarities, but only confusion can accrue from the attempt to equate the two kinds of activity. In the case of an aesthetic sport such as figure-skating the suggestion is at least initially plausible because of the widespread failure to recognise the important distinction between the aesthetic and the artistic, and because figure-skating, unlike, for instance, football, can so easily become an art form. But in the case of the purposive sports, which constitute the great majority, there is not even a *prima facie* case, even though there may be many movements in such sports which are superb aesthetically.

Rather ironically, the fact that sporting activities and the movements of athletes have been the subject for art, for instance in painting and sculpture, is sometimes adduced, at least by implication, in support of the contention that sport is art. For example, Lowe (1976) writes:

> Among sculptors, R. Tait McKenzie has brought a fine sense of movement to his athletic studies cast in bronze. There is no question about the aesthetic qualities of these art works: hence they provide intrinsic clues to our grasp of the elusive nature of beauty in sport.

I say that it is ironic because examination reveals that this kind of argument achieves the very opposite of what its authors intend, since it makes the point which could also be regarded as a summary of my distinction between the aesthetic and the artistic. For whereas sport can be the subject of art, art could not be the subject of sport. Indeed, the very notion of a *subject* of sport makes no sense.

Bibliography

1. Anthony, W.J., 'Sport and physical education as a means of aesthetic education', *British Journal of Physical Education*, vol. 60, no. 179 (March 1968).
2. Bambrough, J.R., 'To reason is to generalise', *The Listener*, vol. 89, no. 2285 (11 January 1973).
3. Best, D., *Expression in Movement and the Arts* (London: Lepus Books, Henry Kimpton Publishers, 1974).
4. Carlisle, R., 'The concept of physical education', *Proceedings of the Philosophy of Education Society of Great Britain*, vol. 3 (January 1969).
5. Keenan, F., 'The athletic contest as a "tragic" form of art', in *The Philosophy of Sport*, ed. R.G. Osterhoudt (Springfield, Illinois: C.C. Thomas, 1973).
6. Lowe, B., 'Toward scientific analysis of the beauty of sport', *British Journal of Physical Education*, vol. 7, no. 4 (July 1976).
7. Reid, L.A., 'Sport, the aesthetic and art', *British Journal of Educational Studies*, vol. 18, no. 3 (1970).
8. Scruton, R., *Art and Imagination* (London: Methuen, 1974).
9. Wittgenstein, L., *Philosophical Investigations* (Oxford: Basil Blackwell, 1953).

Sport, Art, and Particularity: The Best Equivocation

TERENCE J. ROBERTS

David Best (1; 3; 4; 5; 6) has mounted a consistently strong attack against too closely associating most sports with the aesthetic or any sport with art. His position consists of two main arguments: first, that the aesthetic cannot be central to most sports because, unlike art wherein the aesthetic is central, most sports have an aim or purpose which can be identified independently of the way that aim or purpose is accomplished; and second, that, unlike all art forms, no sports have the capacity to express a conception of life situations. While there are important ways the two arguments interrelate, this paper attempts to overcome the obstacle posed by the first by demonstrating that it rests upon a fundamental equivocation.[1]

Before that argument can proceed, it is necessary to outline Best's position.[2] In the chapter entitled ''The Aesthetic in Sport'' in *Philosophy and Human Movement* (3), Best begins by asking whether all sports can be considered from the aesthetic point of view. He affirmatively responds, ''any object or activity can be considered aesthetically—cars, mountains, even mathematical proofs and philosophical arguments'' (3: p. 99). The af-

firmation does nothing to advance the case of an intimacy between sport and the aesthetic: it's true, but trivial, that sport is aesthetic in this sense. With respect to the nontrivial claim, Best argues that an examination of the respective natures of the aesthetic and most sports reveals that an intimacy between them is impossible. Employing works of art, specifically paintings, as paradigms of that which is primarily of aesthetic interest, Best contrasts the aesthetic way of looking with the functional, purposive way:

> To take a central example again, when we are considering a work of art from the aesthetic point of view we are not considering it in relation to some external function or purpose it serves. It cannot be evaluated aesthetically according to its degree of success in achieving some such extrinsic end. By contrast, when a painting is considered as an investment, then it is assessed in relation to an extrinsic end, namely that of maximum appreciation in financial value. (3: p. 101)

It is the nonpurposive, nonfunctional character of the aesthetic that Best thinks precludes the possibility of a close relationship between sport and the aesthetic[3] because most sports are assessed in terms of an extrinsic end:

Reprinted from *Journal of the Philosophy of Sport*, XIII, (1986), pp. 49–63. Copyright 1987 by the Philosophic Society for the Study of Sport. Reprinted by permission.

there are many sports, indeed the great majority, which are like the painting considered as an investment in that there is an aim or purpose which can be identified independently of the way it is accomplished. That is, the manner of achievement is of little or no significance as long as it comes within the rules. For example, it is normally far more important for a football or hockey team *that* a goal is scored than *how* it is scored. In very many sports of this kind the over-riding factor is the achievement of some such independently specifiable end, since that is the mark of success. (3: p. 101)

Art, and more generally the aesthetic, Best argues, are much different:

> The end cannot be identified apart from the manner of achieving it, and that is another way of saying that the presupposition encapsulated in the question, of explanation in terms of purposive action is directed onto an external end, is unintelligible in the sphere of aesthetics. In short, in an important sense the answer to "What is the purpose of that novel?" will amount to a rejection of the question. (3: p. 103)

That is, an understanding and an appreciation of the so-called "purpose" of an art work cannot be separated from an understanding and an appreciation of the art work itself. The means are the end, and consequently any change in the means will change the so-called end. As Best puts it,

> there is a peculiarly intimate connection between the form of an object of aesthetic appreciation, i.e. the particular medium of expression, and its content, i.e. what is expressed in it. So that in art there cannot be a change of form of expression without a corresponding change in what is expressed. (3: p. 102)

Whereas on the other hand, he argues, something

(e.g., most sports and paintings considered as investments) is appreciated primarily as a means to an end, the means employed become relatively unimportant and can be altered without affecting the nature of the end attained. For instance, Best points out, if a painting is valued exclusively as a means of attaining maximum appreciation in financial value, what sort of painting it is matters little. Similarly, in most sports there are many ways of achieving the end (i.e., scoring); how it is achieved is relatively unimportant.

Notice that Best restricts his comments to "most" sports. He does admit of another class of sports (i.e., the "aesthetic" sports) whose purpose, unlike that of the "purposive" sports just described, "cannot be specified apart from the aesthetic manner of achieving it" (1: p. 157). Similar to the arts, these sports (e.g., gymnastics, diving, figure-skating, synchronized swimming) have "an intrinsic end which cannot be identified apart from the means" (3: p. 104). Consequently, in these aesthetic sports,[4] as contrasted with the purposive ones,[5] "the way in which the appropriate movements are performed is not incidental but central" (3: p. 104). He argues that while "it would make perfectly good sense to urge a football team to score goals without caring how they scored them" (3: p. 104), it would make no sense to urge a gymnast to perform a vault without caring *how* he or she did it. Not *any* way of getting over the box could count as even a bad vault, whereas "*any* way of getting the ball between the opponents' posts, as long as it is within the rules, would count as a goal, albeit a very clumsy or lucky one" (3: p. 105).

At first glance Best's argument appears sound: sport and art do seem to differ radically with respect to their means–end relationships. Goals in sport are identifiable apart from how they are accomplished. This is borne out by the frequency with which participants in and observers of sport appear to be more concerned with the fact *that* goals are scored rather than with *how* goals are scored. Alternatively, the "sadness" of a painting is indissolubly linked to the way it is expressed;

not only can it not be expressed in a better or even a different way, it cannot be understood or even identified apart from that way.

On closer inspection, however, I think it can be shown that the veracity of Best's argument is more apparent than actual. The "fundamental" differences between sport and art are not fundamental at all. Rather, they are simply and trivially a function of the equivocal way Best characterizes sport and art. If that can be demonstrated, groundless will be his claim that the aesthetic can be only incidental to most sports.

The plan is to first outline Best's "particularity thesis,"[6] a device he uses to demonstrate the particularity of response appropriate to works of art. Employing the same thesis, it will then be shown that many of Best's statements about sport and art are equivocal or misleading or both. More specifically, it will be demonstrated,

1. That under certain descriptions, art too can be characterized as "having an aim or purpose which can be identified independently of the way in which it is accomplished";
2. That Best's argument inappropriately equates "having an aim or purpose which can be identified independently of the way in which it is accomplished" with "having an external aim or purpose which it serves";
3. That Best understands goals only in the trivial sense and that this way of understanding is no more inappropriate for art than it is for sport;
4. That the claim "there are many ways to score a goal" is correct only in certain respects and that in those same respects similar claims can be made of art;
5. That Best's failure to realize all of the above is a function of his exclusive viewing of art in particular terms while equivocally viewing sport exclusively in general terms.

In the chapter "The Particularity of Feeling" in *Feeling and Reason in the Arts* (1), Best discusses a "general-particular" spectrum within which can be placed emotional responses to works of art and, for that matter, many other aspects of life:

> Emotions can be seen as forming a spectrum with at one extreme those feelings which are relatively undifferentiated and at the other those which are highly particular. Placing on the spectrum depends upon the variety of intentional objects, that is, the possible objects on to which typical behavior may be directed, and by which each such emotion is identified. (1: p. 141)

Best explains that feelings at the undifferentiated or general extreme of the spectrum may be identified in widely different ways because there are many different objects onto which the fear of, say, people or reptiles would be directed. In the middle of the spectrum the feelings are more particularized. That is, there are fewer possible objects of, for instance, the fears of aggressive people and snakes than the previous, more general, fears of people and reptiles (1: p. 141). At the most particular extreme of the spectrum, Best argues, the intentional object of the feeling can be but one:

> At the other extreme of the spectrum are those highly particularized feelings each of which can be experienced and identified in only one way. In the case of such a feeling it would make no sense to suggest that there could be another intentional object since, apart from its relation to *this particular object,* the emotion could not intelligibly be said to exist. An example might be fear of a particular person with a peculiarly sneering and sarcastic manner, or, more obviously, love or friendship for a particular person. In these cases the emotion is directed on to and is identified by only one object. (1: p. 141)

It is clear that Best wishes to place works of art at the most particular end of the spectrum. The sadness of Mozart's 40th Symphony, he argues, can be identified only by that piece of music: "to change the particular form of the expression, whether within the same artistic medium or into another, would be to change the object of the emotion, and consequently the emotion itself" (1: p. 142). Best makes similar claims elsewhere. For instance, he argues that the impossibility of expressing *King Lear* emotions in another play is a logical one, not a practical one: "it simply does not *make sense* to speak of expressing *King Lear* emotions in another play, since it is the language of that play which identified the emotions" (2: pp. 315-316). Elsewhere he claims,

> if anyone thought that the purpose of Picasso's Guernica could be expressed as "man's inhumanity to man," or "the horrors of war," or any such trite phrase, he or she would thereby reveal a failure to understand it. Such phrases *are* trite and commonplace. The work is not. (5: p. 36)

Yet virtually whenever Best advances this particularity claim with respect to art and what it expresses, he makes what I take to be a very important qualification which suggests that what is expressed in a work *can* be identified and understood (albeit generally) independently of the particular work. For instance, in countering Boxill's (7) position and arguing against the possibility of different works expressing the same thing, Best admits,

> In a very trivial sense, of course, that may be true. One could say that Tolstoy's *Father Sergius,* and Shakespeare's *King Lear* are expressing the same idea, namely that renunciation is not a form of self-interest. (5: p. 36)

While Best is careful to point out that such a characterization is decidedly inadequate, it is, as will be explained later, nevertheless *an* understanding of them, albeit a very general one. The qualification is made yet more forcibly:

> clearly the response to a work of art could be specified in a general way, for example as

"sad," or, according to the theme of the work, it could be specified with varying degrees of particularity. It could be placed at any point on the spectrum according to the way in which it is specified. That is, it will always be possible to redescribe a 'particular' response in more general terms. (1: p. 142)

Best argues that such an admission does not damage his thesis since, unlike many emotions characterized in general terms, such as the fear of snakes, responses to works of art will always be capable of specification at the particular extreme. Yet once again, that a work can be described as sad generally implies that what is expressed can be understood, albeit generally, apart from the work. And neither are such general descriptions as trivial, trite, commonplace, and heretical as Best makes out. If so, Best himself is guilty of an heresy of the highest order when he describes, in fairly general terms, an aspect of Beckett's play, *Not I*:

> The character in this play, of whom it is significant that only her mouth can be seen, pours out a stream of incidents which have happened to her during her life. She appears to be engaged in a desperate but vain search for the essence of what she is, or at least for some essential aspect of her life. Yet each of the incidents she recounts seems to be only *contingently* related to what she is, since it might not have happened to her, or it might have happened differently. This seems to leave her with nothing that is essential, and therefore with the despairing feeling that she has no identity. Thus she finds it confusing, abhorrent and terrifying to refer to herself in the first person. (2: p. 309)

But the heresy of heresies comes with Best's next statement: "Francis Bacon is, I think, making a similar point in his painting *An Accidental Being*." Both "heresies" are tacit admissions of precisely what Best denies! The first is a description of the meaning of a work, or at least part of that meaning, apart from the work itself. The second demonstrates that what is expressed (at the level of generality in which Best has described it) in one work *can* be expressed in another. It is clear that what has been described has been identified independently of both works. Having seen neither (to admit my ignorance), I nevertheless can understand the description to be a correct statement about the meaning of both. Of course it still could be argued that the description is trite, commonplace, and trivial, and so, consequently, must be my understanding of them. While I would argue to the contrary, such a claim is really beside the point. Of both works I now have *an* understanding—an understanding of their meaning which has been identified and described independently of them.

Best has consistently argued that complete identification of means and end is an important distinguishing feature of the concept of art. That claim can now be seen in a different light. While complete identification of means and end is necessary to a complete understanding of works of art, less particular characterizations and understandings of them are always possible as well. And, as the characterizations become more general, so that which is described as expressed (e.g., sadness) becomes more independently identifiable from the work, that is, from how it is expressed peculiarly by the work. So whether the aim, purpose, or meaning of a work of art can be identified independently of the way it is accomplished is not a function of the nature of an art work itself, as Best would argue, but rather is a function of the *way* it is described, particularly or generally. Described particularly, the sadness of the work cannot be understood nor even identified independently of the work. But under other levels of description, that is, general ones, the sadness can be identified independently of the work.

Best has been blinded by his *way* of looking. His overriding reluctance to view art in other than exclusively particular ways blinds him to the realization that under more general modes of description which, depending on our interest, are equally legitimate, what is expressed by a work can be identified and understood (albeit generally) apart from the work. This reluctance is only the first side of the two-sided fundamental equivocation to which I earlier alluded. Before that second facet is revealed, however, I would like to suggest how the reluctance just described may be the hidden cause behind Best's misconception that an object's "having an aim or purpose which can be identified independently of the way in which it is accomplished" is equivalent to the object's "having an external function or purpose it serves."

An examination of several statements by Best reveals he does assume such an entailment. For instance, he claims that "there are many sports, indeed the great majority, which are like the painting considered as an investment in that there is an aim or purpose which can be identified independently of the way it is accomplished" (3: p. 101).

Earlier, however, Best has made it quite clear that a painting considered as an investment is a paradigm case of considering something "in relation to some external function or purpose it serves" and of assessing it "in relation to an extrinsic end" (3: p. 101). Later when contrasting aesthetic and purposive sports, he implies the entailment by arguing that because aesthetic sports have means-end identity, they, unlike purpose sports, have an *intrinsic* end (3: p. 104). Absence of means-end identity in an object or event must then mean for Best that the object or event serves an extrinsic purpose.

Although it may be correct to claim that both paintings considered as investments and most sports (under certain descriptions—more on this later) have an aim or purpose which can be identified independently of the way it is accomplished, that does not necessarily mean that therefore both have or serve external aims or purposes. That can be true only if all instances of independently identifiable ends are instances of external ends. To be sure, many of the former are instances of the latter, as exemplified by the painting considered as an investment. But many are not, and I argue that sport (and art under certain descriptions) is just such a case.

My argument that the scoring of goals is not an external purpose of sport but rather an internal purpose within sport is virtually identical to Joseph Kupfer's (9; 10), and I am indebted to his precise formulation of it. Kupfer argues that the common overemphasis on scoring/winning as something somehow apart from the game is a result of a mistaken understanding of scoring/winning as *the purpose of* playing. The consequence of this mistake, he argues, is that the playing of games is devalued to the point at which it is viewed as merely a means to the attainment of the dominant end of scoring/winning. In an effort to explain this mistake, Kupfer employs the Kantian distinction between purpose and purposivity. Kupfer admits that art, purely purposive, may contain within it aims or purposes, and as such appear to have something in common with purposeful objects such as telephones and cars. But the critical difference is that in contrast to such purposeful objects, the purely purposive serves no external purpose. He concludes,

> The purely purposive then may include purposes within it without as a whole being subservient to any extrinsic purpose or end. Sport is like art in being purposive but without external purpose. (9: p. 204)

So, for Kupfer, scoring/winning are purposes to be sure, but purposes within sport and akin to such other internal purposes as " 'taking tricks' in bridge; singing a harmonic in a barbershop quartet; or achieving validity in an argument'' (9: p. 121).

Such internal purposes abound in art. Instances can be taken from Best's work itself. For example, in his attempt to distinguish between the aesthetic and the artistic, Best argues that a critical appreciation of a work such as Shakespeare's *Measure for Measure* might consider a number of questions relating to the characters of Angello and Isabella. For our purposes, principal among these are,

> whether their learning from their experiences is central to the play, or whether the inten-

> tion is rather that those reading or watching it should learn from the inability of the characters to recognize their own weaknesses. (1: p. 162)

Admittedly, the answer to the question of whether the intention is to have the readers learn from the inabilities of Angello and Isabella can be resolved only in terms of the play itself. But that is beside the point because it only shows the purpose is an internal one. The fact remains that such an intention, such a meaning, such a purpose, *can*, in an important sense and as Best has done, be identified apart from the way it is accomplished.

Best's failure to recognize the above can be seen as a result of his penchant to characterize art exclusively under the particular level of description which precludes the possibility of discovering an important counter-example to the common but facile conclusion that all instances of independently identifiable ends are instances of external ones.[7] In the absence of any important counter-examples, it is understandable to conclude that a newly discovered object or event (e.g., sport) that has an independently identifiable purpose (under certain descriptions) must be like all those other objects or events that also have independently identifiable purposes which are *external* to the object or event (e.g., paintings viewed as investments and social surveys). That is, if all known cases of X are also cases of Y, there is no good reason to believe that a newly discovered X is not simply just another instance of Y. But art, under certain descriptions, is the counter-example that renders suspect all such facile ''X, therefore Y'' judgments. Viewing it exclusively in particular terms blinds one to that discovery.

Of course, to show up the incorrectness of Best's apparent assumption that all independently identifiable purposes are external ones does not yet get sport off the hook. It has to be proven, not just claimed, that scoring/winning is not external. Once again Kupfer's work is helpful. He argues that sport is unlike common purposeful activities, such as shingling our roofs or taking medicine, which came into existence for the sake of keeping homes dry and restoring health, respectively. Without those prior desires there would be little reason to shingle or to take medicine. But it is ludicrous to suggest that the scoring of goals was the previously desired purpose for which the playing of sport was brought into existence. Prior to sport no one ever needed goals. Prior to basketball no one ever needed balls passing through netted hoops. Yet, not only can the scoring of goals not be the raison d'être of competitive sport but, unlike the purposes of shingling and taking medicine, it cannot be achieved by any other means:

> Practical purposes in the everyday, however, are independent of their means and are rightly said to be the purposes *of* their activities since they are attainable by some other means. The practical activity is itself subordinated to the goal as its instrument. There are other ways besides shingling of keeping homes dry, other ways of restoring health besides taking medicine. These just seem the best, given our circumstances, resources, and know-how. (9: p. 120)

But there are no ways of accomplishing the so-called "purpose" of basketball or baseball other than by playing basketball or baseball. We are always on the lookout for more effective, less costly ways of keeping homes dry and restoring health. But no one is thinking, "Basketball, as a means of getting balls through hoops, is decidedly ineffective. It is imperative that a more cost-effective strategy of getting more balls through hoops be devised." The reason for this is clear:

> Scoring is not an end which could be accomplished by some other avenue because what it *means* "to score" depends upon the particular kind of game being played. Obviously, scoring in tennis is defined by the structure of the game of tennis, and so on for the other sports. (9: p. 120)

It is now clear that scoring/winning is not a purpose external to sport. Whereas under certain descriptions scoring/winning can be identified independently of its means, it, unlike the externality of the appreciation in value of a painting considered as an investment, is not external to sport. But even if Best were to concede this along with the concession that under certain descriptions at least some works of art have independently identifiable but not external purposes, he might still wish to claim that the main thrust of his argument remains intact. That is, even if he does admit that scoring is not external to, say, hockey, because the rules of hockey define what it *means* to score, he may still wish to argue that within those rules there are many ways to score.[8] In other words, it might still be maintained that even if scoring can be viewed as an end or purpose within purposive sports, unlike art there remains an undeniable gap between the achievement of the internal end and the way in which it is achieved. Such a view is highly misleading, entails a trivial view of goals, and is generated by the following equivocation: viewing sport in exclusively general terms while viewing art in exclusively particular ones. We have already exposed the latter face of that equivocation. We can expose the former by examining Best's trivial conception of goals.

Although it is possible to view goals in hockey or soccer as simply the event that occurs precisely at the moment when the ball or puck passes into the net or over the crease, or a run in baseball as simply the event that occurs precisely at the moment when the runner's foot hits home plate, such an understanding of goals is trivial. Yet if Best's view of the place of goals in sport is correct, it is to this trivial understanding of them that we are restricted.

Obviously we do not often view goals in such an empty way. We know and wish to know so much more. Imagine what the video highlights of any game in any sport would be like if such a trivial understanding of goals were operative. We would see only so many pucks passing over creases, feet hitting plates, balls passing through hoops, falling into little holes, or landing in back of nets.

Such "highlights" would be decidedly uninteresting and over in seconds. We would feel cheated; we demand much more. Luckily, normal video highlights cater to those demands—they detail precisely *how* the goals were achieved. Admittedly there is no necessary connection between what is included in video highlights and the nature and place of goals in sport. Yet they do suggest an alternative, at least as legitimate, understanding of goals that includes much more than the trivial view depicted above. The passing of the puck over the crease or the ball through the hoop marks only the completion of a goal. In an important sense they begin much earlier and cannot be distinguished from all those elements directly and indirectly contributing to that completing moment.

How far back we go and how much we include is a function of our interest and the nature of the sport and goal in question. For instance, contrast a gridiron touchdown that is a dazzling runback of the opening kickoff with a ninth-inning, game-winning run in baseball that is the culmination of a full-count base-on balls, three close but unsuccessful attempted pickoffs, a full-count strikeout, another unsuccessful attempted pickoff, a stolen second base, a full-count sacrifice fly to left field with a missed tag at third, and a two-out full-count ground ball single just beyond the outstretched glove of a diving second baseman. And contrast both of the above with that sort of goal characteristic of such fluid games as hockey, soccer, basketball, and Australian Rules football, in which the scoring play seems to imperceptibly flow out of the play itself such that where and when we choose to pinpoint its beginning is fairly arbitrary.

Such nontrivial complete understandings of goals are examples of the inseparability of scoring and the play itself as explained by Kupfer:

As the culmination of play scoring helps determine its form and completeness. The scoring aspect of a play is not detachable from it in that the play is partially defined in terms of the success or failure in scoring. . . . The complete description of the play includes

whether or not it issues in scoring. But just as the play cannot be completely specified independent of scoring, neither can scoring be specified or identified independent of the play. (10: p. 356)

While Kupfer admits that the score, understood in a numerical sense, can be separated from the means employed, its independent specifiability is merely an abstraction from the way in which the goals were achieved. Scoring is not so independently identifiable (10: pp. 356-357).

To attempt to understand a goal as somehow separate from the way it is scored is no less inappropriate than is the attempt to understand the sadness of a work apart from the way that sadness is expressed. The description "that a goal was scored" tells us no more about *the* goal scored than does the description "sadness is expressed" tell us about *the* sadness expressed. Though useful in some situations depending on our interest, such descriptions are no more than trite, trivial, and commonplace understandings of *the* goal and *the* sadness, respectively. By describing art in exclusively particular terms, Best seeks to avoid those general and trivial accounts of the meaning of art works, the implication of which is the supposition that what is expressed in one work could be expressed in another. Such a supposition, Best argues, in an important sense reveals a failure to understand the nature of art. But the implication of Best's exclusively trivial account of goals is to suppose that one goal scored is the same as another goal scored. In that same important sense, such a supposition reveals a failure to understand the nature of sport.

We have at last come face to face with the second facet of Best's fundamental equivocation. He refuses, or at least fails, to describe goals in other than exclusively general terms. That refusal either entails or is entailed by his failure to recognize that goals can be particularly described and must be so described if our understanding of them is to be anything more than trivial. The equivocation can be clearly seen: Best describes art in exclusively particular terms, while he equivocally describes sport in exclusively general terms. With such an equivocation operative, it is little wonder that he sees radical differences between them. But *what* he sees has been determined by the *ways* he looks and in that sense is not there.

I would now like to discuss yet another manifestation of that equivocation, and in the process demonstrate further that the differences Best sees between sport and art are not so much a function of their radically different natures as he assumes but a function of the radically different ways he respectively views them. The manifestation in question is Best's (3: p. 103) claim that, ''in contrast to a work of art, . . . there are many ways of achieving the end, i.e., of scoring a goal, in hockey.'' Although the assertion that there are many ways to score a goal is true in certain respects, in those same respects similar and no less legitimate claims can be made of what is expressed in art.

Viewed particularly, there is only one way to paint the painting painted or express the sadness expressed: the constitutive way it was painted, the constitutive way it was expressed. Any change to any relevant aspect of the way the painting was painted or the sadness was expressed would produce a different painting, a different sadness. Yet because Best fails to apply this particular level of description to sport, he fails to realize that virtually the same can be said of goals scored. Viewed particularly in that nontrivial sense depicted above, there is only one way to score the goal scored: the constitutive way it was scored. Any change to any relevant aspect of the way the goal was scored would result in a correspondingly different goal.

To view goals generally is to separate them from the particulars that constitute them. So separated goals lose what makes them peculiar. One becomes the same as another. Viewed this way, it makes sense to claim there are many ways to score *a* goal. And so it is with art. To view expressions of sadness generally is to separate them from the particulars that constitute them. Separated expres-

sions of sadness lose what makes them peculiar. One becomes the same as another. Thus, it also makes sense to claim there are many ways to express sadness, represent Churchill, man's inhumanity to man and the horrors of war. The protest that such generalized accounts fail to capture the sadness expressed can be mounted just as legitimately on behalf of sport: such generalized accounts fail to capture *the*[9] goal scored. To deny that is to equivocate.

Therefore, Best's claim that there are many ways to score a goal in the purposive sports[10] but only one way to paint the painting can be seen as nothing more than an unfortunate manifestation of a fundamental equivocation. Viewed generally, there are just as many ways to express sadness as there are ways of scoring a goal; viewed particularly, there is only one way to express *the* sadness expressed or score *the* goal scored. Once the equivocation is righted, the differences vanish.

One loose end remains. It might be objected that while the above particularized account of goals may be a legitimate way of viewing them, its occurrence is rare; most players and fans don't really care how goals are scored as long as they *are* scored. In contrast, the argument would claim, the parallel generalized account ''that sadness is expressed'' is relatively unimportant to most artists and viewers of art. For the sake of simplification, this objection will be discussed in two parts: the comparison of the relationships fans and observers of art have to sport and art works, respectively, followed by a similar comparison of athletes and artists.

The claim that most fans don't really care *how* goals are scored but rather *that* goals are scored not only belies the fact of our interest in the detailed depiction of scoring plays as catered to in video highlights, but is more of sociological than philosophical interest. Even if such a claim is correct, and it certainly is not clear that it is, there is no necessary connection between the way something is most often viewed and the nature of the thing itself. Kupfer argues that it may be the case that most observers of sport are as jaded in their appreciation of it as are art dealers who evaluate works of art exclusively in terms of their market value. Nevertheless, we should not "appeal to the priorities of . . . typical audiences to determine the place of scoring or winning within the logic of sport" (10: p. 357).

We need not go to the extreme of jaded art dealers to find parallels in art. They—like those who view works exclusively in such terms as a hedge against inflation, as a means of tying together the disparate colors within a room, or as a means of filling blank or ugly walls—miss or ignore the meaning of those works altogether. I would like to demonstrate that parallels to the common importance of "*that* a goal is scored" in sport can be found in art but which, unlike the examples given above, involve an understanding of the meaning of the work in such a way that, due to the interest operative, the meaning is appreciated at a high level of generality such that, for instance, "*that* sadness is expressed" is more important than *how* it is expressed. Novels, poems, plays, and movies, for instance, are often employed as aids in the teaching and discussion of moral issues. If the issue to be discussed, for instance, is "man's inhumanity to man," those responsible for selecting the works to be employed may be much more interested in *that* the issue is expressed by the works than in *how* it is expressed. Or, to choose an example from Best, if the issue to be discussed is "why people should be cognizant of their own weaknesses," one might choose, among others, Shakespeare's *Measure for Measure*, being more concerned with *that* it expresses the idea than with *how* it does it. Similarly, the principle concern of those in libraries and museums who classify works on the basis of subject matter is whether "such and such" is expressed, represented, or discussed and not the intricacies of how that is done.

In all these cases the interest in the works' meanings is at a more general level. Admittedly, if the interest remains at that level we might think it unfortunate because so much will be missed. And just as we should not let the jaded interest of so-called "typical" fans determine the place of scor-

ing within the logic of sport, we would not let such generalized, and in that sense trivial, accounts determine the place of meaning within the arts. There is so much more to be seen, known, and appreciated.

Turning now to the producers of those goals and works, I argue that, similar to those athletes who sometimes value "that a goal is scored" more than how it is scored, some artists, at least sometimes, are more concerned with, for example, *that* a painting is painted or sadness or beauty expressed rather than with how it is accomplished. Ironically, Best provides the backdrop for an example of such:

It has been said, with some justification, that beauty is what the bourgeoisie pays the artist for, that is, that he or she has to take time off from serious art in order to produce beauty for a living. (5: p. 35)

Faced with the threat of eviction from an irate landlord for his failure to pay the last 2 months' rent, a down-and-out painter who normally prides himself in not pandering to the common taste may come to the grim realization that he'd better paint something that sells. Knowing that beautiful (but dreary!) "works" recently have been selling like hotcakes down at the local flea market, he might exhort himself thus: "Look, I don't care how you do it, you've just got to get in that damn studio and paint some paintings that are beautiful." Viewed from that perspective, once they are painted, *that* they are beautiful will be their mark of success.

Such sacrifices of "how" for "that," I would argue, are fairly typical in the arts. Yet I would not want to argue, as Best has done with sport, that such sacrifices reflect the true nature of art even though it would be no less legitimate to do so. Certainly there are times when many, perhaps most, athletes will take any goal they can get and show little concern for how it is achieved. But just as our proud artist above could take little pride in his beautiful paintings, little pride can be taken in the scoring of such goals. Most artists and athletes most of the time care very much for the *how* of it, for it is only through such a concern that their true prowess can be realized and displayed.

In summary, it has been shown that under an unequivocal application of the general mode of description, both sport and art can be characterized as having respective aims or purposes that can be identified independently of the way they are accomplished without it being entailed that those ends or purposes are external. Concomitantly, the claim "there are many ways to score a goal" is correct, but no more correct than the claim "there are many ways to express sadness." It was also revealed that this general mode can produce nothing but equally trivial, trite, and commonplace accounts of goals and that which is expressed or represented by a work of art. Since Best's view of goals is restricted to this level, it was shown to be a trivial one.

An unequivocal application of the particular mode or level of description to both sport and art revealed that just as *the* sadness expressed by a work cannot be identified or understood apart from the way it is expressed, neither can *the* goal scored be identified or understood apart from the particular way it was scored. It was shown that, in that important sense, not only is there only one way to paint *the* painting painted or express *the* sadness expressed, but only one way to score *the* goal—*the* way they were painted, expressed, or scored. And just as it was accepted that under the particular mode of description a failure to understand the above reveals a failure to understand the nature of art, it was argued that Best fails to understand the nature of goals as constituted by and unidentifiable apart from their particulars.

Best has told the truth, but only half of it. What he says of art is correct but misleading in that its correctness is a function of the application of a certain mode of description: the particular mode. The application of the general mode of art reveals a much different picture—a picture Best fails to see and is unable to describe. Most of what he says

of sport is also correct but, once again, correct only with the context of a limited way of looking: the general way. His failure to view them particularly has blinded him to their other side, a side that is not dissimilar to art particularly described.

Best has strongly and consistently maintained that the differences between sport and art with respect to their relationship with the aesthetic is a consequence of their fundamentally different natures in terms of form–content, means–end identity. It has been shown, however, that those "fundamental" means–end identity differences are simply and trivially the result of an equivocal application of radically different modes of description to sport and art. Once the equivocation is righted, the "differences" evaporate.

In conclusion, although there still may be substantial differences between sport and art in their relationship to the aesthetic, they cannot be for the reasons Best gives us. Although this paper contributes little to the advancement of a systematic theory of the sport aesthetic, it at least removes a major obstacle to the successful advancement of any such theory.

Notes

1. A subsequent paper will attempt to counter Best's second argument that, unlike all art forms, no sport forms have the capacity to express a conception of life situations.

2. Since nowhere is there any indication to the contrary, I have assumed that Best understands the position he advances in all his works discussed here (1; 3; 4; 5; 6) to be a consistent whole. Consequently, my discussion of his position frequently jumps from one work to another.

3. While it is sometimes referred to by Best as a difference between sport and the aesthetic, I think the difference he advocates is more fundamentally and properly a difference between sport and art.

4. Best argues that the gap between means and end is never completely closed in the aesthetic sports because they have an externally identifiable aim (e.g., in gymnastics, the requirements set by each particular movement) to which the performances must conform if they are to be successful.

5. Since my argument is with Best's position, and since the "aesthetic" sports are immune to that position, unless otherwise indicated all future uses of "sport" or "sports" are references to the "purposive" sports.

6. Although Best employs this term only in "Logic, Particularity and Art" (2), where he discusses it fully, it is operative in a less detailed way in his other works.

7. It is difficult to guess which came first. Either his exclusively particular treatment of sport has blinded him to the realization that art, under the general level of description, provides an important counter-example to the claim that all independently identifiable purposes are external ones, *or*, for fear that otherwise art could be characterized as having an external purpose, his assumption that all independently identifiable purposes are external ones has led him to describe art in exclusively particular terms. Either way, the result is the same.

8. While he has never admitted that scoring is internal to sport, he has always maintained that those many ways in which a goal can be scored must be understood as within the rules (e.g., 3: pp. 101, 103).

9. Note the importance of the definite article here. While there are many ways to score *a* goal, there's only one way to score *the* goal. Best (1: p. 144) makes a similar point elsewhere.

10. With respect to this issue, the purposive sports may have a closer affinity with the arts than do the aesthetic sports. Just as "the poet may take liberties with the sonnet form without necessarily detracting from the quality of the sonnet" (3: p. 106), athletes in most "purposive" sports may take liberties with established conventions of style and strategy without necessarily detracting from the quality of performance. Contrastingly, as Best points out, "if the gymnast deviates from the requirements of, for instance, a vault, however gracefully, then that inevitably does detract from the standard of performance" (3: p. 106). So while the ways to score goals, express sadness, and perform a particular vault are infinite, the range of infinity of the last is more restricted. Related to this is the "aesthetic" sports' peculiarity of having a built-in standard of perfection such that a performed dive or vault can be said to be perfect. The same sense of perfect doesn't seem to operate in art or the "purposive" sports; in that sense there are no perfect expressions of sadness or perfect goals. These issues need further examination.

Bibliography

1. Best, David. *Feeling and Reason in the Arts*. London: George Allen and Unwin, 1985.
2. Best, David. "Logic, Particularity and Art." *British Journal of Aesthetics*, 23 (1983), 306-318.
3. Best, David. *Philosophy and Human Movement*. London: George Allen and Unwin, 1978.
4. Best, David. "The Aesthetic in Sport." *British Journal of Aesthetics* (1974), 197-221.
5. Best, David. "Sport is Not Art." *Journal of the Philosophy of Sport*, XII (1985), 25-40.
6. Best, David. "Sport is Not Art: Professor Wertz's Aunt Sally." *Journal of Aesthetic Education*, 20 (1986), 95-98.

7. Boxill, J.M. "Beauty, Sport, and Gender." *Journal of the Philosophy of Sport,* XI (1984), 36-47.

8. Goodman, Nelson. *Ways of Worldmaking.* Indianapolis: Hackett Publ., 1978.

9. Kupfer, Joseph H. *Experience as Art.* Albany: State University of New York Press, 1983.

10. Kupfer, Joseph H. "Purpose and Beauty in Sport." *Sport and the Body: A Philosophical Symposium. Second Edition.* Edited by Ellen W. Gerber and William J. Morgan. Philadelphia: Lea & Febiger, 1979.

Beauty, Sport, and Gender

J.M. Boxill

With a head fake to the right, Dr. J takes a long stride left toward the basket, glides upward from his left foot, is airborne with the basketball high over his head, and in one fluid motion slams the ball through the hoop. It is the human body at its best, operating against obstacles set by nature and obstacles artificially created. It is the ultimate one-on-one move at its most beautiful.

Kareem Abdul-Jabbar receives a pass at the low post and is quickly double-teamed. With a pass fake, he takes a drop step toward the basket, holds the ball high over his head, and in one flowing movement lets go a "sky hook." This is Kareem's "patented" shot; it is the hook shot as only Kareem can do it. There is no question that these movements have great aesthetic value. But can we thereby conclude that they are art? A bird in flight, a beautiful sunset, a beautiful waterfall—these have aesthetic value, but we do not thereby conclude they are art. Louis Reid (3: p. 249) maintains that "many movements in games or athletics or gymnastics have great positive aesthetic value; but it is wrong to jump to the conclusion that they are *art*, any more than the flight of a bird is art."

In a similar vein, David Best (1: p. 211) maintains that, "The aesthetic applies, for instance . . . to sunsets, bird song and mountain ranges, whereas the artistic is limited, at least in its central uses, to artifacts and performances intentionally created by man." And Paul Ziff (4: p. 45) maintains that "mechanical efficiency may or may not be aesthetic but such efficiency is not intended by the athlete to be beautiful. A lack of intention to be beautiful thereby disqualifies sport as potentially aesthetic."

These positions resist the idea that sport can be an art form. However, there are those of us who wish to place sport in the realm of art. Perhaps one of the boldest positions is set out by C.L.R. James in *Beyond a Boundary* (2). The book deals specifically with cricket, but can be extended to all sports. "The aestheticians," he says, "have scorned to take notice of popular sports and games—to their own detriment. The aridity and confusion . . . will continue until they include organized games and the people who watch them as an integral part of their data" (2: p. 192).

Thus, that sport is an art form is not a new idea. So why another paper? Because I think my position differs from the others—it answers the critics and goes beyond. To establish my position, I must answer those critics. Ziff, Best, and Reid maintain that certain features that are essential to sport preclude its consideration as an art form or an aesthetic experience. They grant that there may be aesthetic qualities to sports and games, but these are only by-products. As Reid (3: p. 252) puts it, "The aesthetic qualities of games and sports are by-products. . . . They can be important and precious by-products, but by-products they are none the less."

The main features which are claimed to keep sport outside the realm of art are these:

Reprinted from *Journal of the Philosophy of Sport*, XI, (1984), pp. 36–47. Copyright 1985 by the Philosophic Society for the Study of Sport. Reprinted by permission.

1. The concern for skill in the form of technical efficiency overshadows the essential art ingredients of style, grace, and form.
2. The strong desire for victory in competitive sports overshadows the aim of beauty.
3. Even if one of the aims of sport is beauty, it is not the sole aim.
4. Finally, even when athletes aim at beauty, they are not consciously making any statement about the human condition.

So, given these features that appear to be undeniable, why try to elevate sport beyond its simple importance as a source of pleasure and meaning to its millions of participants and spectators? Why indeed? Because it is precisely these aesthetic qualities that account for the pleasure and meaning of sports to its participants and spectators. If "elevating" it is what I am doing, then so be it; I simply aim to place sport in its proper position.

I will contest each of the reasons for claiming that sport is not art. I will argue that the concern for efficiency in sport is paralleled by a concern for efficiency in the acknowledged art form, and in neither case does it overshadow the concern for beauty; that similarly the desire for victory in competitive sport does not necessarily overshadow the concern for beauty; that even if beauty is not the sole aim of sport, neither is it the sole aim in the acknowledged art forms; and finally, that it is a false assumption that sport makes no statement about the human condition. More positively I will argue that just as art is self-expression, so too is sport; that in both art and sport, self-expression is hampered by a lack of skill; and finally, that sport is as valid a means of self-expression for women as it is for men.

For various, mostly false, reasons, women have been denied access to the single most available means of self-expression. In referring to beauty in relationship to women, it is usually referred to in terms of women as objects of beauty, not as creators of beauty. Women's bodies were deemed aesthetic in themselves, and to be viewed in the same way as any other object of natural beauty. To go beyond this "natural beauty," and to create beauty is to destroy the female-feminine object of beauty.

"Feminine" beauty can be retained only in such art forms as dance or in the "form" sports such as gymnastics, swimming, and diving. The other so-called "masculine" sports destroy feminine bodies; they present dangers to the female body. But many of these form sports are not available or suitable to all women and, as a result, a great many women have had no vehicle for self-expression. Hence, in establishing that sport is an art form, I further maintain that just as sport provides a vehicle for self-expression in men, it too provides a vehicle for women. Indeed, sport is the single most available means of self-expression for both men and women.

I

Let me now examine the interrelationships among skill, technical efficiency, and beauty in sport and in art. Nobody denies that skill and technical efficiency are necessary to sport. In order to play any game well, one must develop to a certain skill level. Fledgling athletes look clumsy and perform clumsily because their bodies are developing, and they are just beginning to learn the skills. Basketball is a sport that exhibits clearly the athlete's developmental process from its beginnings to the level attained by Dr. J or Abdul-Jabbar. It also illustrates the position I hold regarding women in sports.

Basketball played at the junior high level—boys or girls—is painful to watch. Most of the players are not in tune with their bodies, and their coordination level is low. As a result, their skill level is low. They are playing an "adult" game with a regulation-size ball at a regulation height, and getting the ball down court and making a basket are major accomplishments. There is little strategy, pattern, or style in the game at this level. At the high school level, the coordination and technique are beginning to commensurate with the skill necessary for aesthetic appeal. Of course, some players are significantly better than others, and this is true for both boys and girls. But because of size differential, the boys develop more of the skills necessary for aesthetic appeal. Further, the boys' training at this level is much more intensified than the girls', whose lack of training also contributes to a lower skill level. It has certainly improved over the years, but a deficit still remains.

At the college level the skills are more finely tuned and a high efficiency level is reached. Athletes at this level of skill begin to improvise and add personal style to the game, which then becomes their "signature." These additions are impossible without the requisite mastery of basic techniques. For only when the basics are mastered as the skill is performed efficiently, with the least expenditure of resources, can a performer aim at beauty or make an aesthetic response. At this level of efficiency the acquisition and improvement of technical skill are no longer ends in themselves: Here the performer as athlete aims at beauty.

As basketball is played today, at least, the skill, accuracy, and grace displayed by males are superior to those displayed by women. This is why spectators usually prefer to watch men play rather than women. Even though women can be graceful, add a basketball and a different kind of grace is required. To see what the human body can do with a round ball and hoop is often awe-inspiring. What Dr. J, Kareem Abdul-Jabbar, and James Worthy can do with a basketball is breathtaking.

The women are only beginning to display this type of bodily excellence. It is interesting to note that beginning with the 1984–85 season the collegiate women will be using a smaller ball—although the same height hoop. This, in my opinion, will enhance the skill level, because hand size is very important in basketball. Players with small hands have difficulty handling the ball; the larger the hands, the better the control. Obviously, women have smaller hands, so their ball control

is less proficient than men's. For most women dunking is impossible even if they can jump high enough; they need to be able to "palm" the ball with ease. Only a few women can do this. Most men can, however, and this is a significant factor in developing a high skill level.

In gymnastics there is little difference between skill levels for men and women. However, there are significant differences in their performances. The women perform on uneven parallel bars and a balance beam, whereas the men perform on even parallels, rings, and a high bar. The skills required are different, and men and women both display bodily excellence at high skill levels. The women's events generally emphasize the qualities of flexibility, coordination, and grace. The men's events emphasize other qualities such as strength and agility. While both men and women do floor exercises, the performances differ. Nevertheless, a high level of skill and efficiency is still required for a performer to aim at beauty or make an aesthetic response in the audience. And, the aesthetic response is greater in those who understand and appreciate the intricacies of this sport as well as others. Gymnastics is also a sport in which efficiency and beauty are inseparable. There is a streamlining which is itself beautiful. Other examples of this are ski-jumping, high-jumping, and pole-vaulting. Of these, it is hard to say that efficiency is the sole aim, since to be efficient is to be beautiful. In other cases such as basketball, once efficiency is attained, style is added where the aim is beauty.

All of what I have said about the relation between efficiency and beauty in sport may be applied to the relation between the two in art. Just as in sport, it is undeniable that skill and technical expertise are important in the acknowledged arts, for example, music, painting, and dance. Does this preclude their being art? Clearly, skill and technical expertise are as necessary to art as they are to sport.

It can scarcely be said that a musician's performance which lacks technical efficiency or skill has aesthetic appeal. We suffer through our children's piano recitals, dance recitals, art shows, and beginning orchestra concerts. Some display a certain potential. We see a *potential* for aesthetic appeal, but the lack of skill or techniques renders any aesthetic appeal slim. (This is not to say, of course, that the "young artists" themselves do not have an aesthetic experience). We attend these events out of loyalty or parental pride, not for any aesthetic appeal. Only when a certain skill level is attained can there be an aesthetically beautiful performance. At first the concern is mastering basics and achieving a skill level; in playing an instrument, for example, hitting the right note is the primary concern, then hitting the right notes in a certain pattern and speed. Only when this is achieved can style be considered and only then can there be any aesthetic appeal. There is no wasted energy, no superfluous movement.

In literature, the writer's end is to express a certain thought. The resultant writing is efficient if the thought is expressed with no waste of words; every word counts in that each says something. The end result is beautiful precisely because it is efficient. Verbosity is not efficient, nor is it beautiful. In music the connection between beauty and efficiency may not be quite as strong. When playing a composition efficiently, you waste no energy; now you can begin to add style and grace in trying to produce the aesthetically pleasing rendition. Efficiency and beauty may not be identical, but efficiency is necessary for the beautiful. Thus, in art there is a definite and important relation between efficiency and beauty. In some cases they too are inseparable, and in others efficiency is as necessary a condition as beauty.

Thus the development of technique, skill, and efficiency is as important to acknowledged art forms as it is in sports. This development in sport parallels that of art, and I conclude that, contrary to Ziff (4), it cannot be the case that concern for technical efficiency overshadows the essential art ingredients. Indeed, skill and technical efficiency are necessary to these ingredients. Thus this first feature does not preclude sport from being an art form.

II

The argument in Section I establishes a parallel between sport and art with respect to efficiency and beauty, but it is not enough to show that sport is an art form. There are still many respects in which sport fails to parallel the acknowledged art forms. One of these is the strong desire for victory in sports. This has no parallel in other art forms, and this, it is argued, excludes sport from the realm of art. It is allowed that there may be some aesthetic appeal to these sports whose main concern is victory, but if there is any it is a by-product, or is incidental to the sport and is subordinate to the main purpose of victory. As "proof" of this claim, Best (1: p. 201) poses this question to a player: "Which would you prefer, to score 3 goals in a clumsy manner, or to miss them all with graceful movements?" The answer, he feels, is obvious.

Let's pose a similar question to a musician performing Beethoven's Fifth at a recital: Which would you prefer—to hit right notes awkwardly or hit the wrong notes smoothly? Let's ask the gymnast at a competition a similar question: Which would you prefer—to perform a double flip with a half-twist clumsily, or a simple walk-over with graceful movements? Are the answers obvious? No, the answers aren't obvious in any of these cases including Best's. In posing the question to begin with, he is assuming the peculiar psychology of winning at all costs, and that is a bold assumption for this is not always the case. Most assuredly the desire for victory is strong in every competitive event, yet that is not the only object. Some athletes would prefer to lose with a well played performance than win in a lousy performance. Some coaches would rather that their teams lose through a well played game than win by a fluke or with a lousy game. Where the well played game is stressed, victory takes a back seat. Where winning at all costs is stressed, the well played game is secondary. This is especially true where victory is tied to money or some other external aim.

But, let's take some examples: In basketball, except for the pros, men's basketball allows for a stall game. This maneuver allows weaker teams to compete with stronger teams at a more even level. Now some coaches use it to win and some shun it in favor of a well played game which attempts to display bodily excellence. This same holds true for athletes. Some want to play the stall game to go for the win, and some would prefer to display their skills with style with the possibility of losing. Of course, a stall game can demonstrate its own elements of style! Often, however, the stall is justified because of the diverse skill levels of teams, so that a lesser skilled team is not made to look bad by a more highly skilled team. In the pros, where the level of skill is the highest, a 24-second clock precludes any stall. Interestingly, in college women's basketball, there is a 30-second clock to prevent the "boring," usually unaesthetic, stall-game.

In basketball someone must win; that is a feature of the rules. However, not every player or coach aims solely at winning. What about cases in which, say, Larry Bird puts up an awkward shot at mid-court to win and it goes in? Would he not prefer that to losing with a "beautiful" attempt? First of all, this is only one shot out of an entire game, a game which requires great efficiency. For the entire game to come down to this one shot, both teams must have performed well and displayed a great amount of bodily excellence. And second, to be able to make that shot, a player must have prior skill. It is a one-in-a-million shot! Yet is this any different from, say, a painter who tries some new technique or medium that might fail or might achieve just the expression he wanted in the painting? Both show great skill.

Let me illustrate with another example that the answer to Best's question is not obvious. Let us say that USC is playing UCLA in football, the score is 21–18 in favor of UCLA, and USC has the ball on UCLA's 35-yard-line with 30 seconds to go in the game. The options are to go for the tie with a field goal or to go for a win with a touchdown. Now some coaches and players would go for the win and perhaps lose, and others would prefer not to lose and go for the tie. The point is, a well played game that is aesthetically pleasing is often the primary aim and is preferred to winning "at all costs." Thus, I do not believe Best's question has the obvious answer that he believes it does.

There are further confusions in the question and the conclusion he draws from it. Granted, many differences exist in sport and acknowledged art forms. But there are also a great many differences among acknowledged art forms themselves. What accounts for many of these differences is the medium through which the art is displayed. The medium provides the vehicle for self-expression. The abilities and skills required are also very different for each. Dance requires tremendous bodily strength, coordination, and grace. Instrumental music requires a good ear and finger dexterity. Sculpture demands artistic hands, good visual perception, and a steady hand. Poetry requires a tremendous facility with words. And as I said earlier, a definite skill level is necessary if the works are to produce an aesthetic response. In fact, if there is an aesthetic response, we assume a high level of skill.

The more we understand the more we appreciate the difficulties and intricacies involved that enhance the aesthetic response. Further, certain restrictions within the chosen media provide a specific discipline within the various art forms. These serve to enhance the art itself. For example, a sonnet puts limits on the number of lines; there is great flexibility within this form, but to be able to express oneself effectively within the framework of the sonnet the poet must possess great skill to produce a work of art that is aesthetically pleasing.

Now, the medium for sports is competition—competition involving people against people, as in games, competition involving people against nature, as in mountain climbing, and competition involving people and animals against other people and animals, as in equestrian events or horse racing. But critical to the competition is victory: In most cases someone must win and someone must lose.

A significant feature of the competitive games is the set of rules that define the game and the process of victory. These rules can be very strict, as in basketball, football, soccer, or baseball, yet they allow for much creativity and provide a vehicle for self-expression. The rules are so designed as to require bodily excellence, to provide a vehicle to display beauty. The rules provide a discipline in which skill and efficiency are required, not simply brute strength and size.

In sports requiring only brute strength or size, there is limited spectator appeal, which is part of the reason why rules are made or revised—to reward spectator appeal (i.e., aesthetic appeal). Some rules may be added or revised for safety reasons, but most are revised to ensure technical skill or bodily excellence over mere strength and size, which I argue increases aesthetic appeal and thus spectator appeal. This is done in various ways. The aesthetic response is best when two teams are somewhat evenly matched, where each team is challenged and the outcome is not a foregone conclusion; so rules are revised to try to bring about this situation. But in every one of these revisions the concern is always for bodily excellence. For example, the 3-second lane in basketball was widened to prevent a 7-footer from just standing next to the basket waiting for a lob pass inside. We still have the lob pass inside, but either it has to be one move around a defender, which requires timing, coordination, and accuracy, or it requires a move or shot away from the basket. The rule designers are well aware of this; they are deliberately establishing a challenge, and it is this challenge which forces bodily excellence that produces an aesthetic response and an aesthetic experience.

As stated in Section I, the player's first concern is getting the basics mastered and/or figuring out a shot selection. However, once this is done, he or she is concerned with style, with aesthetics. Dr. J doesn't simply score—he does it with style, with a fluid, graceful style and often with a flourish to enhance the beauty of the movement. Abdul-Jabbar adds style to a normal hook shot; he is challenged, and these challenges provide opportunities for his patented sky-hook.

One may object that the player's concern is still for efficiency; that is, what is the most efficient way of scoring, dribbling, catching, or batting? This is true enough. But the most efficient method is usually one that displays bodily excellence and exhibits the body in harmony with the equipment and/or the factors of nature. When the body is moving efficiently, it displays a fluidity and grace that is its beauty. The running of Emil Zapotek was not aesthetically pleasing even though he won; but this doesn't undermine the aesthetics of sport. At the time of his victories little was known about bodily efficiency; as more technical knowledge was gained, runners were trained to get the body moving efficiently. The greater the efficiency, the more it approaches the aesthetics of the body, to a point at which efficiency and beauty fuse into one. This is demonstrated by the grace, beauty, and efficiency of athletes like Mary Decker, Wilma Rudolph, Francie LaRue, Sebastian Coe, Evelyn Ashford, and Greg Scott. It is repeated in swimming, where efficiency and beauty fuse into one. Mark Spitz displayed this beautifully; Mary T. Meager displays it now in her record-breaking butterfly events. As swum by Tracy Caulkins, the breaststroke achieves a high level of aesthetic appeal.

Now there is a further confusion by Best. He says that in sport the aim is victory. We have seen that this is not necessarily true for the player. But it is necessarily false for the designer of the game, who aims at designing the rules so that skill becomes a necessary condition for beauty. Continual changes in the game are made to rule out victory of the unskilled, that is, the unbeautiful. Thus, even if the player is concerned with efficiency, this must be within the discipline of the rules designed to bring out the beautiful. The designers of the rules have little concern for efficiency and can have no concern with victory; the designers' main concern is spectator appeal (i.e., aesthetic appeal), an appeal that requires and enhances bodily excellence.

There is also an intermediary—the coach (the choreographer). The coach's job is to harmonize the players in accordance with the game design. Players must be coached to play their parts, much as the director of a play must coach the actors to play their parts. He or she does this by ''walking through'' and by breaking the pattern into segments and drilling these separately, much as a music conductor breaks a composition into bars. Then the coach puts all the parts together in harmony. Each player must attain a complementary level of skill, and when it looks good it leads to success. The coach sets the tone and plays a significant part in determining the style of play. Only when there is harmony can there be beauty.

Without a doubt, some coaches aim at winning at all costs; others aim at a well played game. Generally, a well played game achieves victory but this is not always the case. One thing is sure though: A well played game that is aesthetically pleasing can only take place in competition that involves a desire to win. Without the desire to win, there is a lack of concentration and of artistic performance. A mediocre performance seldom portrays beauty in any art form. The desire to be good, and in the context of competitive games the desire for victory, does not subordinate aesthetics; it often enhances it. And in some cases this is necessary for beauty to emerge. The desire for victory is not necessarily a desire to win at any cost. The desire for a well played, aesthetically pleasing game need not be subordinate to the desire for victory.

III

The third feature claimed to exclude sport from art allows that beauty can be an aim of an athlete, but not the sole aim. But is beauty the *sole* aim of the artists in the acknowledged art forms? Does not the poet or novelist aim at getting a point across? May not the composer of musical compositions want to reflect a social situation? May not the artist in his or her painting aim at expressing an idea, however commonplace or trite? Best (1: p. 200) does not deny this, but maintains that these ends cannot be identified apart from the

manner of achieving them. The end is inseparable from the means of achieving it. In sport, in particular competitive sports, the end can be specified independently of the manner of achieving it *as long as it conforms to the rules of the game* (1: p. 201, emphasis mine). In other words, there are very many ways of achieving the desired end, and the various means do not affect or change the end.

In art, however, ''there cannot be a change of form of expression without a corresponding change in what is expressed'' (1: p. 200). Does Best mean by this that a work of art cannot be improved, that any attempt to rework a piece is itself a different piece altogether? There are different versions of *The Rubiyat*; when A.E. Houseman's notes were examined, different versions of the same poem were found, indicating an attempt to rework and improve the one poem. Yet are they different versions or are they different works altogether? According to Best, they would be different works, with each expressing something different. However, I doubt if that was Houseman's feeling. He was trying to improve the original; the message was the same. He was merely trying to convey it in the most beautiful, most effective manner. Now it may be that all the early versions conveyed the same message, but the final version did so in the most vivid and most beautiful way.

To illustrate his point, Best (1: p. 200) showed a disanalogy between a social survey report and a work of art. The report is evaluated by how effectively it conveys the information, whereas this would be irrelevant to the *aesthetic* judgment of a novel. In a report, however, the aim is to convey the information most effectively where the appeal is intellectual, where the information is set out logically, and where logical conclusions may be drawn. Style may be important if it makes a stronger appeal to the intellect, that is, if it makes the information more understandable. Thus, the sole aim is conveying the information. In a work of art there is more. The artist wishes to convey a message not by an appeal to our intellect but by an appeal to our emotions or our sense of beauty. And this is the aim of the aesthetic. The artist uses beauty to get his or her message across. This is why it takes less time to write a report on social conditions than to write a novel expressing the social conditions. The artist is not simply concerned with beauty; if he or she were, then while he/she may reflect aspects of life situations, he/she would not consciously be making any statement about the human condition.

Thus, the sole aim of the artist is not beauty; he or she wants to express something as well—not just in *any* way—only in a beautiful way. But he/she wants to express it nonetheless. The artist may in addition want to sell his/her works. Does this make it any less art?

Now, I agree that when the athlete's aim is beauty it is not the sole aim. The athlete wants to win, not necessarily in *any* way, but in a way that displays his or her skill and bodily excellence. The athlete in this sense uses beauty to achieve his or her goals, much as the artist does. The rules of the game play a significant part here as they are designed to bring out bodily excellence, that is, the aesthetic performance. Obviously, sometimes victory is achieved in a nonaesthetic way, and sometimes this is not satisfying to either the athletes or the spectators. After a successful defense of his title, former boxing champion Johnny Bumphus was quoted as saying that although he won, he was not at all satisfied with his performance because it was not artistic.

Thus, I believe I have shown that while athletes may aim at beauty, it is not the sole aim, nor is it the sole aim of the artist. In both cases, beauty is not only an aim in itself but also a means to achieve some other aim; for the artist it is a means of self-expression; for the athlete it is a means to victory and in this may also be a means to self-expression.

IV

The feature that Best feels clearly excludes sport from art is that art forms are limited to artifacts or performances intentionally created by humans in which there is at least the possibility of a close involvement with life situations.

The novels of Charles Dickens express the social conditions of the England of his time. Beethoven's Fifth Symphony expresses the awesomeness of death. Dylan Thomas in "Poem to his Father" expresses a defiance of death. These are all creations by men which definitely involve life situations. Then there are dramatic plays. For example, in *Cyrano de Bergerac*, Rostand is clearly making a statement about love; it is also the old theme of beauty and the beast. Just as Cyrano uses Christian in the play to express his love for Roxanne, Rostand uses the characters to express his theme. The actors who play the various roles are not themselves consciously making the statement, but through their self-expressions put together as a whole, the statement is conveyed to the audience.

The play is the vehicle for the theme of love; it is also the vehicle for self-expression by the actors. To successfully portray Cyrano, the actor must put a lot of himself into the role. It must be played with style; it cannot simply be a speaking of words. It can be played successfully in many personal styles, but it cannot be played by everyone. This style is the actor's self-expression—his way of achieving an aesthetic experience. He wants to make the part of Cyrano believable, and he wants it to be beautiful. The combined contributions of the playwright and the actor account for the aesthetic experience. It is especially so when his performance has evoked an aesthetic response from his viewers. In this, let it be remembered that the performer is not consciously making a statement about love, although through his self-expression he portrays or reflects the statement of the playwright.

I maintain there is a parallel situation in sports. In Section II I made a distinction between the designer and the performer, and there is this same distinction in plays, as already shown. In competitive sports there is no question that the games themselves are intentional creations of the human being. Like art in general, they are spawned from leisure. But they are not simply play activities;

they are artificially created, rule-governed activities set apart from the work-a-day world, and they have their own boundaries in time, and space. The rules and boundaries vary in restrictiveness. Basketball is played in a limited space (96 ft × 50 ft), has specific time periods, and has a set of restrictive rules that are explicit about what can and cannot be done in an attempt to score. The rules are fewer and less restrictive in cross-country skiing. They are nonetheless performances intentionally created and not *"objets trouvés."*

For the parallel to work, at least the designers must consciously be making a statement about the human condition. To a certain degree there must be the possibility of a close involvement with life situations. I maintain there is much that is being said intentionally. In every competitive sport, several things are taking place. Each game displays relationships that are or ought to be found in society. There is competition, yet cooperation—cooperation among players as well as cooperation of each according to the promulgated rules. If a rule is broken, there are immediate consequences. The impartial referees and umpires determine when a rule is broken, and the designers of course determine the rules. The designers are definitely concerned with establishing rules that stress achievement through effort, with the rules designed to reduce achievement through raw talent alone. Rules are designed to require that discipline, self-sacrifice, and technical efficiency be exhibited to achieve success. When done at its best—with style—athletes achieve aesthetic experiences for themselves and evoke aesthetic responses from the audience.

The aesthetic appeal is minimal when the skill level is low, as when lack of skill hampers self-expression, or when success is achieved through mere strength or innate, undisciplined talent. This may account for the high spectator interest in women's tennis and in men's basketball as opposed to women's basketball. In tennis, strength is the determining factor of success for men; in the women's game, a high level of skill, efficiency, and strategy combines for a beautiful performance. In women's basketball, the skill level is still some-what low and thus there is a correspondingly low aesthetic appeal. In the men's game, however, the skill level is significantly higher and reaches its peak in the National Basketball Association. Because the skill level is so high, players have the qualifications to add style and aim for beauty. This evokes aesthetic responses in viewers and achieves the aesthetic experience for the athlete.

The definers of the rules that characterize and sustain a game intend both that there be a concern with life situations and that the performances exhibit this aesthetically. James (2) maintains that certain features ought to be included in cricket to express the social history of the time. In basketball the 3-second lane was widened to prevent success without hard work. This expresses the idea of success through effort and is a concept constantly stressed by coaches—usually by referring to parallel real-life involvements. It is interesting to note that the New Games evolved because their creators did not like the social conditions expressed or taught in the usual competitive games. They generally feel that competition is stressed to the detriment of cooperation; besides, at the end of competition there is always a loser. But in New Games cooperation is stressed because it is felt that cooperation is what sustains a society. Rules are deliberately created for this purpose, and the performers learn this very important lesson in playing these games.

The expressions of life situations are manifested differently in sports than in the traditional art forms, but there are deviations among the other art forms as well. Thus, it is wrong to say that sport has no involvement with life situations or that it makes no statement about the human condition.

V

The previous sections have answered the main criticisms used in excluding sport from art. Given that the essential features of sport and of art are compatible, I maintain that sport is an art form. Not only are they compatible, but in some cases they enhance one another. The essential feature of efficiency is necessary for both sport and art; the feature of sport that concerns the desire to win is required for beauty; the aim of beauty is not the sole aim of either sport or art; and sport, like other art forms, maintains a close involvement with life situations. In this concluding section, I will discuss one other feature which is as essential to sport as it is to art—self-expression. Since much has been said already, I will only put together what has gone before.

First of all, self-expression literally means to express oneself. There are different ways of doing this in one's work or one's play: through words, body movements, music, pictures. Art certainly provides a vehicle for self-expression. The individual's desire is to create beauty. It is the desire for an aesthetic experience, and the experience is accomplished when the expression of oneself is achieved. Poets use words; artists use visual media. We allow actors to use scripts to express themselves and achieve an aesthetic experience. This is paralleled by the athletes. Athletes must perform at their best, and then they may add style to their performance. Their style and success are their self-expressions. In both art and sport, self-expression is hampered by a lack of skill. The actor playing Cyrano must know the words, expressions, and movements before he can add his own flair. The athlete must do the same.

Dr. J, Abdul-Jabbar, James Worthy, Walter Payton—they must have control of the basics before they can perform with style. This is true for all athletes and artists, be they men or women. A performance or work cannot be beautiful unless the basics are mastered. Women are just beginning to achieve the skill level necessary for self-expression and for an aesthetic performance. Until recently, this means of self-expression was not available to them. That is, certain "form" sports were available and considered feminine, but these were not suited for all. In fact, we are finding that the so-called masculine competitive sports can be played just as skillfully and efficiently by the women as they are by men. This does not mean women have to compete with men. I believe there is an aesthetic reason for women generally not to compete with men, and this follows from my position that aesthetic experiences and aesthetic responses are found in evenly matched, well played games. This is why boxing, for example, has different weight classes. There is no contest between a heavyweight and a flyweight.

In other sports the men's game and the women's game emphasize different qualities, as in gymnastics; or different styles of games, as in basketball. In some sports it may be aesthetically pleasing for men and women to compete together, as in diving or in equestrian events. And some women may have the ability to compete against a man in a masculine sport. But generally women need not compete with men to achieve an aesthetic experience or evoke an aesthetic response. However, opening up sports equally to women shows that developing one's skills is as aesthetically pleasing for women as for men. It illustrates that for women, as for men, there is a potential for success through discipline and hard work; and it indicates a level of equality that was previously denied. This helps make sense of Marx's notion that we are all artists; we are all capable of having aesthetic experience. This is not possible for all of us when art is restricted to the acknowledged art forms. But, by accepting sports as an art form, we have provided a vehicle for self-expression and aesthetic experience to a large group of people who previously had no such vehicle.

Bibliography

1. Best, David. (1974). "The Aesthetic in Sport." *British Journal of Aesthetics,* 14, 197-213.

2. James, C.L.R. (1983). *Beyond a Boundary.* New York: Pantheon.

3. Reid, Louis A. (1970). "Sport, the Aesthetic, and Art." *British Journal of Educational Studies,* 18, 245-258.

4. Ziff, Paul. (1974). "A Fine Forehand." *Journal of the Philosophy of Sport,* 1, 92-109.

A Commentary on Jan Boxill's "Beauty, Sport, and Gender"

JOSEPH KUPFER

With much of Professor Boxill's analysis of what makes sport aesthetic I am in agreement. But as Tolstoy noted about happy families in contrast to those that are conflict-ridden, agreement tends to be less interesting than argument. So, I'll spend most of my time questioning and quarrelling.

The main flaw in Boxill's discussion is that she feels compelled to argue that sport is an art form in order to establish it as a rich vein for aesthetic experience. While art forms do indeed provide a strong source of aesthetic experience, sport need not be an art form to do so. In short, Boxill can have everything that she and I want for sport as aesthetic without going to the lengths she does to argue that it's art.

In all fairness, she takes her cue from a confusion of Paul Ziff's. He writes, "A lack of intention to be beautiful thereby disqualifies sport as potentially aesthetic" (cited on p. 2). Well, this is just plain silly. Lots of things have lots of aesthetic values without being beautifully intended (if intended at all): sunsets, cornfields, streetlamps, people. Things of nature and things man made may in fact be *more* aesthetically worthwhile than many

works of art even though they are not intended to be beautiful while the latter are.

Boxill allows herself to be drawn into Ziff's confusion of art and the aesthetic when she says that he, David Best, and Louis Reid "maintain that certain features which are essential to sport preclude it from being considered *an art form as an aesthetic experience*" (p. 2, my italics). She is so concerned to show that sport has the artistic aim or intention that Boxill overstates the case in at least two ways.

First, by mistakenly identifying effect with aim, Boxill notes that "Something is efficient when it produces its desired ends with the least expenditure of resources. . . . In some cases efficiency and beauty are inseparable" (p. 6). Yes, but this doesn't show that beauty is intended or aimed at. A runner may aim at health and produce large calf muscles. A gourmet may aim at taste pleasure and produce a fat gut. An athlete may aim at excellence or efficiency and produce beauty. While I agree with her that beauty may accompany efficiency, it need not be aimed at. What's more, who cares? Maybe athletes are more beautiful, like people in their everyday lives, when they do not consciously aim at beauty.

Second, Boxill gets carried away to the point of claiming that young athletes admire grace and

Reprinted from *Journal of the Philosophy of Sport,* XI, 1984, pp. 48–51. Copyright 1985 by the Philosophic Society for the Study of Sport. Reprinted by permission.

style more than winning. It's *more* worthy of contemplation when the athlete is effective in scoring, she says. But this just seems to be wrong. We admire the graceful athlete *when* successful, sometimes even the successful *graceless* athlete such as Pete Rose, Larry Bird, or Dick Butkus. Those who are graceful but can't put the ball in the hoop, throw the runner out, or hang on to the football don't last and don't receive much admiration. The dance troupe beckons.

In her effort to establish sport's artistic credentials, Boxill distorts the way people actually see sports. She claims "that contrary to Ziff, it cannot be the case that concern for technical efficiency overshadows the essential art ingredients" (p. 10). Why not? It may be unfortunate, but concern for technical efficiency not only can but often does in fact overshadow the aesthetic aspects of sport. Not only for professionals, but for most amateur participants and spectators, succeeding at the competition certainly appears to be more important than aesthetic appreciation. What Boxill probably meant to say was concern for technique and success *ought* not put our aesthetic perceptions in the shade, or we will be the worse for it.

She need not go as far as she does. Sport need not *be* art in order to have varied and intense aesthetic qualities. A sunset is no less aesthetically rich and moving for not being "art." Why worry so about that label? Again, I agree with Boxill that the demand for skill and concern for victory need not diminish the aesthetic delight we take in sport. But where aesthetic goals seem primary in the creation of art, for most people they are not dominant in the appreciation of sport. Why not? What is the main purpose of engaging in or viewing sports? The following sorts of things come to mind: to play; to compete; to physically exert oneself. Perhaps these three can be combined: to physically exert oneself in playful competition (or watch others do so). Even if this is the main reason for engaging in or watching sport, it doesn't mean that the result can't be aesthetically wonderful or that the aesthetic cannot contribute to our repeated return to the sporting arena.

Since Boxill emphasizes the resemblance between sport and art, downplaying the competitive side of sports, I was surprised that she did not go into the noncompetitive sports at greater length. For it is there, in the formal or stylistic sports, that her best case can be made. In art, appearance is the chief purpose: the sound of the notes, the play of lines and colors, the contours of the marble. In formal sports such as diving, gymnastics, and figure skating, success is measured *only* in aesthetic terms. If a case is to be made that sport is art, then surely these sports make it best. The fluidity of the dive; the grace and controlled power of the gymnastic routine; the seamless pattern of glides, jumps, and spins in figure skating. All we care about are the aesthetic features; there just *is* nothing else to appreciate in these sports.

It's probably worth noting that spectator interest is high in female performances of these sports. Perhaps, as Boxill argues, this is because women's skill level is high in these formal sports. Perhaps . . . it is because distinctive female athletic virtues —such as flexibility and grace—are nicely exhibited in these sports. In analyzing the differences between men's and women's basketball, for example, gender differences such as these should be taken seriously. However, Boxill seems to think that spectators prefer men's basketball over women's simply because women play at a lower level of skill. This may be part of it (although women shoot for a higher percentage than men). A larger part of the difference in the level of play seems to me to stem from physical differences between the sexes, and not just the upper body strength. . . .Men seem to run more quickly, jump higher, and hang in the air longer. If Bill Russell is right, and basketball is "played in the air," then these physical differences would help explain the superiority of the men's game and its greater aesthetic appeal to audiences.

In contrast to the formal or stylistic sports just mentioned are those sports that require opposition for their performance. These competitive sports provide that aesthetic aspect in which the formal sports are deficient—what Boxill calls sports' "close involvement with life situations" (p. 21). Here I find her accurate, especially when she notes that competition is complemented by cooperation and that, as in life, the rules of the game are set up to reward effort rather than raw talent alone. What I would like to suggest is that the parallels with real life run even deeper and that a great deal of sport's aesthetic can be found in them. I have in mind all the dramatic qualities that emerge from the interplay of people in conflict. Like a novel, film, or theatrical play, competitive sports show us the complication of characters as well as their *character*, their inner fabric. And this yields aesthetic dividends. Consider the way fortunes are reversed, how the hero one minute may become the goat the next. Or the way some athletes rebound from adversity and some don't; the way one play can give rise to a stirring victory, a wonderful season, even a whole career.

And of course there is the inevitable role of luck in sport, as in life: the bad-hop single; the golf ball hitting a rock in the ocean and bouncing on to the green; the fortunate carrom of the hockey puck. Sport parallels life not only by rewarding effort but also by rewarding us for just happening to be at the right place to benefit from accident. Our imaginations fill in "what might have been" as we sketch alternate scenarios, sporting events, the careers of athletes, as well as our own lives. Such scenarios have shapes, patterns which, like so many artistically crafted stories, harbor aesthetic delights.

Then, too, sport often molds and tests character. We literally see the maturation of a Joe Namath or a Jimmy Connors: brash young men who learned to control their tempers and egos in the swirl of competition (not to mention the fast lane). Sport publicly exhibits athletes' fatal flaws—both in character and talent. Thus did Ivan Lendle crumble against Jimmy Connors after building a two set advantage in the 1983 U.S. Open Championship, not from lack of talent but from lack of heart. (His stunning redemption against McEnroe in the '84 French Open, in the exactly reversed situation, may have marked a

toughening of will.) On the other hand, former middleweight boxing champ Bobo Olsen's flaw was one of talent rather than character. He was a notoriously "slow starter"; vulnerable in the early rounds, he strengthened as a fight progressed. Sugar Ray Robinson, realizing this after an earlier match, quickly dispatched Bobo in two fights, first to reclaim and later to retain the crown. With tennis court and boxing ring as its stage, sport publicly disclosed a weakness of character in the first case, a decisively flawed talent in the other.

This is the very stuff of drama, found in art and real life. Not only do competitions have form, but so do people. The changes in their character, *how* the character is revealed in competition, the way they respond to adversity or fortune, all take shape before us in the physical interaction of the contest. But *how* the character changes, or *whether* a serious flaw will prove fatal in this particular outing—these concerns carry with them a tension essential to aesthetically rich drama. We delight in our own uncertainty, awaiting the outcome of the clash of forces—athlete against athlete, but also the athlete against herself in the midst of mounting pressure. Not only do we relish the suspense of games, series, and seasons, but character itself is often in doubt. Consider how different athletes respond to pressure.

Some great athletes rise to that once-in-a-lifetime occasion while others falter. Thus did Roberto Clemente field and hit, run and throw with such timely flair that he brought the Pittsburgh Pirates to a come-from-behind victory in the 1971 World Series. Thus did Gil Hodges fail miserably, going 0 for 21, for the old Brooklyn Dodgers against the Yankees in the 1952 World Series. The rising and falling each provide a distinctive aesthetic quality as character, replete with its history, confronts momentous situation. We savor the form of the reliable Hodges' plummet from his starry height, the weight of the Series seeming to crush him, as much as we marvel at the almost carefree Clemente soaring in the spotlight. In such pressure-packed contexts, our usual appreciation of physical performance is compounded by the character of the particular athlete confronting a magnificent challenge. Sport shrinks the dimensions of real life situations to manageable proportion, providing sharper focus, perhaps enabling us to appreciate similar drama in the real world.

The way athletes rise to the occasion, or are instead subdued by it, conveys some of the drama of sport, and this drama is a large part of sport's aesthetic appeal. But Boxill mistakenly identifies the aesthetic with the emotional; she claims that an appeal to the emotional sense is *the* aim of the aesthetic (p. 19). While I don't deny that such an appeal to the emotions is important, I do deny that it exhausts the aesthetic.

As the brief discussion of the parallels with life should indicate, sport's aesthetic attraction includes intellect, desire, and imagination as well as emotion. It takes thought to analyze the twists and turns of sporting events and then synthesize them into a moving pattern. It takes imagination to see into the athlete's character, or project possible scenarios for a contest, or diagnose what went wrong with a game plan. What's more, these intellectual and imaginative operations are aesthetically rewarding. And the mirroring of real life surely includes reference to real life desires or purposes. Thus did Cedric Maxwell of the Boston Celtics just recently say that the main difference between the Celtics and the Lakers in the 1984 NBA Championship series was that the Celtics "wanted it" more—had a more intense desire to win. That intensity was exhibited in the fierceness of their rebounding, continuity of concentration, and tenacity in defense, all of which were ingredient to the aesthetic of the individual games and the shape of the series as a whole. We witnessed

a struggle during which each team's character was tested and that testing provided a host of aesthetic qualities.

Returning briefly to the formal sports discussed earlier, we see that their aesthetic valuing also amounts to more than simply an emotional appeal. Both intellect and imagination are appealed to when we appreciate the gymnast's grace or the diver's fluidity. For both involve form and form is as intellectual and imaginative as it is emotional. Following the complicated movements, seeing how they relate to one another, and grasping them as a whole, engage thinking and imaging in aesthetic play.

So, once again I agree with Boxill, but argue with her in doing so. I agree that sport has great potential to echo real life and that this can be a source of aesthetic delight. But, again, it need not do so in order to provide aesthetic experience—as evidenced in the formal sports and sometimes even the competitive ones. What's more, and more ironic, is that art itself *need* not display similarities with real life situations. Architecture, abstract painting or sculpture, and a good deal of music (Bach fugues, for instance) afford intense aesthetic experience with little or no paralleling of real life situations. Boxill prejudices the case by choosing examples from the literary arts whose representational nature makes such parallels likely, often central.

Again, Boxill makes a telling observation. But in an effort to show how sport is an art, she has emphasized a feature that art itself does not always exhibit. As I've said repeatedly, this is her main flaw. She correctly discusses many of the aesthetic features of sports, but mistakenly thinks that she must show that sport is an art form to do so.

Context and Intention in Sport and Art

S.K. WERTZ

David Best has recently argued that the context of sport is not appropriate for art and vice versa.[1] For Best, it is the context alone which determines the genre of an action. If we wish to determine what constitutes the specific character of a dance or sport movement, what is required is not to consider it in isolation, nor to try to locate what lies behind it, but to consider what lies around it.[2] Intentional action (like that seen in dance or sport movement) usually carries institutional or conventional implications. And these so-called "implications" are the ones Best wants to substitute for the intentional in "intentional action." Best elaborates:

> . . . of what makes a movement a dance movement, it can now be seen that the solution to the problem is given by the context of its occurrence. This movement takes place as a part of a dance, in a studio unlike that precisely similar physical movement which occurs as part of a gymnastics sequence in a gymnasium. It is the context which determines the difference between the two intentional actions. And where a movement is performed in isolation yet is still clearly recognizable as a dance movement, its character is given by the normal context of its occurrence. That is, it is recognized implicitly as the sort of move-

ment which normally occurs in dance. This possibility of extension also justifies the description of some gymnasts as dancers and some dancers as gymnasts. The descriptions derive from the normal context of the respective styles of movements, even although they are now performed in a different context (p. 82).

For Best, then, in the final analysis, it is the context of any action which determines its description. An agent *performs* an action *a* just in case there are institutions and conventions which surround *a*. What makes a movement an *X* movement is the context of *X*'s occurrence. The context provides "a sense of place," which originates and is sustained by its conventions and institutions being practiced by those who participate in them. So the difference between two seemingly similar movements, a dance movement and a gymnastics sequence, for example, is their sense of place, the differential being the actual, physical location; one movement may occur in a studio and another may occur in a gymnasium. A dance or a gymnastic sequence connotes a sense of place, and this is how two intentional actions, which are similar (if not identical), are differentiated.

I shall argue that this analysis is extreme. Instead of finding identifying marks within the nature of the action itself, Best has looked to the context. This is the philosophical notion on which Best bases his objection to Toller Cranston's and

Reprinted from *Southwest Philosophical Studies*, VIII(5), (Spring, 1984), pp. 144–147. Reprinted by permission.

David Curry's pronouncements that figure-skating is art.[3] Best would say that the "character" of the figure-skating movements is prescribed by the normal context of their occurrences. The intentions of their "author" do not contribute to their character. These movements, regardless of the author's intentions, are simply categorized by their physical setting. Since they appear in an ice rink, furthermore, they are sport movements, and can never become something else.

In other words, the place where an action is performed is the deciding factor for Best as to whether or not it can be described in a certain manner. That a given set of movements is performed in a studio or in a gymnasium or in a stadium determines why these actions are classified as dance, gymnastics, and sport, respectively. This hardly seems an adequate criterion for making such heavy-weight decisions. After all, much that goes on within the confines of a stadium would not be called "sport." Many things happen on a football field which are not normally part of football. Outright physical conflict or confrontation is not "tackling" in football; it exceeds the appropriate actions of tackling.

We do not know whether we are within the confines of the conventions and institutions of a sport through an examination of its context or surroundings. Rather, it is the participants' reasonable care in carrying out those conventions and institutions which make up a game like football. Also, a dancer may not have a studio available to her for dancing so uses a gymnasium instead. Would Best suggest in such circumstances that she does not know what she is talking about when she informs him that the action performed was not sport or gymnastics, but dance? If we accept what she says, then we allow for more than the context of an action to determine its type. That is, an appeal to intentions has been made which helps us pick out the right conventions or institutions.

It seems, in instances such as these and in the figureskating case, that to determine the genre of an action more is required than location or surroundings. I suggest that intention is what is called for. To make classificatory decisions—especially

like the ones we want to make here—we need both intention and context. The authorship of actions is as important as their context. Authorship contributes to the conventions and institutions which make up a given context for an action.

Indeed, as I have suggested, authorship enables us to account for conceptual change, as in the Cranston-Curry case. We do not conclude that because Cranston and Curry do not perform in a studio their activity could not possibly be art. Cranston may have been marked down on occasion for deliberately performing figure-skating as an art form in competitions, but this must have been in front of conservative judges; times have changed since then. There have been other occasions when his and other skaters' performances were not marked down. On the contrary, high marks were given, e.g., Peggy Fleming's performances and routines at the 1968 Grenoble Olympics. So again it seems that deciding whether sport is or can be art is a contingent matter. In other words, we must examine individual cases.

Let me sum up. The contextualist demand that Best has made seems to me to be unreasonable and unsympathetic. Intentions do need to be consulted in such matters. Best's methodological proposal is too restrictive for the purposes at hand. And yet at the same time, it is too broad because it allows actions which should not be counted, such as the tackling example cited above. Intention, then, is as likely a candidate for determining the meaning of an action as the context is. Both intention and context are features of actions which are necessary in order to ascribe meaning to them.

Another, related difficulty I have with Best's solution is his idea of what counts as "context." He wants a "normal" context, although he does admit varying contexts (p. 82). How did the "normal" become normal, except through some sort of change in circumstance which a given community decided to accept as a type? These circumstances are not given; they are made. So why could sport performances not be admitted in a different context? What happens when the same set of physical movements begins to express a different set of intentional actions? For example, Fleming, Cranston, and Curry perform their movements in figureskating; yet their discussion of the routine includes statements not ordinarily or normally used. They ascribe artistic predicates to their actions. These statements, in effect, constitute a conceptual change because the intentional actions which surround the performance have changed. If Fleming, Cranston and Curry are unhappy by the way the audience behaves in a skating area, it is because the audience does not appreciate what these skaters take their surroundings to be. For them, the skating rink is no longer just a rink, but a dance floor, an artistic arena. Perhaps audiences (and judges) have to be educated to see that performers no longer conceive of their activities as merely athletic or sporting, but as artistic. A new set of conventions is being employed, and has been established at the rink. Fleming, Cranston, and Curry want the context of their intentional actions changed. And they are changing it by insisting on the rink as an art space. The sense of place has been altered.

A Russian writer, Natalia Arkina, has speculated that sport and art are being combined in several activities to bring about a new form of human expression.[4] Music is what links sport and art together for Arkina. Music brings life to sport by freeing it from the seconds and the meters by which champions and records are measured. Music draws our attention to the artistic quality of sport performances. Music can be a unifier, as Arkina suggests, between sport and art, and I would want to add that this is the case whether it is physically present or imagined. Musical themes or other artistic devices (like choreography) may *aid* athletes in their performances. Certain quarterbacks and ends may envision pass patterns along these lines in order to help coordinate and synchronize the plays. Anything which

enables the athlete to enhance his performance will be encouraged by his coach—even if it comes from art. Best wants to prohibit the athlete from taking advantage of this option.[5]

Notes

1. David Best, *Philosophy and Human Movement* (London: George Allen and Unwin, 1978), ch 7; "Art and Sport," *Journal of Aesthetic Education*, 14 2 (April 1980), 69-80; and "The Aesthetic and the Artistic," *Philosophy*, 57, 221 (July 1982), 357-72.
2. Best, *Philosophy and Human Movement*, p. 81.
3. Ibid., pp. 120-121. Cranston and Curry are world-class skaters from Canada and England who have conceived of their skating as art. Best thinks they are confused because "the *context* of sport, even an aesthetic sport, is not appropriate for art" (p. 121; my italics). Earlier (p. 82) Best allowed for the possibility of extension, but here he flatly denies it.
4. Natalia Arkina, "Sport and Art: Figure-Skating and Classical Ballet," *Cultures*, 4, 2 (1977), 123-36. This article appears in translation and was translated from Russian by J. Delamotte.
5. For further discussion of this topic, see my "A Response to Best on Art and Sport," *Journal of Aesthetic Education*, 18 (1984), and "Artistic Creativity in Sport," in *Sport Inside Out: Readings in Literature and Philosophy*, David L. Vanderwerken and Spencer K. Wertz, eds. (Fort Worth: Texas Christian University Press, 1985).

Sport Is Not Art

DAVID BEST

In this paper I shall consider responses to my argument that sport is not art, beginning with arguments proposed in various papers written by Spencer Wertz.[1] First let me correct the strange way in which he construes my philosophical work, in terms of a sort of despotic Dickensian headmaster. For instance, he accuses me of having "forbidden" the raising of certain questions, of "ruling out" artistic possibilities in sport, of "disallowing" conceptual change, of "prohibiting" athletes from certain options, and other iniquitous Hitlerisms. I plead not guilty. I am innocent of these charges of overbearing interference with the liberty of others. I am engaged in no such tyranical impositions, but rather in the humble task of considering philosophical issues. If I point out that it makes no sense to speak of four-sided triangles, I am certainly not prohibiting, disallowing, or ruling out anything. If someone feels that his or her untrammelled freedom requires his/her proclaiming the existence of four-sided triangles, I have no wish to impose any limitation on that person. Not guilty. Spencer Wertz has framed me.

Of course, the question we are considering is more complex, but the triangle example indicates something of the character of philosophy in which I engage. To cast me into the role of a dictatorial beak is likely to evoke an adversarial polemic rather than a disinterested philosophical consider-

Reprinted from *Journal of the Philosophy of Sport*, XII, (1985), pp. 25–40. Copyright 1986 by the Philosophic Society for the Study of Sport. Reprinted by permission.

ation of the issues. I shall be regarded as an overbearing sergeant major, and discussion with me rather like a cabinet meeting chaired by Margaret Thatcher.

I

I shall consider primarily Wertz's papers "Context and Intention in Sport and Art" (12), "A Response to Best on Art and Sport" (13), and "Sport and the Artistic" (14). But first let me make some brief comments on three additional points in his unpublished symposium paper, delivered at the 1984 Olympic Scientific Congress.

(I) In appealing for support to the work of J.L. Austin, Wertz reveals a fundamental misunderstanding. For Austin certainly does not say that as long as a word is used commonly in certain ways there is no further question about whether it is correctly used. On the contrary, Austin is best known for pointing out the distinctions of meaning which are lost in general usage, and that the loss of such distinctions incurs a loss of concepts. For example, Austin gives a series of words such as "accidental" and "unintentional," which are commonly used synonymously, and he shows that this is incorrect *despite* common usage, because it blurs distinctions. Austin's emphasis is on our being more sensitive to differences, so that conceptual distinctions are not lost. Thus, contrary to Wertz's claim about the use of "art" in sport-

527

ing contexts, Austin would strongly have *opposed* the contention that just because a word is commonly used in certain ways there is no further question about whether it is correctly so used. To give an obvious example (which is not Austin's), "disinterested" is commonly used to mean uninterested. But that is an incorrect use.

(II) Wertz has misunderstood Wittgenstein's statement: "Practices give words their meaning." Wittgenstein refers here to the practice in which the use of a word is embedded, and which gives meaning to that word. For example, such practices give sense to expressions such as "Thank you" and "I promise." That is, in relation to its meaning we have to consider the practice, the context of actions in which a word is set. This relates to the preceding point, for just because people do something different on ice does not imply that they are justified in using the term "art" to describe it.

(III) Wertz frames me again by falling into what I call "the disease of the dichotomous mind." He sets up a simple disjunction of semantic theories— Putnam/Kripke versus Frege—and dumps me conveniently on one side of it. He even says that I "advocate" a Fregean model. I challenge anyone to find any such advocacy in any of my work. I have never been such an advocate. In fact, I have fundamental doubts about the possibility or usefulness of holding a semantic theory, so I certainly do not subscribe to any particular one.

But more important, semantic theory is irrelevant and merely obscures the issues. Wertz raises the matter in relation to my contention that the meaning of an action is given by its normal context of occurrence. For example, if I perform a backhand action in a conference room, it is recognizable as such in that context only because it is normally performed in the context of tennis or squash. It may be objected that perhaps it could be a dance action. But my point is that we can discuss such questions without resort to semantic theory. It is no help to bring in technicalities. Philosophers notoriously create technical terms to explain phenomena of ordinary life and language, and then expend considerable time and ingenuity

arguing about the meanings of these terms. An example is the extensive debate over whether the term should be "intentionality" or "intensionality." I suspect that the very use of technical terms and formal methods in philosophy, at least often, is already a symptom of underlying error.

II

On the question of action, intention and context, Wertz has massively missed the point I was making. He says, for instance, "Instead of finding identifying marks within the nature of the action, Best has looked to the context," and, on my view, "The intentions of their 'author' do not contribute to their character. These movements, regardless of the author's intentions, are simply categorised by their physical setting. Since they appear in an ice rink. . .they are sport movements and can never become anything else" (12: p. 145).

I shall make just two points here. First, it is a caricature to attribute to me what Wertz calls (12: p. 145) "the extreme" view that actions, regardless of the author's intentions, are determined simply by their physical setting. This completely ignores pages 79 to 82 of my book *Philosophy and Human Movement* (3), in which I give an account of how an action can be a dance action despite being isolated, or in a physical setting quite different from the normal. In short, of course I do not deny that one can dance in a gymnasium, on a beach, in fields. Conversely, of course I do not suggest that everything which occurs on a stage is necessarily drama or dance.

Wertz (12: p. 145) says that this context of physical location hardly seems an adequate criterion for making such heavyweight decisions (i.e., about whether sporting actions can be art). This reflects again Wertz's conception that my philosophical work consists in despotic impositions, rather than a disinterested consideration of conceptual questions. For there is no question of decisions heavy or lightweight. Wertz (12: p. 147) objects that Best *wants* to prohibit athletes from artistic options, and that Best *wants* to reject sport as an art form. In a similar vein, he objects (12: p. 146) that my contextualistic demand is ''unsympathetic'' to sportspeople. Whatever may be the validity of this speculative psychology, it is irrelevant. Even if I were engaged in a sinister plot to undermine the artistic pretensions of sport, what matters is the validity or invalidity of the arguments, not any supposed psychological motivation.

To repeat, I do *not* propound the obviously silly thesis that the character of an action is determined solely and simply by the physical location of its occurrence. What I *do* say—and this is significantly different—is that the character of an action is inextricably related to the normal context of occurrence. To explain that significant difference takes me to the more important, and second, issue about which Wertz has missed the point of chapters 5, 6, and 7 of my book (3). It is related to the preceding point in that it stems from oversimple conceptions (a) of what is meant by ''context'' here, and (b) of how the character of an action is derived from its normal context of occurrence.

Wertz's contrast of intention and context reveals a misunderstanding of my central argument concerning their relation. For example, he writes (12: p. 145), ''To make classificatory decisions [sic] . . . we need both intention and context. The authorship of actions is as important as their context. Intention is as likely a candidate for determining the meaning of an action as the context is. . . . Both intention and context are necessary in order to ascribe meaning to them.'' In fact, I do not deny the relevance of intention. Quite on the contrary. My point is that the very possibility of intentions *depends upon* normal context of occurrence; if such a context did not exist then the supposition of the relevant intention would be unintelligible. (Incidentally, this brings out something of the inseparable relationship between aesthetics and philosophy of mind.)

It is essential to clear up Wertz's misunderstanding of what I mean by a context here. He states

that by a context I mean simply a physical setting. But, as I made very clear, I mean far more than that. Indeed, I give a series of examples of the way in which the same physical movement, of signing my name, could be various intentional actions according to which context it occurs in (3: p. 79). It could be a donation, or buying a car, if I were signing a check, an agreement to accept employment if I were signing a contract, a protest if I were signing a petition, and so on. I point out that it is the context of the practices of banking and financial exchange that gives the possibility of the intention to give a donation by signing a check. Clearly I do not mean by a context merely a physical setting. It is not simply the physical setting of a bank which constitutes the requisite context. Similarly, when I refer to the context of a gymnasium I do not mean simply ropes, wall bars, vaulting horses, and so forth in some aseptic physical sense. So I certainly do not deny that a gymnasium could be used as a theatre or for dance. (It is significant, however, that dance teachers in schools often strongly object if the only space available for dance is the gymnasium, since they believe, justifiably, that such a setting detracts from the kinds of sensitivity they are trying to develop in their students.)

It would be irrelevant to consider here the complexities involved in the notion of a context, but I shall outline three related ways in which the meaning of an action depends upon a context.

In the first, the context is where the action is taking place. This is not simply a physical setting in the aseptic sense in which Wertz understands it. It may be illuminating to consider an analogue to a central misconception of behaviorism (which I discussed in another paper at the Olympic Congress [7]). The behaviorist tries to operate with a notion of pure behavior, that is, of physical movements of muscles and joints, of which a robot would be capable. Yet what gives his or her thesis plausibility is that, inevitably, he/she has implicitly to presuppose what he/she explicitly denies, namely that such behavior is that of a human being, which already involves intentions, feelings, thoughts, and so forth. Analogously, talk of the physical context of a gymnasium or theatre implicitly includes the kinds of practice for which it is normally used.

In the second sense, the context is the whole sequence or setting of actions. To take a simple case, in normal circumstances it would be incoherent to say "Thank you" to someone who had just punched you on the nose. To consider the more complex kind of case that concerns us, there is clearly no problem, for instance, about the inclusion of handsprings as part of a dance. But if a performance were to consist exclusively, or almost exclusively, of handsprings, forward rolls, vaults, and so forth, that would cast serious doubt on whether it could legitimately be regarded as dance. In general, it constitutes a criticism of dance, for instance by reviewers, to say that it is gymnastic. Clearly the context in this sense, of the setting of an action in surrounding actions, allows for dance in gymnasia, fields, and on beaches.

In the third sense, the context is the practice of dance. To use the simple case again, it is the context in this sense, of expressing gratitude in this way, which gives sense to our saying "Thank you." This is the sense in which the practice of banking and financial exchange is the context which gives meaning to my intention of buying something by signing a check.

Wertz denies any logical relation between intention and context. For him an intention is the logically free decision of the performer. But a prehistoric cave dweller could not have had, still less *decided* to have, the intention to buy something by signing a check. To regard the intention as a logically distinct mental event is unintelligible. It makes no sense to suppose that my intention in tackling someone on a Rugby field could be that of performing a checkmate move in chess.

Moreover, contrary to what Wertz (12: pp. 146-147) suggests, merely adding music to a sporting activity does not make it artistic. On a parity of argument, the turgid pop and sentimental music that assaults our senses in every supermarket these days would make shopping an art form. Wertz

goes so far as to say that the music need not be physically present, but only imagined. That would turn this paper into art, for as I write I have Bach's *Goldberg Variations* in mind. Whistling as one walks? Singing in the bath? The mind boggles at the huge variety of art forms—almost anything can be art on that basis.

Wertz (12: p. 147) adds here, "Musical themes or other artistic devices may aid athletes in their performances. Anything which enables the athlete to enhance his performance will be encouraged by his coach—even if it comes from Art." But this is irrelevant, and does not help his argument at all. It is claimed that music aids increased production on assembly lines. Does that turn factory work into an art form? Well-designed running shoes are an aid to some athletic performances. Does that turn the Olympic Games into a form of shoe designery?

Despite Wertz's assumption to the contrary, I certainly do not deny the possibility of conceptual change. There is far more to be said on this question than I can include here.[2] But, briefly, there are limits of intelligibility. Certainly a performer *may* be able to bring about at least the beginnings of a change of concept. Indeed, it is strange that Wertz attributes to me the view that concepts are eternally and rigidly fixed, since I give the example (3: p. 21) of how Cranston, Curry, and others have created an art form of theatre or dance on ice. But such an art form grows out of, derives its sense as an art form, from artistic concepts which we already have. I cannot simply decide, arbitrarily, that blowing my nose, even to music, is an art form.

The main question here can be illustrated by showing how, when certain contexts change, the very possibility of certain intentions may be lost. A deep malaise in Western society is reflected in this loss of contexts, and the respective intentions, in relation to religious belief. One cannot have the intention of showing profound reverence for the dead in the absence of a religious context. And there is no sense in the notion that we could simply *decide* on an alternative. At the very least, alternative modes of expression of reverence would have to evolve. Intending is not a sort of context-independent subjective wishing or willing. It would make no sense to suggest that I can intend what I am writing now to be mathematics, or nuclear physics. Similarly, we could not simply decide that eating fish and chips would in the future be a mark of profound reverence for the dead. Not *anything* could count as an expression of the meaning of a human life. It is wildly implausible to suppose that, with the progressive loss of the old religious customs, people could simply get together and decide on new ways of marking the significance of a human life, except perhaps as a development of conceptions and practices which are already endowed with the requisite gravity. (This is a huge topic, of profound significance for our society. I believe, for instance, that it is central to the deep causes of the appalling tragedy at the May 1985 Brussels soccer match. . . .)

In Wales, not so many years ago, the coffin was carried through the streets, the mourners all walked with slow solemnity to the funeral service. Then we had a hearse, and the mourners in cars, proceeding slowly. Now things have speeded up to the fairly normal pace of traffic, and the funeral procession mingles with other vehicles. Soon, what? Is it possible to show reverence for the dead with the hearse and cars traveling at 80 mph on a freeway? Later still, perhaps, simply a telephone call to the garbage collector to remove the body.

My central point is that with the loss of the context of these practices we are losing the possibility of certain intentions of showing profound reverence for the dead. We cannot simply *choose* alternatives. The loss of those contexts incurs the loss, perhaps irrevocably, of certain conceptions of the meaning of life, and of certain related intentions that an individual may have. However, the question of whether we need to take as decisive what the athlete says about what he or she is doing will arise more clearly in Section III, where I discuss whether anything whatsoever can be art.

III

On the more general question of sport and art, Wertz has radically changed his position (13 and 14). In his first paper, to which I replied with "Art and Sport" (4), he accepted my distinction between what I call "purposive" and "aesthetic" sports. He accepted that purposive sports cannot be art, but believed that aesthetic sports could be art. He now argues that even purposive sports, such as football, are art. I have no wish merely to repeat previous arguments, but it does seem to me unquestionable that the purposive sports, that is, the great majority, are not even plausible candidates for art forms. Briefly, in purposive sports there is a means/end distinction (3: chap. 7). For instance, the end which at least largely defines the character of soccer, namely scoring goals, can be achieved by various means. It makes perfectly good sense for a soccer manager to tell his team that he doesn't care *how* they score, how ugly and clumsy are their methods, as long as they *do* score more goals than their opponents.

By contrast, it would make no sense to say to an artist that it does not matter how she achieves the purpose of her work. And similarly, it would make no sense to say to a gymnast or diver that it does not matter how he or she achieves the purpose of the activity, since achievement in such aesthetic sports is inseparably bound up with the manner in which one performs. These actions do not have a purpose that can be specified independently of how one performs them. In short, in the arts and aesthetic sports there is no intelligible distinction between means and ends, whereas there is such a distinction in the case of purposive sports. This is sufficient to show that these sports, which comprise the great majority, cannot be art. However, there are also other arguments to support this.

I have to say, with regret, that Wertz seriously misrepresents my arguments in several places. So may I urge anyone who reads his papers to read especially chapter 7 of my book (3) in order to distinguish what he says I say from what I *do* actually say. For instance, he asserts that "Best thinks he has found a criterion which allows us to distinguish art from sport by a single *fundamentum divisionis*" (13: p. 105). Yet nowhere have I said anything of the sort! He claims that my argument "can be condensed into a syllogism." But I should hardly have taken the trouble to write lengthy papers, and a chapter of a book, if all that I had to say could have been expressed in a simple syllogism. Wertz ignores most of my argument and misrepresents that aspect of it which he does consider. He even misquotes me. I had argued that it is a central characteristic of an art form that it allows for the expression of a conception of life issues, such as conceptions of war, or social injustice of various kinds. Of this he says, "Best is not totally unaware of the difficulties; he admits that 'the expression of a conception of life issues seems intolerably forced and absurd'" (13: p. 106). In the way Wertz quotes me, this clearly implies a blatant self-contradiction. But to use the quotation in this way is a gross misrepresentation. I inserted this qualification with respect to *certain* works of art, to bring out that such a characteristic applies to an art *form*, and certainly not to every work of art in that medium. Wertz quotes it as if I were making a general or universal point about works of art, thus misrepresenting my argument as simply self-contradictory.

One of Wertz's most extraordinary misrepresentations is that the concept of art to which I refer in arguing that sport is not art "covers only the nonperforming arts," whereas, as he rightly says, sport's best case as a candidate for art is as a performing art (13: p. 105). Yet the arts on which I quite *explicitly* concentrate principally, as the basis of my case against sport as art, are dance and drama, that is, performing arts (see, e.g., 3: pp. 116-122).

Wertz is also strangely confused about imagination. I wrote, "In art, unlike sport, the object of one's attention is, to put it roughly, an *imagined* object" (4: p. 78). According to Wertz, this is a version of what he calls the "dual object theory," which he explains as follows:

the work of art is one thing and what it signifies or means is another. . . .So what we have now is not one object making up the work, but two. We now have a mysterious, inferred object, one which is somehow removed from the actual art object. What is the ontological status of this "imagined object?" Why are two objects necessary? . . . Best has created a problem by divorcing the imaginary content of the works of art from those artworks themselves. (13: p. 105)

On the contrary, with respect, the only mystery is why *Wertz* has created a spurious problem by assuming that my writing of an imagined object commits me to a "dual object theory." Admittedly there are problems here, hence the qualification "to put it *roughly*," the object is an imagined object. But these are certainly not the problems Wertz creates. His argument here frankly is just silly. If I imagine a unicorn, or little men from outer space, does this commit me to there being actual objects, in addition to these imagined ones? (Think of the creatures in fairy tales and *Alice in Wonderland*.)

The point I was making, which is highly significant for my argument and which Wertz completely ignores, is that in drama, for example, we respond not to John Smith, the actor playing the part, but to the character in the play, Othello. At the end of the play it is Othello, not John Smith, who dies. Similarly, in the repertoire of the Alvin Ailey Dance Theatre some years ago was a moving piece called *Adagio for a Dead Soldier*. One responded to the grief of the character being portrayed, not to that of the dancer. The significance of the point is this: In sport, even sports of the aesthetic kind, there is no such distinction. There is no "imagined object" in this sense. (I am now even more unhappy with this term than when I used it as a rough characterization, but I cannot here give a detailed explanation of this [see 8, chapter 12] and I cannot think of another term that will make the point so clearly. It is sufficient, however, to refute Wertz's argument.) On the stage it is King Lear, not the actor, who suffers. We cannot say, similarly, "On the football field it was the fullback, not John Smith, who was playing in that position, who broke his leg.'' And the same applies to aesthetic sports such as gymnastics and diving.

Contrary to Wertz's assumption, then, it is the performing arts, of dance and drama, that provide the most powerful *support* for my argument that sport, even of the aesthetic kind, is not art. Thus Wertz's argument does not even overcome the problems inherent in his oversimple syllogized caricature of my argument.

The criterion by which I distinguish the aesthetic and the artistic is closely related. For the possibility of an imaginative portrayal, expression of a conception of life issues, applies only to the arts. As I put it, sport can be the subject of art, but art could not be the subject of sport. Indeed, the very notion of a subject of sport makes no sense. As I pointed out, this distinguishing feature of the artistic as opposed to the aesthetic is what gives humorous point to Oscar Wilde's characterization of a sunset as only a second rate Turner. Wertz ignores this central part of my thesis. Yet he needs to confront it directly to have any hope of making a convincing case for sport as art.

Wertz's claim that sports are performing arts because the rules of sport are like artistic texts seems to me a desperate attempt to prop up a hopeless case. He says, ''what sets performances off from other activities, (like creations) is that the actions which make up a given performance must satisfy antecedent requirements. The performing arts, to sum up, are actions governed by antecedent works or texts'' (13: p. 107). First, it is false that performances of dance and drama necessarily require texts. More important, since there are implicit or explicit rules (or antecedent requirements) for almost every activity, that would make almost anything an art form, and thus the criterion is vacuous. For instance, are the laws of a country artistic texts? When one drives on the right in the United States and on the left in the United Kingdom, is one offering an artistic interpretation of a text? (Speed patrolmen would not be much impressed by appeals to poetic licence.)

Wertz suggests that Roberts has produced a convincing case for viewing sporting actions as representing other actions, as in fakes or feints (13: p. 108). But, to judge from what Wertz says, so far from being convincing as a reason for accepting that sport is art, this suggestion seems to me hopelessly implausible. For even if one should wish to use the term ''represent'' in this context (and it seems to me intolerably forced), a sport feint certainly does not represent in the same way an actor might be said to represent Hamlet. The insuperable objection to this suggestion is the same as the one I raised above in relation to the imagined object or subject matter of art.

If I may say so, it would be helpful if further discussion were carried on with reference to my argument, rather than to one that is unrecognizable as mine. Since Wertz's argument in this paper (and to some extent in others) is directed not against my case but against a caricature, there is nothing he says that touches my thesis. Hence he provides no reason for reconsidering my conclusion that there is no valid case for the claim that sport is art.

IV

Wertz (14) quotes Cranston as saying that when sport is most creative it is *consequently* artistic. But that is a nonsequitur. That something is creative does not in the least imply that it is artistic. He also says that if any of such things as an interest in creating new and different routines, in music and style, is attended to, then we *do* have subject matter in sport. But if this notion makes sense at all, it is clearly not the sense in which I use the term in relation to the arts. In Wertz's sense any interest whatsoever would have a subject matter. For example, an interest in playing the stock exchange would have the subject matter of making money. That is clearly quite different from the way in which Athol Fugard's plays have as subject matter the social and personal effects of apartheid. To repeat, whereas sport can be the subject matter of art, it makes no sense to say that art could be the subject matter of sport. The very notion of a subject matter of sport is incoherent.

Wertz writes (14), "If an athlete's performance is to be improved. . .by the artistic manipulation of his or her medium (the body on ice or on a tennis court . . .) then who are we (Best) to say that sport is not artistic?" This is either irrelevant or question-begging. The manager of a well-known soccer team used to claim that ballet dancing improved his team's soccer performance. But that did not imply that soccer became ballet. On the other hand, if Wertz means that the artistic can become intrinsic to the performance of the *sport*, this merely begs the question, for we return to the original question of whether sport can be art.

Wertz clearly thinks that what the sportsperson says about his or her intentions is definitive; if he/she says his/her intention is artistic then it *is* artistic. This is a manifestation of the persistent misapprehension that one is necessarily in the best position to say what one's own intentions are. Yet, notoriously, we can be mistaken about our own intentions. Moreover, the question of whether what a person says about his or her own mental states is decisive is a philosophical question. Thus, contrary to what Wertz (14) claims, what philosophers have to say *is* more relevant than what nonphilosophical, even if "accomplished and reflective," athletes have to say.

To repeat, I do not of course suggest that art can be rigidly defined, or that the concept cannot change. But to say that a concept has vague and changeable boundaries is not to say that it has no boundaries and thus that we can arbitrarily decide what is art.

Wertz asks what else there is for a tennis player to do when he has become the best. There are innumerable answers. Two of the most relevant, perhaps, are that he can continue to improve his tennis, and that if he really is ambitious to become an artist he can learn to play the piano, or paint, or act, or dance.

V

Jan Boxill (9), in another commentary upon my works, completely ignores that central aspect of my argument, the crucial and usually overlooked distinction between the aesthetic and the artistic. (For a detailed account see 8: chapter 11; and 6). The confusion of the two concepts runs throughout her paper and destroys her argument for sport as art. Moreover, as a result, she seriously misrepresents me in several ways. For example, she writes (9: p. 36), "Ziff, Best, and Reid maintain that certain features that are essential to sport preclude its consideration as an art form or an *aesthetic experience*" (my italics). I strongly protest. I really don't know what to make of this, for the paper of mine which she quotes ends by explicitly stating that sport can *undoubtedly* be superb aesthetically. And I spend a considerable proportion of it examining what it is which *makes* sport such a superb aesthetic experience. Again, may I urge readers to read what I wrote (improved in 3: chapter 7) rather than Boxill's misrepresentation of what I wrote.

Consequently Boxill includes me in with philosophers with whom I have explicitly disagreed—she quotes C.L.R. James (9: p. 36): "The aestheticians . . . have scorned to take notice of popular sports and games—to their own detriment." I protest again. I am an aesthetician, and my record shows very clearly that, so far from "scorning to take notice," I have written and spoken *extensively* on the aesthetic in sport. It really is totally unjustifiable, unfair, and exasperating that I am cast into the ranks of philosophers who denigrate or deny the aesthetic in sport, when in fact I have spent much time and energy arguing *for* it, and disagreeing with the kind of philosopher Jan Boxill has in mind.

So what leads Boxill to this extraordinary misrepresentation? I can only assume that, despite its centrality to my argument, she still fails to understand the crucial distinction between the aesthetic and the artistic. I too have argued strongly for the aesthetic qualities of sport. What I deny is that sport is art. Boxill's argument is directed against a straw man, for in supposing that she is opposing me, she constantly adduces arguments that refer, for example, to the *beauty* of sport. Much of her argument is concerned to show the relationship between beauty, and skill and efficiency. Again, that is precisely what *I* argue in the paper she quotes. But it has no relevance to the case for sport as art.

Boxill (9: p. 36) quotes Ziff: "A lack of intention to be beautiful thereby disqualifies sport as potentially aesthetic." As Joseph Kupfer (10: p. 48) points out, "This is just plain silly. Lots of things have lots of aesthetic values without being beautifully intended (if intended at all): sunsets, cornfields, streetlamps, people." Although I agree with Kupfer here, and with most of his criticisms of Boxill, he has failed to diagnose the source of Ziff's obvious mistake, which is the same fundamental mistake as Boxill's, and which is shared by Kupfer. That source is, again, the common conflation of the aesthetic and the artistic. Thus it is understandable that Ziff insists that the relevant kind of intention is required for something to be "aesthetic," when what he should really have said was "artistic."

Boxill (9: p. 36) also seriously misrepresents me by including me with Ziff and Reid: "They grant that there may be aesthetic qualities to sports and games, but these are *only by-products*"(my italics). Again I protest! A considerable proportion of my paper is devoted to showing the crucial distinction between purposive and aesthetic sports which I mentioned above. While I maintain that the aesthetic is not necessary (even if desirable) in the purposive sports, I argue that the aesthetic is logically inseparable from the aesthetic sports—hence the title I gave them. In the aesthetic sports, that is, I explicitly deny that it would make sense to regard the aesthetic as a by-product.

Boxill's conflation is also revealed in her pervasive assumption of the place of beauty (even if it is not the sole aim) in art. For instance, "The artist uses beauty to get his or her message across"; "The sole aim of the artist is not beauty" (9: p. 43), and "This helps to make sense of Marx's notion that we are all artists; we are all capable of having aesthetic experience" (9: p. 46). But it certainly does not follow that if one is capable of an aesthetic experience one is an artist. Moreover, an artist may not be concerned with beauty at all. On the contrary, he or she may deliberately repudiate in his/her work, even with disgust, the whole notion that beauty has anything to do with serious art, as in the case of Mönch and Dada. And one would hardly call the powerful works of Francis Bacon "beautiful." It has been said, with some justification, that beauty is what the bourgeoisie pays the artist for, that is, that he or she has to take time off from serious art in order to produce beauty for a living.

Referring to my distinction between purposive and aesthetic/artistic (she conflates them), Boxill confuses my logical point with a psychological one. To be fair, in the paper she quotes I had not put the point as clearly as I might have done, and I have since rectified this (3: chap 7). She says that I assume "the peculiar *psychology of winning at all costs*" (my italics, 9: p. 40). Again, I have said nothing of the sort. Later, supposedly as a criticism of me she writes: "However, not every player or coach aims solely at winning." Nowhere have I denied it. My point is the logical one I made above, that in a purposive sport such as soccer, it makes perfectly good sense for a coach to urge the team to aim solely at winning without any regard for aesthetic considerations. This would make *no sense* in an aesthetic sport, such as gymnastics, since winning requires a concern for the aesthetic. The point has nothing to do with competition, despite the common assumption that the aesthetic is somehow to be contrasted with the competitive.

Similarly, as I pointed out above, it makes no sense to say to an artist that it does not matter *how* he or she accomplishes his/her work, as long as he/she achieves its purpose. That is, by contrast with purposive sports (the great majority), there is no means/end distinction in art, or in the aesthetic sports. Boxill misunderstands my argument here, and it is admittedly complex. I have written a separate paper precisely on this question (5) and cannot deal with it adequately here. However, I shall offer a brief sketch.

Boxill again misrepresents me. She writes, "May not the artist in his or her painting aim at expressing an idea *however commonplace or trite?* Best does not deny this" (9: p. 43). Best most emphatically *does* deny this! It is hard to imagine any artist worthy of the name actually *aiming* at expressing a commonplace or trite idea. More important, it is precisely this way of writing that reveals a fundamental confusion about form and content in the arts. Boxill seems to think that there is no problem about identifying the purpose of, or what is expressed in, a work of art independently of the particular work. But if that were true, substitution would be possible, that is, quite different works could be said to express the same thing. In a very trivial sense, of course, that may be true. One could say that Tolstoy's *Father Sergius*, and Shakespeare's *King Lear* are expressing the same idea, namely that renunciation is not a form of self-interest. But anyone who thought that that was even remotely adequate as a characterization of its "purpose" could not have the slightest appreciation of either. Hence the crucial significance of the so-called "heresy of paraphrase" in the arts. The "heresy" is that any attempt to capture what is expressed in a work of art independently of the work itself is bound to fail *because* it will be merely commonplace or trite. This is why artists of all kinds tend to be so reluctant to talk about their work, and why they cringe at the attempts by critics to give accounts of it. One well-known dancer, asked what her dance was expressing, replied, "Do you think I should take the very great trouble of dancing it if I could express it in so many words?"

It is, of course, possible to go to the other extreme, which many artists and philosophers of the arts have done. As I have put it elsewhere (1: p. 160), while it is crucial to recognize that the aim of a nonverbal work cannot be adequately characterized in words, that does not imply that *nothing* useful can be said in words. Roughly, the verbal explanation may, as it were, help to point one in a certain direction.

To put it more simply, if anyone thought that the purpose of Picasso's Guernica could be expressed as "man's inhumanity to man," or "the horrors of war," or any such trite phrase, he or she would thereby reveal a failure to understand it. Such phrases *are* trite and commonplace. The work is not.

This does not commit me, as Boxill (9: p. 43) assumes, to the view "that a work cannot be improved, and that any attempt to rework a piece is itself a different piece altogether." This reveals an oversimple conception of logic and identity, for which I have criticized two other philosophers in the paper mentioned (5). Briefly, although there may be changes, within limits, without a change in what the work is expressing, those changes are given their sense only in terms of an identity given by that particular work. By contrast, the aim of a purposive sport, for example scoring a goal, can be characterized quite independently of any particular way of achieving it. Hence Boxill's example of the Rubiyat supports, rather than constitutes a counter-example to, my case. (I realize that this is an inadequately brief account of a complex issue, but I cannot trespass on the clemency of the editor to write what would require another paper.)

Finally, that one can express oneself in sport as well as in art is no argument at all for the claim that sport is art. There are innumerable ways of expressing oneself which are not art.

Although I largely agree with Kupfer's criticisms of Boxill, since he too conflates the aesthetic and the artistic (see 10: p. 50), I do not entirely agree with his argument. However, I have other disagreements with him. He writes, "Like a novel, film, or theatrical play, competitive sports show us the complication of characters as well as their *character*, their inner fabric" (10: p. 50). While this is true, it is importantly confused as an argument for sport as art. The point is one I brought out above, namely that it is the character of the athlete which is shown in sport, whereas in drama it is the character not of the actor but of the person he or she is portraying.

This fundamental confusion is again, and more clearly, illustrated in Kupfer's remarks about drama, in sport and life (10: pp. 50-51). That there is undoubtedly drama in sport does not in the least show that sport is art in the sense of theatrical drama. Again, in sport the drama happens to the athlete, that is, John Smith, the football player, whereas in the theatre it happens to Hamlet, being played by John Smith. "Drama" and its cognates are used in a wide variety of real-life situations, without in any way implying that the situations are the art of theatrical drama. As I have shown above (and more clearly in 3: chapter 7), the term is used in a different sense in the theatre context. For instance, to speak of a dramatic car crash does not imply that the car crash was art.

B.C. Postow (11: p. 52) also reveals throughout her paper the aesthetic/artistic confusion, for instance when she writes "artistic performers in musical or theatrical ensembles *are* expected to do what they can to enhance the aesthetic quality of the whole performance." Not necessarily. Sometimes artistic considerations require that performers should ignore aesthetic considerations, or even produce a performance that is strikingly, abhorrently ugly.

More important, Postow (11: p. 53) appeals to Wittgenstein's notion of family resemblances as support for "the case for classifying oppositional sports as artworks." Again, there is much more to be said about this than I can include here (see 1: pp. 29-32). But whatever may be the point of the notion of family resemblances (and I have increasing doubts about it), it certainly cannot provide any support for the contention that sport is art. For resemblances can be found between any two objects or activities—and even great resemblances between many activities—without it being the case that one just *is* of the same kind as the other. For example, imagine the final of a competitive music festival in which there are two rival male voice choirs, with 15 in each. Similar to Rugby in many respects. Is it then Rugby?

What is required is that the similarities be of the relevant kind. But family resemblances cannot explain what counts as a relevant similarity since, to put it paradoxically, we need to presuppose what counts as a relevant similarity *before* we can recognize that this counts as a family resemblance. So the whole enterprise is viciously circular. But again, I can only apologize that this is intolerably condensed. I cannot here explain my point at greater length.

May I, with great respect, again plead for greater care if this general question of sport and art is to be further discussed. I have given considerable thought to the undoubtedly complex issues, and have tried to express my arguments with care and precision. It is a waste of time, for them and for me, if my critics merely misrepresent my arguments, ignoring whole sections and grossly oversimplifying detailed arguments. This paper consists largely of correcting misrepresentations and repeating my arguments in different terms, which, I hope, may stimulate further, constructive debate on an interesting issue.

VI

Perhaps the principal question is why some people are so strongly inclined to contend that sports are art forms. Wertz and Boxill, to name but two, clearly assume that to be regarded as art would raise the status of sport. In the former this is combined with the sense of "art" which is ascribed to accomplished performance of any activity. For example, Wertz writes (14) that an athlete might reach a level of performance at which improvement would be measured in terms of artistic considerations, that is, sport becomes art when it reaches a sufficiently high level. But this offers no support for the contention that sport is art in the sense required. It is significant that I have never heard it argued that art is sport. And it would not be congenial to those of Wertz's persuasion to accept the inevitable consequence of his thesis that if art reaches a low enough level it becomes sport.

Ironically, those who, like Wertz, try to elevate the status of sport by contending that it is art would, if successful, achieve the very opposite of what they intend. Notice first how Wertz misconstrues my argument here. He attributes to me the assertion that when athletes refer to sport as art "they endow sport with greater respectability than should be allowed" (14). In fact that is the opposite of what I say. What I wrote was, "I do not see why it should be thought that sport would somehow be endowed with greater respectability if it could be shown to be art" (3: p. 116). Indeed, it would devalue sport to regard it as art.

In an earlier unpublished paper, Wertz quotes some modern activities which are claimed as art, and accuses me of having an old-fashioned 18th-century conception of art. How he reconciles this with my examples of Athol Fugard, Beckett, Pinter, modern dance, Dada, Picasso, and so forth, I do not know. He says that he does not know what kind of world Best has been living in, and enlightens me: "Having looked at art works done in human excrement . . . sport as art seems downright tame." Well, I don't know what is your view of excrement sculpture as art, but I think it stinks.

Seriously, this misrepresentation, like the others, merely obscures the issues. When I was in the United States a few years ago, a group had created the new "art form" of sitting naked, each contemplating his or her own navel. My present point is that if we were to accept this as an art form, it would be a very poor one. There could be no sense of profound meaning here. Although some people have deep navels, this is hardly the same sense.

Similarly, if we were to accept that sports should be regarded as art forms, then they would be very poor art forms. Before people jump to misconstruing me again, let me emphasize that this is *not* to say that sports are of little value. It *is* to say that judged by the criteria of *art* they could count only as poor. A principal criterion of the depth and value of art is its insight into—the light it casts on—the most profound aspects of the human condition. This is why Shakespeare, Tolstoy, Dostoievsky, are great artists. Such a possibility is not open to sport in the same sense, no matter how high the level of performance.

Much misconception stems from a confusion of senses of "art," hence Wertz's misapprehension that if sport reaches a high enough level of performance it becomes art. But it is not the case that

a sufficiently high level of tennis can become art in the requisite sense, any more than a high enough level of poker can transform it into chess. Admittedly the term is used in the sense of high level of achievement, so that a variety of achievements, such as cookery, hairdressing, and lawn-mowing are referred to as artistry. But this is obviously not the sense in which drama and dance are art forms. (I even saw a book entitled *The Womanly Art of Breast Feeding*.)

Paradoxically, Wertz at least twice refers to his argument as the case for the *analogy* between sport and art. But if A is analogous to B that entails that A is not the same as B. That is what analogy means. So if he argues that there are analogies between sport and art, he ipso facto concedes my case that sport is *not* art. And the same applies to Boxill's argument for the parallel between sport and art. Incidentally, I nowhere deny, nor would I deny, that there are interesting and illuminating analogies or parallels between sport and art.

VII

Let us be clear how self-defeating it is to accept that because art cannot be strictly defined then *anything* can be art. If it applies to everything, it can meaningfully be applied to nothing, in which case since there would be no sense in the term "art," there would be no sense or point in claiming that sport is art. Those who argue in this way fail to recognize how self-defeating is their own argument. It is only if there are some boundaries, even if vague and changeable ones, that there can be a concept of art. To argue that there are no boundaries is to argue for the destruction of any point in claiming that sport, or anything else, is art.

I have had to omit much; there is far more to say. Perhaps a short book is required. I remain, if anything, even more convinced that sports are *not* forms of art. That does not in the least devalue sport. On the contrary, to judge it by artistic standards (if that made sense, which I deny) would devalue sport. Superb aesthetically, sport can undoubtedly be. Why not judge sport by its own standards, including aesthetic standards?

Notes

1. This paper is partly based on refutations of Wertz which will appear in *Philosophy* ("The Limits of Art"), *Southwest Philosophical Studies* ("Context and Intention") and *The Journal of Aesthetic Education* ("Sport Is Not Art").
2. See (8: chap. 4) for a more extended discussion.

Bibliography

1. Best, David. *Expression in Movement and the Arts.* London: Lepus Books, Henry Kimpton Publishers, 1974.
2. Best, David. "The Aesthetic in Sport." *British Journal of Aesthetics,* (1974), 197–221.
3. Best, David. *Philosophy and Human Movement.* London: George Allen & Unwin, 1978.
4. Best, David. "Art and Sport." *Journal of Aesthetic Education,* 14 (1980), 69-80.
5. Best, David. "Logic and Particularity." *British Journal of Aesthetics,* 23 (1983), 306-318.
6. Best, David. "The Dangers of 'Aesthetic Education'." *Oxford Review of Education,* 10 (1984), 159-167.
7. Best, David. "Body, Mind and Sport." Unpublished paper delivered at the 1984 Olympic Scientific Congress in Eugene, Oregon, 1984.
8. Best, David. *Feeling and Reason in the Arts.* London: George Allen & Unwin, 1985.
9. Boxill, J.M. "Beauty, Sport, and Gender." *Journal of the Philosophy of Sport,* XI (1984), 36-47.
10. Kupfer, Joseph. "A Commentary on Boxill's 'Beauty, Sport, and Gender'." *Journal of the Philosophy of Sport,* XI (1984), 48-51.
11. Postow, B.C. "Sport, Art, and Gender." *Journal of the Philosophy of Sport,* XI (1984), 52-55.
12. Wertz, S.K. "Context and Intention in Sport and Art." *Southwest Philosophical Studies,* 8 (1984), (Spring), 144-147.
13. Wertz, S.K. "A Response to Best on Art and Sport." *Journal of Aesthetic Education,* 18 (1984), 105-108.
14. Wertz, S.K. "Sport and the Artistic." *Philosophy,* in press.

Bibliography for Sport and Aesthetics

Aldrich, Virgil C. "Art and the Human Form." *Journal of Aesthetics and Art Criticism,* 29 (1971), 295-302.

Anthony, D.W.J. "Sport and Physical Education as a Means of Aesthetic Education." *Physical Education,* 60 (March, 1968), 1-6.

Arkina, Natalia. "Sport and Art: Figure-Skating and Classical Ballet." *Cultures,* 4, (1977), 123-136.

Arnold, Peter J. "Aesthetic Aspects of Sports." *International Review of Sport Sociology,* 13 (1978), 45-61.

Arnold, Peter J. *Meaning in Movement, Sport and Physical Education.* London: Heineman, 1979.

Arnold, Peter J. "Aesthetic Aspects of Being in Sport: The Performer's Perspective in Contrast to That of the Spectator." *Journal of the Philosophy of Sport,* XII (1985), 1-7.

Aspin, David N. "Sport and the Concept of 'the Aesthetic'." In *Readings in the Aesthetics of Sport.* Edited by H.T.A. Whiting and Don W. Masterson. London: Lepus Books, 1974.

Bammel, E., and Bammel, L.L. "Aesthetics of Play." *Physical Education,* 32 (December, 1975), 192-193.

Baumbach, Jonathan. "The Aesthetics of Basketball." *Esquire,* 73 (January, 1970), 140-146.

Best, David. "The Aesthetic in Sport." *British Journal of Aesthetics,* 14 (1974a), 197-213.

Best, David. *Expression in Movement and the Arts.* London: Lepus Books, 1974b.

Best, David. *Philosophy and Human Movement.* London: George Allen and Unwin, 1978.

Best, David. "Art and Sport." *Journal of Aesthetic Education,* 14 (1980), 69-80.

Best, David. *Feeling and Reason in the Arts.* London: George Allen and Unwin, 1985.

Bouet, M. "Contribution a l'esthetique du sport." *Revue d'Esthetique,* 1 (1948), 180-194.

Bouet, M. "The Phenomenology of Aesthetics of Sport." In *Sport in the Modern World—Chances and Problems.* Edited by Ommo Grupe, Dietrich Kurz, and Johannes Teipel. New York: Springer-Verlag, 1973.

Brown, George S., and Donald Gayner. "Athletic Action as Creativity." *Journal of Creative Behavior,* 1 (1967), 155-162.

Brown, Joe. "Movement and Figurative Sculpture." *Quest,* 23 (January 1975), 84-87.

Cady, Edwin, H. "The Public Art Form." In *The Big Game: College Sports and American Life.* Knoxville, TN: University of Tennessee Press, 1978.

Carlisle, Robert. "Physical Education and Aesthetics." In *Readings in the Aesthetics of Sport.* Edited by H.T.A. Whiting and Don W. Masterson. London: Lepus Books, 1974.

Castle, Ted. "Carolee Schneeman: The Woman Who Uses Her Body as Art." *Artform,* 19:2 (1980), 64-70.

Chastel, Andre. "The Element of Play in Twentieth Century Art." *Diogenes,* 50 (Summer, 1965), 1-12.

Cheney, Gay. "Kine-Aesthetics." *Proceedings of the National College Physical Education Association for Men/National Association for Physical Education of College Women National Conference,* Orlando, Florida, January 6-9, 1977.

Cooper, W.E. "Do Sports Have an Aesthetic Aspect?" *Journal of the Philosophy of Sport,* V (1978), 51-55.

Cordner, C.D. "Grace and Functionality." *British Journal of Aesthetics,* 24 (1984), 301-313.

Dubois, P.E. "The Aesthetic of Sport and the Athlete." *The Physical Educator,* 31 (1974), 198-201.

Dufrenne, M. "La Philosophie du Sport." *Education Physique et Sport,* 1 (1950), 4-6.

Edgell, C.H. *Sport in American Art.* Boston: Museum of Fine Arts, 1944.

Elliott, R.K. "Aesthetics and Sport." In *Readings in the Aesthetics of Sport.* Edited by H.T.A. Whiting and Don W. Masterson. London: Lepus Books, 1974.

Fetters, Janis L. "The Aesthetic Experience of the Body in Sport." Unpublished doctoral dissertation, Ohio State University, 1976.

Fetters, Janis L. "The Body Aesthetic: A Symbolic Experience." *Proceedings of the National College Physical Education Association for Men/National Association for Physical Education of College Women Conference,* Orlando, Florida, January 6-9, 1977.

Fisher, Marjorie. "Sport as an Aesthetic Experience." In *Sport and the Body: A Philosophical Symposium.* Edited by Ellen W. Gerber. Philadelphia: Lea & Febiger, 1972.

Gablewitz, E. "Aesthetic Problems in Physical Education and Sport." *Bulletin of the Federation International d'Education Physique,* No. 3, 1965.

Galvin, Richard F. "Aesthetic Incontinence in Sport." In *Sport Inside Out: Readings in Literature and Philosophy.* Edited by David Vanderwerken and S.K. Wertz. Fort Worth: Texas Christian University Press, 1985.

Gaskin, Geoffrey, and Masterson, Don W. "The Work of Art in Sport." *Journal of the Philosophy of Sport,* I (1974), 36-66.

Gray, Miriam. "The Physical Educator as Artist." *Quest,* 7 (December, 1966), 18-24.

Groos, Karl. *The Play of Man.* New York: D. Appleton and Company, 1901.

Hazelwood, R. "Nature of Concepts and Its Importance for Understanding the Aesthetic." *Physical Education Review,* 3 (Autumn, 1980), 111-120.

Healy, John William. "Art and Sport: A Comparison." Unpublished doctoral dissertation, Columbia University Teachers' College, 1977.

Hein, Hilde. "Play as an Aesthetic Concept." *Journal of Aesthetics,* 27 (1968), 67-71.

Hein, Hilde. "Performances as an Aesthetic Category." *Journal of Aesthetics and Art Criticism,* 28 (1970), 381–386.

Hohler, V. "The Beauty of Motion." In *Readings in the Aesthetics of Sport.* Edited by H.T.A. Whiting and Don W. Masterson. London: Lepus Books, 1974.

Hohne, E. "Coubertin on the Place of Art in Modern Olympism." *Bulletin of the National Olympic Committee of the German Democratic Republic,* 14:4 (1969), 31-40.

Holme, B. "Sport as a Challenge to Artists." *Design,* 61 (1960), 125-127.

Ingram, A. "Art and Sport." *Journal of Health, Physical Education and Recreation,* 44 (February, 1973), 24-27.

James, C.L.R. "The Relationship Between Popular Sport and Fine Art." In *Readings in the Aesthetics of Sport.* Edited by H.T.A. Whiting and Don W. Masterson. London: Lepus Books, 1974.

Jokl, Ernst. "Art and Sport." In *Readings in the*

Aesthetics of Sport. Edited by H.T.A. Whiting and Don W. Masterson. London: Lepus Books, 1974.

Kaelin, E.F. "The Well-Played Game: Notes Toward an Aesthetics of Sport." *Quest,* 10 (May, 1968), 16-28.

Kapreliam, Mary Haberkorn. "A Comparison of Two Aesthetic Theories as They Apply to Modern Dance." Unpublished doctoral dissertation, University of Wisconsin, 1969.

Keenan, Francis W. "The Athletic Contest as a 'Tragic' Form of Art." In *The Philosophy of Sport: A Collection of Original Essays.* Edited by Robert G. Osterhoudt. Springfield, IL: Charles C Thomas, 1973.

Kellar, Hans. "Sports and Art—The Concept of Mastery." *Readings in the Aesthetics of Sport.* Edited by H.T.A. Whiting and Don W. Masterson. London: Lepus Books, 1974.

Kent, Norman. "Art in Sports." *American Artist,* 32 (March, 1968), 45-47, 55.

Kleinman, Seymour. "Effort/Shape: Heightening Aesthetic Awareness of the Self and the Other." *Proceedings of the National College Physical Education Association for Men/National Association for Physical Education of College Women National Conference,* Orlando, Florida, January 6-9, 1977.

Kleinman, Seymour. "Art, Sport, and Intention." *National Association for Physical Education in Higher Education Proceedings..* Champaign, IL: Human Kinetics, 1980.

Kovich, Maureen. "Sports as an Art Form." *Journal of Health, Physical Education, and Recreation,* 42 (October, 1971), 42.

Kuntz, P.G. "The Aesthetics of Sport." In *The Philosophy of Sport: A Collection of Original Essays.* Edited by Robert G. Osterhoudt. Springfield, IL: Charles C Thomas, 1973.

Kuntz, P.G. "Aesthetics Applies to Sports as Well as to the Arts." *Journal of the Philosophy of Sport,* I (1974), 6-35.

Kuntz, P.G. "Paul Weiss on Sports as Performing Arts." *International Philosophic Quarterly,* 17 (June, 1977), 147-165.

Kuntz, P.G. "From Ziff to Zen: A Defense of the Aesthetics of Sport." *Philosophy in Context,* 9 (1979), 22-32.

Kupfer, Joseph. "Purpose and Beauty in Sport." *Journal of the Philosophy of Sport,* II (1975), 83-90.

Lenk, Hans. *Die Achte Kunst: Leistungssport-Breitensport.* Zurich: A. Fromm Verlag, A. Fromm, 1985.

Littlewood, P.K. "An Inquiry Into the Aesthetic Nature of Play: Philosophic Bases and Current Concepts." Unpublished master's thesis. Washington State University, 1981.

Lowe, Benjamin. "The Representation of Sports in Painting in the United States: 1865-1965." Unpublished master's thesis, University of Wisconsin, 1968.

Lowe, Benjamin. "The Aesthetics of Sport: The Statement of a Problem." *Quest,* 16 (June, 1971), 13-17.

Lowe, Benjamin. *The Beauty of Sport: A Cross-Disciplinary Inquiry.* Englewood Cliffs, NJ: Prentice-Hall, 1977.

Maheu, Rene. "Sport and Culture." *Journal of Health, Physical Education and Recreation,* 34 (October, 1963), 30-32, 49-50, 52-54.

Martland, T.R. "Not Art and Play, Mind You, nor Art and Games, but Art and Sports." *Journal of Aesthetic Education,* 19 (1985), 65-71.

Masterson, Don W. "Sport, Theatre and Art in Performance." In *Topical Problems of Sport Philosophy.* Edited by Hans Lenk. Koln: Bundesinstitut für Sportswissenschaft, 1983.

Masterson, Don W. "Sport and Modern Painting." In *Readings in the Aesthetics of Sport.* Edited by H.T.A. Whiting and Don W. Masterson. London: Lepus Books, 1974.

Meakin, Derek C. "Aesthetic Appraisal and Human Movement.'' *Physical Education Review,* 3 (Spring, 1980), 41-49.

Meredith, Lawrence. ''Aesthetics and Kinesthesis: Meditations on Metaphysical Education, or Graffiti in the Gameroom.'' *Arete: The Journal of Sport Literature,* 2 (Fall, 1984), 11-24.

Metheny, Eleanor. *Connotations of Movement in Sport and Dance.* Dubuque, IA: W.C. Brown, 1965.

Metzi, E. ''Art in Sports.'' *American Artist,* 26 (November, 1962), 30-37.

Mitchell, Robert Thomas. ''A Conceptual Analysis of Art as Experience and Its Implications for Sport and Physical Education.'' Unpublished doctoral dissertation, University of Northern Colorado, 1974.

Mitchell, Robert Thomas. ''Sport as Experience.'' *Quest,* 24 (Summer, 1975), 28–33.

Nahm, M.C. ''Some Aspects of the Play-Theory of Art.'' *Journal of Philosophy,* 39 (March, 1942), 148-159.

Nasmark, H. ''Aesthetics and Sport.'' *Bulletin of the International Federation d'Education Physique,* 1, 1963.

Osborne, Harold. ''Notes on the Aesthetics of Chess and the Concept of Intellectual Beauty.'' *British Journal of Aesthetics,* **4** (1964), 160–163.

Osterhoudt, Robert G. ''An Hegelian Interpretation of Art, Sport, and Athletics.'' In *The Philosophy of Sport: A Collection of Original Essays.* Edited by Robert G. Osterhoudt. Springfield, IL: Charles C Thomas, 1973.

Perry, R. Hinton. ''The Relations of Athletics to Art.'' *Outing,* 49 (1902), 456-463.

''The Poetry of Football.'' *The Arts of Sport and Recreation.* Edited by Derek Stanford. London: Thomas Nelson and Sons, 1967.

Postow, B.C. ''Sport, Art and Gender.'' *Journal of the Philosophy of Sport,* XI (1984), 52-55.

Pouret, H. ''Is Sport an Art?'' *Report of the Tenth Session of the International Olympic Academy,* Athens, Greece, 1970.

Racy, R.F. ''The Aesthetic Experience.'' *The British Journal of Aesthetics,* 9 (1969), 345-352.

Rau, Catherine. ''Psychological Notes on the Theory of Art as Play.'' *Journal of Aesthetics and Art Criticism,* 8 (1950), 229-238.

Reid, Louis A. ''Human Movement, the Aesthetic and Art.'' *British Journal of Aesthetics,* 20 (1980), 165-170.

Reid, Louis A. ''Sport, the Aesthetic and Art.'' *British Journal of Educational Studies,* 18 (1970), 245-258.

Roberts, Terence J. ''Sport and the Sense of Beauty.'' *Journal of the Philosophy of Sport,* II (1975), 91-101.

Roberts, Terence J. ''Languages of Sport.'' Unpublished doctoral dissertation, University of Minnesota, 1976.

Roberts, Terence J. ''Languages of Sport: Exemplification and Expression.'' In *Sport and the Humanities: A Collection of Original Essays.* Edited by William J. Morgan. Knoxville, TN: University of Tennessee, 1979a.

Roberts, Terence J. ''Languages of Sport: Representation.'' In *Sport and the Body: A Philosophical Symposium* (2nd ed.). Edited by Ellen W. Gerber and William J. Morgan. Philadelphia: Lea & Febiger, 1979b.

Santayana, George. *The Sense of Beauty: Being the Outline of Aesthetic Theory.* New York: Dover, 1955.

Saraf, M.J. ''Sport and Art.'' *International Review of Sport Sociology,* 15 (1980), 123-131.

Saraf, M.J. ''The Aesthetics of Sport.'' *Dialectics and Humanism,* 11 (1984), 87-96.

Schiller, Friedrich von. *On The Aesthetic Education of Man: In a Series of Letters.* Translated by Reginald Snell. New York: Frederick Ungar, 1965.

Sdun, W. ''Zum Begriff des Spiels bei Kant und Schiller.'' *Kantstudien,* 57 (1966). 500-518.

Seward, George. "Play as Art." *Journal of Philosophy,* 41 (March, 1944), 178-184.

Sheets-Johnstone, Maxine. "On Movements and Objects in Motion: The Phenomonology of the Visible in Dance." *Journal of Aesthetic Education,* 13 (April, 1979), 33-46.

Smith, Hope M. "Movement and Aesthetics." In *Introduction to Human Movement.* Edited by Hope M. Smith. Reading, MA: Addison-Wesley, 1968.

Sonenfield, Irwin. "The Play's the Thing." *Journal of Aesthetic Education,* 19 (1985), 111-113.

Souriau, Paul. *The Aesthetics of Movement.* Translated by M. Souriau. Amherst: University of Massachusetts Press, 1983.

Sparshott, Francis Edward. *The Structure of Aesthetics.* Toronto, Canada: University of Toronto Press, 1963.

Spencer, Herbert. "Aesthetic Sentiments." In *Background Readings for Physical Education.* Edited by Ann Paterson and Edmond C. Hallberg. New York: Holt, Rinehart and Winston, 1965.

Studer, Ginny L. "Perceptual Anesthesis and Movement Aesthetics." In *Sport and the Humanities: A Collection of Original Essays.* Edited by William J. Morgan. Knoxville, TN: University of Tennessee Press, 1979.

Studer, Ginny L. "Movement Aesthetics Summary." *Proceedings of the National College Physical Education Association for Men/National Association for Physical Education of College Women National Conference.* Orlando, Florida, January 6-9, 1977.

Sweeney, James Johnson. "Contemporary Art: The Generative Role of Play." *Review of Politics,* 21 (1959), 389-401.

Thomas, Carolyn E. "The Perfect Moment: An Aesthetic Perspective of the Sport Experience." Unpublished doctoral dissertation, Ohio State University, 1972.

Thomas, Carolyn E. "Toward an Experiential Sport Aesthetic." *Journal of the Philosophy of Sport,* I (1974), 67-91.

Thomas, Carolyn E. "Beautiful, Just Beautiful." In *Being Human in Sport.* Edited by Dorothy J. Allen and Brian Fahey. Philadelphia: Lea & Febiger, 1977.

Thomas, Carolyn E. "The Sportsman as a Tragic Figure." In *Sport and the Humanities: A Collection of Original Essays.* Edited by William J. Morgan. Knoxville; TN: University of Tennessee, 1979a.

Thomas, Carolyn E. "The Tragic Dimension of Sport." *Philosophy in Context,* 9 (1979b), 33-43.

Thomas, Carolyn E. "Sport Contest as Drama." *Journal of Physical Education, Recreation and Dance,* 53 (January, 1982), 39-40.

Thomas, Carolyn E. "Aesthetic Dimensions." In *Sport in a Philosophic Context.* Philadelphia: Lea & Febiger, 1983.

Tilgham, B.R. "Wittgenstein, Games, and Art." *Journal of Aesthetics and Art Criticism,* 31 (1973), 517-524.

Todd, W. "Some Aesthetic Aspects of Sport." *Philosophy in Context,* 9 (1979), 8-21.

Toynbee, Lawrence. "Artists and Sport." *New Society,* 6 (November 8, 1962), 28.

Umphlett, Wiley Lee. "The Dynamics of Fiction on the Aesthetics of the Sport Film." *Arete: The Journal of Sport Literature,* 1 (Spring, 1984), 113-121.

Ward, D.M. "Sport and the Institutional Theory of Art." *Journal of Human Movement Studies,* 3 (1977), 73-81.

Wertz, S.K. "Beauty in Play: Aesthetics for Athletes." *Southwest Philosophical Studies,* 2 (1977a), 77-83.

Wertz, S.K. "Towards a Sports Aesthetic." *Journal of Aesthetic Education,* 2 (1977b), 103-111.

Wertz, S.K. "Are Sports Art Forms?" *Journal of Aesthetic Education,* 13 (1979), 107-109.

Wertz, S.K. "Aesthetics of Sport." In *Philosophy of Art.* Edited by W.E. Steinkrous.

Washington, DC: University Press of America, 1984a.

Wertz, S.K. "A Response to Best on Art and Sport." *Journal of Aesthetic Education,* 18 (1984b), 105-107.

Wertz, S.K. "Representation and Expression in Sport and Art." *Journal of the Philosophy of Sport,* XII (1985), 8-24.

Wertz, S.K. "Artistic Creativity in Sport." In *Sport Inside Out: Readings in Literature and Philosophy.* Edited by David Vanderwerken and S.K. Wertz. Fort Worth: Texas Christian University Press, 1986.

Whiting, H.T.A., and Masterson, Don W. (Eds.). *Readings in the Aesthetics of Sport.* London: Lepus Books, 1974.

Wood, D. "Arts and Sports: An Artistic Inquiry." *Pelops: Studies in Physical Education, Leisure Organizations, Play and Sport,* 3 (1982), 11-18, 27.

Wulk, Nancy G. "A Metacritical Aesthetic of Sport." In *Sport and the Body: A Philosophical Symposium* (2nd ed.). Edited by Ellen W. Gerber and William J. Morgan. Philadelphia: Lea & Febiger, 1979.

Ziff, Paul. "A Fine Forehand." *Journal of the Philosophy of Sport,* I (1974), 92-109.

Zuchova, K. "Closer Ties Between Sport and Art." *International Review of Sport Sociology,* 15 (1980), 49-64.